I0419012

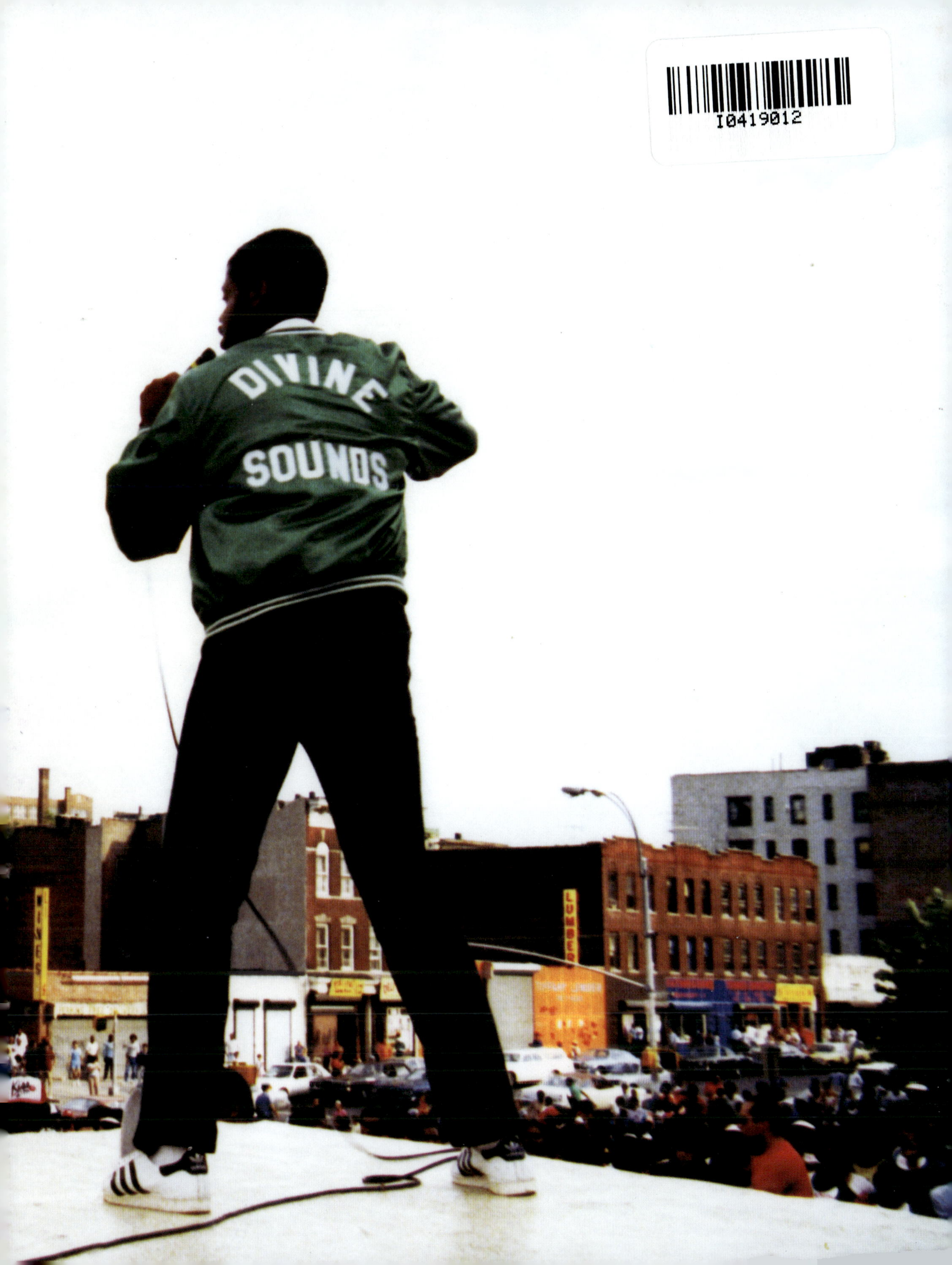

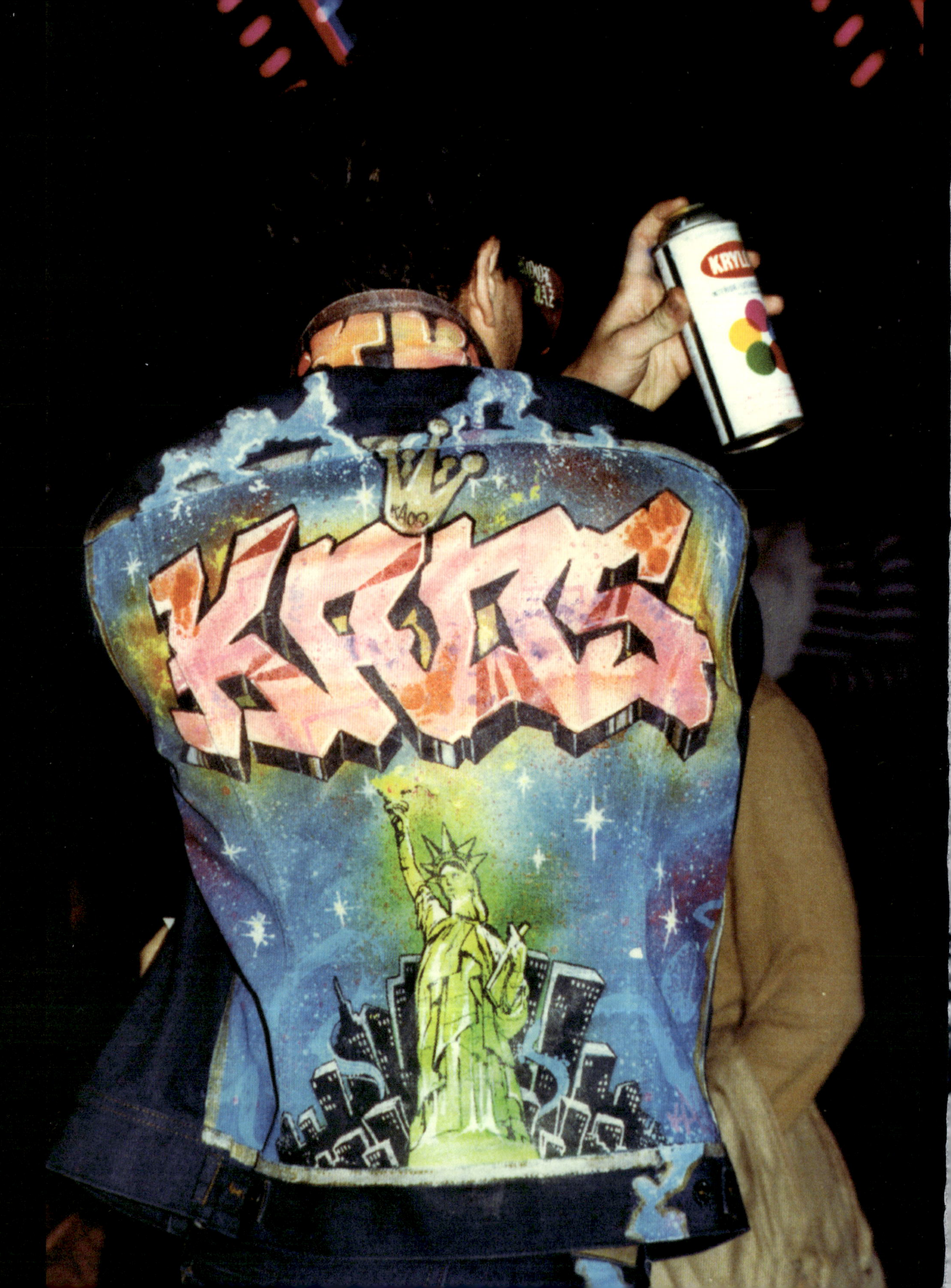

HIP HOP AT THE END OF THE WORLD

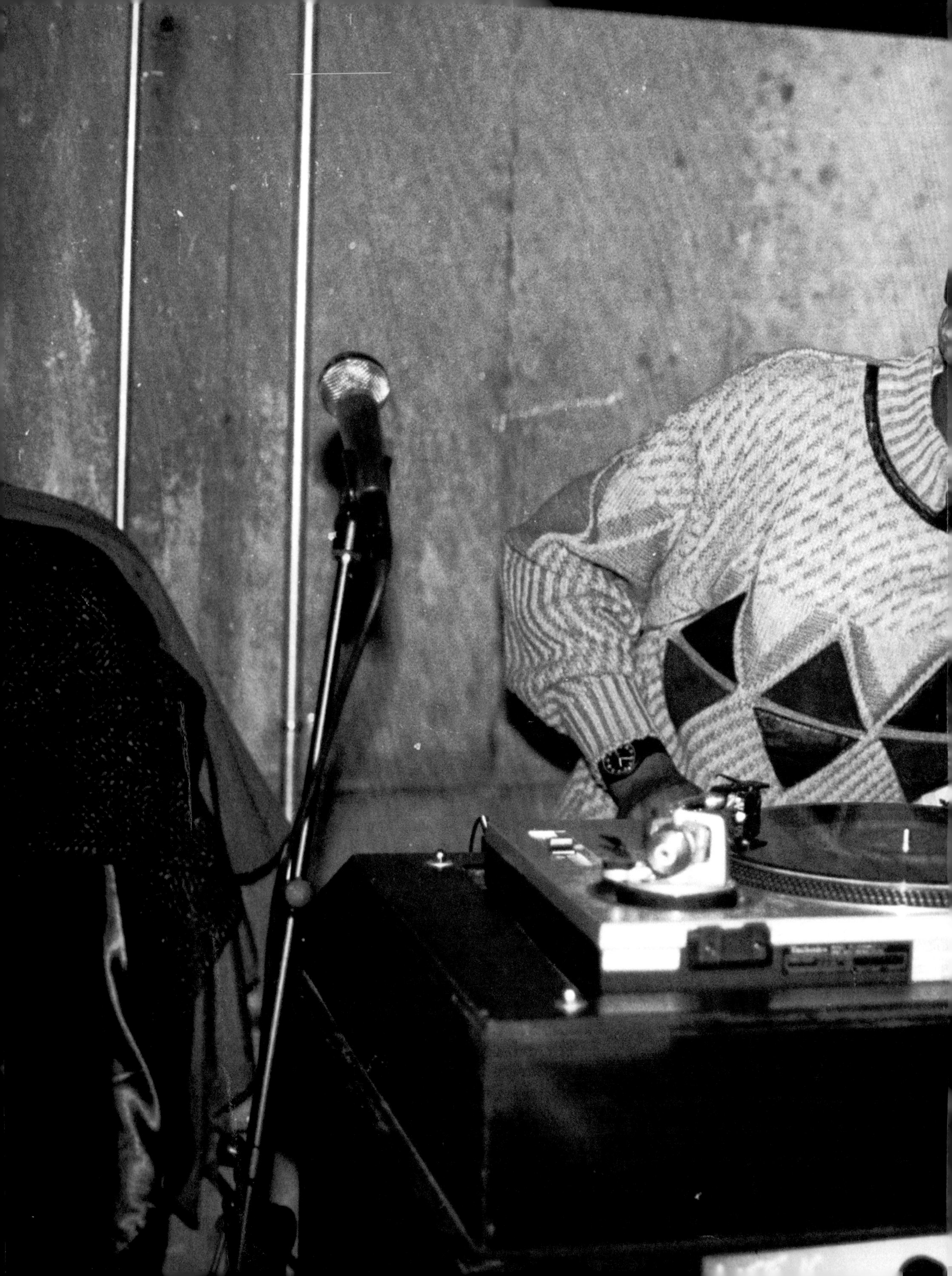

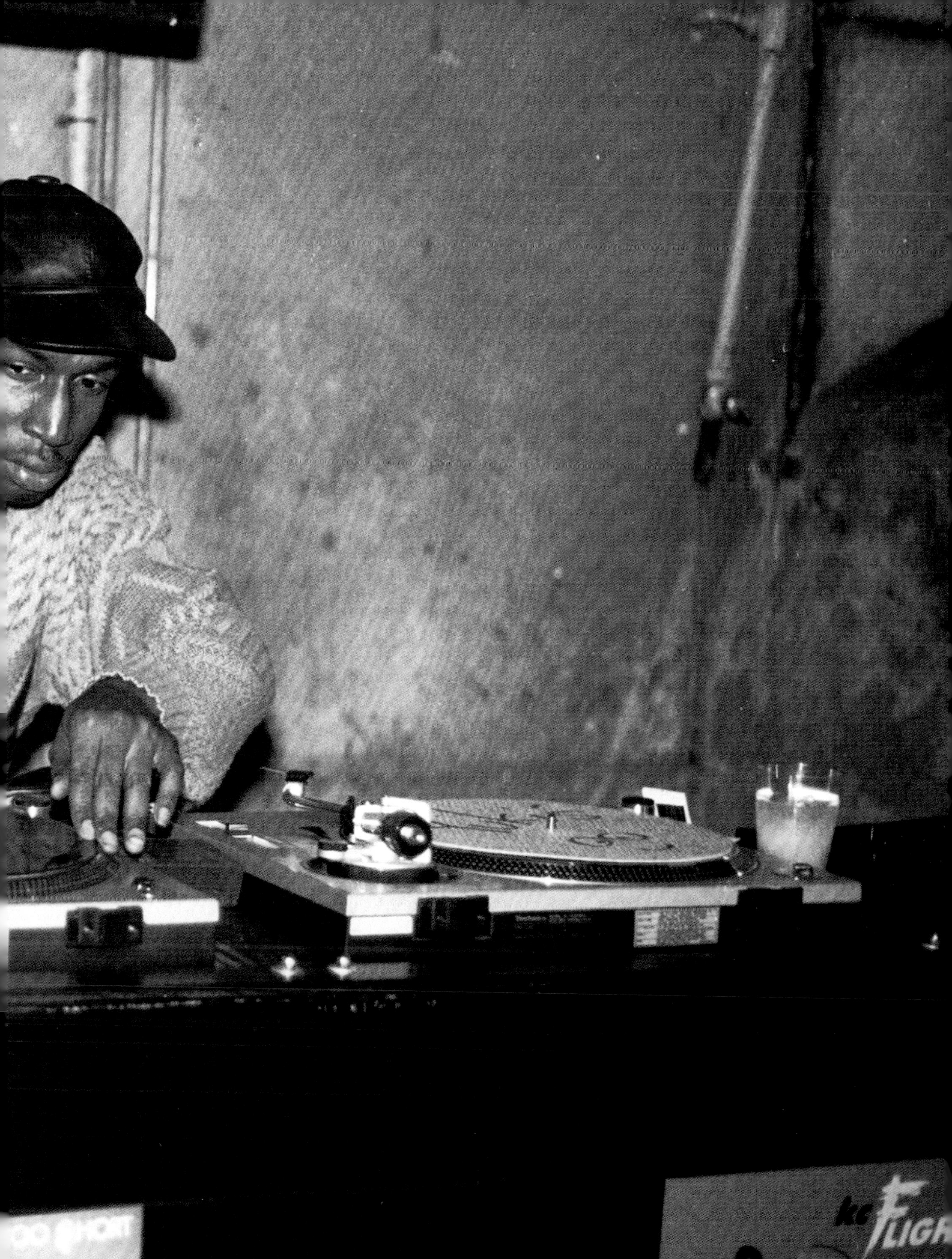

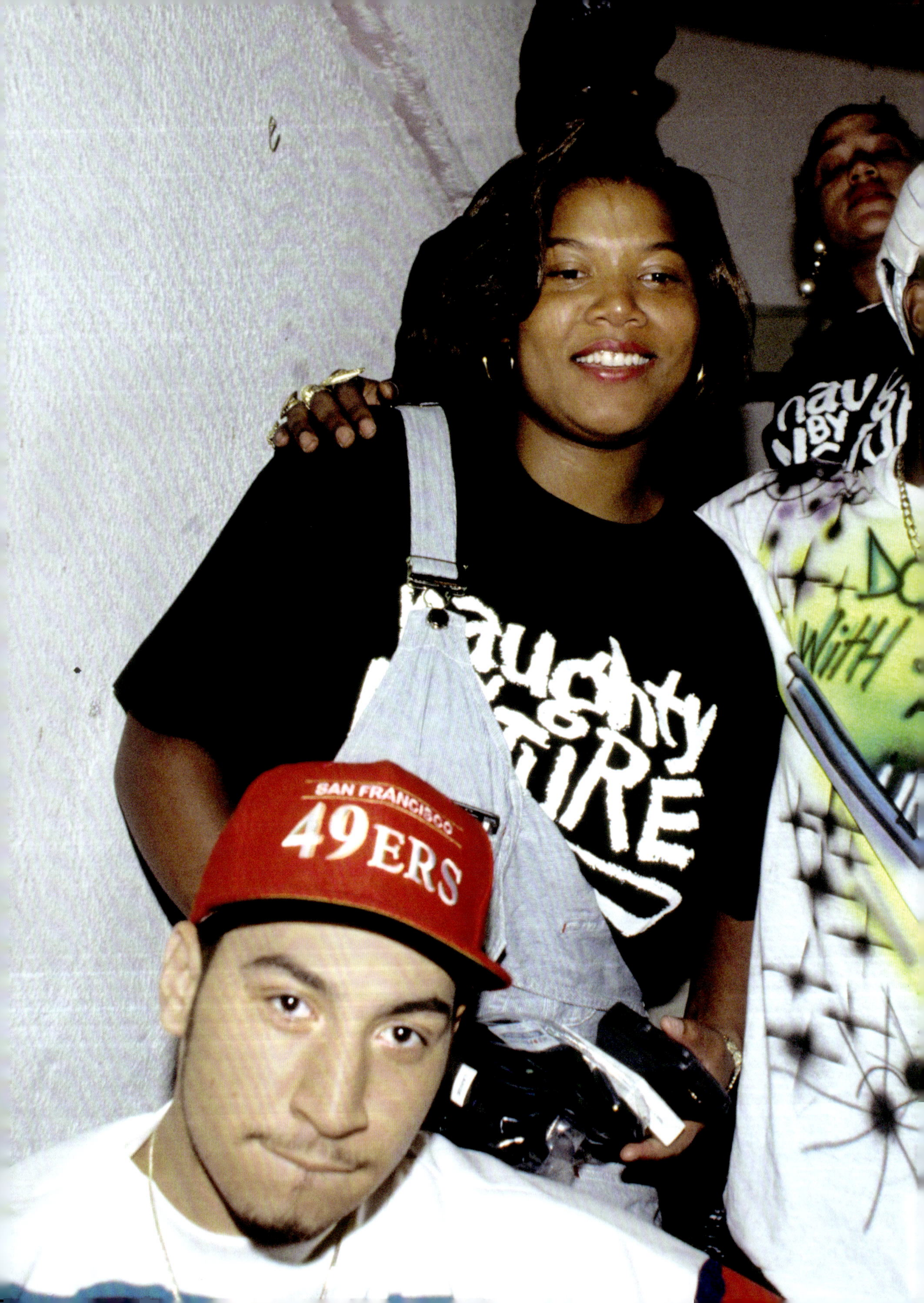
SAN FRANCISCO
49ERS

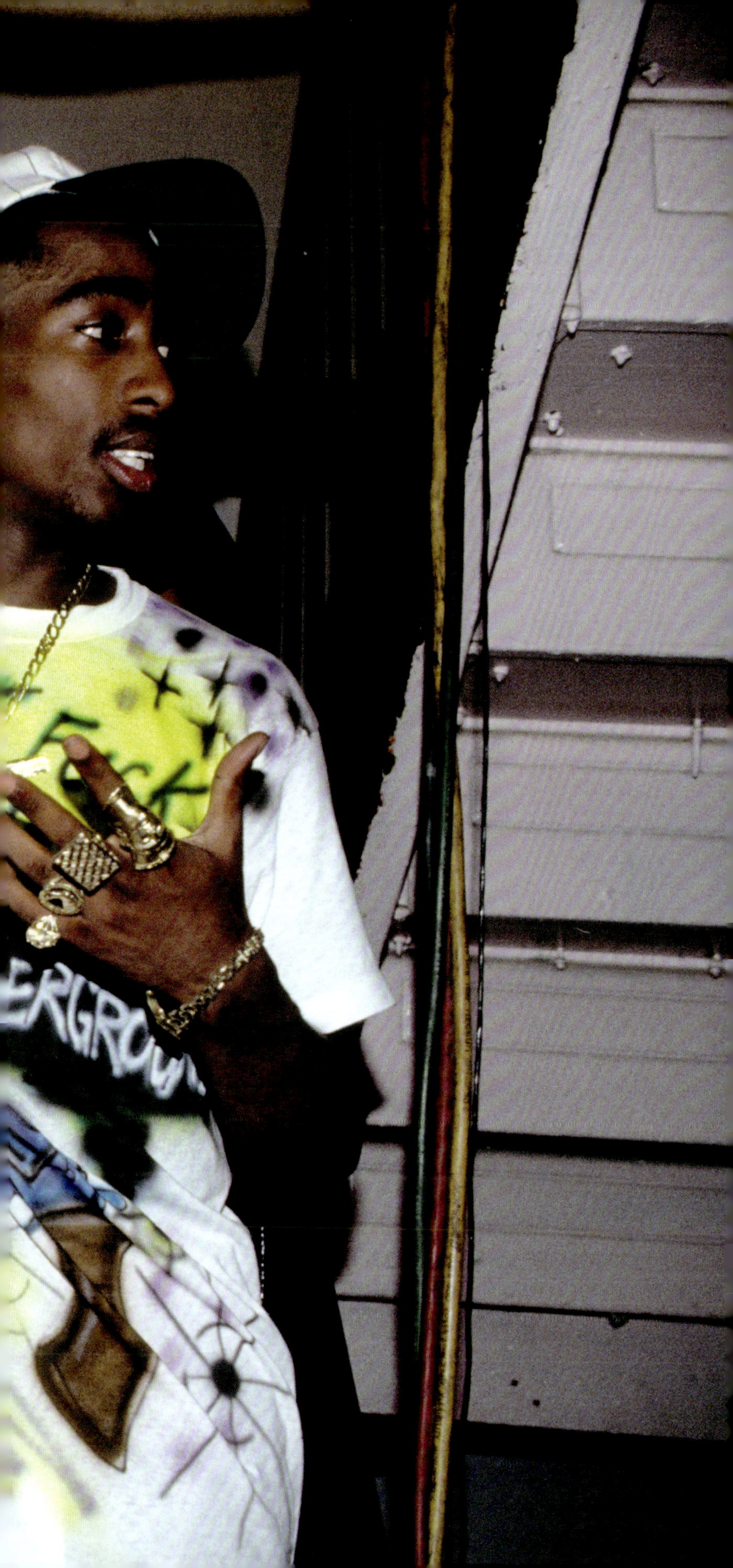

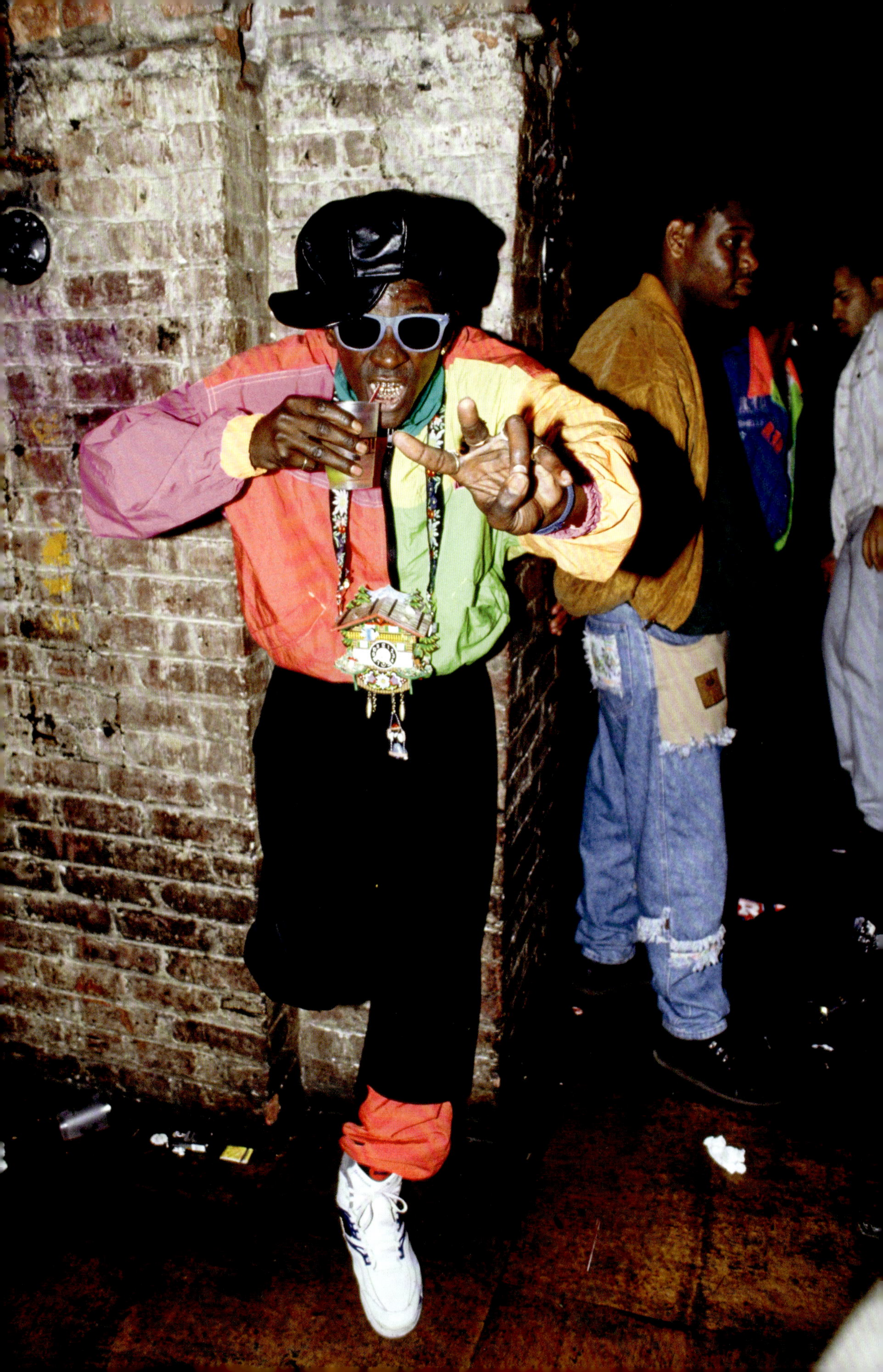

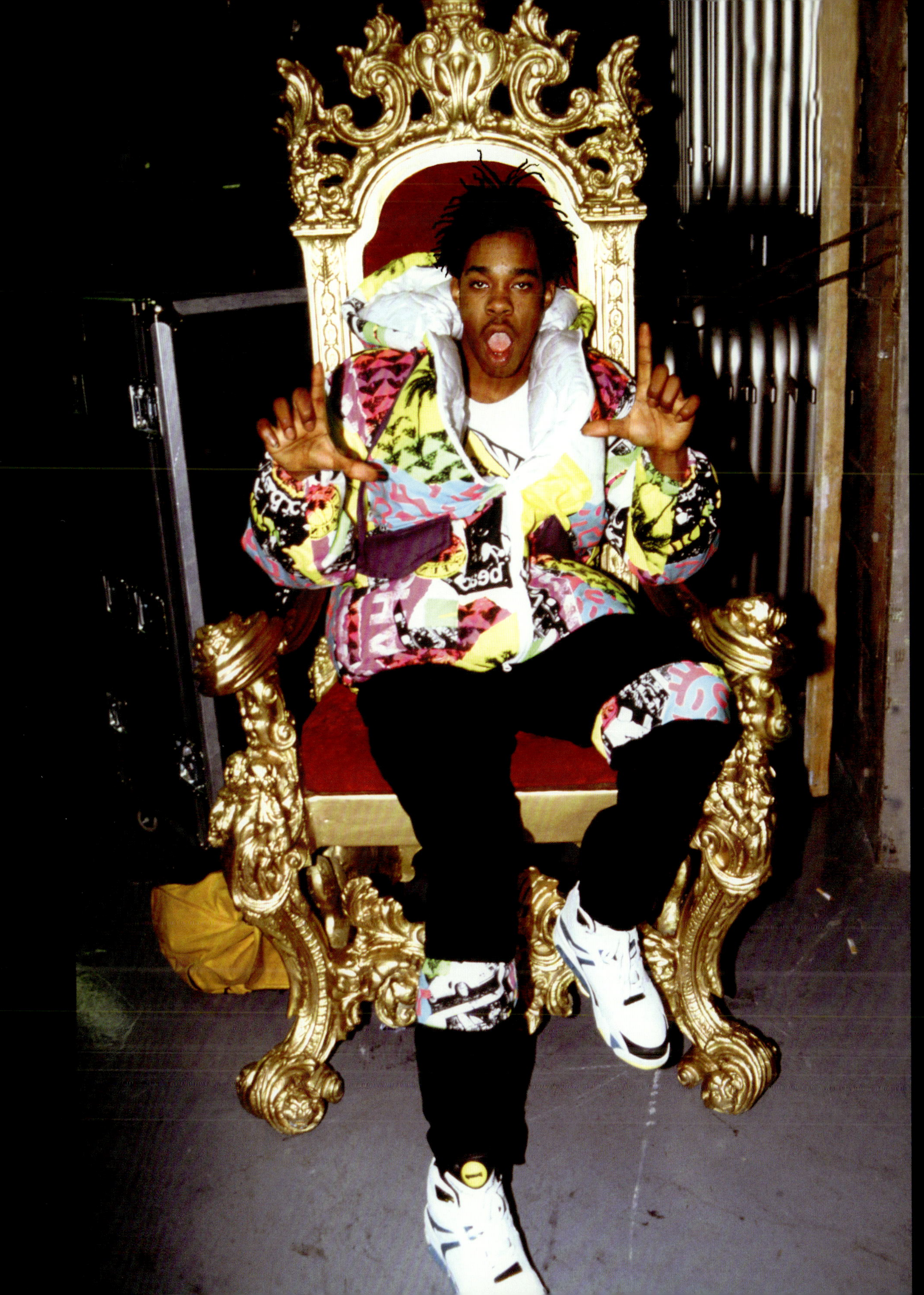

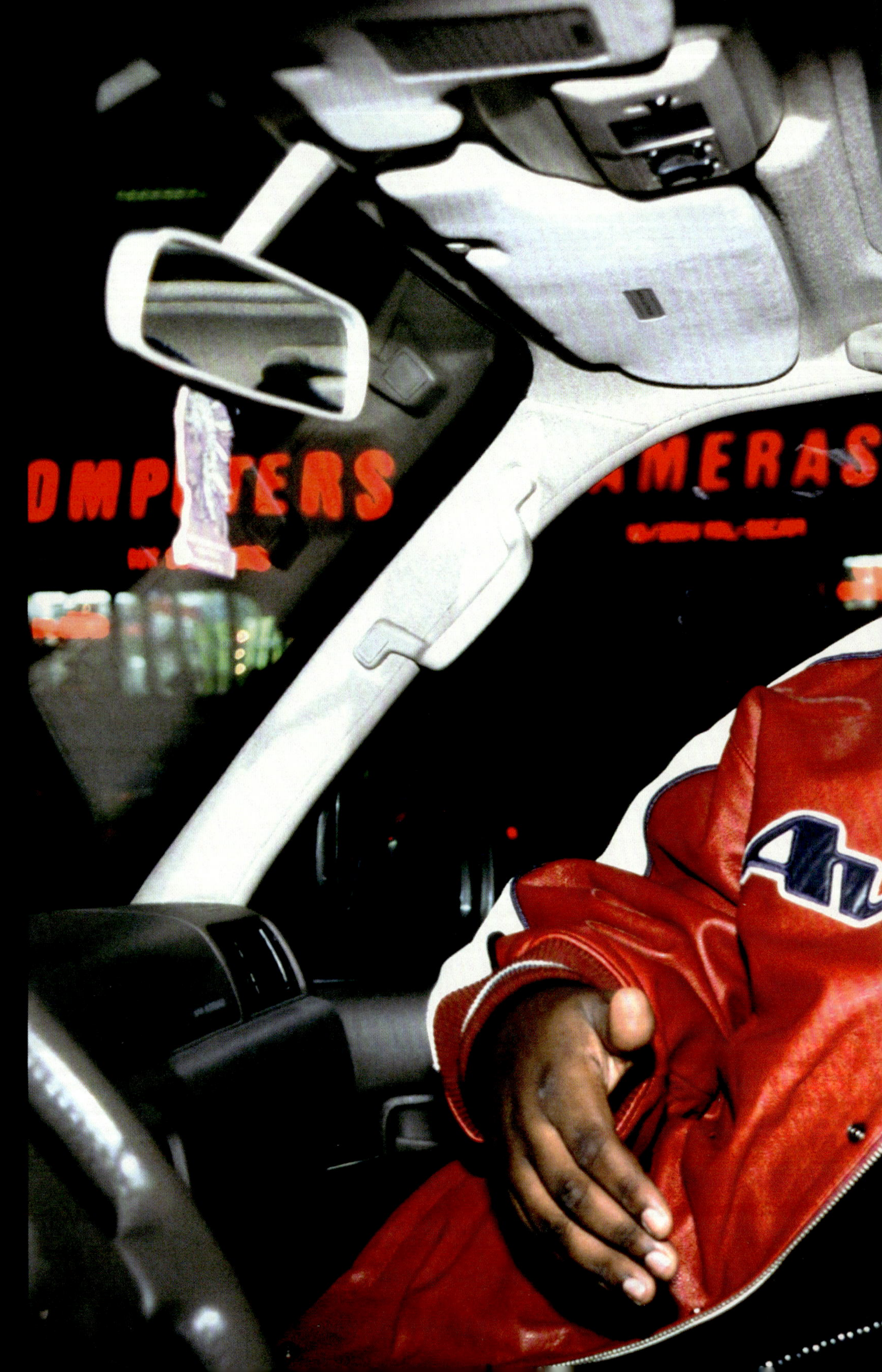

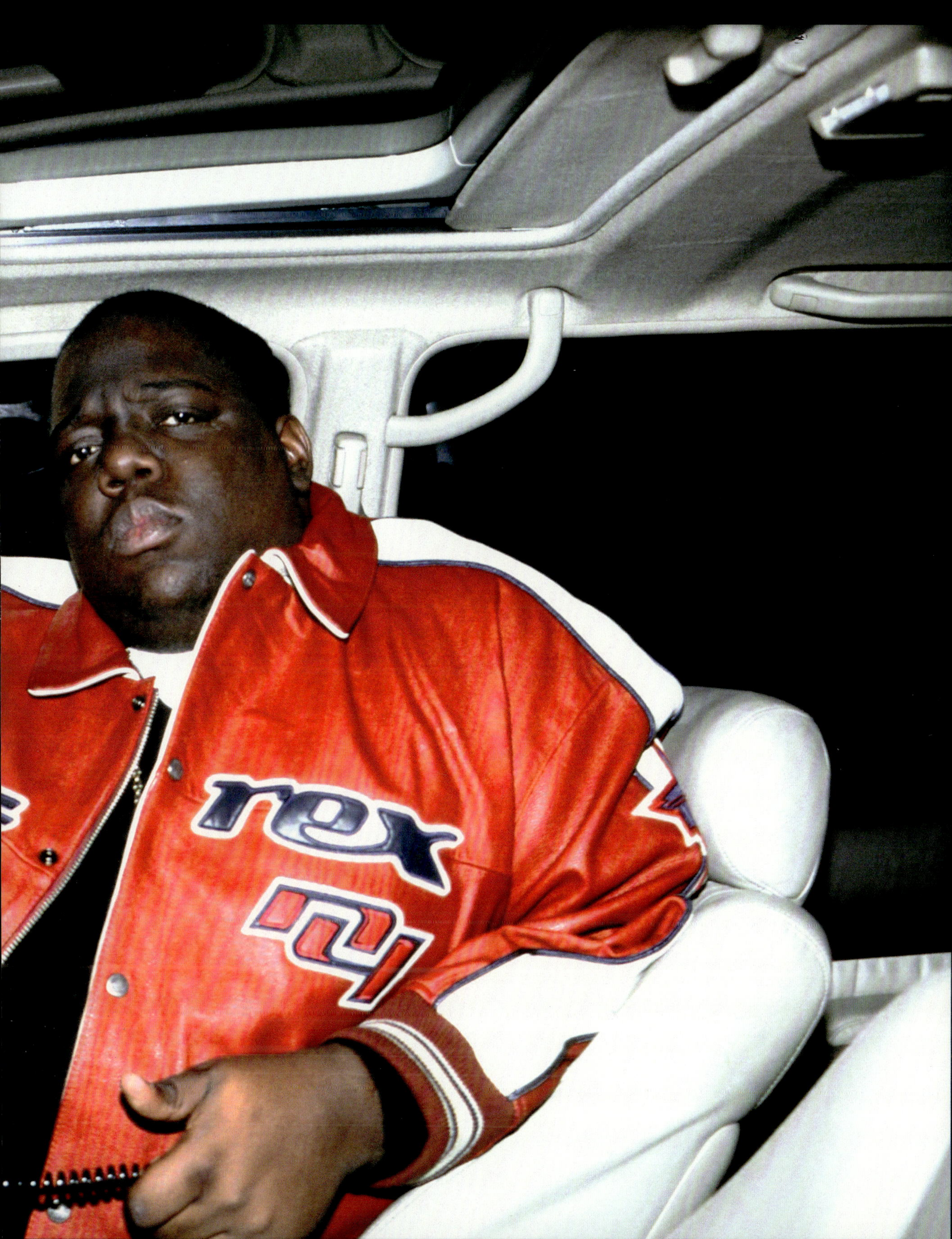
rex

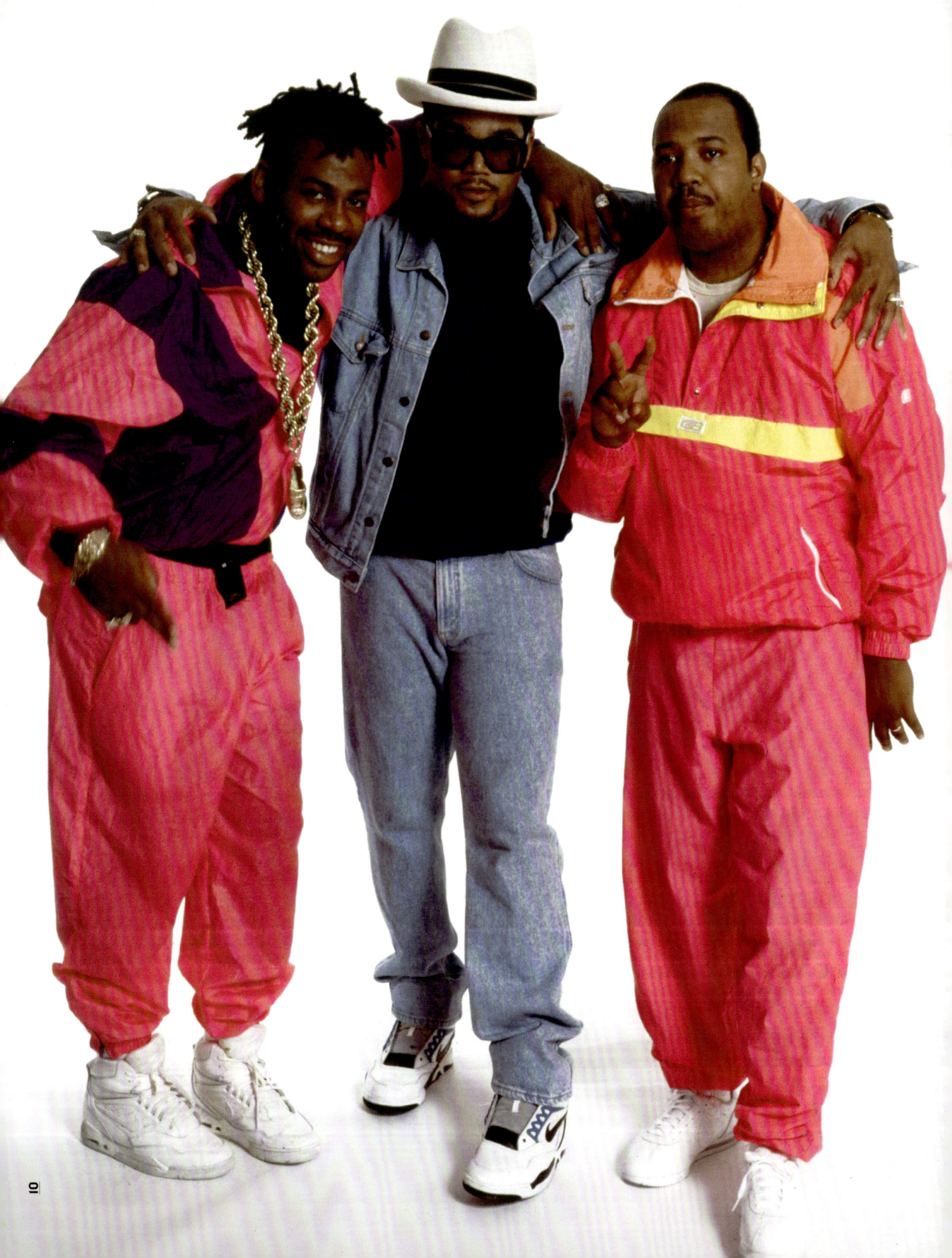

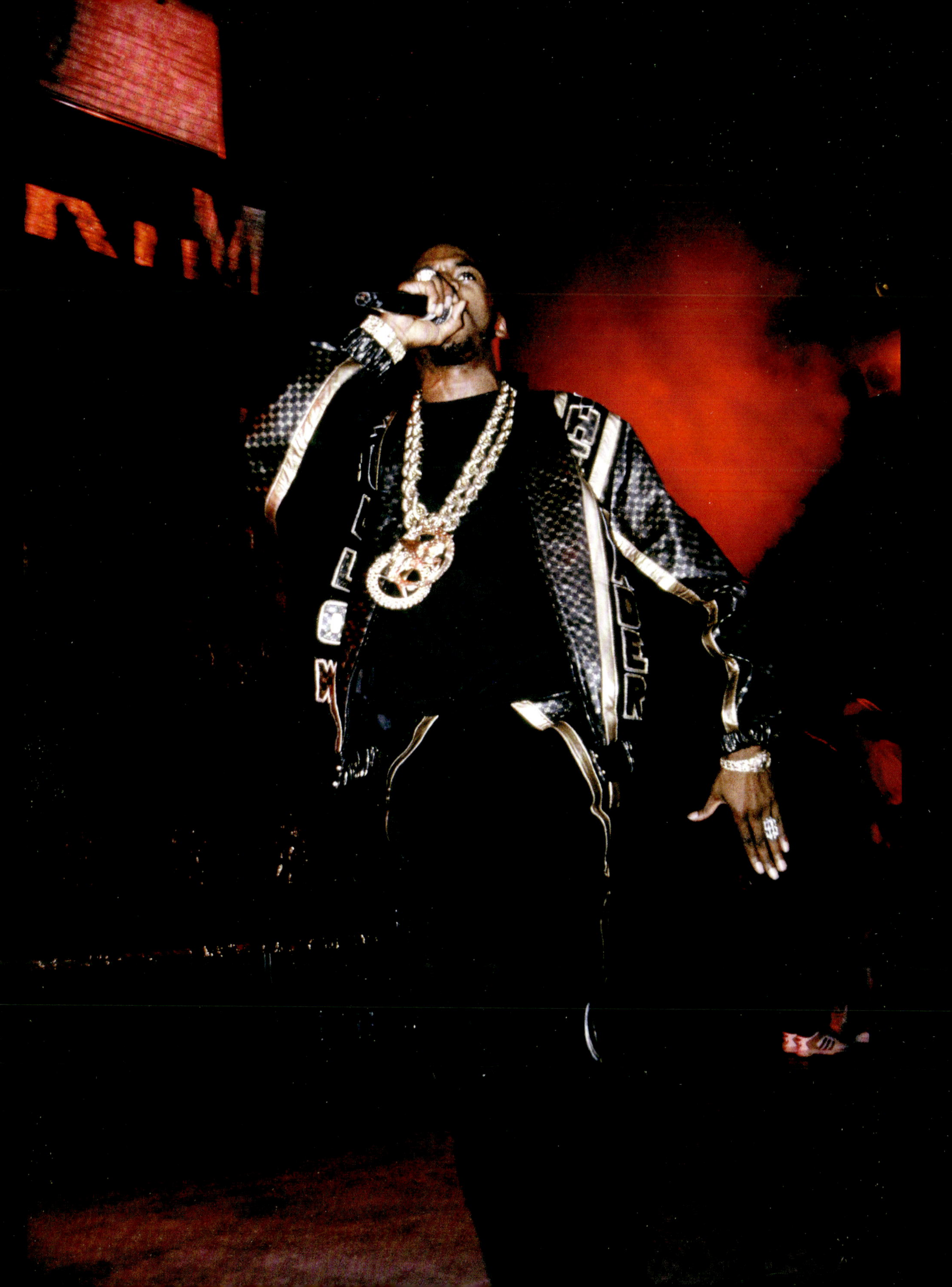

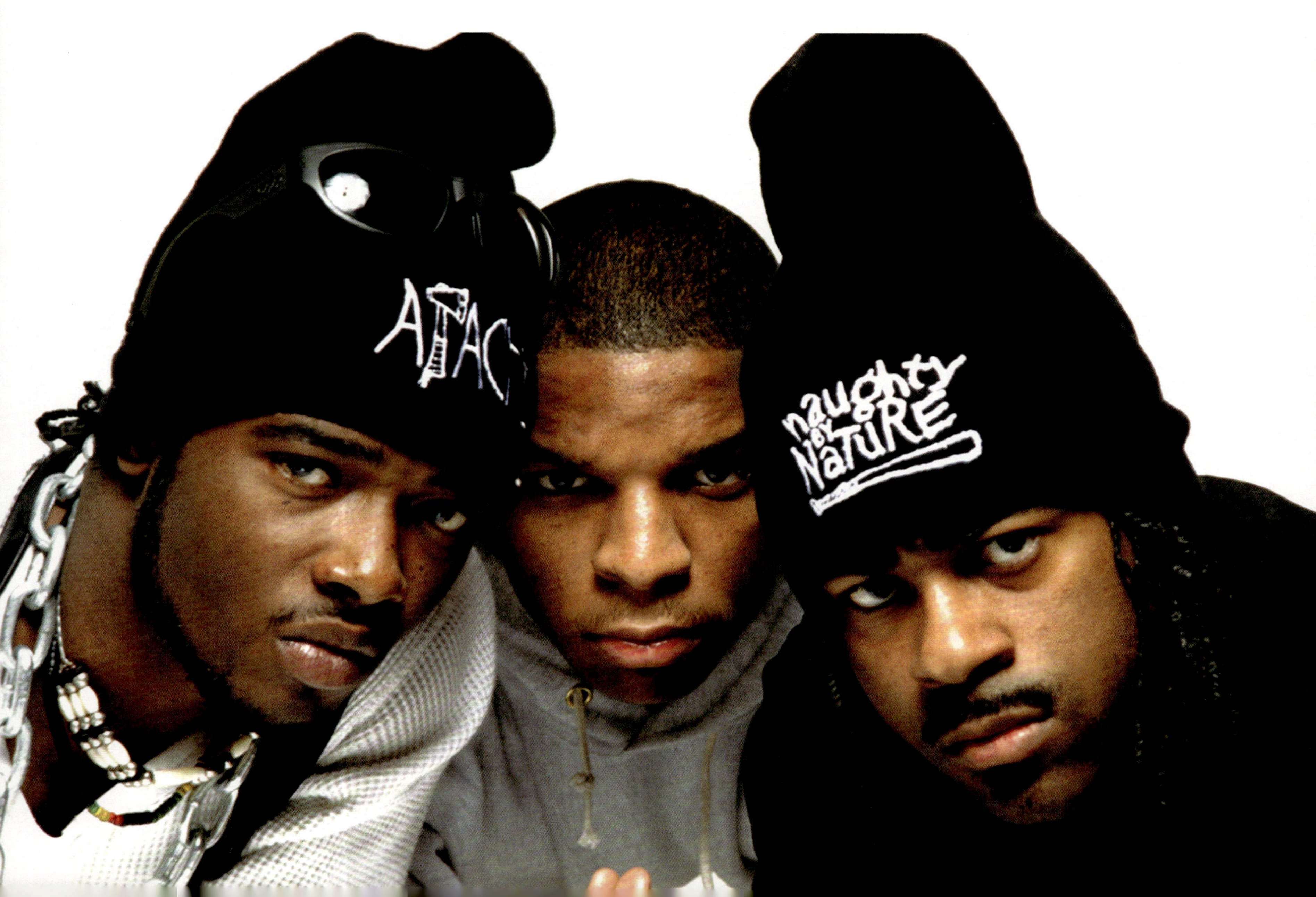
naughty by NaTuRE

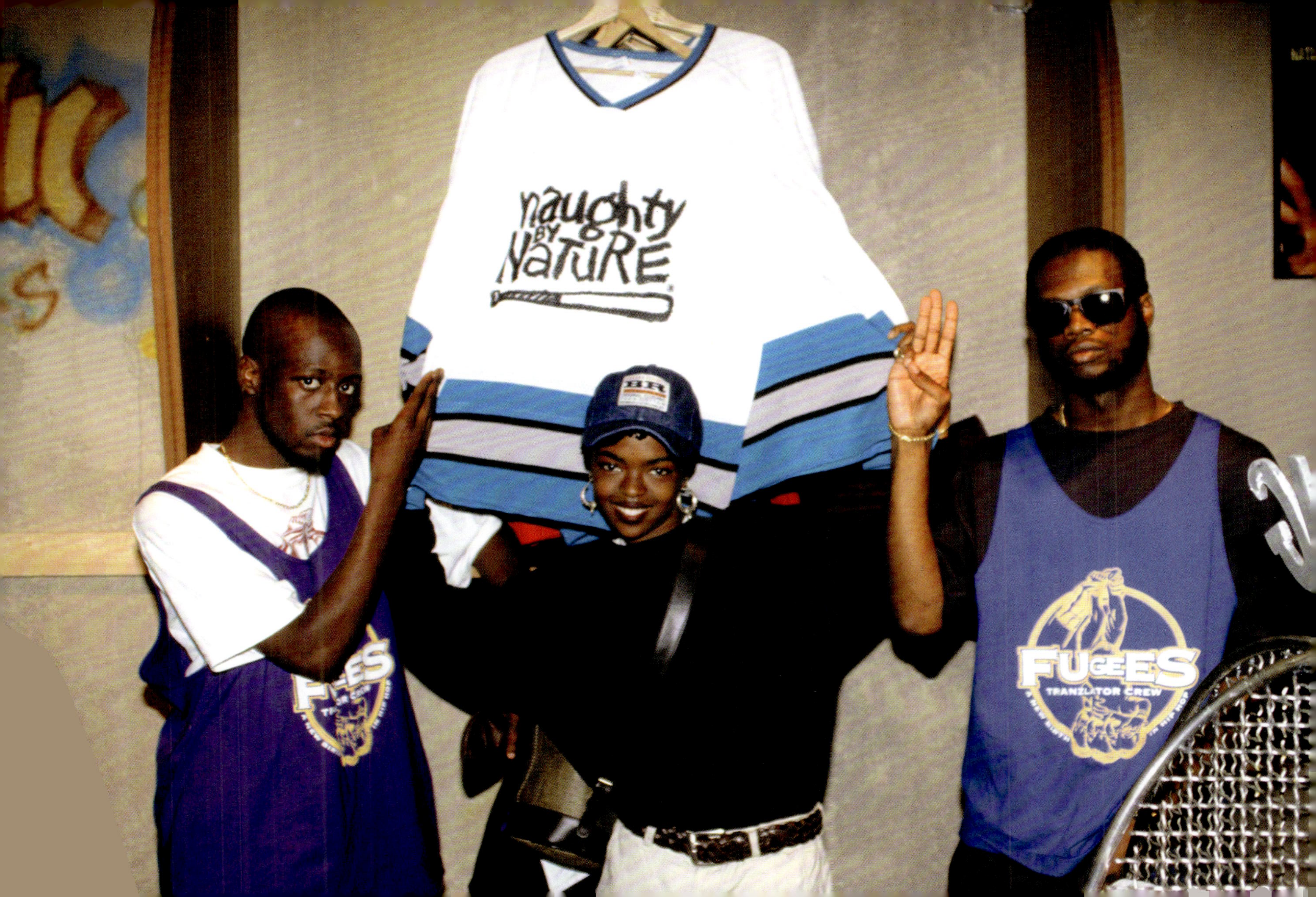
naughty BY NATURE
FUGEES
TRANZLATOR CREW

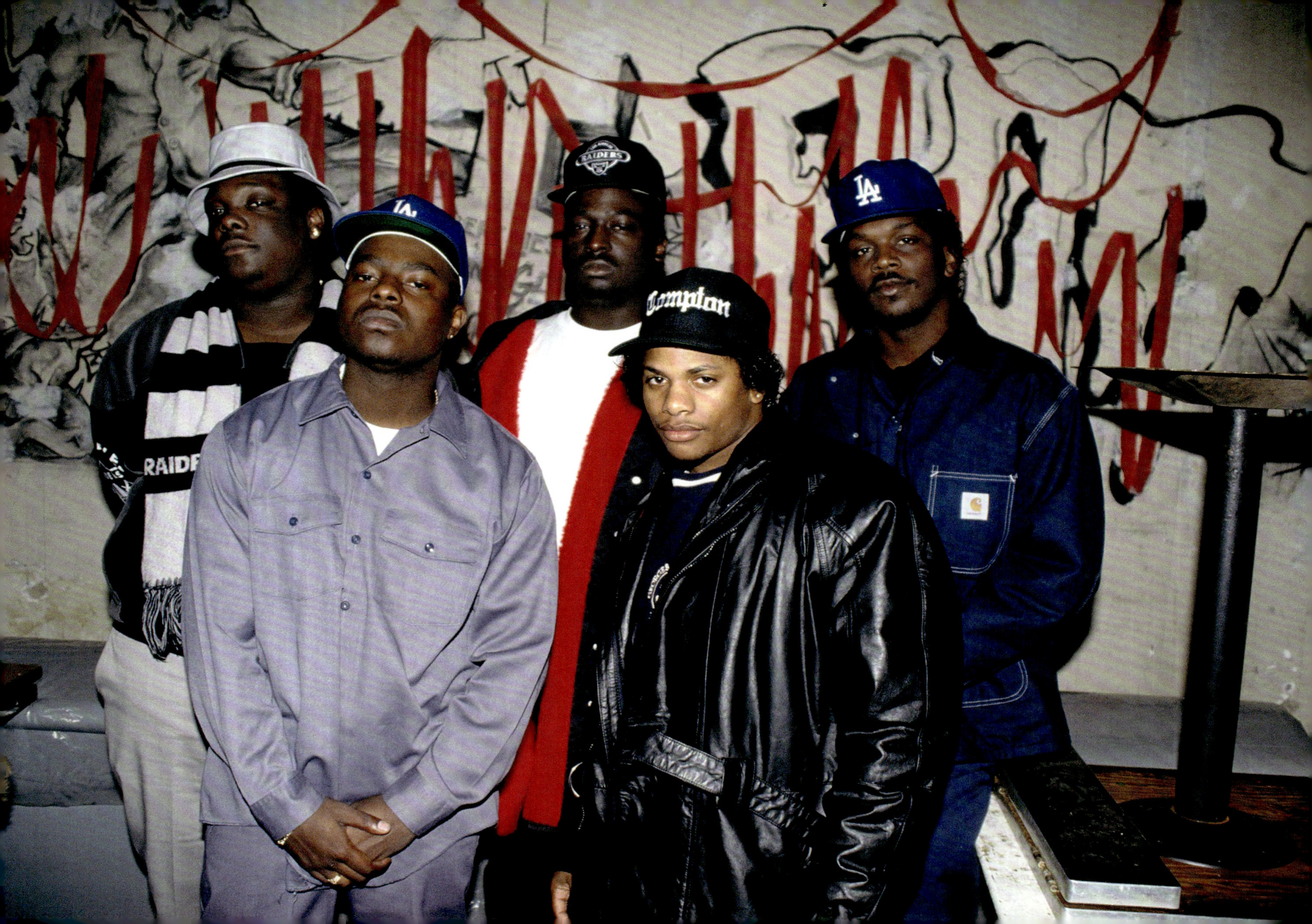
Compton
RAIDERS

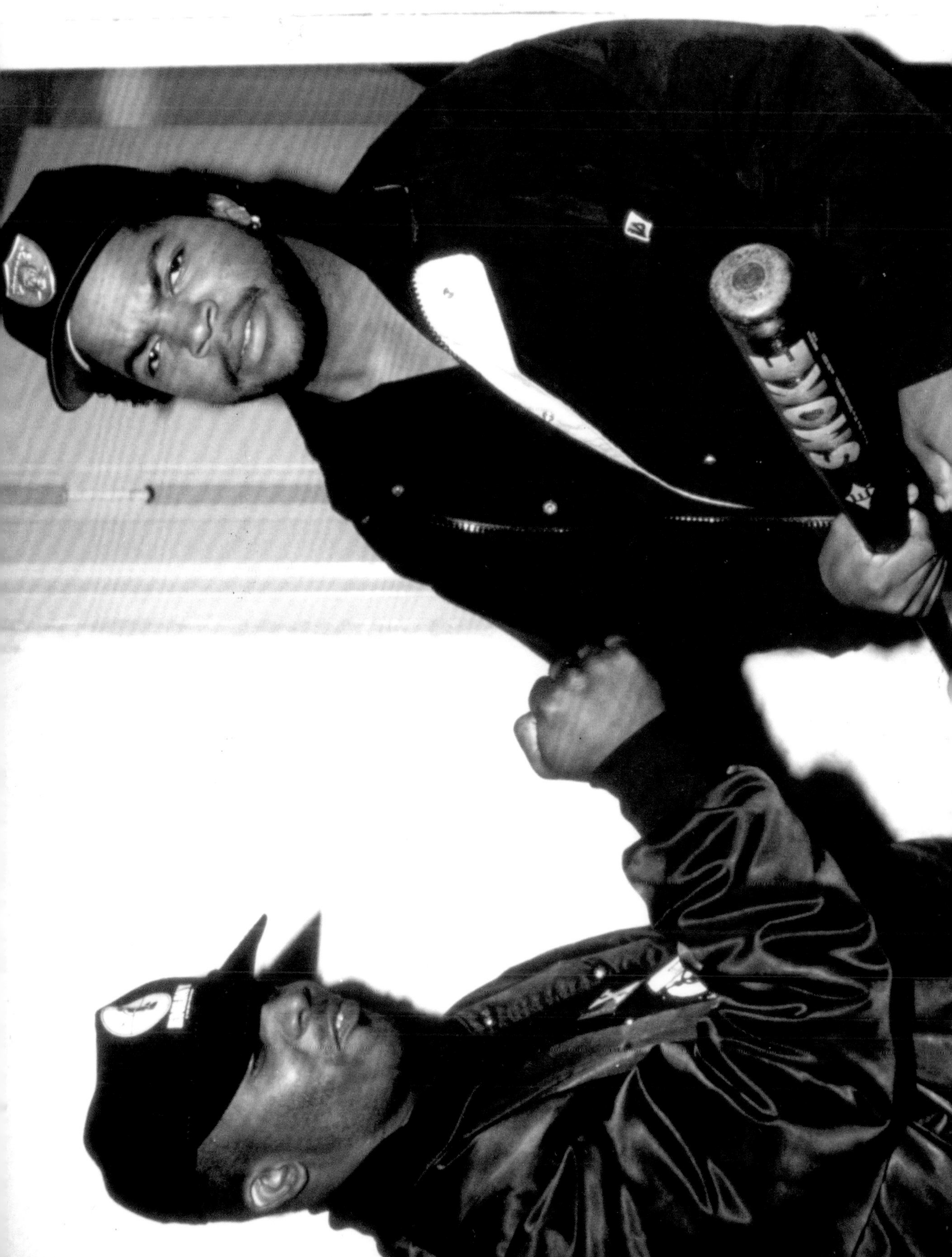

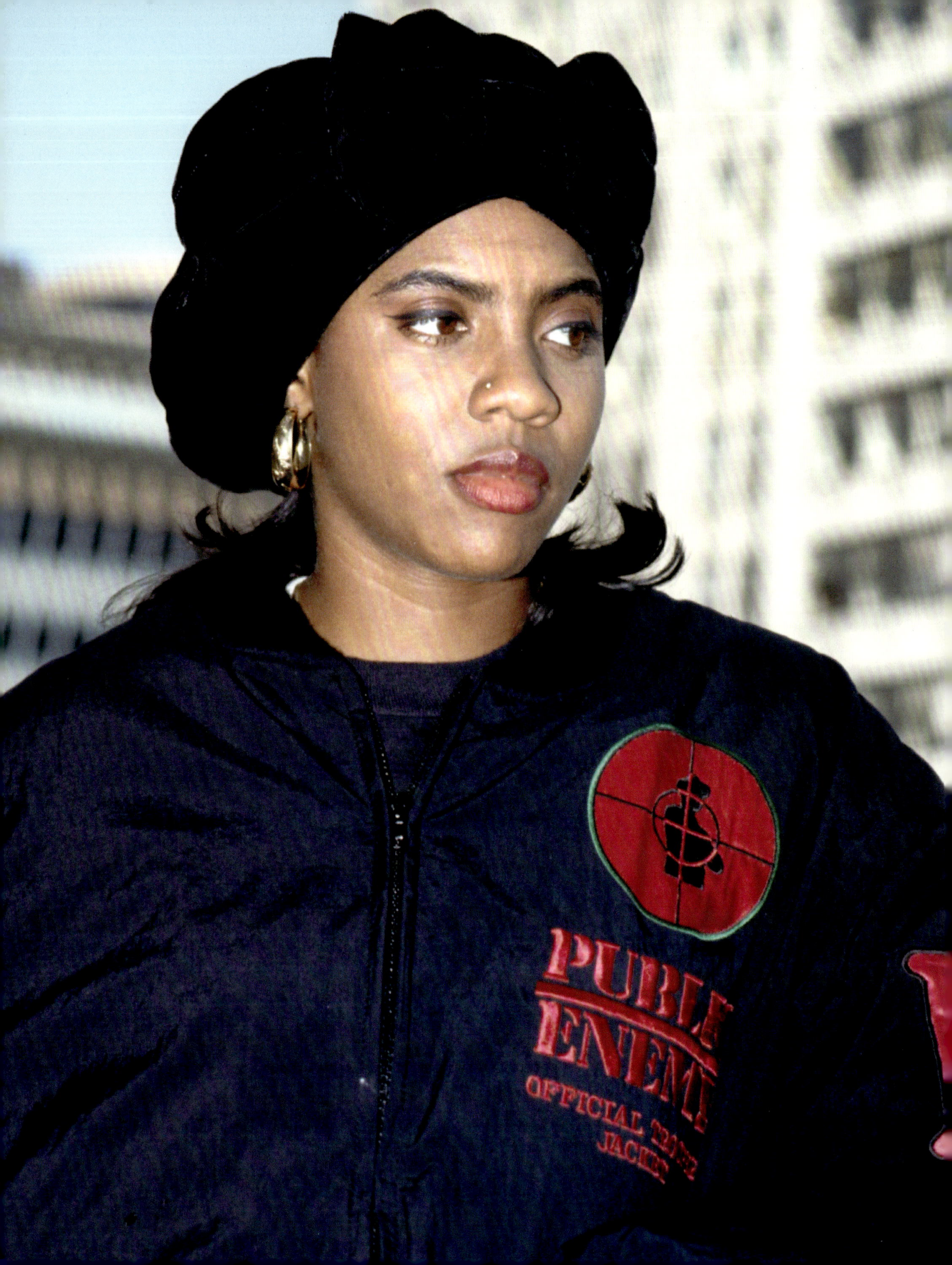
OFFICIAL

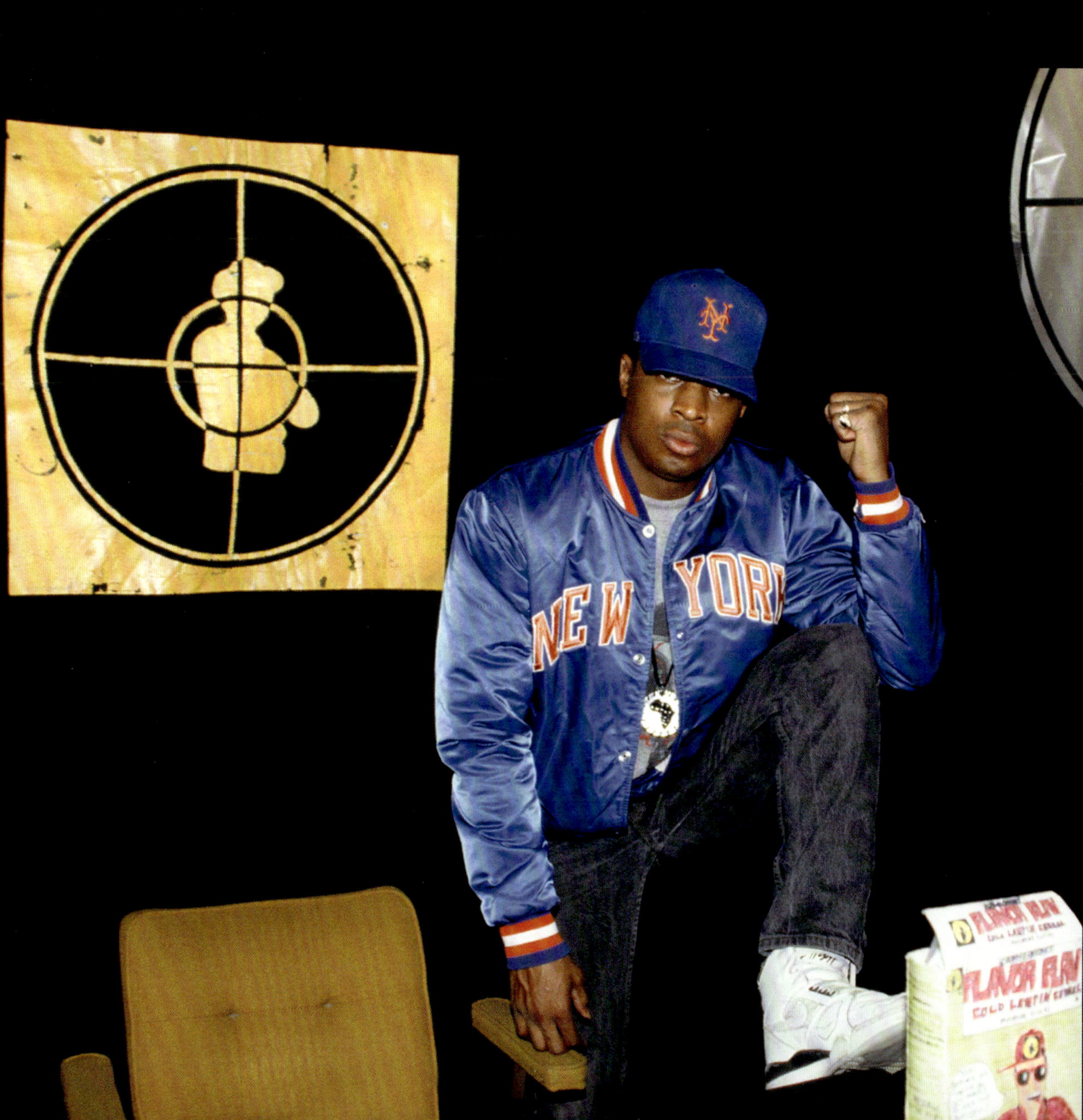
NEW YORK
FLAVOR FLAV

p.02-03 Grandmaster Flash at MARS (formerly on 13th Street and 10th Avenue), NYC, 1989; p.04-05 Queen Latifah, Tupac Shakur and DJ Kid Capri on the stairway of the Apollo Theatre, Harlem, NYC, 1991; p.06 Flava Flav, The Tunnel, NYC, 1989; p.07 Busta Rhymes, The Roxy, NYC, 1989; p.08-09 The Notorious B.I.G., Times Square, 1994; P.10 Run-DMC, Dakota Studio, 1990; P.11 Rakim Allah, performing at the Apollo Theatre for the *Paid In Full* tour, Harlem, NYC, 1987; p.12 Naughty By Nature, Peter Bodtke Studio, Jersey City, New Jersey, 1994; p.13 The Fugees at the Naughty Gear Store, Newark, NJ, 1994; p.14 Eazy-E with Above The Law at Time Café, Union Square, NYC, 1990; p.15 Dre from S1W with Ice Cube, Harlem, NYC, 1991 (S1W, Security of the First World, is part of Public Enemy); p.16 MC Lyte, wearing my Public Enemy jacket with the Chrysler Bldg in the background, NYC, 1991; p.17 Chuck D of Public Enemy, Soho, NYC, 1988; p.18-19 Nas with eagle-shaped clouds on West 42nd Street, NYC, during a break from the video shoot for "If I Ruled the World (Imagine That)," 1996. We saw the clouds and I asked him to mimic them, and we were both moved by the forms they made and saw it as a sign. One of my deepest hip-hop images.

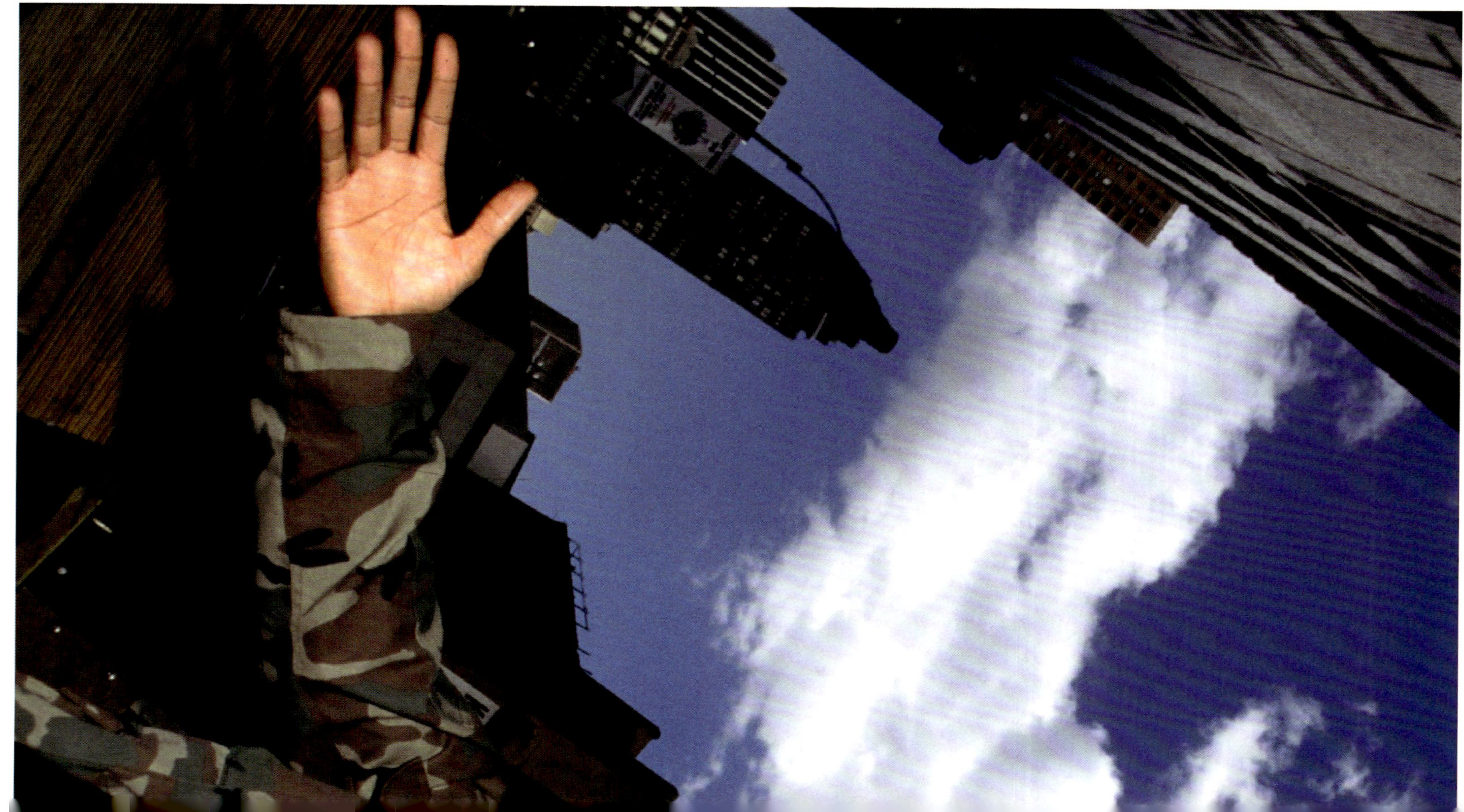

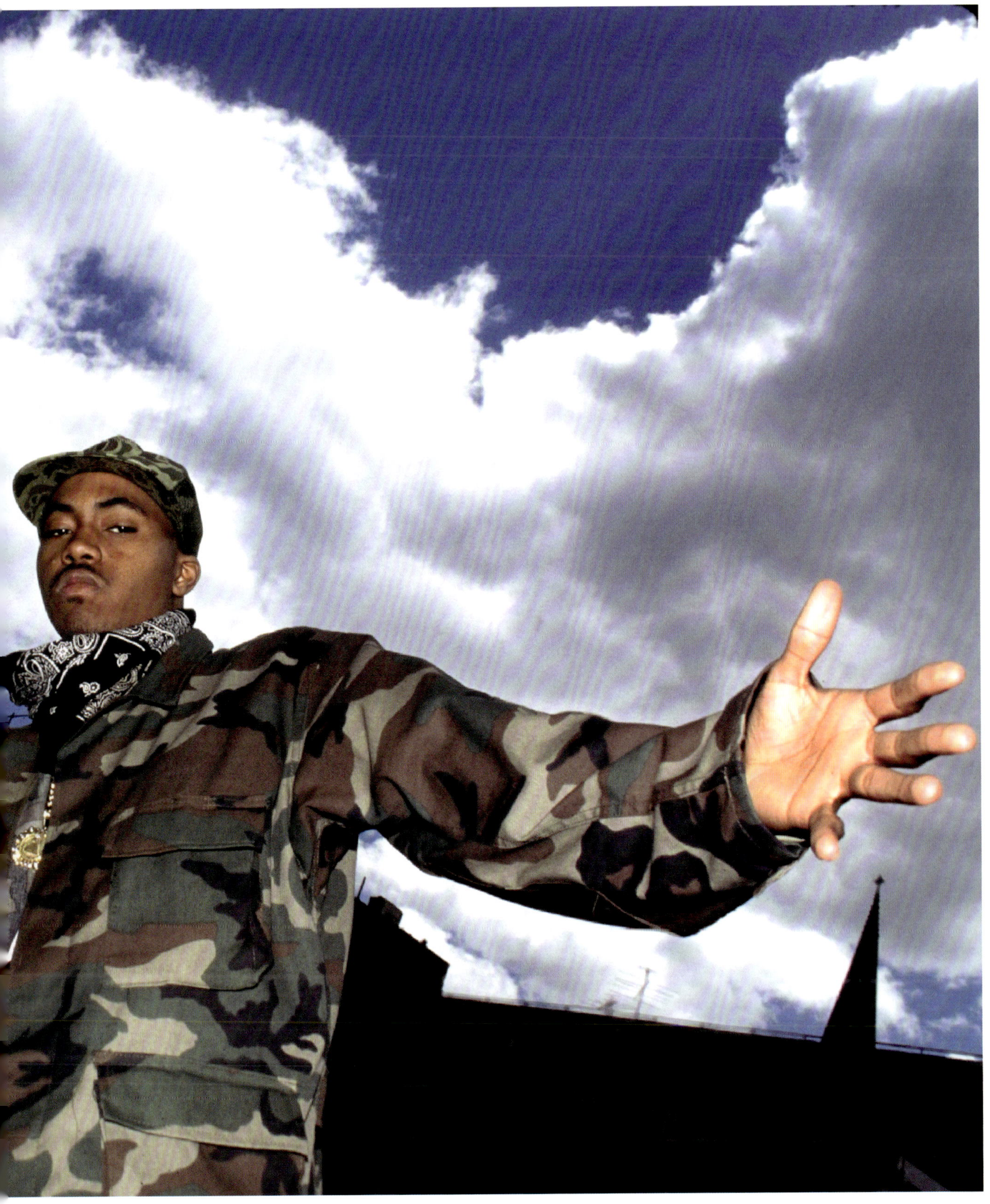

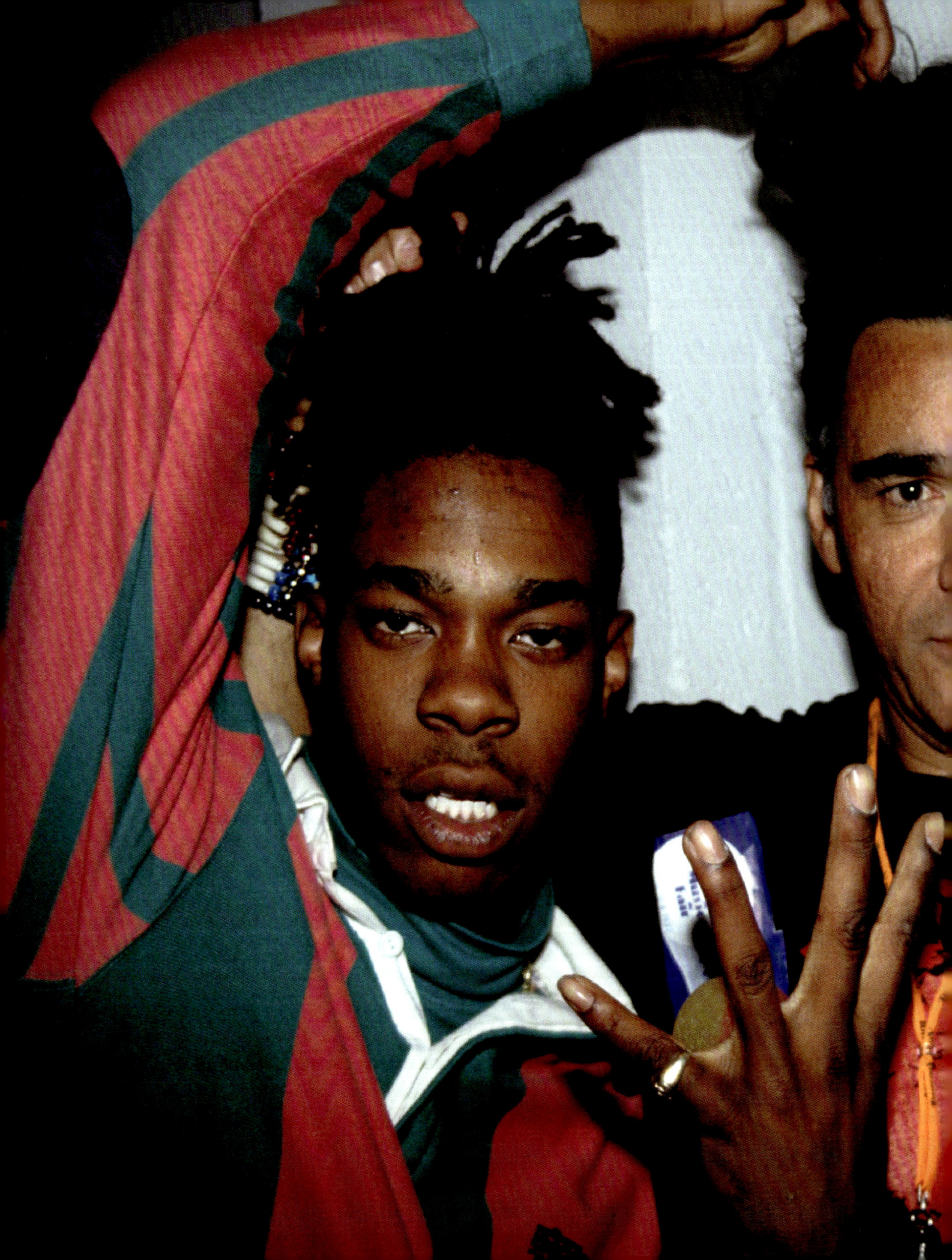

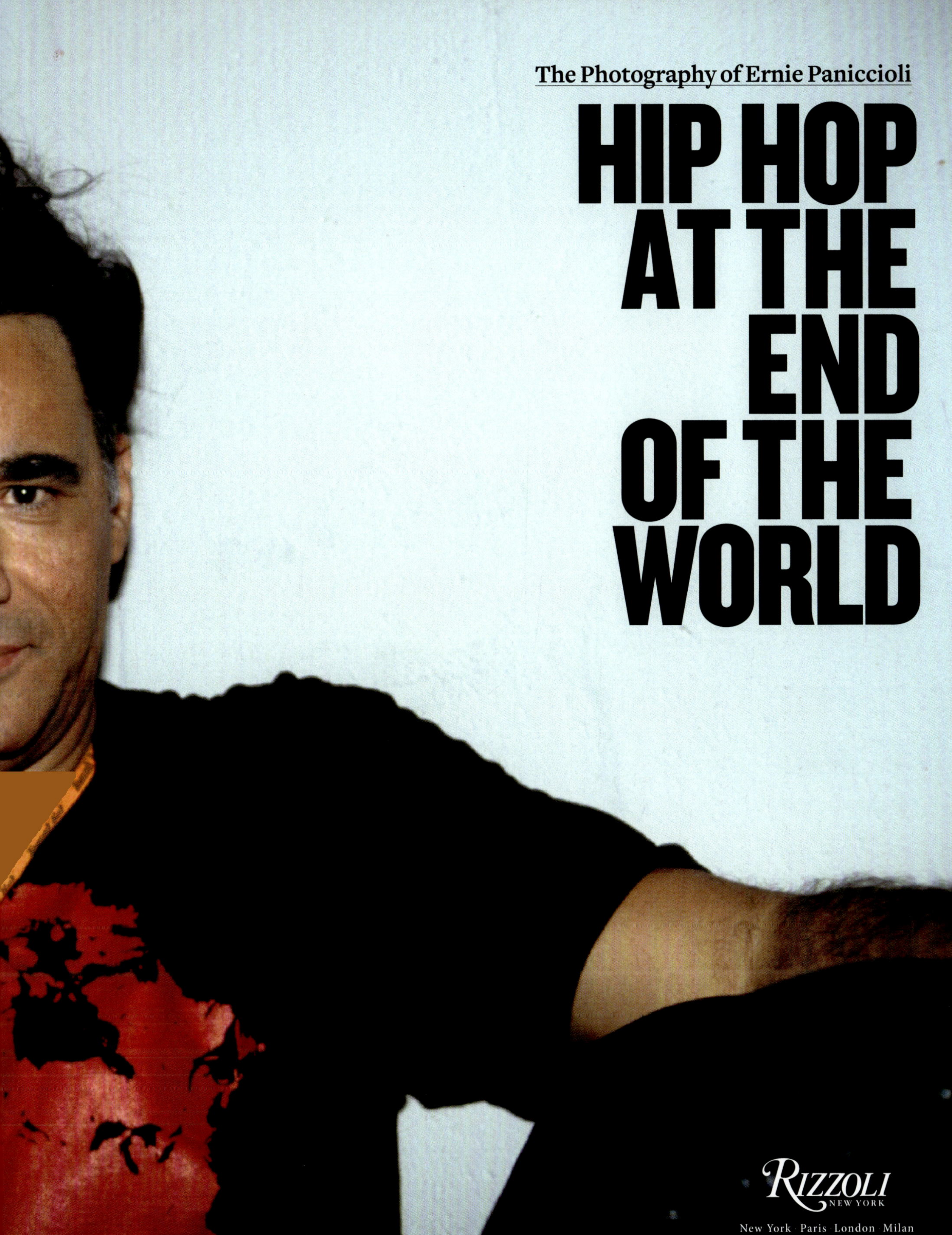

The Photography of Ernie Paniccioli

HIP HOP AT THE END OF THE WORLD

RIZZOLI
NEW YORK

New York · Paris · London · Milan

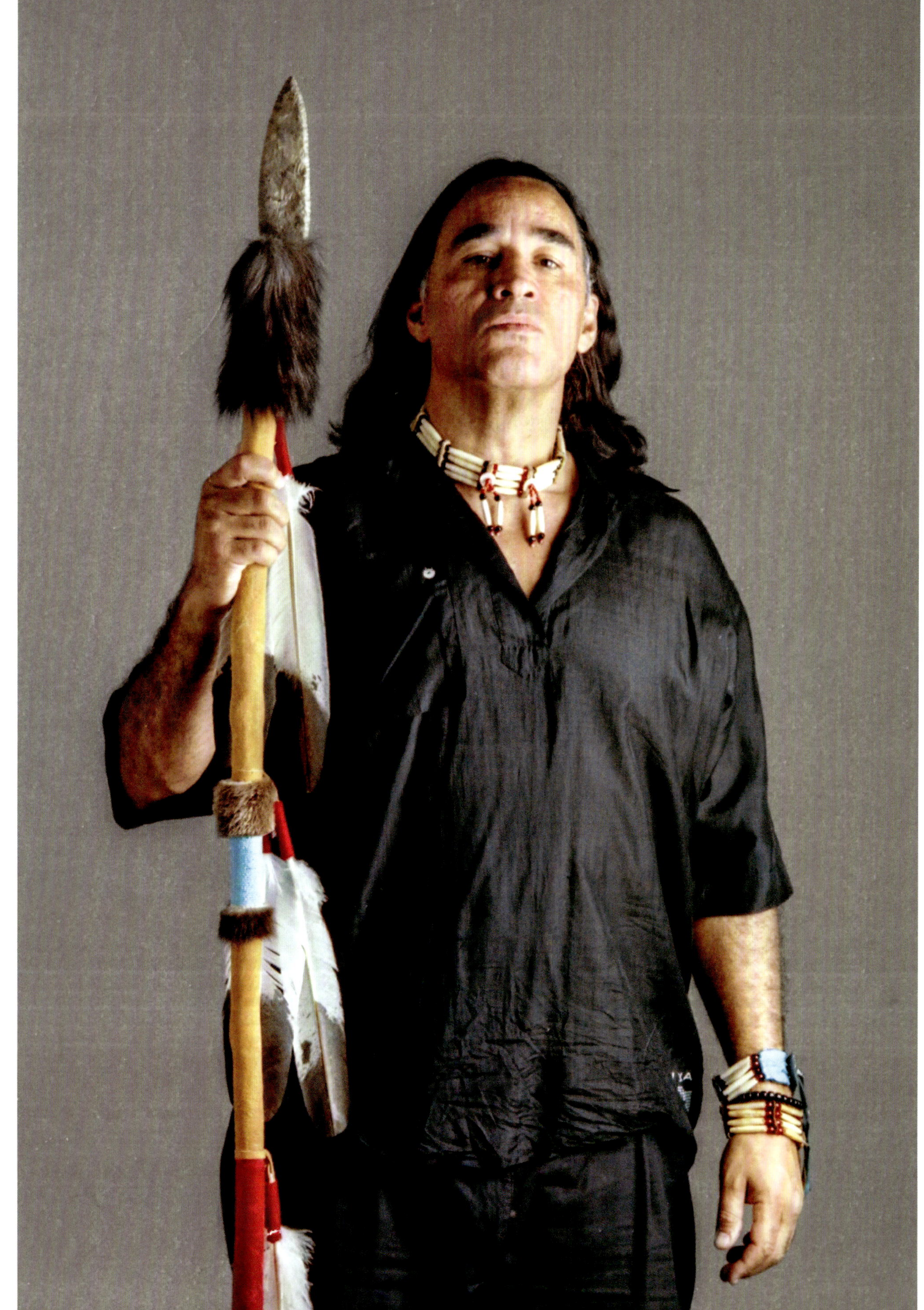

HAIL TO THE CHIEF

A Conversation with Brother Ernie Paniccioli and Ian Luna

In a career spanning over forty years, Ernest "Brother Ernie" Paniccioli amassed what is arguably the largest photographic record of the golden age of hip-hop. Born and raised in Brooklyn, Brother Ernie picked up a camera in 1973 to photograph graffiti art, music, dance and streetwear in the city, and in due course shot nearly every rapper, DJ or group of note for much of the 1980s and 1990s. The principal photographer for magazines such as *Word Up!* and *Rap Masters*, Brother Ernie's archive of nearly 250,000 photographs was acquired for preservation by Cornell University in 2013, and he was inducted into the Hip-hop Hall of Fame the following year (in the same class as the Sugar Hill Gang, Charlie Ahearn, Spoonie G & The Treacherous Three).

A Native-American and First Nations activist, Brother Ernie holds the title of Supreme Minister of Culture for the Universal Zulu Nation, and regularly speaks at colleges and universities on issues affecting indigenous peoples and other communities of color. He sat down with Ian Luna in April 2018 to share some essential biography and many untold stories from a life taking pictures.

Ernie: I'm from South Brooklyn. My mother is Julia. She is native, Cree, and her people are from Canada, and from Pennsylvania, the mines. I am the oldest of three children. Jimmy and Ray were my brothers, and Ray passed away a few years ago.

My father is Tony. I was raised without a father so I have no links to him whatsoever. And the few times that I've tried to talk to him was literally like talking to a person from Mars. So I had to keep inventing fathers, you know. I'd walk down the street, be in a good mood, see a man holding a little boy's hand and break out in tears.

Brooklyn where I grew up, on Union and Fifth, was pretty cool except that I didn't look like everybody else and they would call me Geronimo or half-breed or spic and every day would be a fight. I was not a big kid, and around 10 or 11 I joined a black gang, the Bishops, because one day they saw me getting my ass whooped by about six guys. And three of them came over and beat the shit out of the six. And they said "do you want to join a gang?" I'm standing there all bloody and shitty and I said they didn't have to ask twice. From that day on nobody ever put a hand on me.

p.20-21
Busta Rhymes and Brother Ernie, Westbury Music Fair, Long Island, New York, 1989.

Left:
Portrait of Brother Ernie at Maggie Trakus Studio, Soho, NYC. Photo by Maggie Trakus, 1991.

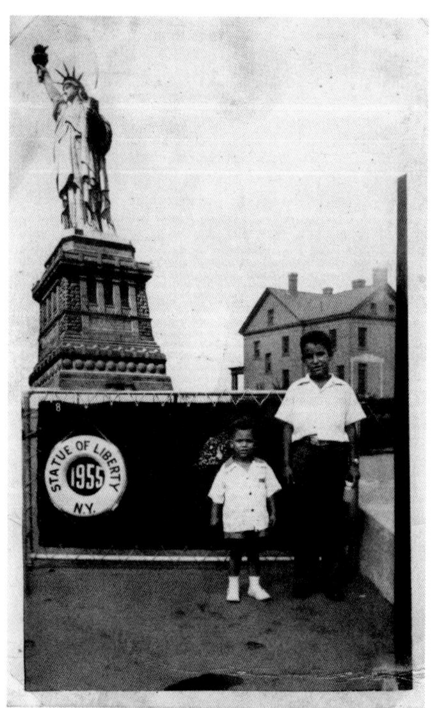

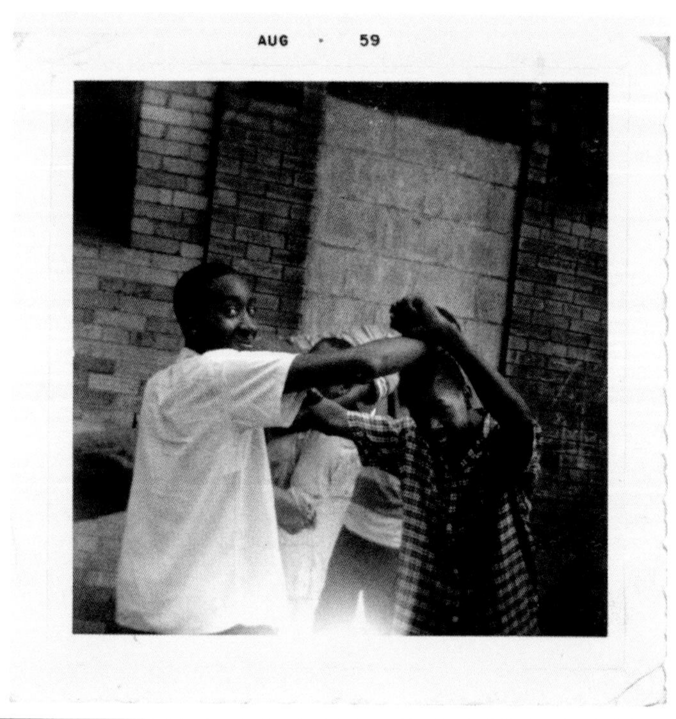

(Left) Ernie at eight years old, with his late brother Ray, who passed away in 2016. Liberty Island, NYC, 1955; (Right) Leroy Barnes and James, members of the Bishops, a gang that Ernie joined. St. Marks Avenue, Brooklyn, NY, 1959.

I went to Catholic school. And a lot of times my mother had a choice between food and rent. You know that movie *Sophie's Choice*? Well that was Julia's Choice. She had three children and when you have a choice between paying rent, feeding your kids, and being kicked out into the street, I don't know how anyone deals with that. I left home at about 13 and I started living in the Village and hanging out. And I met the man who became my personal guru and spirit guide, the musician Richie Havens. We were best friends. I got pictures of him from back then. The day I turned 18, I joined the Navy and I served for six years, from March of 1965.

I BOUGHT A CAMERA AND I STARTED TAKING PICTURES, AND FROM THE GRAFFITI, I STARTED MEETING THE GRAFFITI KIDS WHO INTRODUCED ME TO THE B-BOYS WHO INTRODUCED ME TO THE DJS

I did that because there was nothing for me in the streets. I wanted that. I saw the world and got an education. The other sailors often called me charismatic. I didn't know what that word meant. I didn't know if it was a skin disease. I really didn't know. But that's what they called me.

Ian Luna: I've seen you whip up a crowd, especially in that YouTube video where you were invited by then minister Conrad Muhammad [of the Nation of Islam] to help mediate in the beef between Wreckx-n-Effect and A Tribe Called Quest at Mosque No. 7 in 1993. You were wearing a bone choker and more importantly, a t-shirt with a picture of the warrior Chief Joseph [of the Nez Perce] on it. You were picked on for being "native" as a kid, but when would you say you acquired the consciousness of being native?

EP: In the first grade because every time I would go to school I would come home and my mother would say what did you learn today? And I would tell her and she would deconstruct it. And she only had a third-grade education because she was kicked out of school for not saluting the flag and not believing the pledge of allegiance, "one nation under God, with liberty and justice..." She said that didn't apply. They threw her out, and yet she had read every book in the library on her own. She was one of the brightest women I know. All that deconstruction made me an activist, it made me look at slavery. Back when I was growing up, slavery was like a skin rash. It was never mentioned in school, not Catholic school, not public school—like colonization and raping of the land and so on.

I was always that one person that would ask these questions. You know if Christians believed in God and that you know all of the wonderful things they say about us all being

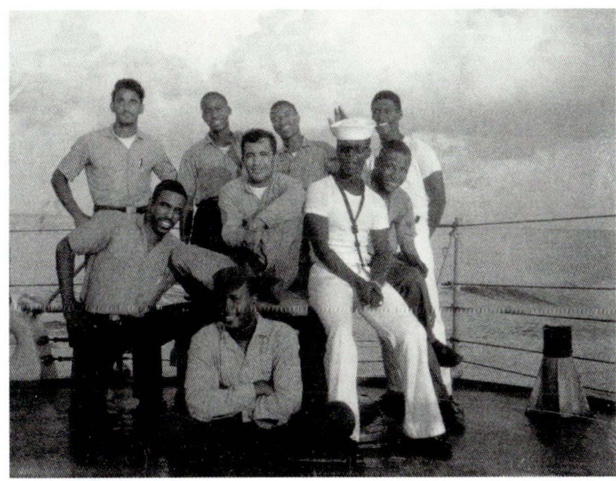

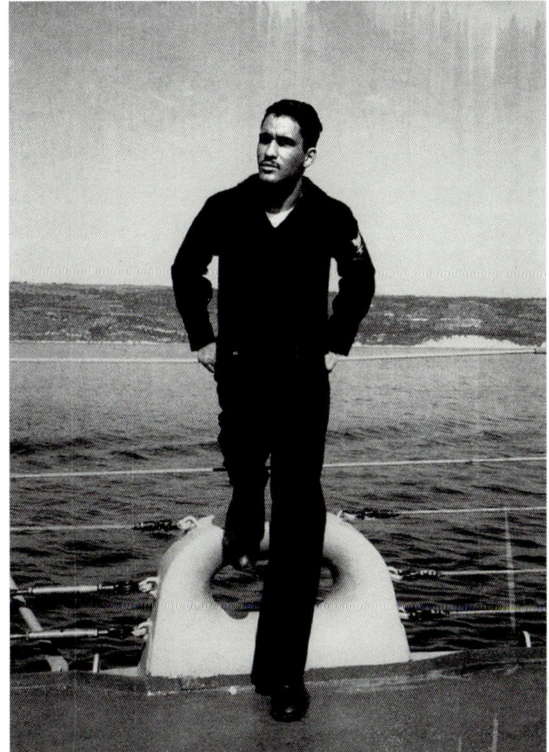

(Top left, middle left, top right, and lower right) Ernie on board the guided missile destroyers USS *Lawrence* (DDG-4) and USS *Ricketts* (DDG-5) 1966-69, where he served as a fire controlman (photographers unknown); (lower left) Richie Havens in his apartment, taken by Ernie, Lower East Side, NYC, 1966.

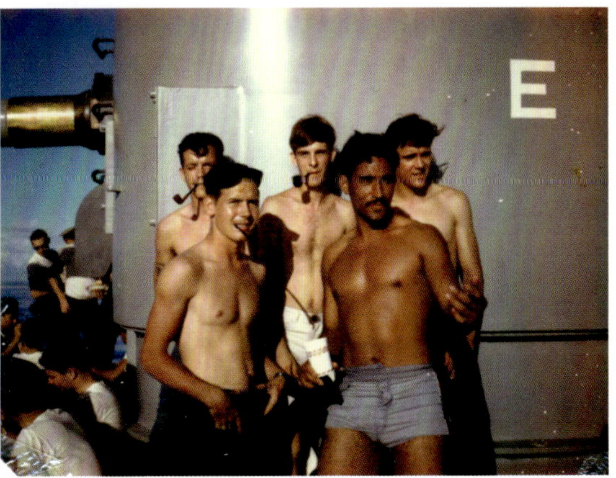

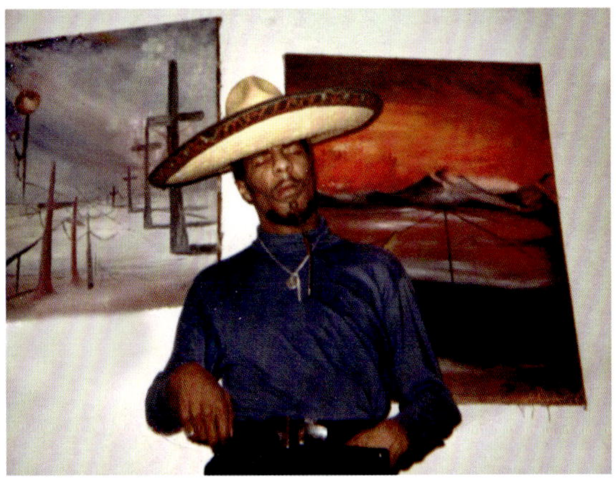

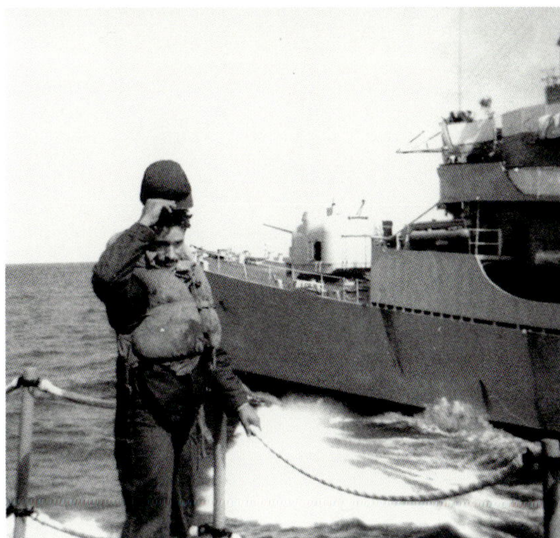

children of God, how could one group enslave another? How could one group colonize another? You know I'd ask these questions, and they went "you'll get that in high school." And in high school, you'll get that in college. In college it's like, "well, that's not relevant."

IL: And then you enlisted. When you got back from the Navy, how did you get into photography?

EP: What happened is that I saw graffiti everywhere. And I'd take people to see it the next day and it was gone and that drove me crazy. So I bought a camera and I started taking pictures, and from the graffiti, I started meeting the graffiti kids who introduced me to the B-boys who introduced me to the DJs who introduced me to the parties and I started going and it became like a passion. And along the way there would always be that one person from a TV station or a magazine or a newspaper that would say, "wow, I wish my editor would focus on this instead of just the crime and the bullshit."

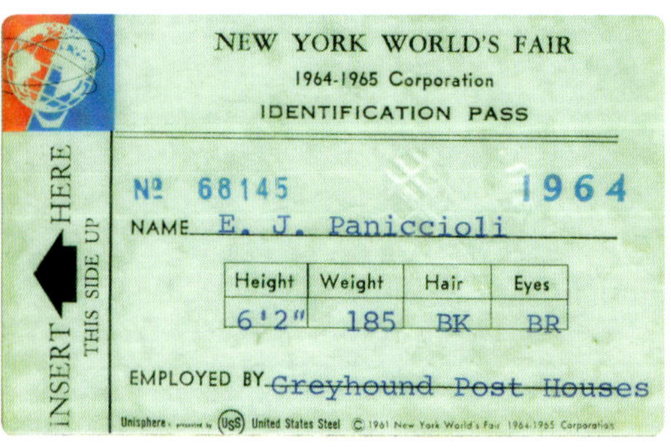

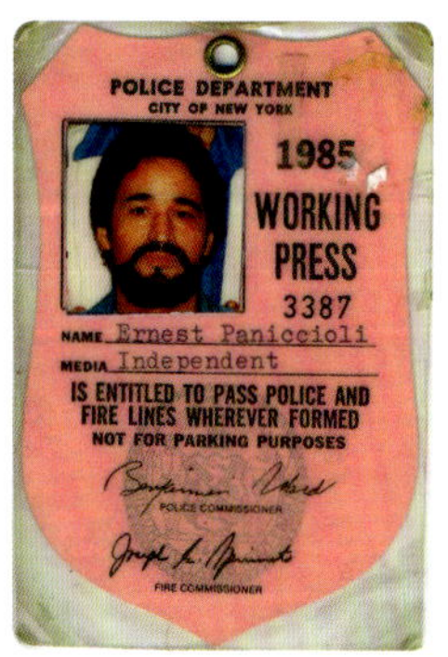

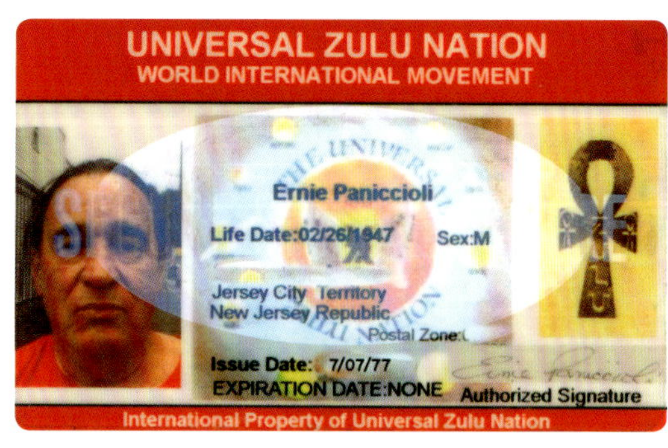

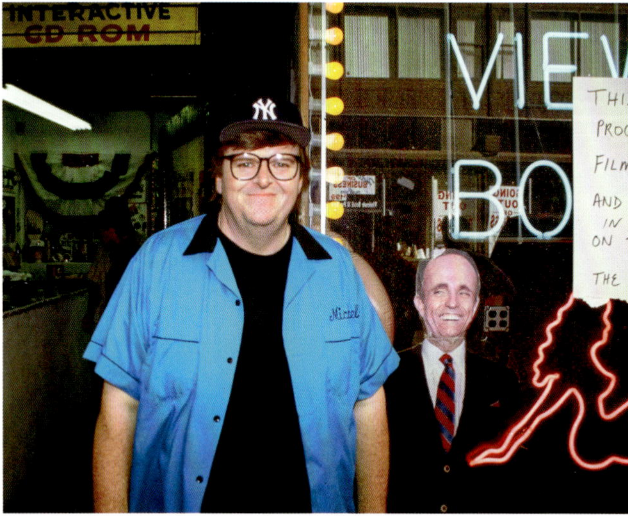

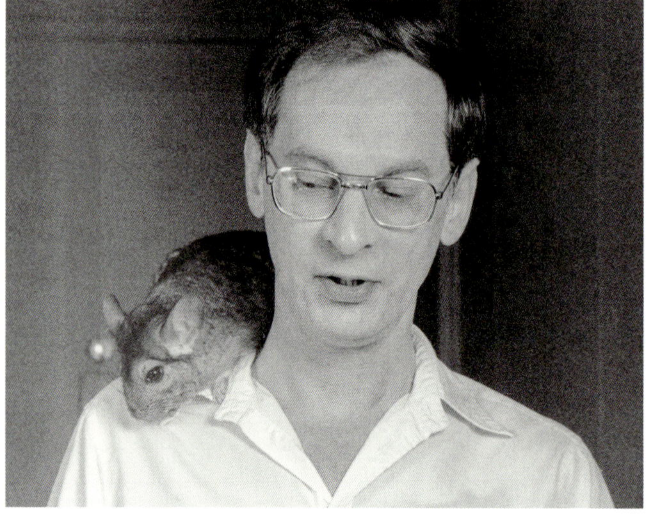

And I became known as the one to go to. I then got a gig with WNBC around 1980, and another with Channel 5, WNEW. [Editor's note: WNEW-TV would later change its call sign to WNYW Fox 5 after it was acquired by Rupert Murdoch's News Corporation.]

And my daughter, Melissa Dawn, came along in 1980, and by the time she was three or four, like every other Spanish girl in the world, she loved Menudo. So I started going to their events and just taking pictures. And I was selling the 4 x 6 pictures for a dollar quicker than I could get them printed to the fan clubs. And sometimes I'd go out just to the little rallies and come home with $1,000 in one-dollar bills. If the cops ever stopped me they'd think I was selling dope or something.

This was in 1983 or '84, but going back a little, my son, Krishna, who was born in 1969, was roller-skating in New York in 1978 and '79, at the Roxy. Everybody was at the Roxy, everybody, Flash, LL, Roxanne Shanté, Run-DMC, they'd all perform. And I'd be there with my camera just doing my thing. So I started getting known as "Ernie the Photographer" which was pretty cool because you could make 100 bucks. Shit I'd work all week and not make 100 bucks after taxes. So it happened like that. Plus my size, you know I never realized this but people looked at me like I had bravado, and they're like, "well, we'll send Ernie."

SEND ERNIE TO THE SOUTH BRONX. SEND ERNIE TO BROWNSVILLE. YOU KNOW BECAUSE ERNIE WAS THIS FEROCIOUS CAT, AND YOU KNOW HE'LL GO ANYWHERE

"Send Ernie to the South Bronx. Send Ernie to Brownsville. You know because Ernie was this ferocious cat, and you know he'll go anywhere."

IL: You're six foot two.

EP: Yeah, and 260 pounds. A martial artist, and an ex-boxer, and growing up where I grew up, that was no big deal, you know. Anywhere I went was fucking better than where I grew up so...

IL: So how did you get to the political work? Do you recall the moment when you started covering municipal politics? The mid- to late 1980s saw a succession events that brought

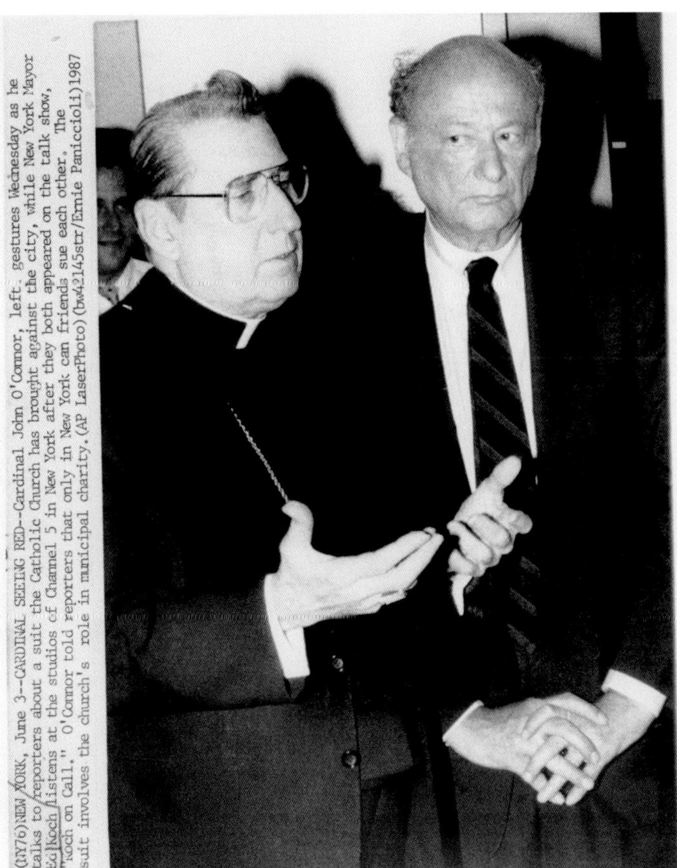

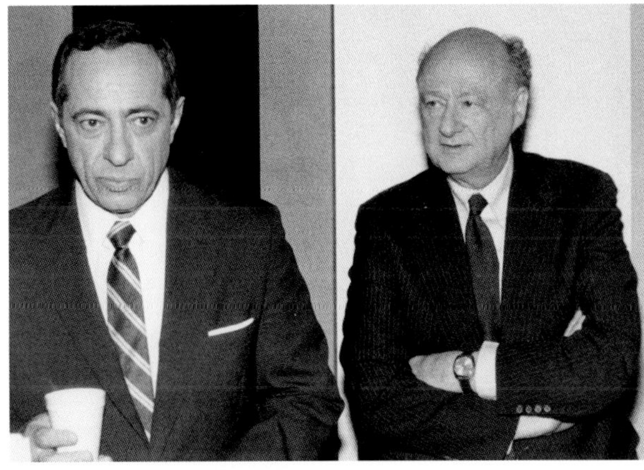

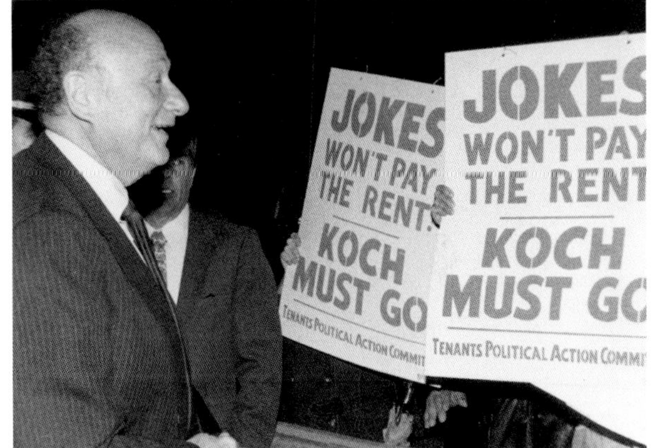

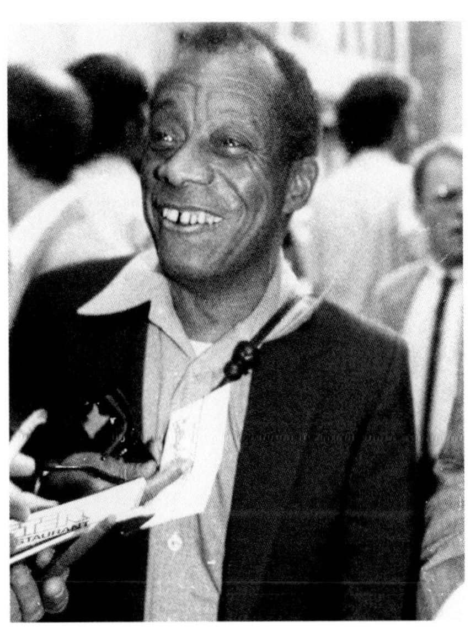

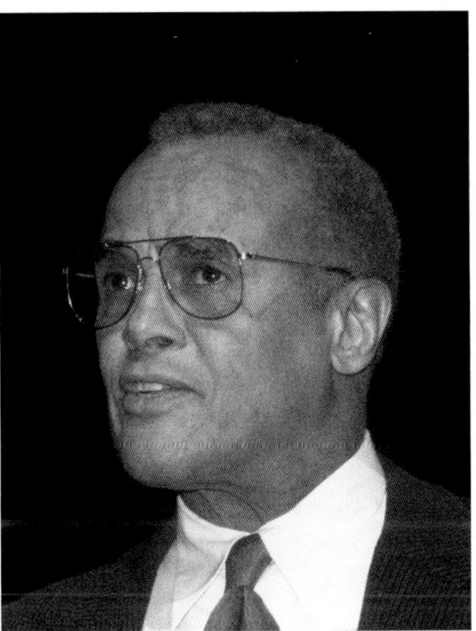

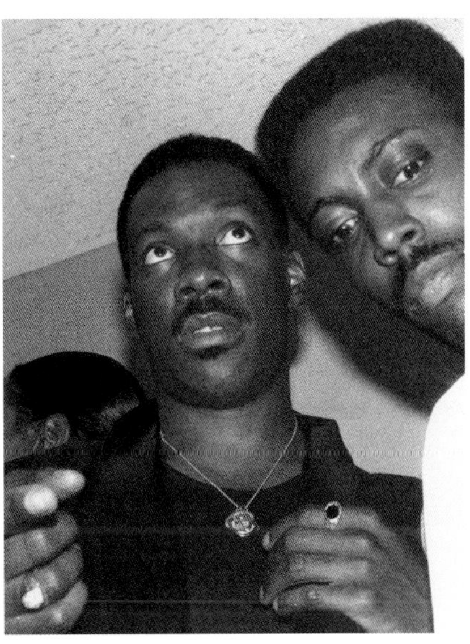

p.26 (Top row, left to right) Ernie's ID for the Greyhound Post Houses, the restaurant concession operated by Greyhound Lines inside the 1964 World's Fair in Queens, NYC; Ernie's 1985 press pass, issued annually through the NYPD; Brother Ernie's current Universal Zulu Nation ID, first issued to him in 1977. He holds the title of Supreme Minister of Culture in the movement; (bottom row, left to right) Still by Ernie of the pilot of *The Michael Moore Show*. Times Square, NYC, 1997; Ernie's portrait of the "Subway Gunman" Bernard Goetz, in his living room on West 14th Street with a guinea pig, where he spent hours discussing ferret feces. NYC, 1985 or 1986.

p.27 (Top left, top right, middle right) Ernie worked for a time as the still photographer on the WNEW-TV Channel 5 show *Koch on Call* featuring Mayor Ed Koch, seen here with two of his nemeses, Cardinal John O'Connor and Governor Mario Cuomo, NYC, 1988; (bottom row) Ernie's pictures of James Baldwin , Harry Belafonte, Eddie Murphy, and Arsenio Hall, all from the mid to late 1980s.

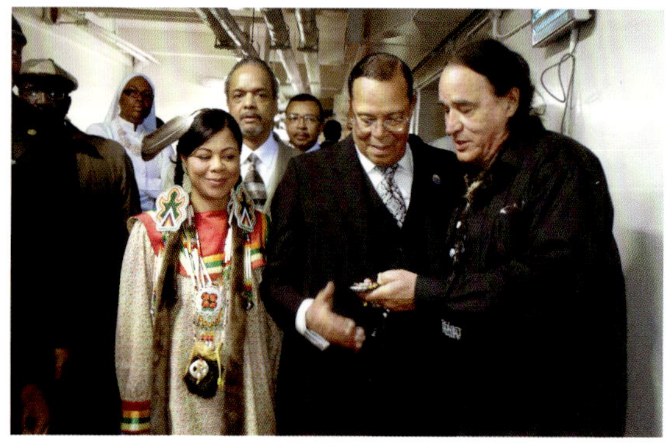

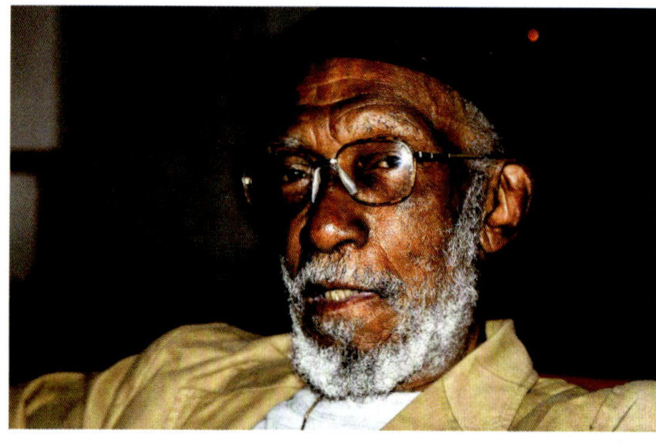

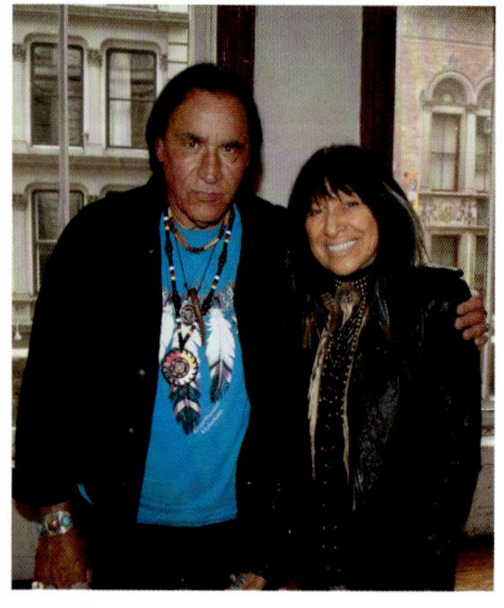

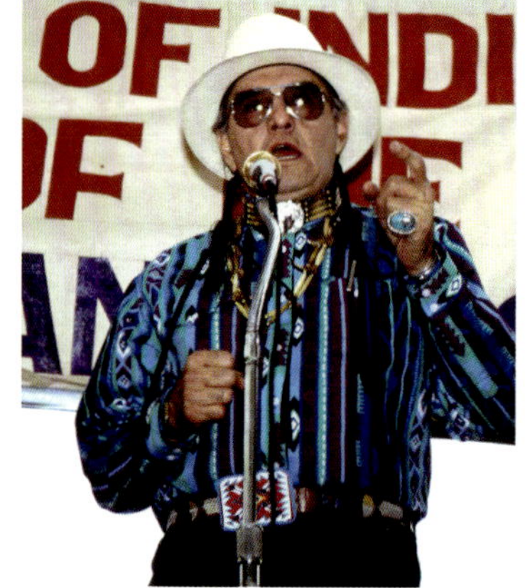

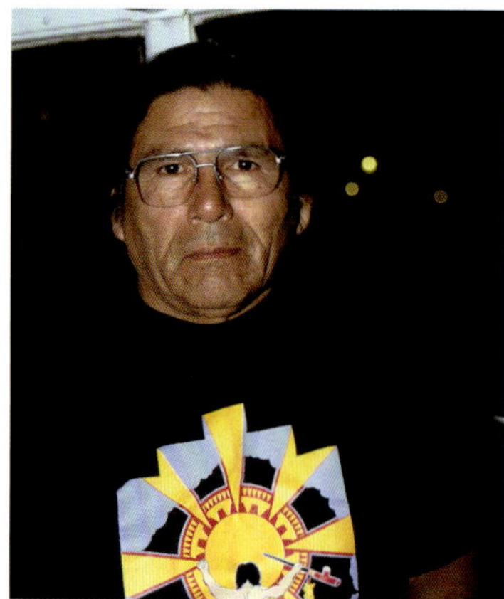

(Top row, left to right) Ernie in discussion with Shinnecock tribal member Nicky Banks and Rev. Louis Farrakhan, leader of The Nation of Islam, Newark, New Jersey, 2016, (photographer uncredited); Ernie's portrait of Sam Greenlee, author of the controversial 1968 novel *The Spook Who Sat By The Door,* about the first black CIA officer, Harlem, NYC, 2015; (bottom row, left to right) Ernie with the legendary Grammy-award winning singer and Native American rights activist Buffy Saint Marie, who was in New York for a concert and to be interviewed by Ernie for *Rumble, The Indians Who Rocked The World*, which won the Documentary Special Award at Sundance, NYC, 2016 (photographer uncredited); American Indian Movement leader Vernon Bellecourt at the United Nations, NYC, around 1980; Dennis Banks was an Anishinaabe Native American activist, teacher, and author. He was a longtime leader of the American Indian Movement (AIM), which he co-founded in 1968, Greenwich Village, 1980.

simmering racial tensions in New York City to a boil, from the fatal beating of Willie Turks, Bernie [Bernhard] Goetz staging *Death Wish* on the IRT, the murder of Michael Griffiths in Howard Beach, the Tawana Brawley rape scandal, and the arrest of the Central Park Five. How did what I would call the "Gabe Pressman metro beat" impact the way you covered hip-hop?

EP: There was a supreme irony before I even answer that question. In the hip-hop world, I was around the top graffiti artists. I would watch them, I would follow them, I would photograph them. And at night I'd be shooting stills for a TV show called *Koch on Call* and I'd be working with Mayor Ed Koch. And the mayor hated graffiti like Trump hates Mexicans. His whole thing was that we need to castrate them, jail them, hang them dogs and criminals. Koch had a fetish about graffiti. I mean he just thought they were wretched, horrible people. "It's not art, it's garbage." And the irony is that during the day, I'm with the graffiti artists and during the night I'm with their nemesis.

And you know some of what he said was correct. And I gave credit to Koch back then, I'll give it to him now. If you were a working person or you had to get on the trains, and back then the sound system either it didn't exist or it sounded like Tibetan. So you couldn't look out the window and see what station you were at because the windows were all painted over. So you basically couldn't sit, you had to stand by the door and watch and hope you got your station right going to work or going home.

There is some serious art-revisionism now, thanks to Henry Chalfant, Martha Cooper, and Charlie Ahern, who were all friends of mine, who did great books and movies about graffiti. It was all beautiful and perfect and artistic. The truth was for every "burner," as they call it, for every great piece of work, there were maybe thousands that looked like dog shit. If you're editing a book and I show you a picture of something that looks like it was done by tying a brush to a dog's tail, you'd be like "Ernie we can't put that in the book."

And I was one of a few people who photographed the real good art but also the pieces of shit. So Koch, as odious as he was towards graffiti artists, still had a point. A lot of it was plain vandalism and it was horrible. I was one of a very few people that had a foot in each camp but that respected the really serious people like Tats Cru and Vulcan and you know Lee...

IL: —Lee Quinones

EP: I had great respect for them but I also had respect people who didn't want their house looking like a shit storm. I was what they would call a moderate.

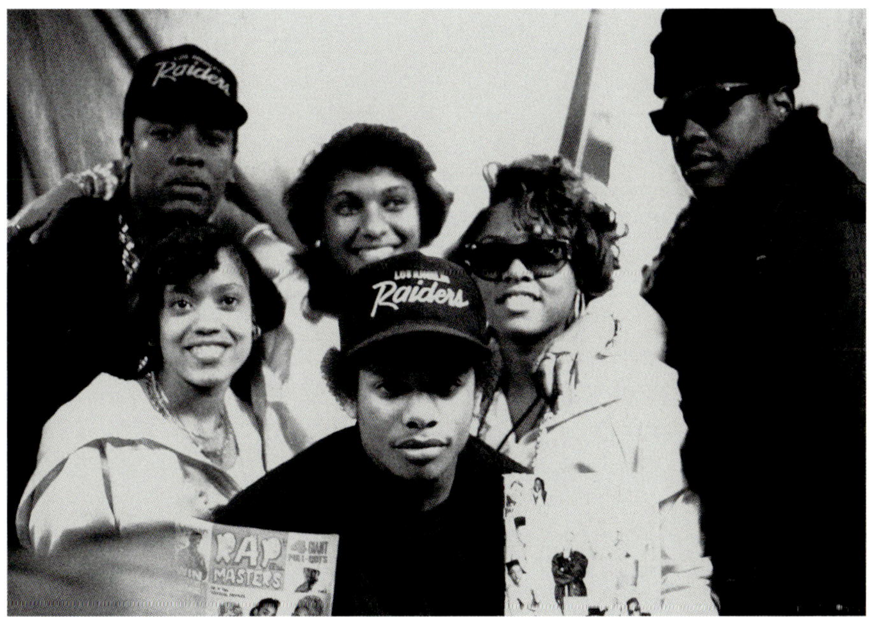

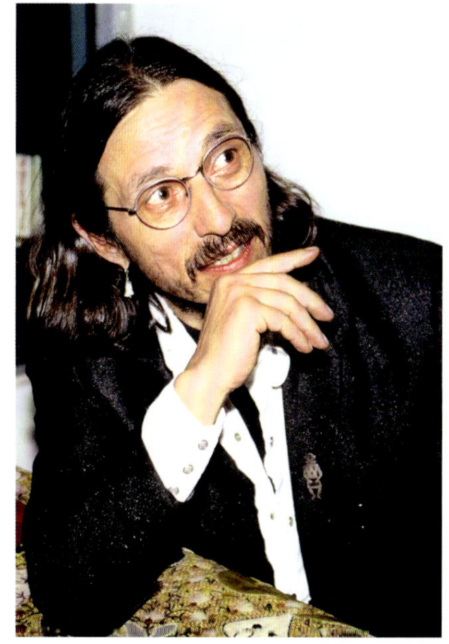

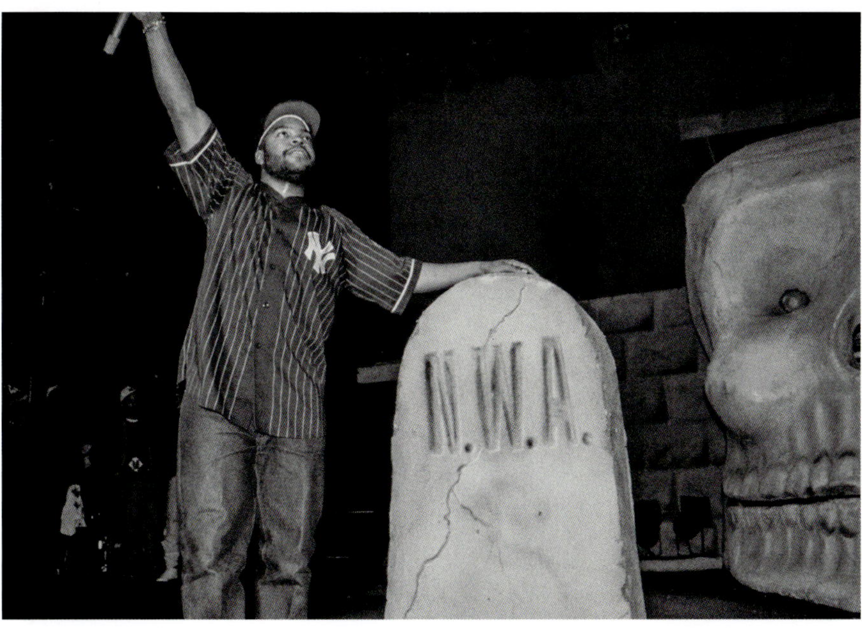

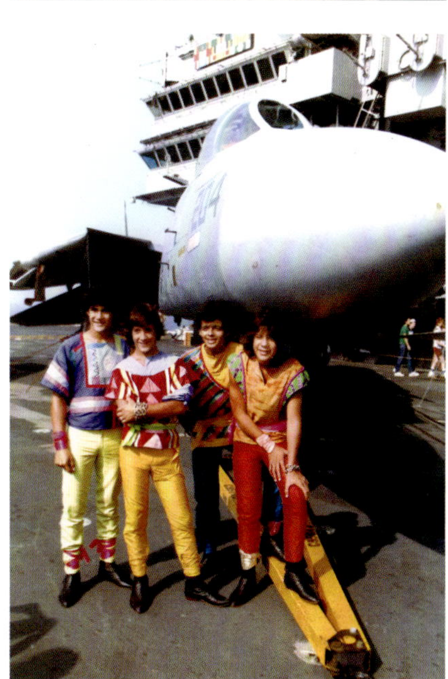

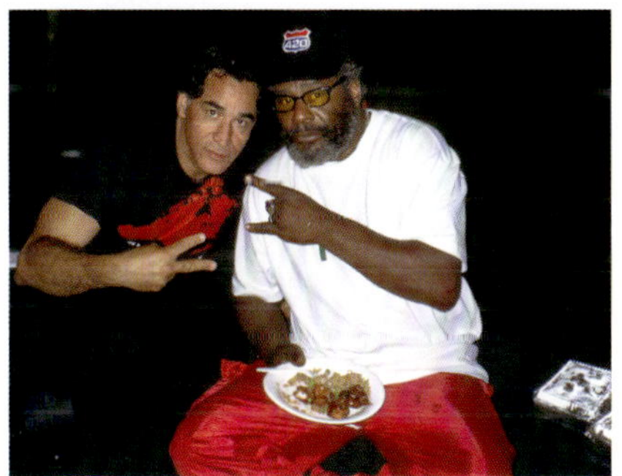

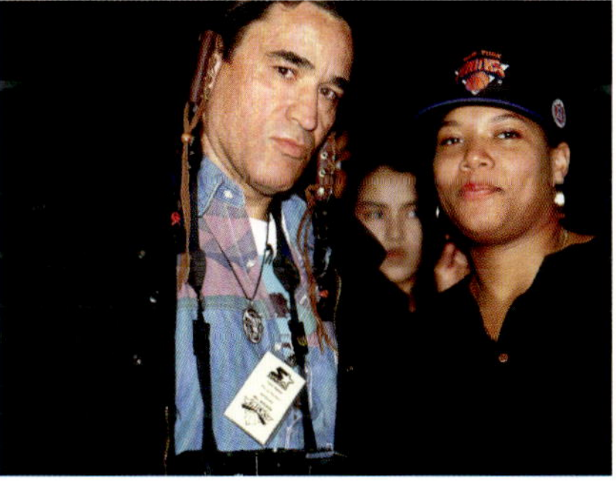

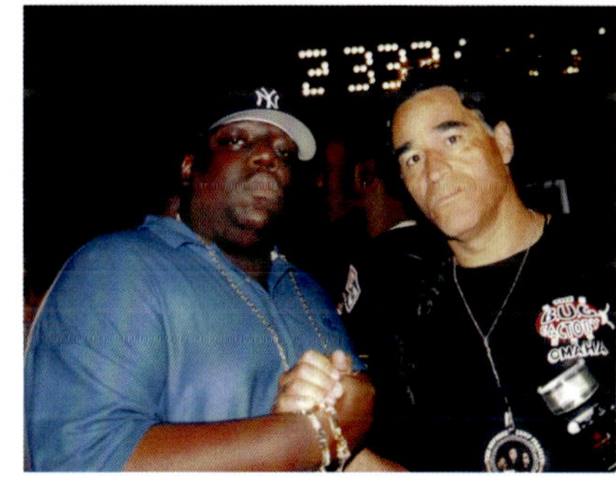

(Clockwise from top left) Dr. Dre, Eazy-E and J. J. Fad, Apollo Theatre, Harlem, NYC, 1987; John Trudell (1946-2015), American Indian Movement (AIM) leader, poet, singer, actor, author and a huge influence on me, 1994; Menudo, the Puerto Rican supergroup, on the USS *Intrepid*, NYC, 1984; Ernie with the Notorious B.I.G., Times Square, NYC, 1996 (Photo by Sean Gutridge); Ernie with Queen Latifah, Sports Café, NYC, 1997 (photographer uncredited); Ernie with George Clinton, shot by Da Brat, Sony Studio, NYC, 2000; Ice Cube, Apollo Theatre, Harlem, NYC, 1990.

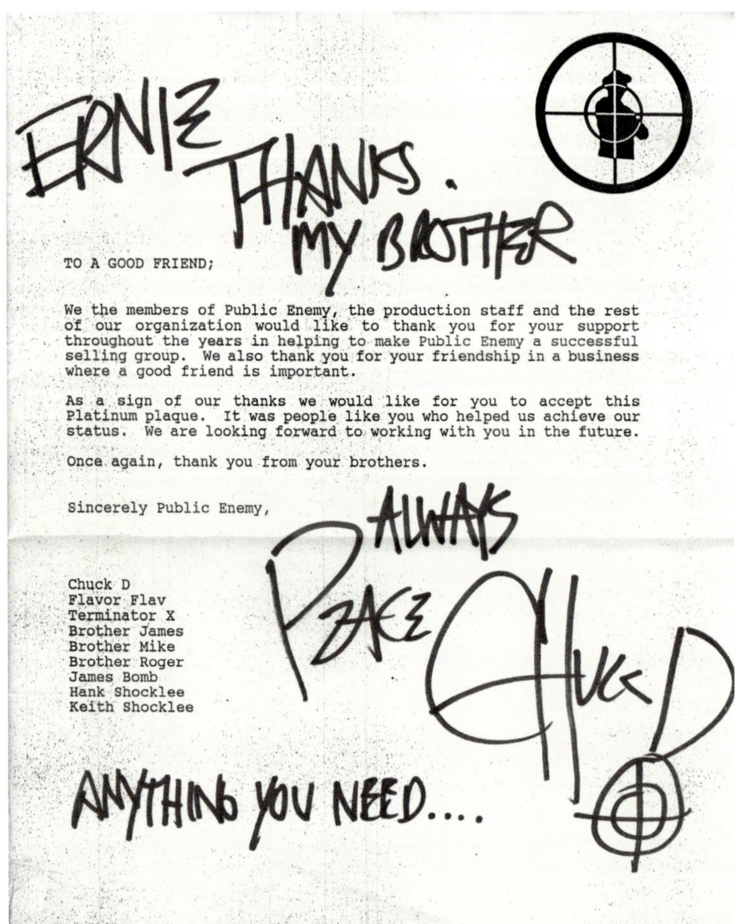

ERNIE THANKS. MY BROTHER

TO A GOOD FRIEND;

We the members of Public Enemy, the production staff and the rest of our organization would like to thank you for your support throughout the years in helping to make Public Enemy a successful selling group. We also thank you for your friendship in a business where a good friend is important.

As a sign of our thanks we would like for you to accept this Platinum plaque. It was people like you who helped us achieve our status. We are looking forward to working with you in the future.

Once again, thank you from your brothers.

Sincerely Public Enemy,

ALWAYS PEACE CHUCK D

Chuck D
Flavor Flav
Terminator X
Brother James
Brother Mike
Brother Roger
James Bomb
Hank Shocklee
Keith Shocklee

ANYTHING YOU NEED....

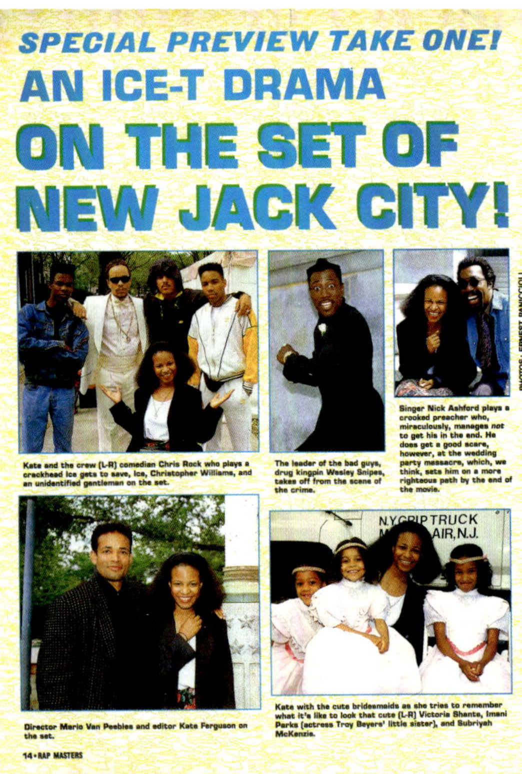

SPECIAL PREVIEW TAKE ONE!

AN ICE-T DRAMA

ON THE SET OF NEW JACK CITY!

Kate and the crew (L-R) comedian Chris Rock who plays a crackhead Ice gets to save, Ice, Christopher Williams, and an unidentified gentleman on the set.

The leader of the bad guys, drug kingpin Wesley Snipes, takes off from the scene of the crime.

Singer Nick Ashford plays a crooked preacher who, miraculously, manages *not* to get his in the end. He does get a good scare, however, at the wedding party massacre, which, we think, sets him on a more righteous path by the end of the movie.

PHOTOS: ERNEST PANICCIOLI

Director Mario Van Peebles and editor Kate Ferguson on the set.

Kate with the cute bridesmaids as she tries to remember what it's like to look that cute (L-R) Victoria Shante, Imani Parks (actress Troy Beyers' little sister), and Subriyah McKenzie.

14 • RAP MASTERS

(Top) Letter from Chuck D of Public Enemy, 1990; (bottom) Ernie's photos from the set of New Jack City as they appeared on *Rap Masters* magazine, 1990.

p.31
(Top) Chuck D, Soho, NYC, 1990; (middle) Doug E. Fresh with mural of Michael Jordan, Harlem, NYC, 1988; Ernie in studio with Naughty By Nature, Jersey City, New Jersey, 1992.

IL: So did the work with Mayor Ed Koch lead to all of the other work where you photograph other newsmakers?

EP: Yes, because what happened is there was a woman who went from one channel to another as a producer and as a publicist, Isabella Fernandez. She wanted to take me on because I'd go anywhere, I'd do anything, and she felt affection for me as a person. She believed in the work, she believed in me. And it was good for her to have a guy you could call, that wouldn't blow you off or fuck it up. You know he'd come back with something.

IL: After Menudo, who was the first person to pay you to start photographing hip-hop? the non-political work?

EP: Believe it or not, the first magazine that printed my hip-hop work was *Teen Machine*. In the mid-80s.

And this goes back to Menudo. My wife is Dominican, who to this day looks like she's twenty, so back then she looked like she was twelve, so she fit in perfectly whenever we'd be at events. She could walk in the crowd and sell the prints I took without the cops hassling us. And you know I obviously looked like a photographer. I'd wear a tie and an overcoat so I'd get into the hotels where Menudo was staying and grab pictures of them in the hallway because I looked official. If I looked like a little Spanish girl that would never happen.

What I did it was probably a great lesson for anybody that reads this. I went to the magazines and I told them that if they'd pay me good, I could get exclusive pictures of Menudo, which was bullshit because at that point, I had not met Menudo. I told them you don't have to pay me until I get the pictures. They were like "why would we publish these pictures of these Spanish kids?" And I showed them pictures of the crowd for thirty blocks in either direction and that schools stopped when these kids were in town. So they were like "oh, okay." I said do you want to sell magazines or you want to just put in the Debbie Gibsons or whoever the fluff-balls are. So they were like holy shit, this guy's serious.

Then I went to Menudo's management and I told them, I said you've got a great thing going. They said "we know that." I then said you could triple your fan base. And they said "well, how could we do that?" And one of them was a real arrogant prick and he said "yeah, Mr. Smart Guy?" I wanted to smack him but instead, I'm going to take money from him. So I told him I said I've got twenty magazines tomorrow, you give me access to these kids, and your pictures will be on the cover of these magazines.

And then everybody shut the fuck up. I just gave them the whole bullshit. But the magazines were going for it.

IL: That's awesome. Menudo was your big break!

EP: I did it on pure balls. I figured the worst they could do was have the goons throw me out. And the worst the magazines could do was tell me to go fuck myself. But when you start talking about money, you know I was serious, and I wasn't giving them a chance to even ask me questions. I just stayed in their face.

THE WORST THEY COULD DO WAS HAVE THE GOONS THROW ME OUT. AND THE WORST THE MAGAZINES COULD DO WAS TELL ME TO GO FUCK MYSELF. BUT WHEN YOU START TALKING ABOUT MONEY, YOU KNOW I WAS SERIOUS

The one magazine I went to first, they were like "okay I'll tell you what, don't even call me." They ended up calling *me*, but I said, "don't call me" because you're going to be the only fucking magazine in town that has no pictures of these kids.

It was all bluff. Then the magazine started really selling, the kids started getting more exposure in a broader sense. Before then they were just in a Latino or a Hispanic thing.

IL: Right. So it was important for you to truly broaden their appeal?

EP: No it wasn't, it was essential that I had a paycheck [laughs].

I was smart enough to realize you know groups come and go. The same thing happened later with New Kids on the Block, with one difference, the manager, Dick Scott was a friend of mine. And they were just a white, Boston version of Menudo.

IL: That's the quote from this interview, the New Kids were "the Boston version of Menudo." [laughs]

EP: Exactly. I mean you have no idea how important emotionally it was to have a Spanish teen group. White people always had somebody. Blacks had the Jackson 5. But Hispanics had nobody.

For Spanish girls, they were bigger than the Beatles. And not just here but in Guatemala, Mexico, Ecuador, Puerto Rico of course... El Salvador, the Philippines, you know and

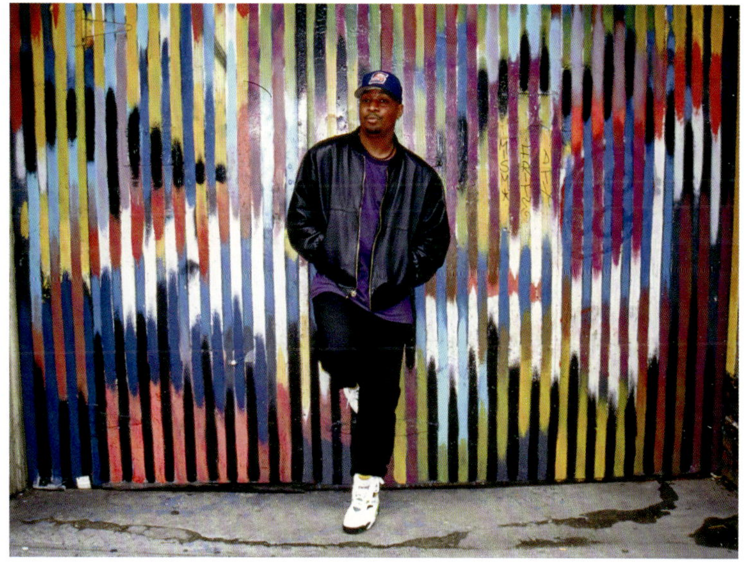

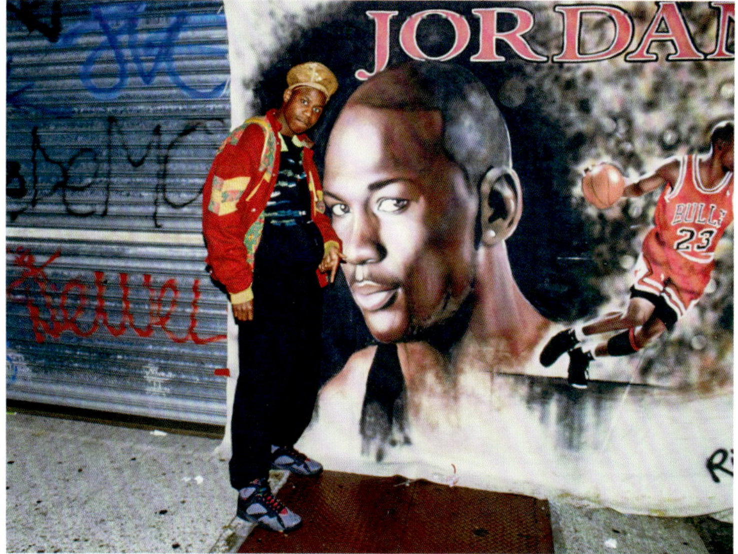

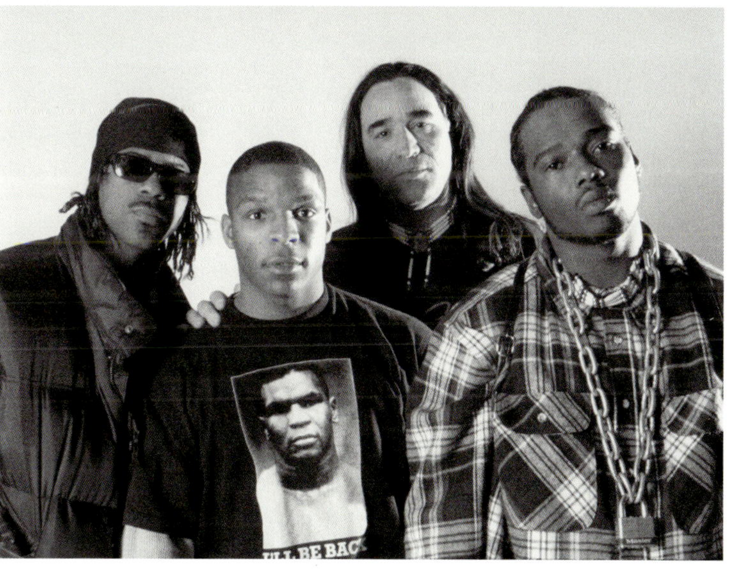

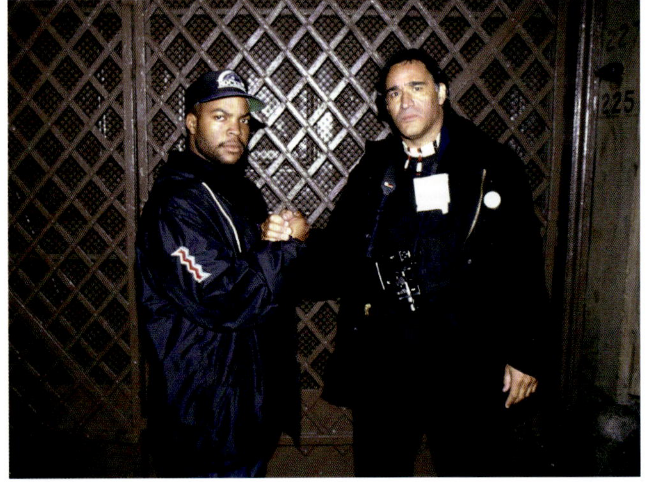

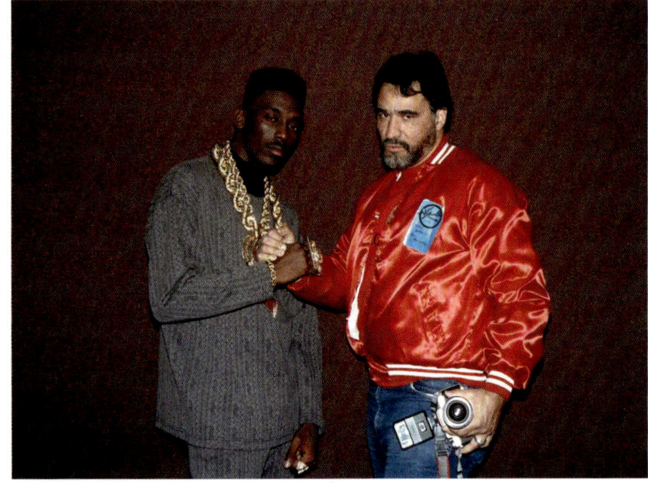

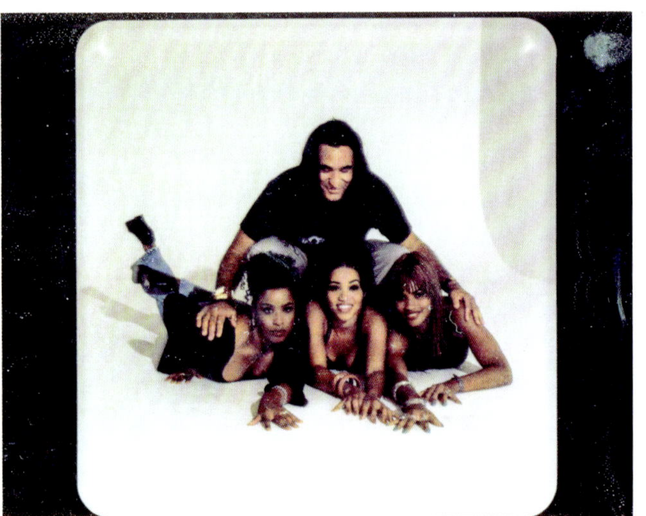

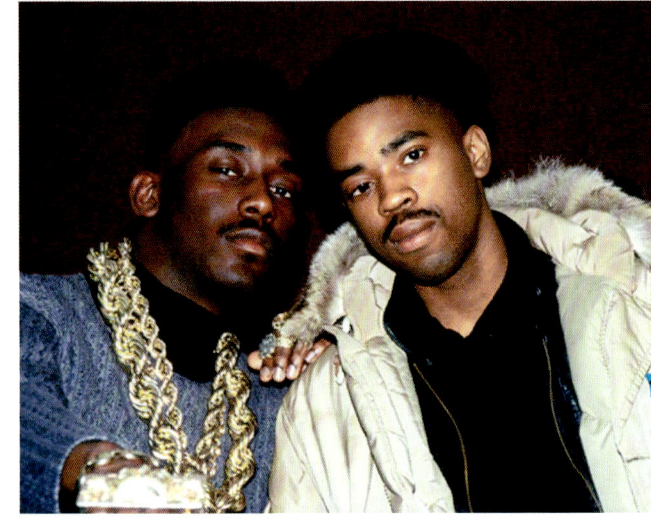

(Clockwise from top left) Ice Cube with Ernie behind the Roseland, NYC, 1991; Big Daddy Kane with Ernie at the Apollo Theatre, Harlem, NYC, 1987 (photographer uncredited); Big Daddy Kane with Slick Rick—without his eyepatch—at the Apollo Theatre, Harlem, NYC, 1987. Polaroid of Ernie with Salt-N-Pepa, Dakota Studios (self-portrait), NYC, 2000.

that's a very important thing and I was lucky and blessed enough to be part of that.

And it was all balls and bluff. That opened up a whole world to me. To *Word Up!* magazine. *Word Up!* wasn't political, it wasn't you know trying to be the blackest or the most hippest sort or most politically conscious. But, the editor, Scott Figman, the reason I wanted to work with him and the reason I stayed with him for 25 years, was he was honest. He paid me.

He said something the day I met him [in 1987] that I felt comfortable with. He said all of these other magazines talk down to their audience. They tell them who to like, who not to like. He said "I want to do it differently. I don't know anything about hip-hop, I don't know anything about rap, I don't know anything. I want the kids to write in and we base the magazine upon fan mail, so that we respect the audience. We look up to them for direction rather than looking down at them just as a commodity." And I was like, "holy shit!"

The only time he and I argued about money is where I'd give him an invoice and he'd say "but you forgot to add this, you forgot to add that." He said to never undercut yourself. I always believe that a fair exchange is no robbery. If you spend $1,100 on film and processing, then that's what you put in. You don't put in $1,300 and you don't put in $900.

That's how I've always been and people respect me for that. There are three things you need to do to earn that respect. Number one, if you say you're gonna do something, you've got to do it. Number two, you've got to keep your promises. Number three, you've got to be aware of people and don't say, "well, he's important, but he's not." Treat everybody with fairness and kindness.

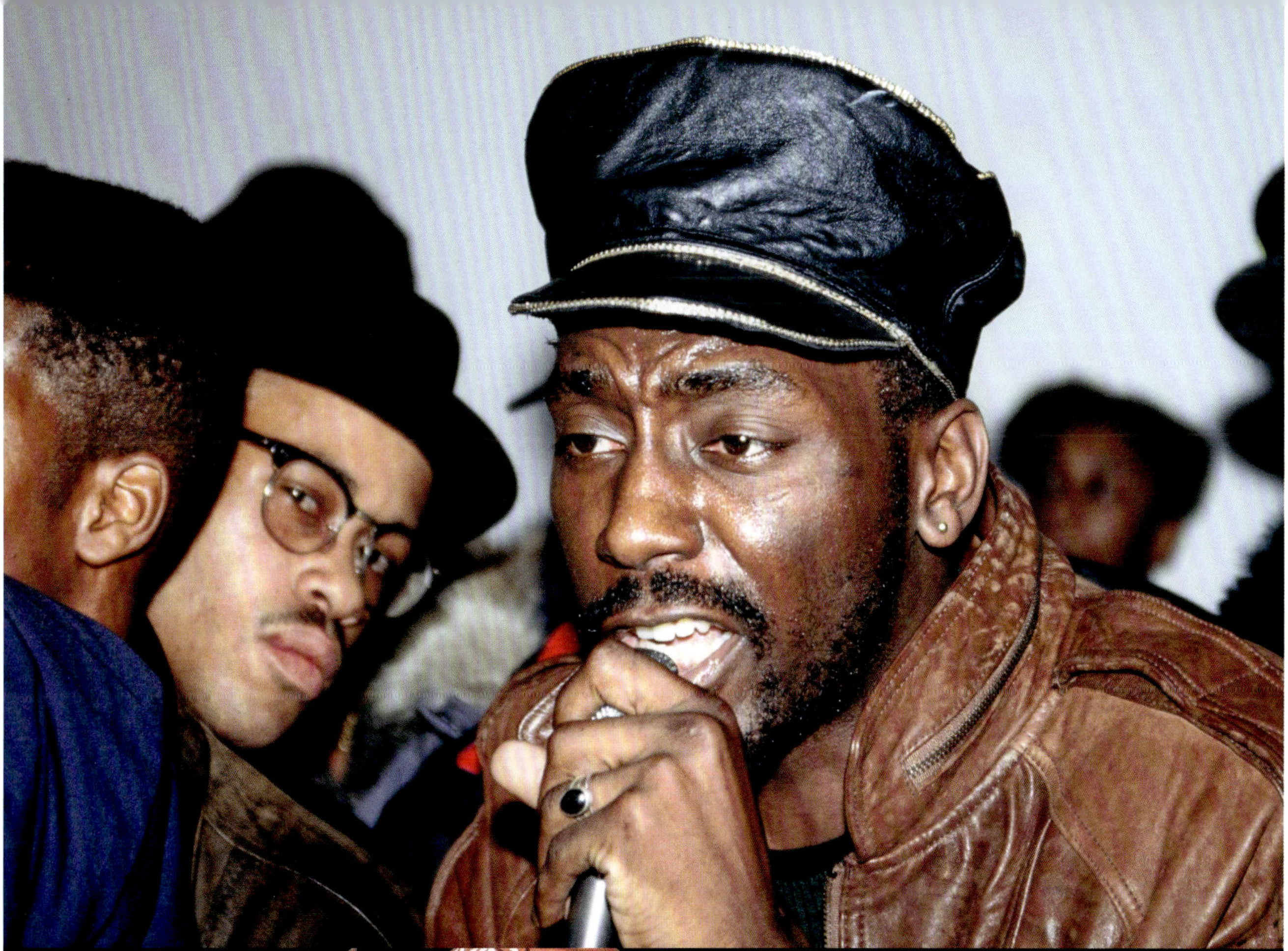

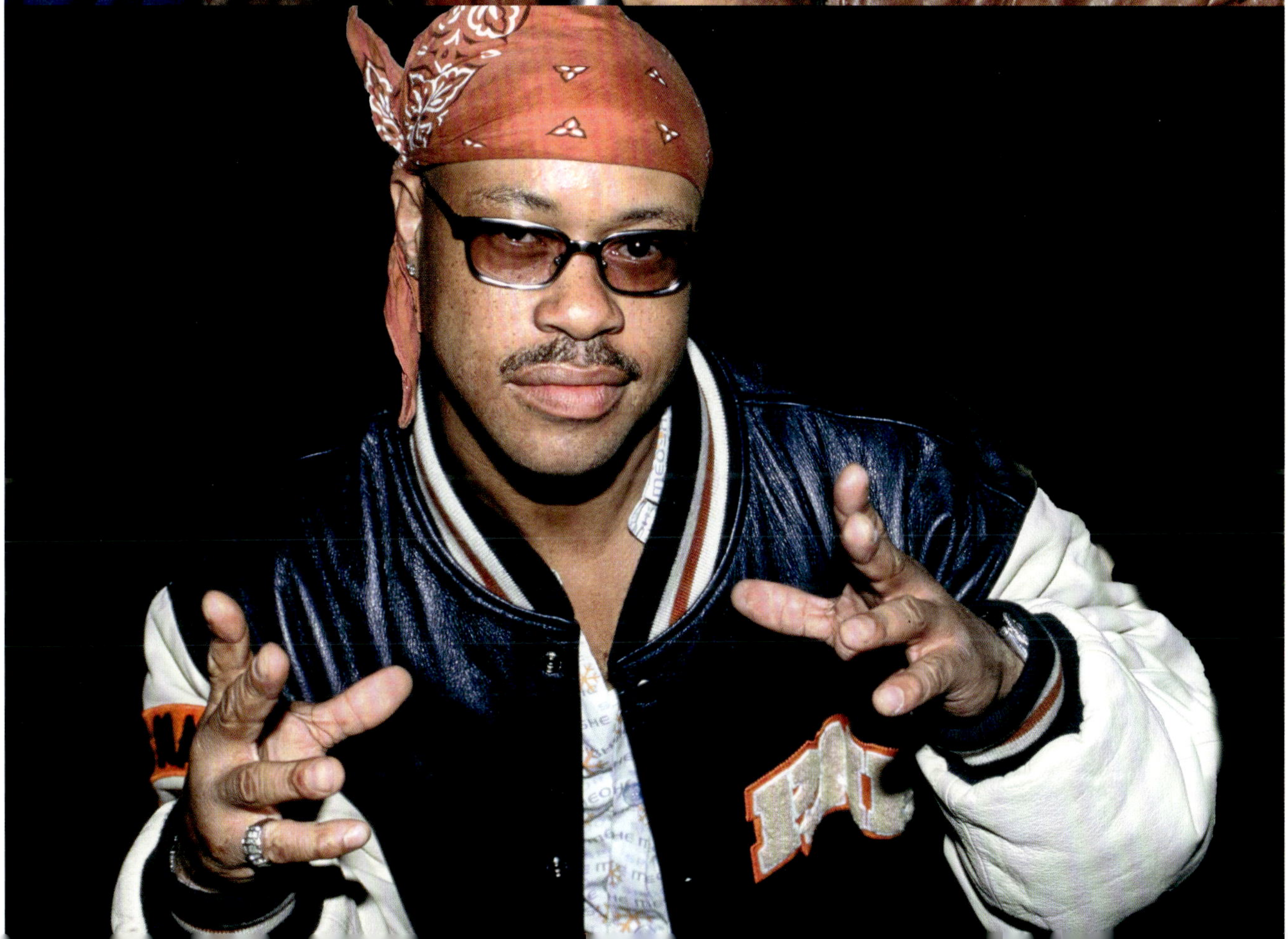

p.33 (top) Big Daddy Kane with the late rapper Guru—Keith Edward Elam (1966–2010)—at Parrish Smith of EPMD's birthday, NYC, 1993; (bottom) Guru, D&D Studios, NYC, 1993.

p.34 (Top) Group shot of EPMD, Das EFX, Kid Capri, DJ Scratch, Apache, and Mister Cee, Lower East Side, NYC, early 1990s; (bottom) Big Pun and Noreaga (aka N.O.R.E.), 1999, NYC.

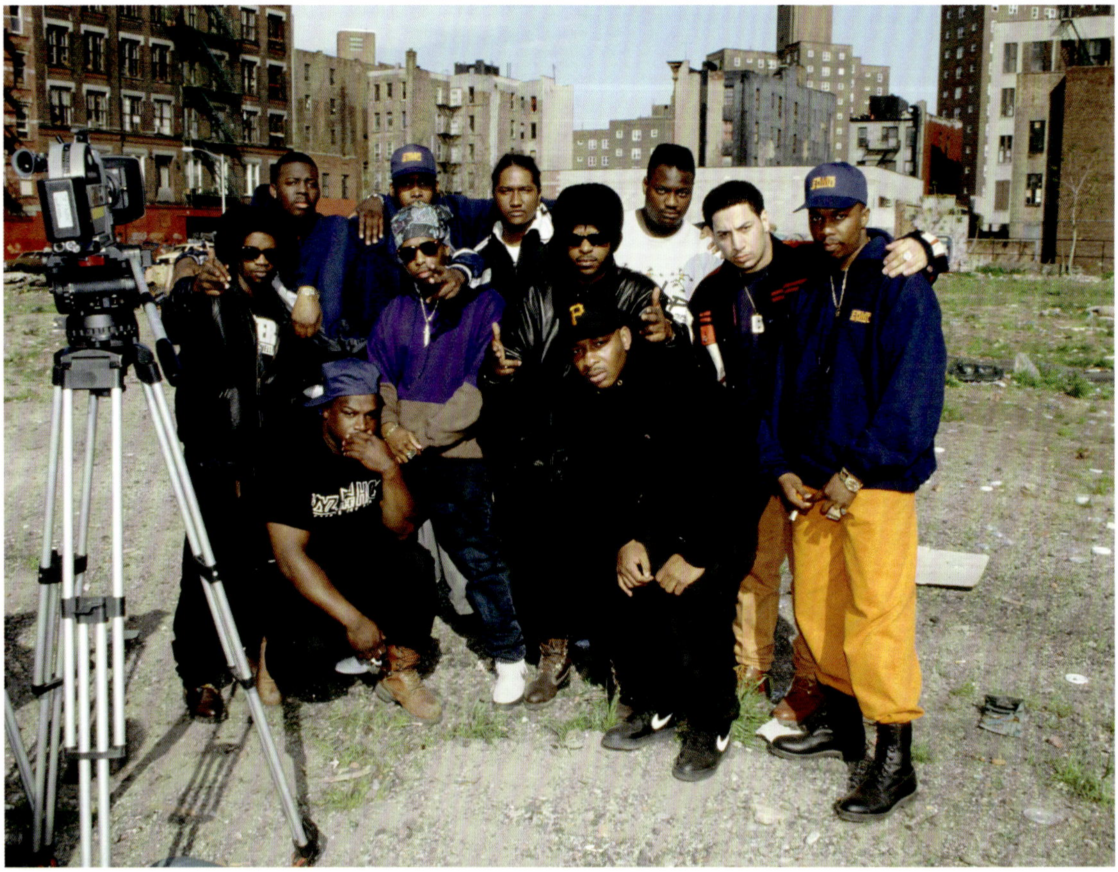

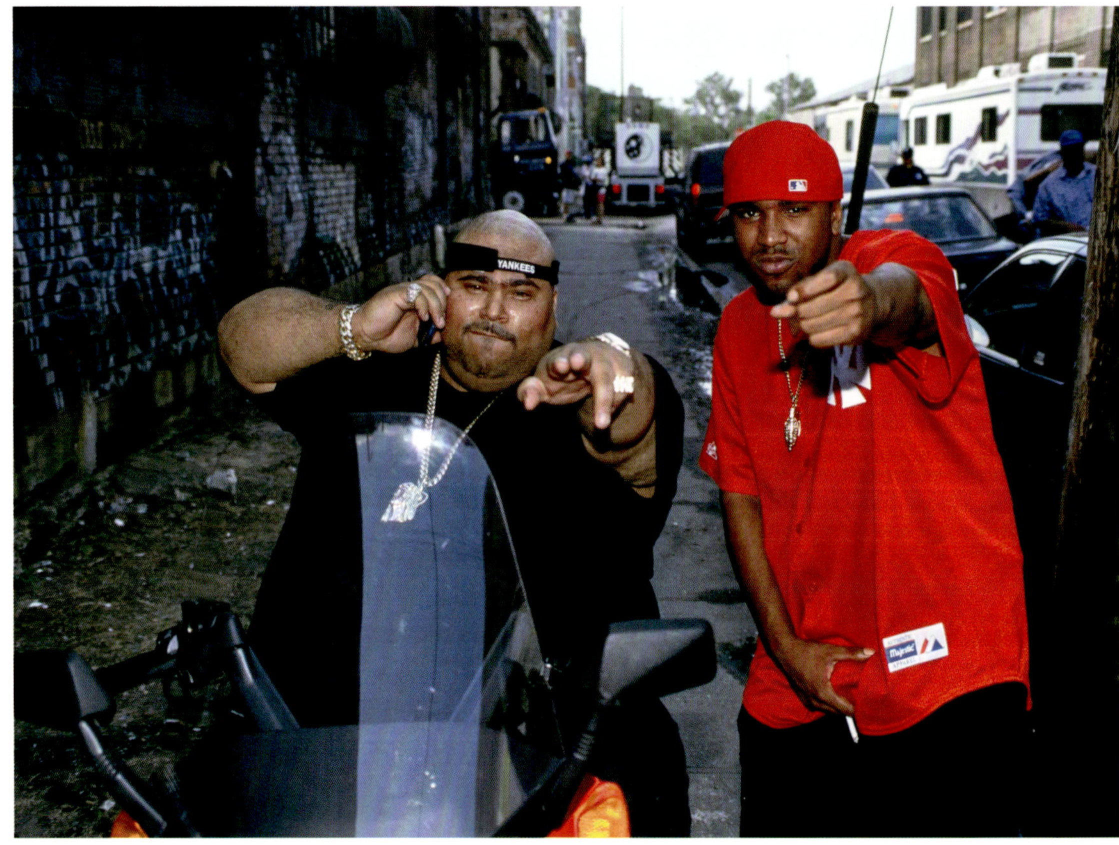

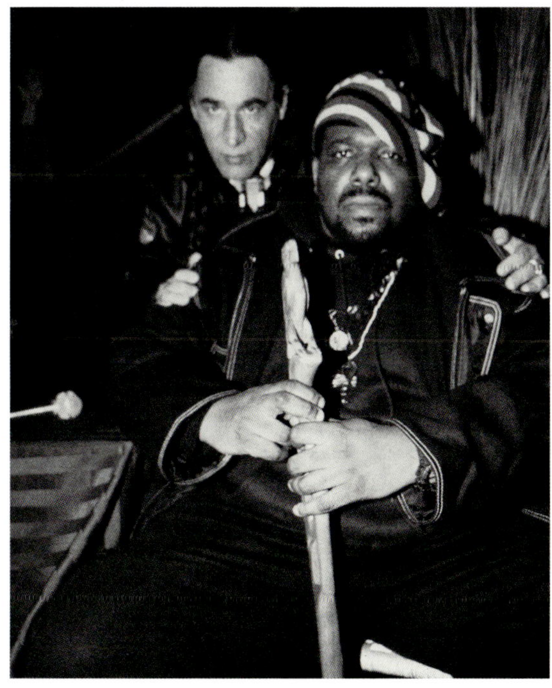

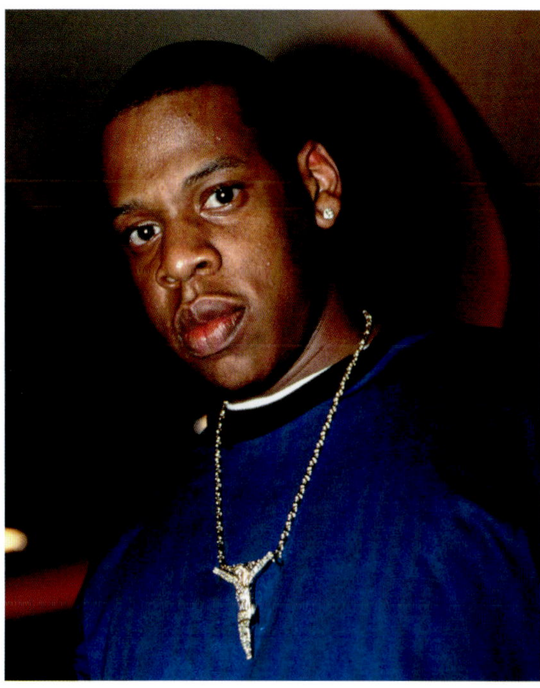

(Left to right) Ernie with Afrika Bambaataa (photographer unknown), S.O.B.'s Night Club, NYC, 2000; Jay-Z, NYC, 1996.

And it doesn't matter who they are because I had Puffy, Jay-Z and Tupac all said the exact same thing to me. And I never forgot it. Puffy came up to me and he said "you should be taking my picture" and this is when he was a fucking intern at Uptown Records with Andre Harrell. So I said "why should I be taking your picture, you a great rapper or what?" He says, "nah, I'm going to be running this shit."

THE KINGS CALL ME DADDY, MOTHERFUCKER. AND I WENT FROM KIND, GENTLE AND SMILING, TO A WAR FACE

And another time I was at a party with Salt-N-Pepa. I think it was Sandra's [Pepa] birthday party. I see this kid, no more than 15, 16, and he's as tall as me and he's got big gold teeth. So I said "hi," and he says "you should be taking my picture." So I said "why, are you a famous rapper?" He said, "no, I'm going to be running this shit, and I'm a great rapper." So I took this picture with Mr. Gold Teeth with Salt-N-Pepa and you know, sure enough, Jay-Z ran that shit. He became the president of Def Jam for a while [in 2004].

The third time I remember was Tupac when he was a roadie for Digital Underground. He says to me, "you better get them pictures now, they're going to increase in value." I said, "oh," I said, "why, are you the greatest rapper?" He said "no, but I'm going to make a difference."

IL: That's an amazing thing for him to have said.

EP: There was a lot of competition out there for photographers. I remember one guy came up to me and he says, "you think you're the shit huh? You think you're all that? You think you're the king of hip-hop photographers?" I just looked at him and said "no, not really. But the kings call me daddy, motherfucker." And I went from kind, gentle and smiling, to a war face.

I've had people come up to me that wanted to try their luck. I'm 71 now, but you can see that I still got a little razor blade under my watch. I would always give people a chance. I'd always tell people that wanted to fight, "are you sure you want to do this right now?" And I'd look them in the eye and I'd smile. That throws people off, because you're either supposed to be intimidated or angry.

They'd be like, this is a different kind of motherfucker. I still do that, you know. Instead of walking away or yelling "fuck you"—none of that dumb shit. You just look them square in the eye and say "are you sure you want to do this right now?" You can hear their balls shrinking.

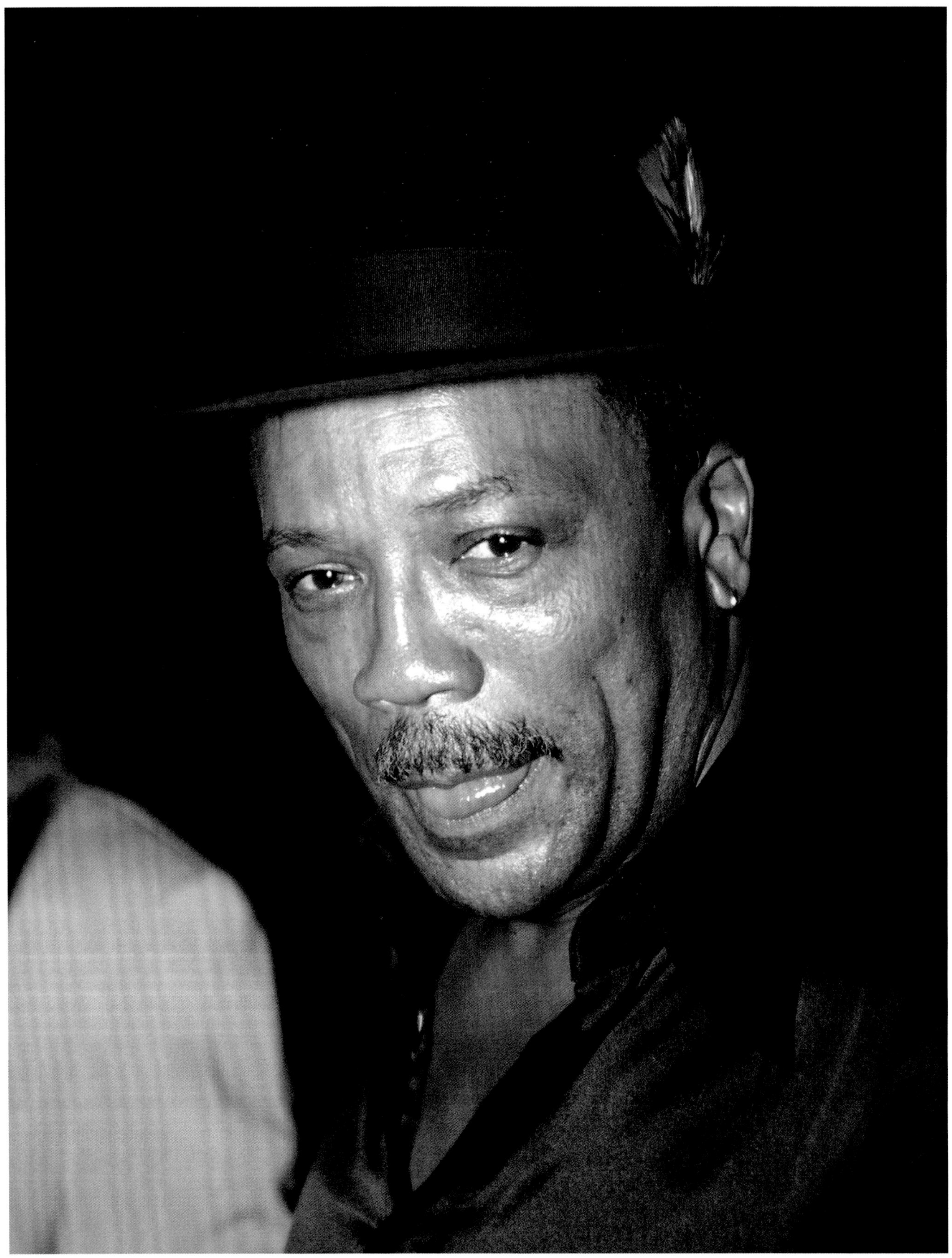

p.36 Quincy Jones, 1990s, NYC; p.37 Afrika Bambaataa with Miles Davis poster on ceiling, NYC, 2000.

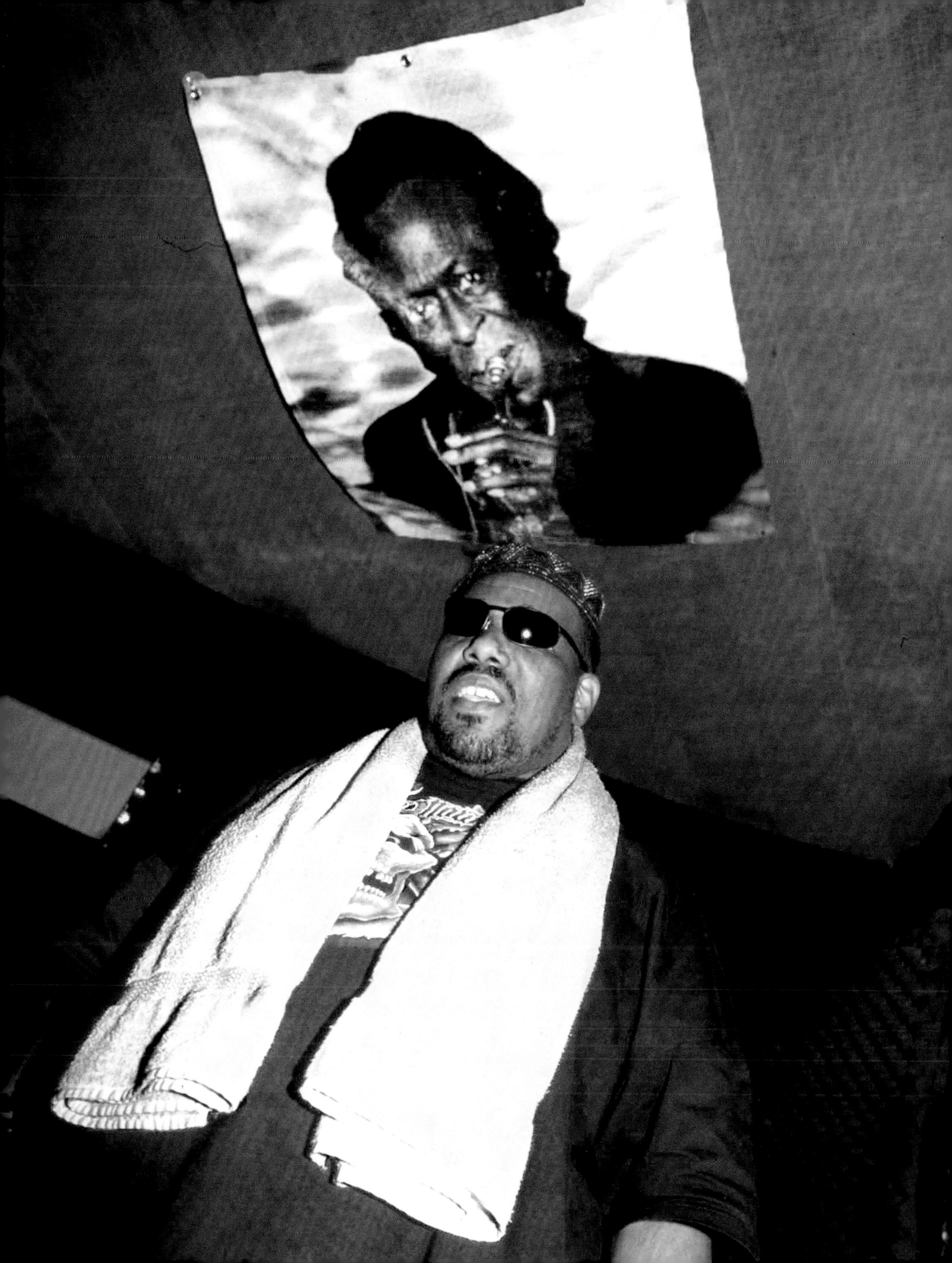

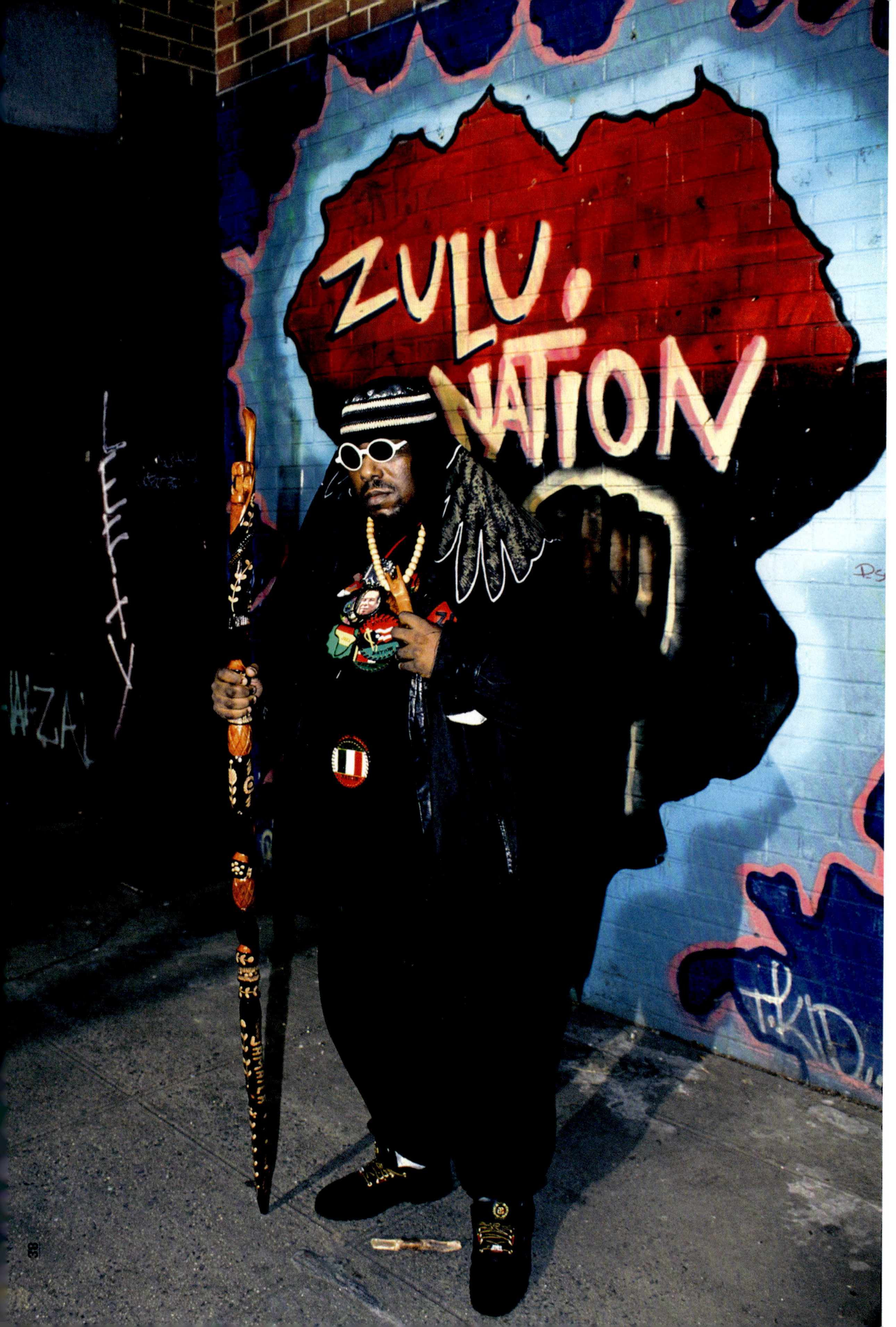
ZULU.
NATION
T.KID

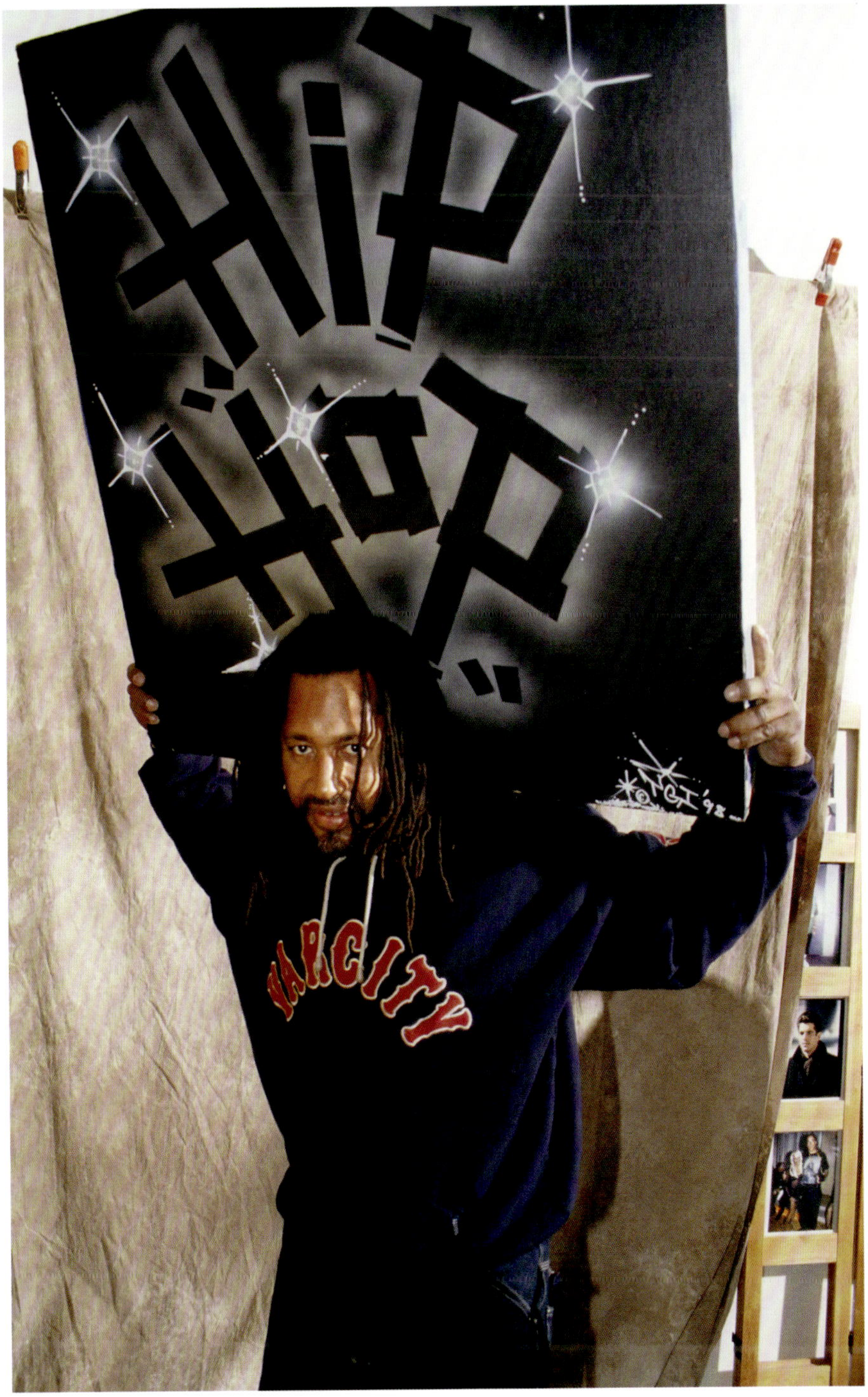

p.38 Afrika Bambaataa, Bronx River Projects, 1994; p.39 Kool Herc, 3rd Eye Studio, NYC, 1999.

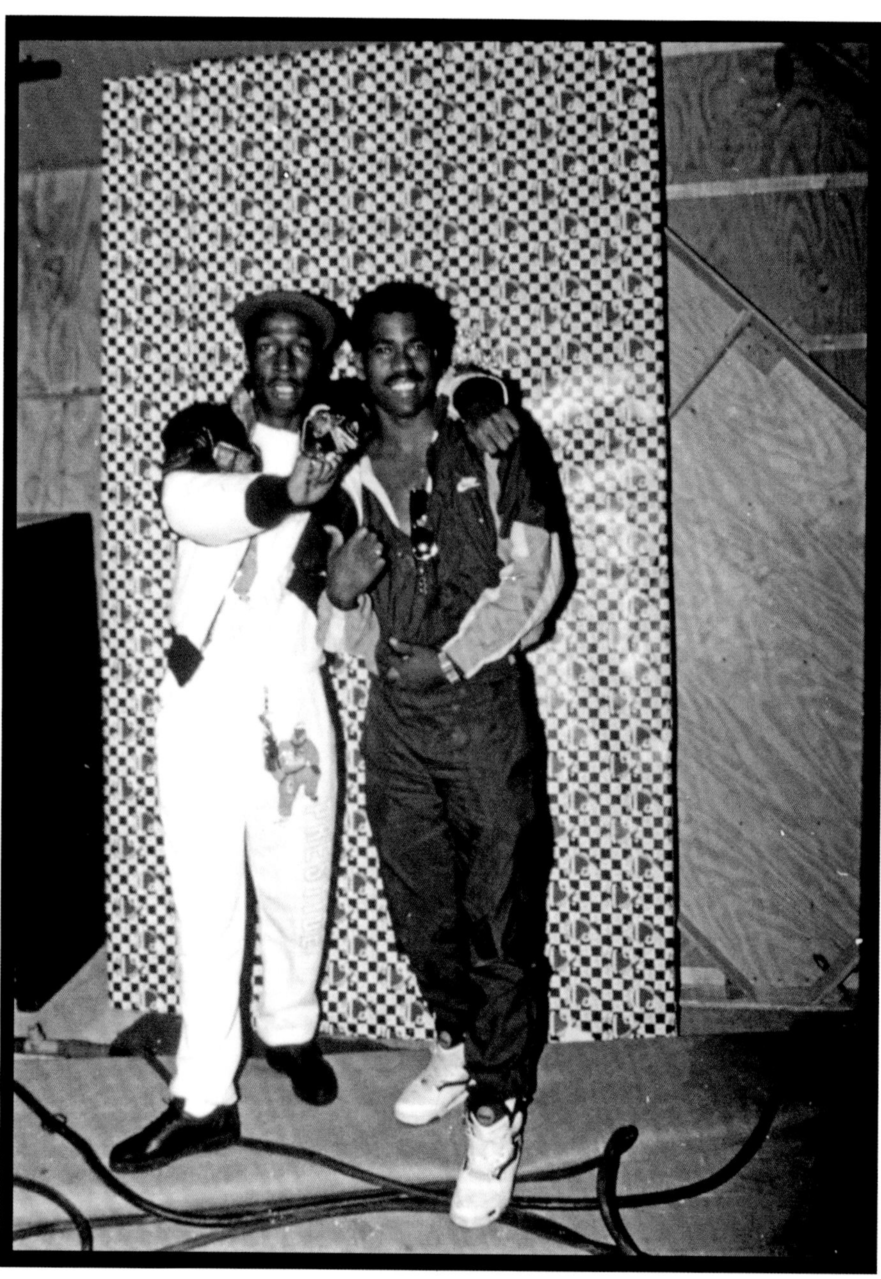

p.40 Grandmaster Flash with Kurtis Blow, NYC, 1991; p.41 Grandmaster Flash with Kurtis Blow, Temple of Hip-Hop, "Hip-Hop Declaration of Peace" Treaty Signing at the United Nations, NYC, 2001.

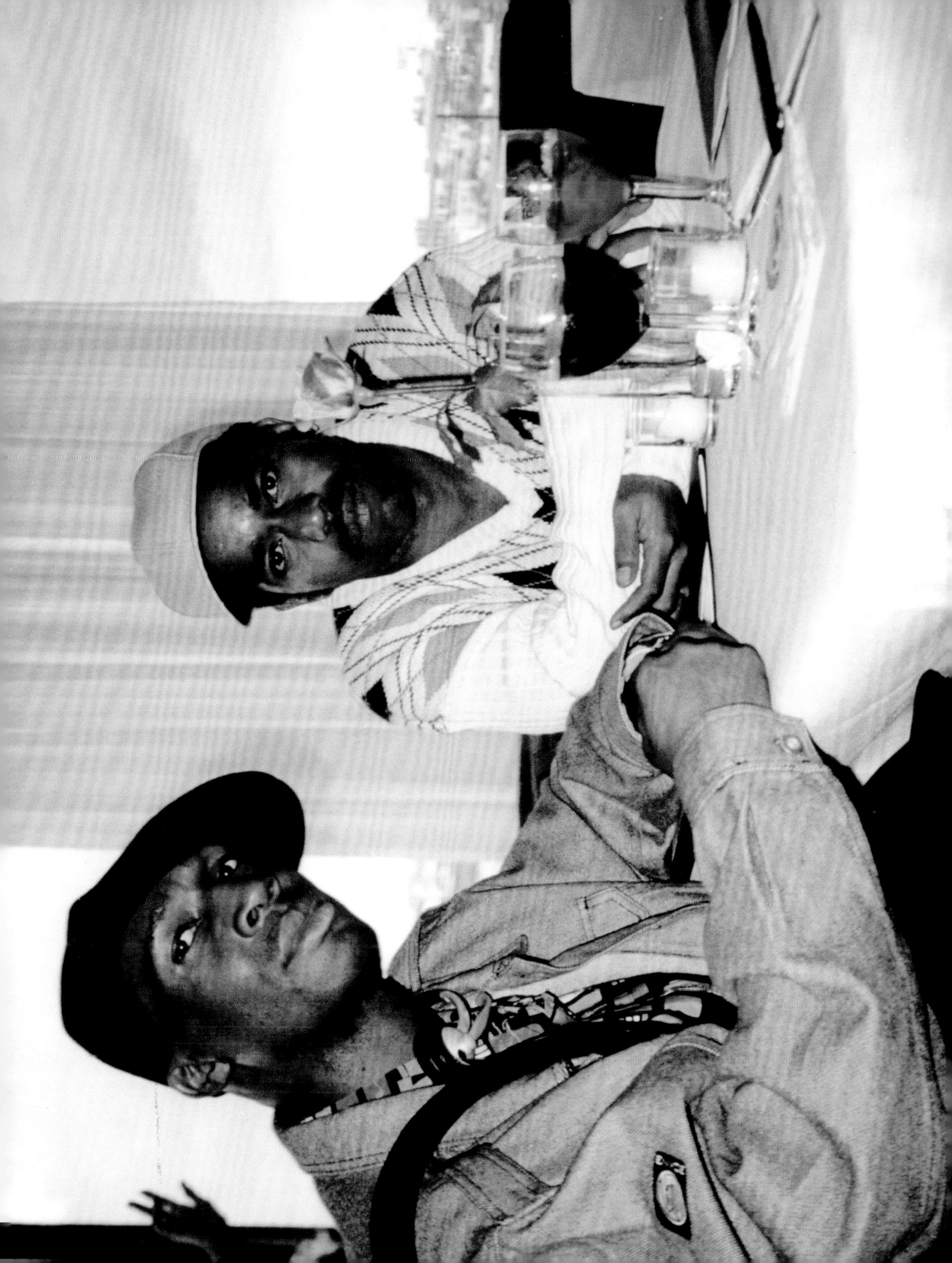

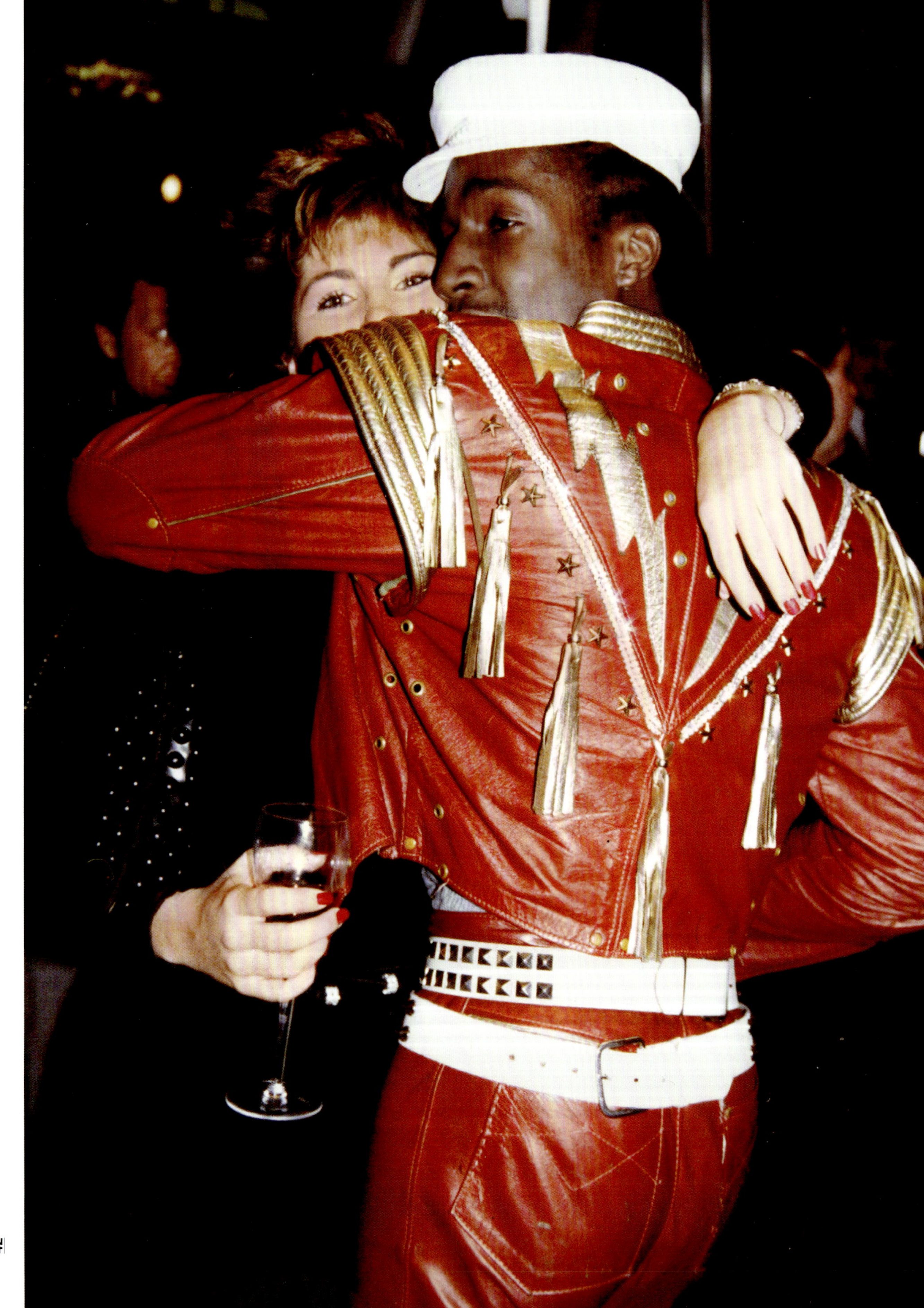

p.42–43 Grandmaster Flash with fan, late 1970s.

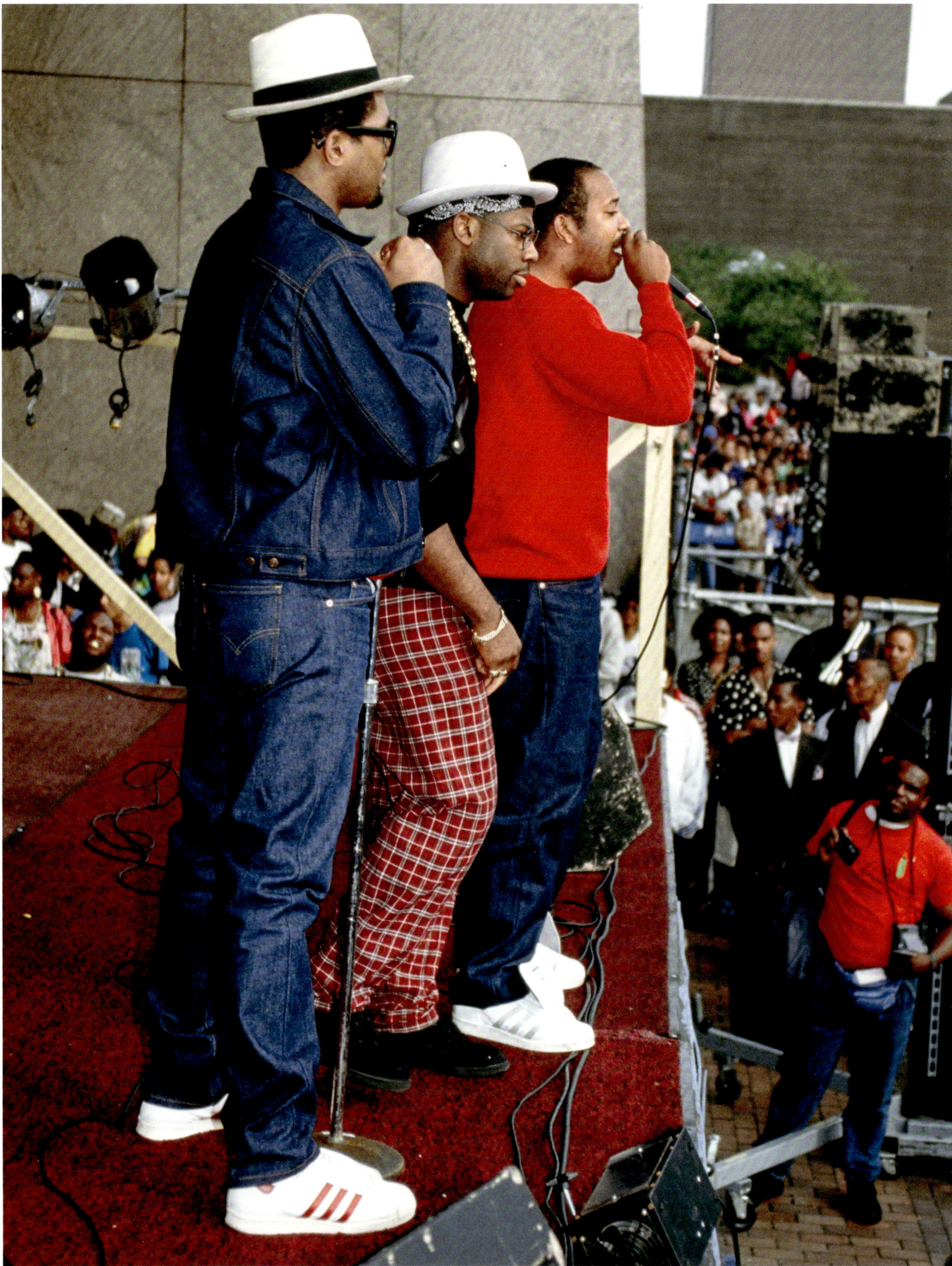

p.44 Run-DMC, “Harlem Rally Against Racism,” 125th Street, 1989; p.45 Run-DMC as they appeared in the early 1990s.

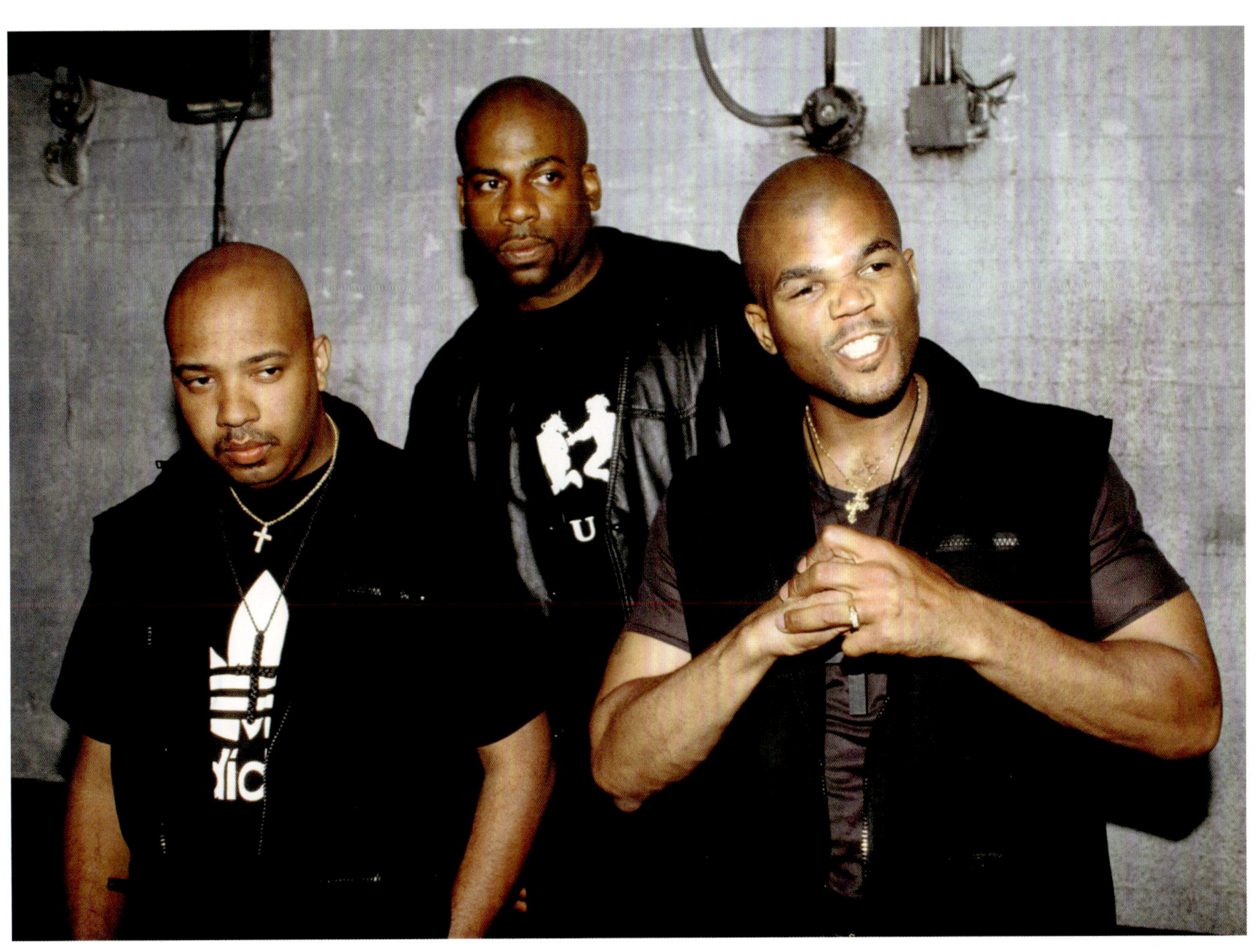

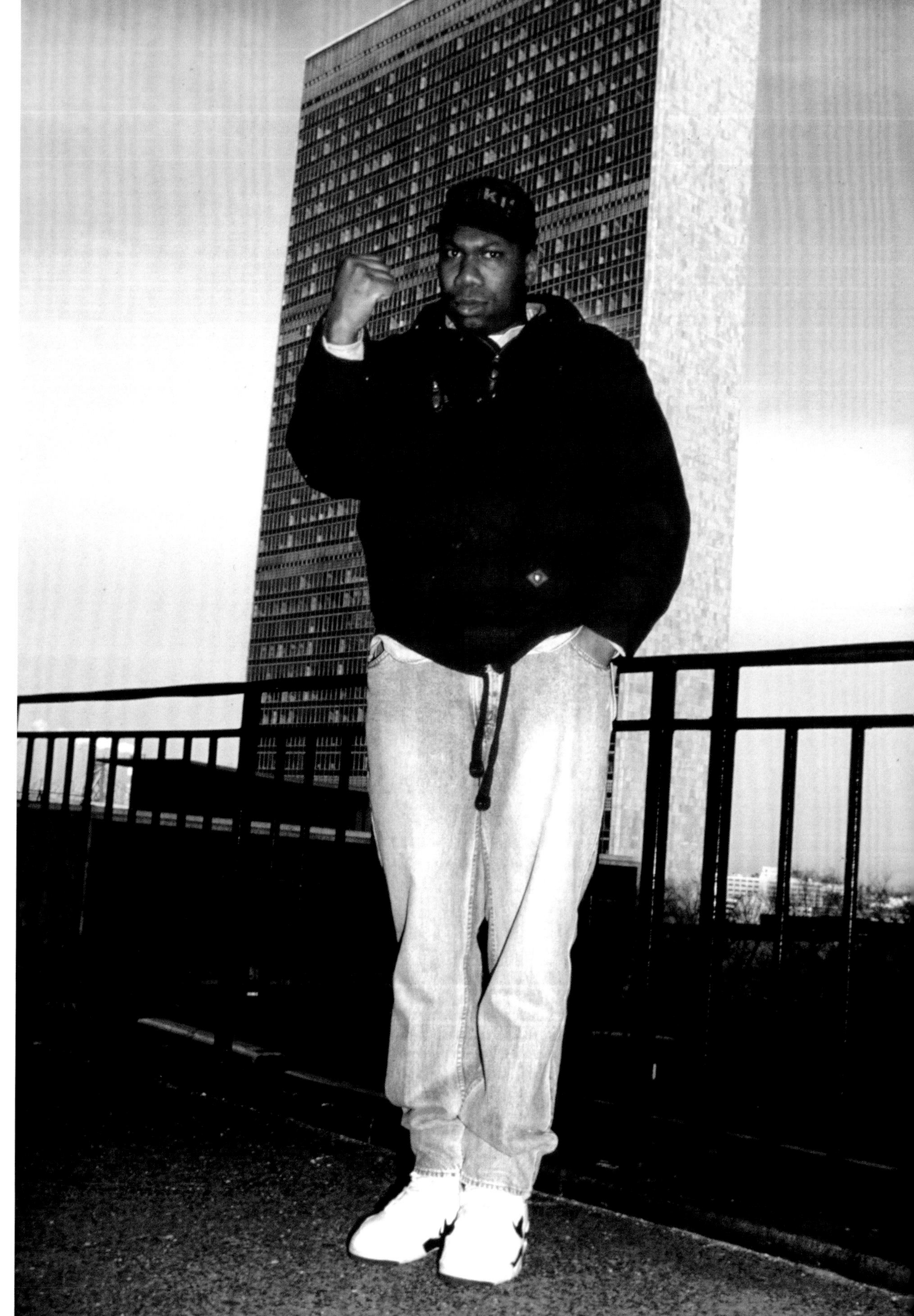

p.46 KRS-One near the United Nations, NYC, early 1990s; p.47 Grandmaster Flash near Chrysler Bldg, NYC, 1991.

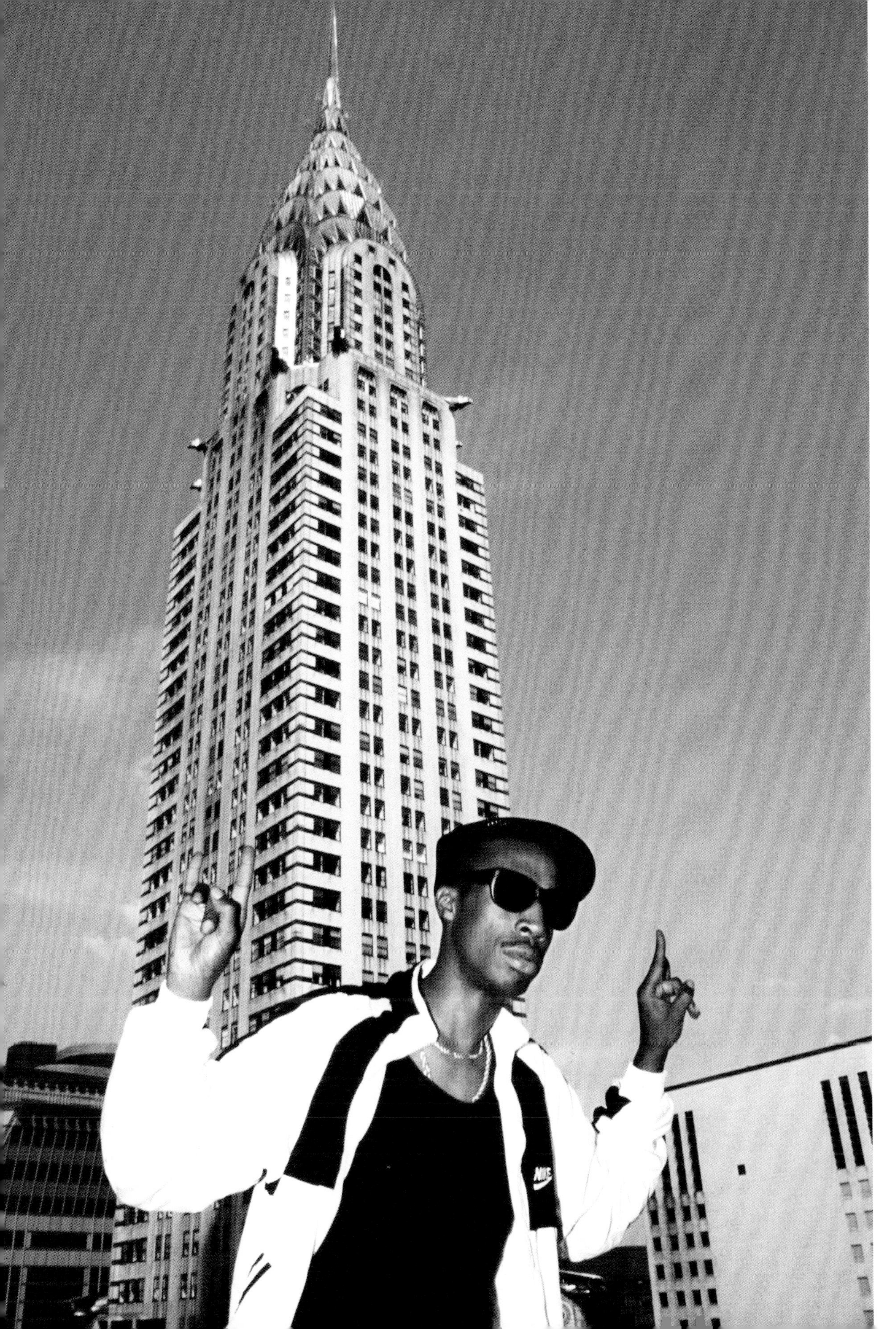
NIKE

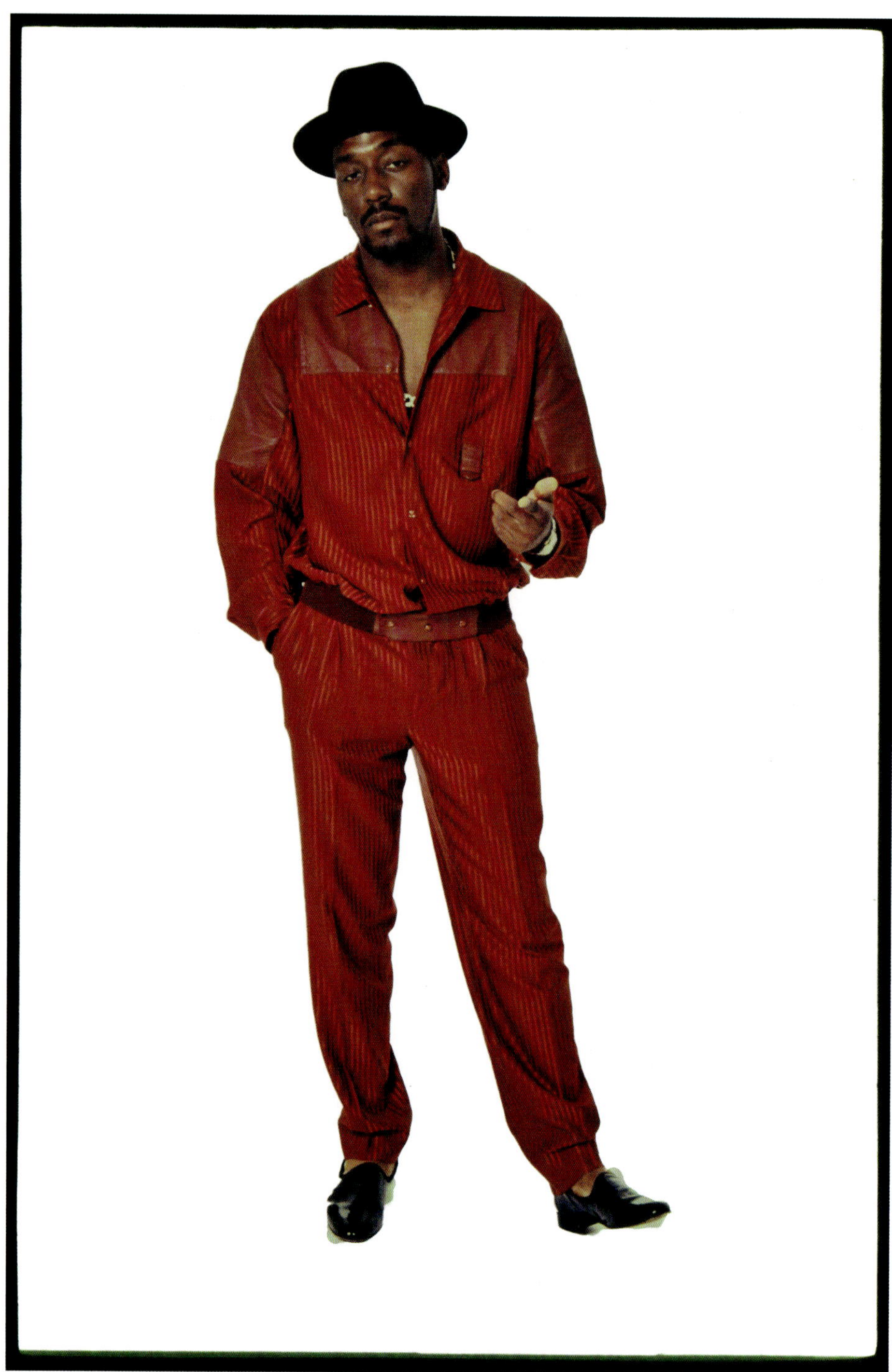

p.48 Big Daddy Kane, Dakota Studios, NYC, 1988; p.49 Rush Management artists: Black Flames, Big Daddy Kane, The Afros, Run-DMC and 3rd Bass, Dakota Studios, NYC, 1988.

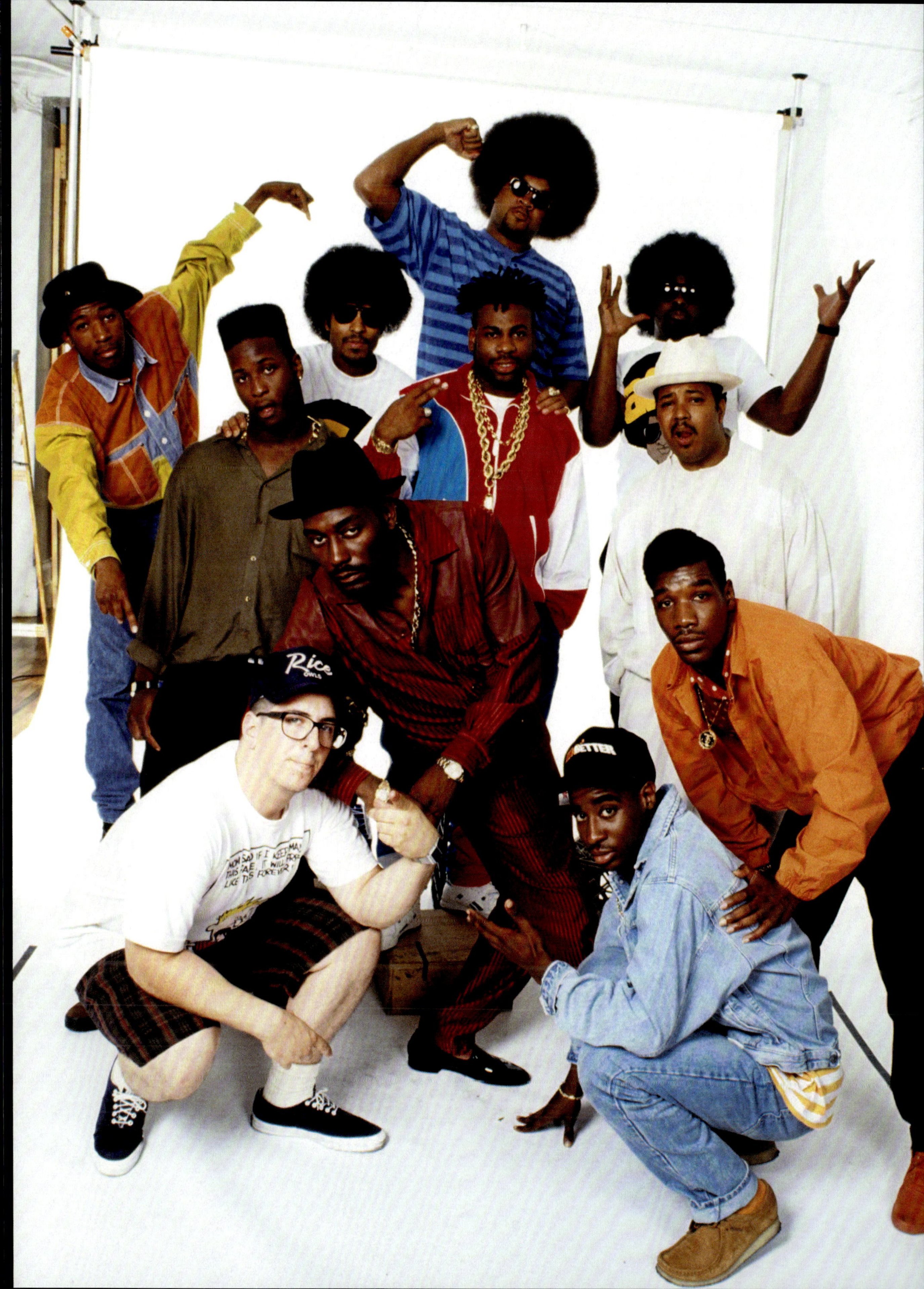
Rice
OWLS
BETTER

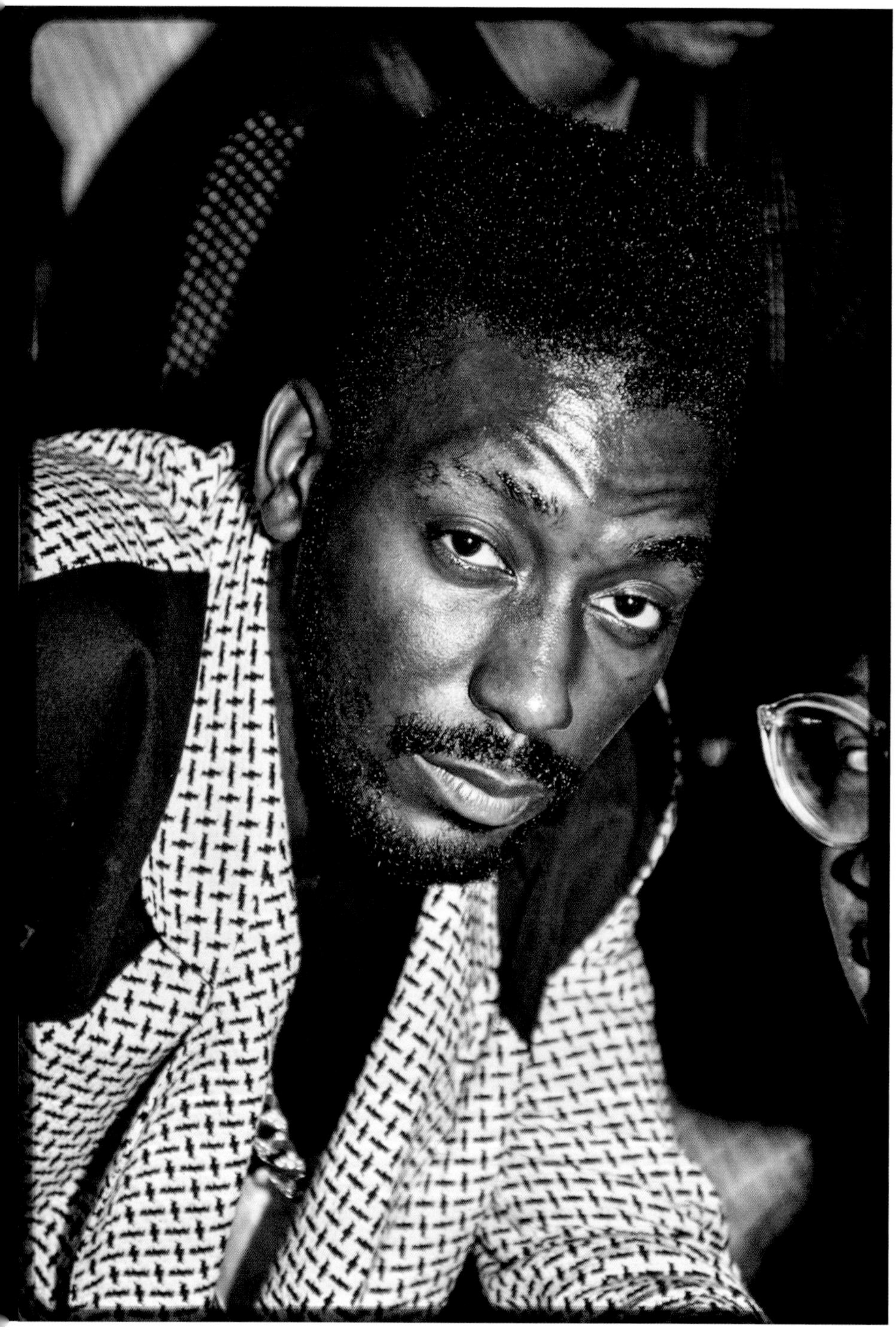

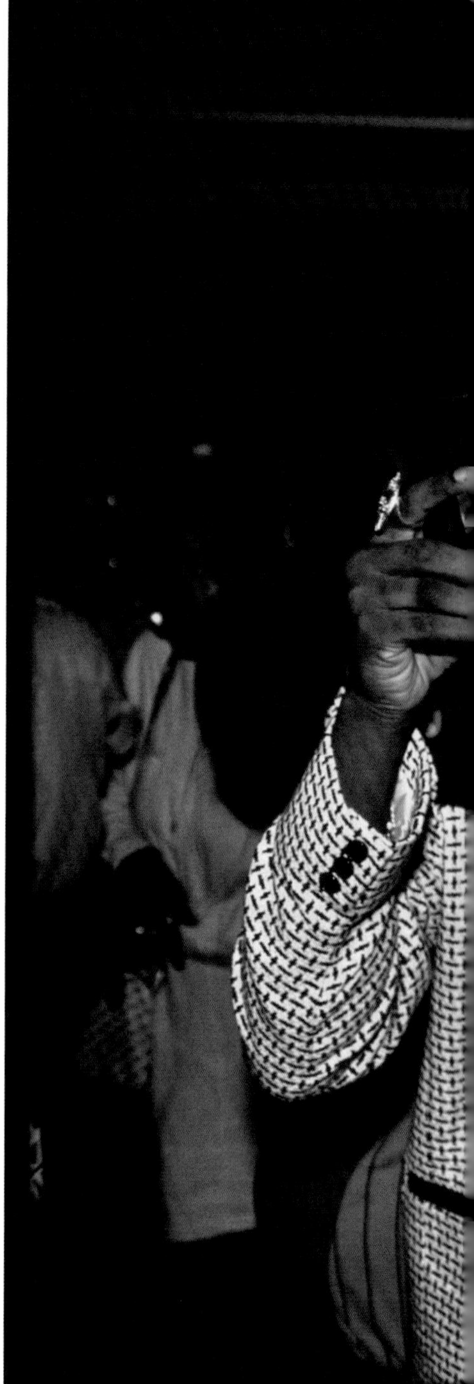

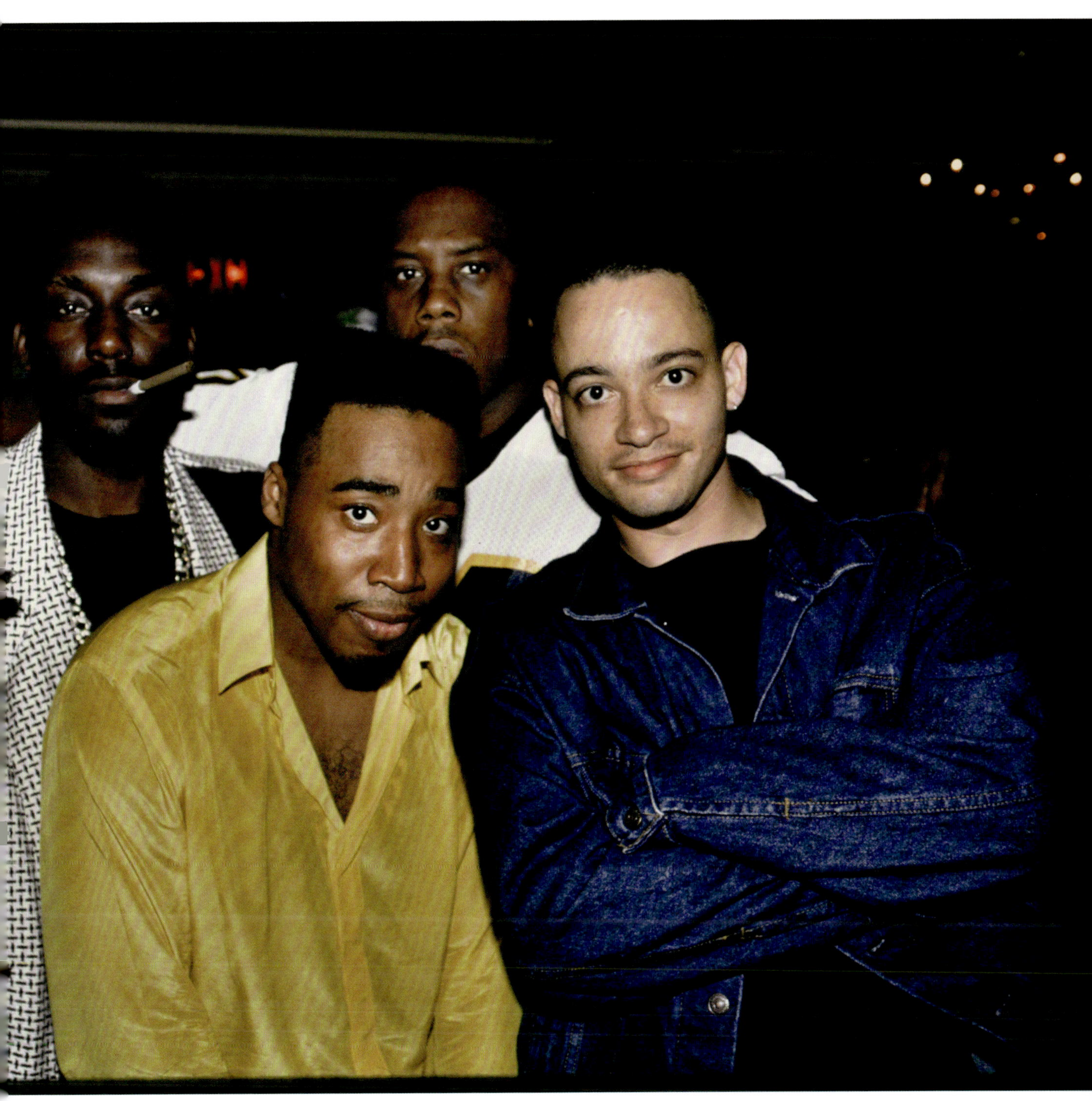

p.50–51 Big Daddy Kane, Positive K and Kid from Kid n' Play, Nell's, NYC, 1994; p.52 Big Daddy Kane at the "Harlem Rally Against Racism," 125th Street, NYC, 1989; p.53 Big Daddy Kane at the Apollo Theatre, NYC, 1991.

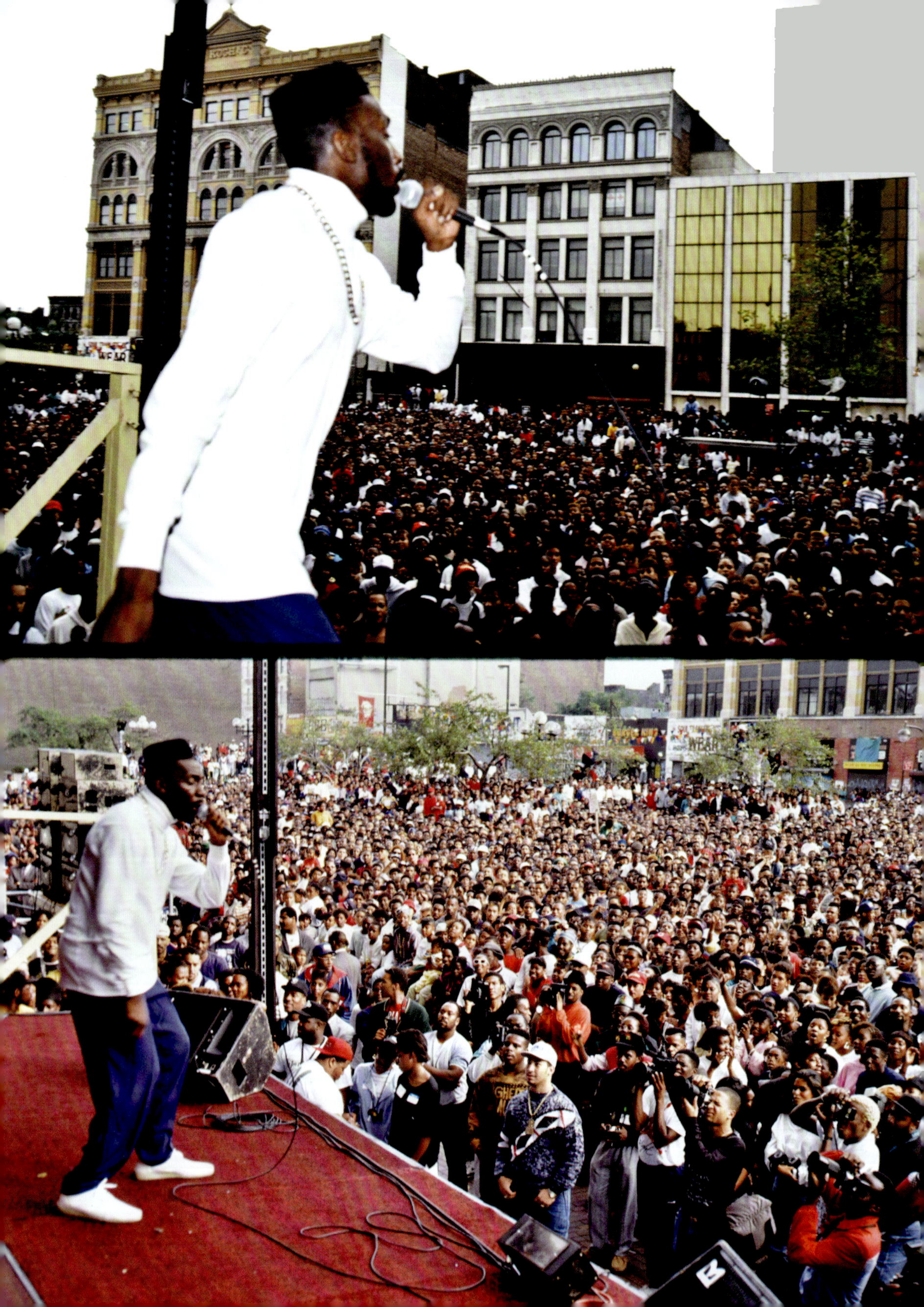

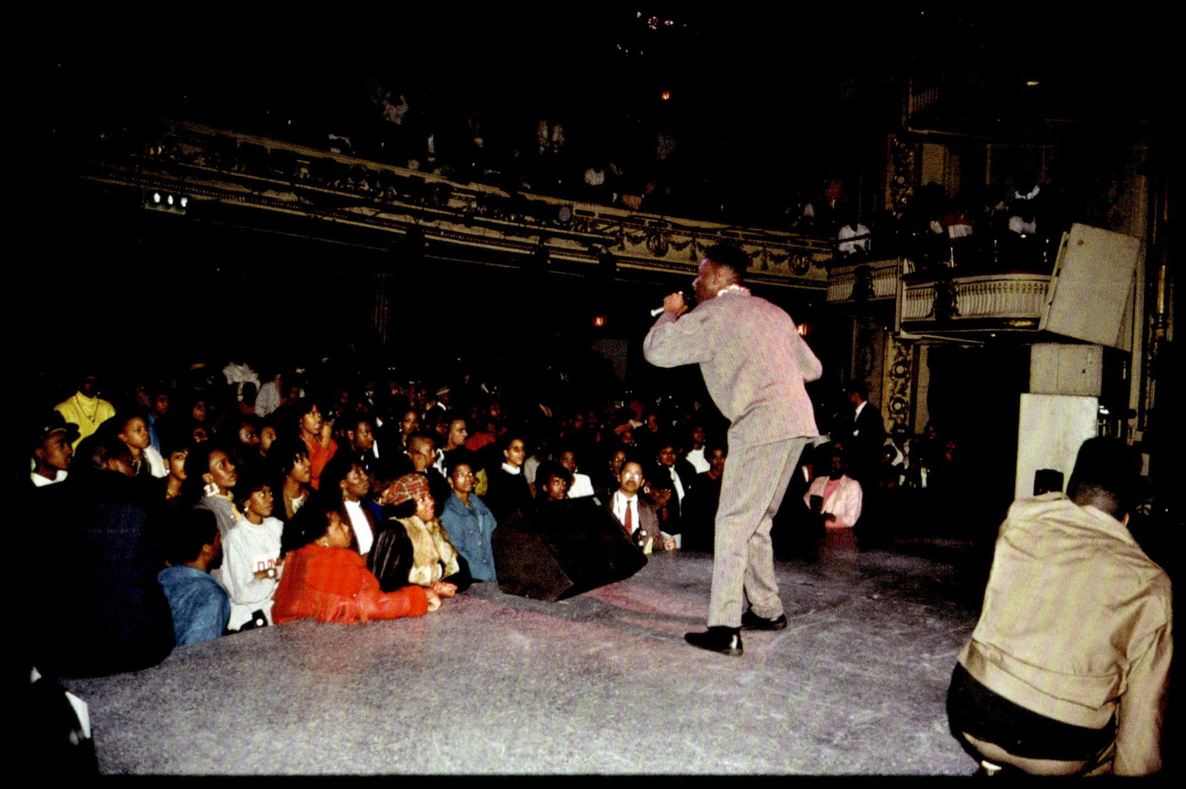

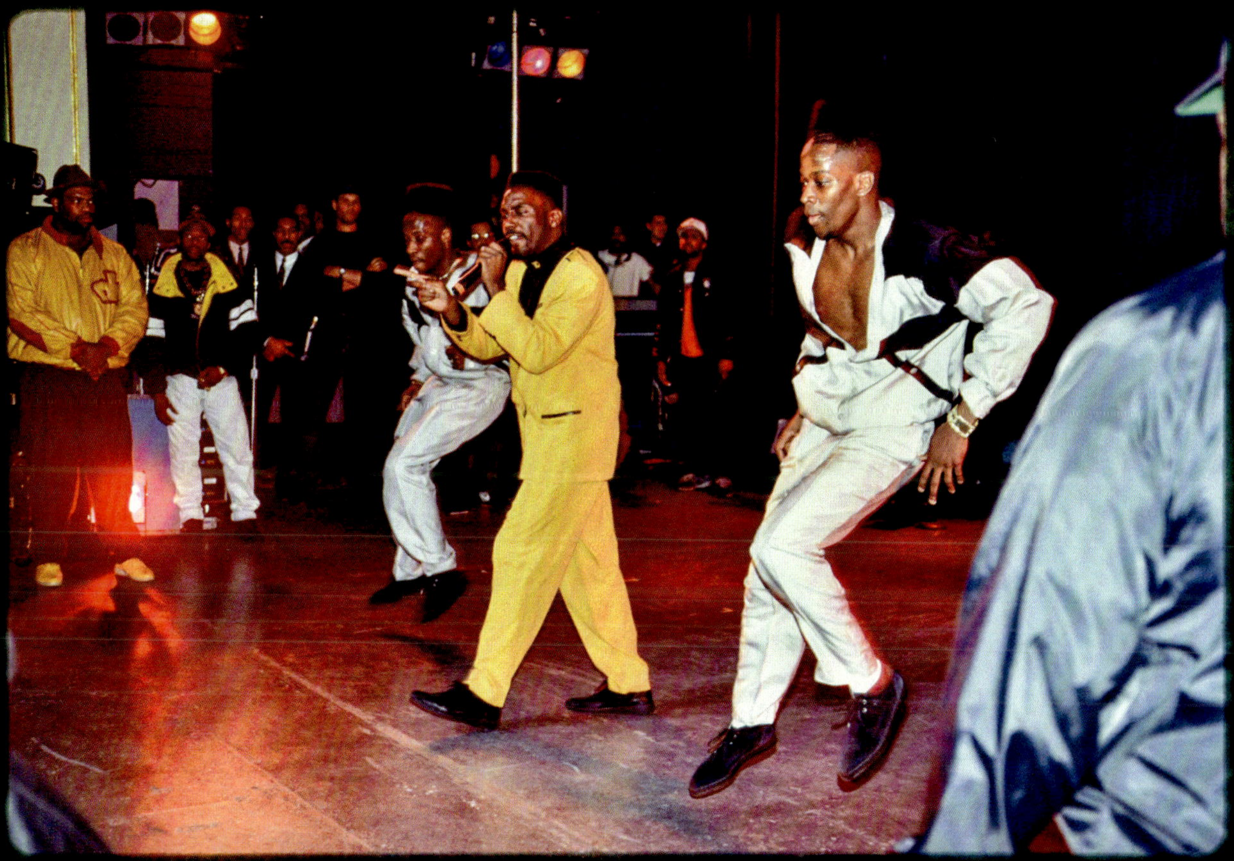

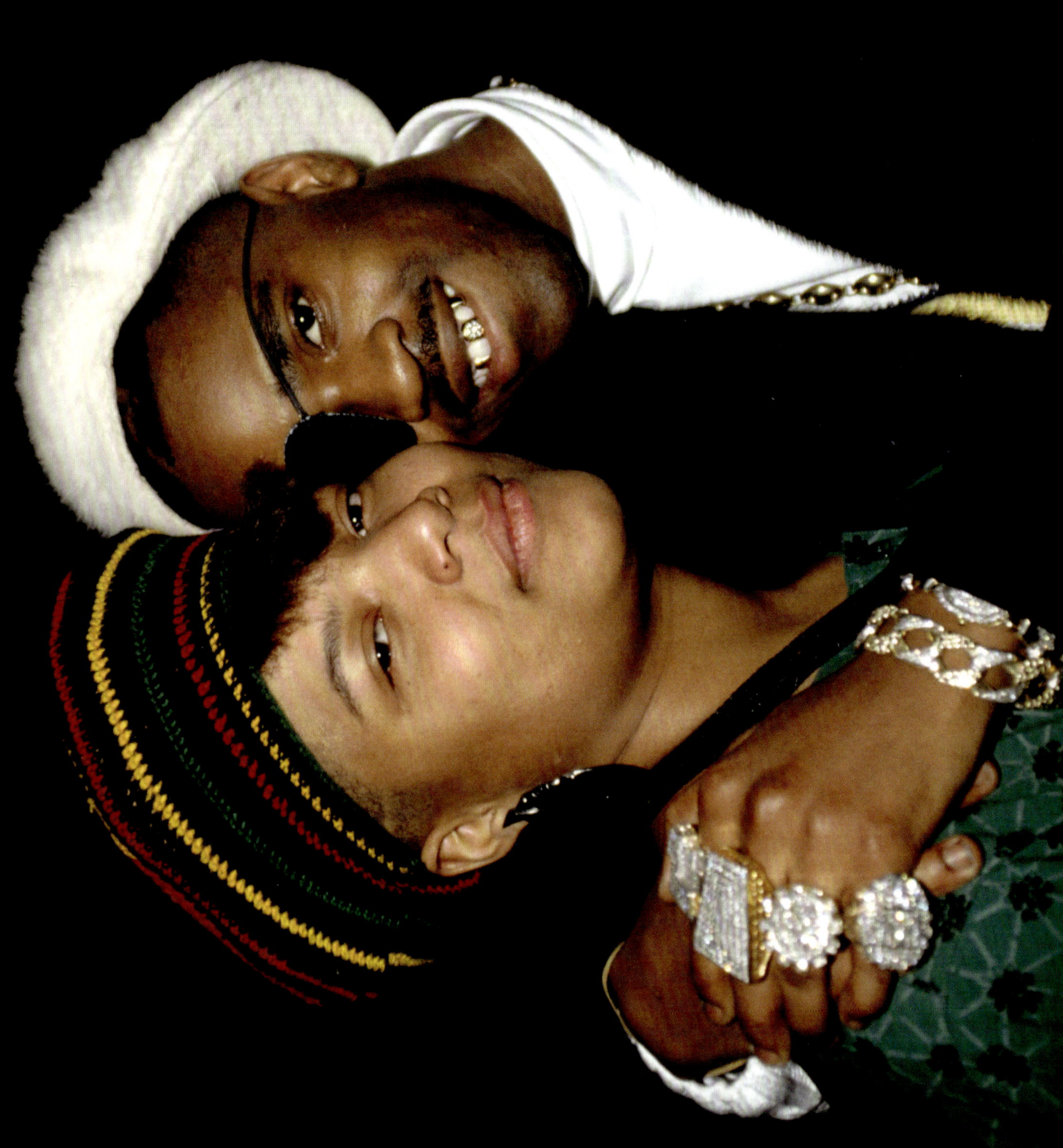

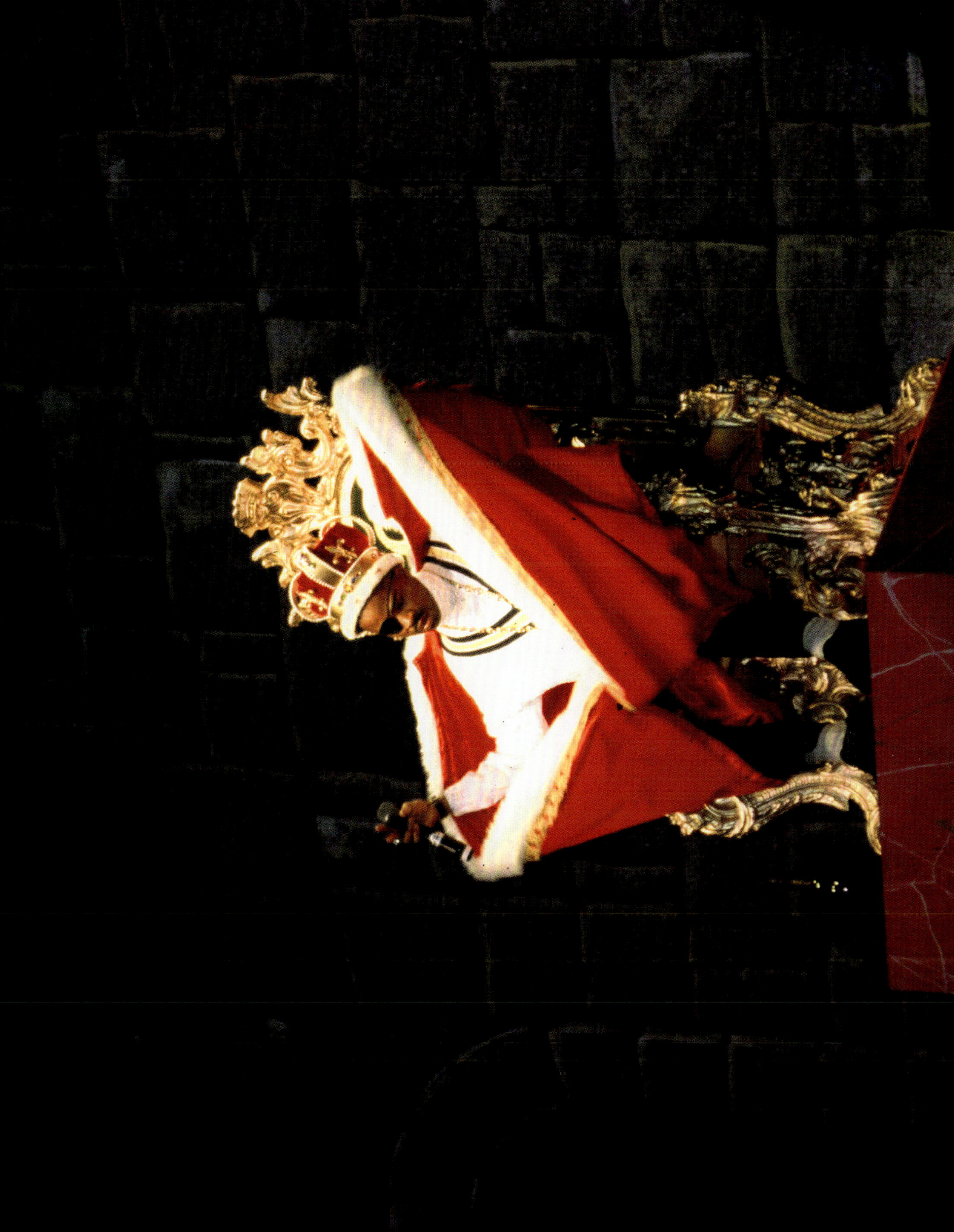

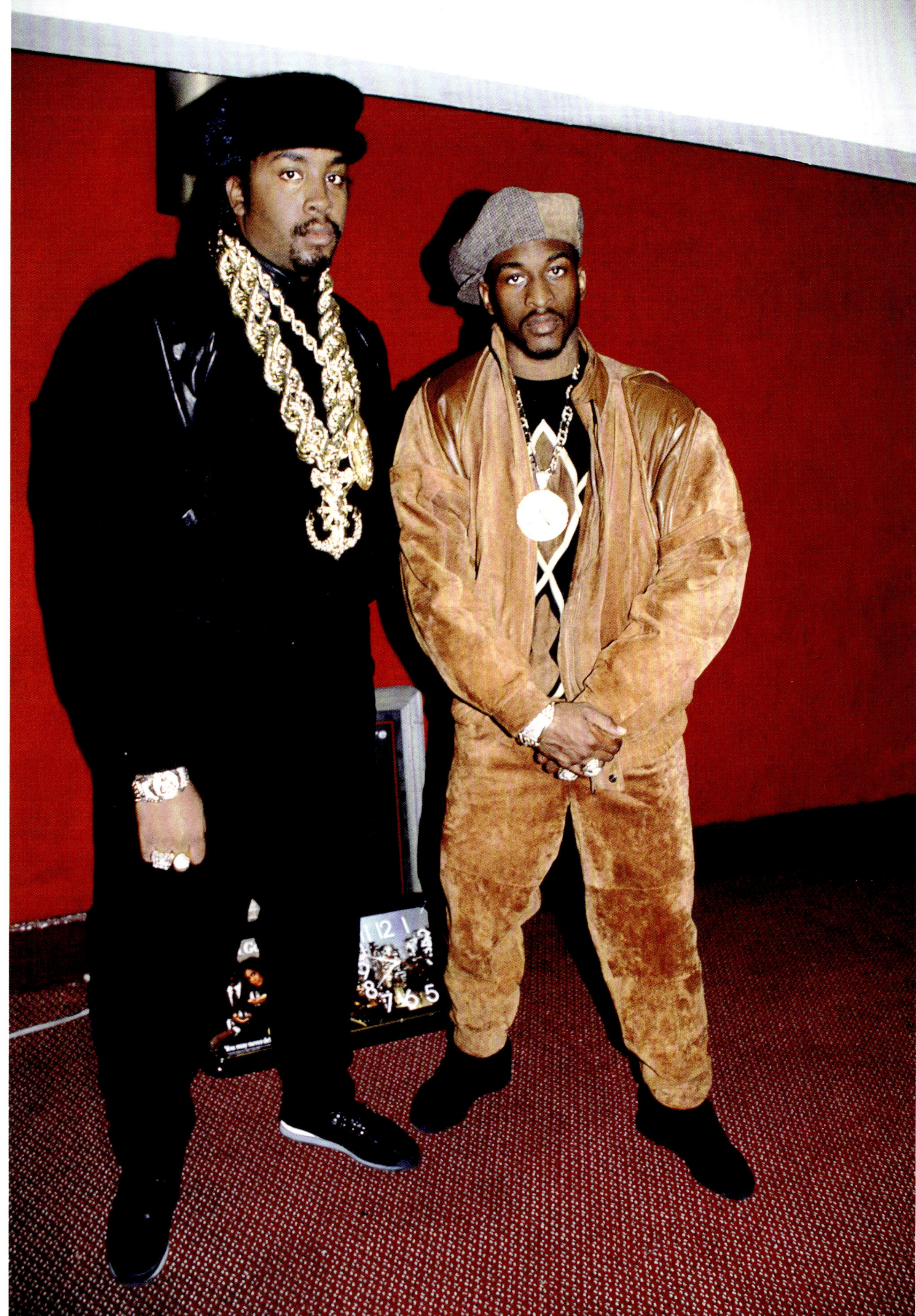

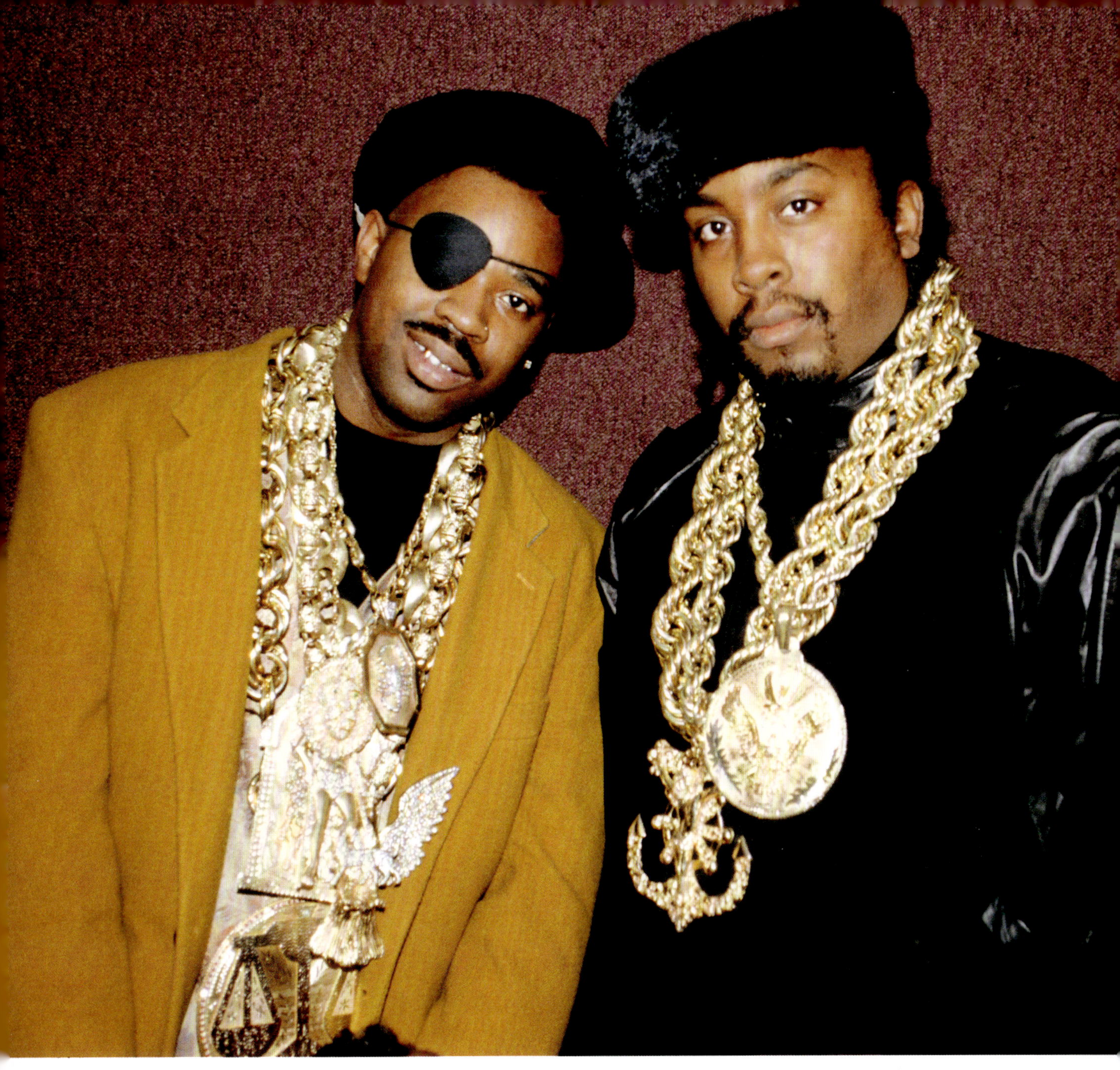

p.54-55 Queen Latifah with Slick Rick; Slick Rick the Ruler enthroned, both at the Beacon Theatre, NYC, 1987.

p.56 Eric B & Rakim, Apollo Theatre, Harlem, NYC, 1989; p.57 Slick Rick & Eric B, the RAPMANIA Show, Apollo Theatre, Harlem, NYC, 1989.

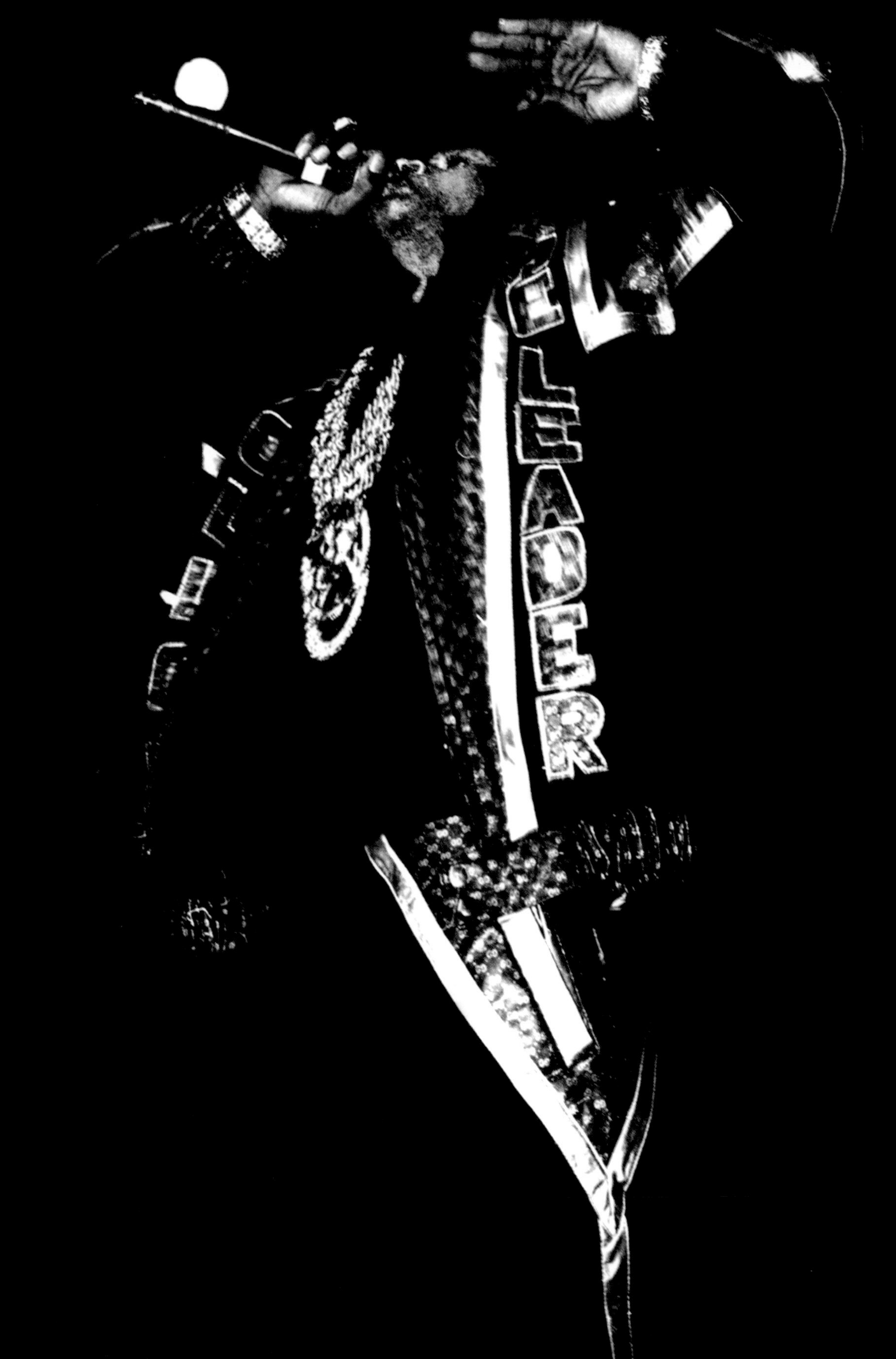
LEADER

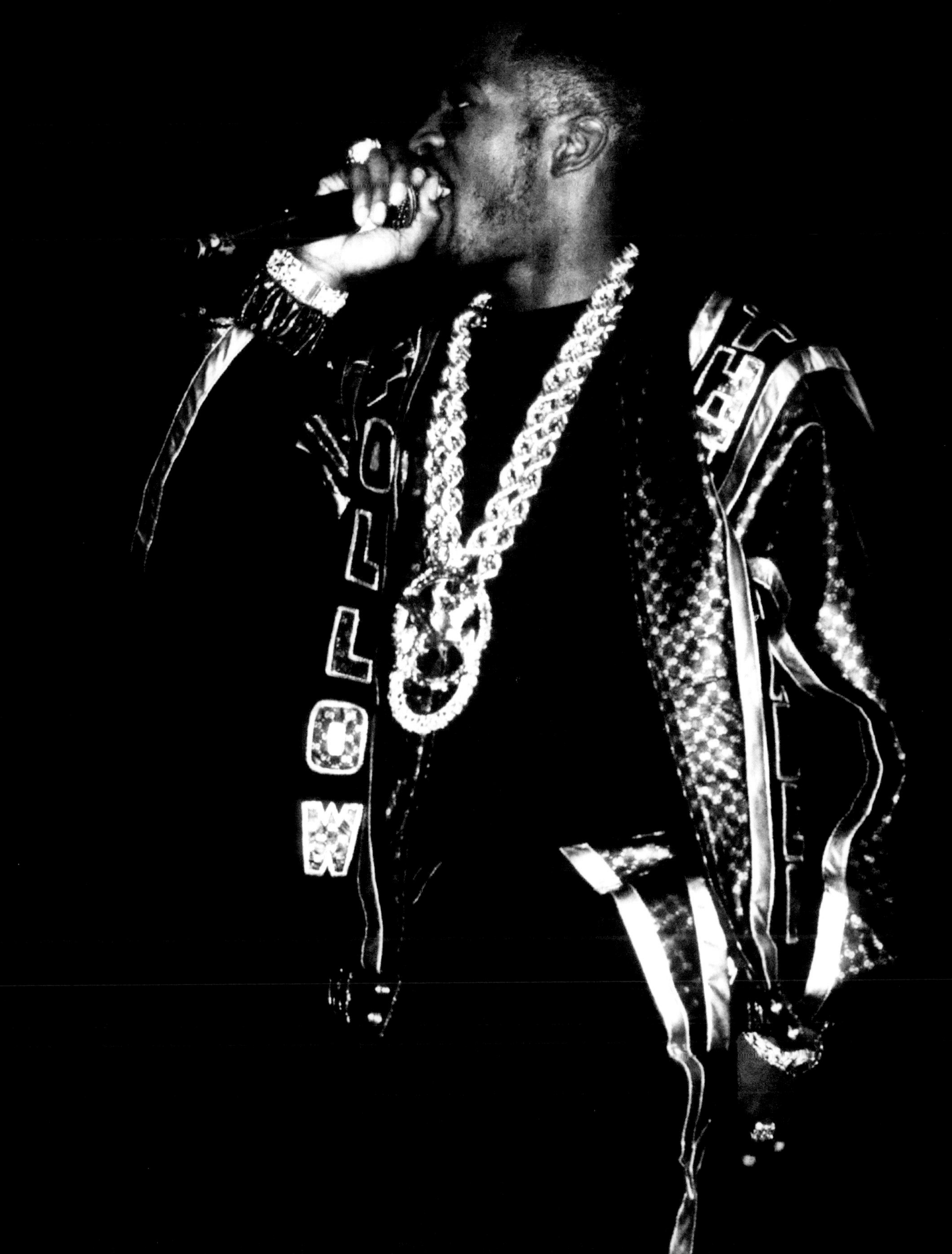

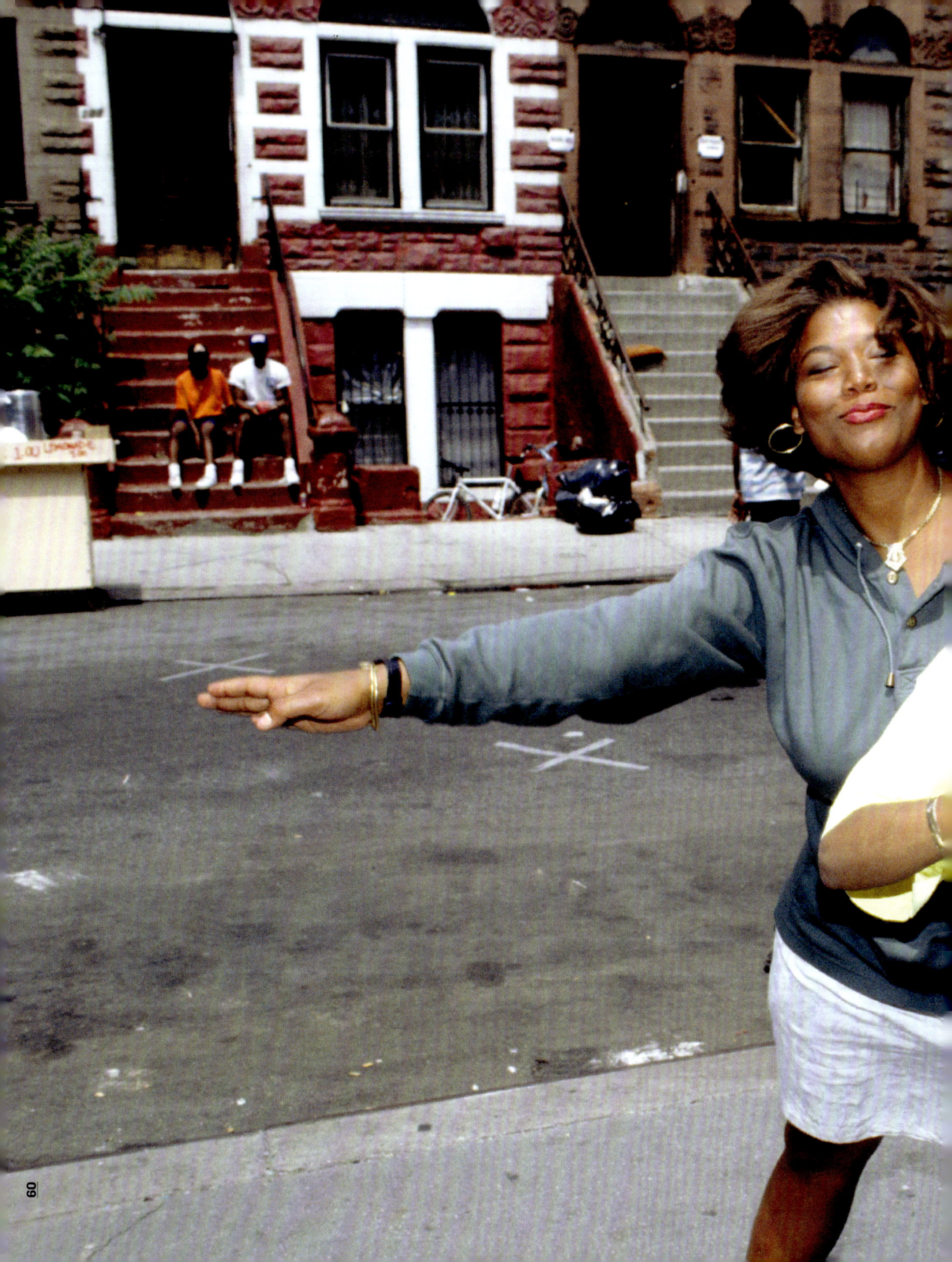

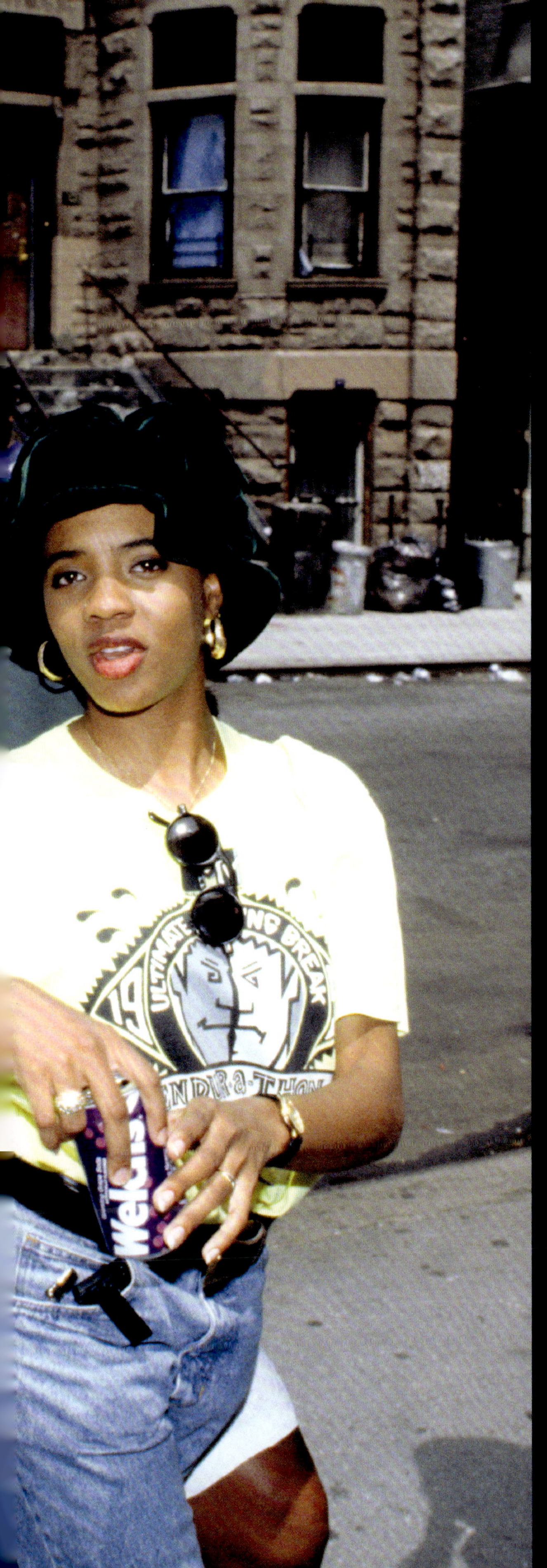

p.58-59 Rakim performing at the Apollo Theatre for the *Paid In Full* tour, Harlem, NYC, 1987.

p.60-p.61 Queen Latifah w MC Lyte on the Harlem location for the video for "Heal Yourself." It was the title track of *H.E.A.L (Human Education Against Lies)*, an 1991 EP produced by KRS-One and D-Nice of Boogie Down Productions (BDP). Carrying a positive message of unity and empowerment through education, the song engaged the talents of Lyte, Latifah, Ms. Melodie, Harmony, Run-DMC, Kid Capri, Big Daddy Kane, Freddie Foxxx, LL Cool J and KRS-One. Harlem, NYC, 1991.

In speaking with KRS-One, his concept in 1991, and now, in 2018, is for "hip-hoppas" to be aware of themselves as part of a "Kultural" identity, and to unify all facets of hip-hop around several core ideals which he defined in his book *The Gospel of Hip-Hop: The First Instrument* (2009). His ideal of unity was also reflected by the varied and massive pool of talent that came together for his first such endeavor, Stop The Violence Movement, with which released a single in 1988 in the wake of the murder of his bandmate and BDP co-founder DJ Scott La Rock the previous year. The 12" single featured raps from BDP, Stetsasonic, Kool Mo Dee, MC Lyte, Doug E. Fresh, Just-Ice, Heavy D and Public Enemy.

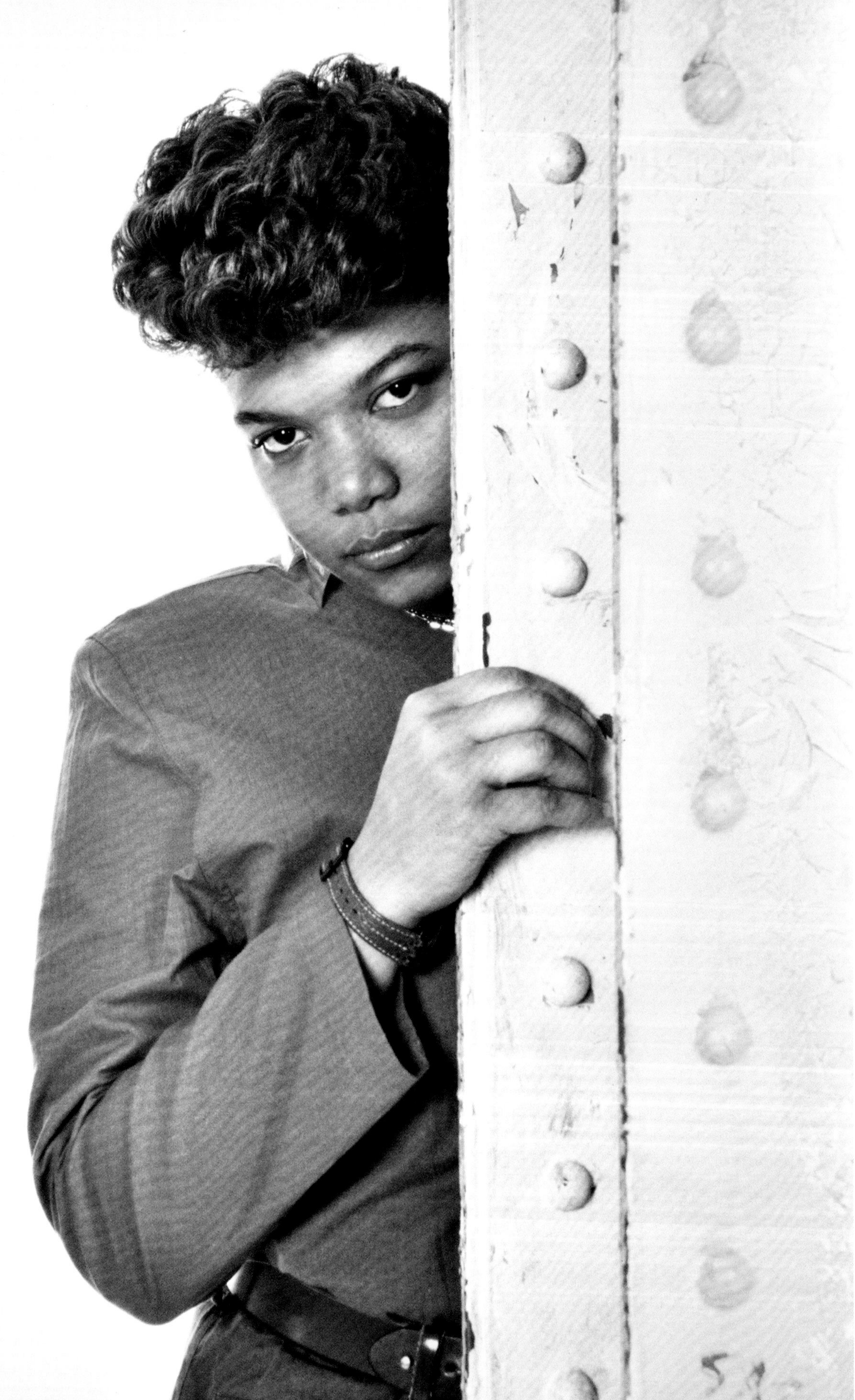

p.62–63 Queen Latifah, Dakota Studios, NYC, 1988.

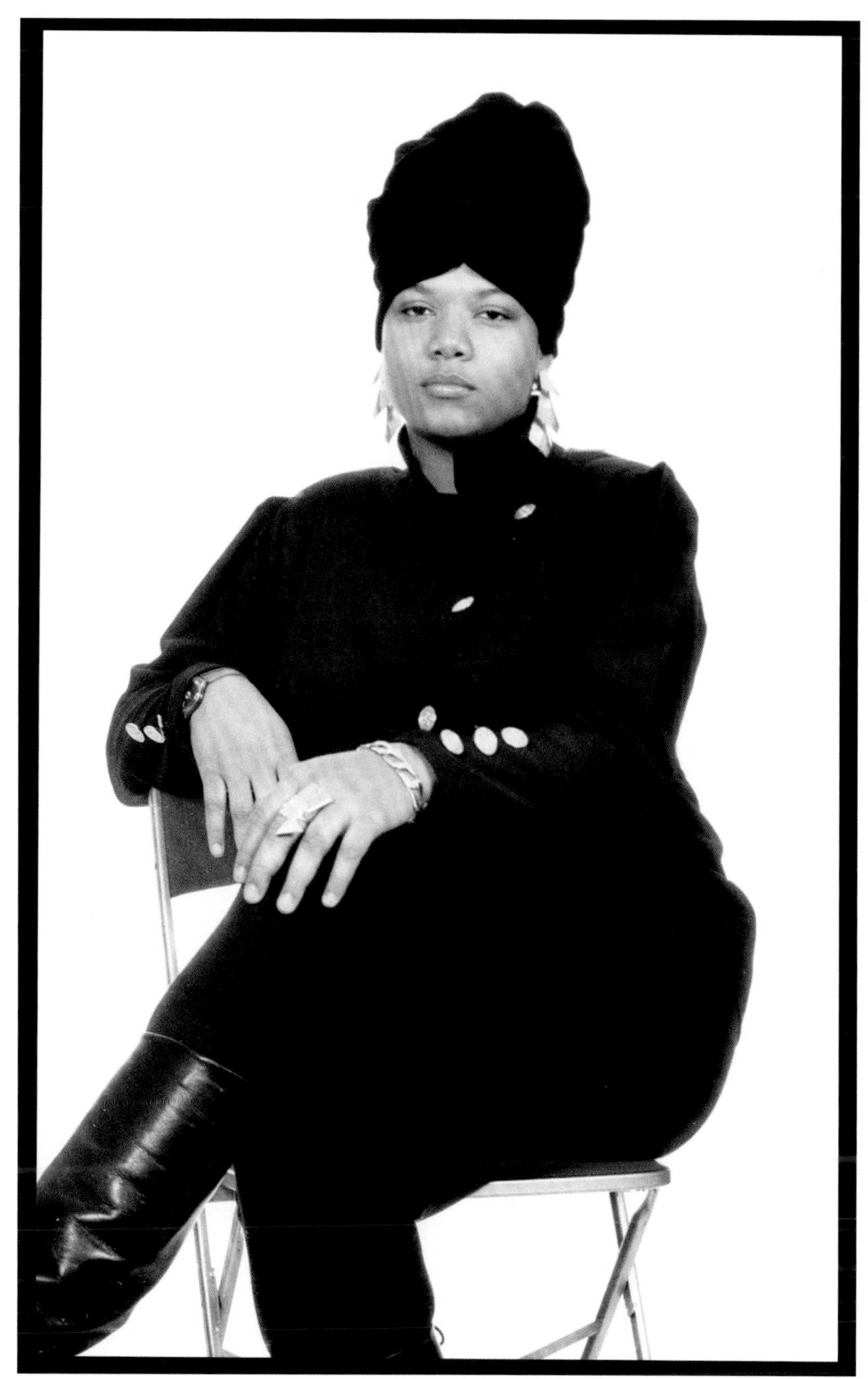

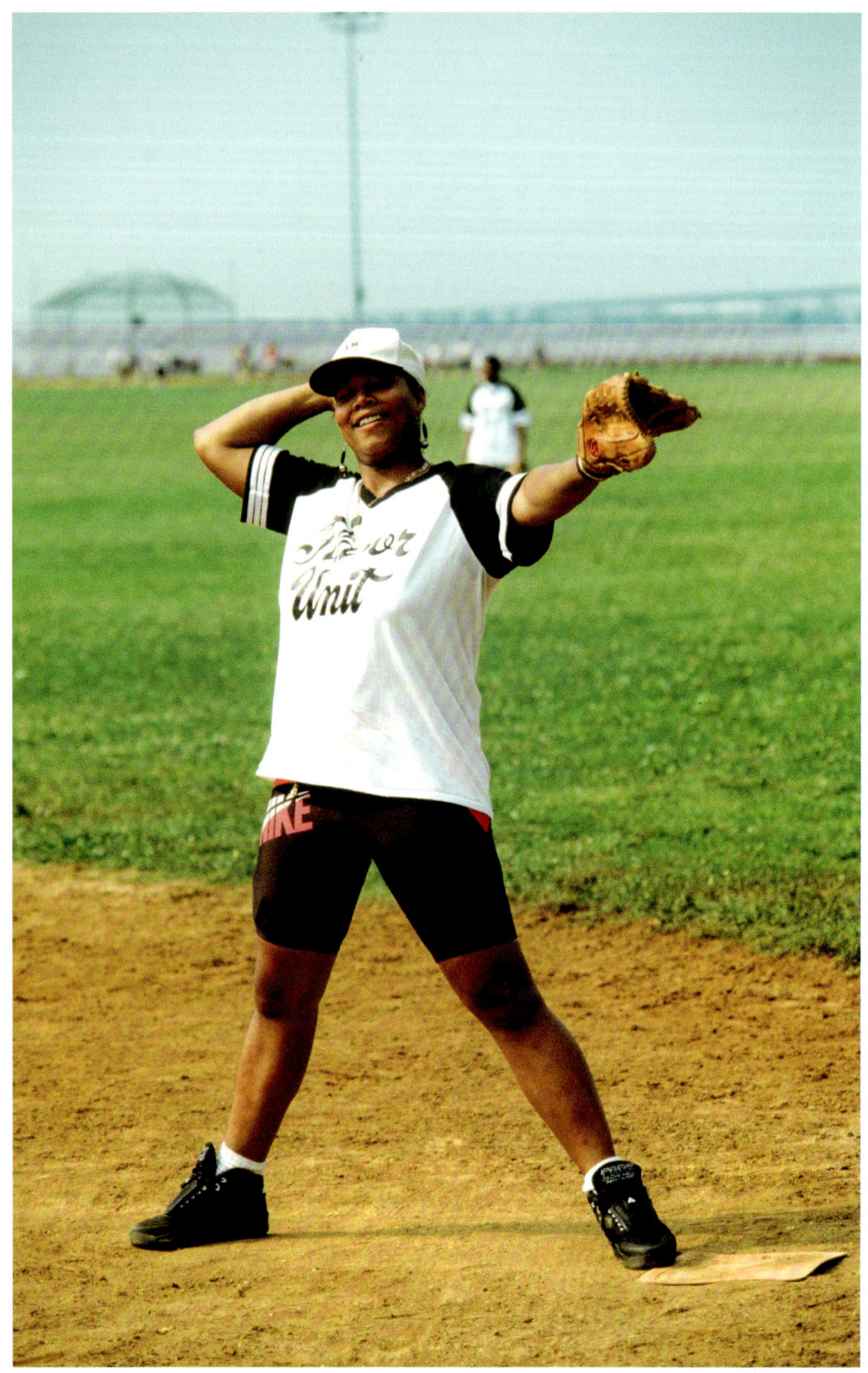

p.64 Queen Latifah in a Flavor Unit vs. Rush Management baseball game in Bayonne, New Jersey, 1992.

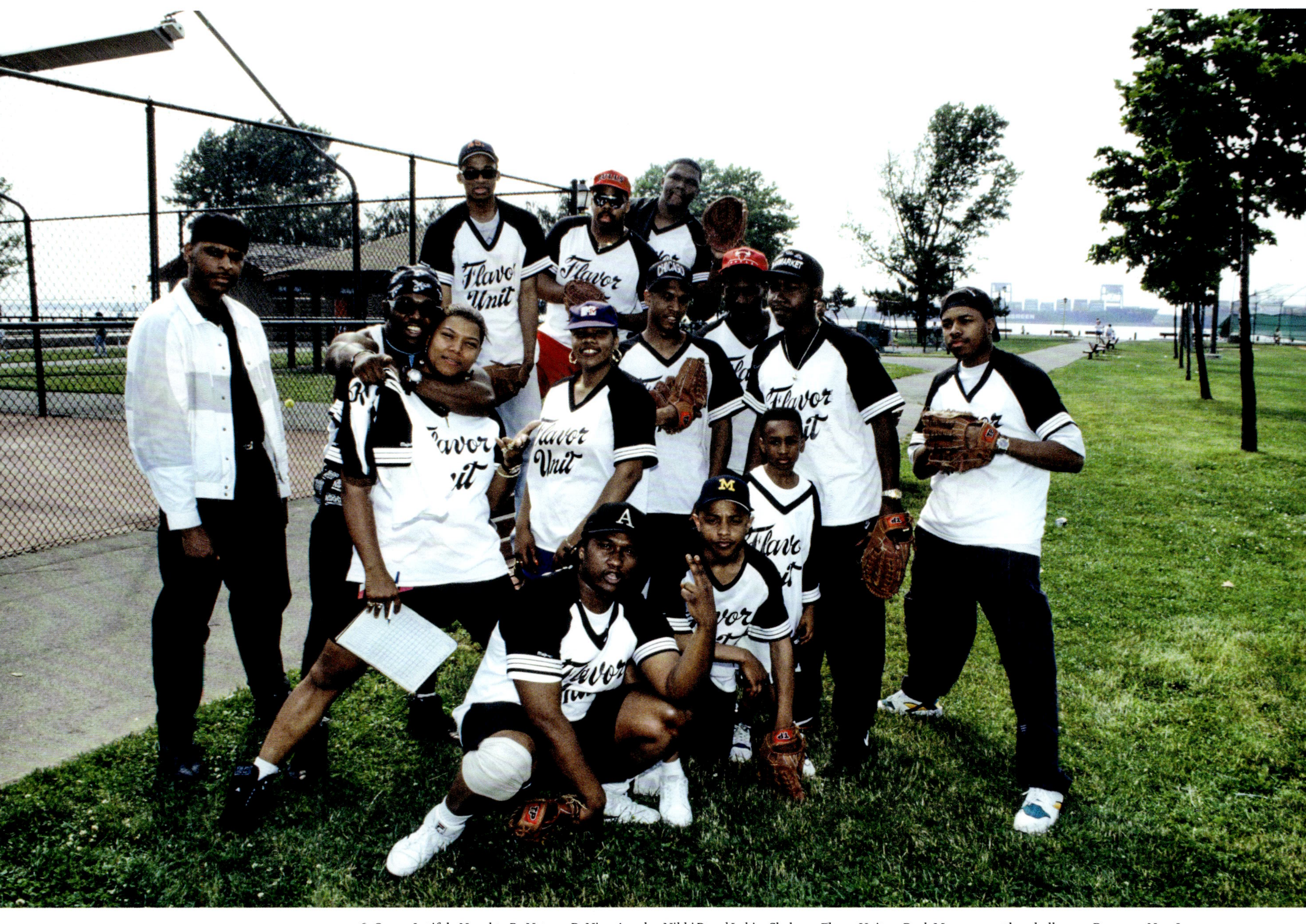

p.65 Queen Latifah, Naughty By Nature, D-Nice, Apache, Nikki D and Lakim Shabazz, Flavor Unit vs. Rush Management baseball game, Bayonne, New Jersey, 1992.

p.66 Fab 5 Freddy, NYC, 1990; p.67 Kool DJ Red Alert, Harlem, NYC, 1990.

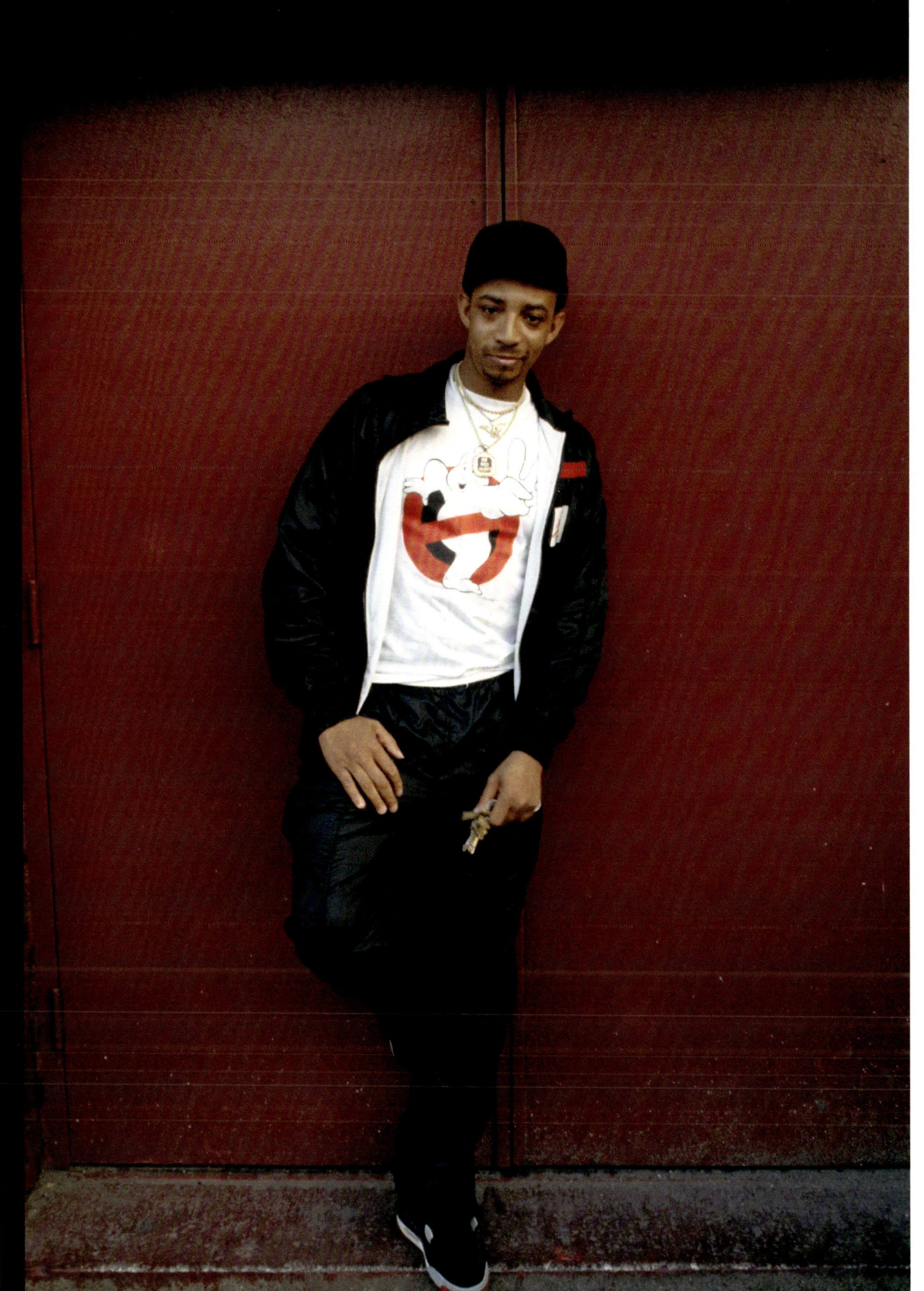

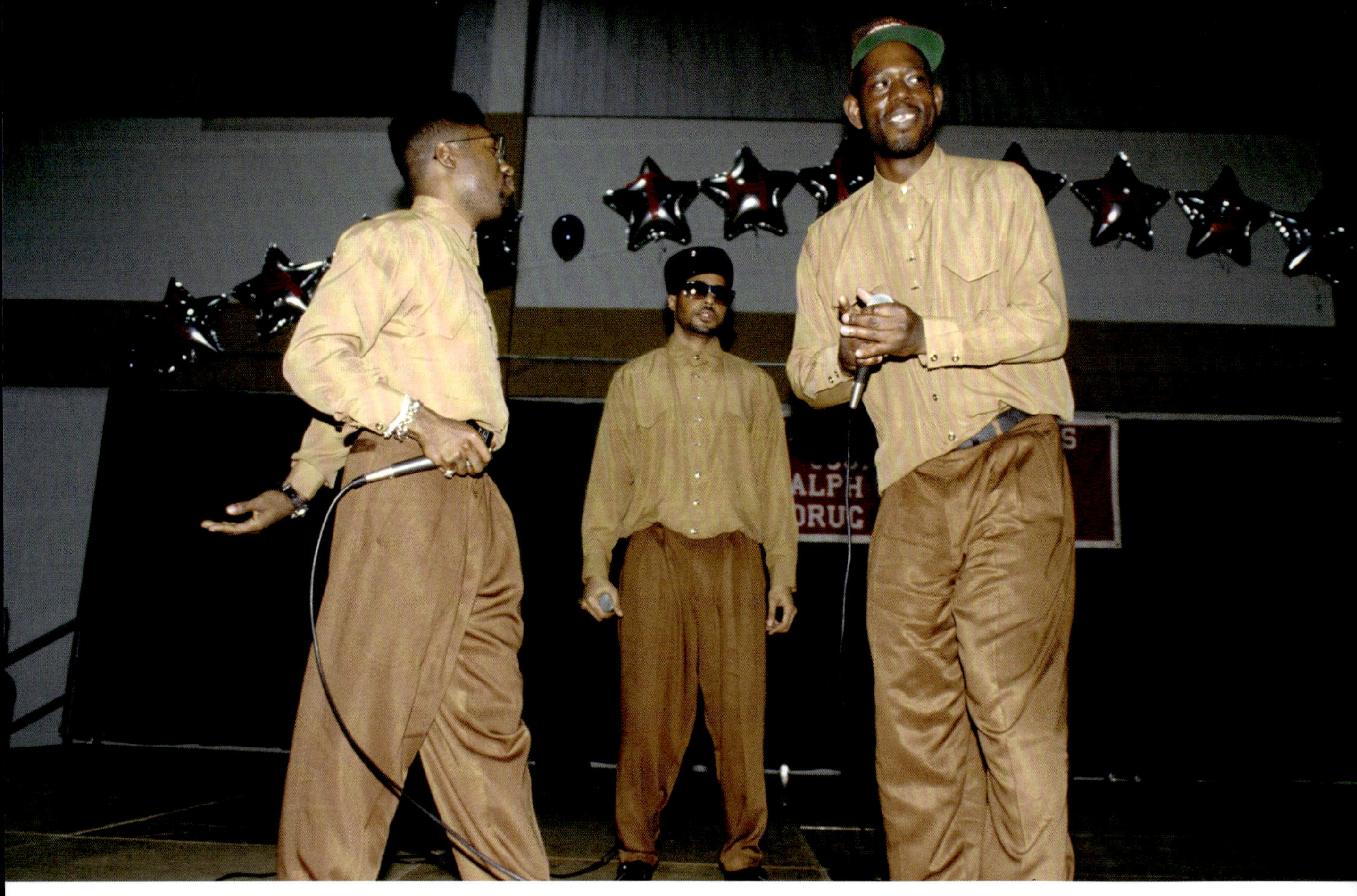

p.68 Stetasonic, Newark, New Jersey, 1989.
p.69 Whodini, NBC Studios, NYC, 1988.

p.71 3rd Bass (MC Serch, Pete Nice, & DJ Richie Rich) in Washington Heights, NYC, 1990.

Notes to page 72:
The New Music Seminar was a music festival and conference that was held annually in New York City from 1980 to 1995 and was recently revived. The New Music Seminar brought out the pioneers of hip-hop, and featured in this picture from the early 1990s are Scorpio, Ice-T, Professor Griff (Public Enemy), Africa Bambaataa, Mr. (Soulsonic Force) Biggs, King Sun and Melle Mel.

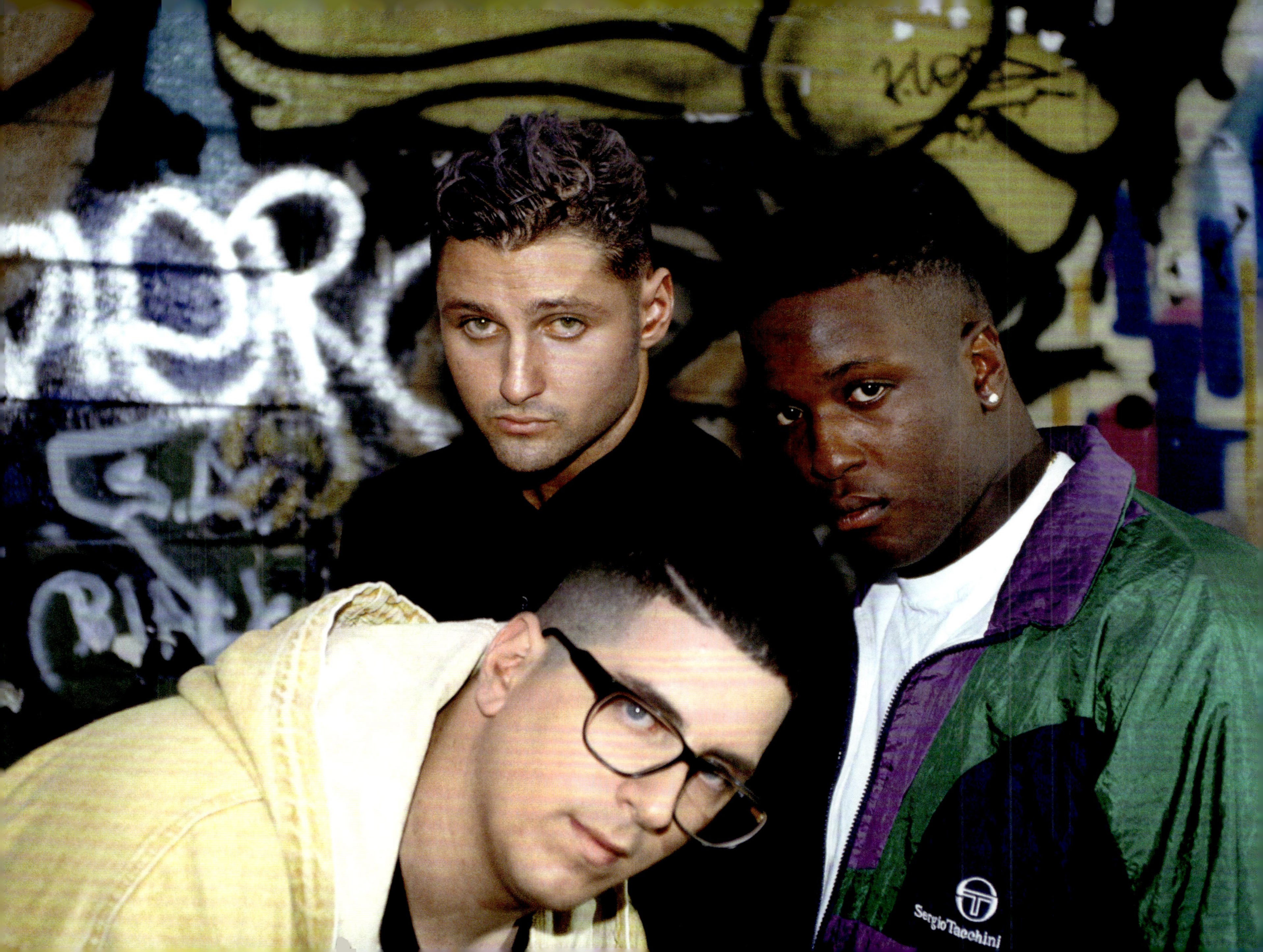
Sergio Tacchini

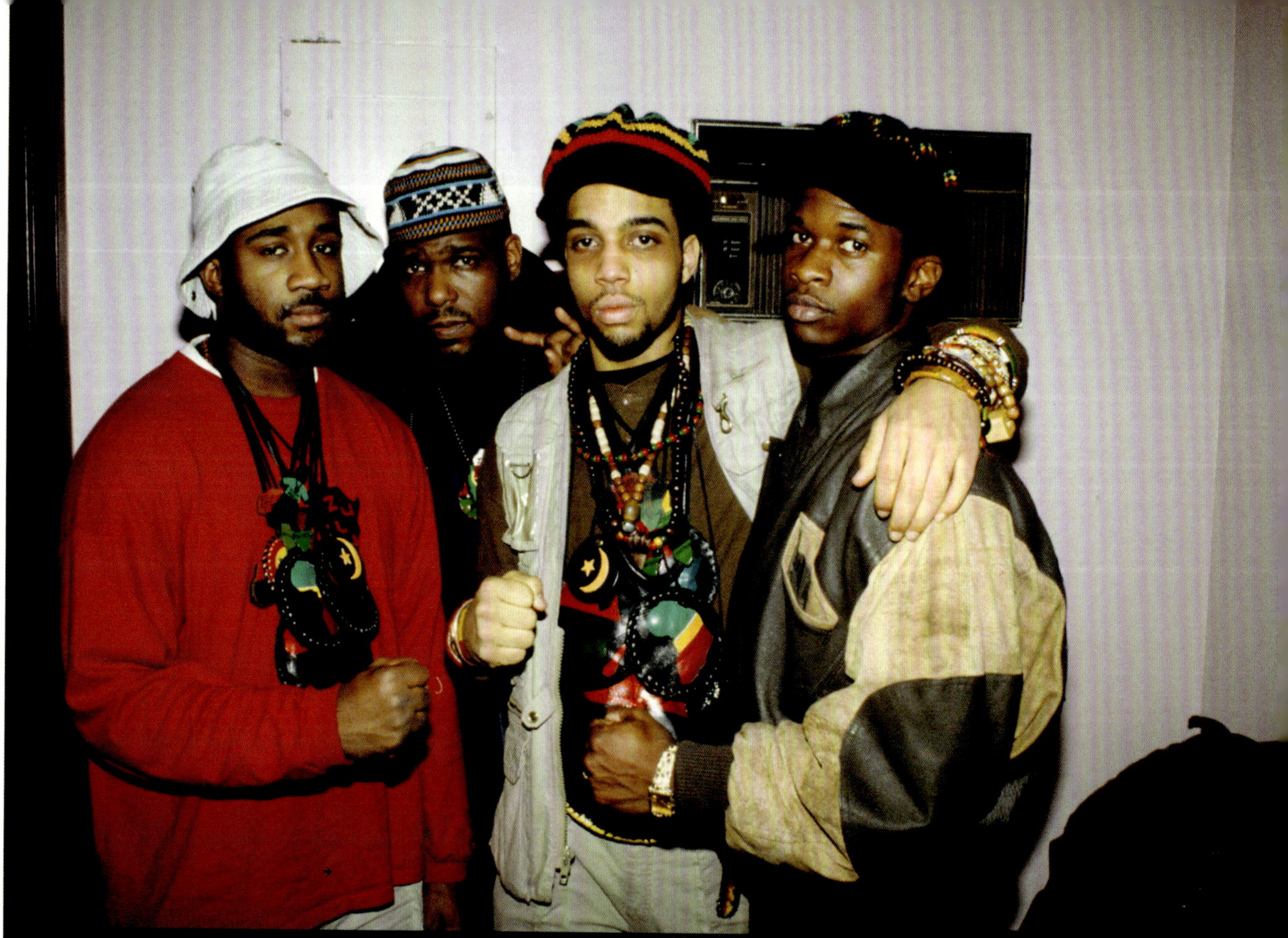

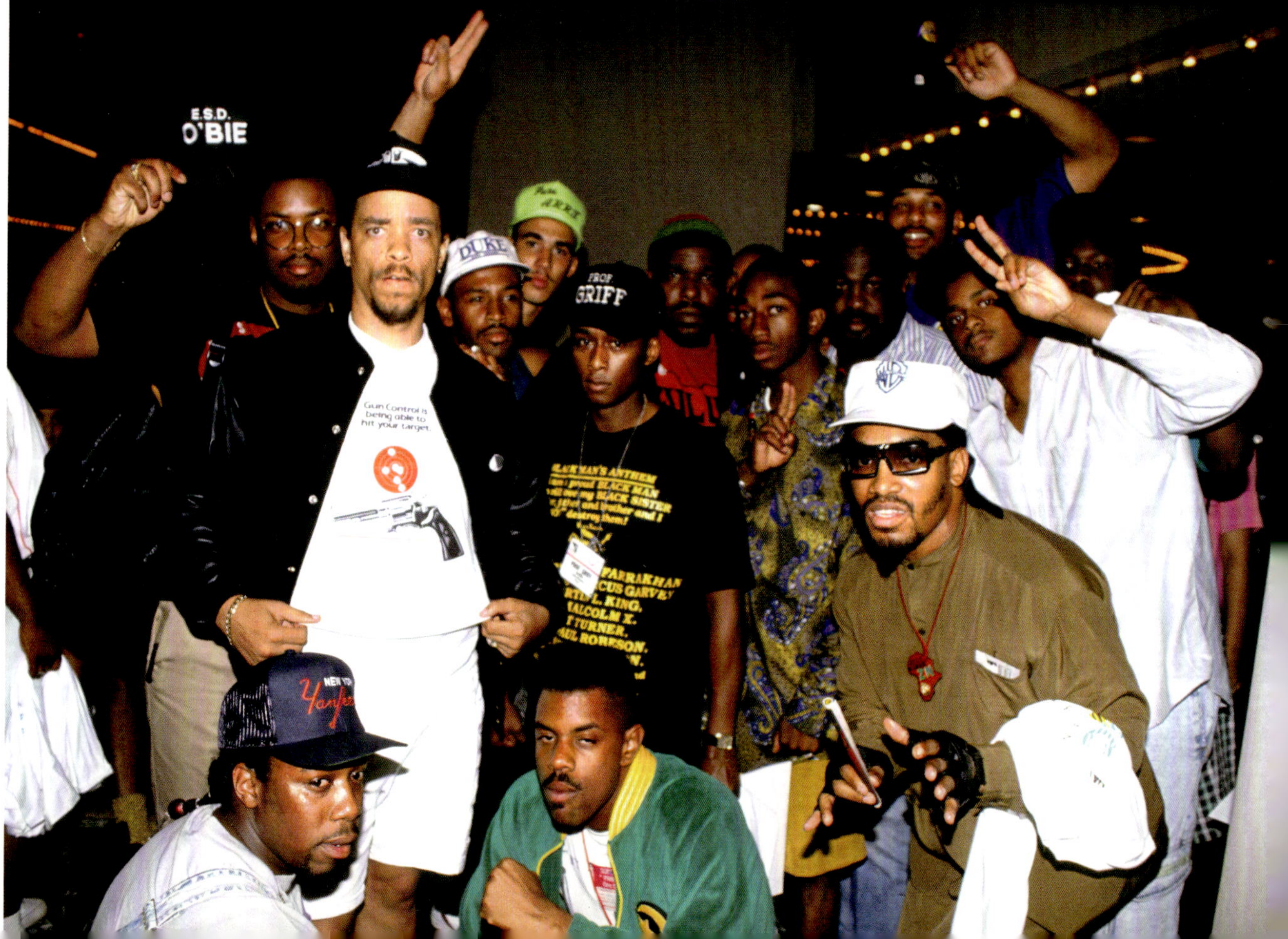

p.72 (top) Afrika Bambaataa with the Jungle Brothers, NYC, around 1989; (bottom) Artists at the New Music Seminar, NYC, early 1990s (see additional notes on page 70).

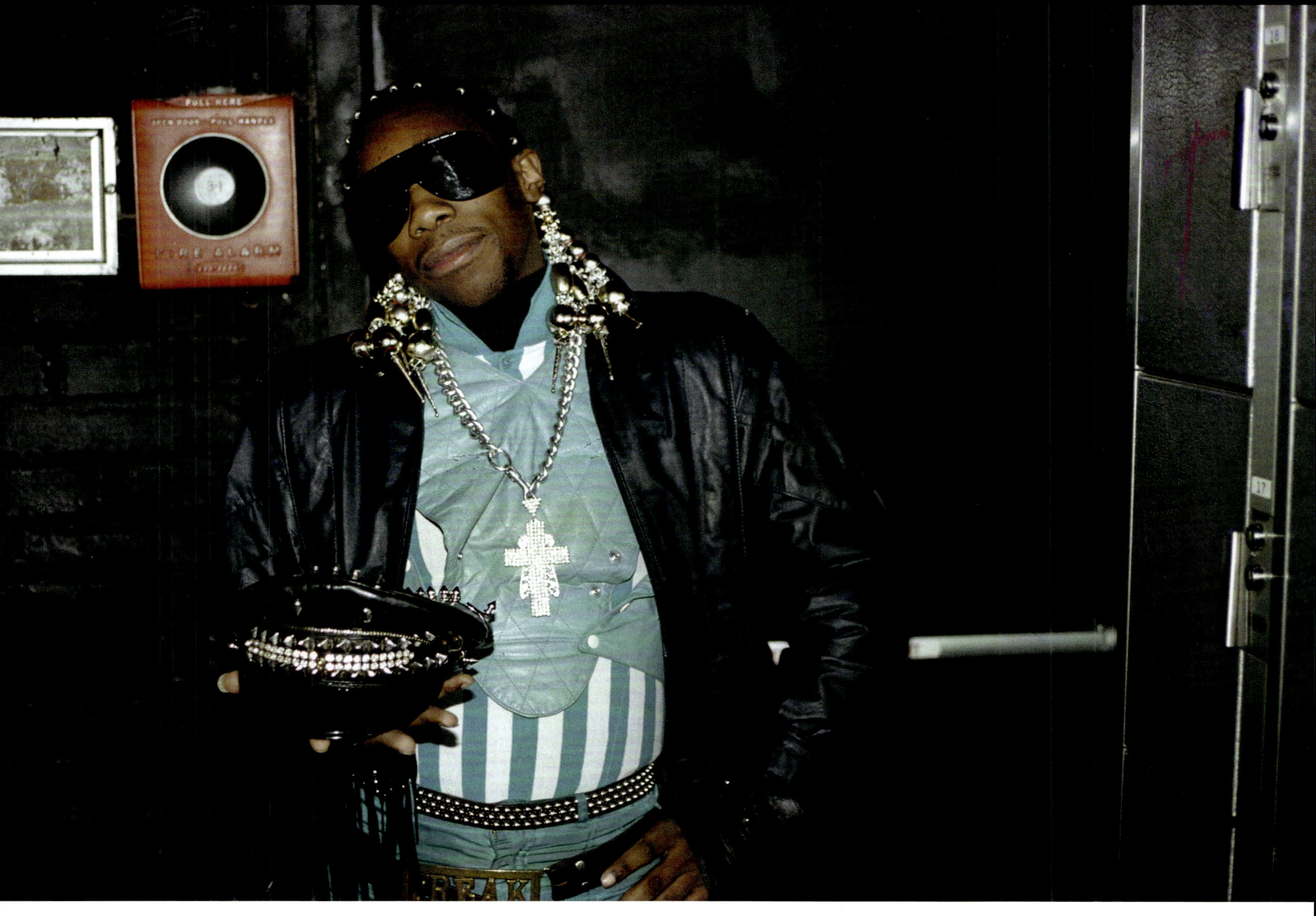

p.73 Scorpio, NYC, around 1987.

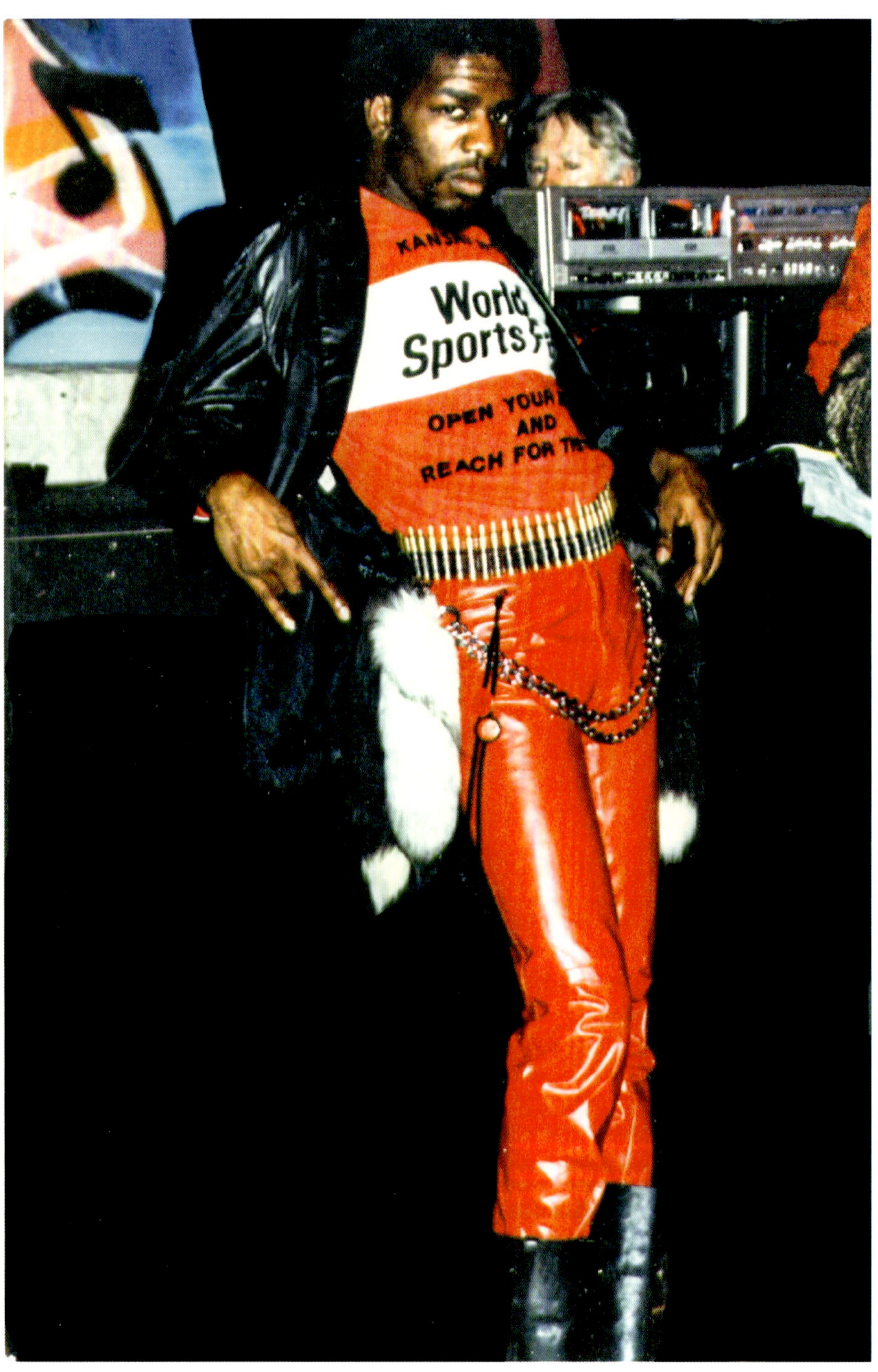
World
Sports
OPEN YOUR
AND
REACH FOR

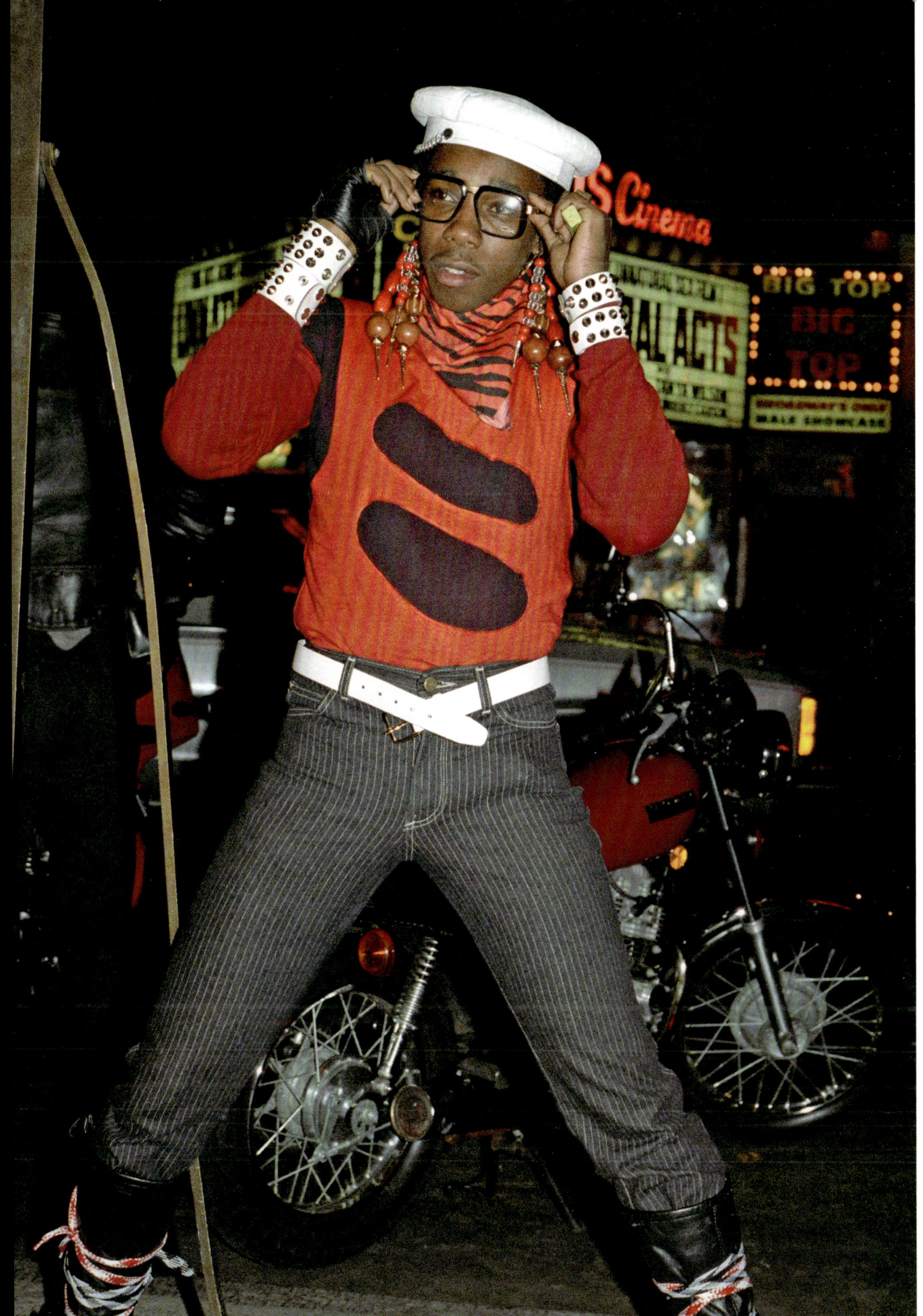

p.74 Tony Tone, The Roxy, 1979; p.75 Scorpio, 42nd Sreet, NYC, 1980.

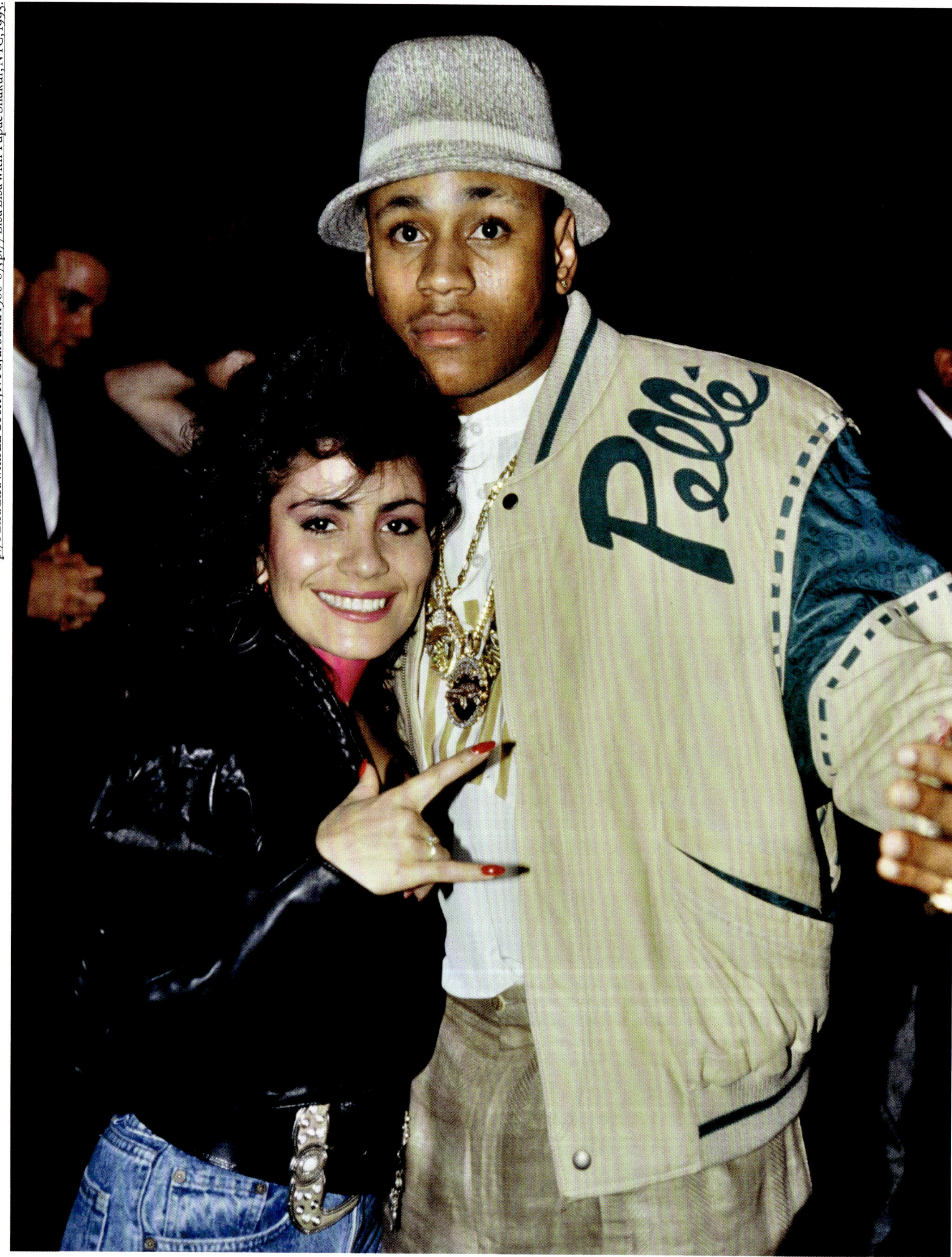

p.76 Lisa Lisa with LL Cool J, NYC, around 1986-87; p.77 Lisa Lisa with Tupac Shakur, NYC, 1995.

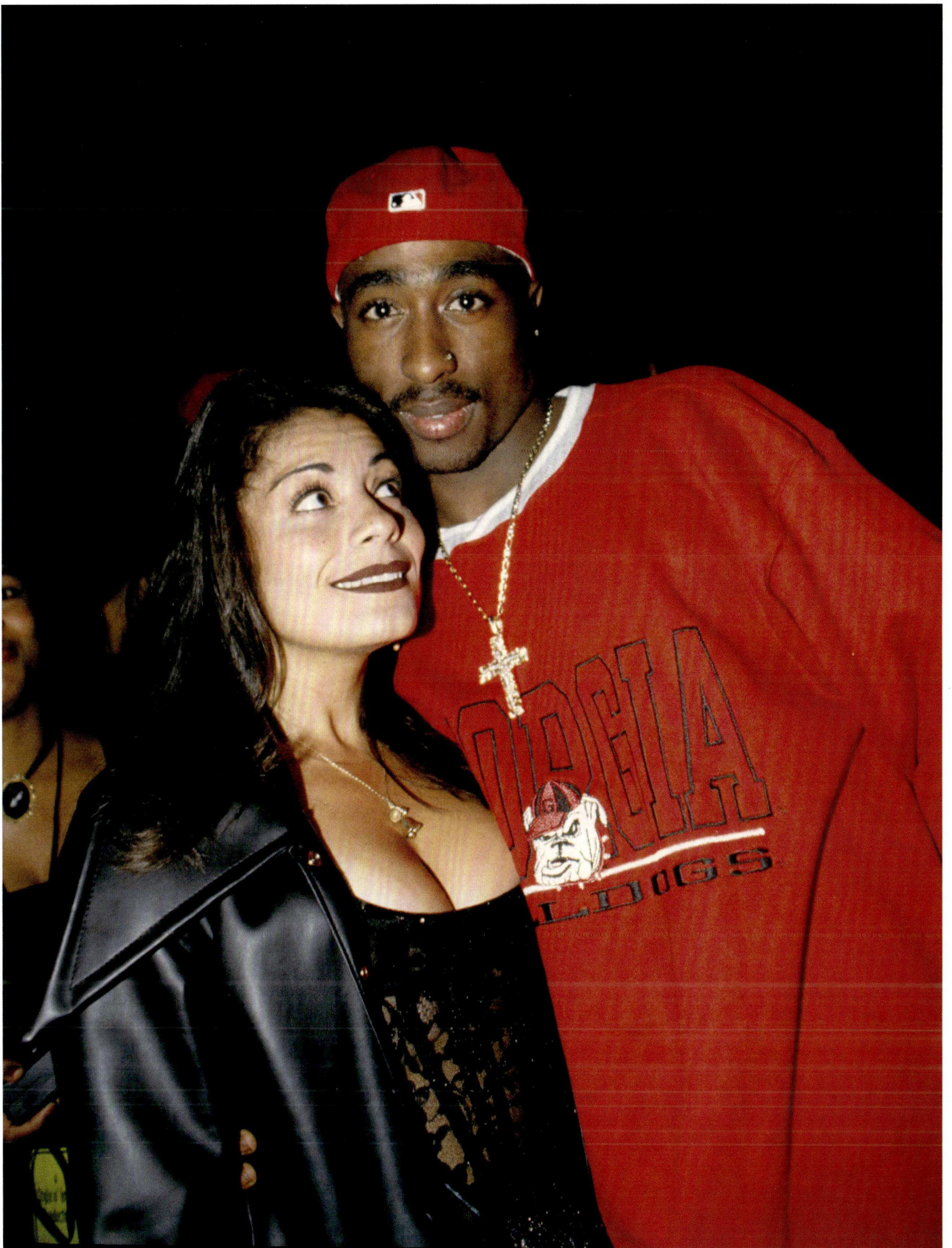

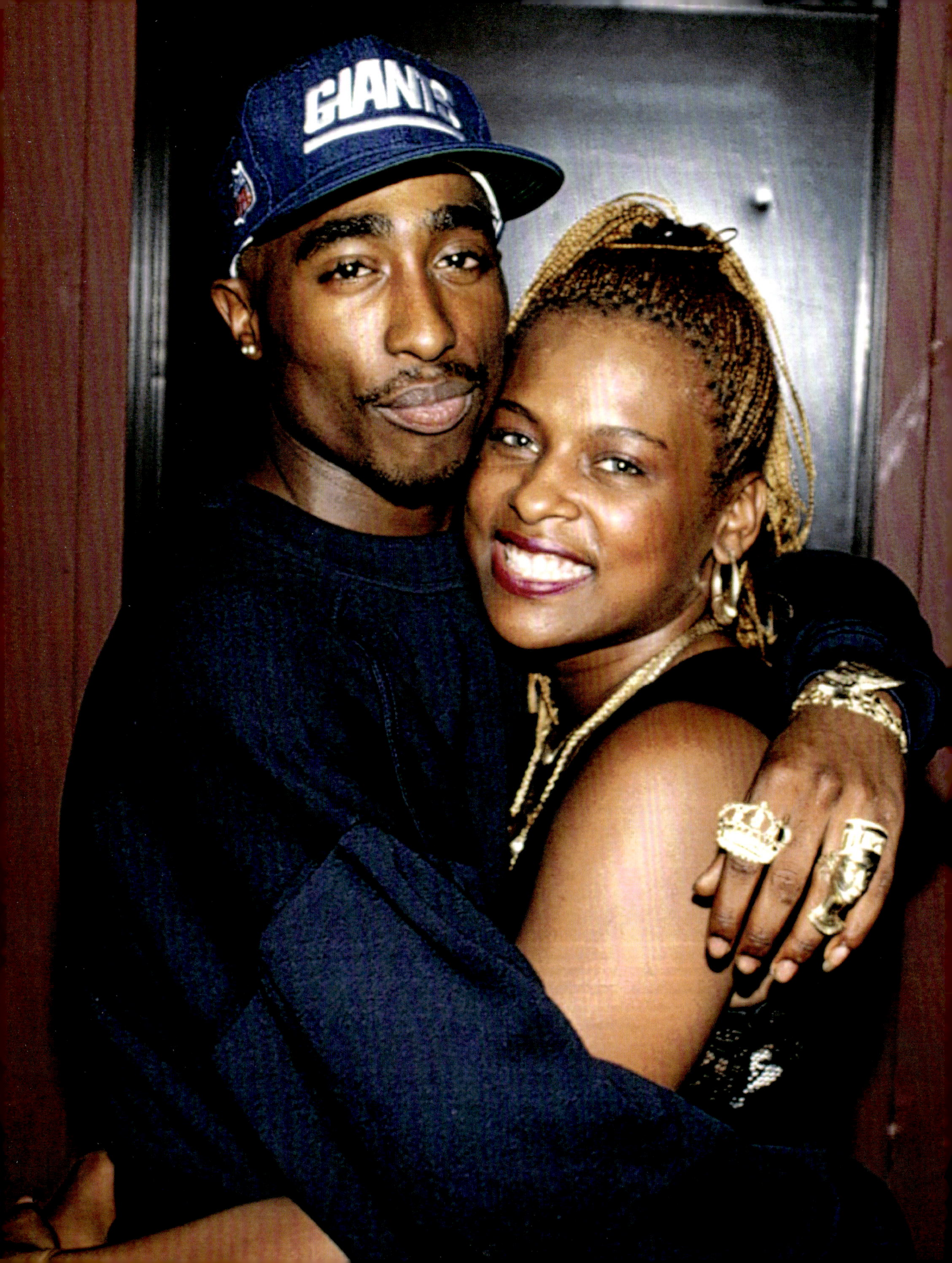
GIANTS

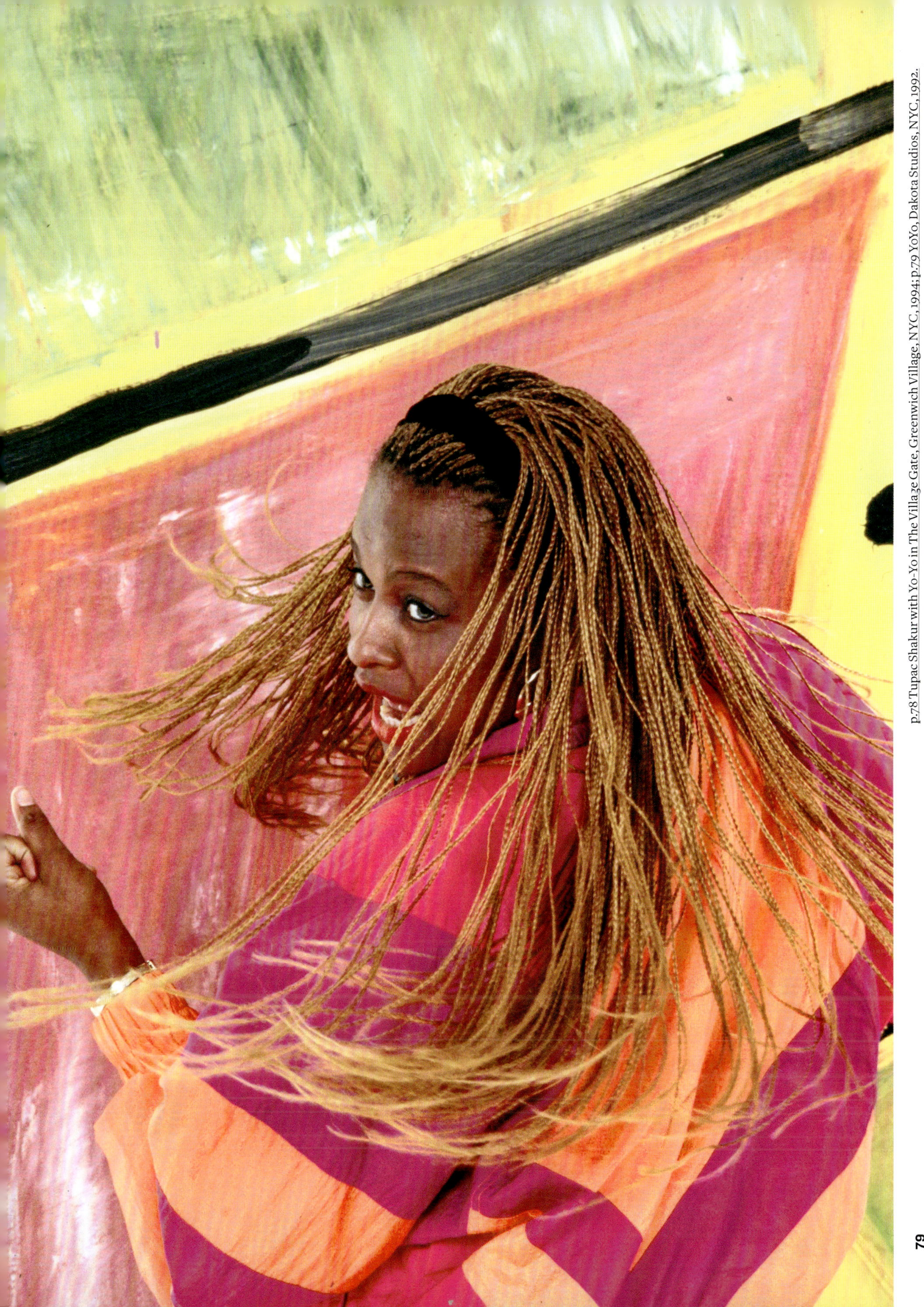

p.78 Tupac Shakur with Yo-Yo in The Village Gate, Greenwich Village, NYC, 1994; p.79 YoYo, Dakota Studios, NYC, 1992.

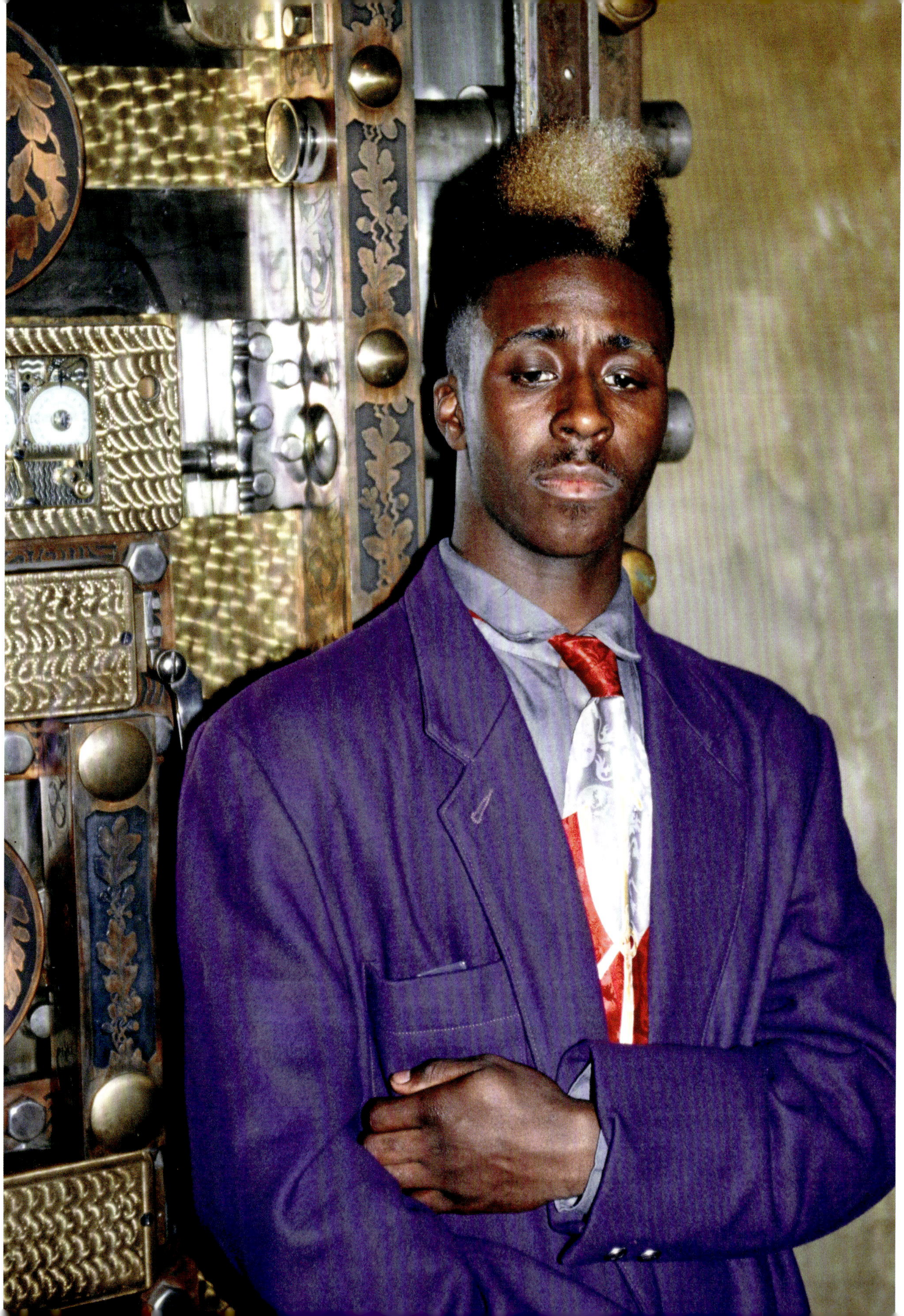

p.80 Kwamé Holland, Club M.K., NYC, 1989

p. 80 This portrait of Kwamé Holland from 1989 was shot inside Club M.K., a former bank on Fifth Avenue and 25th Street. It was a fundraiser for mayoral candidate David Dinkins. Kwamé, Big Daddy Kane, Madonna, Sandra Bernhard, Princess Gloria von Thurn und Taxis and many others were there, and Kwamé and Big Daddy Kane were some of the people that were performing.

This image is notable because Kwamé isn't wearing his trademark polka dots. In the 1994 song "Unbelievable" by The Notorious B.I.G., he and the polka dots go for some ripping:

Hate to blast you, but I have to, you see I smoke a lot
Your life is played out like Kwamé, and them fucking polka dots

When I spoke to Kwamé about it years later, he was clear that Biggie's diss reignited his career because it put his name back on the airwaves and the grapevine.

p.82-83 The producer Hurby "Love Bug" Azor's posse: Mark "DJ Wiz" Eastmond, Kwamé Holland, Cheryl "Salt" Riley, Dee Dee "DJ Spinderella" Roper, Sweet Tee, Kid n' Play, and Sandy "Pepa" Denton, Dakota Studios, NYC, 1990.

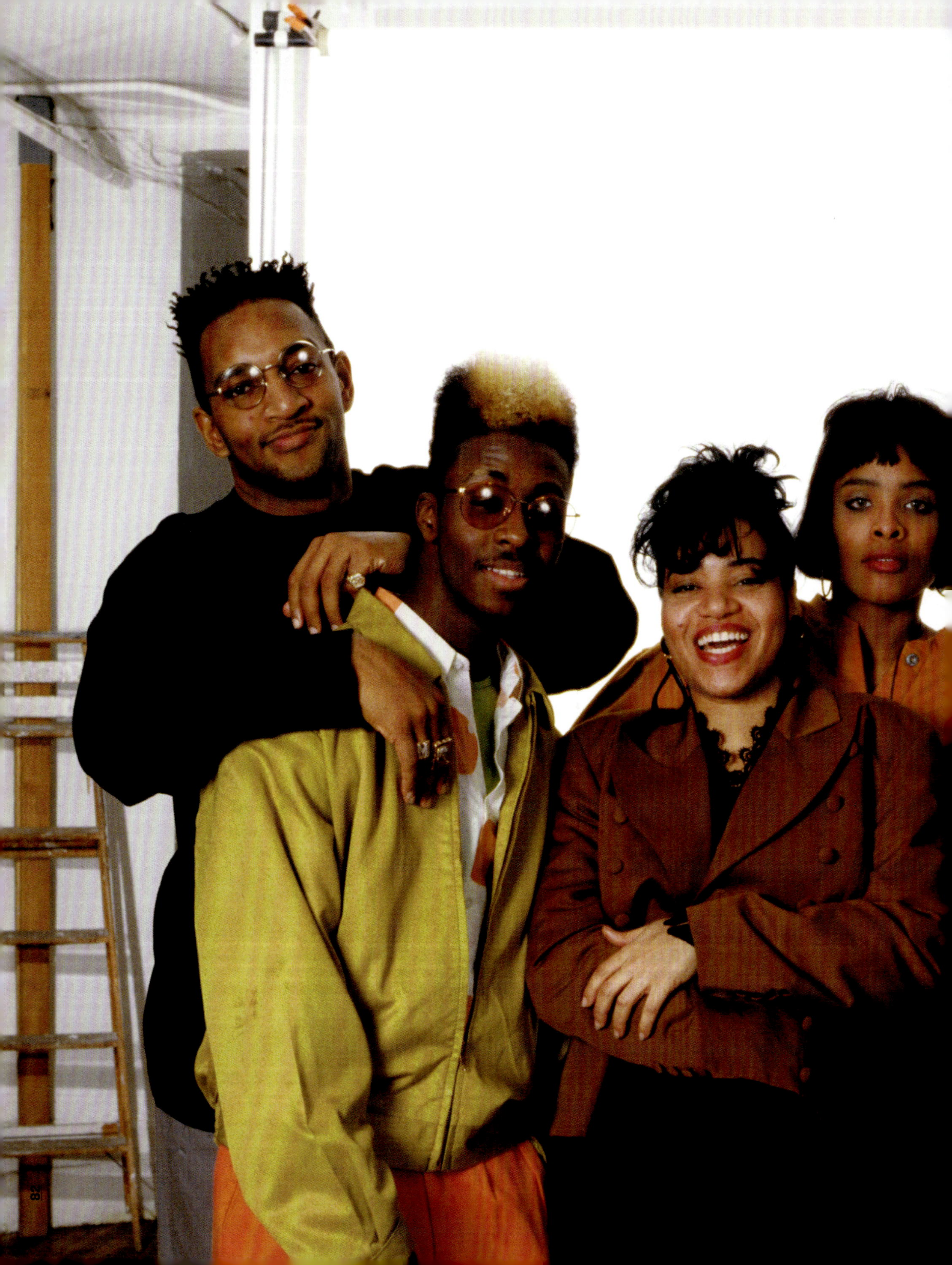

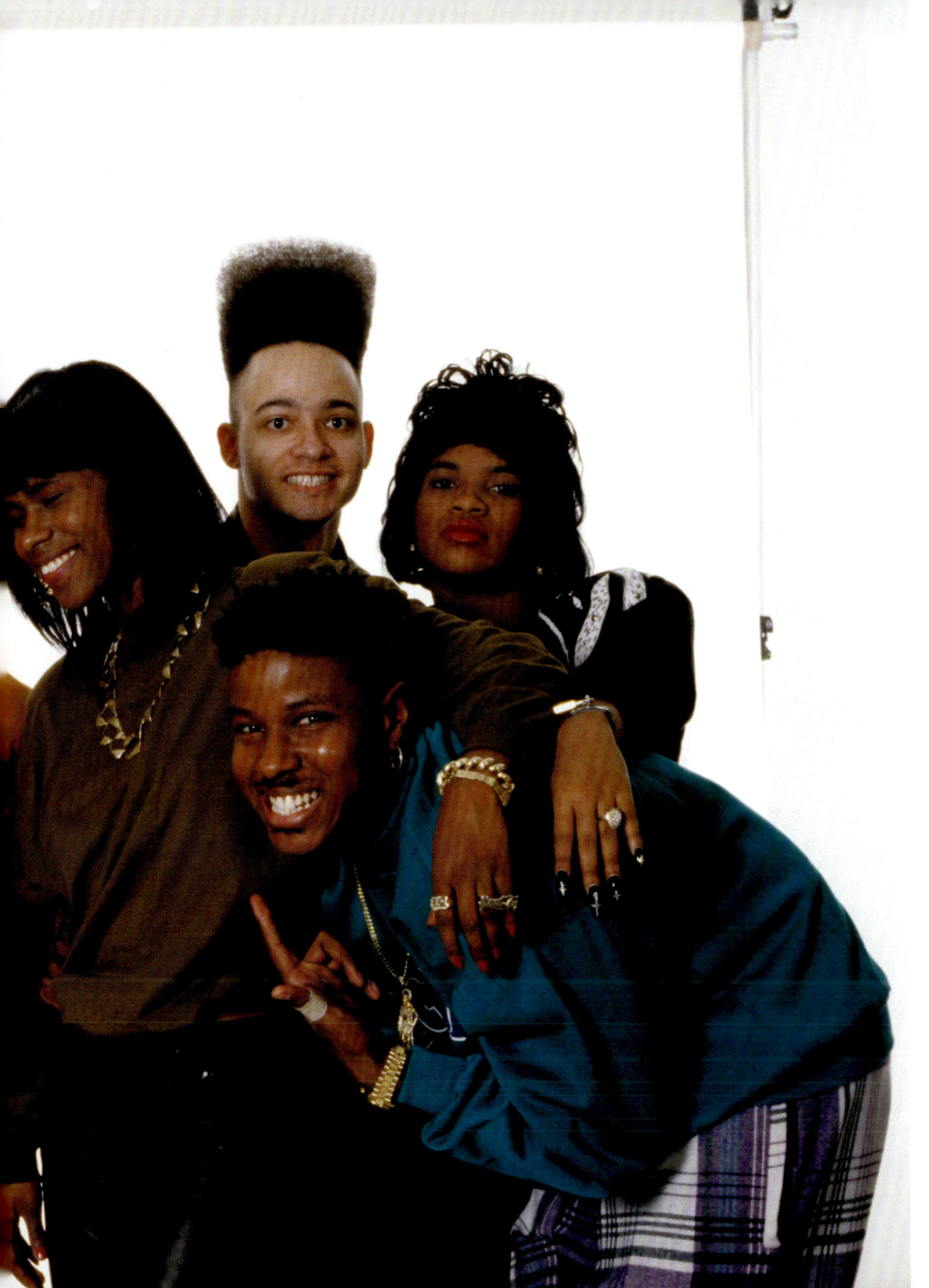

p.84 DJ Wiz, Kid, Slick Rick and Play at RAPMANIA, Apollo Theatre, NYC, 1990; p.85 Kid, Will Smith, Play, DJ Wiz on a shoot for a seatbelt PSA, NYC, 1989.

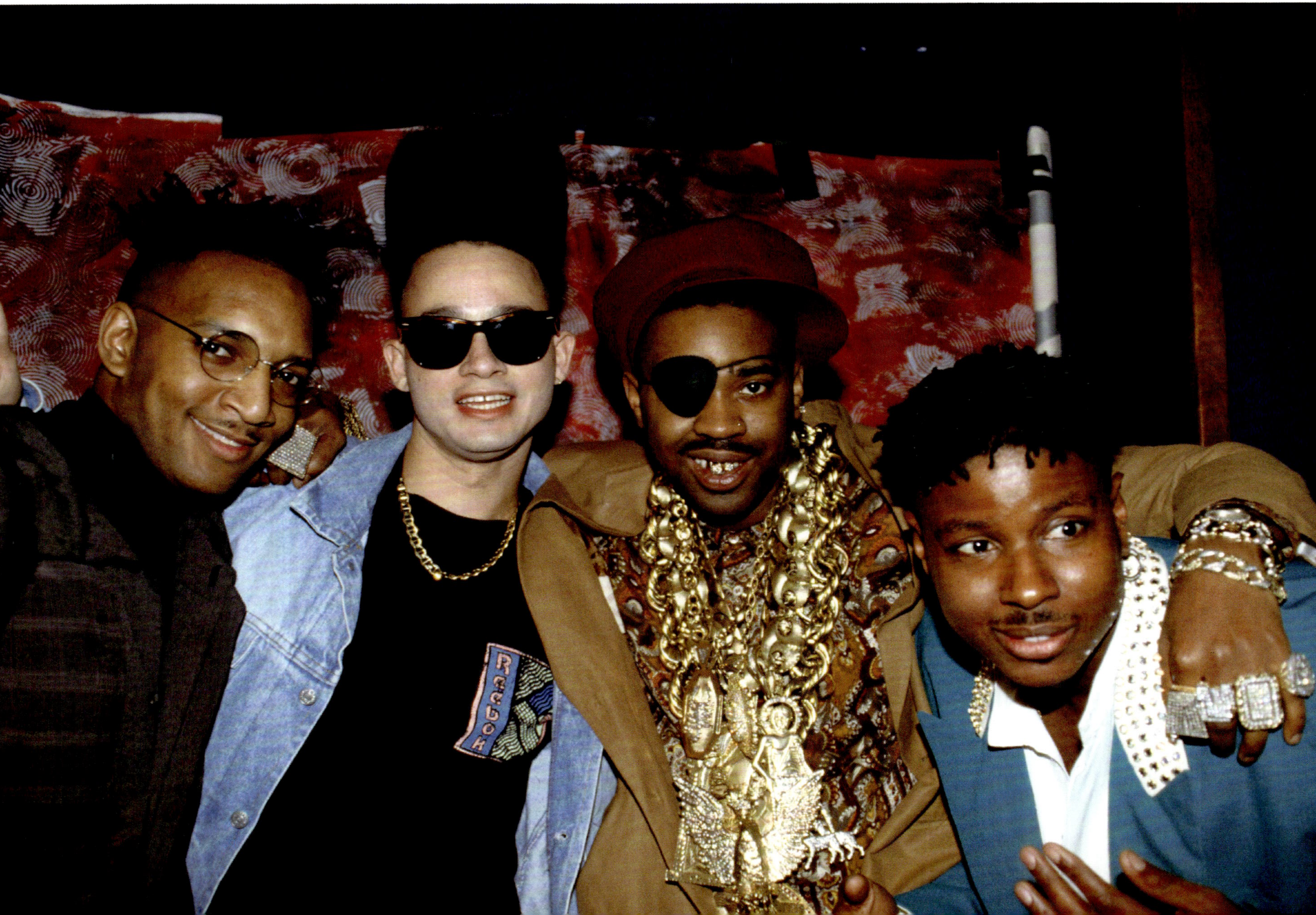

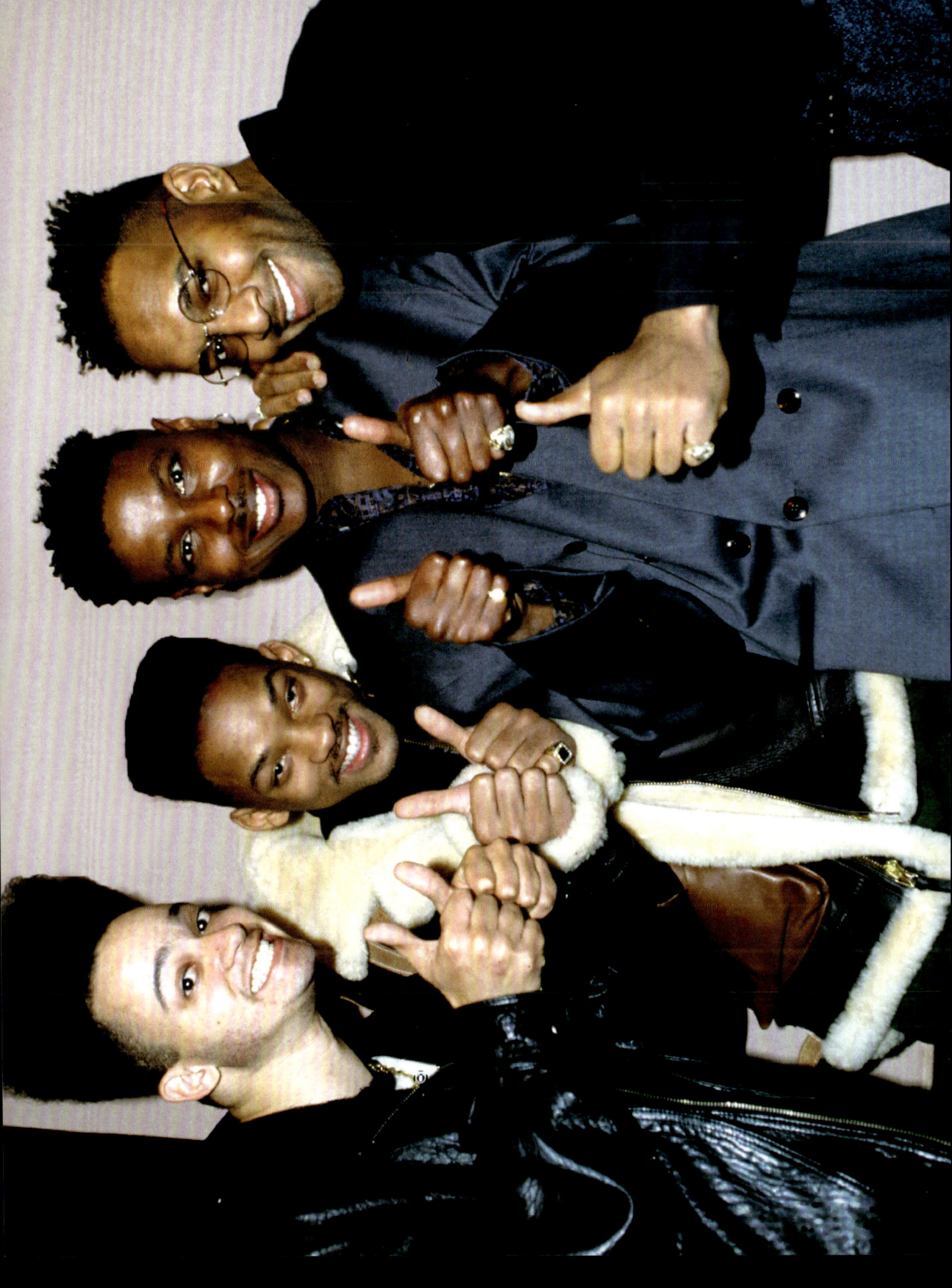

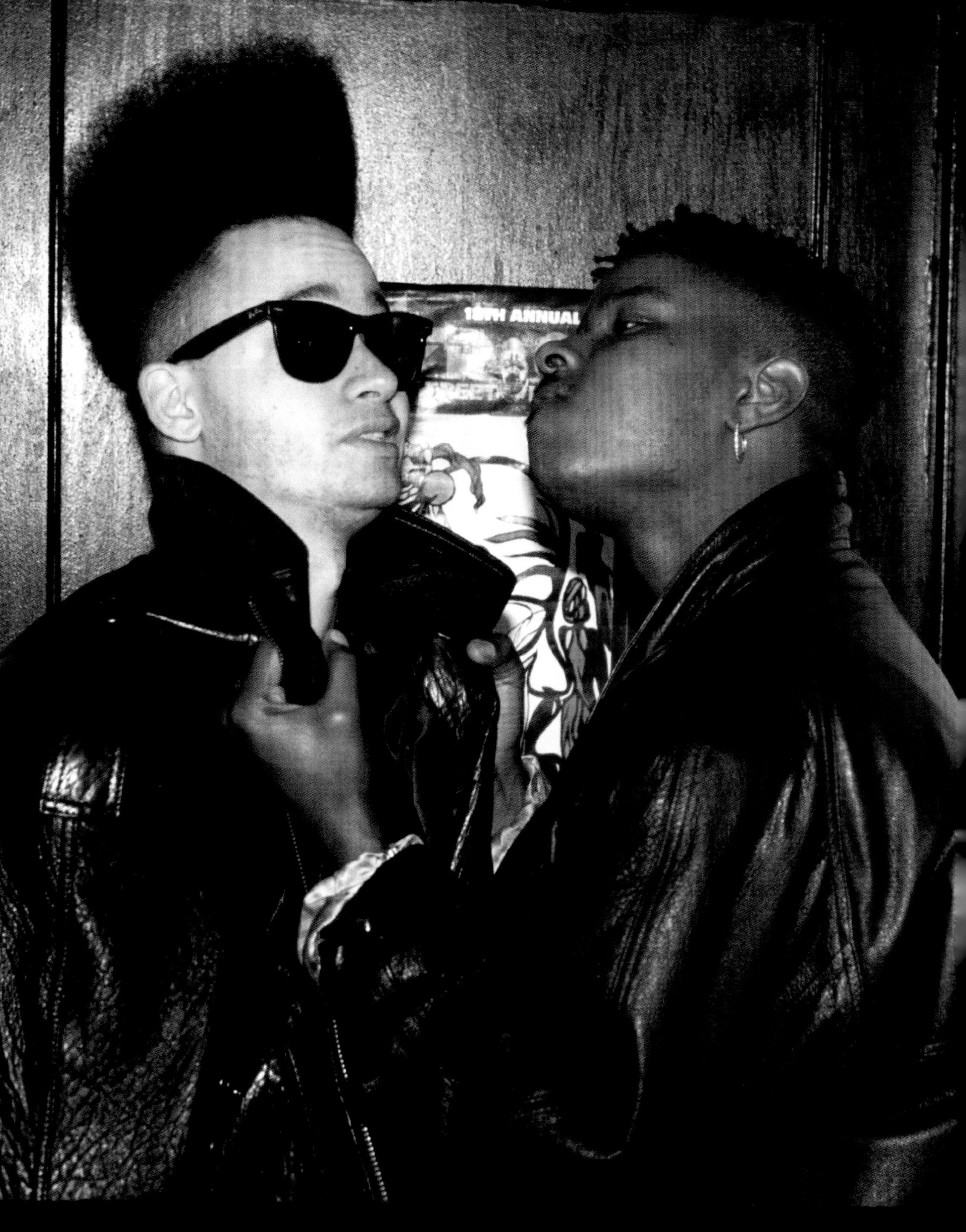
ANNUAL

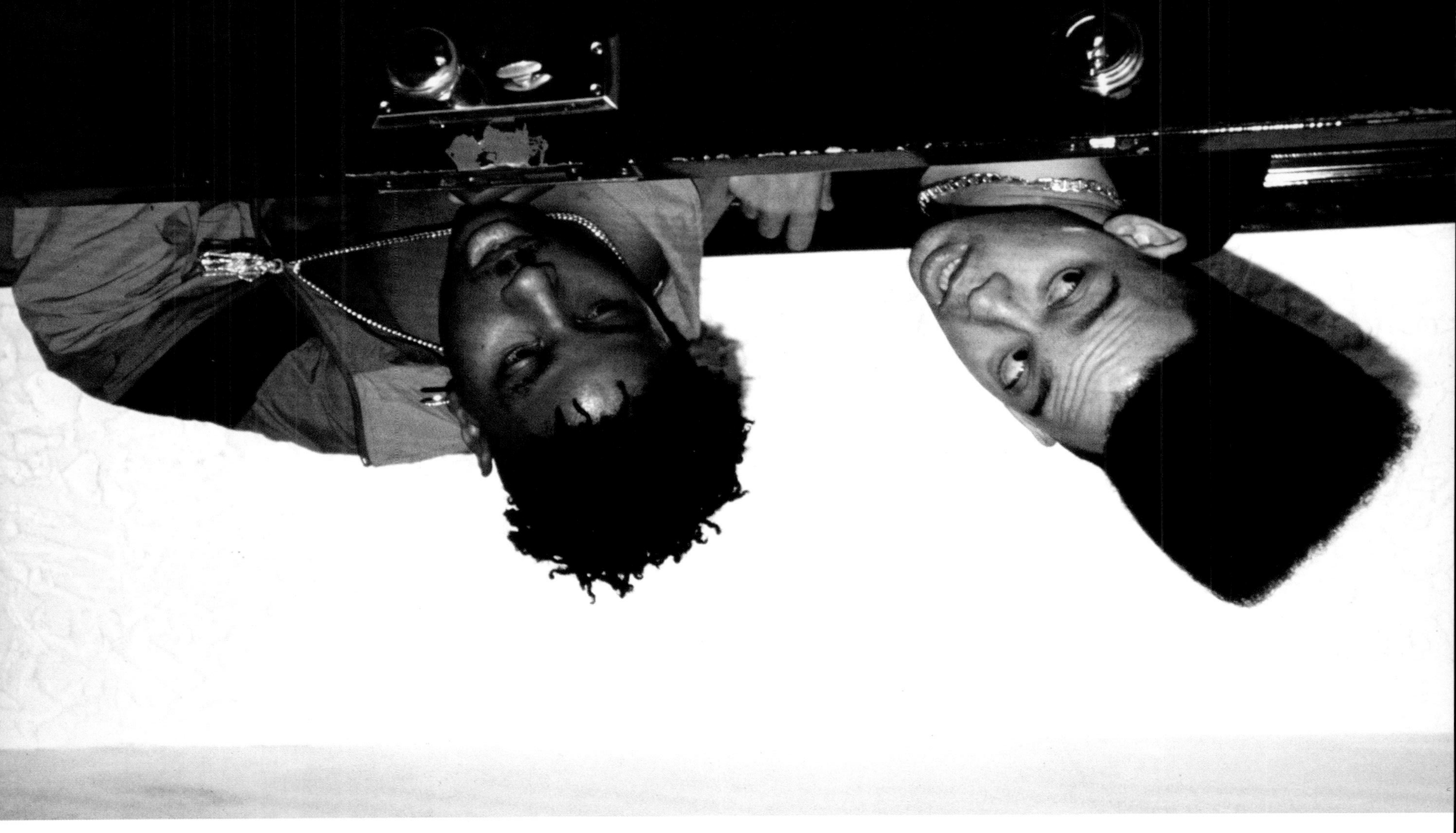

p.86-87 Kid n' Play, Long Island City, Queens, NYC.

p.89 Kid n' Play on a cold High School floor somewhere in Queens NY during their video shoot. One of my favorite shots because it captured both the visual and humorous essence of who they were.

Notes to pages 86-87:
I shot these two images during a photo shoot I did for *Word Up!* magazine, in a Long Island City dance studio where I witnessed them rehearsing their dance moves for well over three hours. They had a natural comic flair and sense of humor as well as warmth. Circa 1993.

p.90-91 Salt-N-Pepa in concert at Club 818, NYC, 1988.

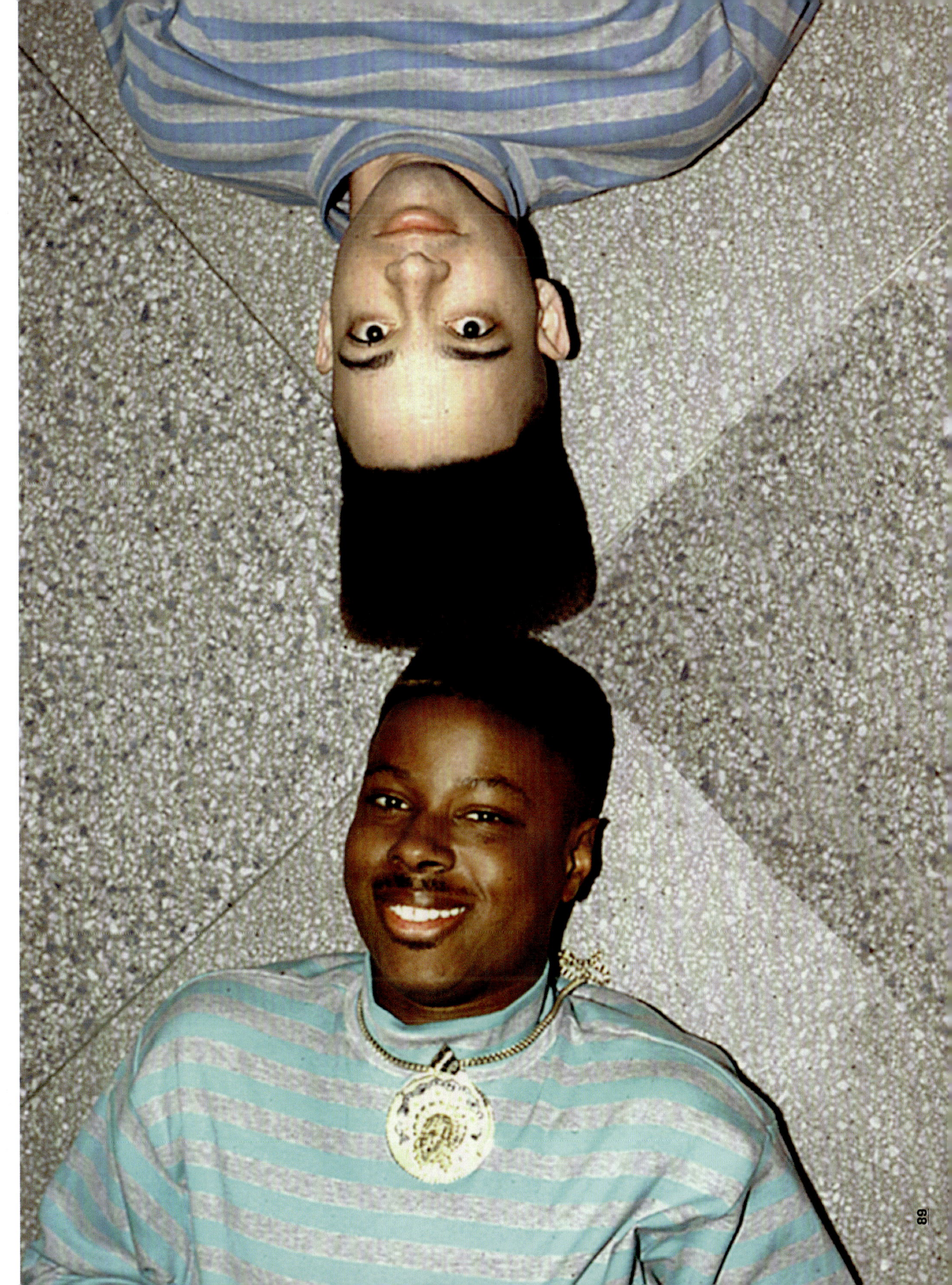

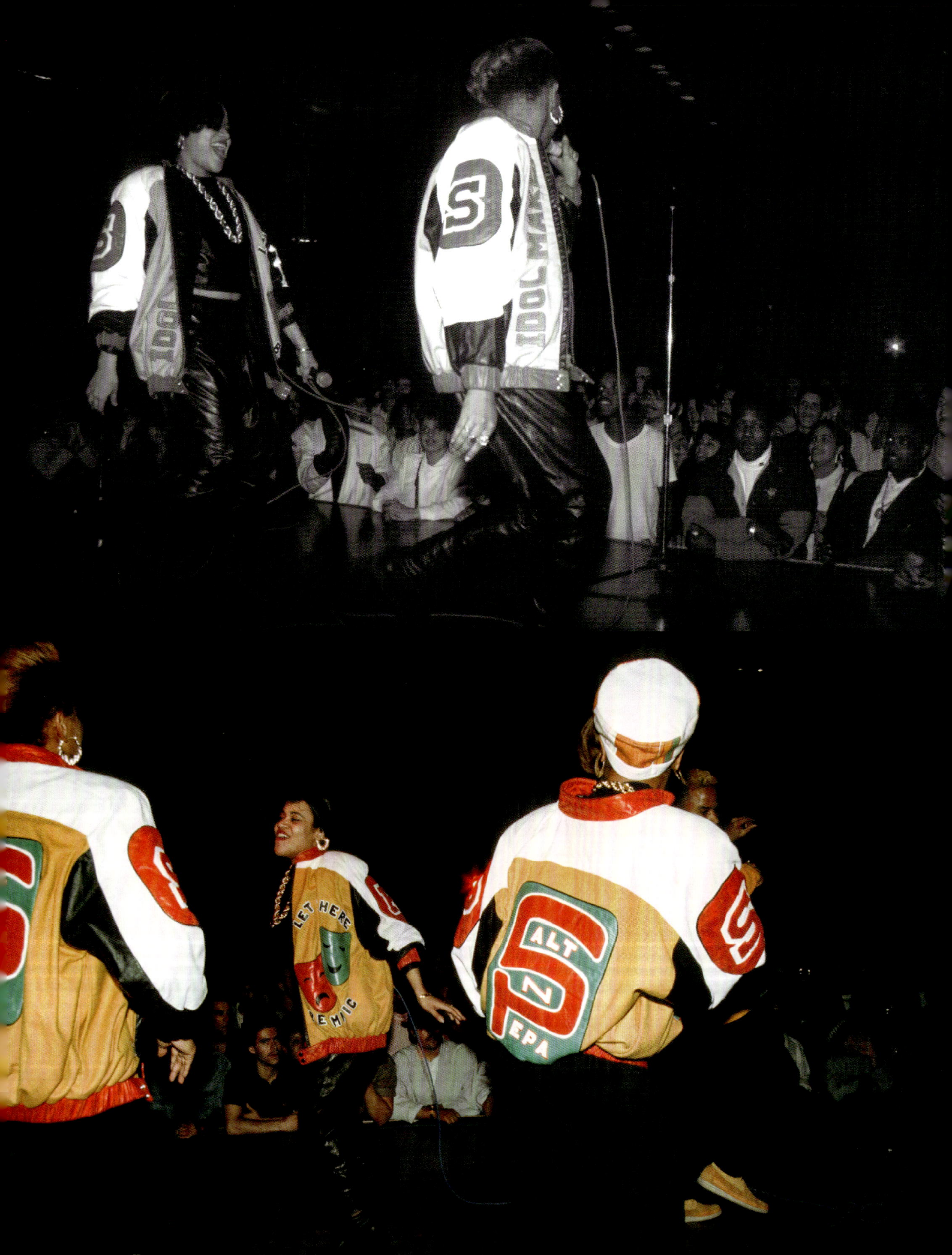
IDOL
ALT
N
EPA

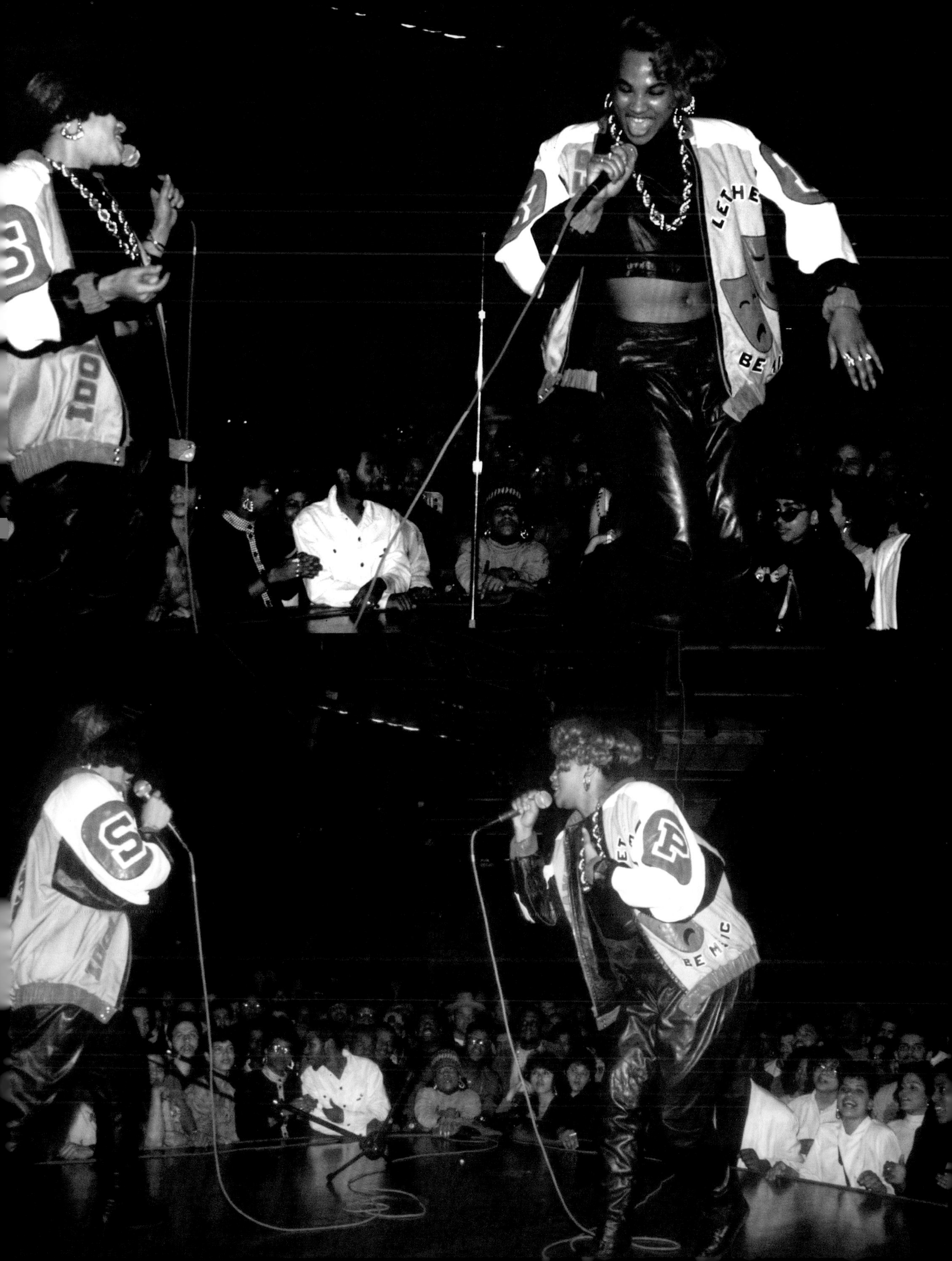

p.92–93 Salt-N-Pepa at Ricky's on the Lower East Side at 7am. I shot this for WNYW Channel 5 News and the host of the segment was Legendary Oldies radio DJ Cousin Brucie, NYC, 1987.

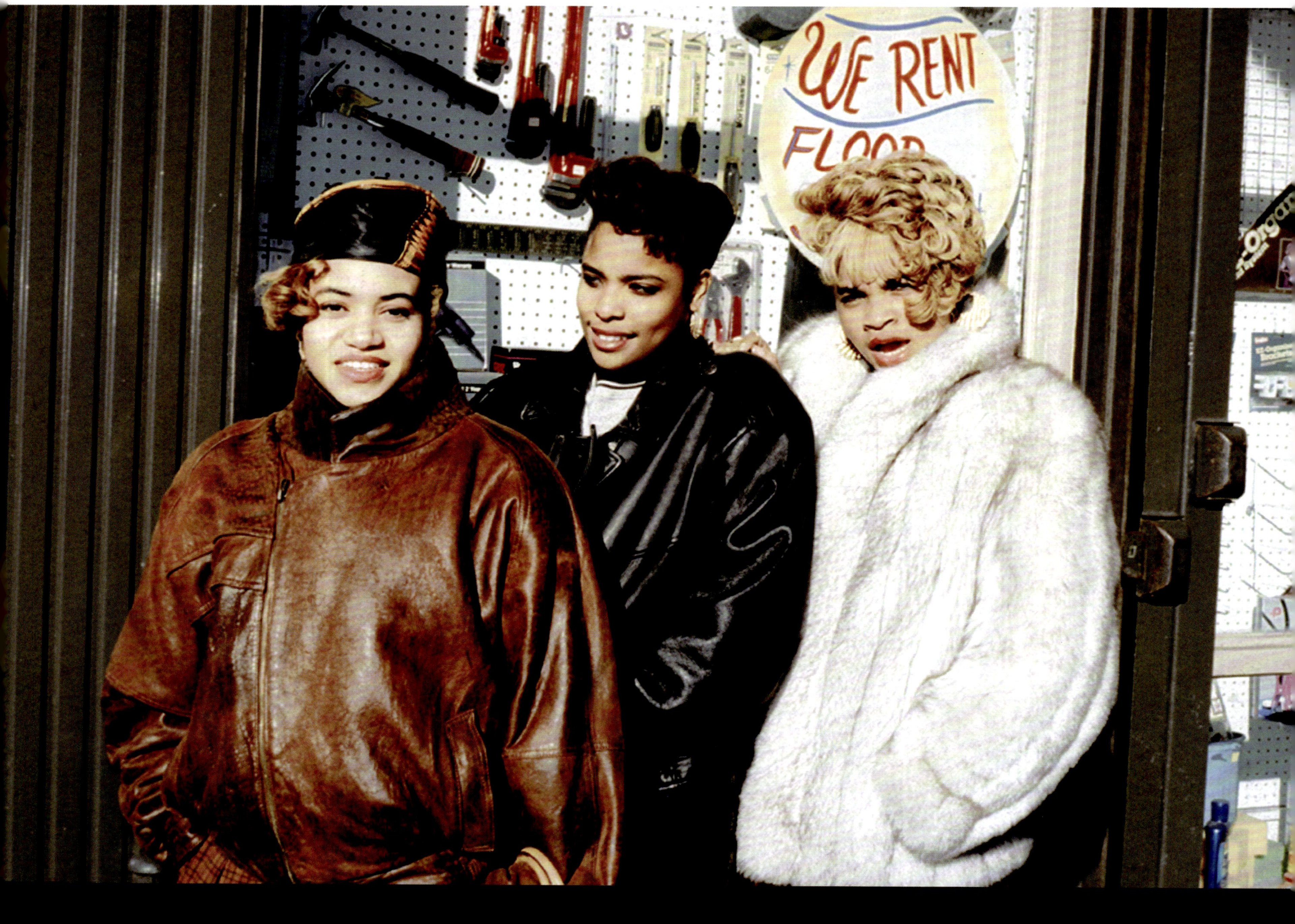

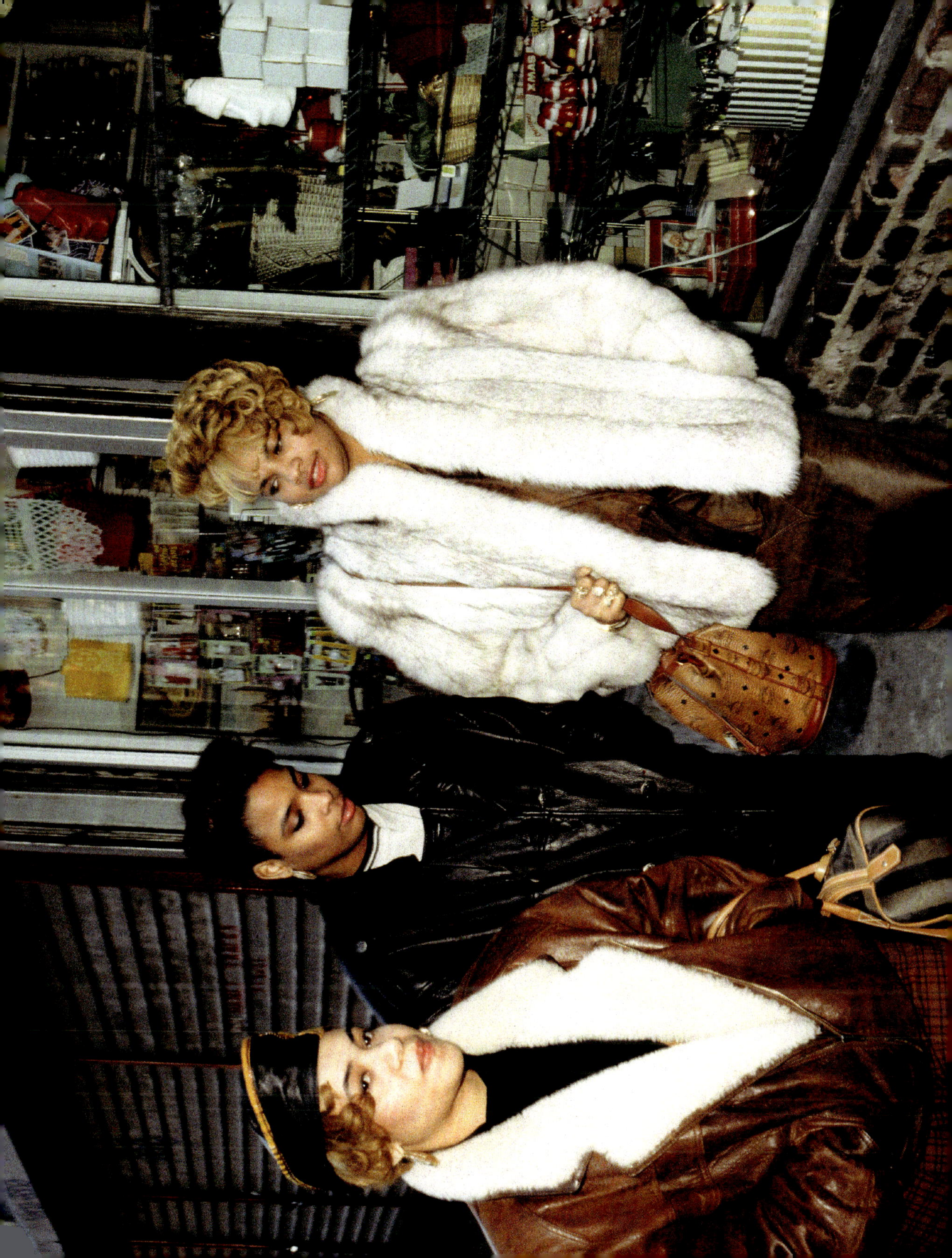

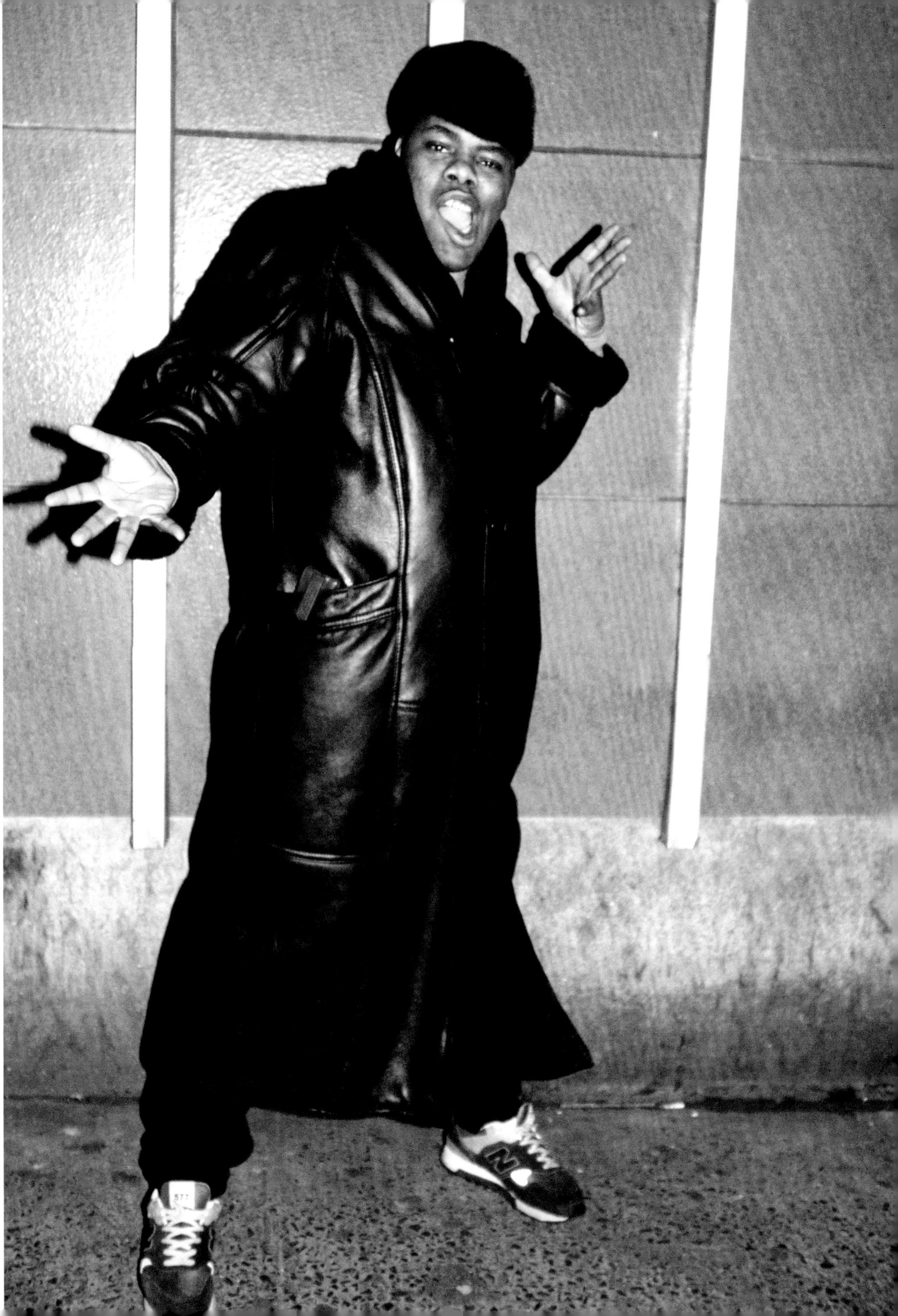

p.94 The diabolical Biz Markie, NYC, 1990 (see additional notes on p.100).

p.95 Jam Master Jay of Run-DMC, Harlem, NYC, 1991; De La Soul, NYC, late 096*-1980s (see additional notes for both images on page 100).

p.96 Queen Latifah, Fab 5 Freddy, Freddie Foxxx, KRS-One, and Big Daddy Kane. Harlem, NYC, 1994 (see additional notes on page 100).
p.97 Justice, LL Cool J, Kool Herc, and The Nigga Twins (aka The Legendary Twins), Apollo Theatre, Harlem, NYC, 1990; Jalil (Whodini), Dr. Ice, Flava Flav (Public Enemy) and Rob Bass, Palladium, NYC, 1991.

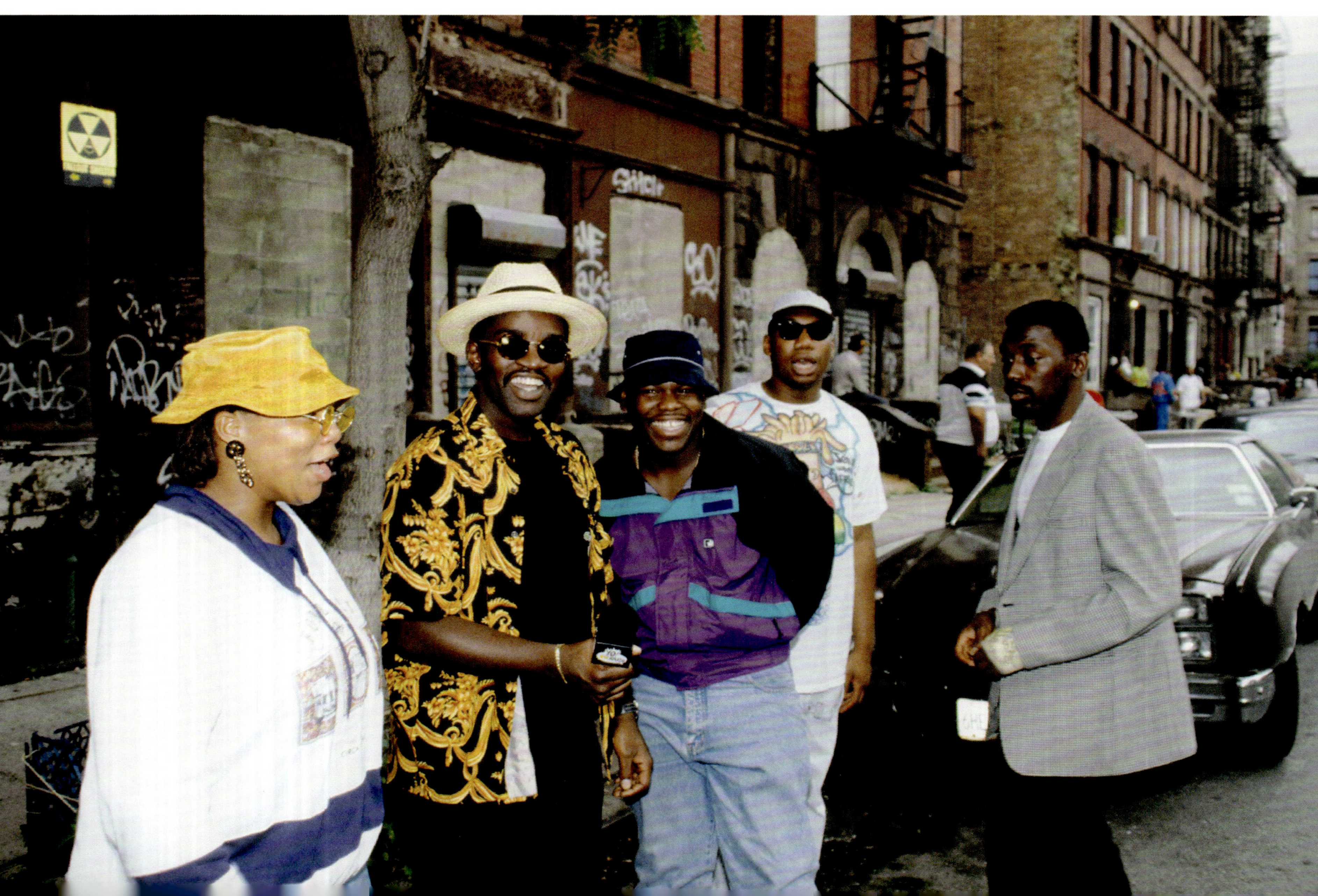

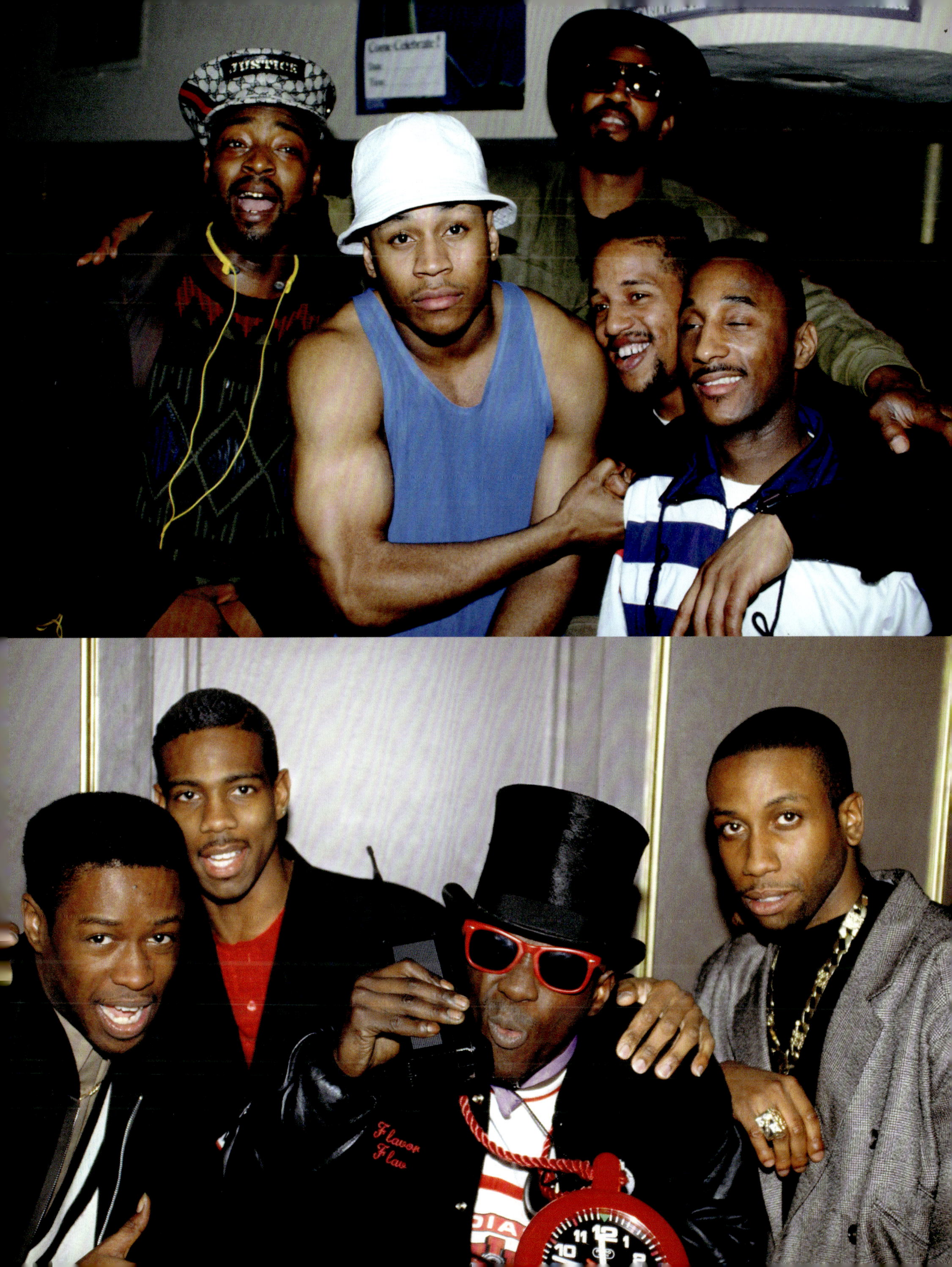
JUSTICE
Come Celebrate!
Flavor
Flav

p.98 Parrish Smith (EPMD), King Sun, LL Cool J and Hank Shocklee, early 1990s, NYC.

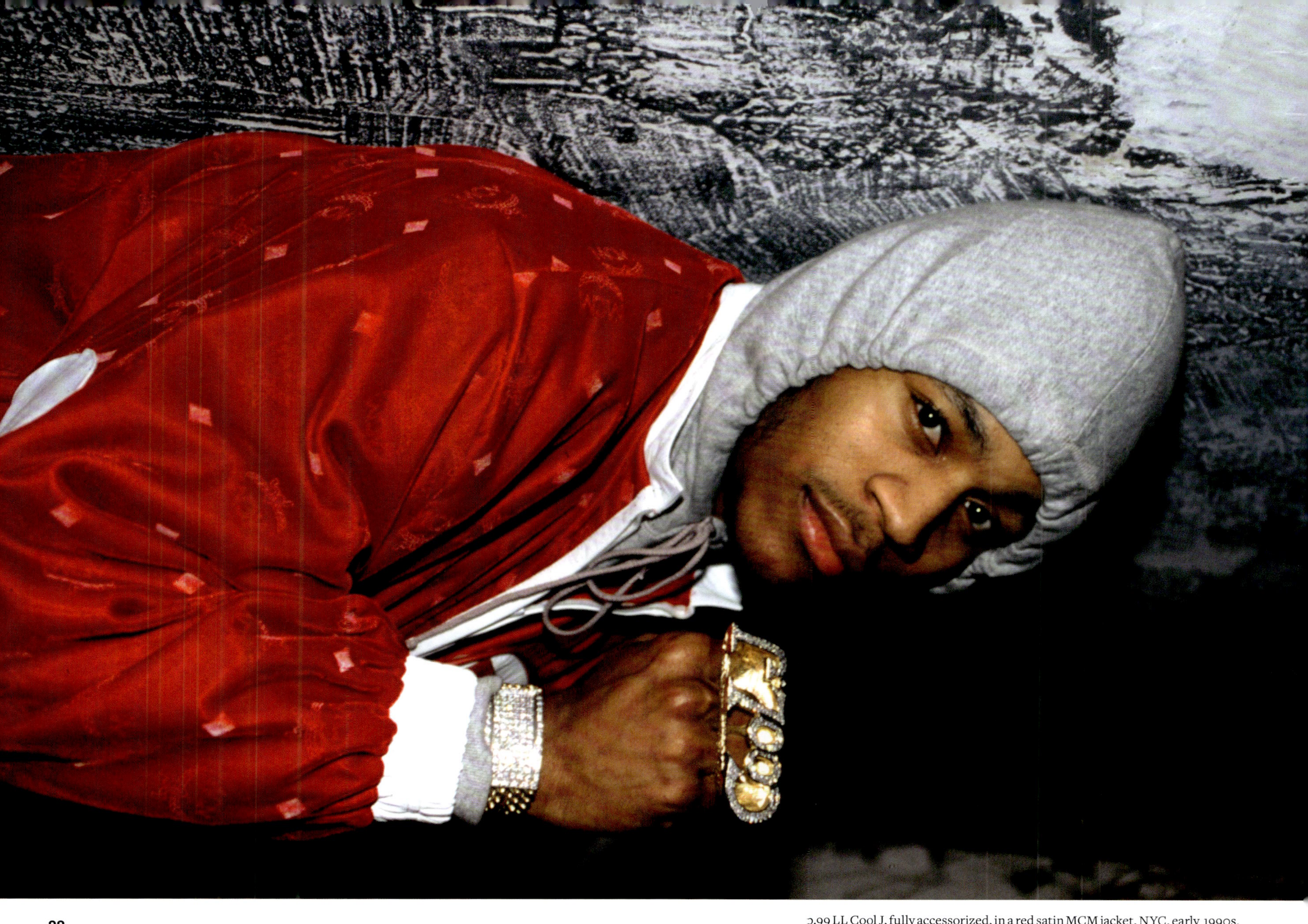

2.99 LL Cool J, fully accessorized, in a red satin MCM jacket, NYC, early 1990s.

p.101 LL Cool J performing at the Apollo Theatre, Harlem, NYC, 1987.

Notes to page 94:
Biz Markie's humor, sense of style, and originality were what guaranteed fascinating live shows of his recorded gems, such as "It's Spring Again," his very manic version of Elton John's "Benny and The Jets," and the all-time classics, "Just a Friend" and "The Vapors." The last one is a potent exploration of fake friendships and romantic encounters brought about by sudden fame.

Notes to page 95 (top):
Jam Master Jay (Jason William Mizell, 1965-2002) was the DJ of the legendary group Run-DMC. Another unsolved murder in hip-hop. He was always warm, funny and energetic. We all miss him.

I took this portrait on the set of the 1991 video for "Heal Yourself," It was the title track of *H.E.A.L (Human Education Against Lies)*, the EP produced by KRS-One and D-Nice of Boogie Down Productions (BDP), and it featured Run-DMC and a half-dozen other acts. The overwhelming dominance of Michael Jordan and the Chicago Bulls at the time led to divided loyalties in New York, one powerfully expressed by Jam Master Jay's outfit here.

Notes to page 95 (bottom):
I first met De La Soul—Pos, Dave and Maseo—at the Beacon Theatre on the Upper West Side with Q-Tip, Latifah and Slick Rick in 1987, and we've been friends ever since.

Notes to page 96:
Queen Latifah, Fab 5 Freddy, Freddie Foxxx, KRS-One and Big Daddy Kane were in Harlem shooting a segment for *Yo! MTV Raps* in 1994, a year before the show ended its seven-year run. The program was the first hip-hop show on the network and was created by Jonathan Demme's nephew Ted. Fab 5 Freddy was host of this particular segment.

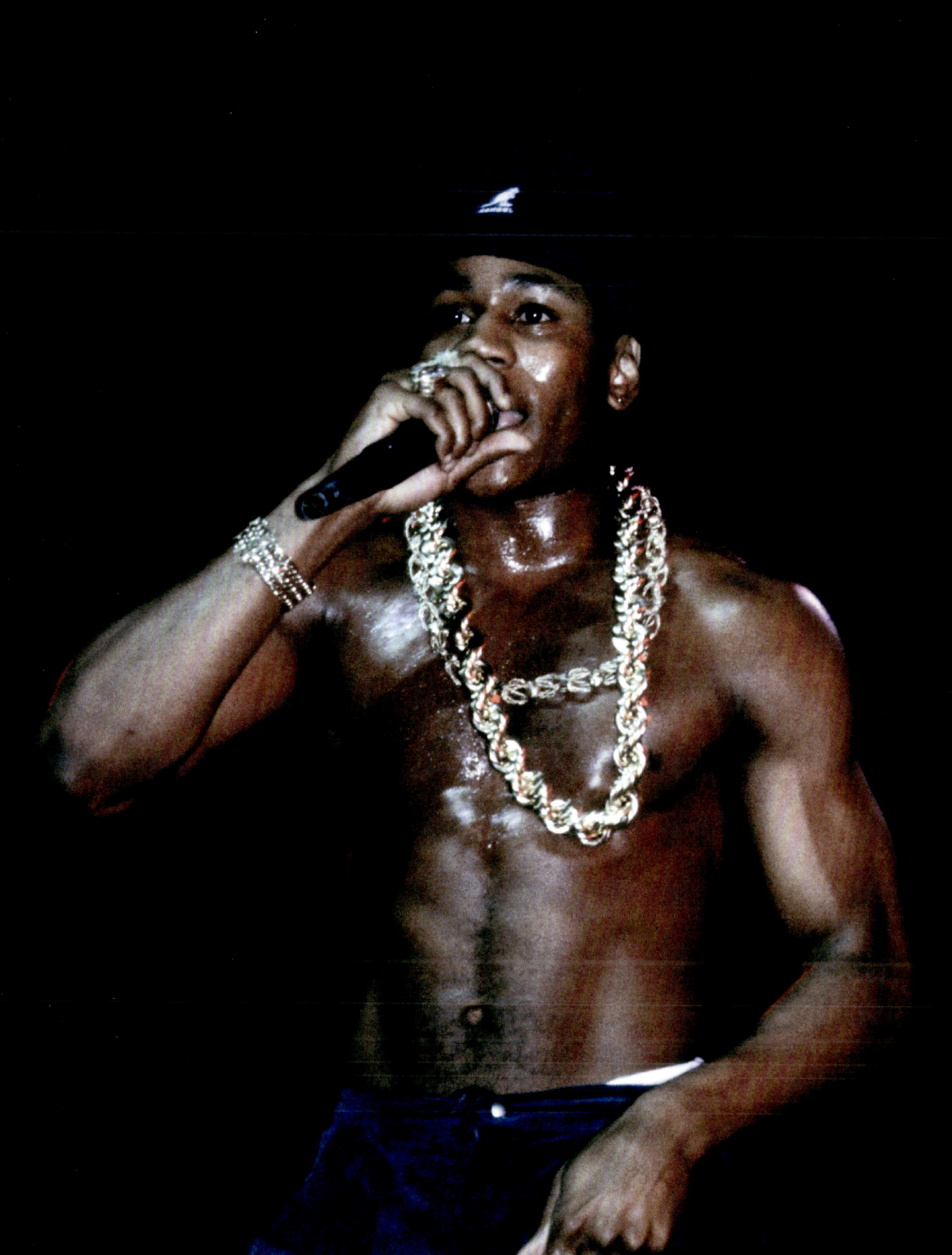

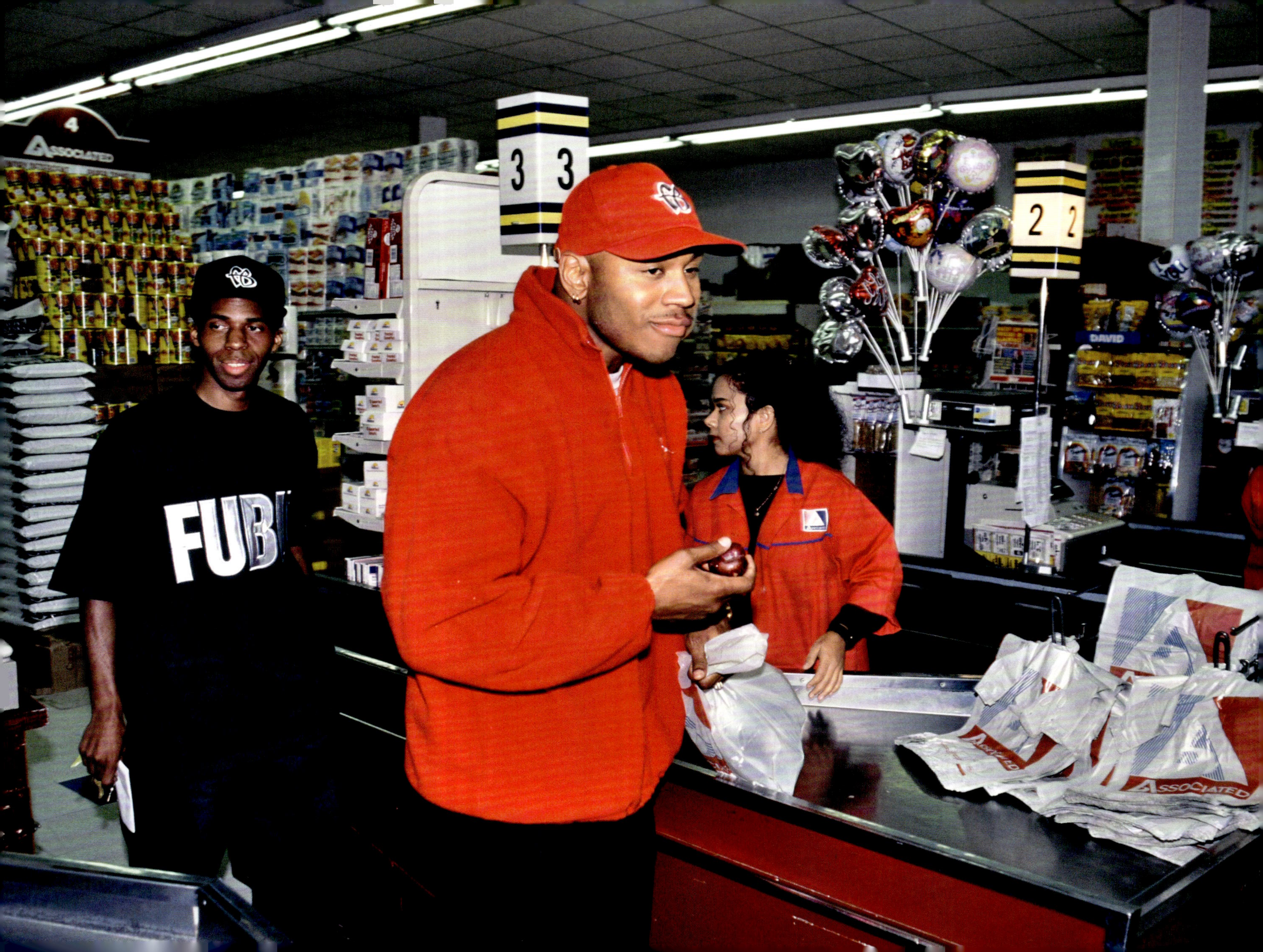
ASSOCIATED

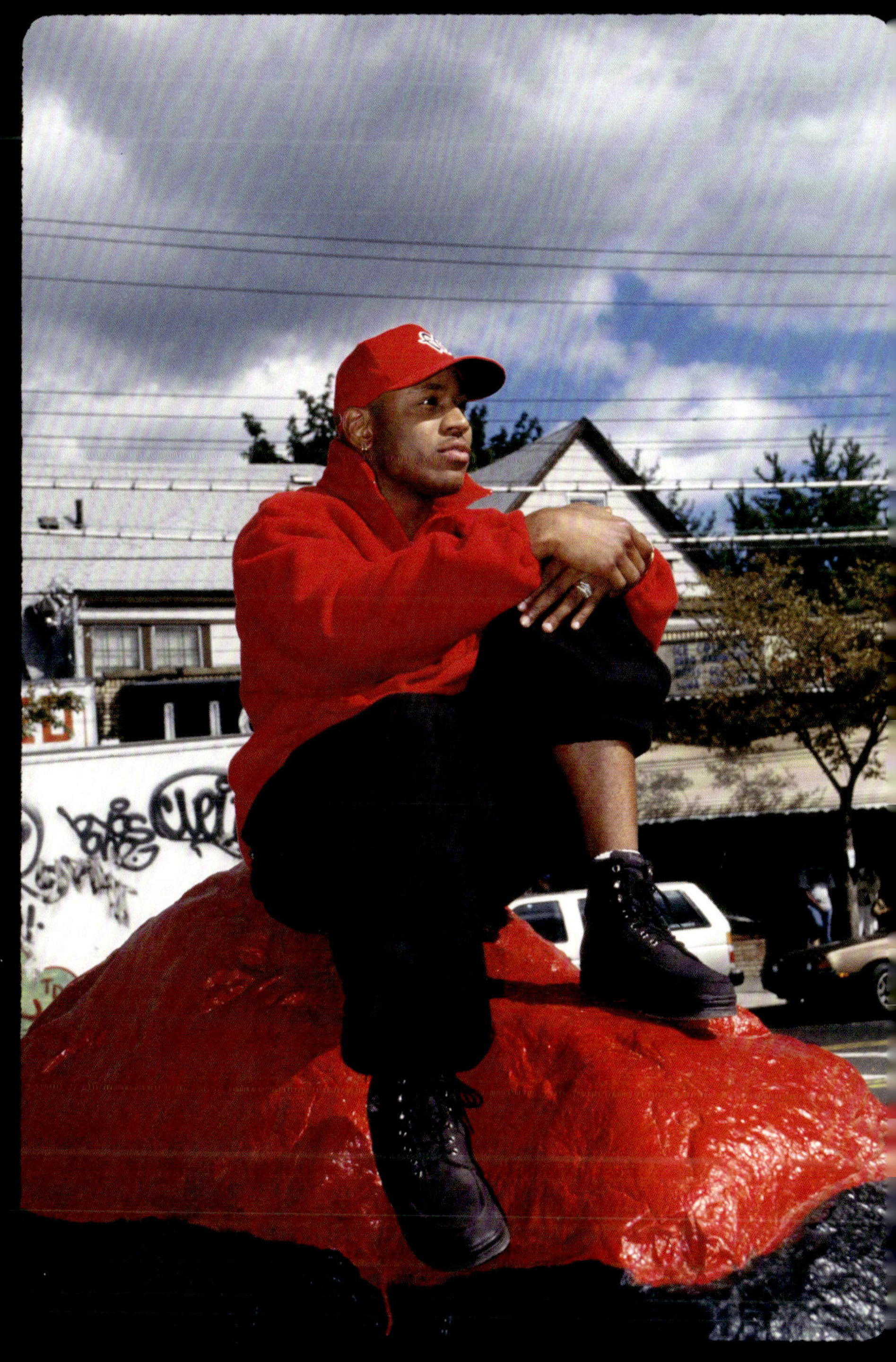

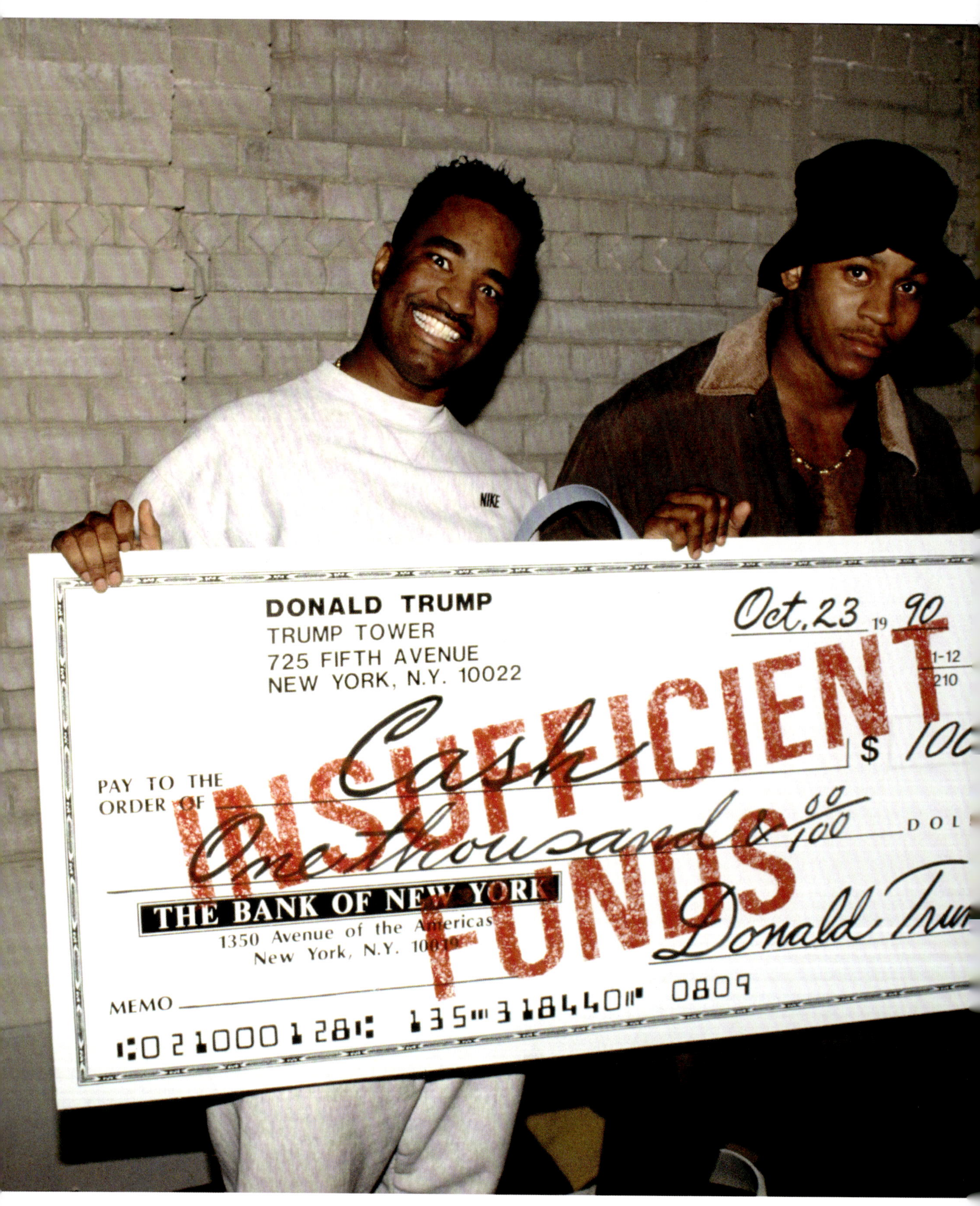

NIKE
DONALD TRUMP
TRUMP TOWER
725 FIFTH AVENUE
NEW YORK, N.Y. 10022
Oct. 23 19 90
PAY TO THE ORDER OF
Cash
One thousand & 00/100
INSUFFICIENT FUNDS
THE BANK OF NEW YORK
1350 Avenue of the Americas
MEMO
0809

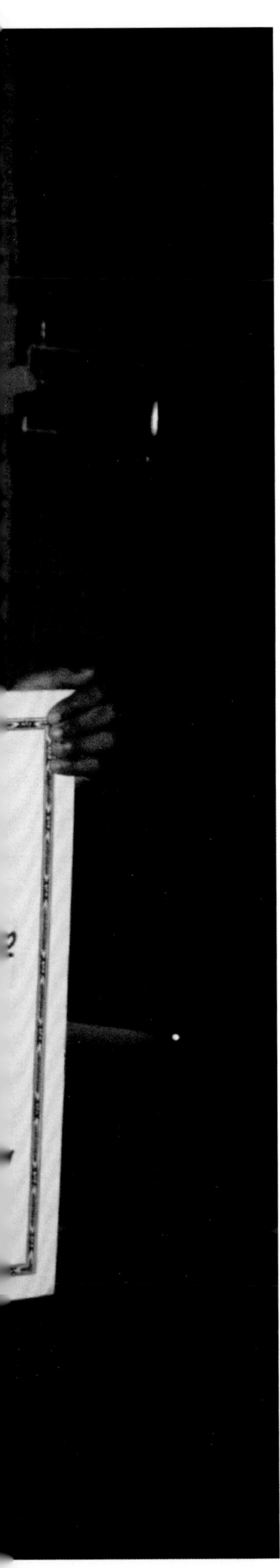

p.104 Marley Marl and LL Cool J backstage at *The David Letterman Show* with a mock up of a bounced check from Donald Trump, Midtown, NYC, 1990.

Notes to pages 102-103:
LL Cool J in an Associated Supermarket, and on Liberty Rock in Saint Albans, Queens, during the shoot for the video for "Hey Lover" ft. Boyz II Men. He would become the face of and hype man for FUBU, and in no small part because of the product placement in this shoot. Queens, NYC, 1994.

p.106-107 LL Cool J, NYC, 1987.

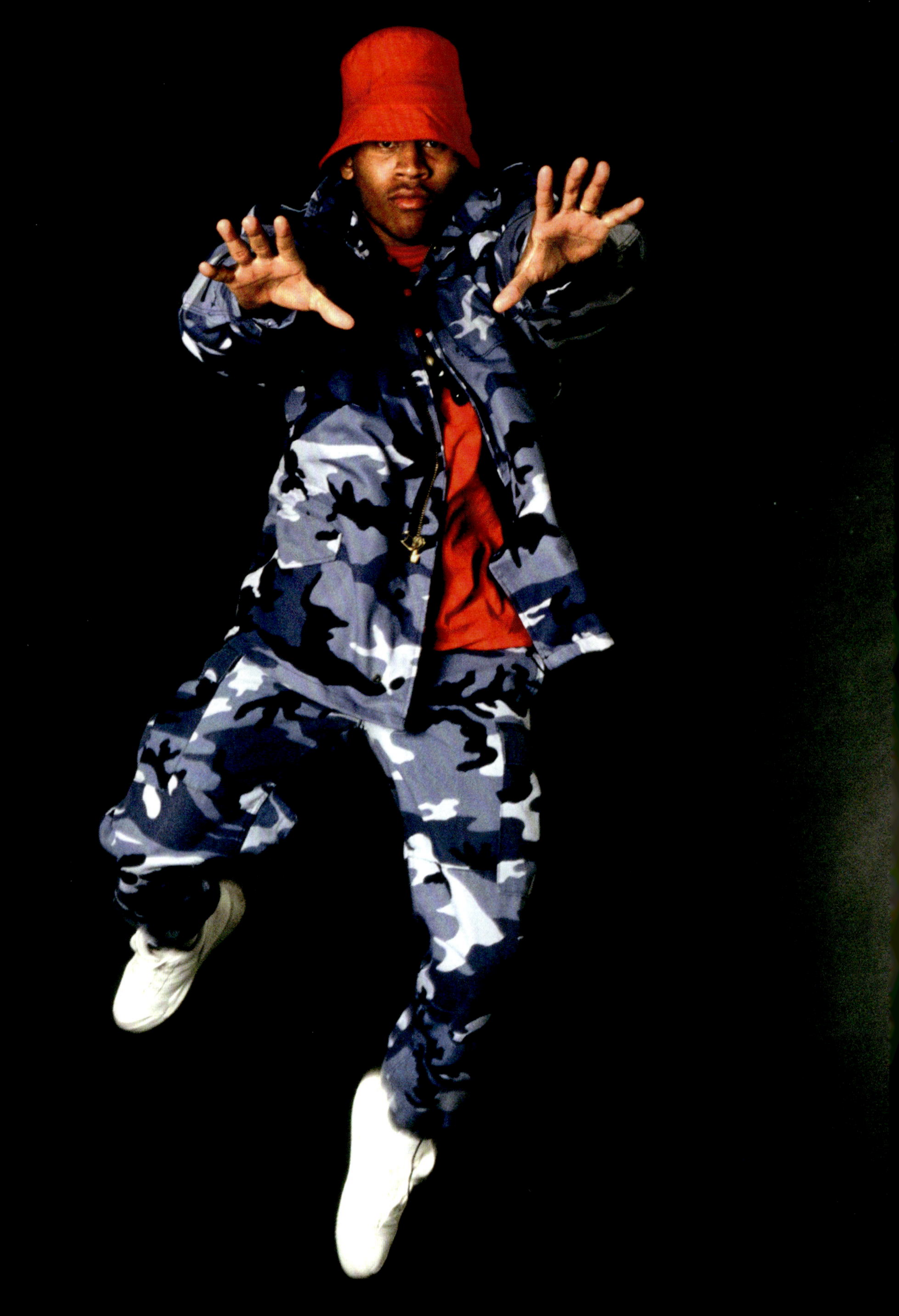

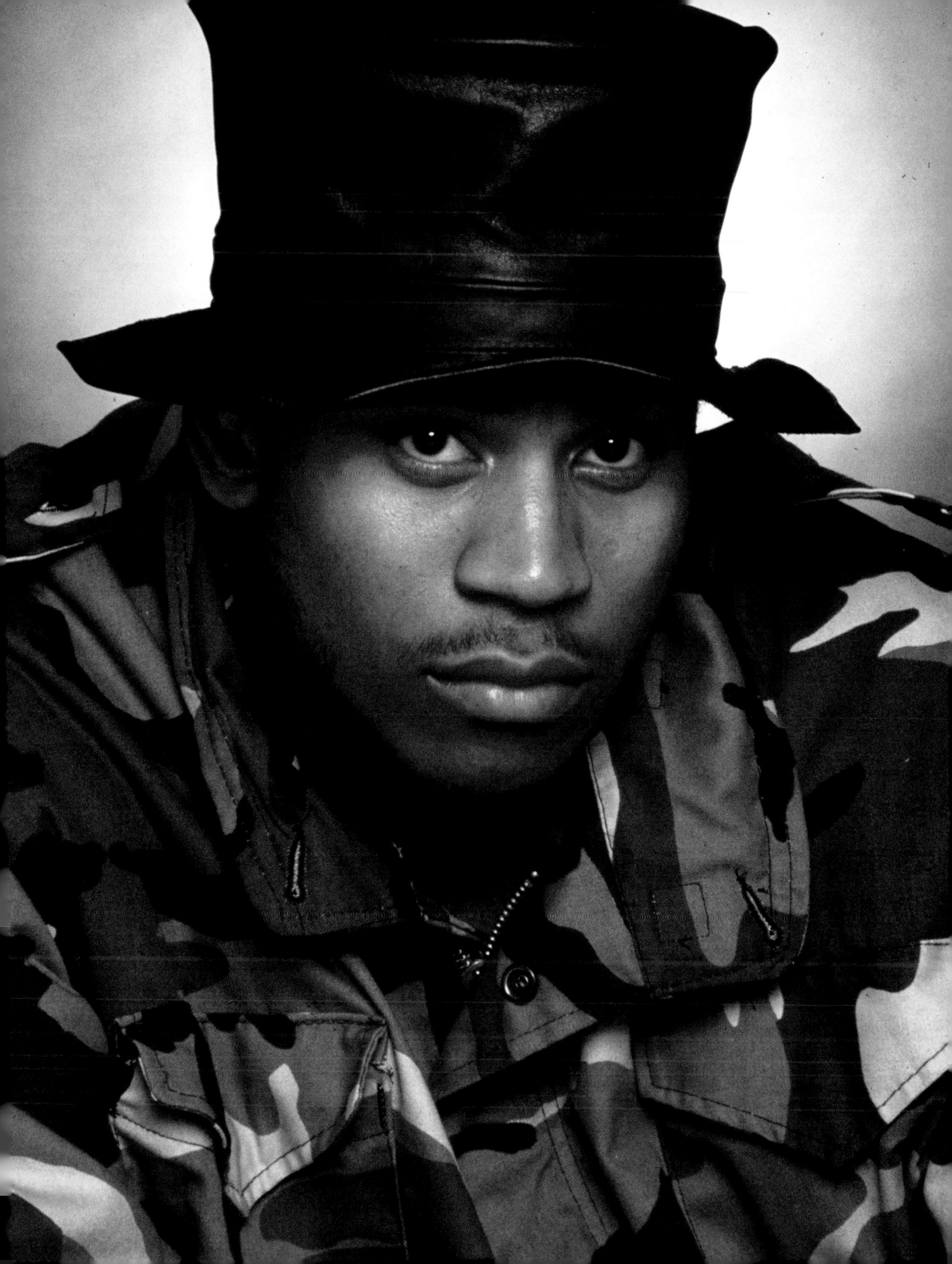

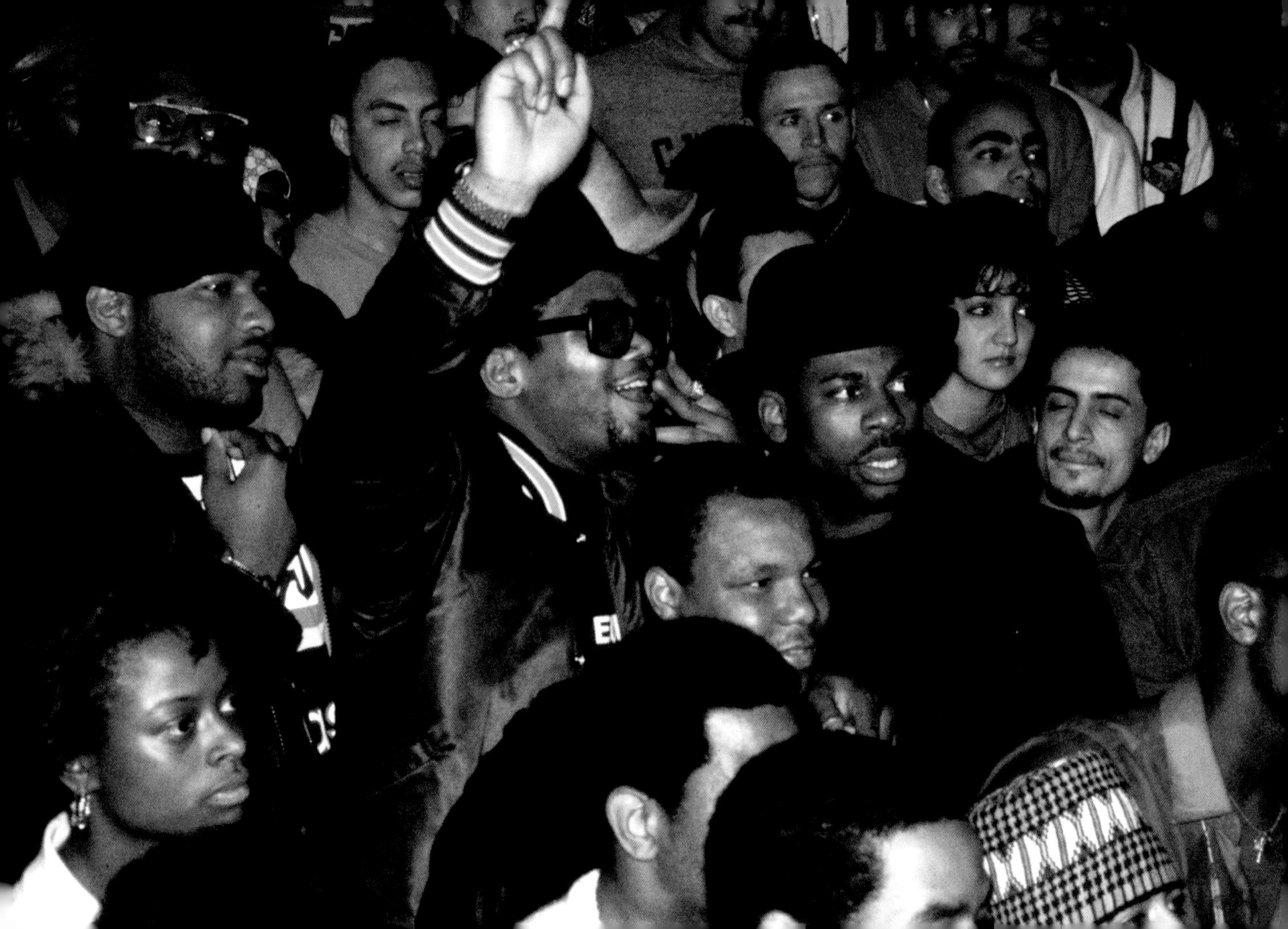

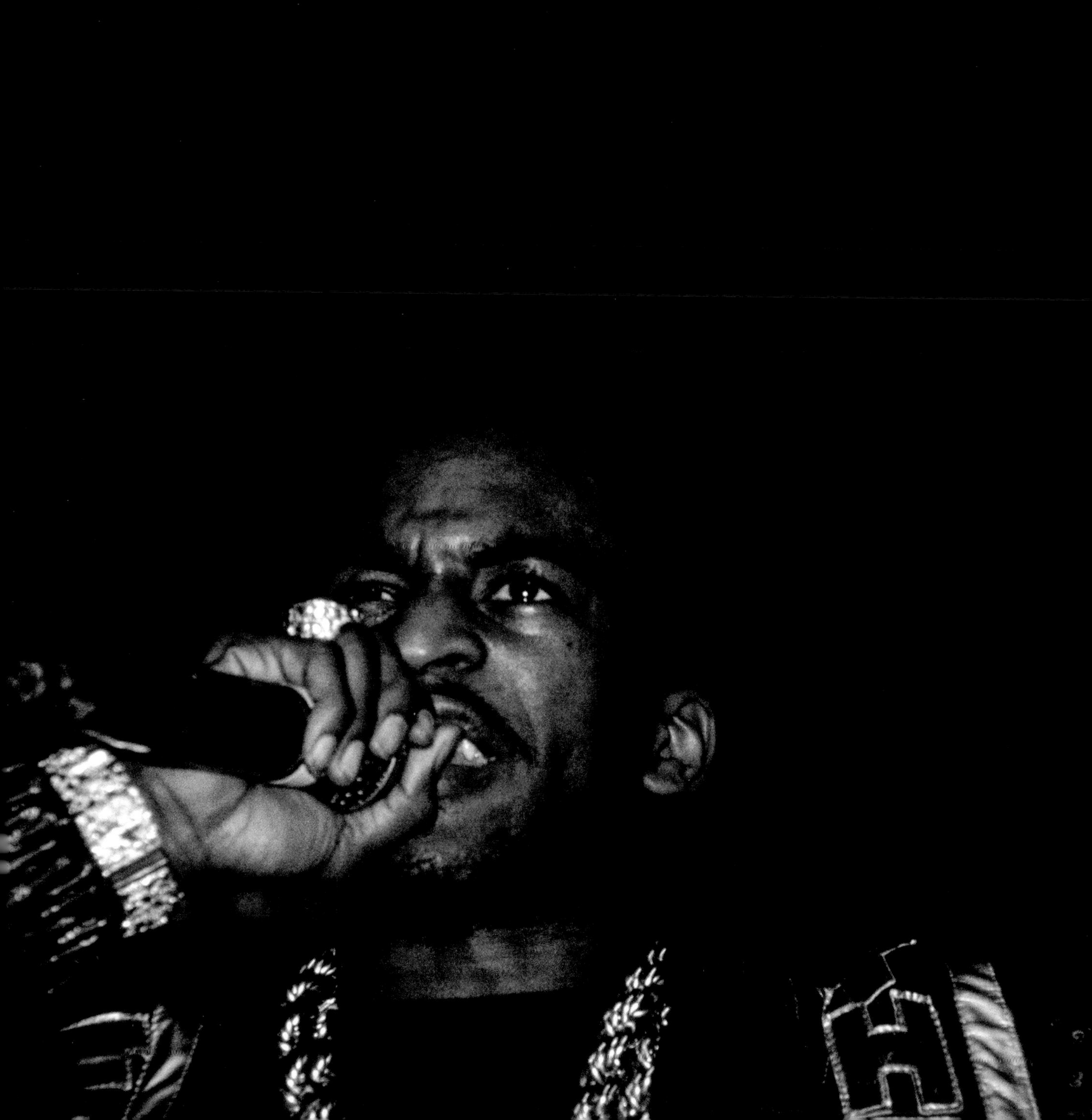

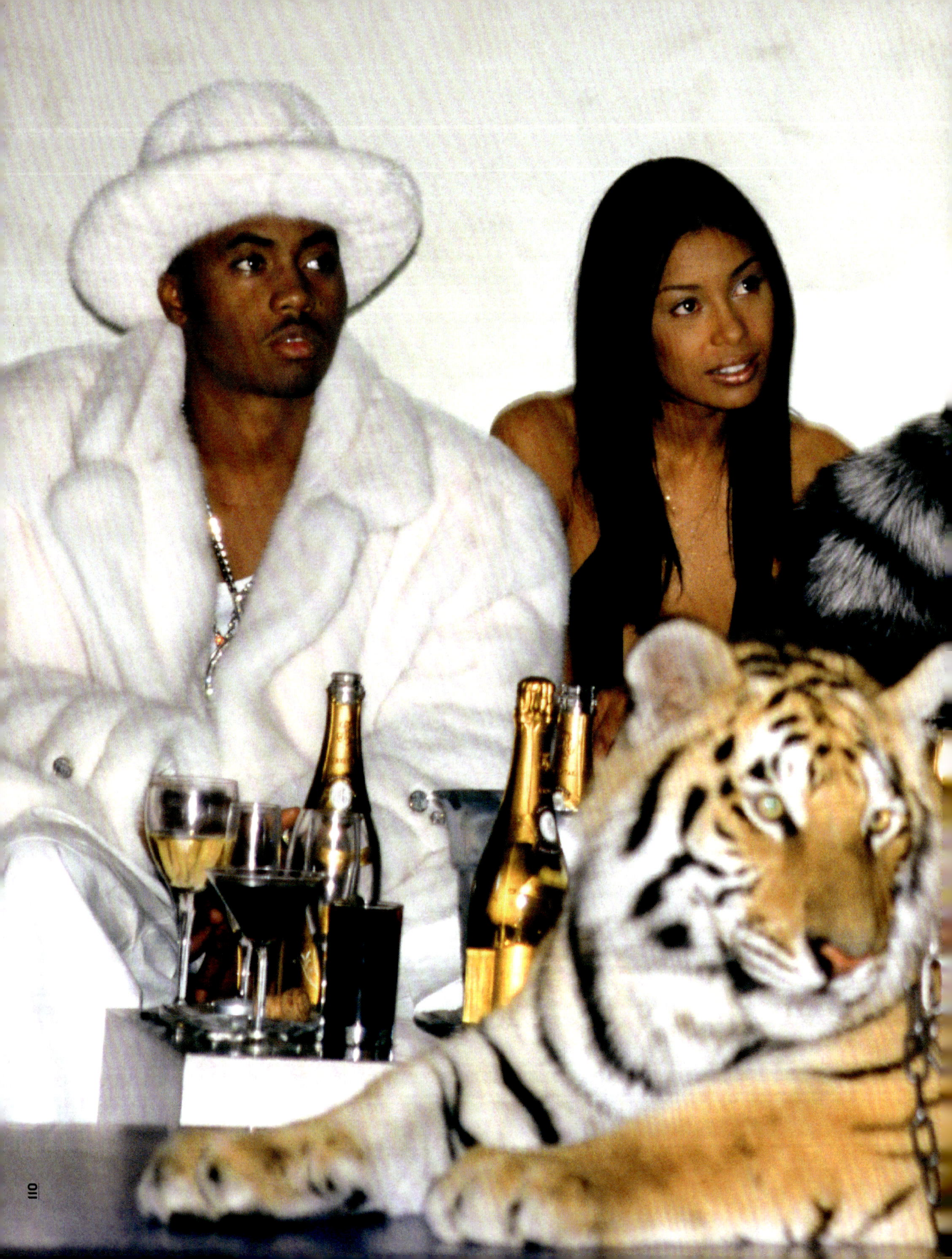

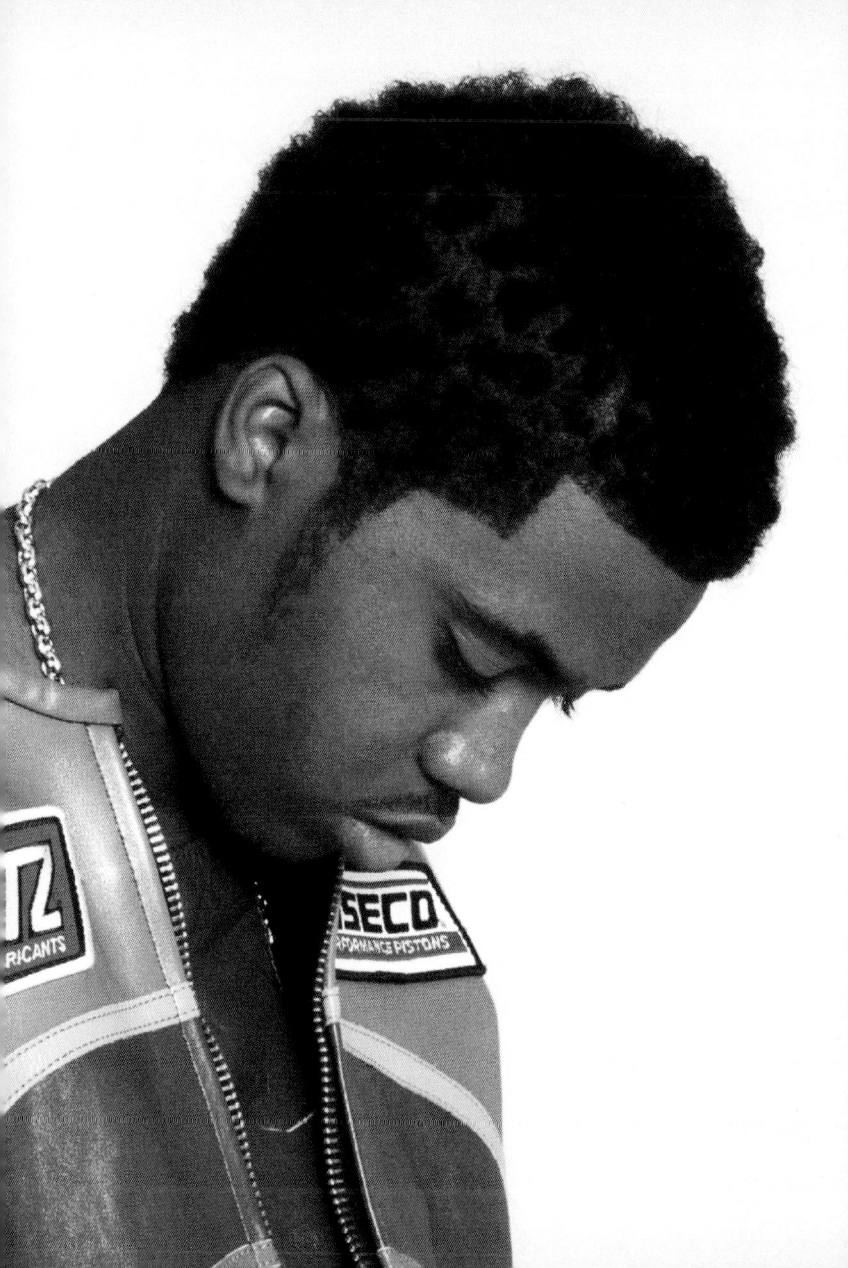
RICANTS
SECO
RFORMANCE PISTONS

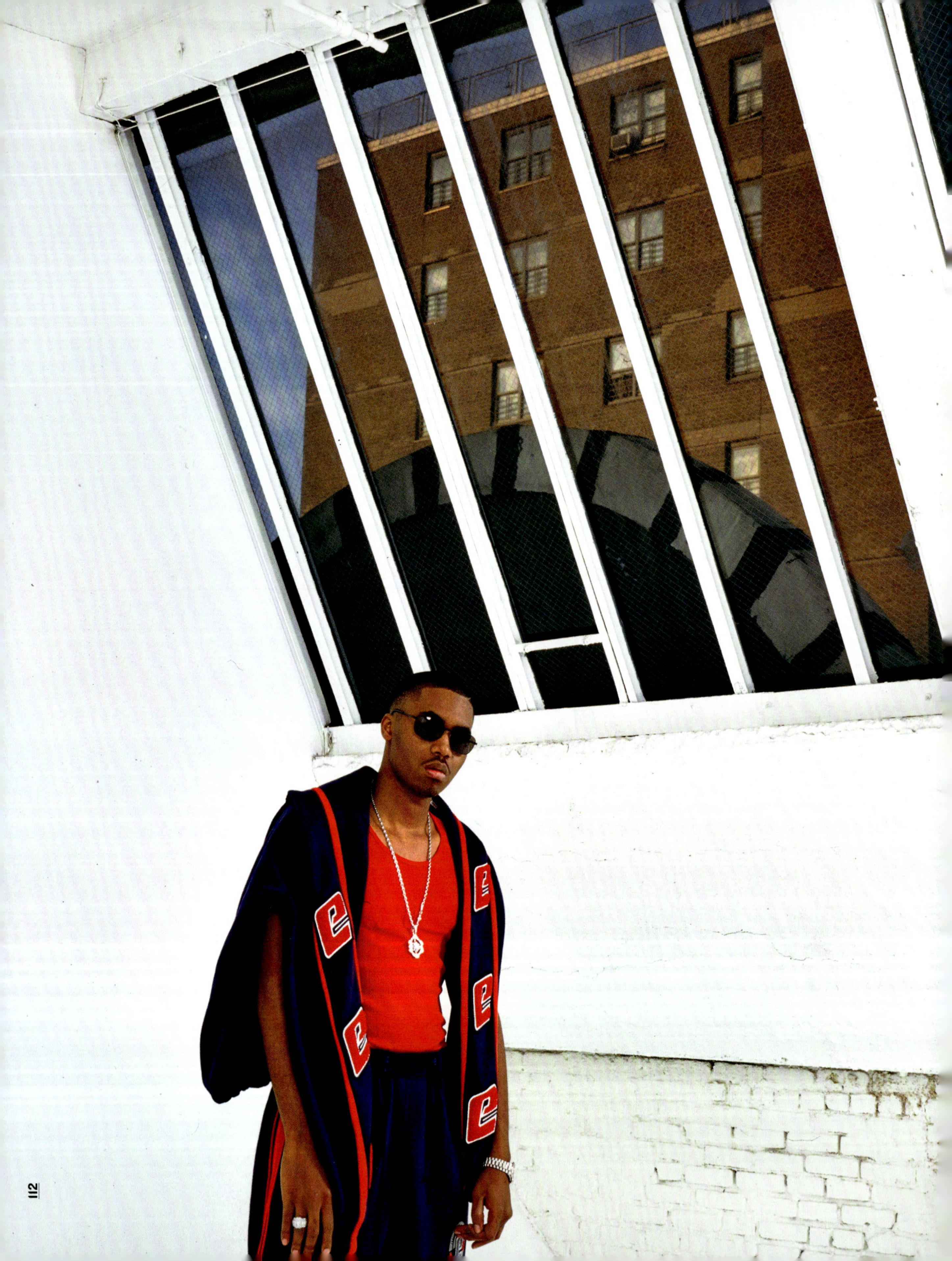

(Opposite Page) Nas in studio shoot for *Word Up!* magazine. I shot Nas in the studio at least a half dozen times and as much in the streets of NY and on music video sets. He was laid back and professional. NYC, 1999.

p.108 Run-DMC watching Salt-N-Pepa in concert at Club 818, NYC, 1988.

p.109 Rakim performing at the Apollo Theatre for the *Paid In Full* tour, Harlem, NYC, 1987

Notes to page 110:
Nas with model and a very live, very large tiger, on the set of the music video for "Hate Me Now," NYC, 1999.

The secret life of tigers. We're in the video shoot for Nas' "Hate Me Now" with Puffy, and this woman with bad hygiene comes in with two tigers. And you could smell her more than the tigers. They walk past me, and I'm looking, and I'm like these are fucking tigers and she goes over and the tigers lay down in front of Diddy. He's arguing with Nas about something and he got on a big fake fur coat and Nas got on a big fake fur coat. I don't know what happened but the bodyguards are sitting next to me across the room. And one of the tigers gets up to Puffy and he just pushes the tiger out of the way so he could continue his conversation.

So I said to one of the bodyguards what are you going to do? He says, "fuck that nigga. If I get ate by a tiger my mother wouldn't even bury me, my family wouldn't even, they'd throw me in the backyard with the dead puppies. Fuck that nigga. If I get shot or beat up you know by some other nigga it's okay I can understand that, they'll you know they'll take care of me, nurse me back to health. But a tiger, a fucking tiger? My mother didn't raise nobody that stupid, fuck that nigga."

But Puffy just pushed the tiger aside like it was nothing. So Puffy gets the award for having the biggest balls in hip-hop ever, period.

p.111 Nas, NYC, 1999.

p.114 Nas on couch. The contrast between a formal, European-style couch and his leather outfit elevated this image above what was then the typical hip-hop mode, NYC, 1999.

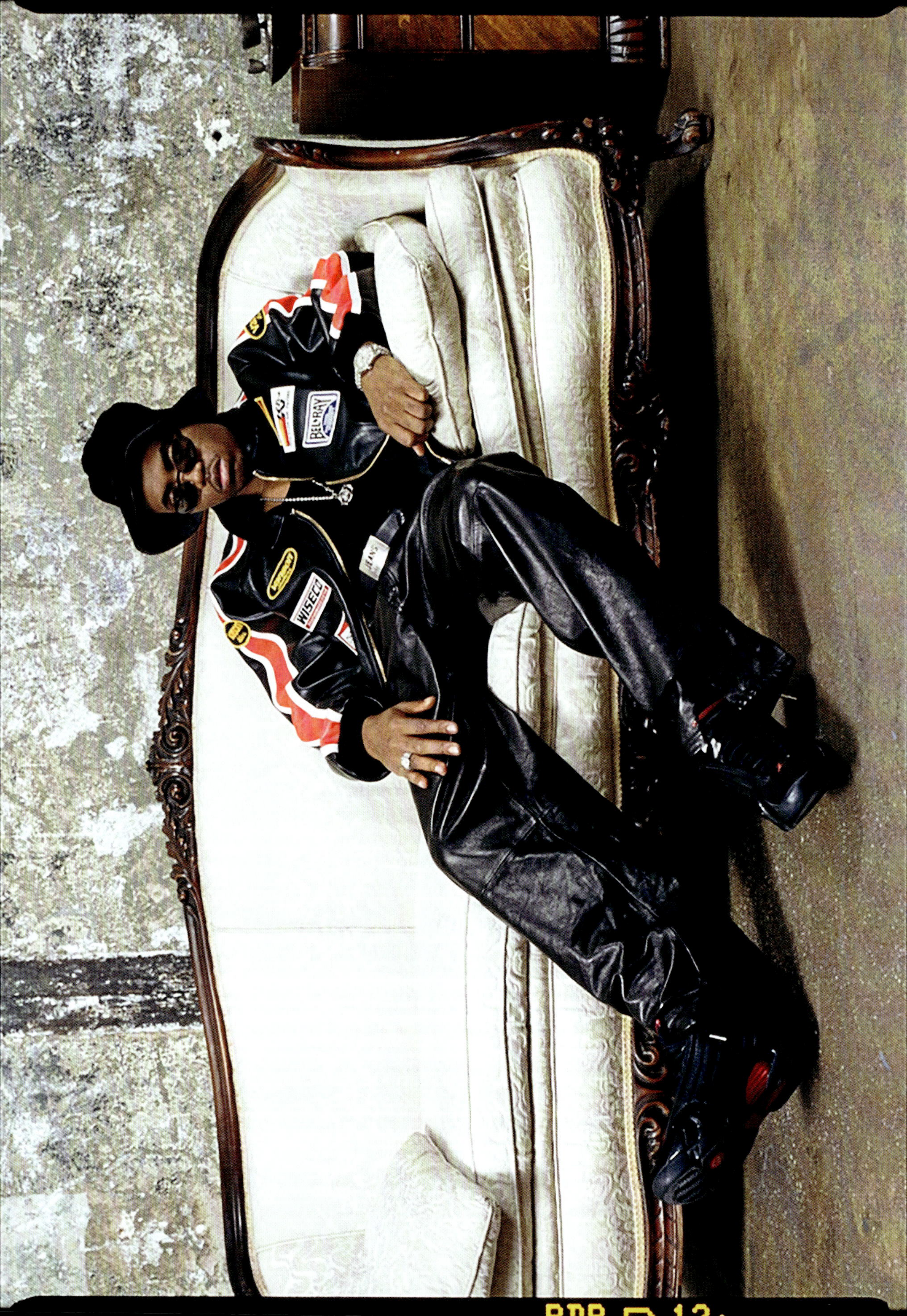

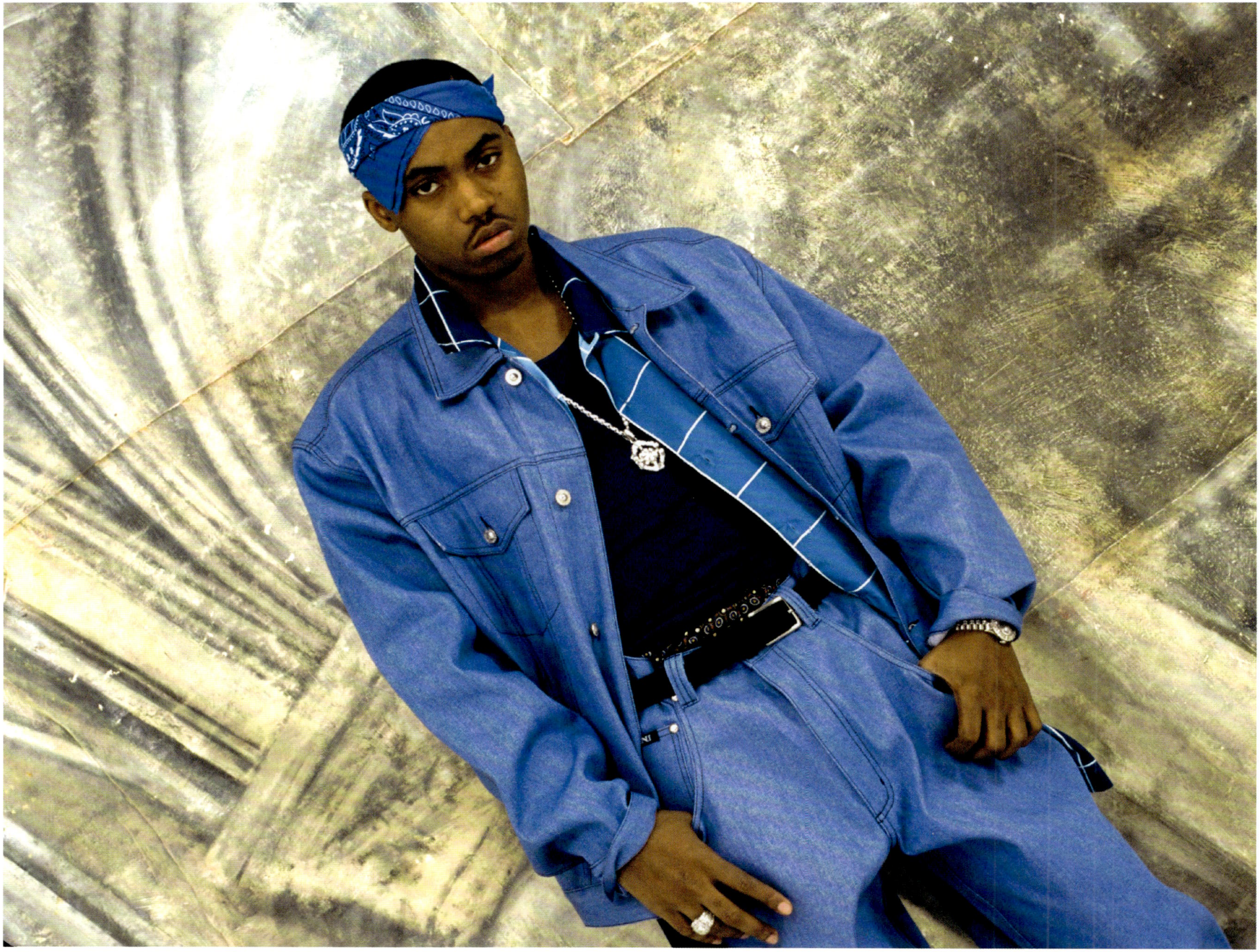

p.115 Nas in blue, contrasted with the yellow painted background, gave this photo an artful, moody vibe, NYC, 1999.

p.116 Nas with the Union Square skyline. Nas seemed contemplative in many of our shoots together that reflected the depth of his lyrics. Dakota Studio, NYC, 2000.

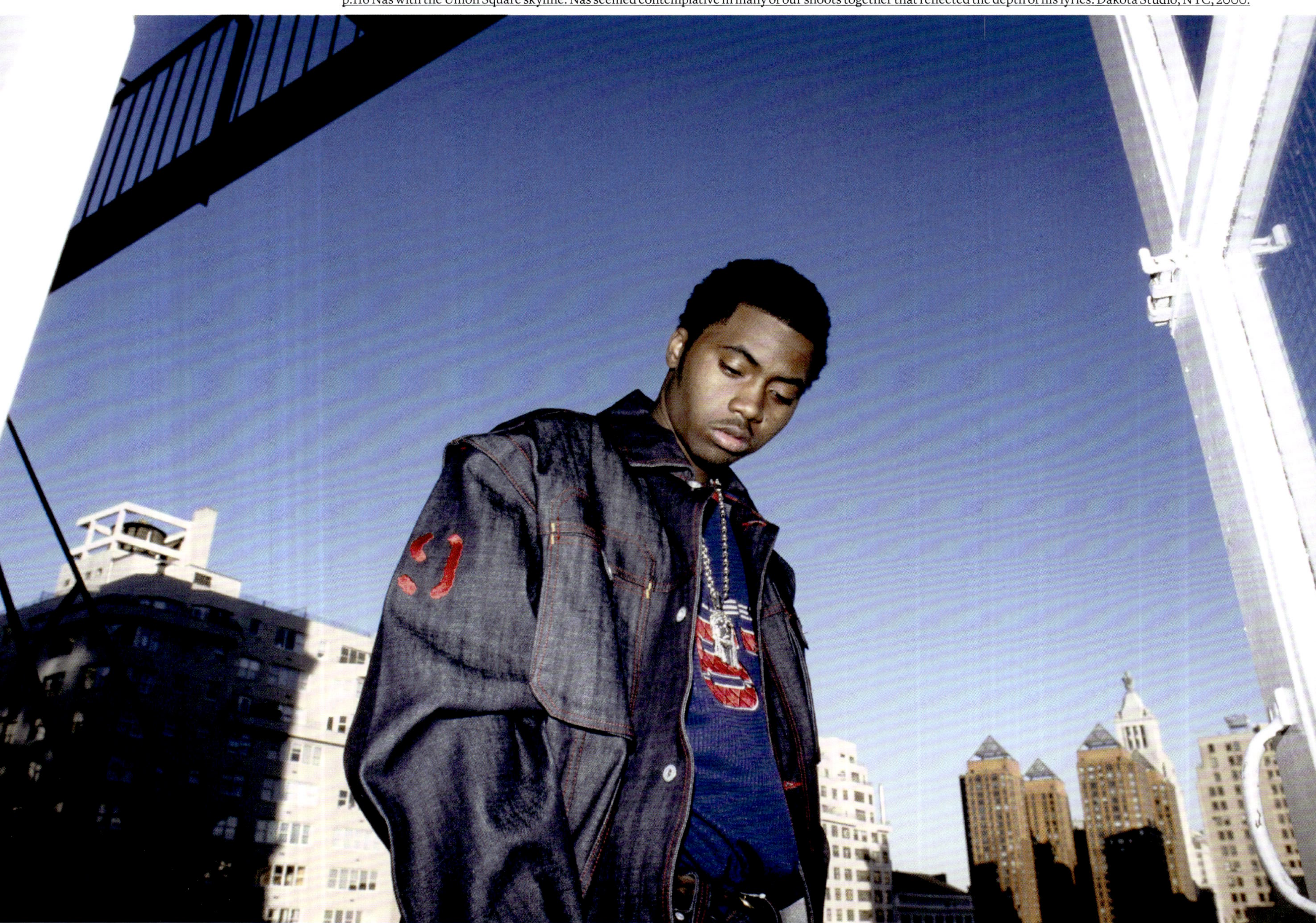

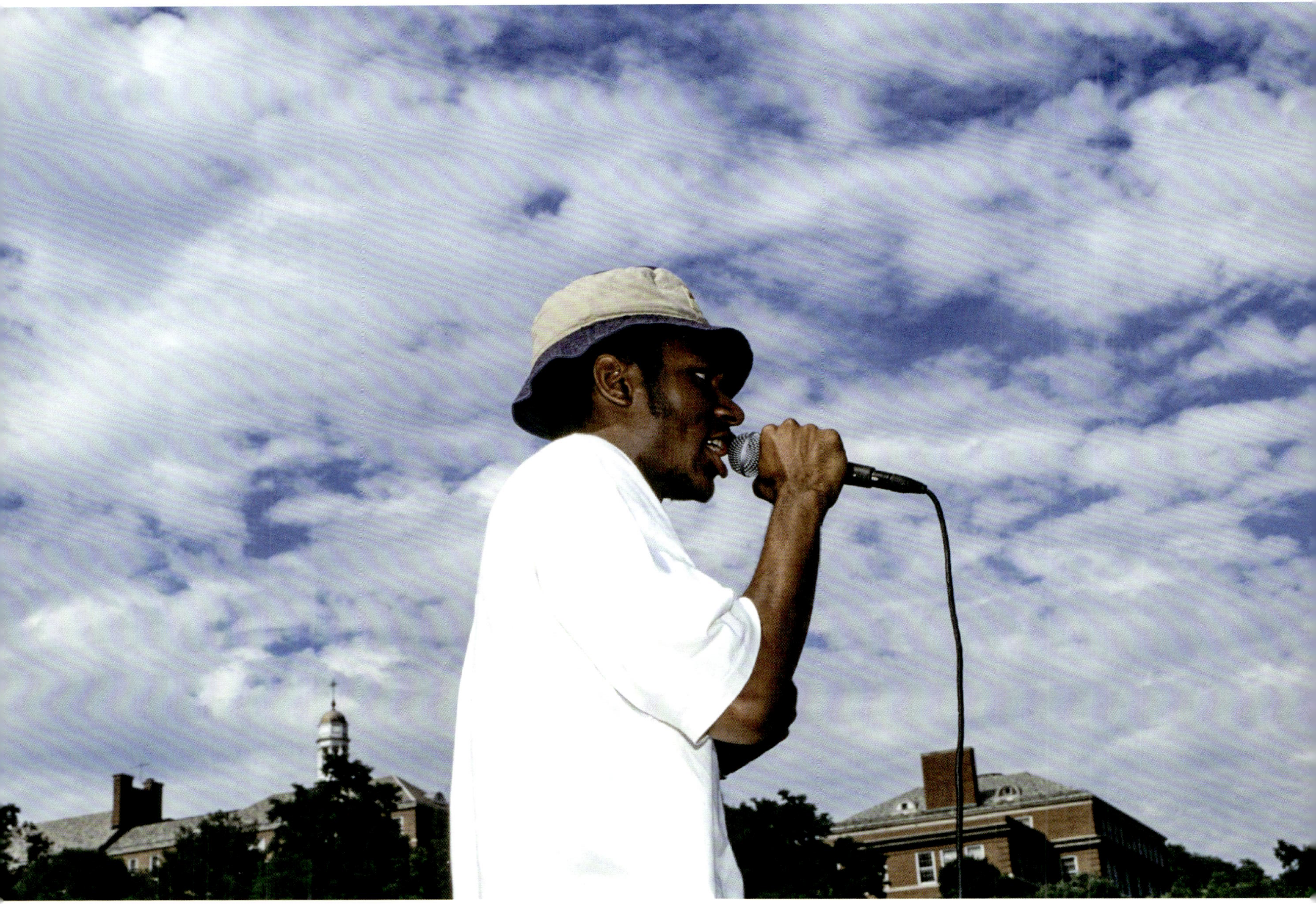

p.117 Mos Def (Yasiin Bey) in concert at a Rock Steady Crew Anniversary, NYC, 1998.

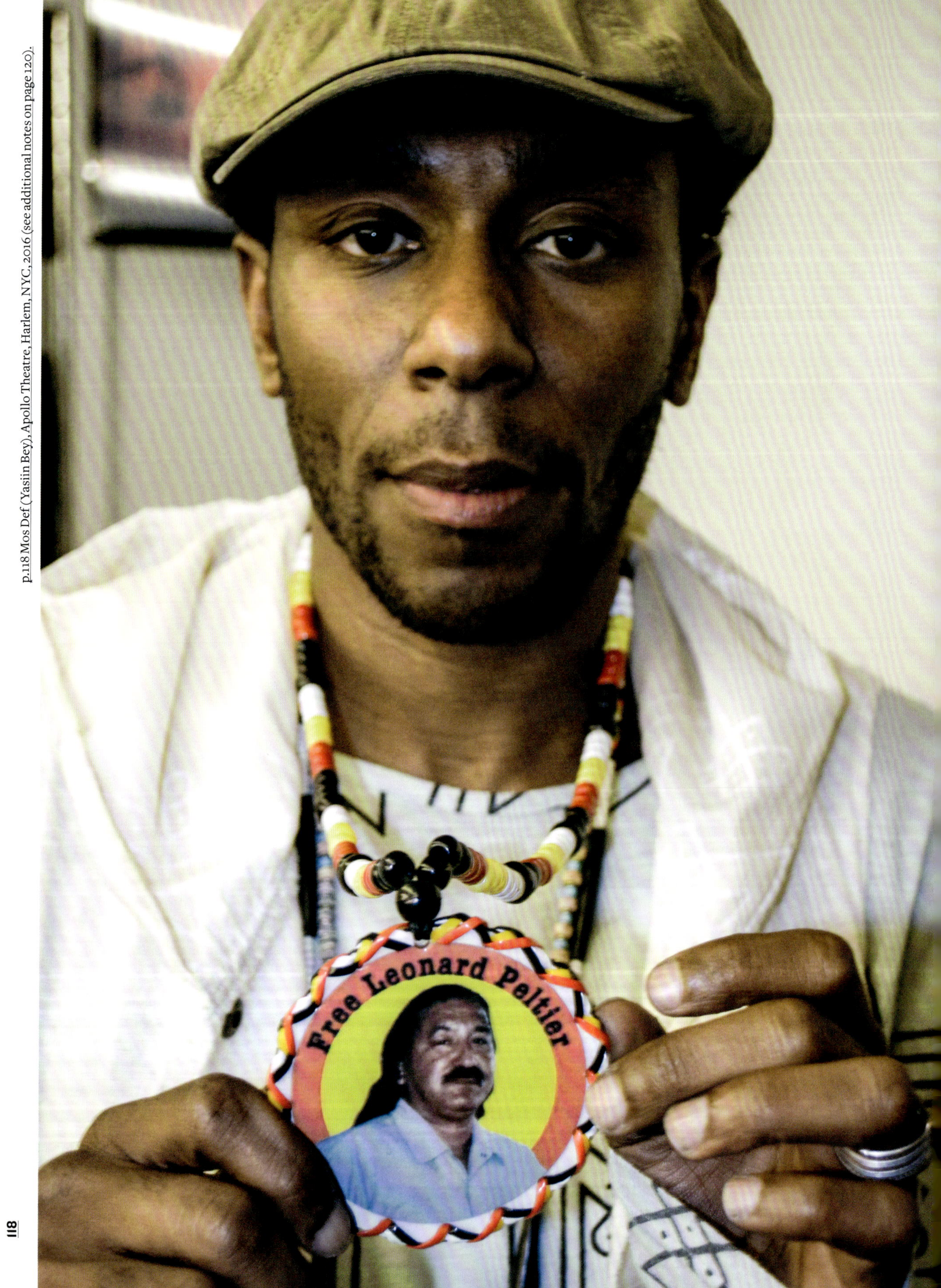

p.118 Mos Def (Yasiin Bey), Apollo Theatre, Harlem, NYC, 2016 (see additional notes on page 120).

p.119 Flava Flav, Roosevelt, Long Island, New York, 1989 (see additional notes on page 120).

p.120 Heavy D & the Boyz, on the set of his video "We Got Our Own Thang," Sony Studios, NYC 1989.

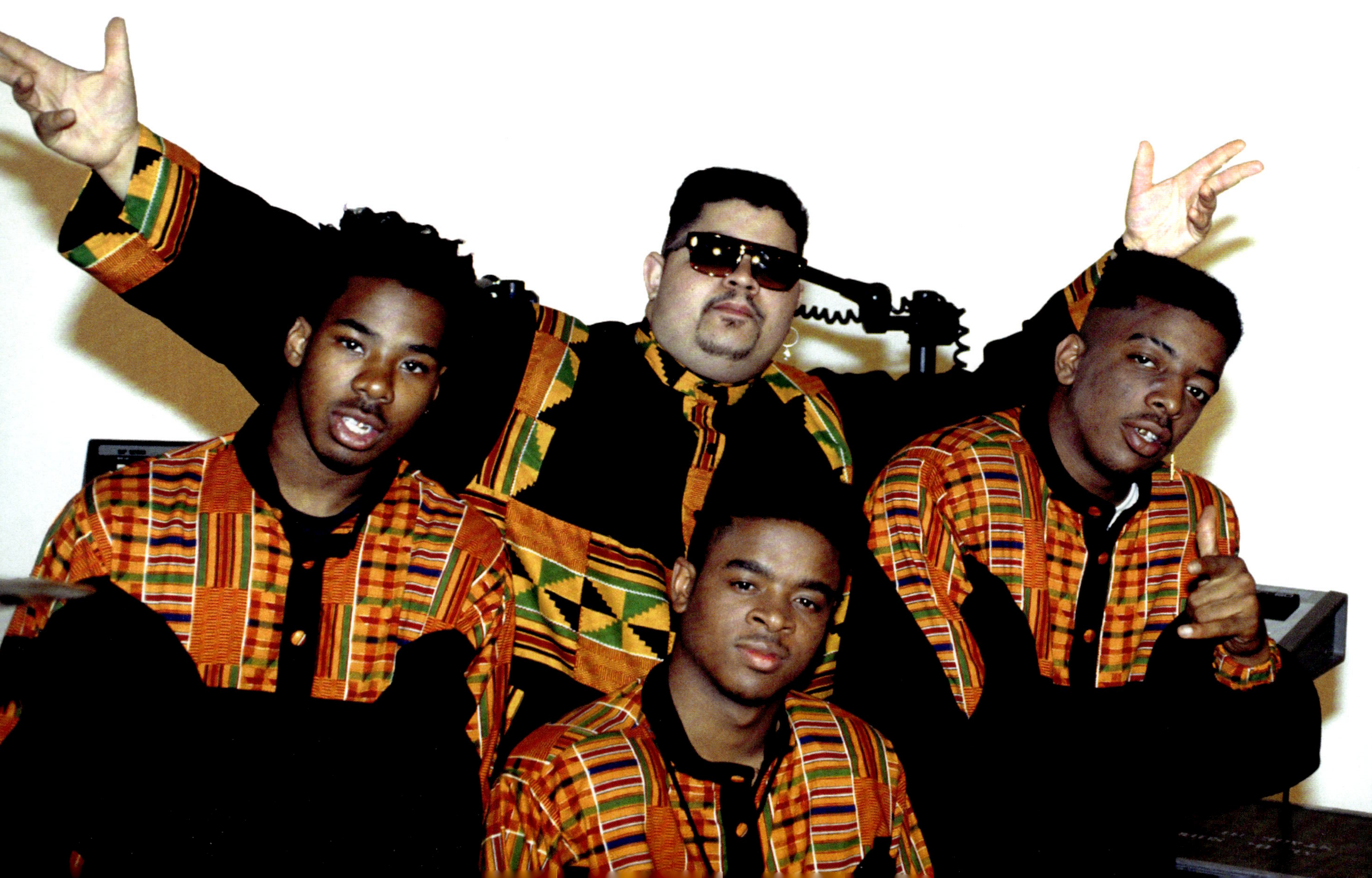

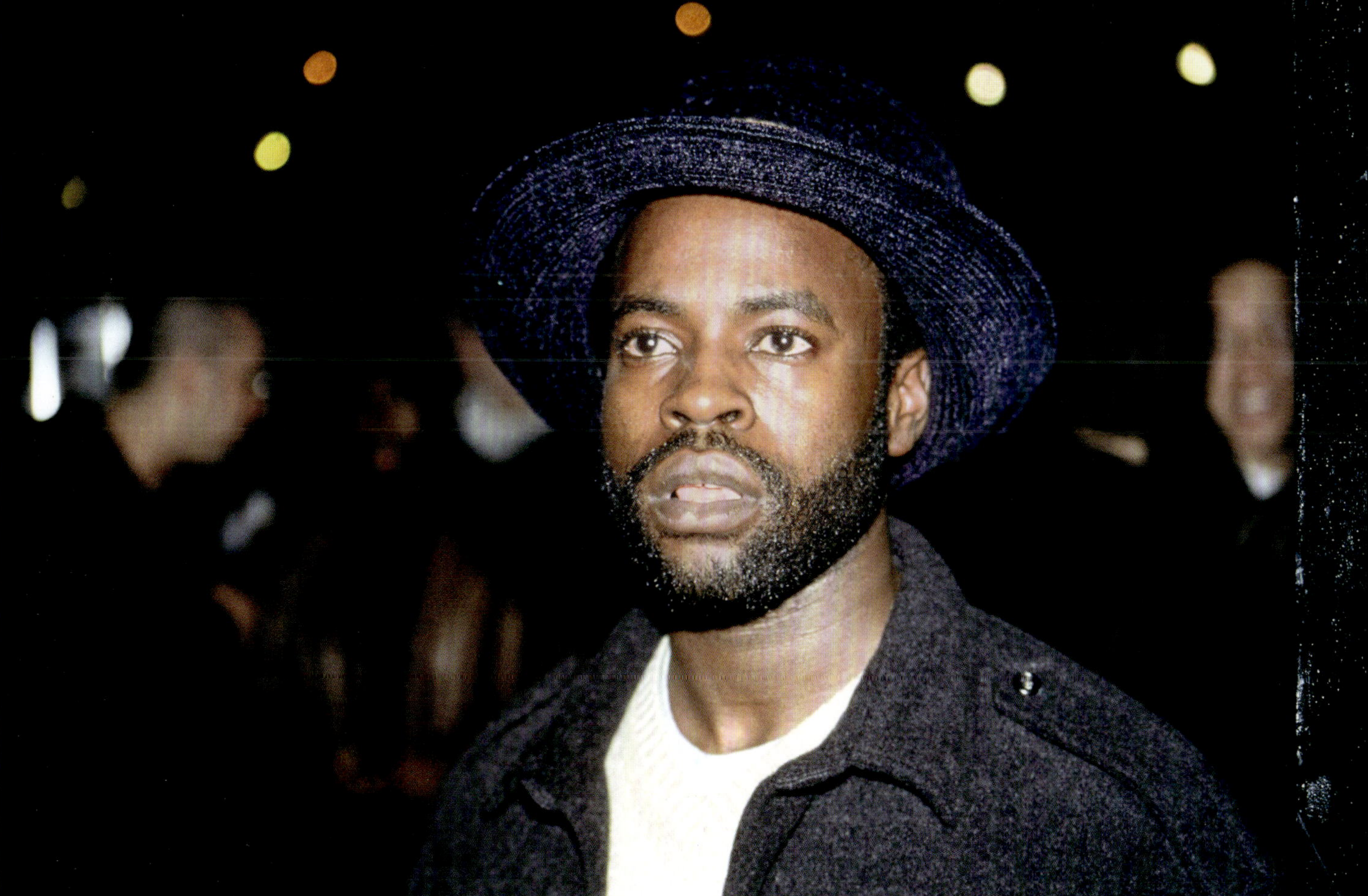

Notes to page 118:
Got a call from Zulu brother Muhammad Islam asking me to be with Yasiin Bey at his very last show at The Apollo. I was blown away by the request because Yasiin occupies a very rare space in hip-hop and rap. When I arrived he was getting out of his SUV behind the theatre. He embraced me and I sensed a great deal of respect and affection from him, and also a degree of pain. I was honored to be there and see him relaxed and happy with friends and family members. He asked permission to wear one of my medallions that had been gifted me by First Nations friends in Canada (Angela Miracle Gladue, Bri Briskool Marie, Jay Robi, and Tristan Shamantan Martell). He wore it while performing a long, intimate, spiritual concert to an intense, loving and packed house. This image of him showing love to a Native American icon, the Anishinaabe and Lakota activist Leonard Peltier, is one of my favorites of all time.

Notes to page 119:
Flava Flav. Perhaps the most obscene hip-hop photo I ever shot. This image invokes so many deeply racist and ugly, historical stereotypes. True to form, Flava is mocking, taunting, forcing viewers to ask themselves if they are part of the solution or part of the problem. This was shot in his mother's house in Long Island.

p.121 Black Thought (Tariq Luqmaan Trotter) from the Roots, a group he founded with Questlove (Ahmir Thompson) in 1987. NYC, late 1990s.

Notes to page 122:
Arrested Development, NYC, 1992. Their song "Tennessee" had a powerful vibe that to this day always gets a club up and dancing. The only rap group comprised of young and old, male and female, their positive and uplifting lyrics and energy stood in stark contrast to gangsta rap, which was enormously popular then.

Notes to page 123:
Digable Planets, NYC, 1994. Conscious, rhythmic, hip and cool. They provided the bridge between jazz, hip-hop, rap and the Native Tongues vibe. Their seminal album *Blowout Comb* (1994) was an instant hit on college campuses, in clubs, coffee shops and among the so-called "backpackers" who wanted more in their lyrics than the encroaching West Coast, Dr. Dre-inspired gangsta stylings.

p.122 Arrested Development, NYC, 1992; p.123 Digable Planets, NYC, 1994 (additional notes on p.121).

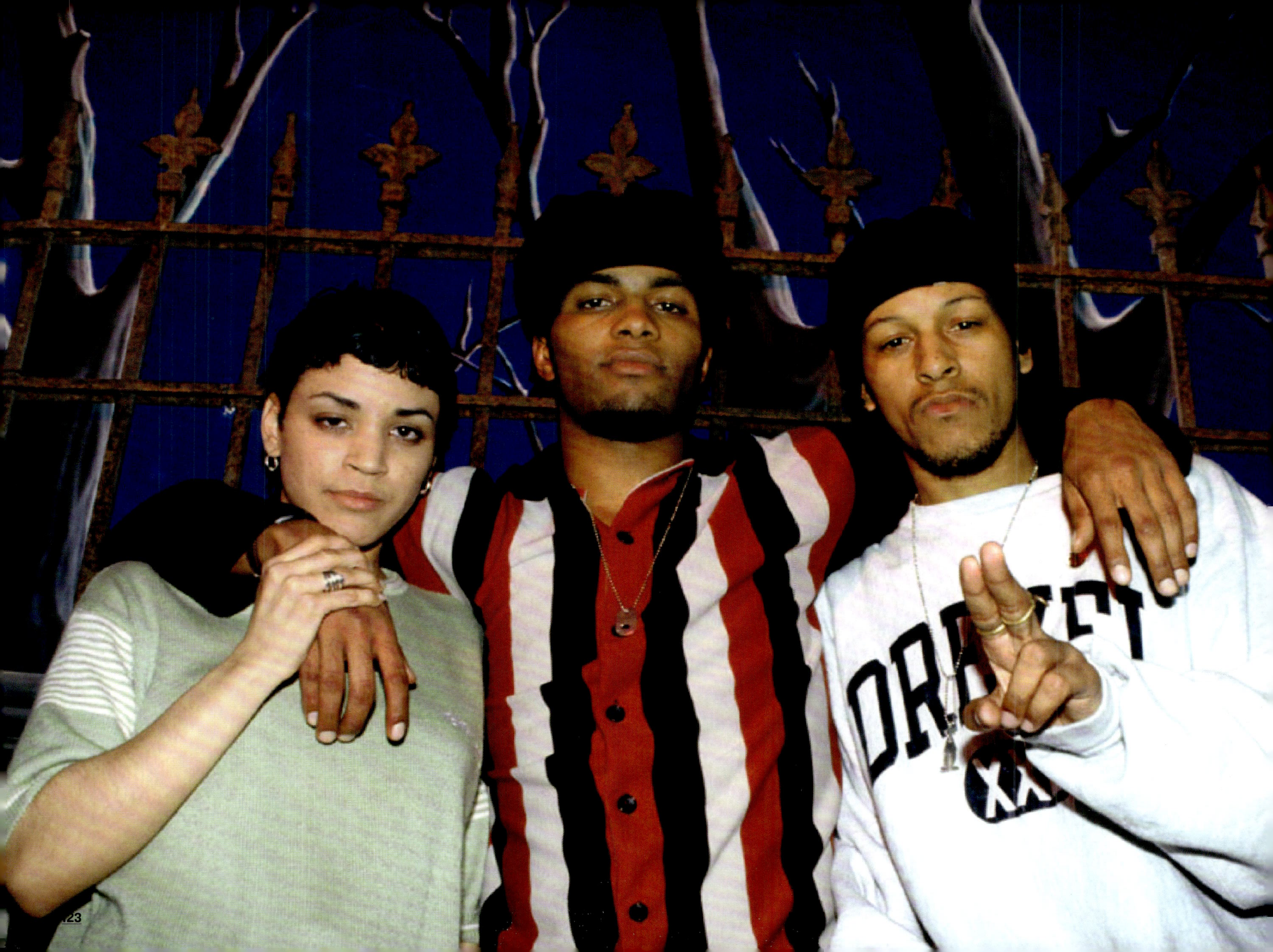

p.124 Ice-T with Body Count and Afrika Islam. Notice that the entire audience is White! The Roxy, 1992.

p.125 Ice-T wearing a Zulu Kings t-shirt. NYC, late 1980s.

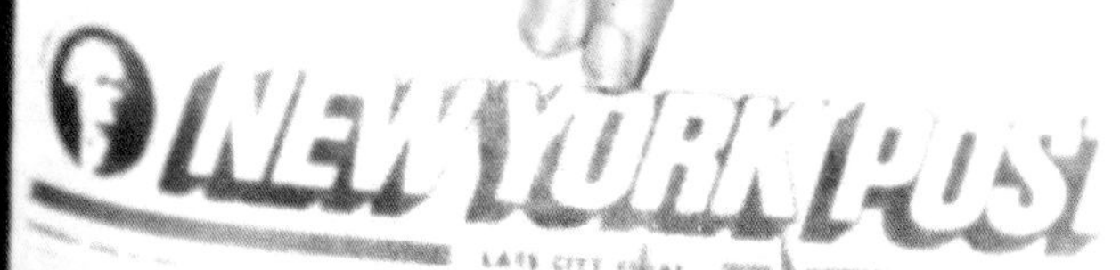

NEW YORK POST

LATE CITY FINAL

COPS PIN RAP ON BATMAN

UPPER E. SIDE MADAM GOES ON THE LAM

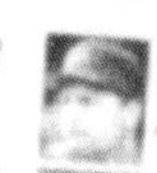

METS, YANKS BOTH LOSERS

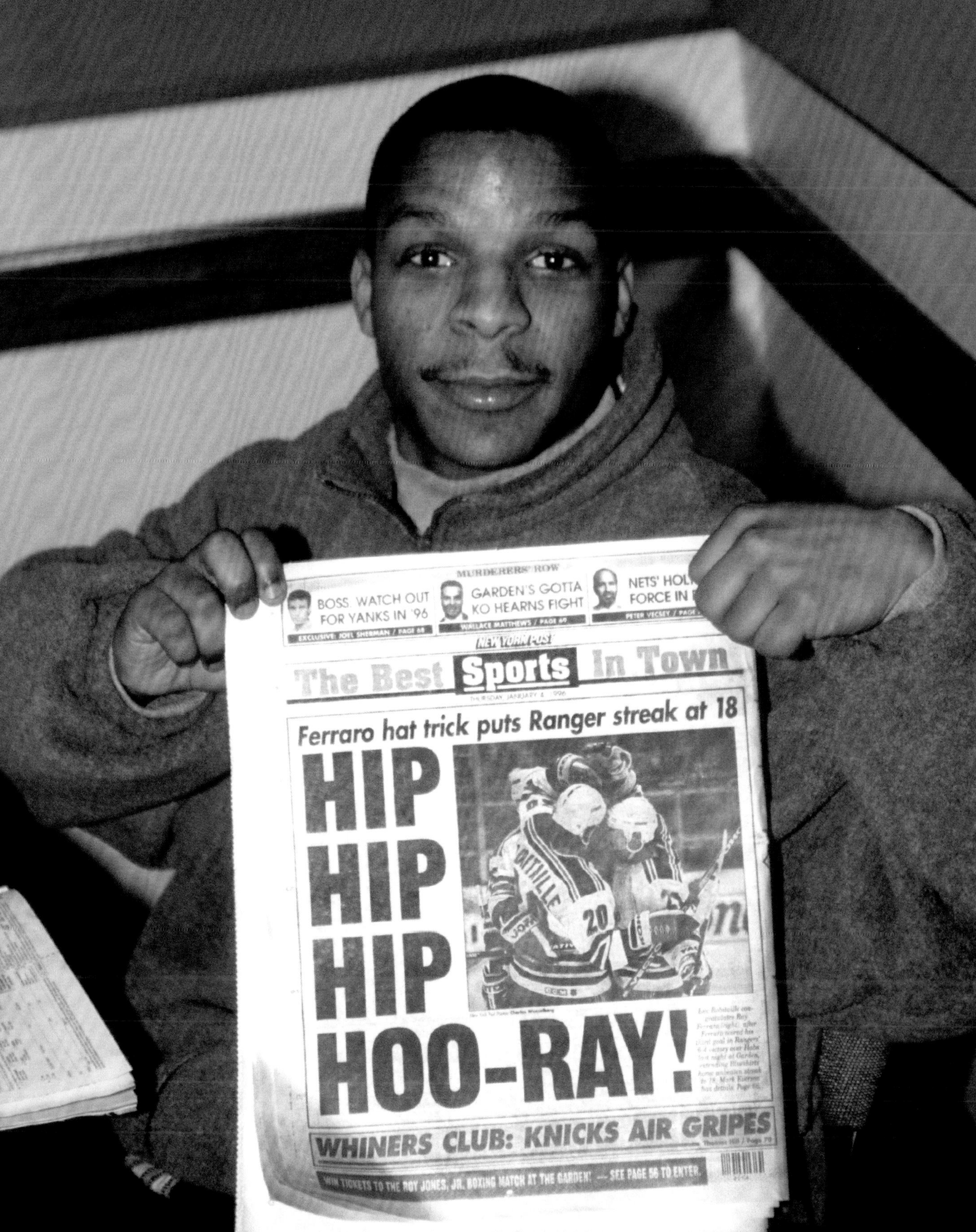
MURDERERS' ROW
BOSS, WATCH OUT FOR YANKS IN '96
GARDEN'S GOTTA KO HEARNS FIGHT
WALLACE MATTHEWS
NEW YORK POST
The Best Sports In Town
Ferraro hat trick puts Ranger streak at 18
HIP HIP HIP HOO-RAY!
WHINERS CLUB: KNICKS AIR GRIPES
WIN TICKETS TO THE ROY JONES, JR. BOXING MATCH AT THE GARDEN! — SEE PAGE 56 TO ENTER.

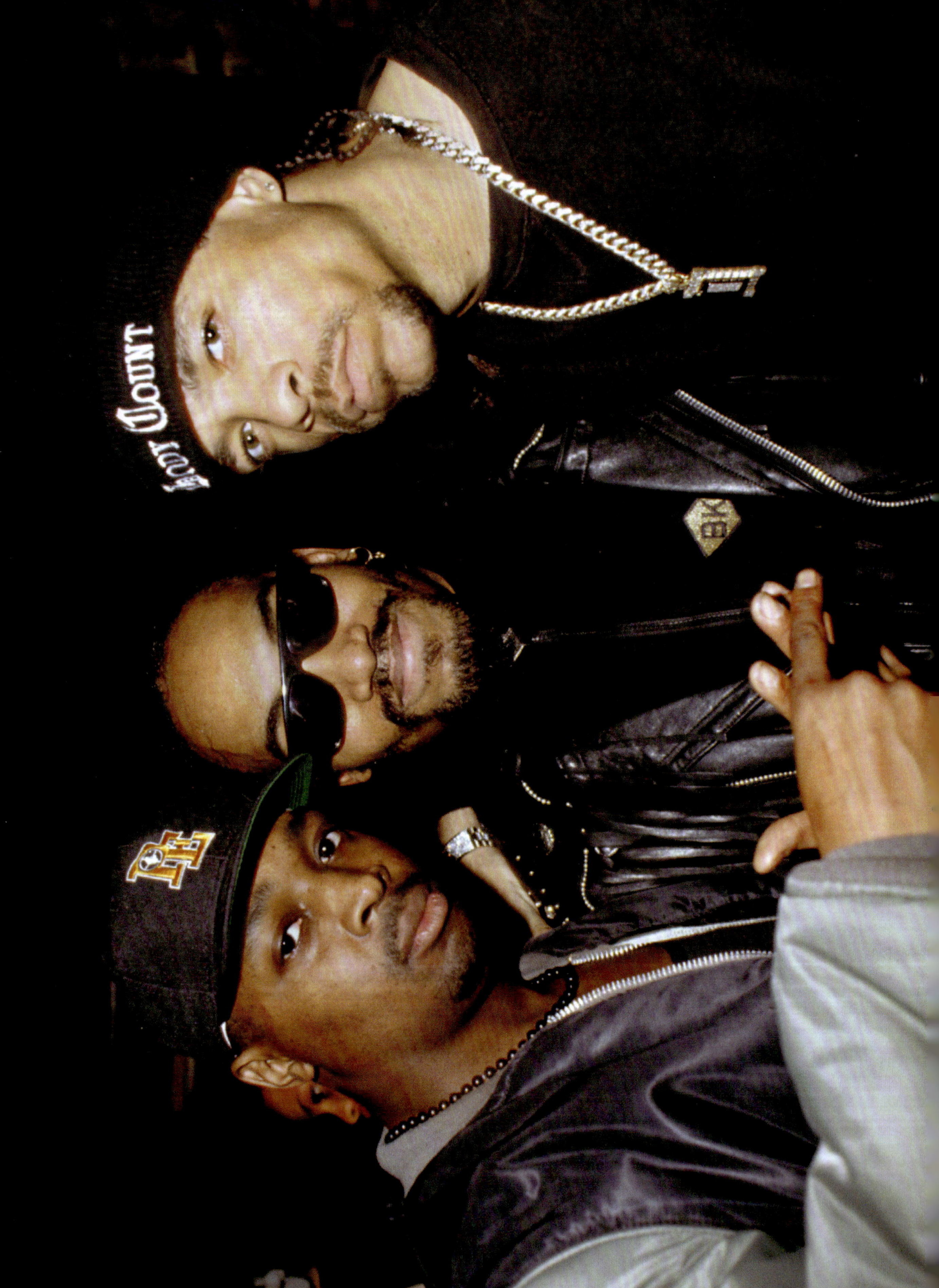

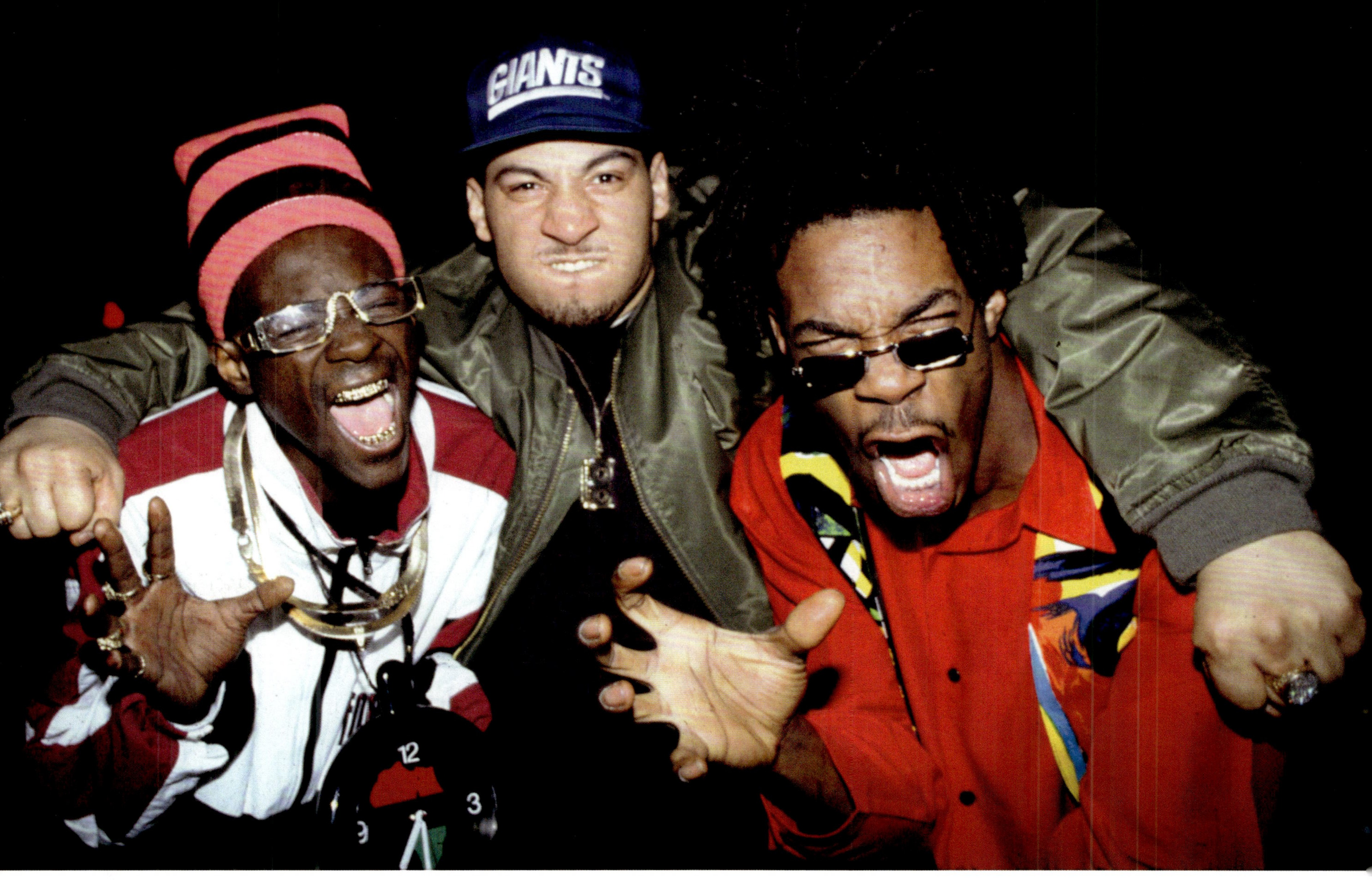

p.126 Ice-T at the New Music Seminar with *N.Y. Post* headline covering the police union boycotting the Time Warner's *Batman Returns* (1992) to protest Body Count's song "Cop Killer." Ice-T and Body Count were signed to Time Warner. New York, June 1992; p.127 Vinny Brown having a laugh at the sports headline which made a pun of his band Naughty By Nature's anthem "Hip Hop Hooray," Newark, NJ, 1993; p.128 Chuck D, Melle Mel and Ice-T. Three schools of Hip-Hop. KRS-One said the photo should be titled "The Storytellers."; p.129 A comic moment with Flava Flav, DJ Kid Capri and Busta Rhymes, Central Park Boat House , NYC, 1993.

p.130 & 131 (top) Flava Flav posing in front of the World Trade Center and Battery Park, NYC, 2000; p. 131 (bottom) And on the day Nelson Mandela came to Harlem, on 125th St, NYC, October 1994.

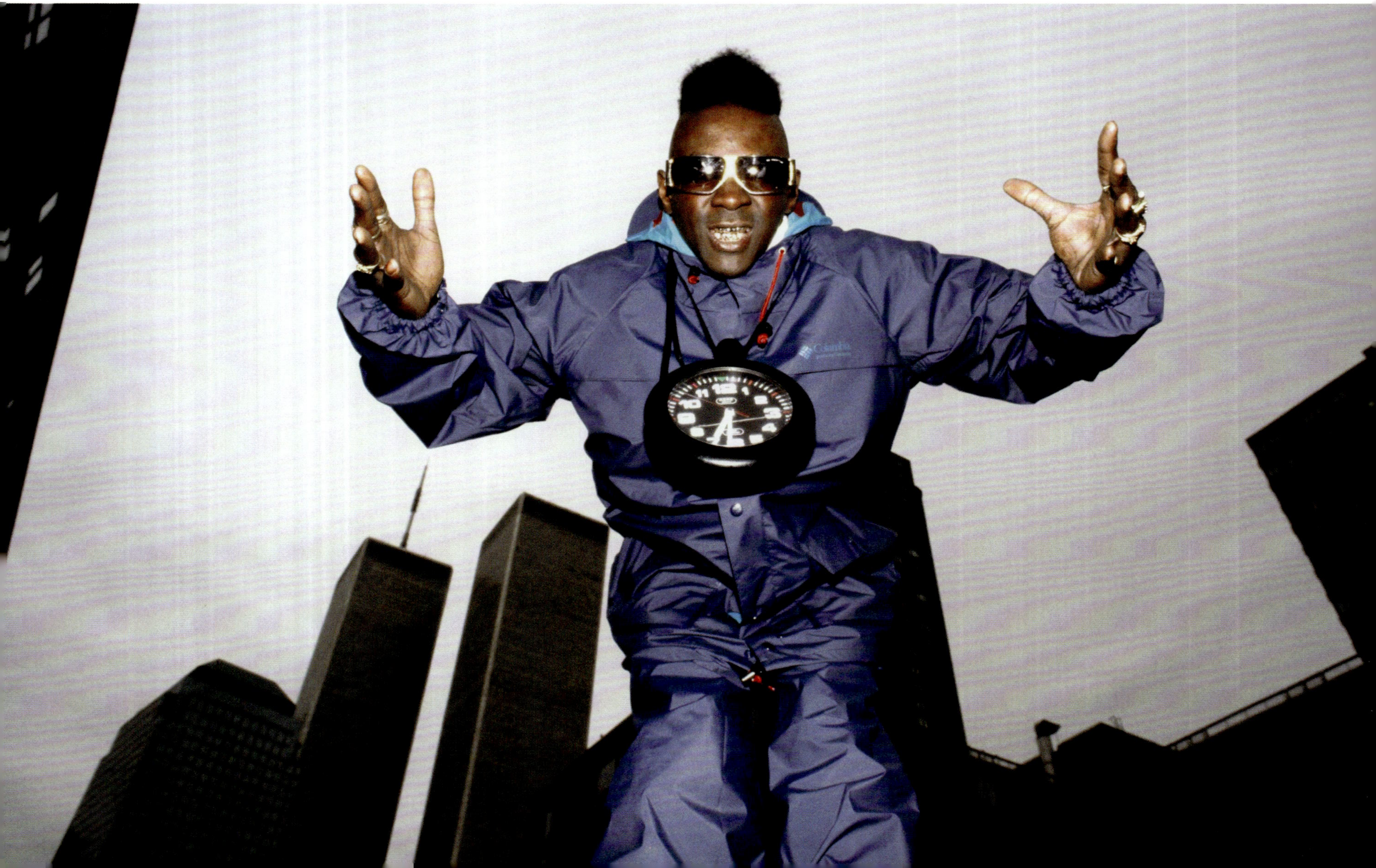

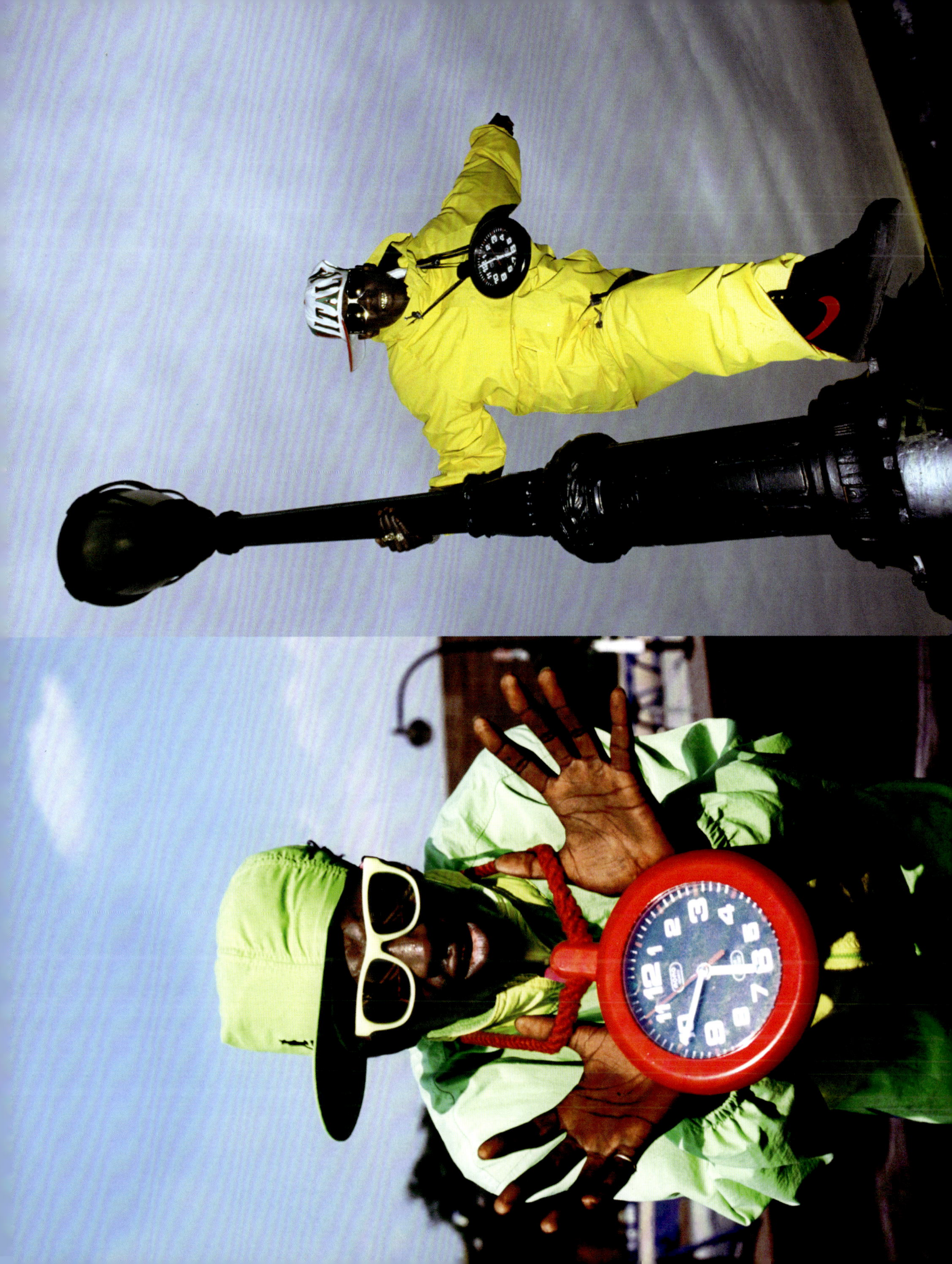

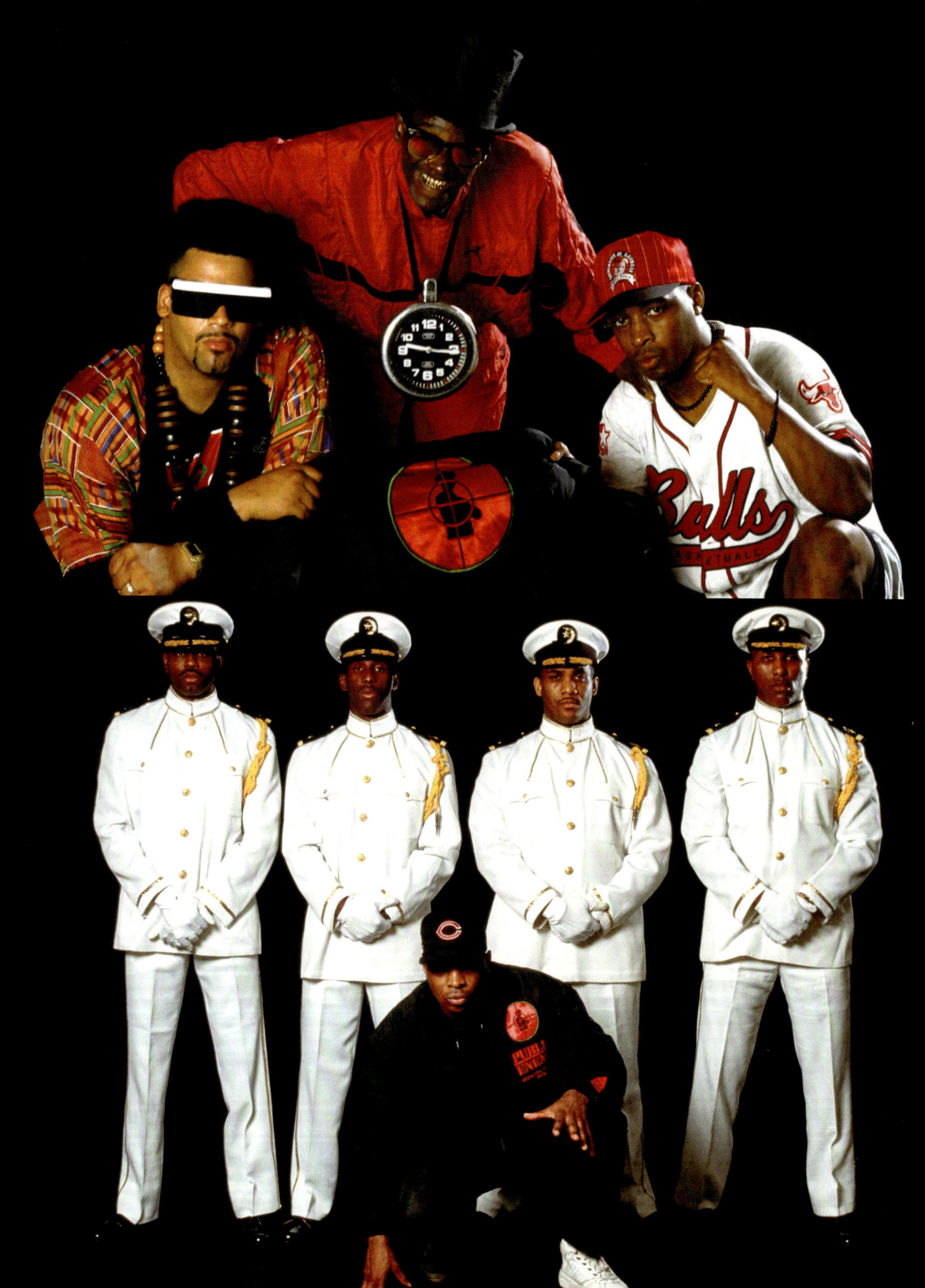
Bulls

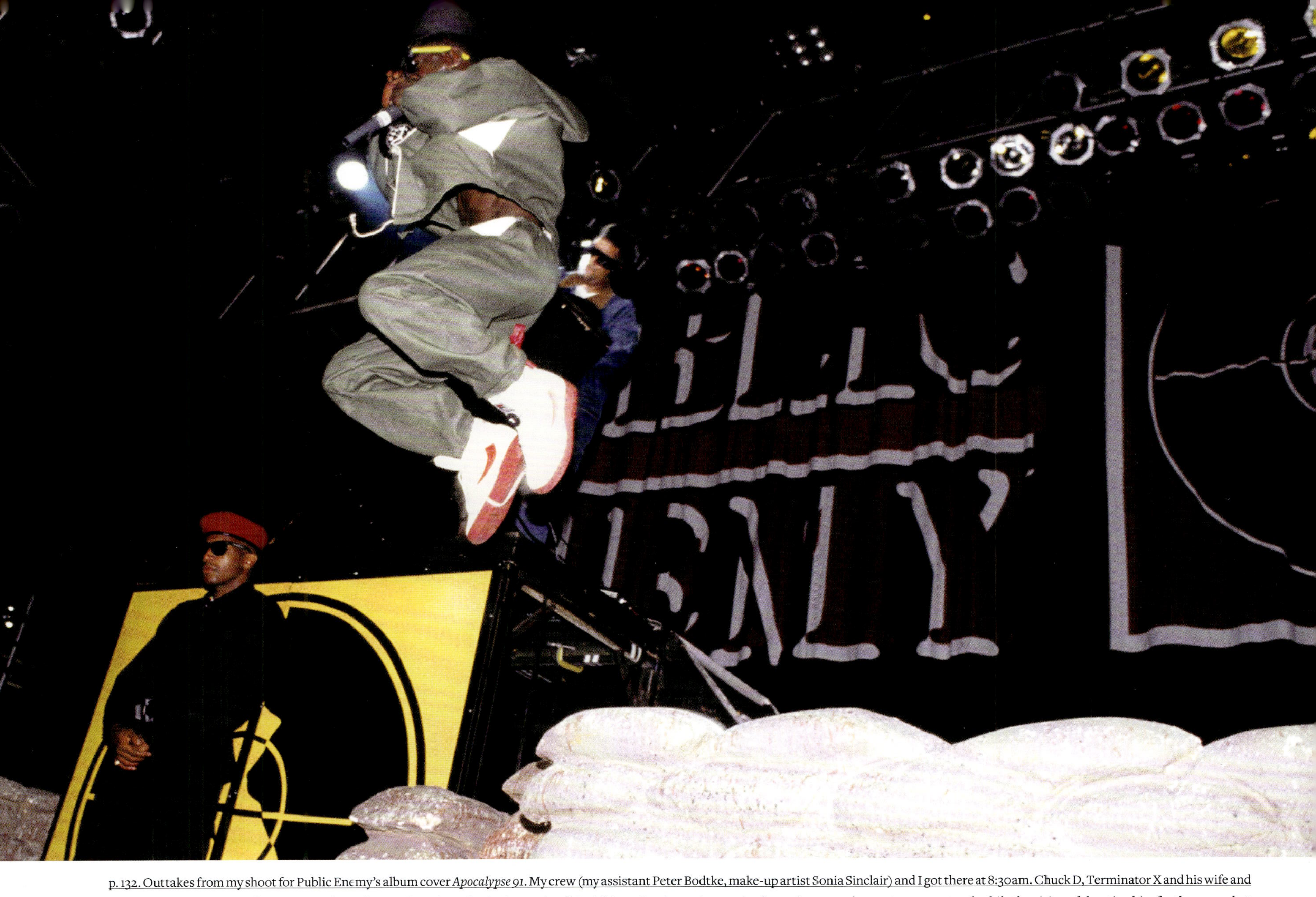

p. 132. Outtakes from my shoot for Public Enemy's album cover *Apocalypse 91*. My crew (my assistant Peter Bodtke, make-up artist Sonia Sinclair) and I got there at 8:30am. Chuck D, Terminator X and his wife and the S1W all arrived punctually at 9am on a hot July morning. Flava Flav had custody of his children that day and spent the day at the zoo and at an amusement park while the vision of shooting him for the cover shot diminished with every hour spent trying to track him down. We had to leave the studio by 9pm and Flava arrived sweaty and disheveled at around 8pm. I had never seen Chuck D as furious as he was that night. He informed Flava that he was no longer in the group and instructed me to finish the shoot without him. As I shot the first few frames, as if by magic Flava jumped into the shoot with a bright orange track suit, a top hat and clock. Chuck acted like nothing happened and we got the cover shot in 30 minutes. Freeport, Long Island, New York, 1990; P.133 Flava Flav and Terminator X, Madison Square Garden, NYC, 1992.

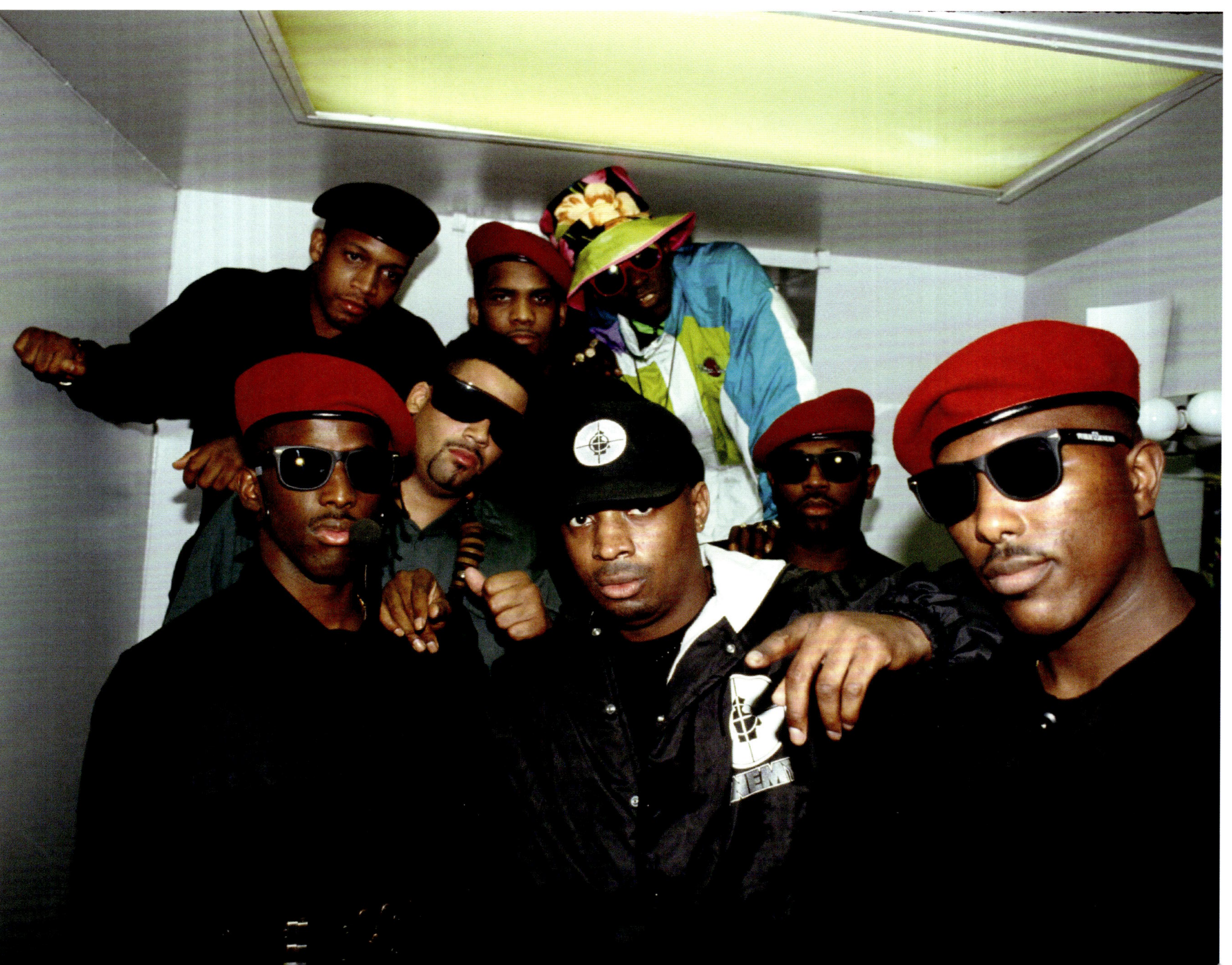

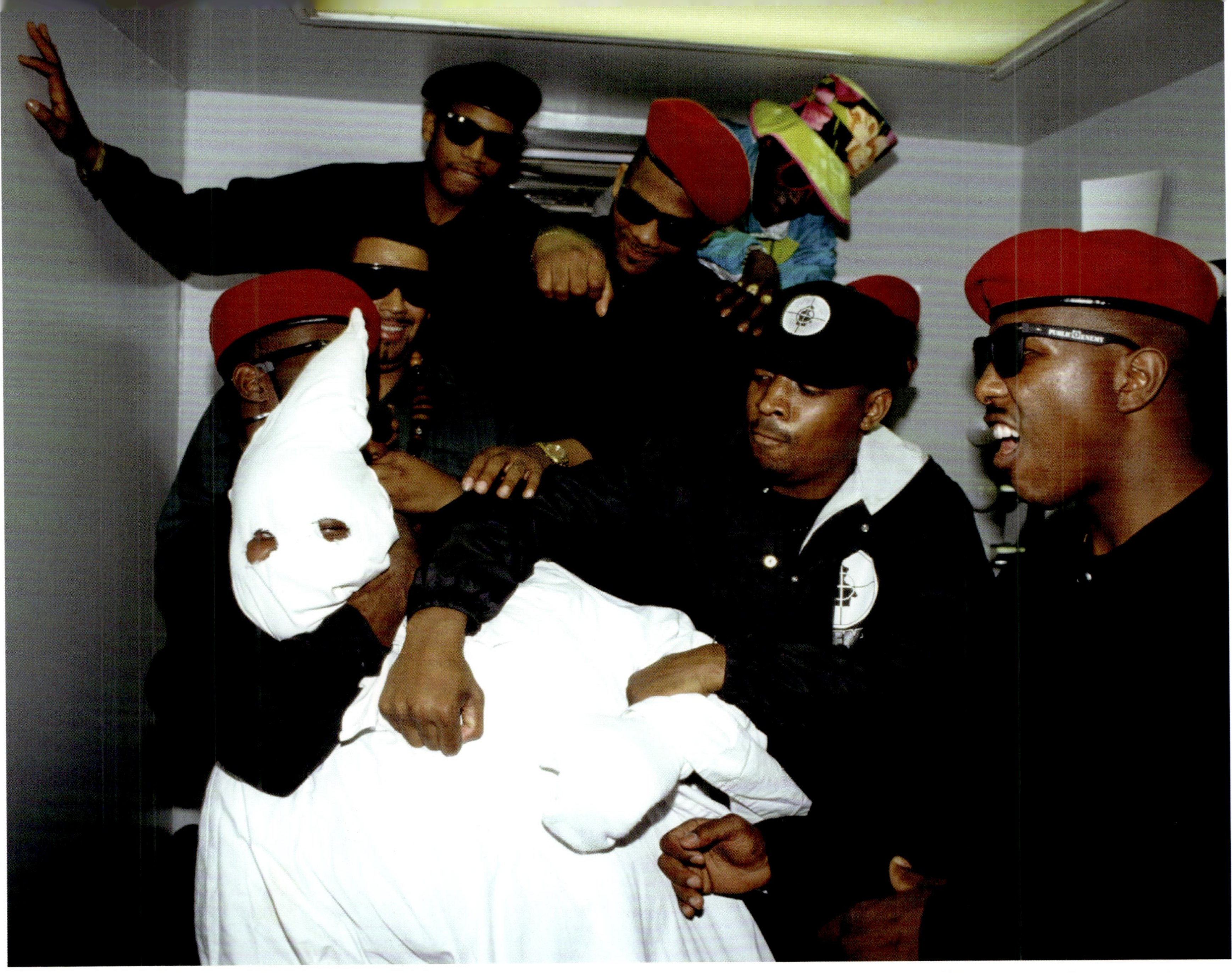

p.134-35 Public Enemy and S1W backstage, Apollo Theatre, Harlem, NYC, 1994.

p.136 My first shoot with S1W at Spectrum, Long Island, New York, 1987.

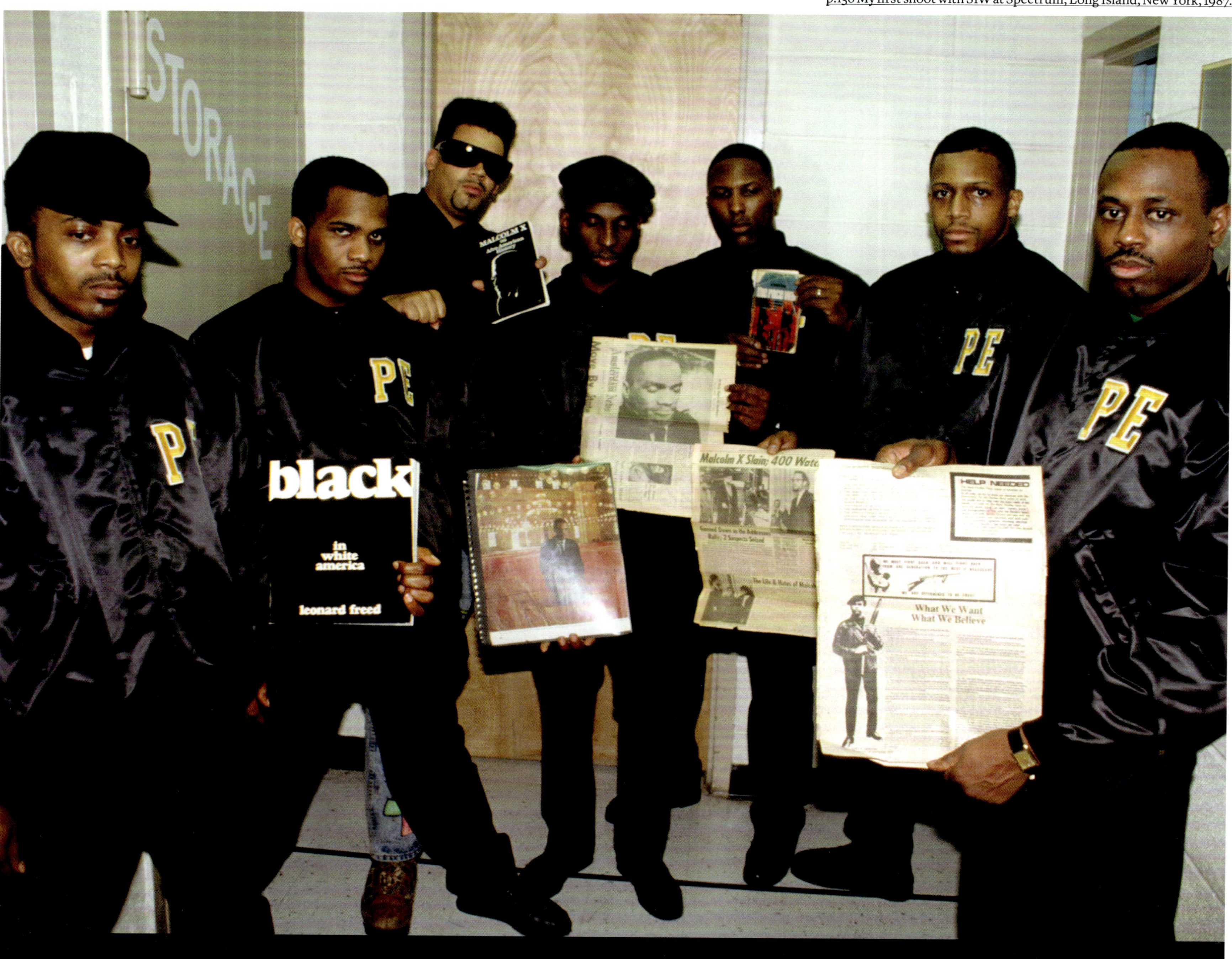

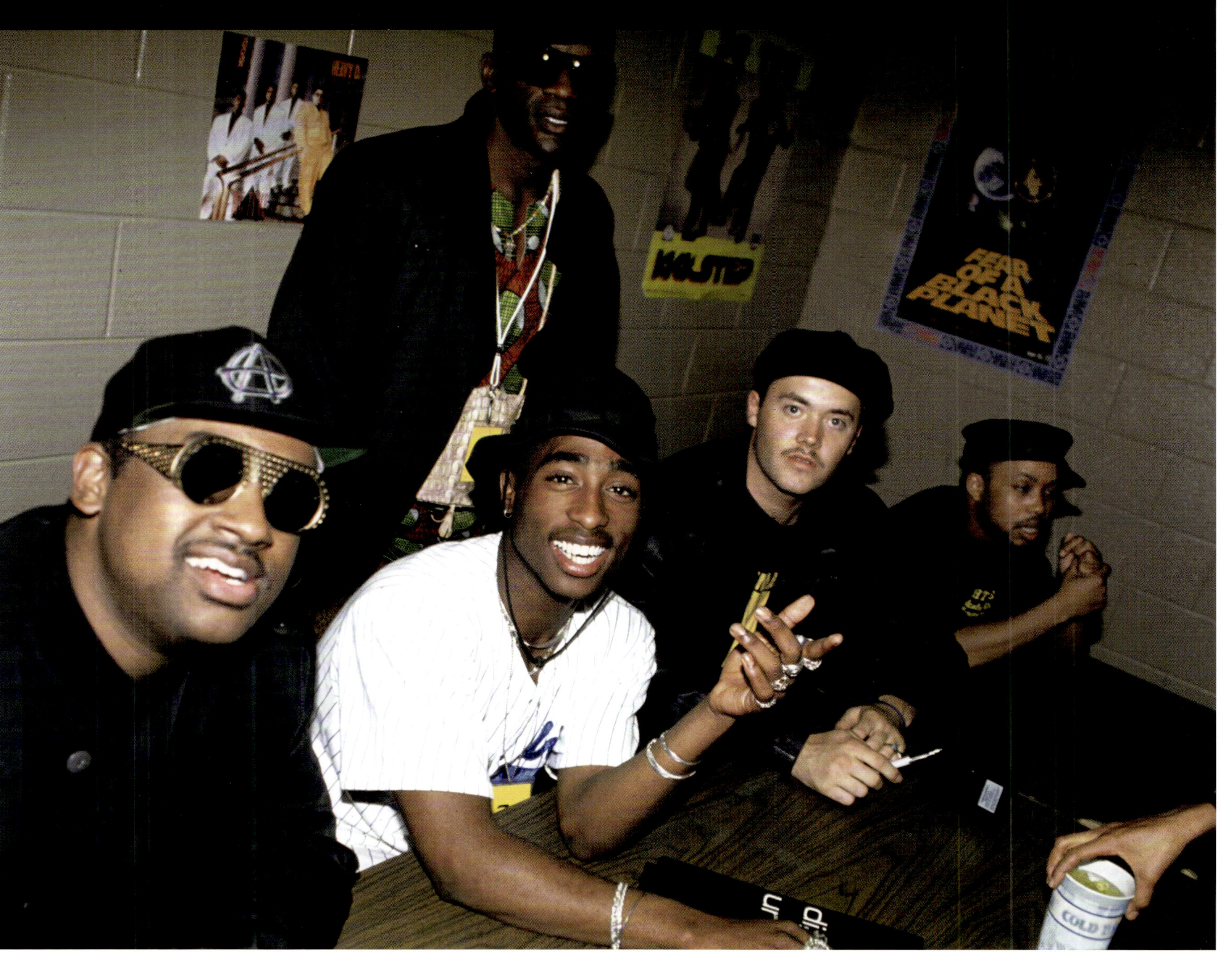

p.137 Tupac Shakur with Digital Underground, Williamsburg, Virginia, 1989. Tupac was a roadie with the group.

p.138-139 Eazy-E, Union Square , NY, 1989. In contrast to his NWA persona he was quiet, polite and respectful to those around him. The photos of him with PBA (policeman's union) cards are ironic because one of NWA's hits was "Fuck The Police." I could not find a magazine in America that would publish these photos.

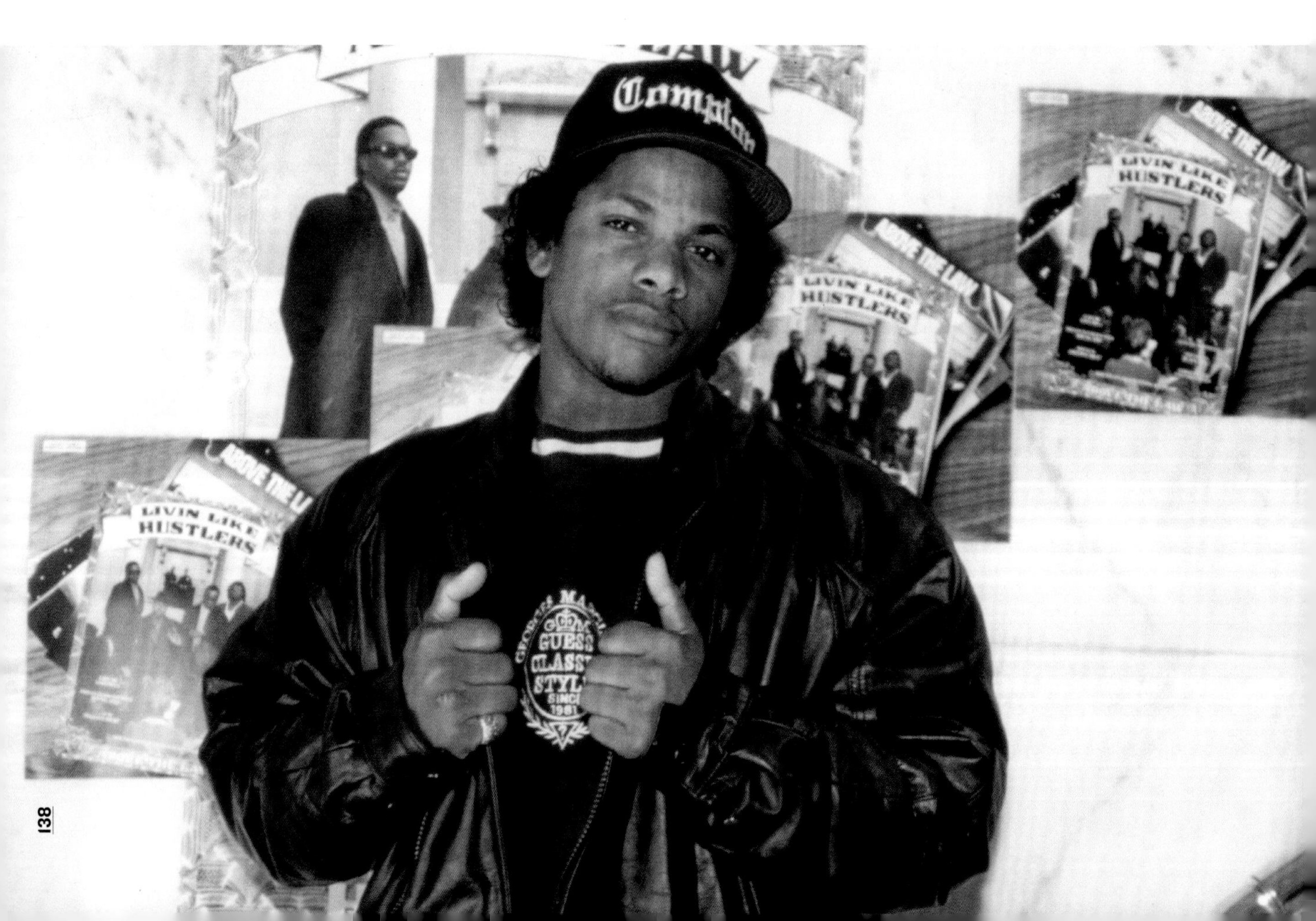

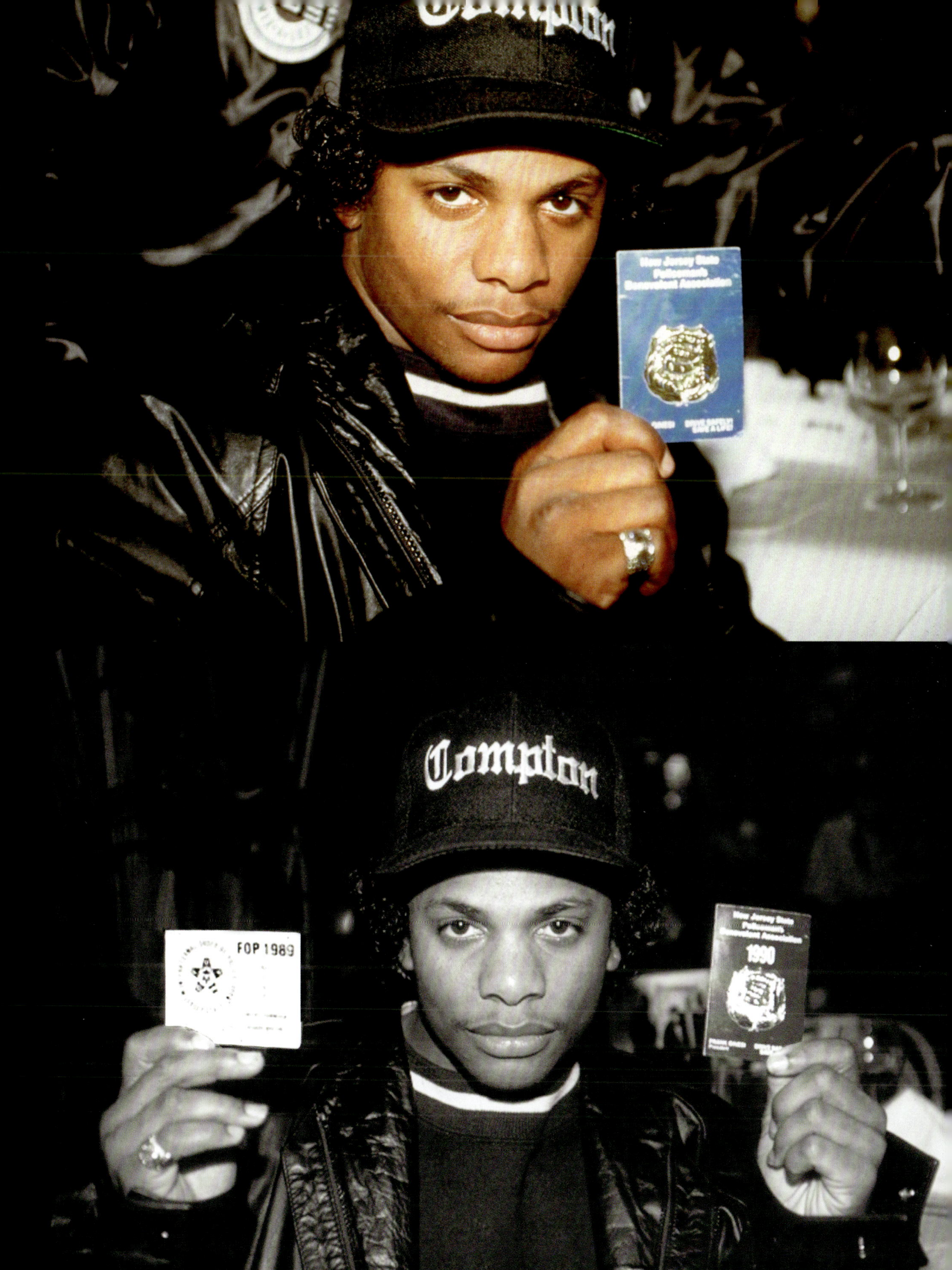
Compton
New Jersey State
Policemen's
Benevolent Association
Compton
FOP 1989
New Jersey State
Policemen's
Benevolent Association
1990

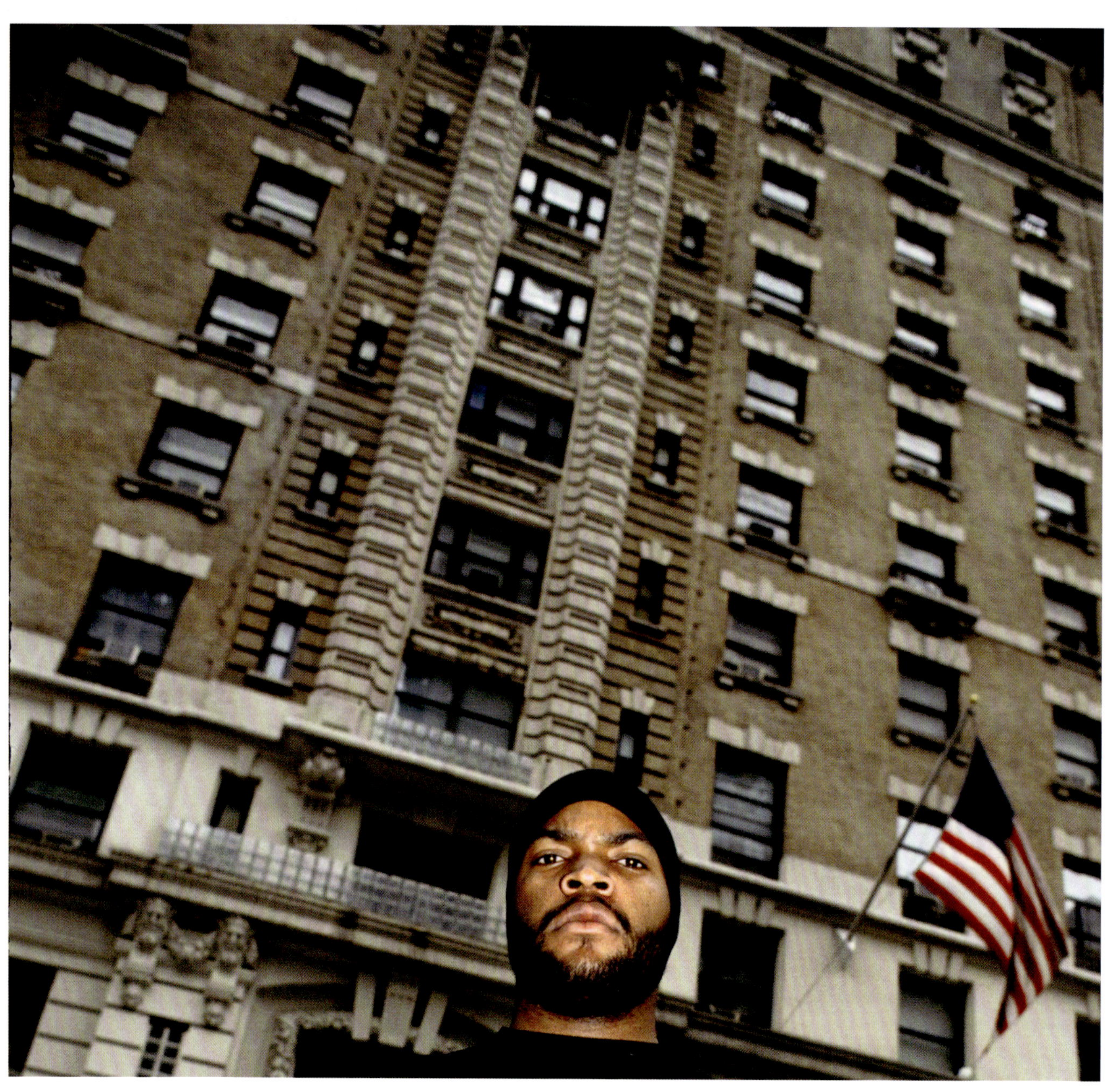

p.140-141 Ran into Ice Cube in midtown Manhattan and spent the next few hours hanging out with him and capturing him walking around the city and greeting fans. He had just been given international exposure from his role as Doughboy in the movie *Boyz n the Hood* and was known as part of NWA and as a solo rapper, yet he walked around the city all by himself, NYC, 1991.

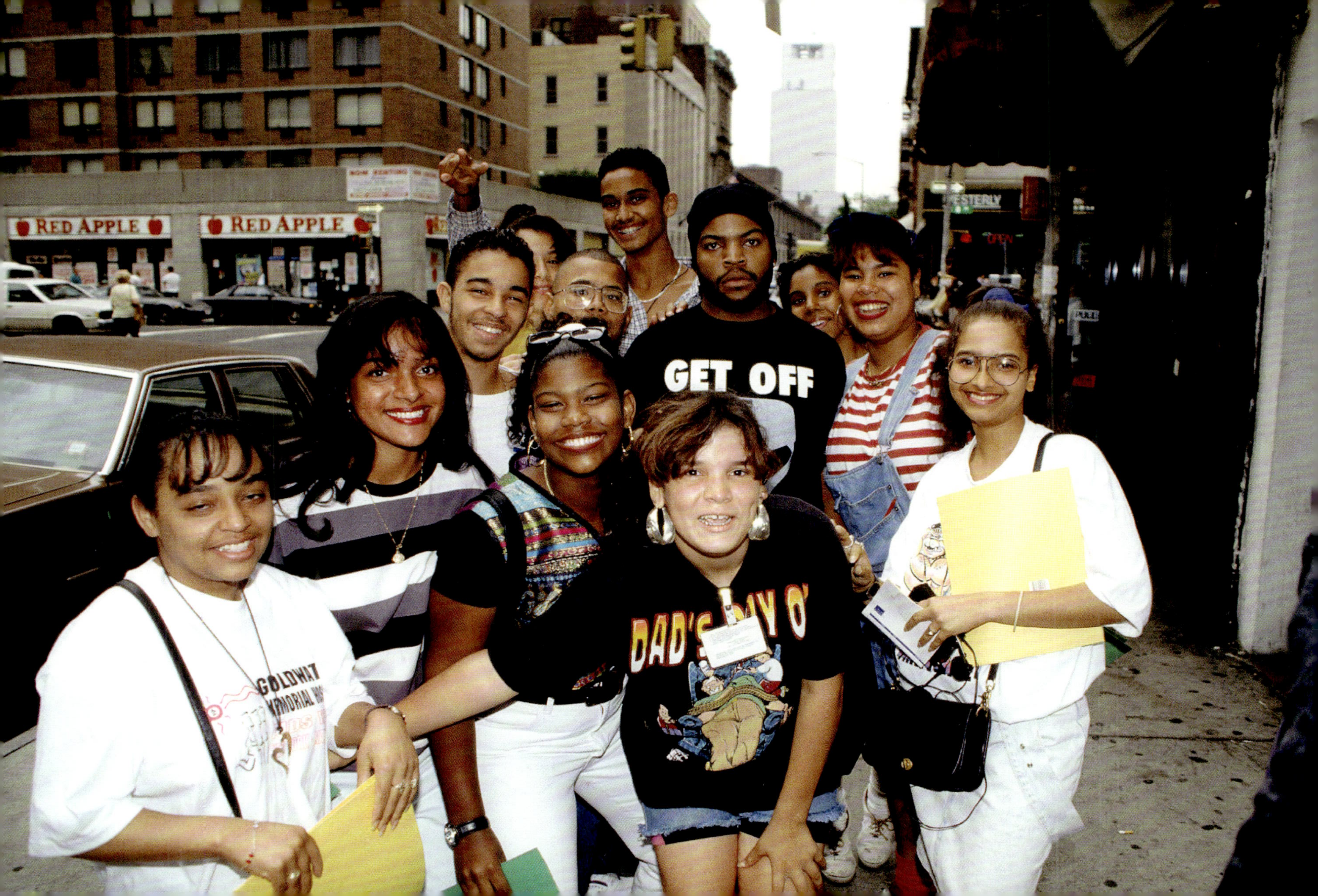
RED APPLE
RED APPLE
GET OFF
OPEN

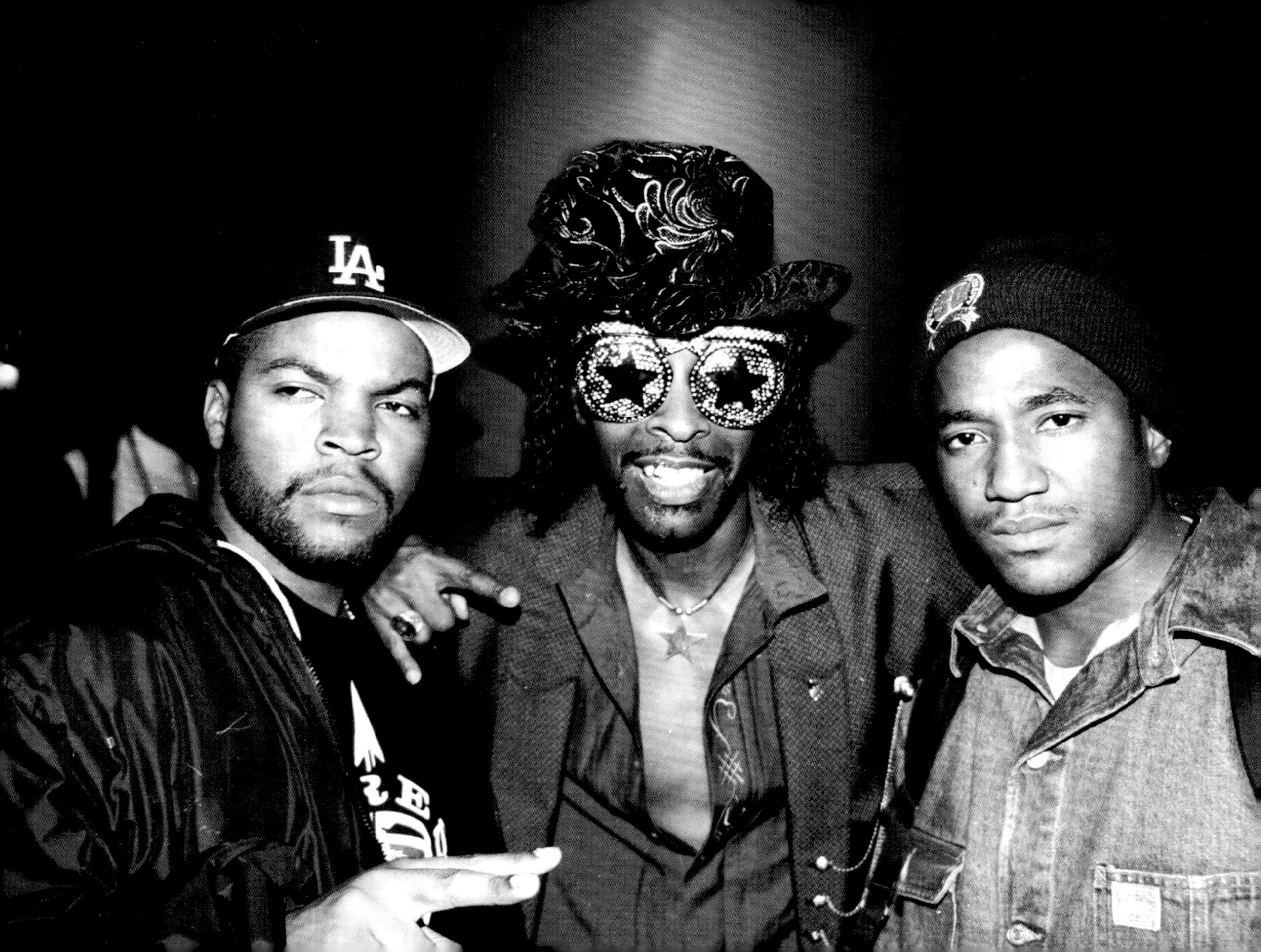
LA

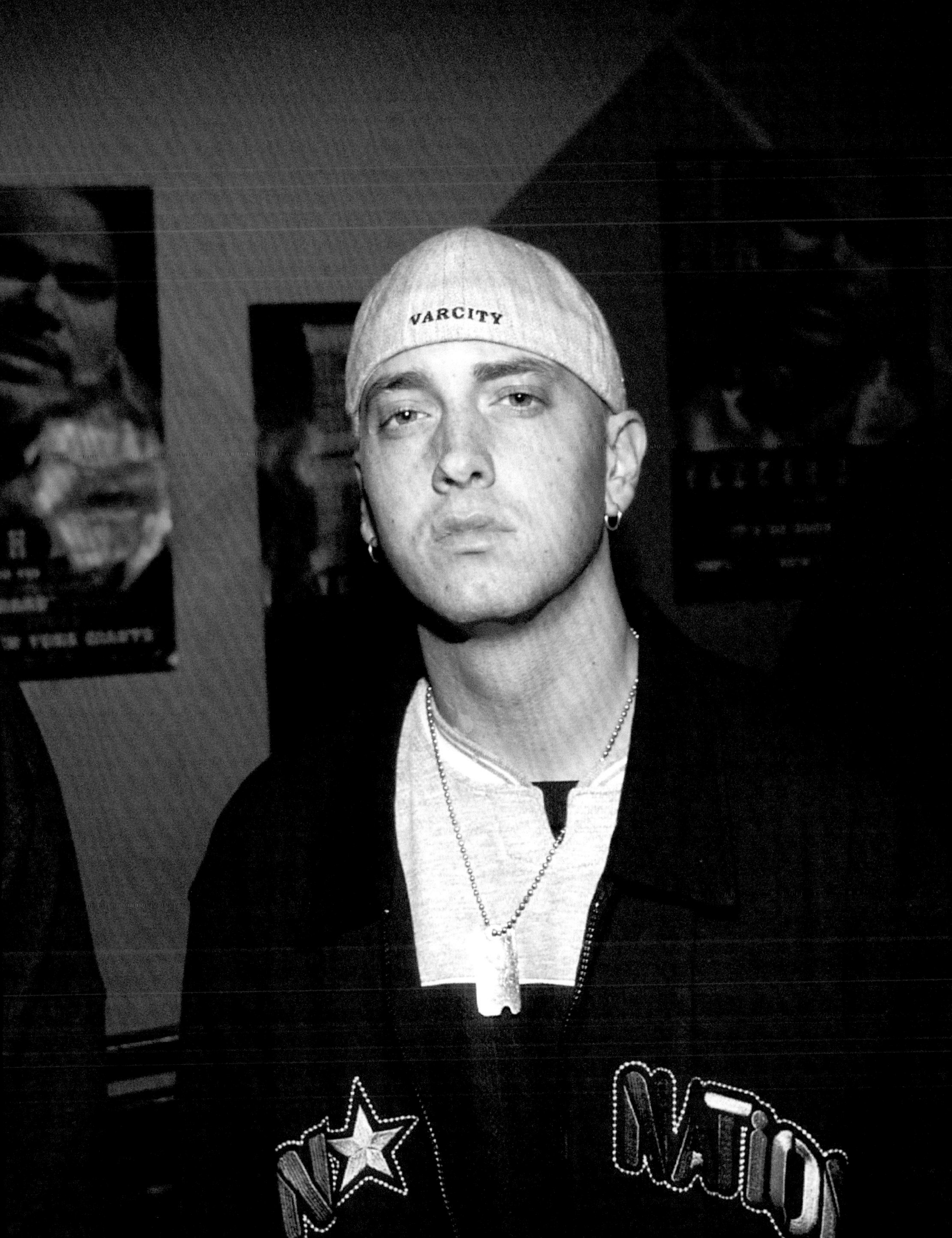
VARCITY

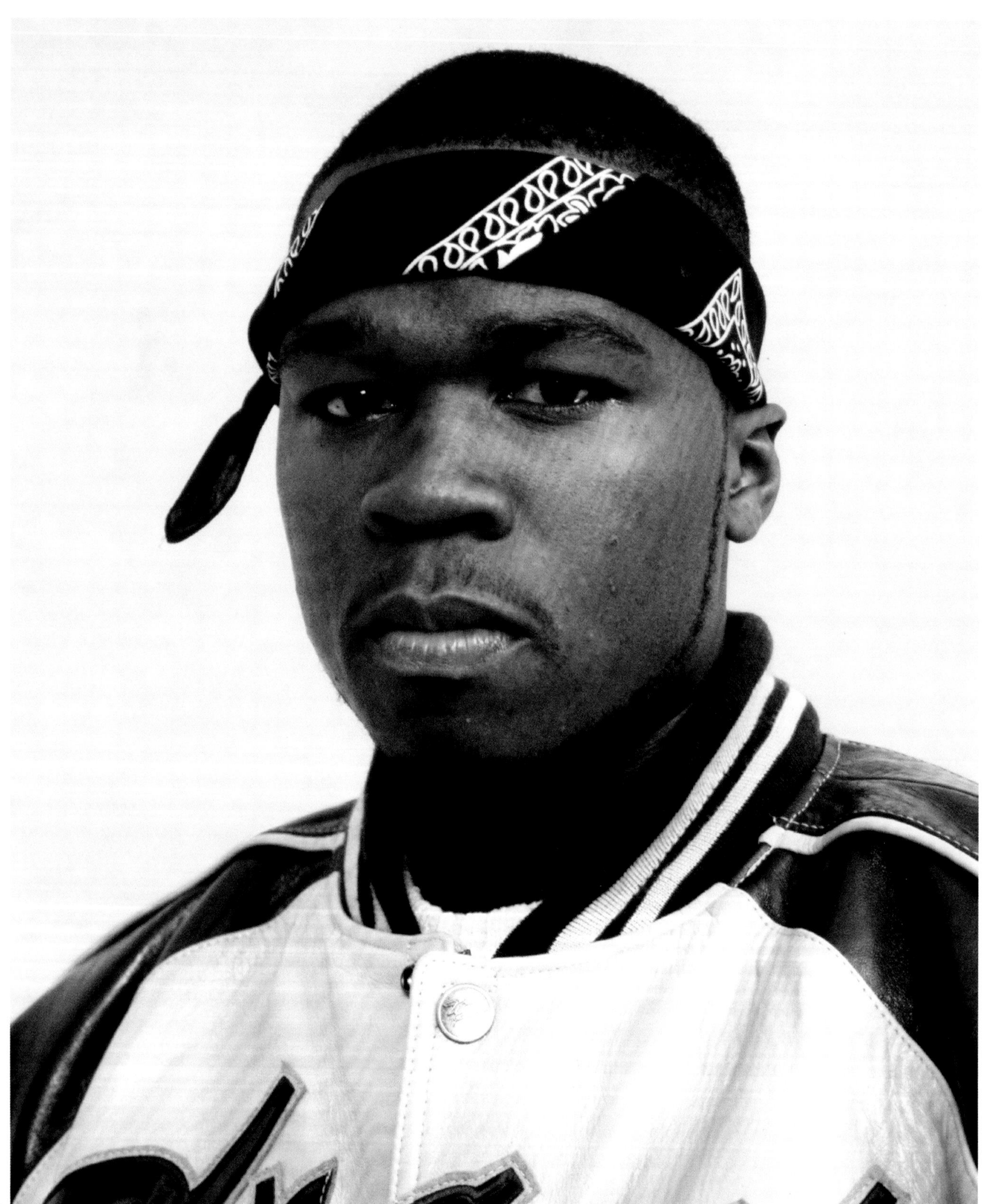

p.142 A vibrant photo of three artists, each with their own style and contribution to hip-hop. Ice Cube, West Coast hardcore rapper and actor; Bootsy Collins, funk bass guitarist; and Q-Tip, Native Tongues icon and Tribe Called Quest member. Wetlands, NYC, 1993.

p.143 Eminem at the funeral of Big Pun who passed away on February 7, 2000. Bronx, NYC, 2000.

p.144 (opposite page) 50 Cent, 3rd Eye Studio, NYC, 2000. He was shot nine times a few weeks after this shoot we did in my studio. He survived and his career went into overdrive because of his increased street cred.

p.146 Lil Wayne, NYC, 1998. Hailing from New Orleans, Louisiana, Wayne was then part of the Hot Boys; p.147 Lil Wayne, 3rd Eye Studio, NYC, 1999.

p.148 TLC (Tionne "T-Boz" Watkins, Lisa "Left Eye" Lopes and Rozonda "Chilli" Thomas), NYC, 1993.

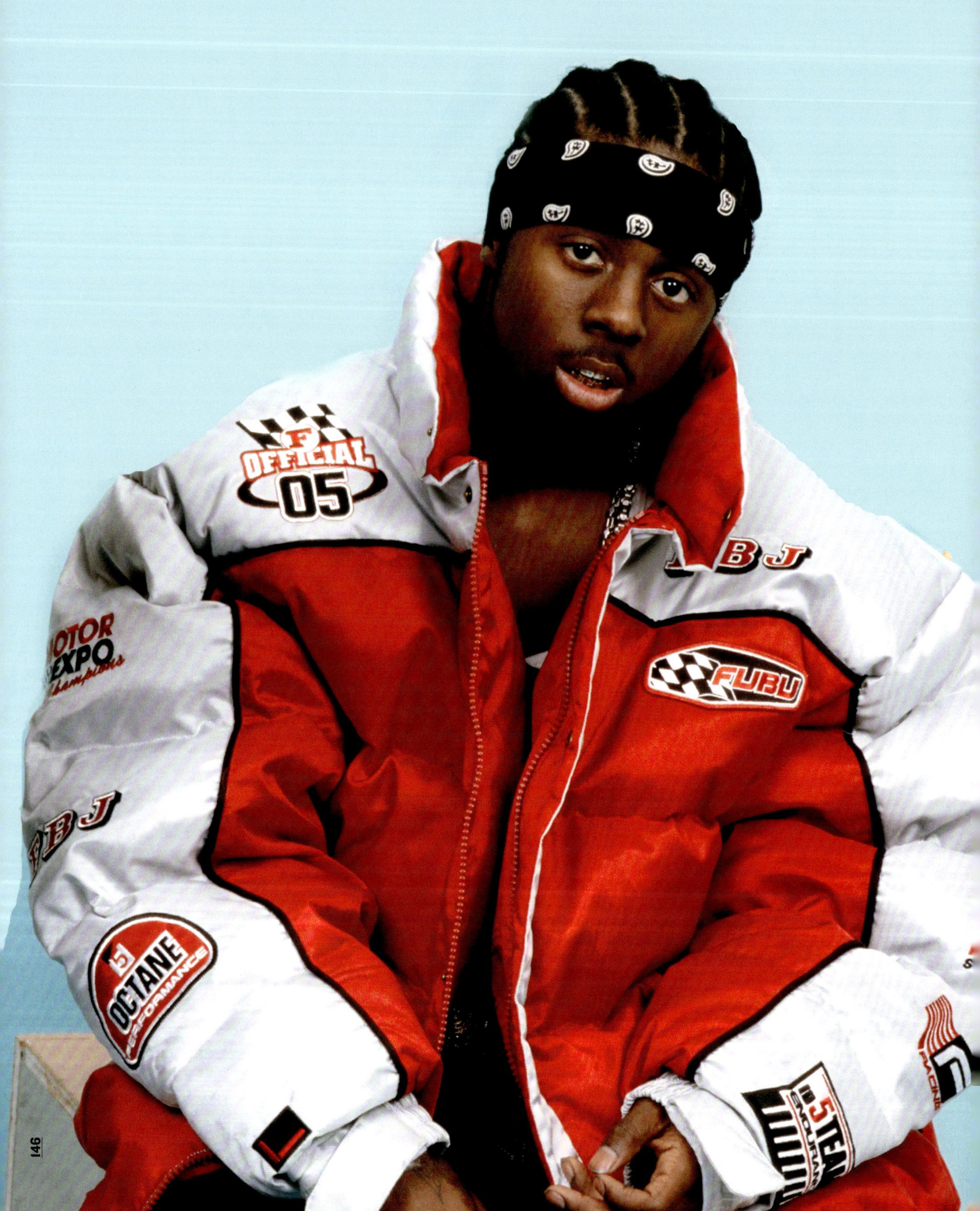
F
OFFICIAL
05
BJ
EXPO
FUBU
OCTANE
PERFORMANCE

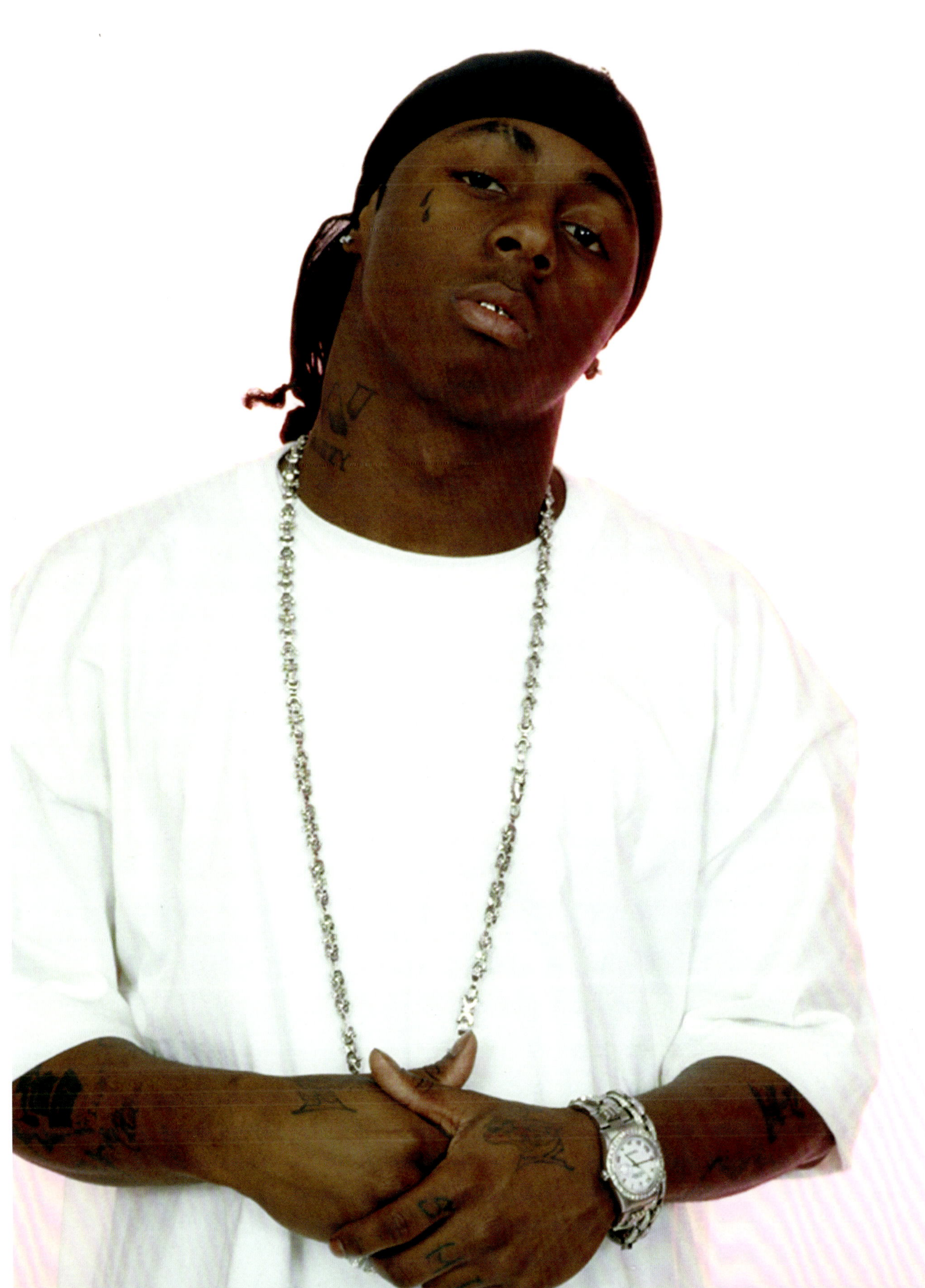

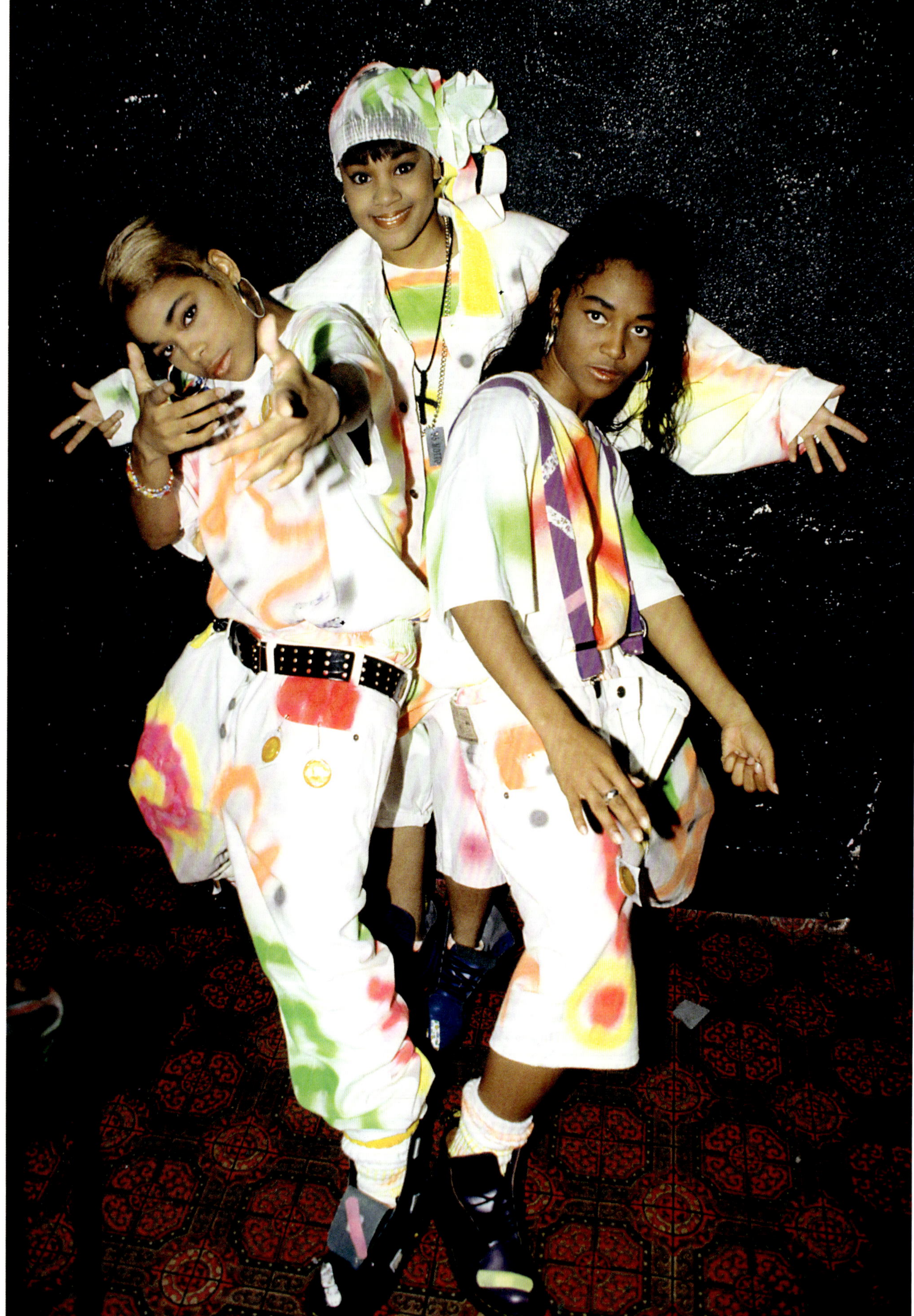

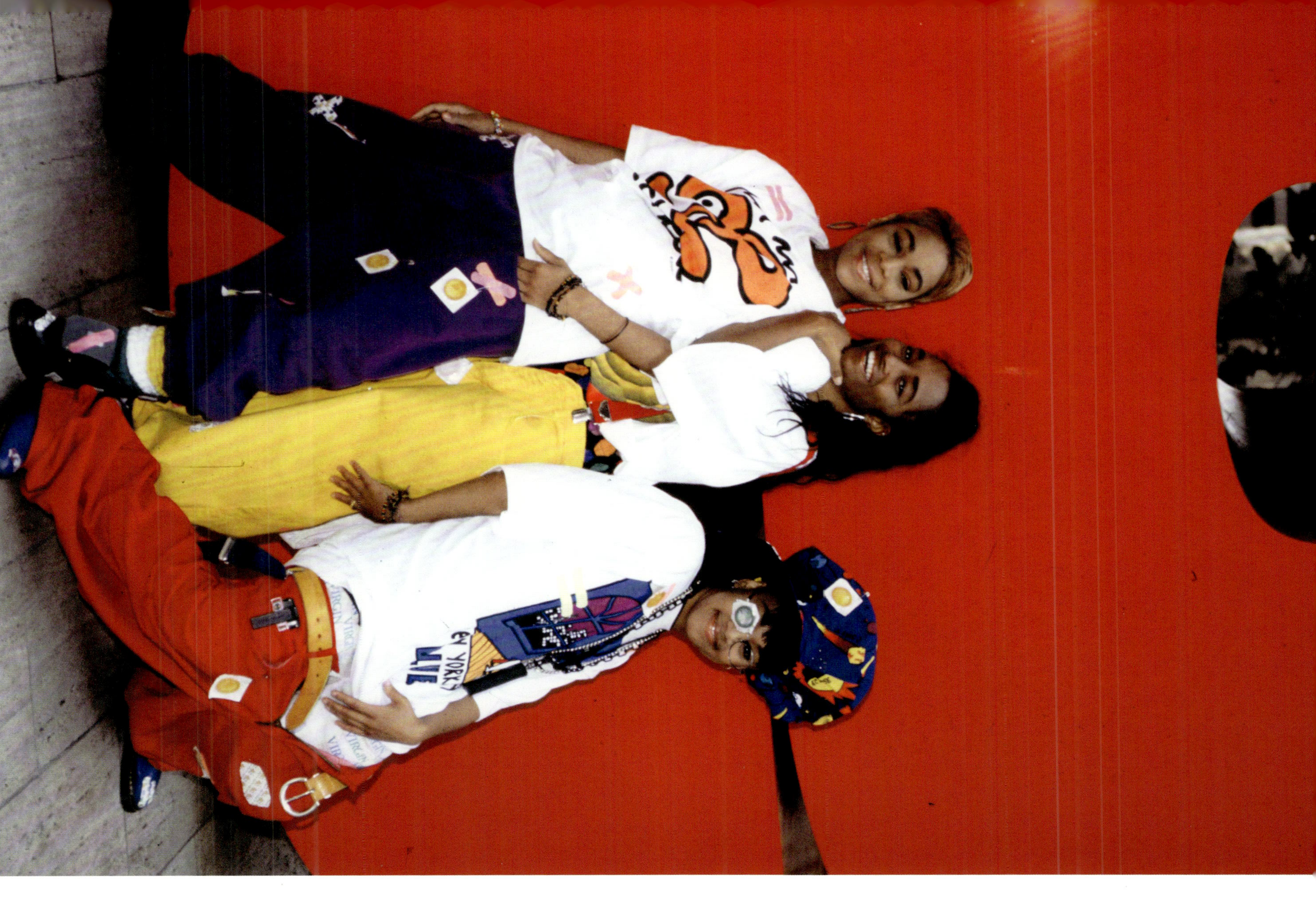

p.149 TLC, West 57th Street, NYC, 1994. I remember them asking if they could braid my hair, and I dozed off while waiting to photograph them. I had been shooting on video sets and studio shoots for about a week non-stop and fell into a deep sleep. When I awoke my hair was laced with little cars, dolls and other hair clip toys. I never expected that but it was so funny and we all laughed our heads off.

p.150 Foxy Brown, NYC, 1998.

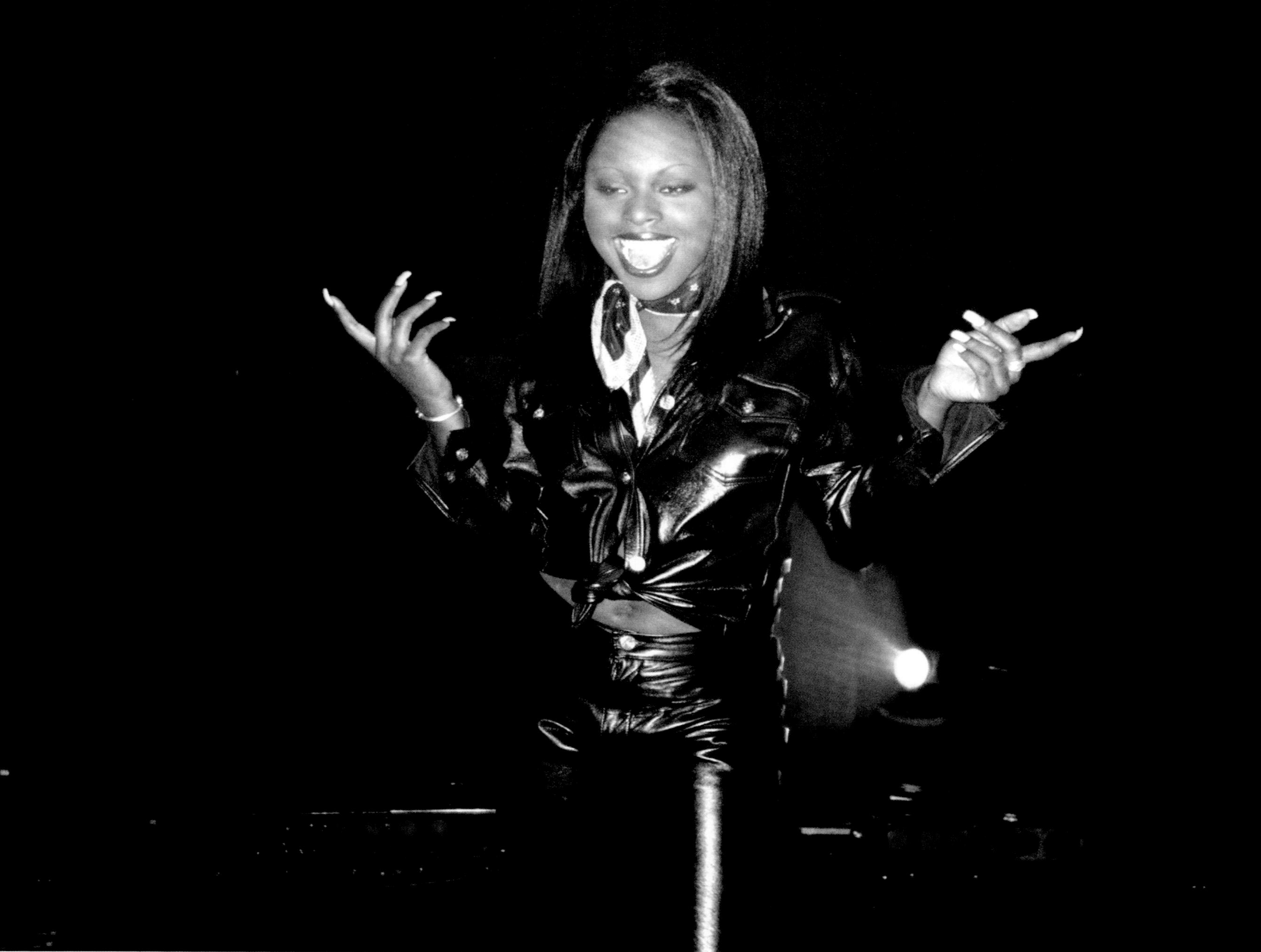

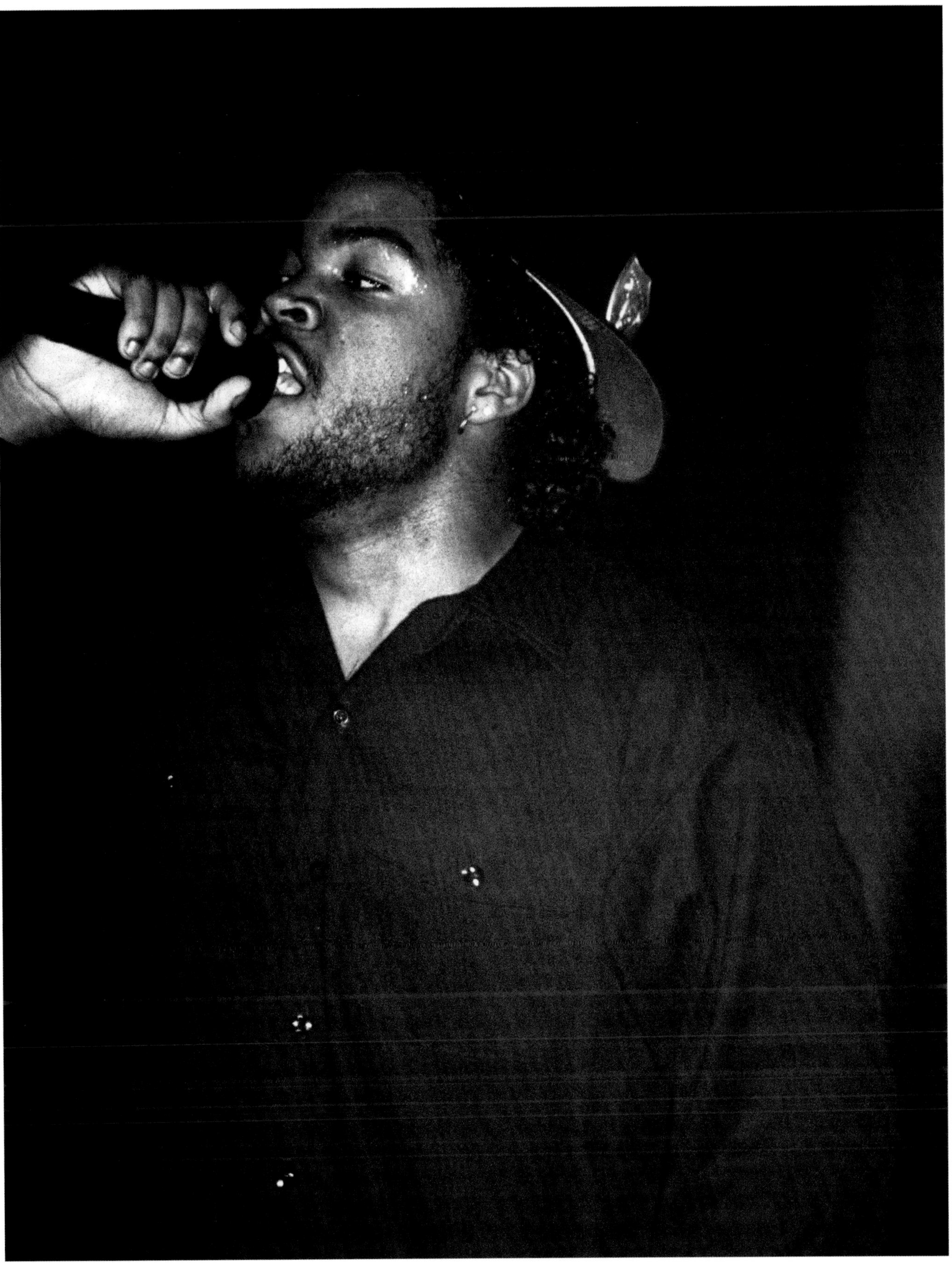

p.151 Ice Cube with jheri curls, The Ritz, NYC, 1989.

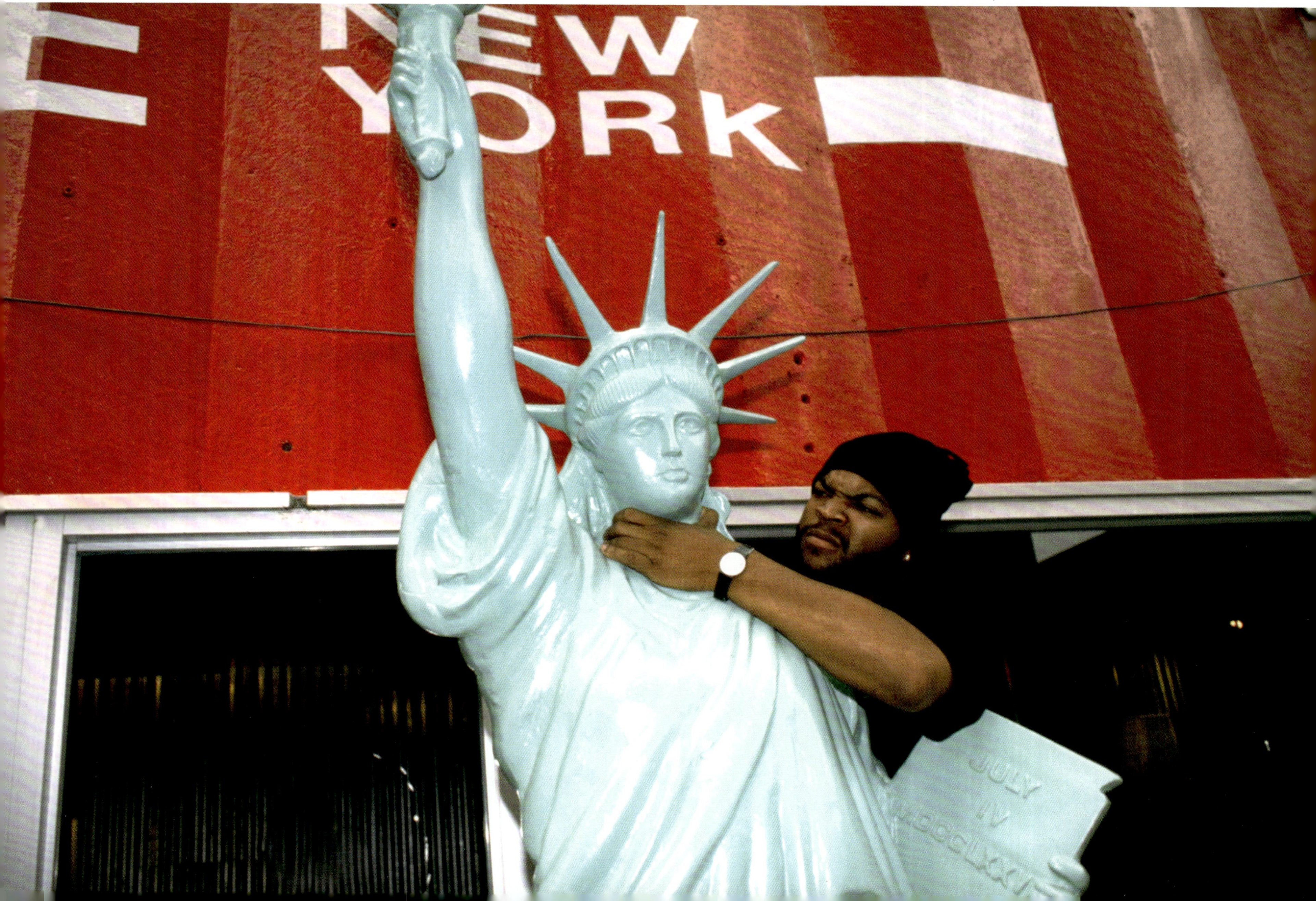

p. 152 Ice Cube and I share a disdain for hypocrisy and felt this image would reflect the gap between the words inscribed on this iconic statue and the reality of a flawed, racially imbalanced system. 8th Avenue, NYC, 1991.

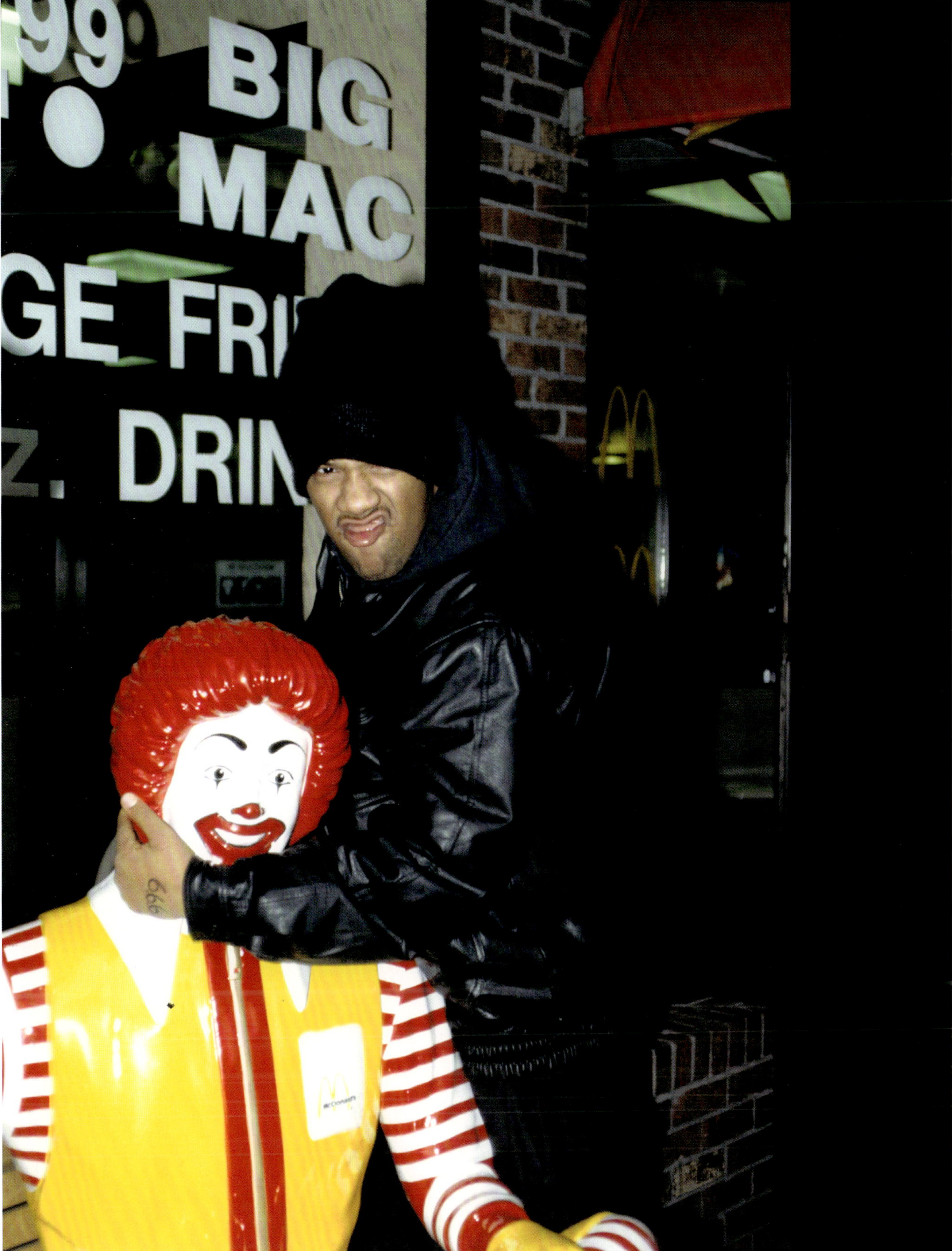

p.153 Redman of the Wu-Tang Clan choking Ronald McDonald. Upper East Side, NYC, 1994.

In 2001 I got a call from Def Jam offering me an all day shoot with Meth and Red. I had known each of them for years, but this was the first time I shot them as a duo. The shoot took place at Def Jam in Midtown Manhattan. I brought my unflappable, unshakeable assistant Dre Fagul Rox Regis, and the shoot was every bit as amped as any of their videos or movies. Through the clouds of exotic herbal mists blared heavy metal tracks turned up to the max; it was the loosest, most organic, most free form shoot in my experience. That shoot could easily have been named "The Contact High Shoot" and yet the images were—no pun intended—totally dope.

p.156-157 Method Man shooting the video for "Shadowboxin," a track in GZA's album *Liquid Swords* in a church in Washington Heights, NYC, 1995. With lyrics like "I breaks it down to the bone gristle," Wu-Tang Clan shoots, either on a video set, on the streets, or in a studio, always provide startling images and this was no exception. Method's fangs and army gear added to one of my favorite and most iconic hip-hop images.

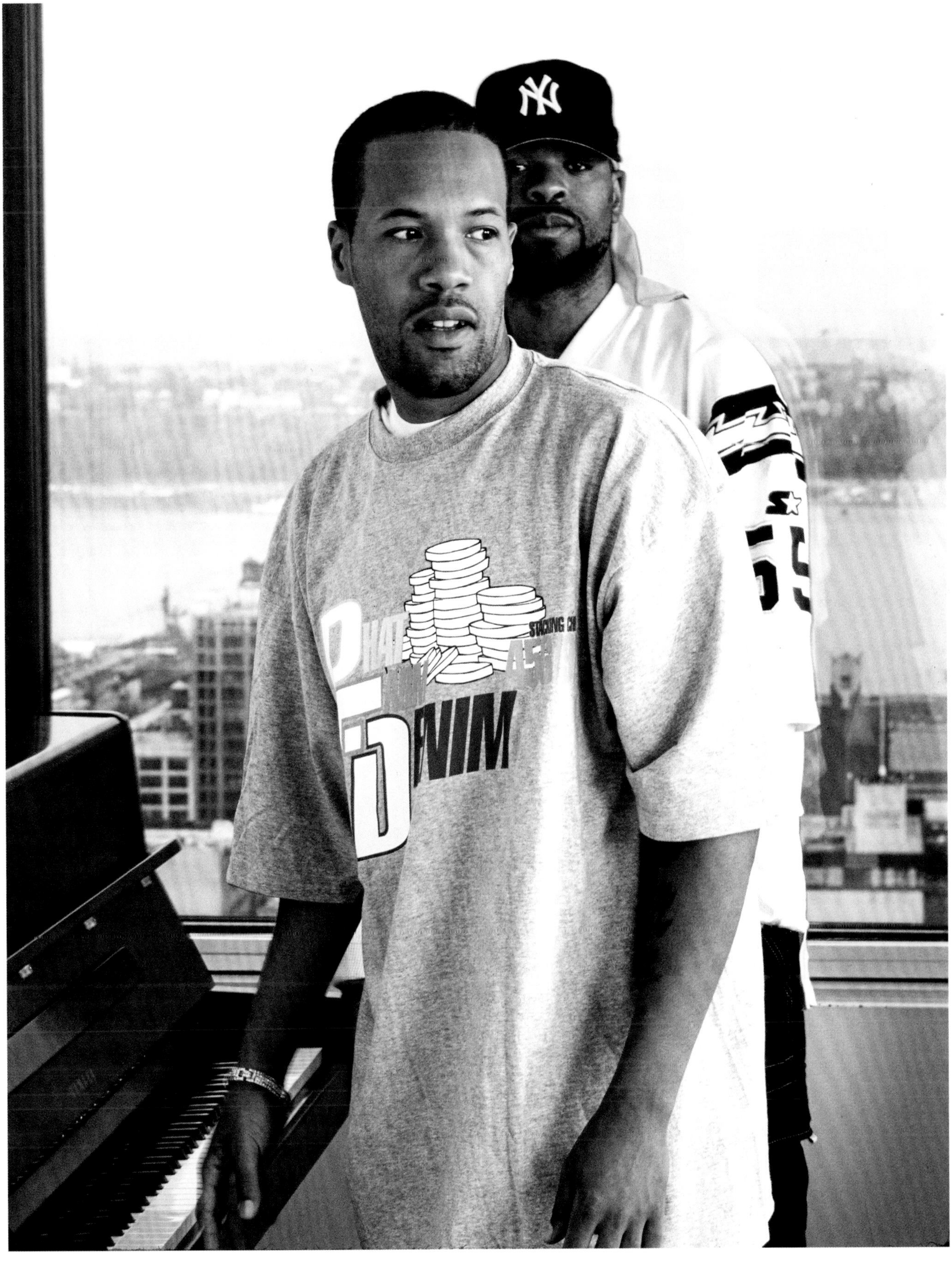

p.155 Redman and Method Man, Midtown, NYC, 2001.

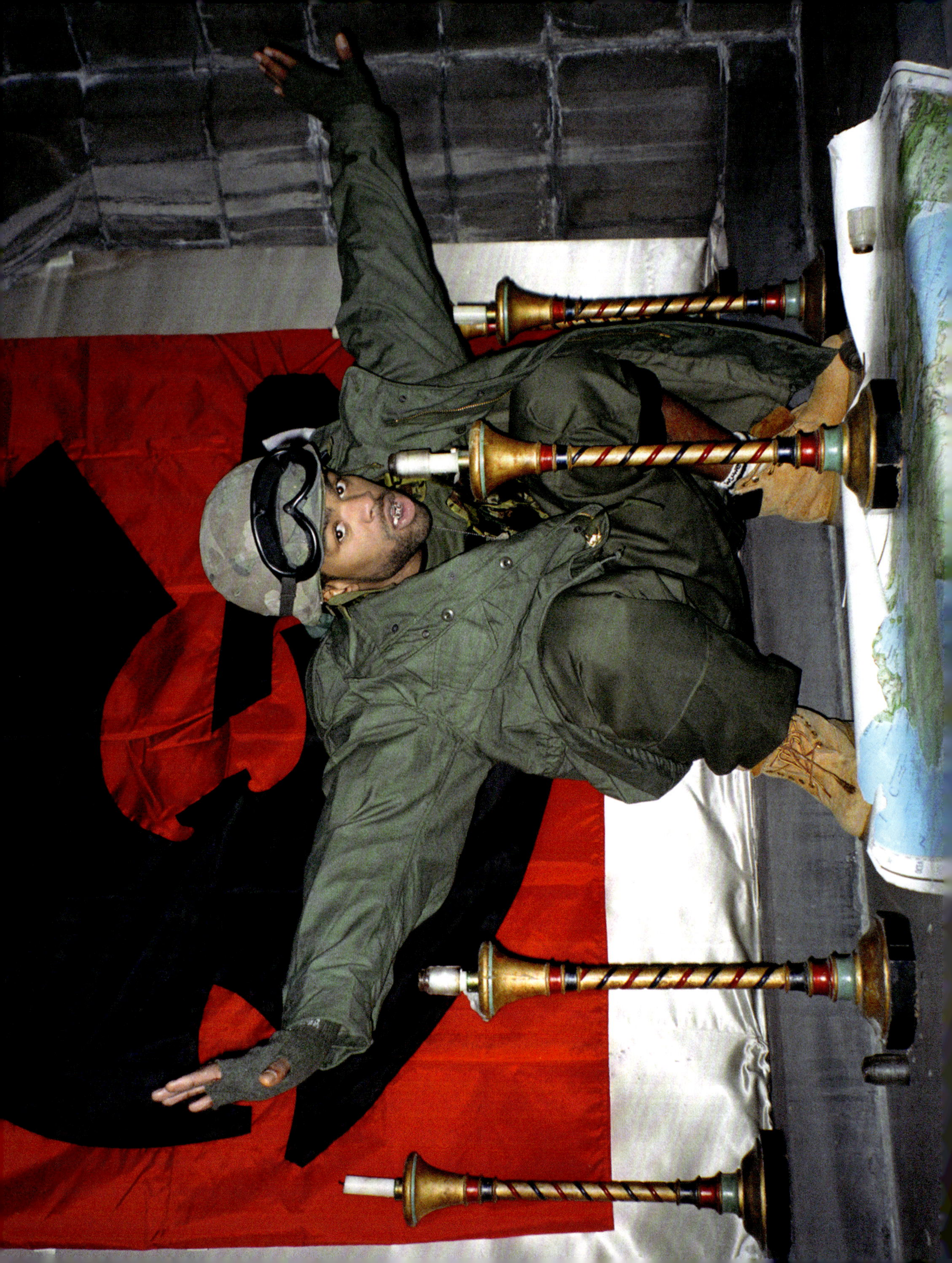

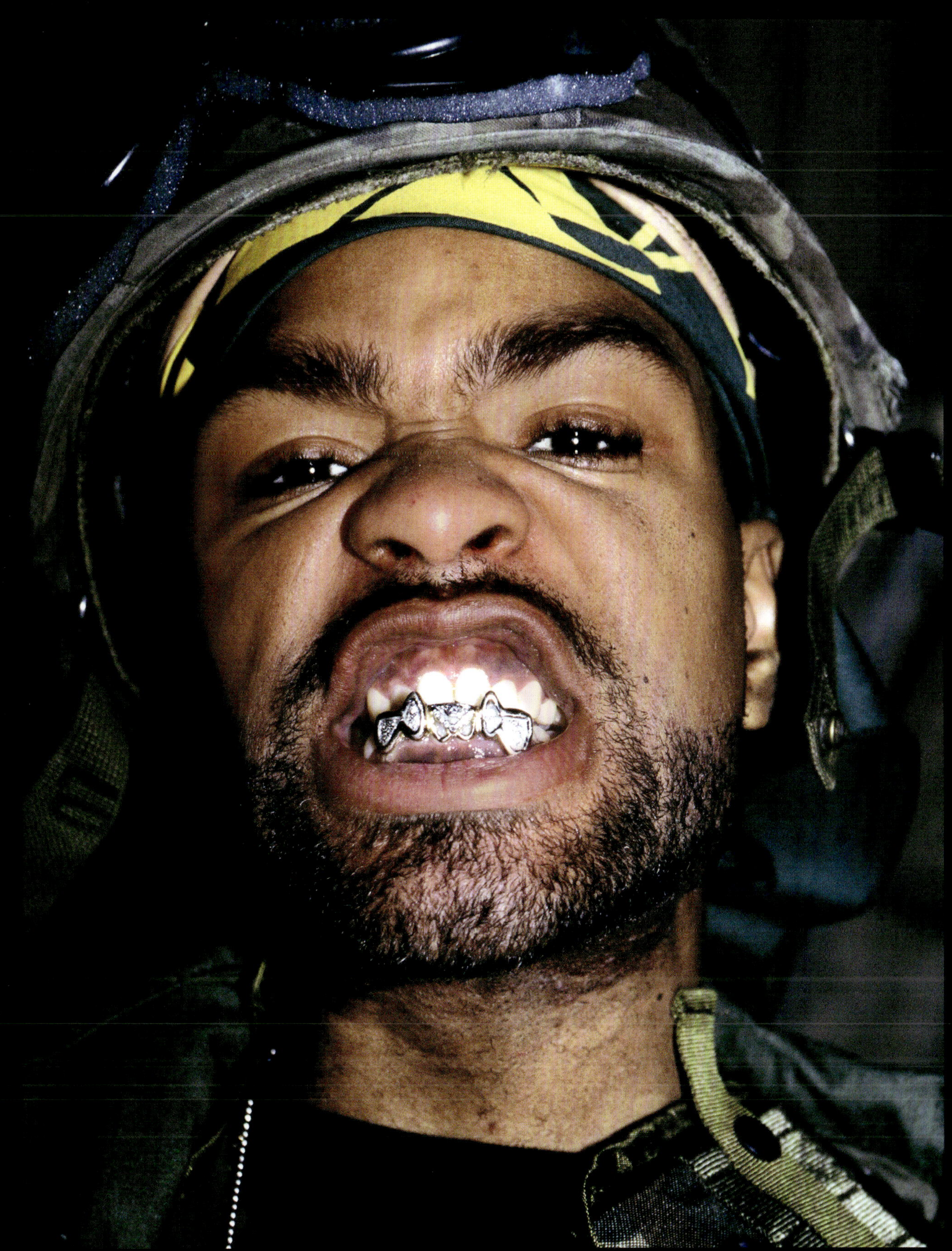

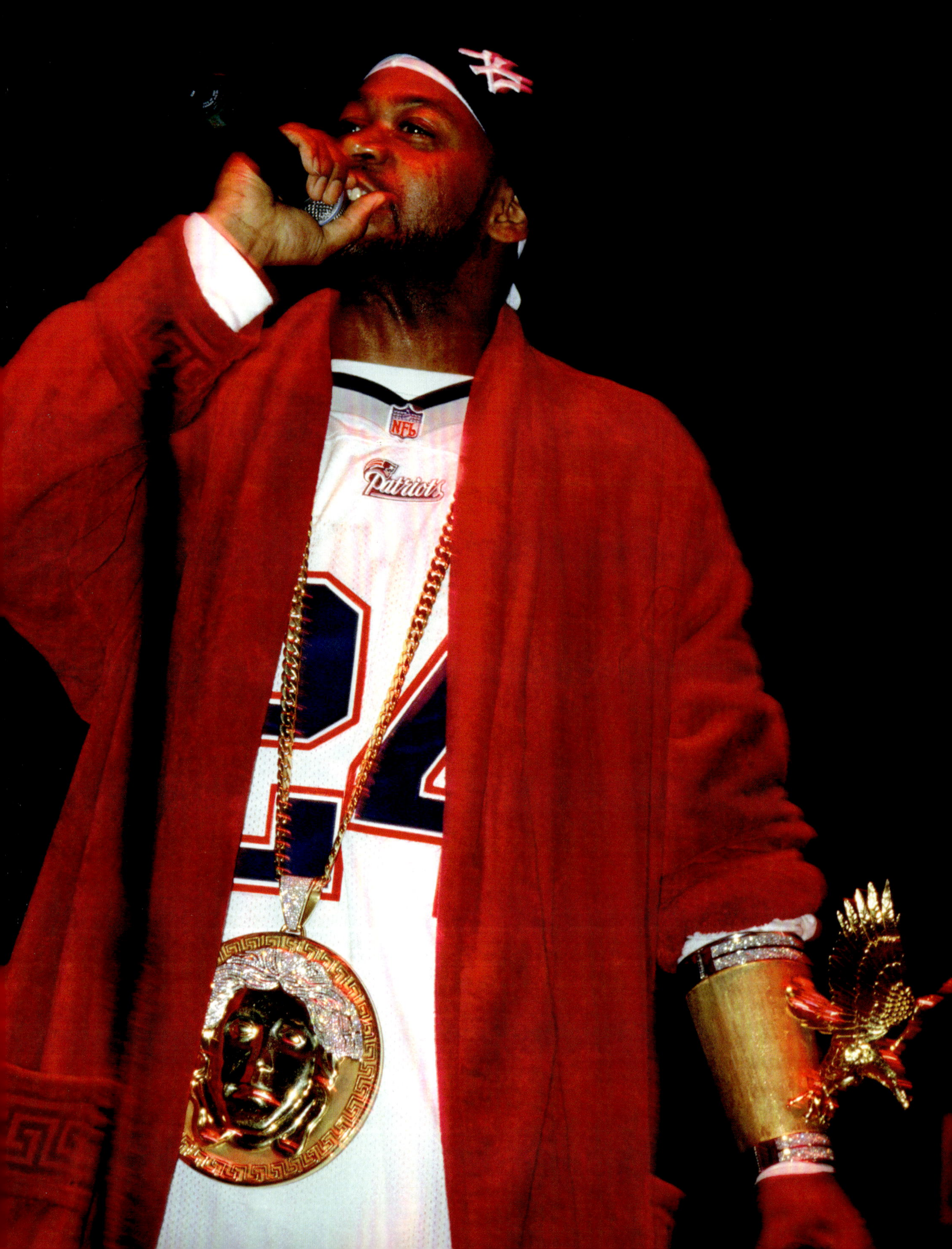
NFL
Patriots
24

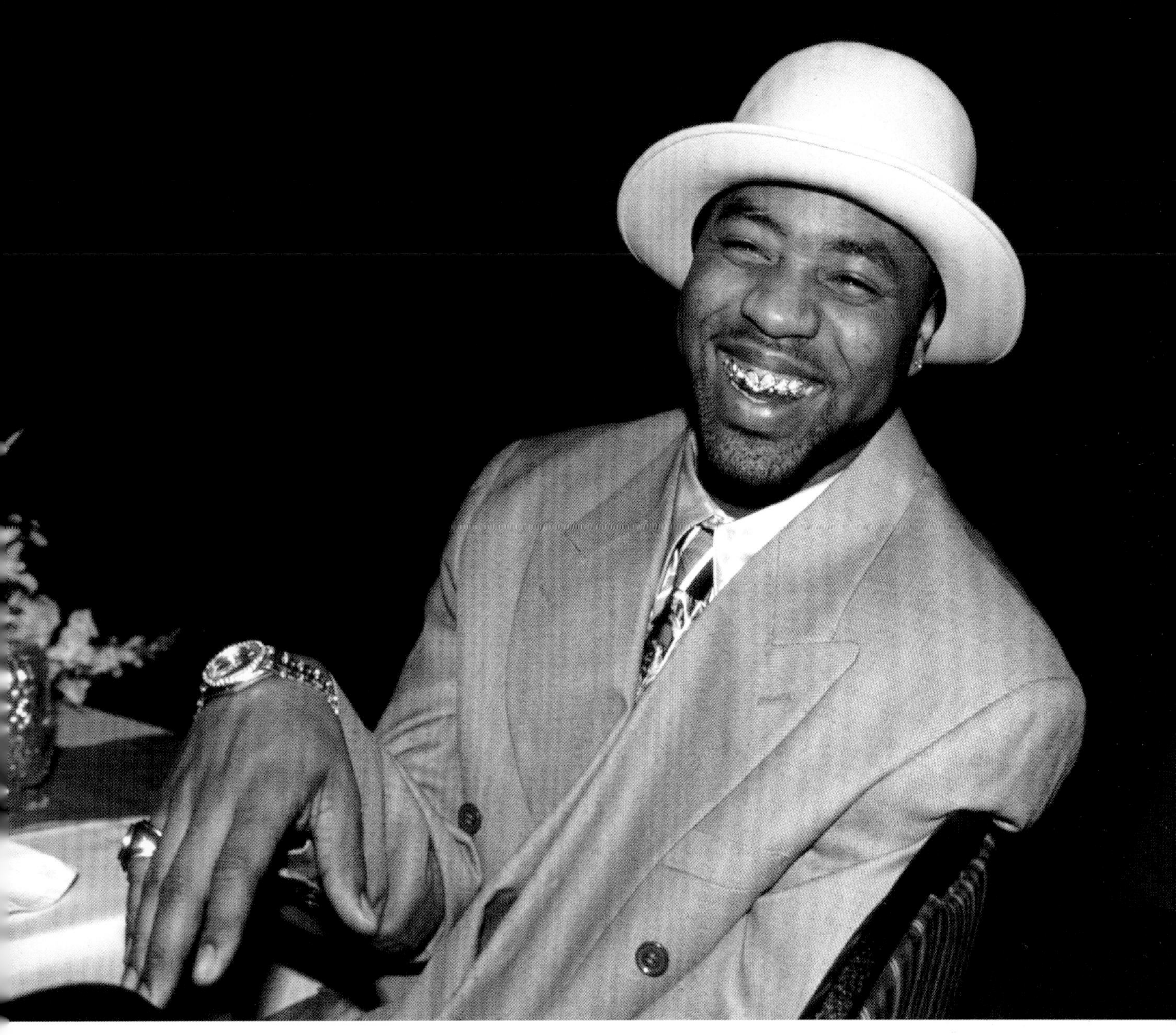

p.158 Wu-Tang's Ghostface, NYC, late 1990s. Everything is wrong with his outfit: red bathrobe, throwback Patriots jumper, Yankees baseball cap, huge Versace medallion, and oversized golden eagle wrist piece. But these things match his lyrics and his energy, so in reality, nothing is wrong. It's simply hip-hop and real hip-hop is always over the top.

p.159 Cappadonna on a yacht where the WuTang did a fundraiser for a Wu charity and I was the cameraman. Catching this smile set the tone for the night. NYC, late 1990s.

Notes to pages 160-161
Wu-Tang's RZA in his incarnation as "Bobby Digital" in a bodega and the streets of New York, 1998. I've known RZA since his start as Prince Rakeem, and his New York studio was one floor above mine. I have always been impressed at both his creativity and his work ethic.

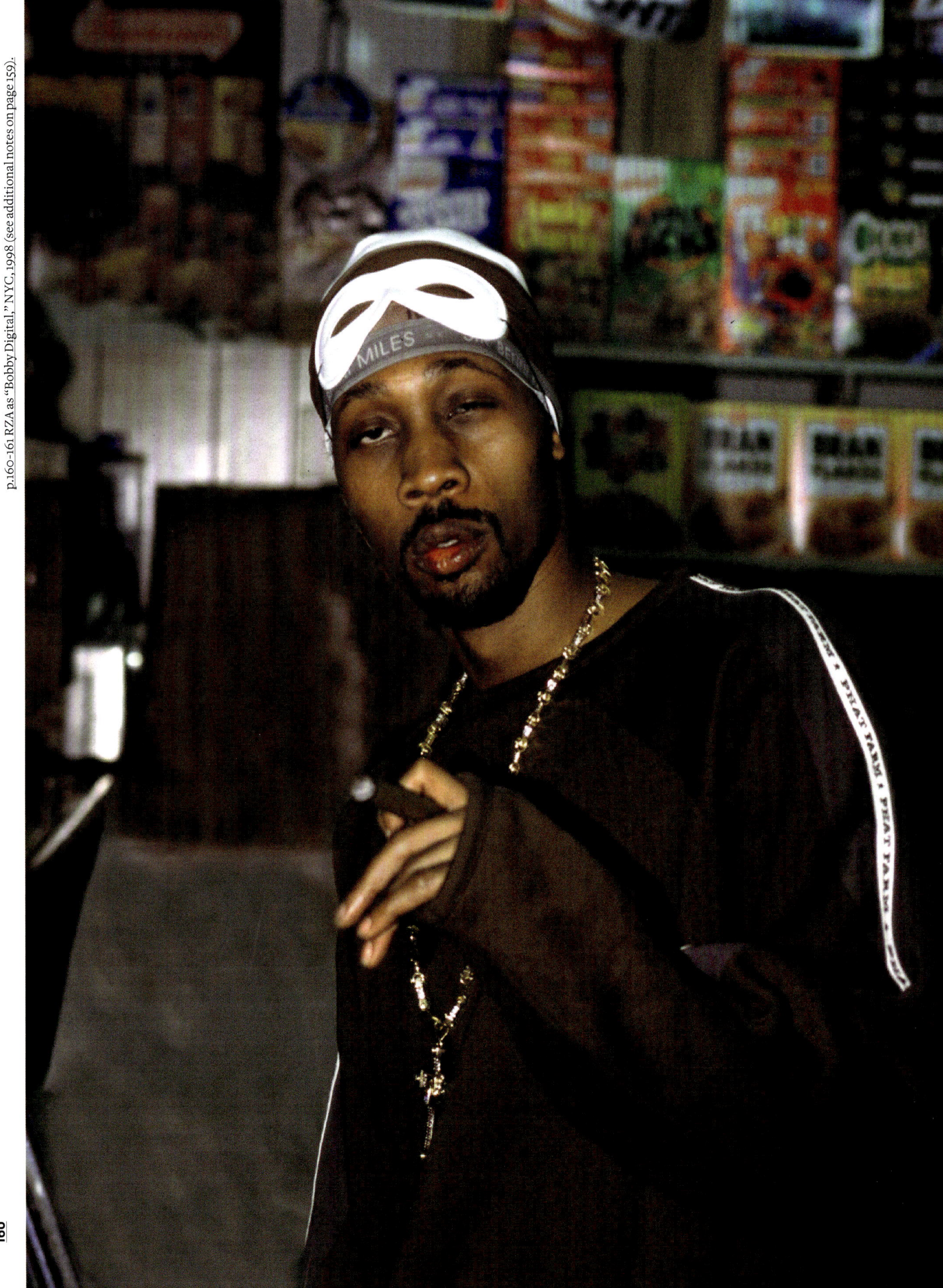

p.160-161 RZA as "Bobby Digital," NYC, 1998 (see additional notes on page 159).

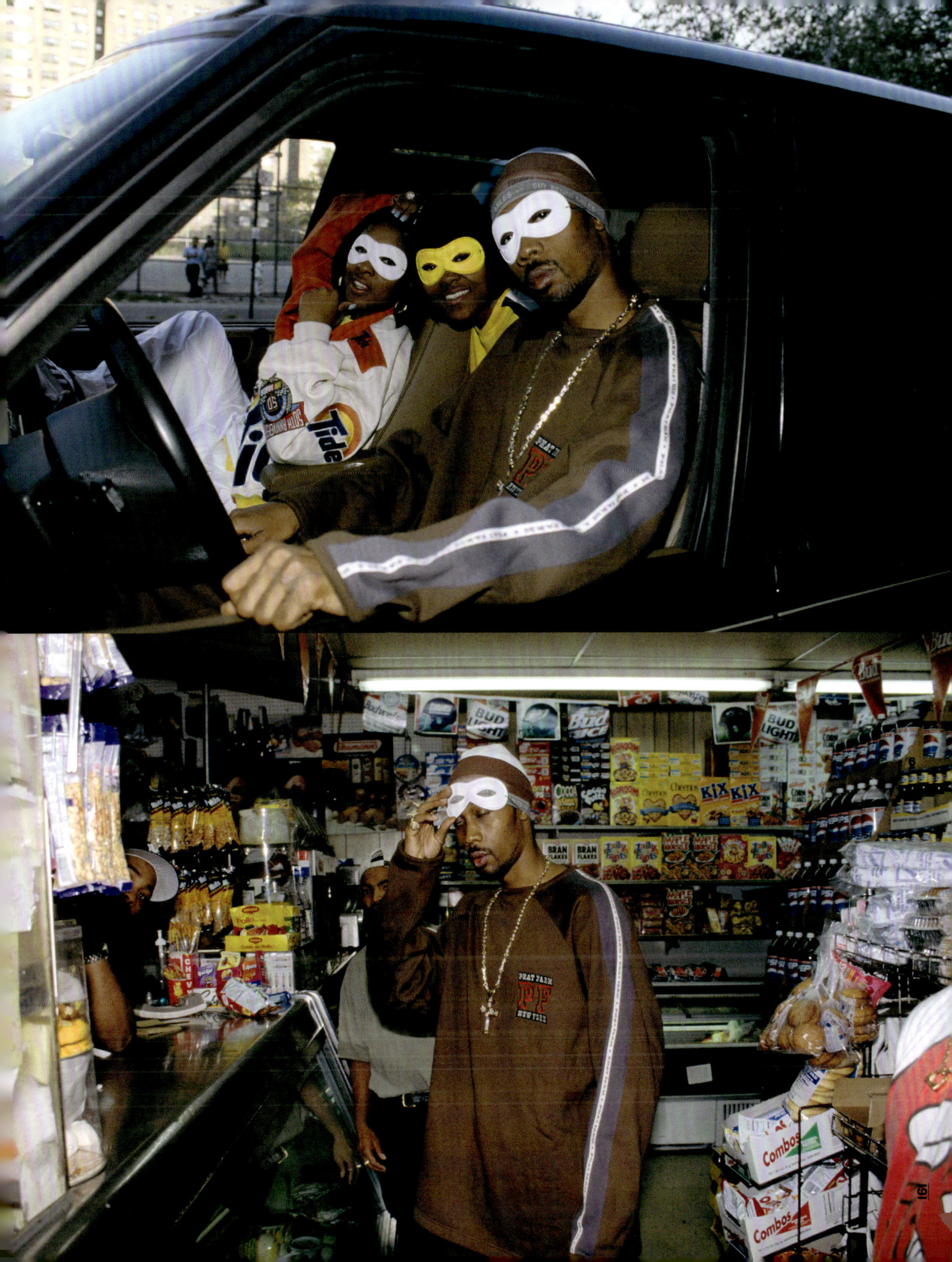
Tide
PHAT FARM
PF
NEW YORK
BUD LIGHT
Bud ICE
KIX
Cheerios
BRAN FLAKES
Combos

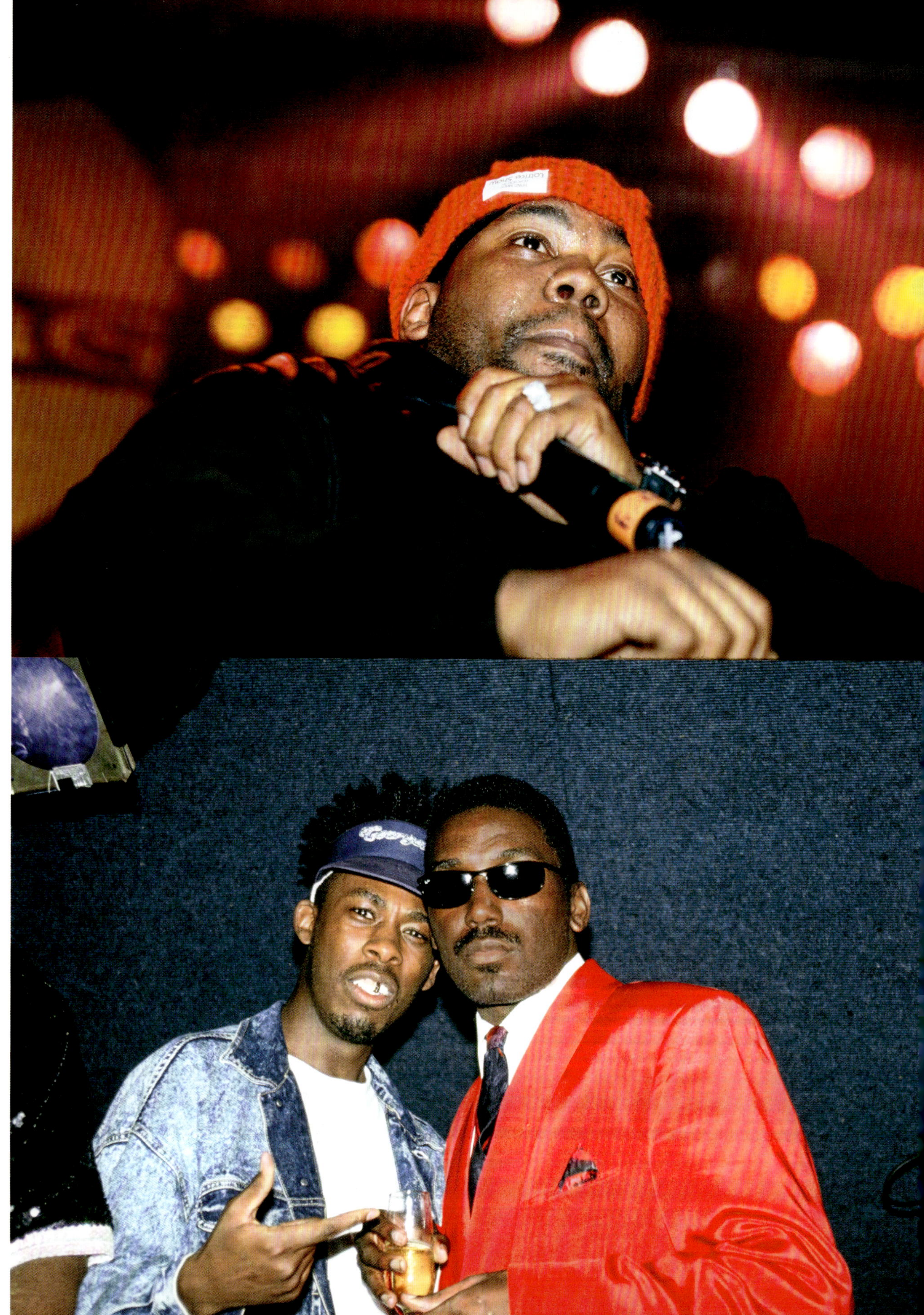

p. 162 (top) Raekwon aka da Chef, late 1990s; p. 162 (bottom) The Genius aka GZA, with Kane, 1991; p. 163 (top) Biggie and Redman, 1995; p. 163 (bottom), RZA with his *sifu*, late 1990s, all NYC (see additional notes on page 165).

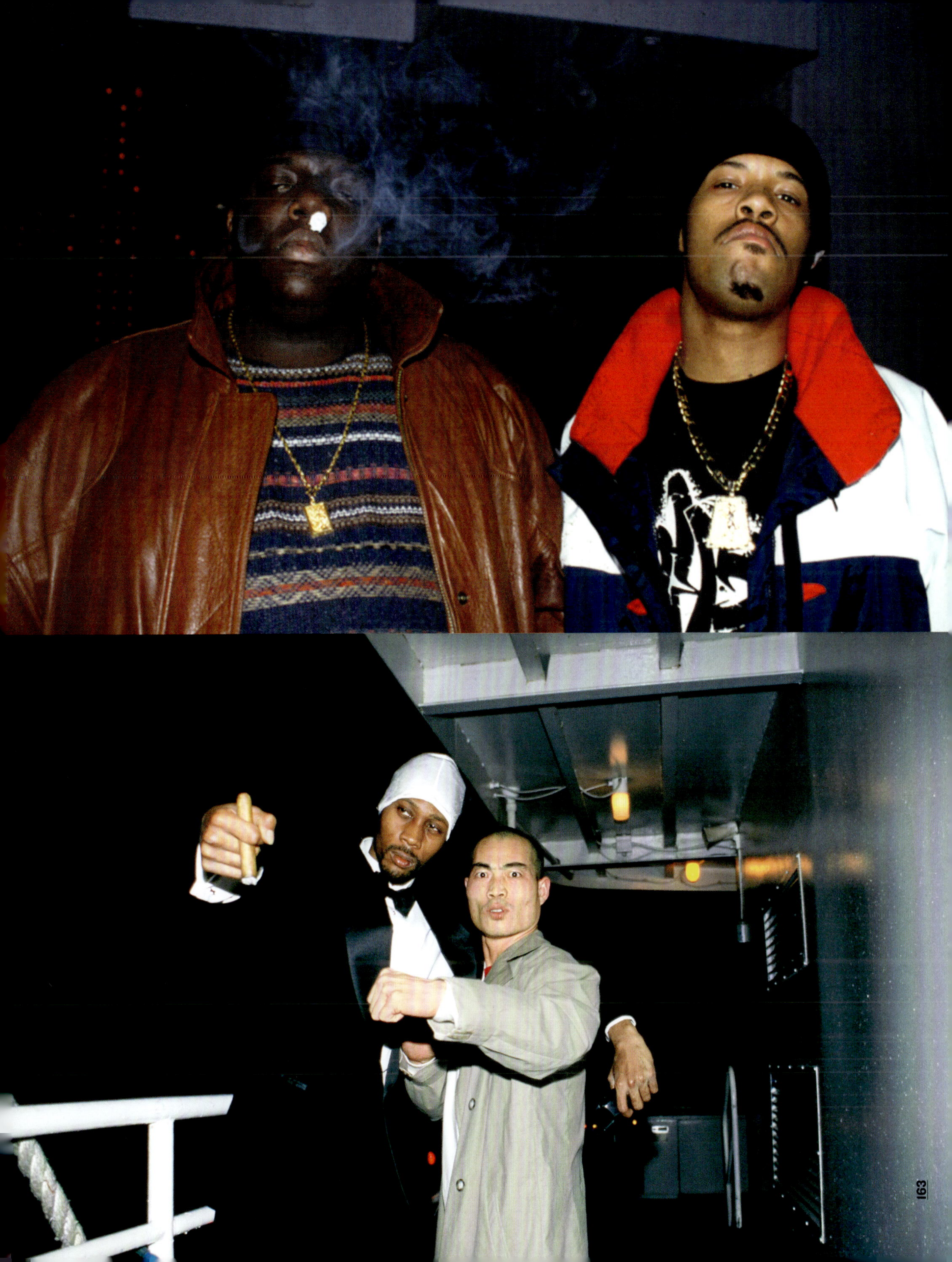

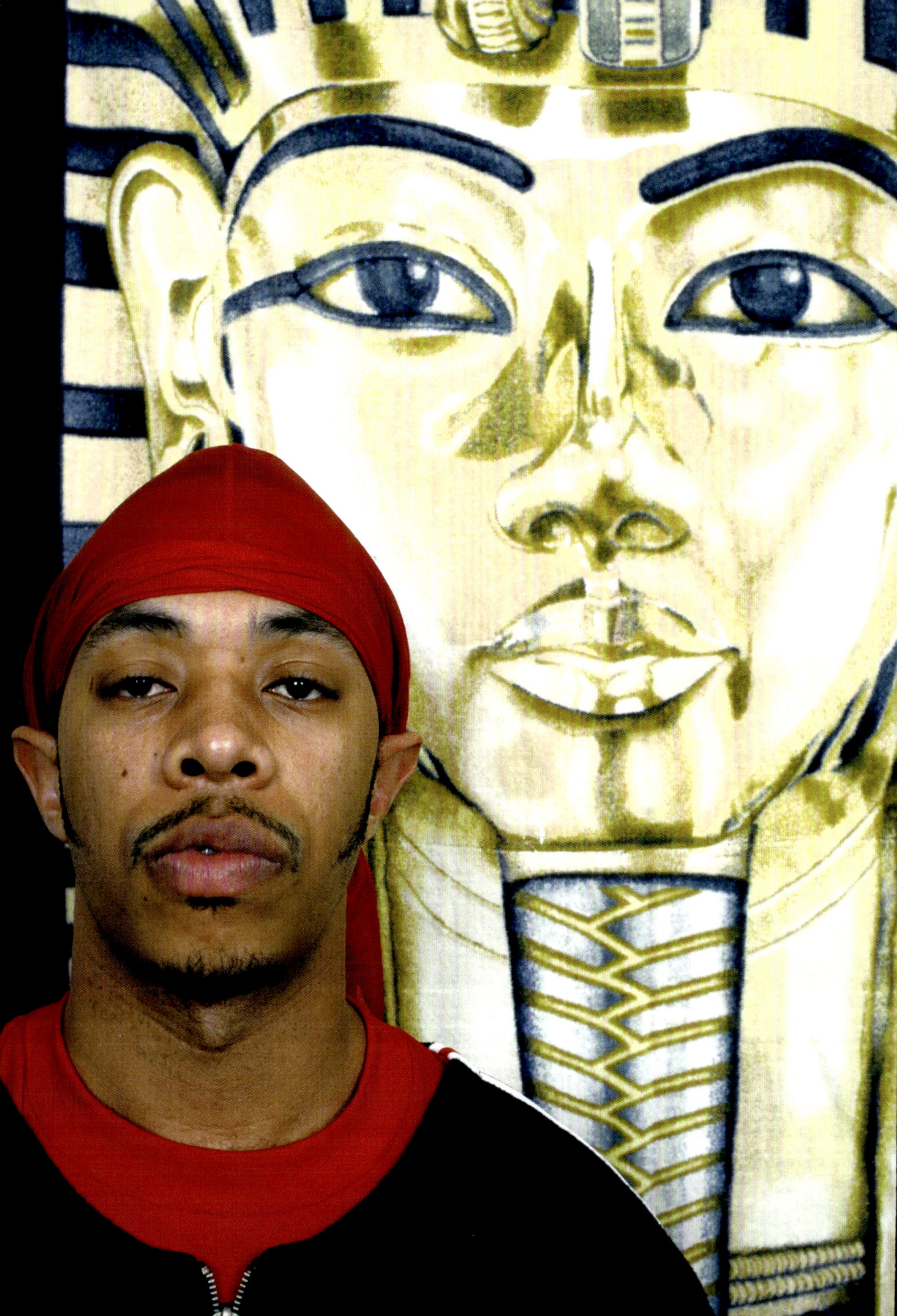

p.164 Wu-Tang's U God, 3rd Eye Studio, NYC, 2000. I had a King Tut poster in my studio and decided to show the uncanny resemblance of the two of them in this photo. His nickname is "Golden Arms."

Notes to pages 162-163:
Raekwon, aka da Chef, in concert, late 1990s.

The Genius aka GZA before he joined the Wu Tang Clan is shown here with Big Daddy Kane, NYC, 1991.

The late Notorious B.I.G., aka Christopher Wallace (1972-1997), seen here with Redman at The Palladium. Biggie was smoking so much weed that his nose started to bleed. I gave him some tissues to stem the bleeding and suggested he stop smoking. His reply to me was "fuck that," and stuffed more tissues up his nose and continued smoking, NYC, 1995.

RZA with his *sifu*, Shaolin monk Shi Yan Ming, NYC, late 1990s.

p.166 The Genius aka GZA, Prince Rakeem aka RZA with Heavy D before the two joined forces with The Wu-Tang Clan, NYC.

p.167 Justice, Sweet Tee, Ice-T. Apollo Theatre, Harlem, NYC, 1987.

Notes to pages 168 -169:
Bobby Brown at the Hotel Le Parker-Meridien, NYC, 1988. After informing his publicist that he did not want to do a photo shoot with me for *Word Up!* magazine and me letting him know I had fifty other people I could shoot who would love a multi-page spread and poster in our monthly magazine, he relented and not only did we get a great and classic shoot but we became friends for decades.

Bobby Brown with Josie and the Pussycats dancers during the video shoot for "Humpin' Around," Brooklyn, NYC, 1992.

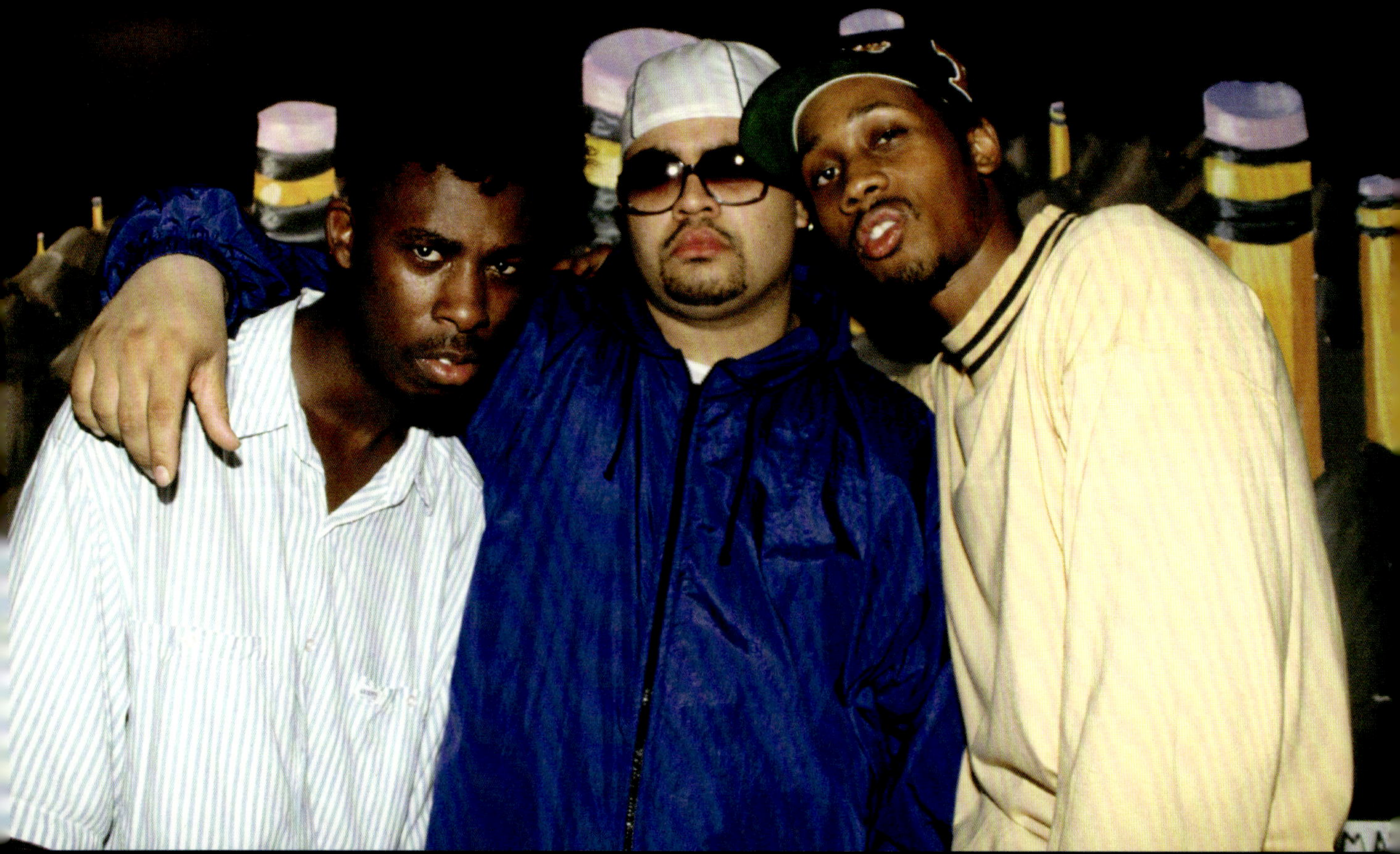

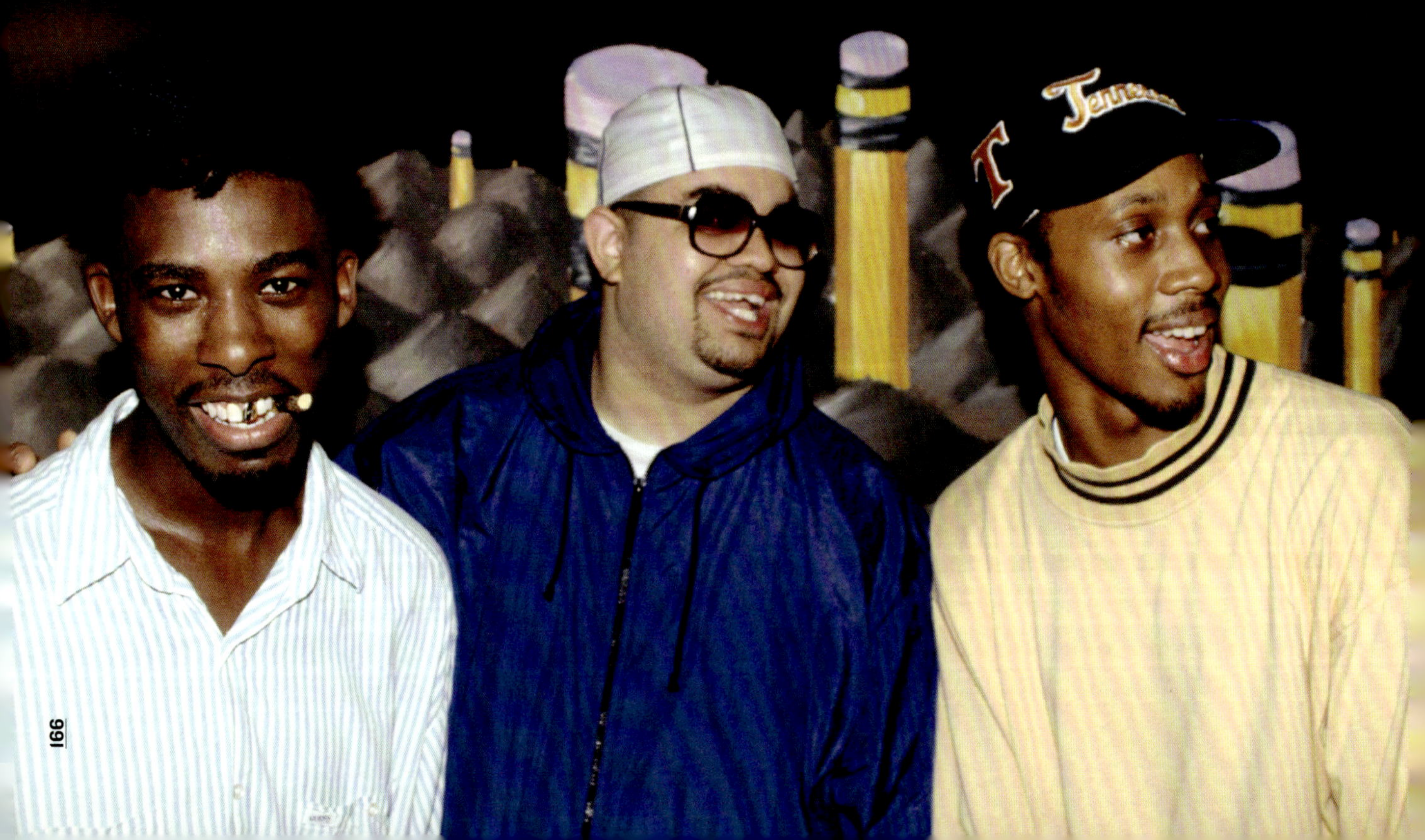

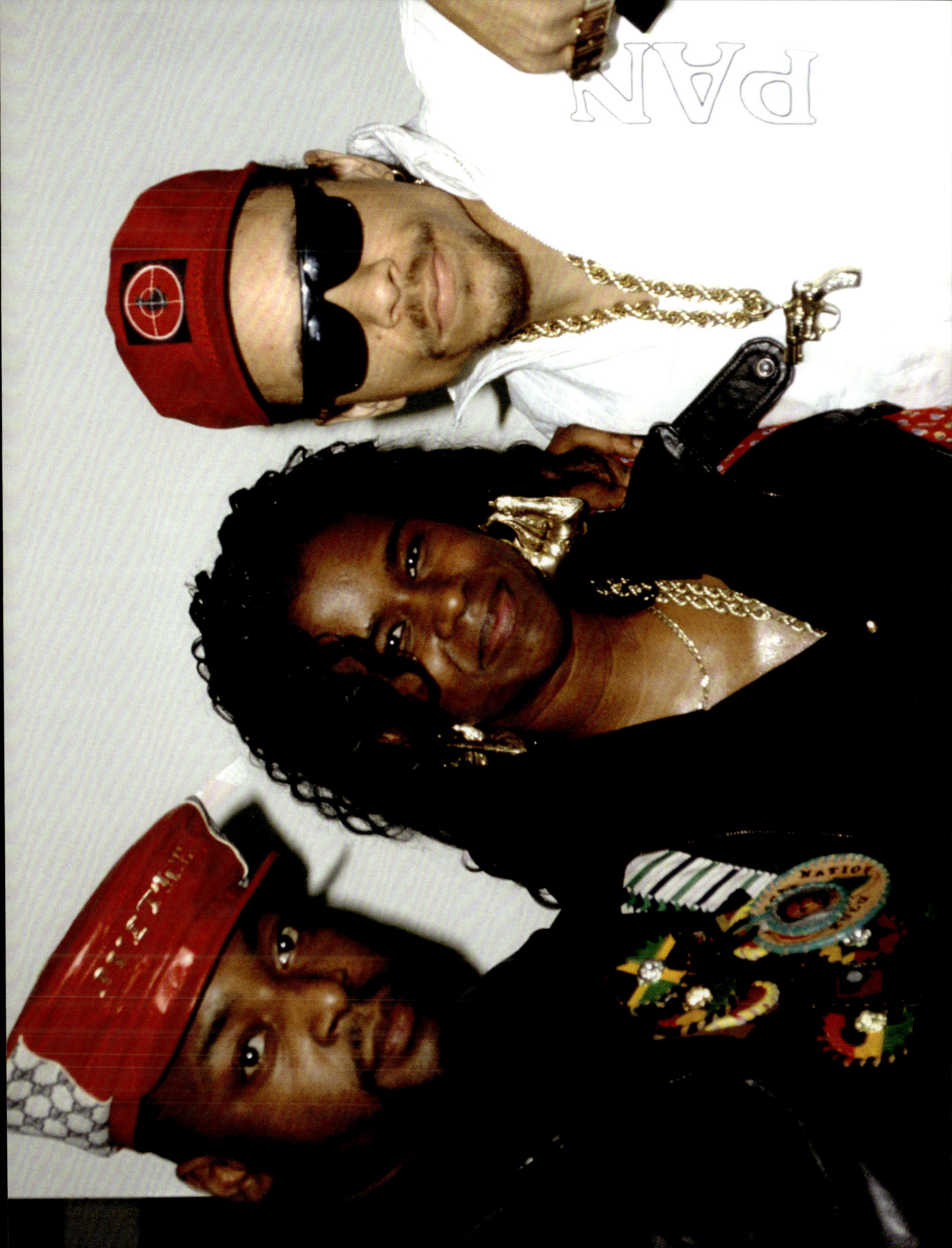

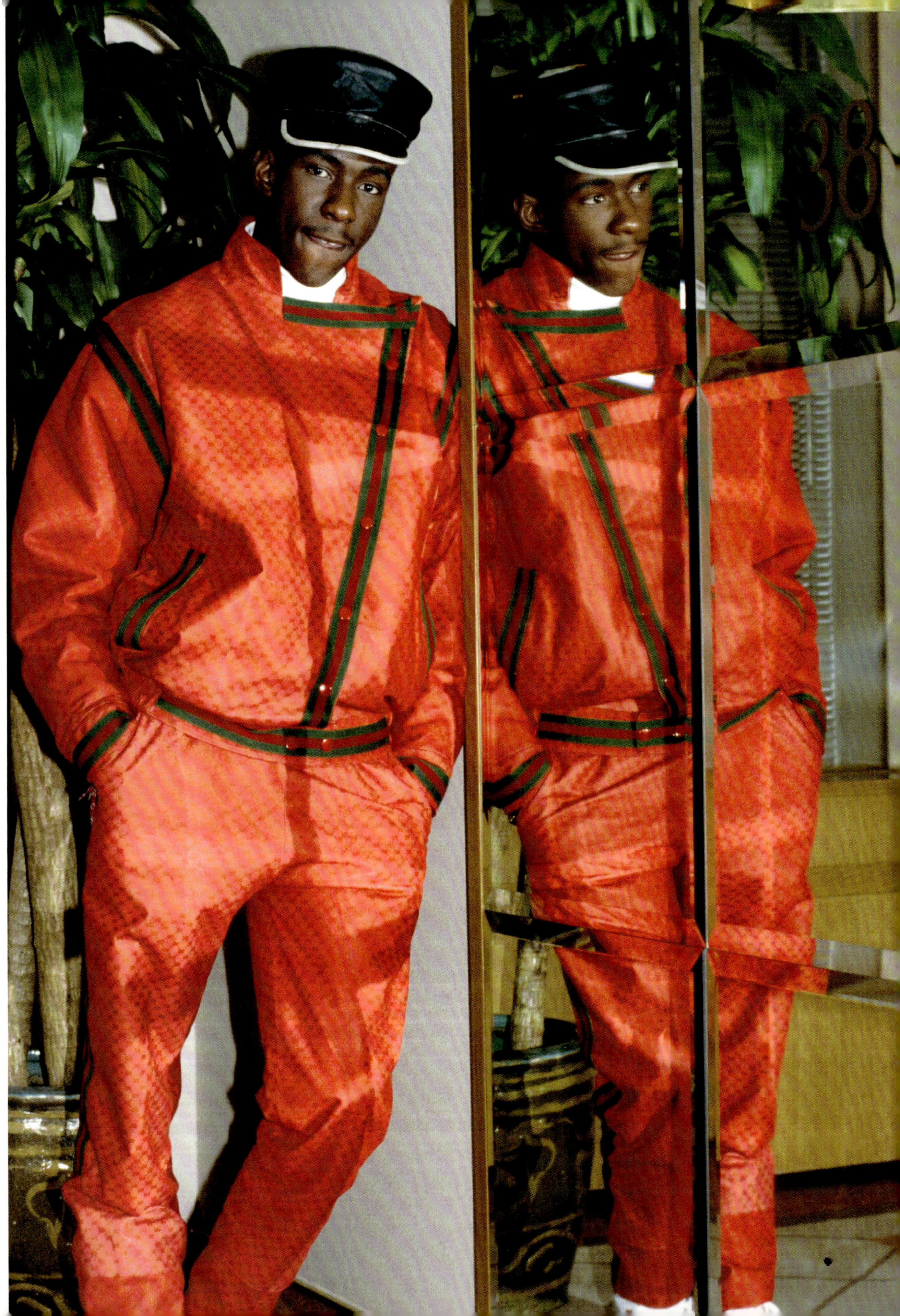

p.168-169 Bobby Brown, 1988; and in 1992 with Josie and the Pussycats dancers, both in NYC (see additional notes on page 165).

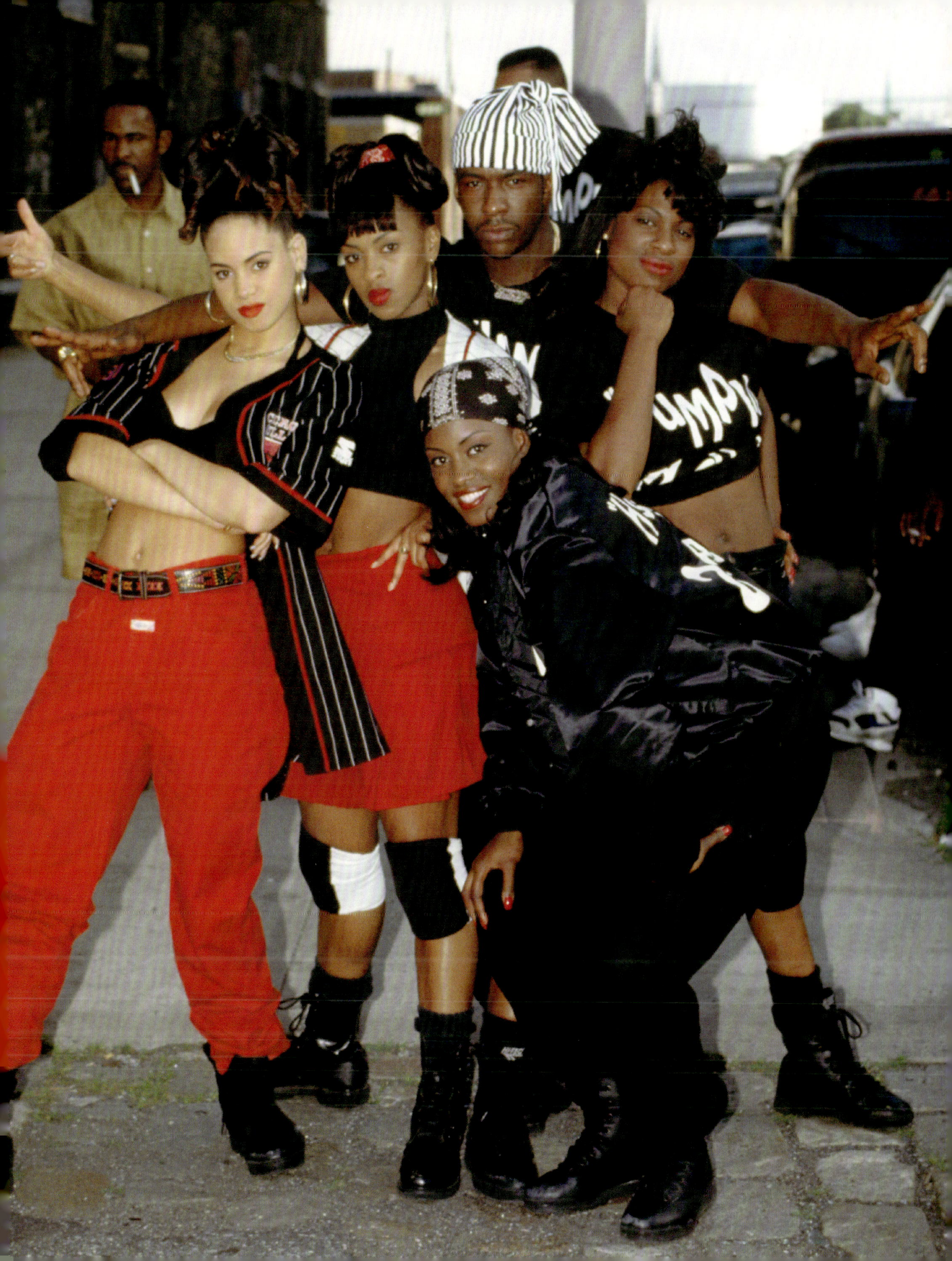

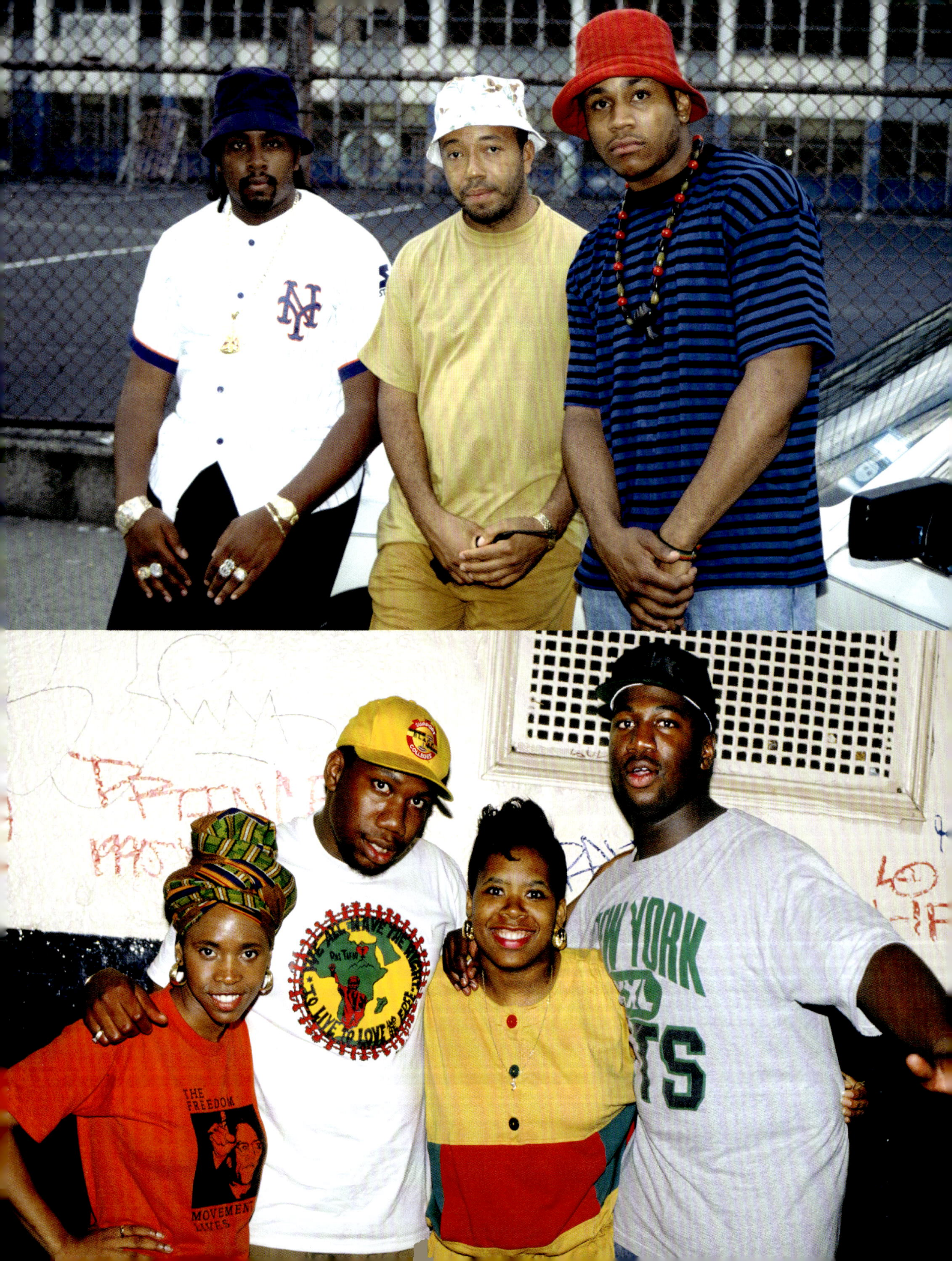
THE FREEDOM
YORK

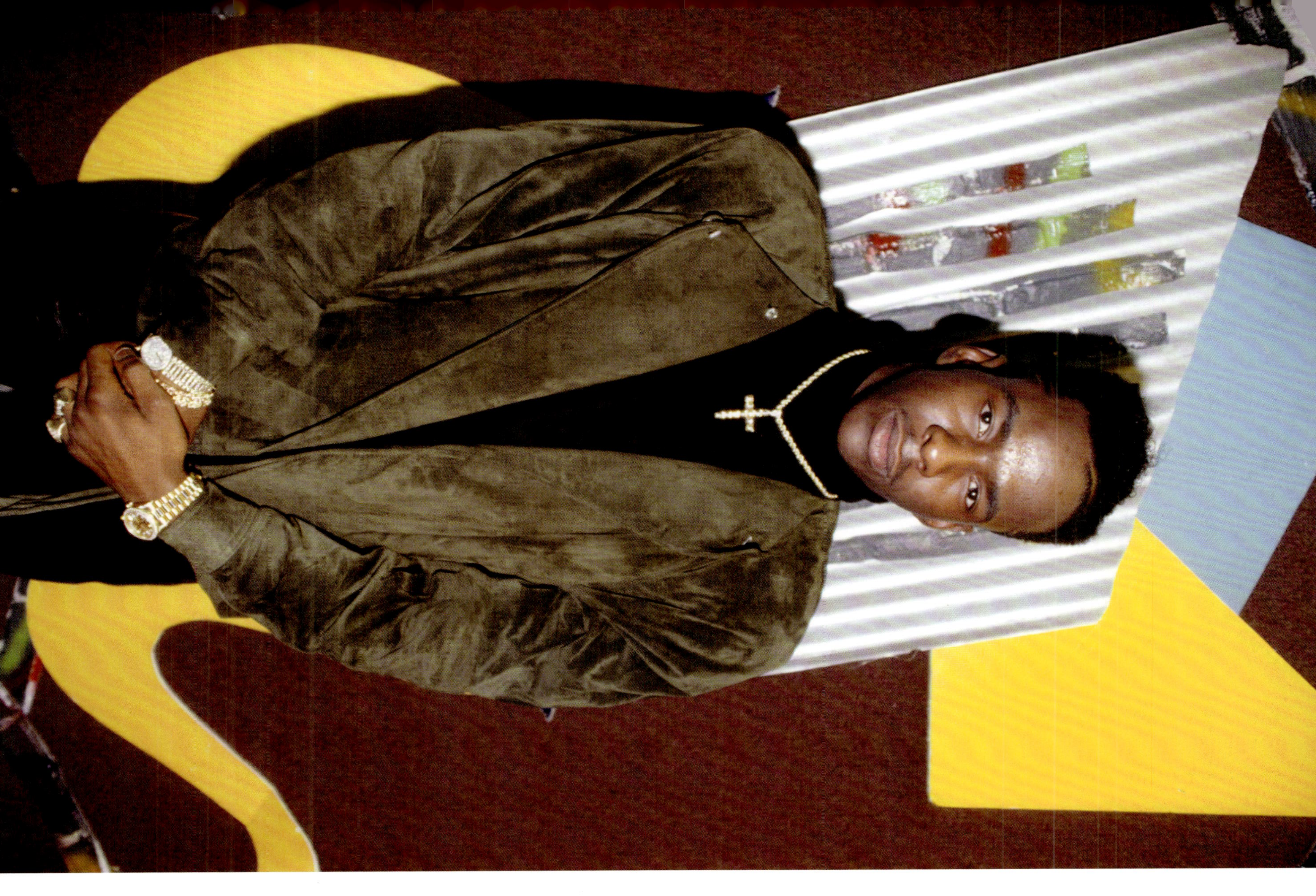

p.170 Eric B, Russell Simmons & LL Cool J, West 126th Street, behind the Apollo, Harlem, NYC, 1989; BDP Crew: Harmony, KRS-One, Heather B, and DJ Kenny Parker, NYC, 1987;
p.171 Bobby Brown, Apollo Theatre, Harlem, NYC, 1987; p.172-173 Whitney Houston, Bobby Brown, and The Notorious B.I.G., NYC, 1995.

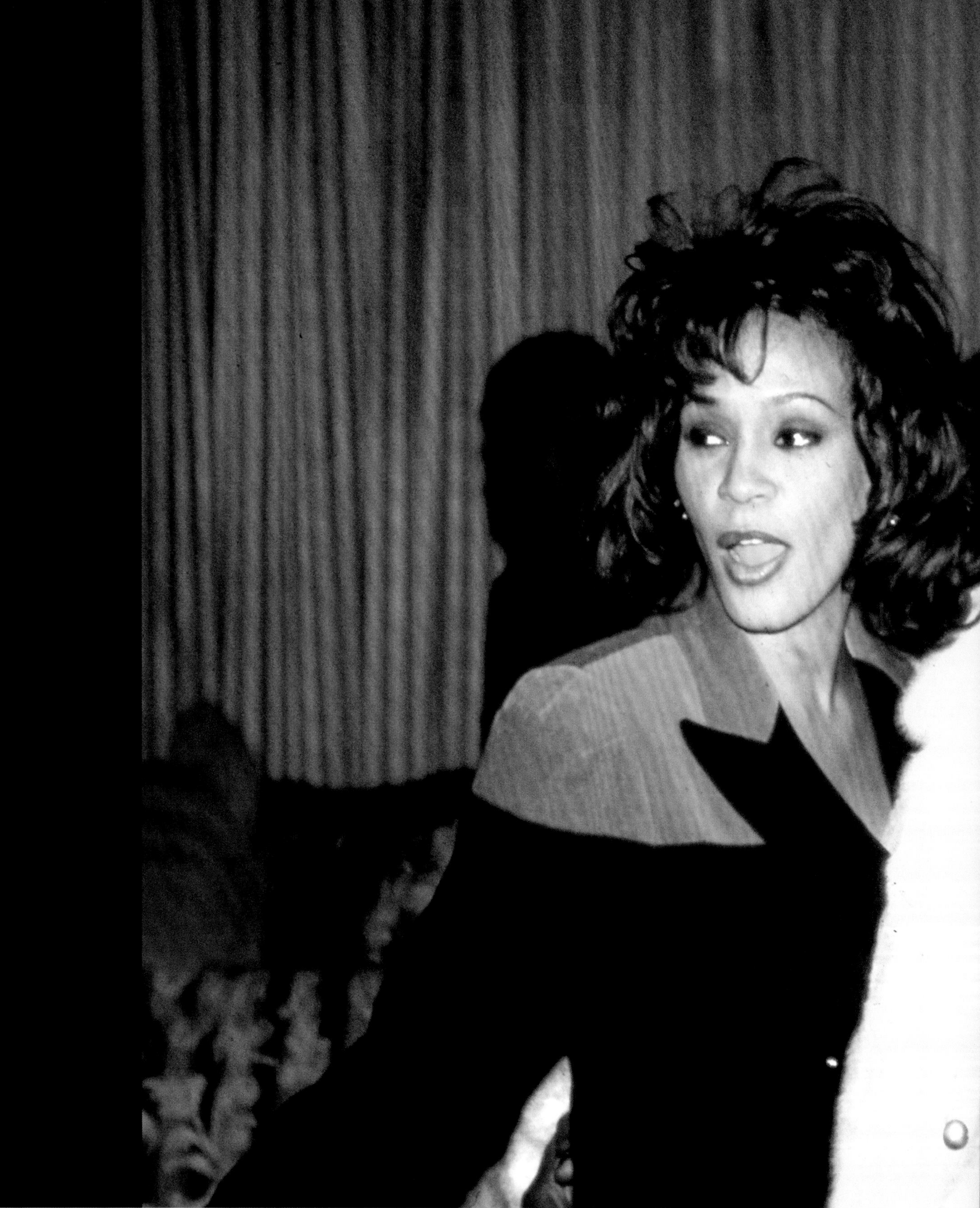

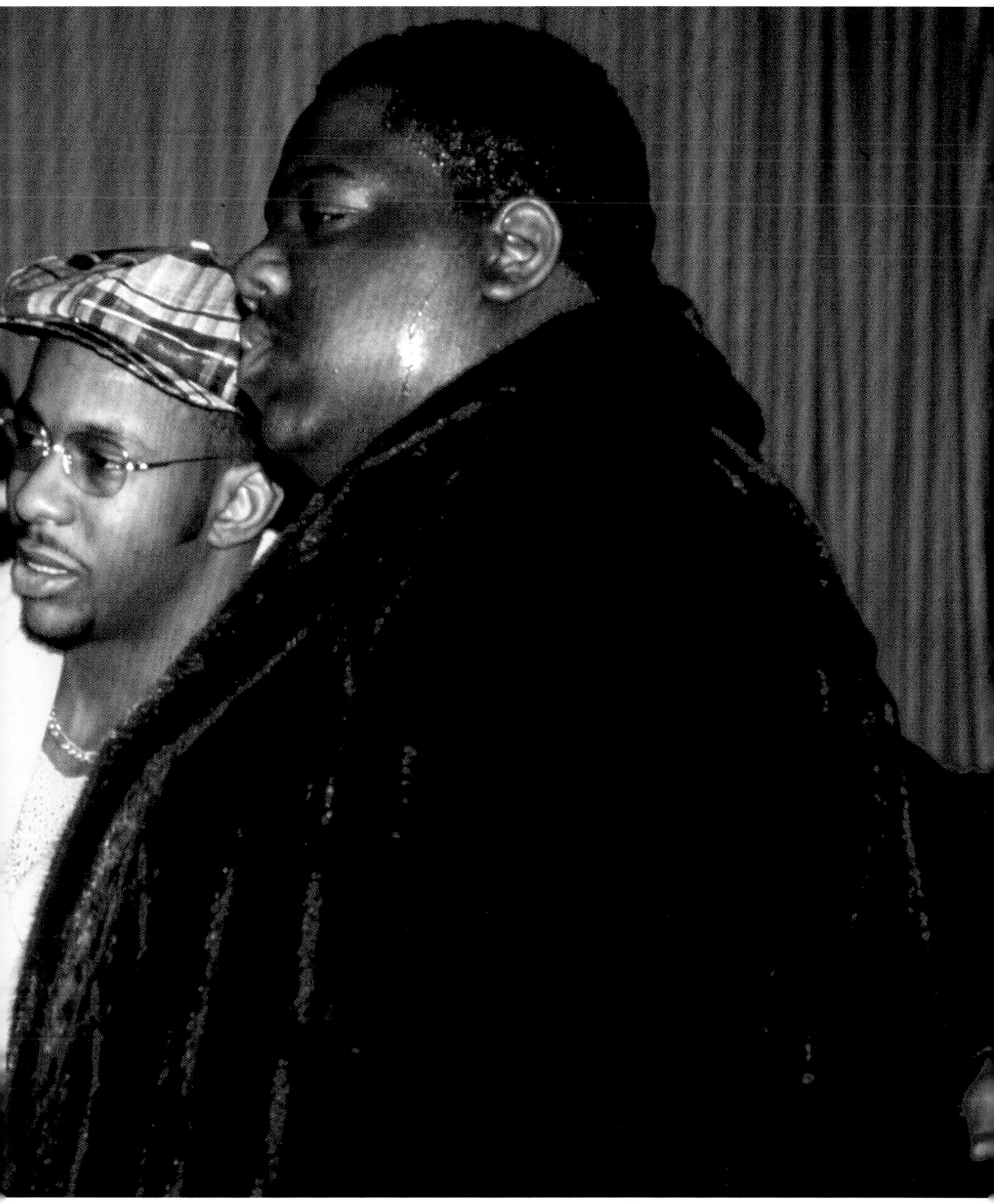

p.174 The Beastie Boys, VHI Hip Hop Honors, Hammerstein Ballroom, NYC, 2004; p.175 Biggie waiting in line to get into the Mary J. Blige Triple Platinum Party at the Copacabana, NYC, 1995.

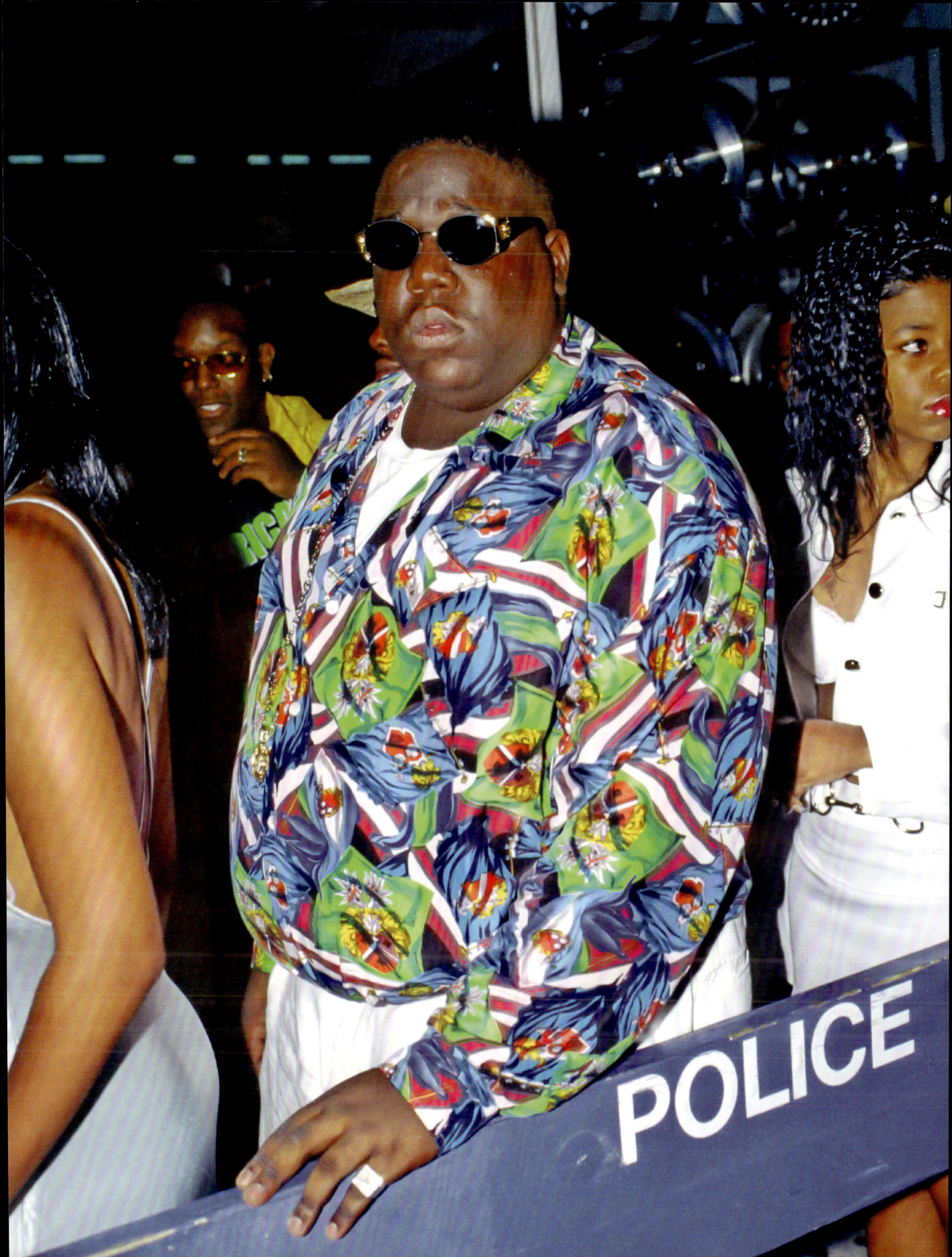
POLICE

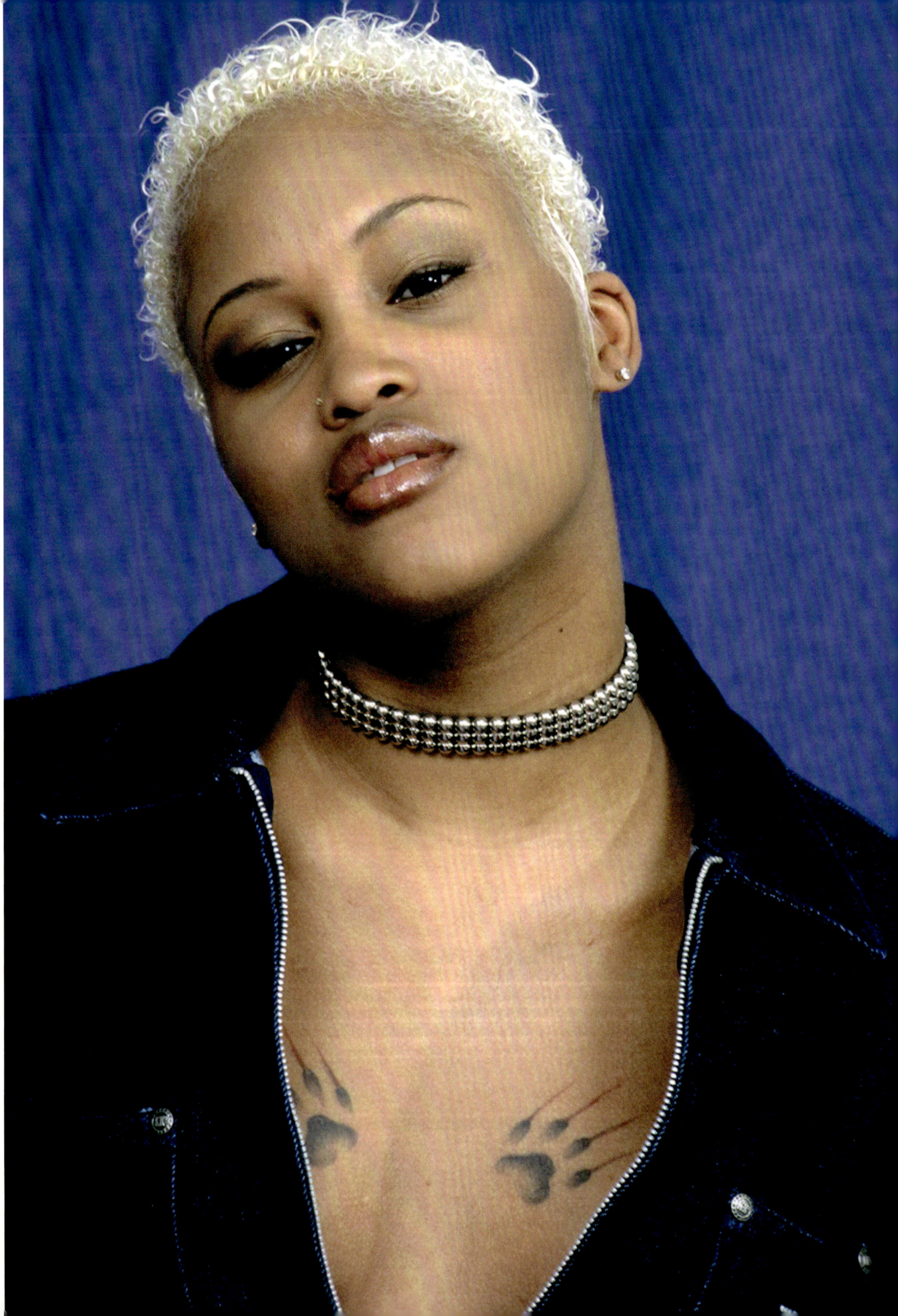

p.176 Eve (Eve Jihan Jeffers-Cooper), NYC, late 1990s; p.177 Faith Evans, NYC, late 1990s.

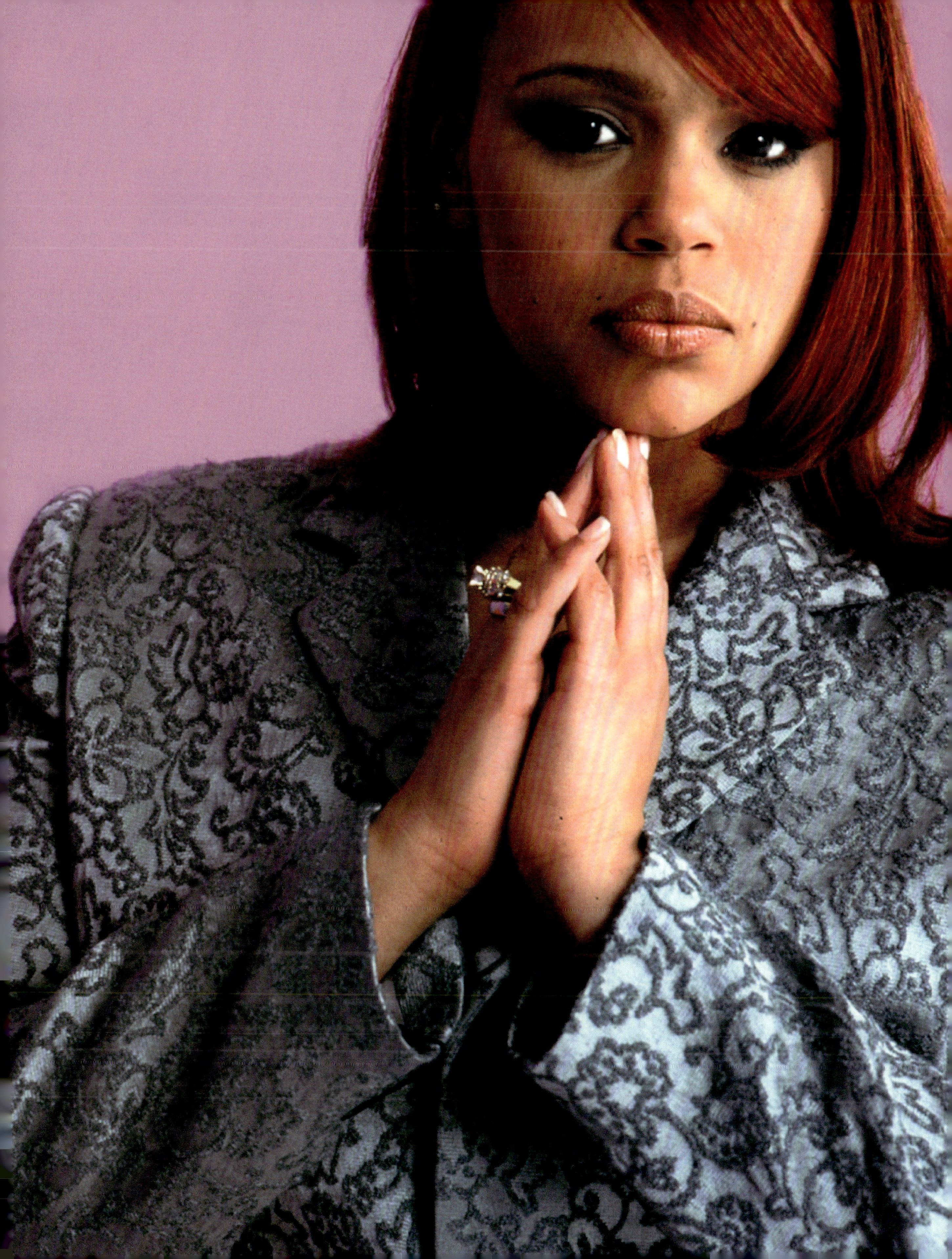

p.178 The Notorious B.I.G., in fur coat toasting me, NYC, 1995.

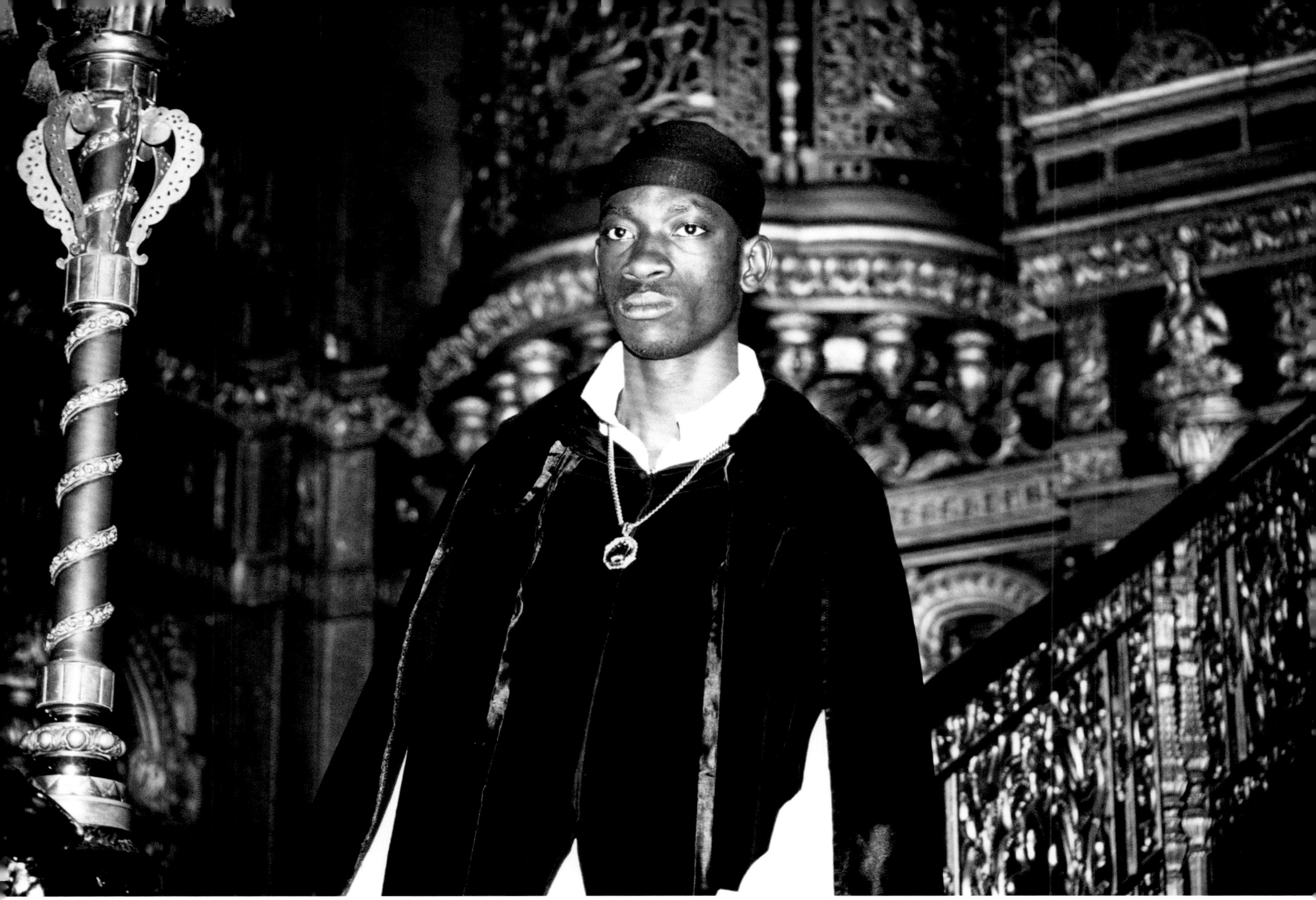

p.179 Bounty Killer at The United Palace, during the video shoot with The Fugees for "Hip-Hopera" ft. the Fugees, Washington Heights, NYC, 1996.

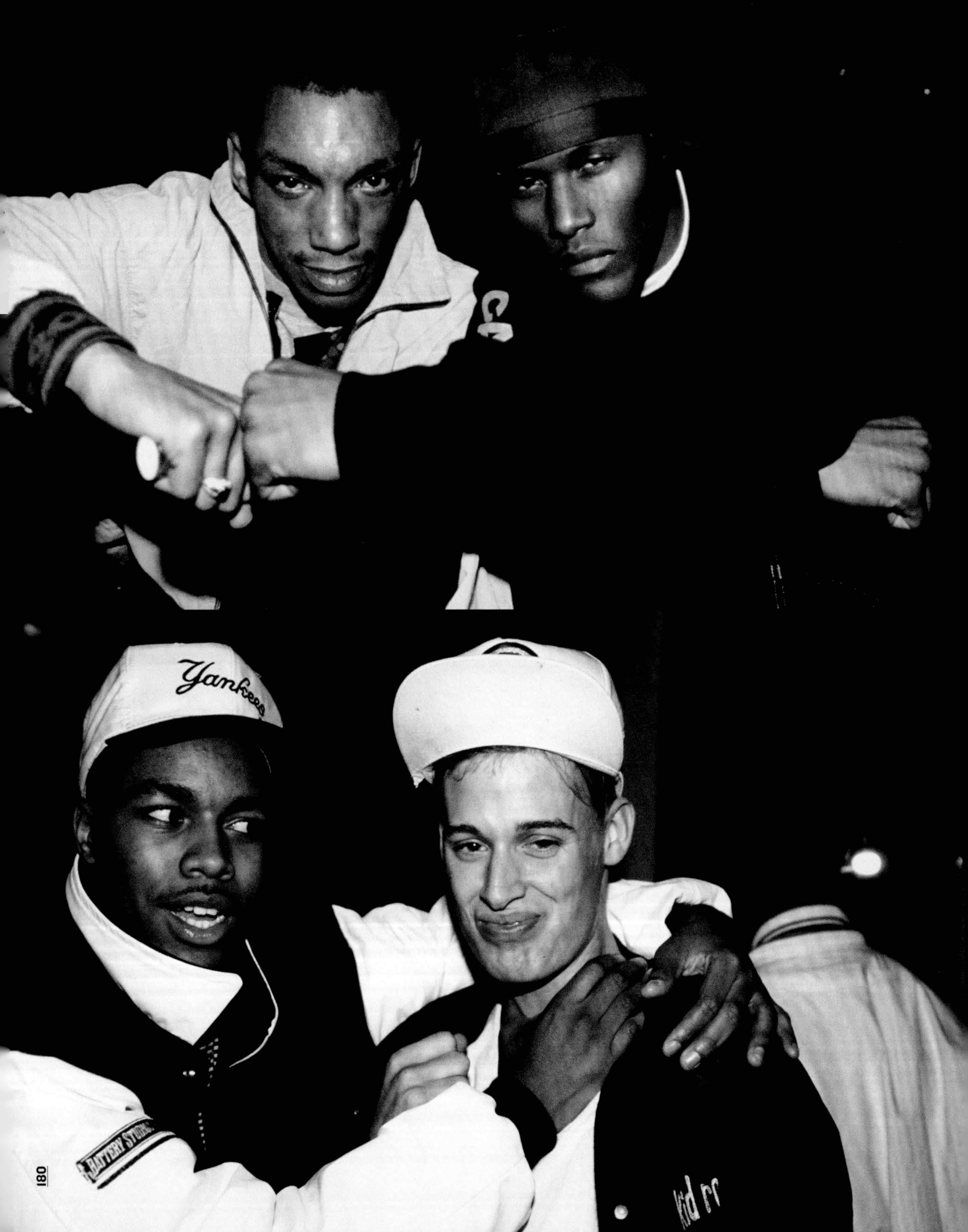
Yankees

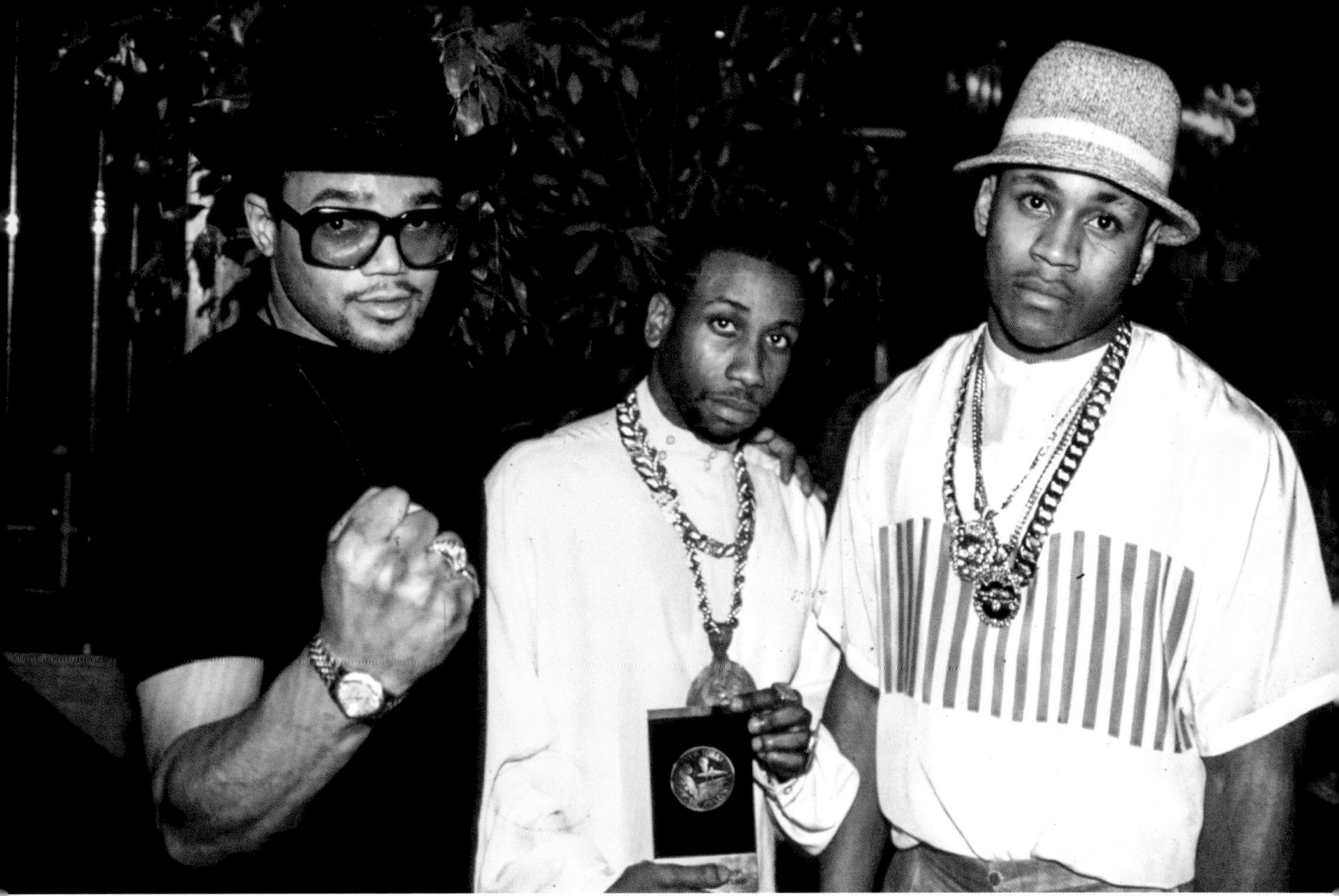

p.180 (top) Tricky and Canibus, NYC, 1998. Only the most aware and devoted hip-hop heads will even have a clue of the intensity of this dual portrait. We were at some music event and I introduced them to each other. Both color outside the lines and have both carved their own unique paths in hip-hop, trip-hop and surreal forms of electronica; D-Nice and Kid Rock, NYC, late 1980s. Under that goofy hat he had grown a Kid from Kid n' Play-style gumby.

p.181 DMC, Rob Bass, and LL Cool J, New York Music Awards, China Club, NYC, April 1989.

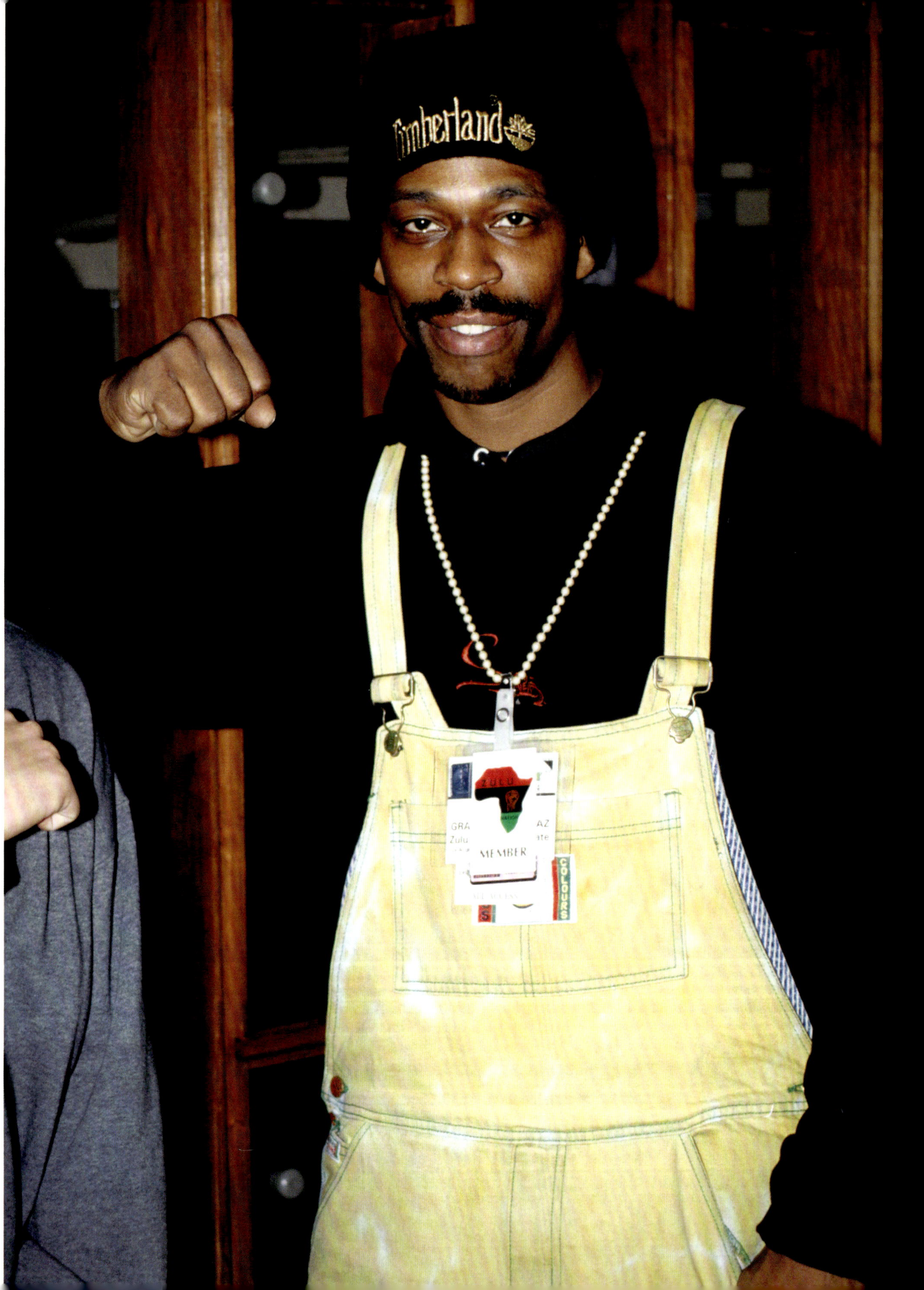

p.182 Grandmaster Caz from the Cold Crush brothers, NYC, 1989. Emcee, DJ, pioneer and Zulu.

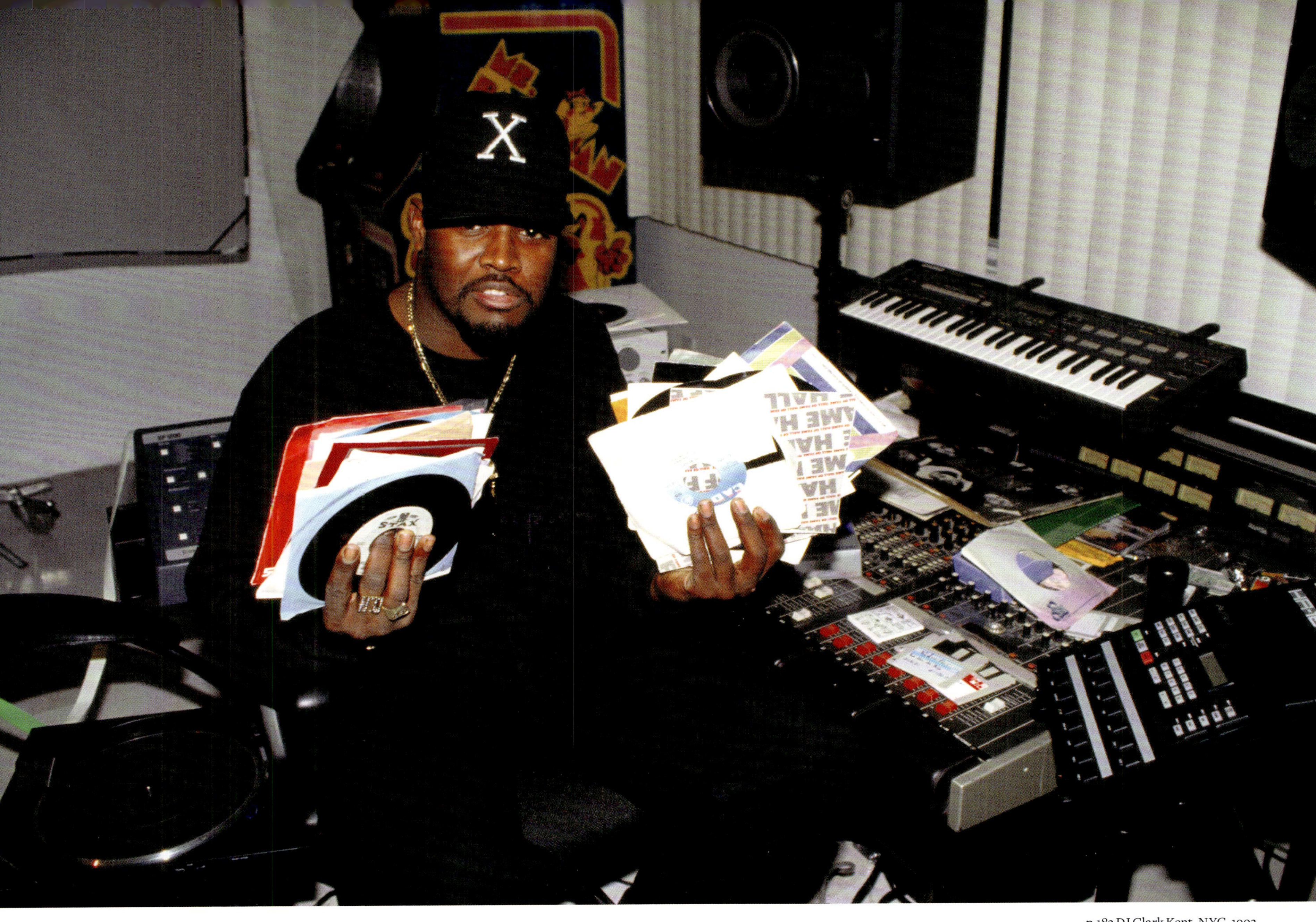

p.183 DJ Clark Kent, NYC, 1993.

p.184 Digital Underground: DJ Fuze, Humpty Hump, and "Shock G" as played by Kent Racker, the younger brother of Gregory Jacobs. Jacobs—the real Shock G and Humpty—regularly employed doubles to play his aliases at concerts, videos, TV shows and even on photo shoots for print media, just to mess with people. NYC, early 1990s; p.185. The real Humpty Hump on stage. Or is it? NYC, early 1990s.

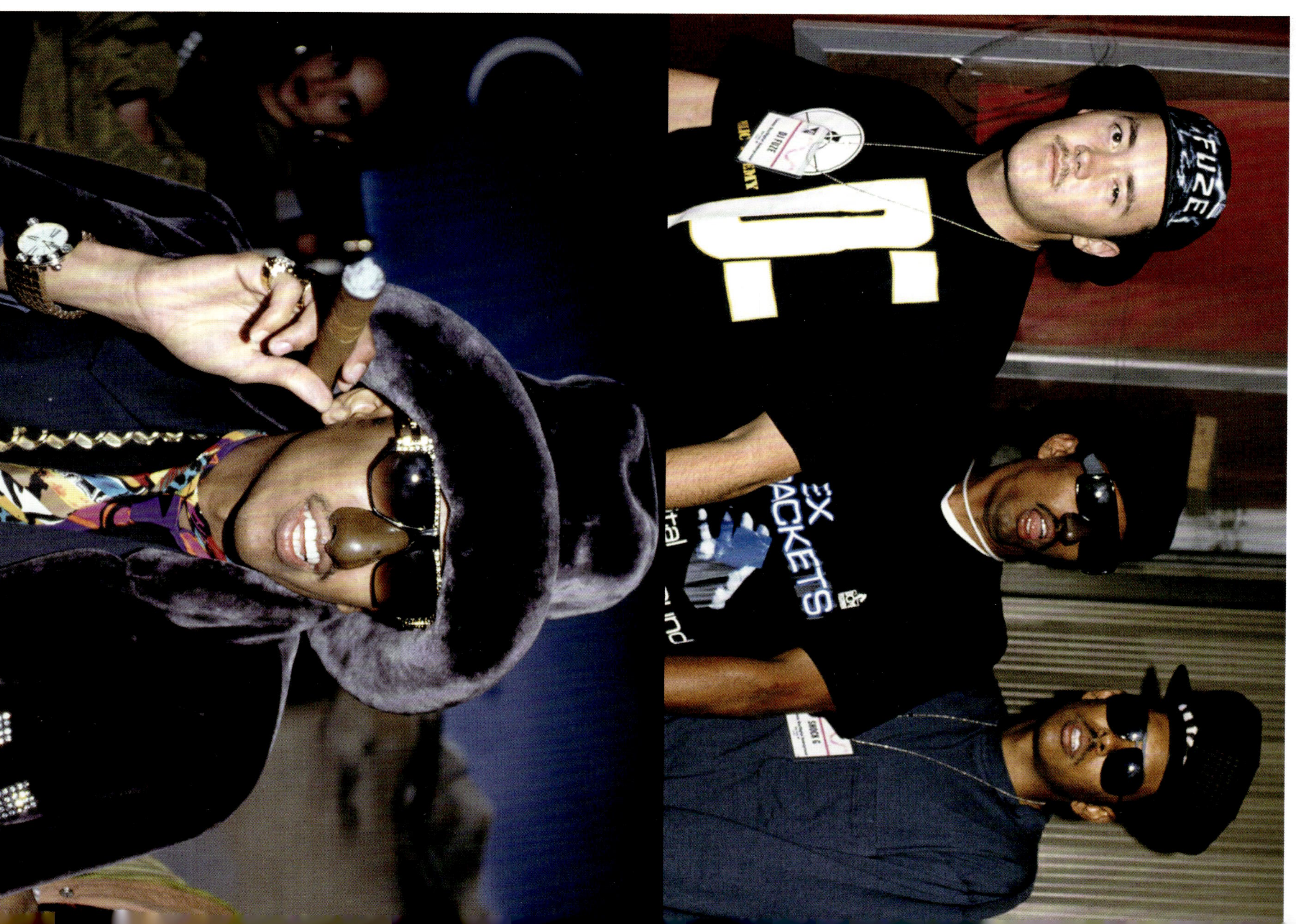

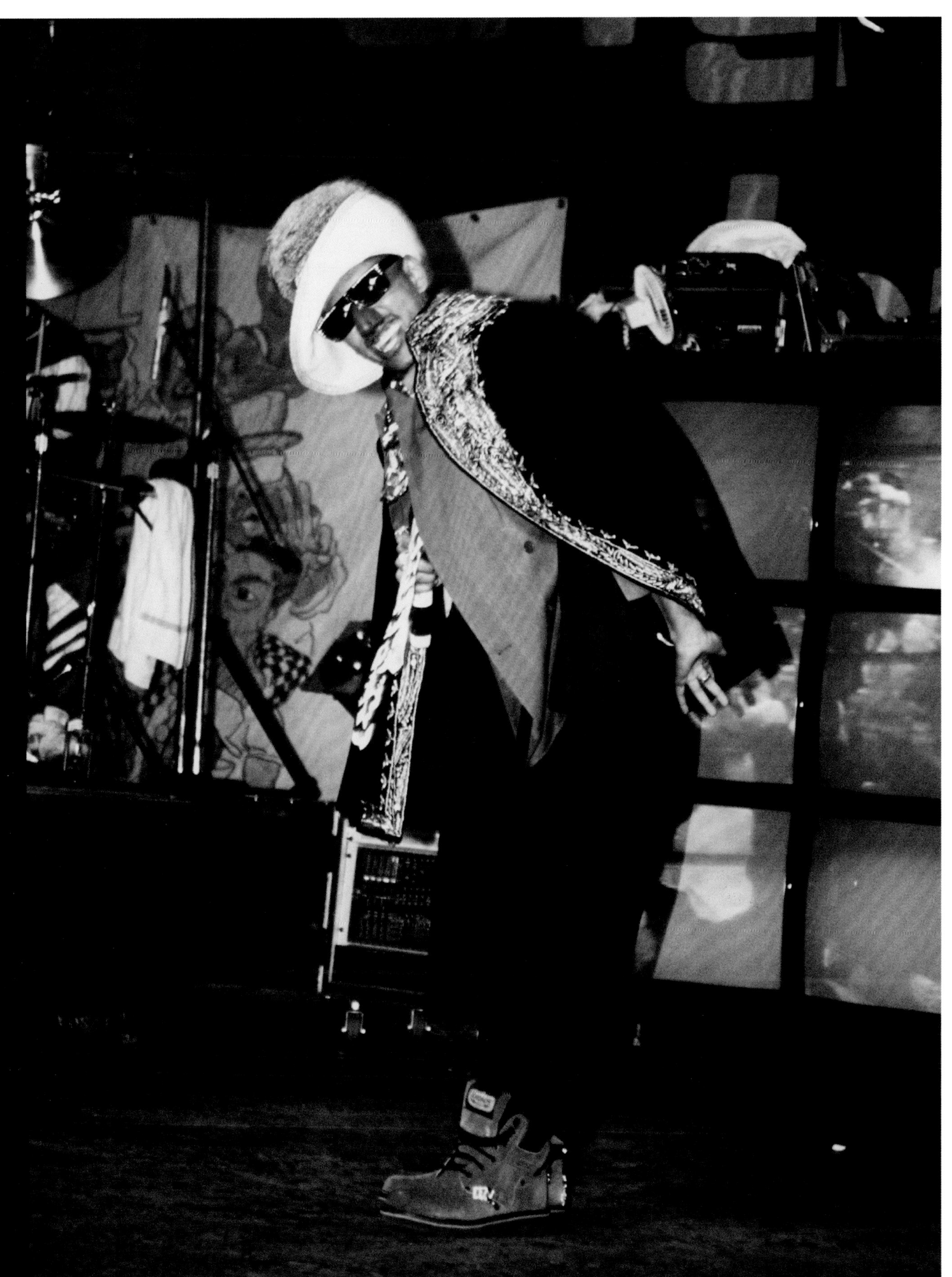

p.186 KMD, NYC, 1991. Yes, that is Zev Love X aka MF Doom, with the baseball cap, and Onyz. That black sambo figure caused a lot of headaches for their album and their label.

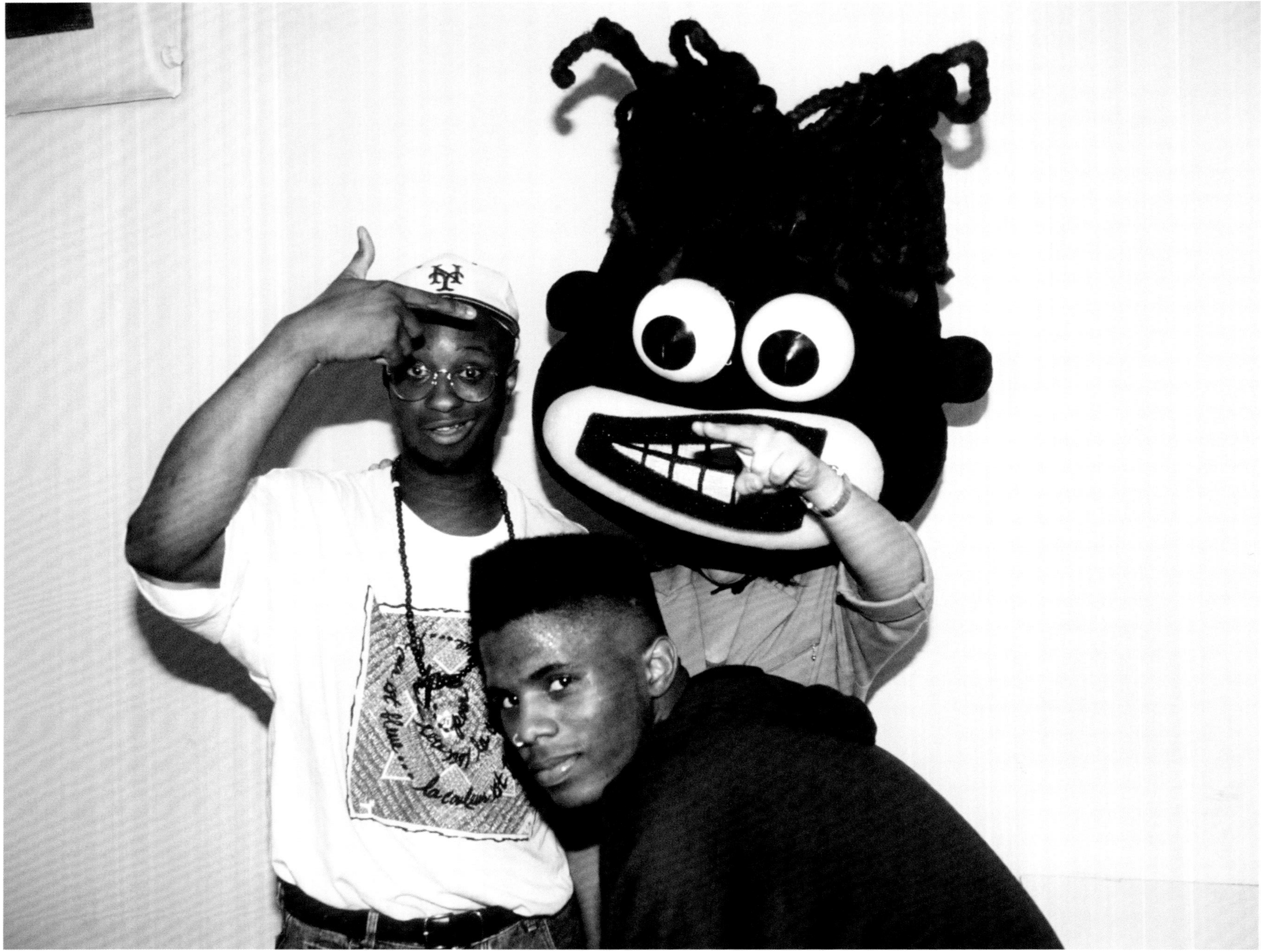

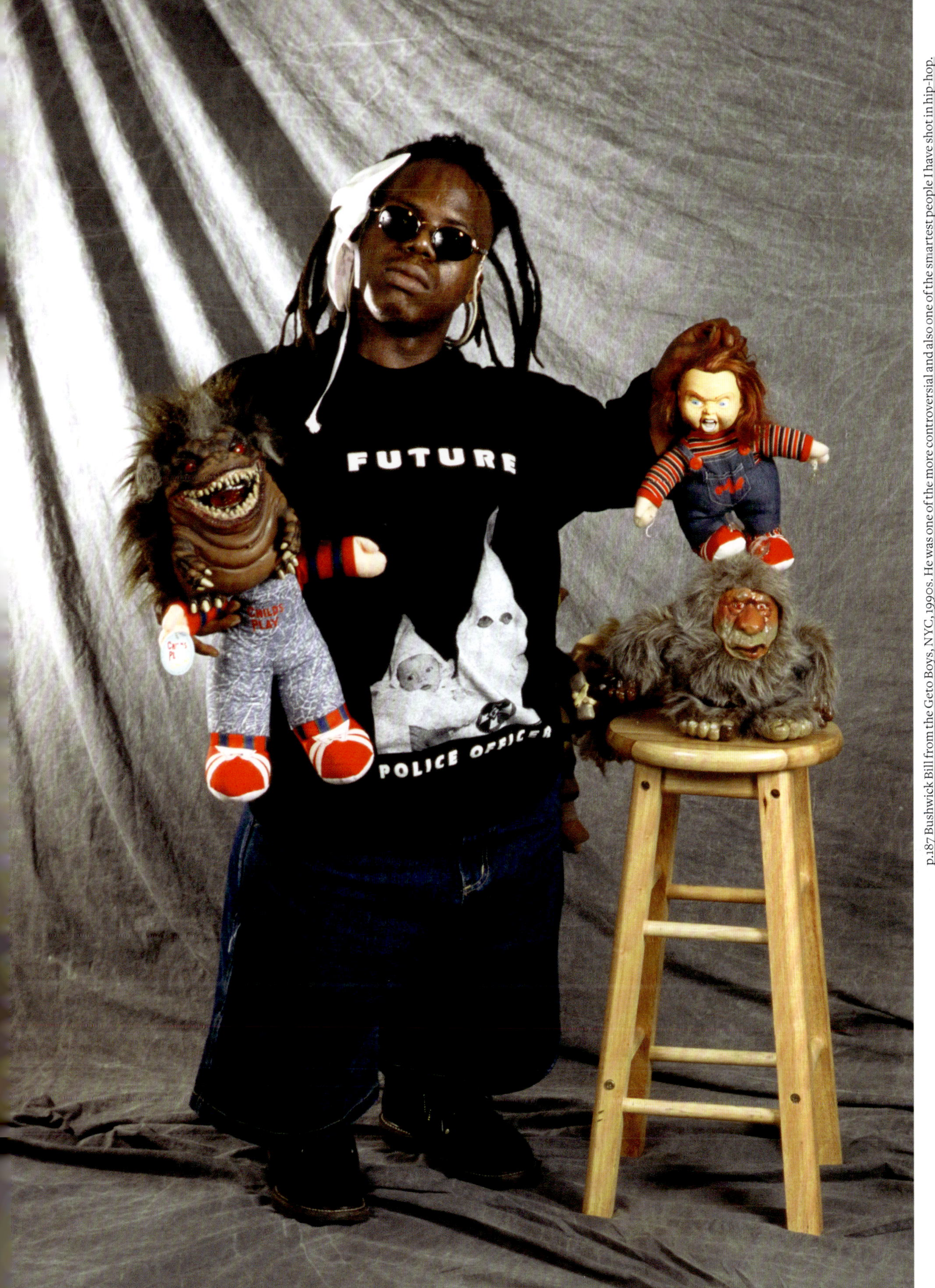

p.187 Bushwick Bill from the Geto Boys, NYC, 1990s. He was one of the more controversial and also one of the smartest people I have shot in hip-hop. Our conversations ranged from poetry to art to sculpture, food and the occult sciences.

p.188 Geto Boys, Apollo Theatre, Harlem, NYC, 1991. A group with three talented rappers, Willie D, Scarface, Bushwick Bill from a place never heard from before in rap—Texas. I recall the first time I saw them perform on 42nd St. in NYC during the New Music Seminar. Their show was to a nearly all-female audience and they did a song about rape and mutilation, murder and necrophilia. The crowd went crazy, booing them and throwing bottles and garbage at them, but they finished the song and went on to make several hit songs, including the classic "My Mind's Playing Tricks on Me."

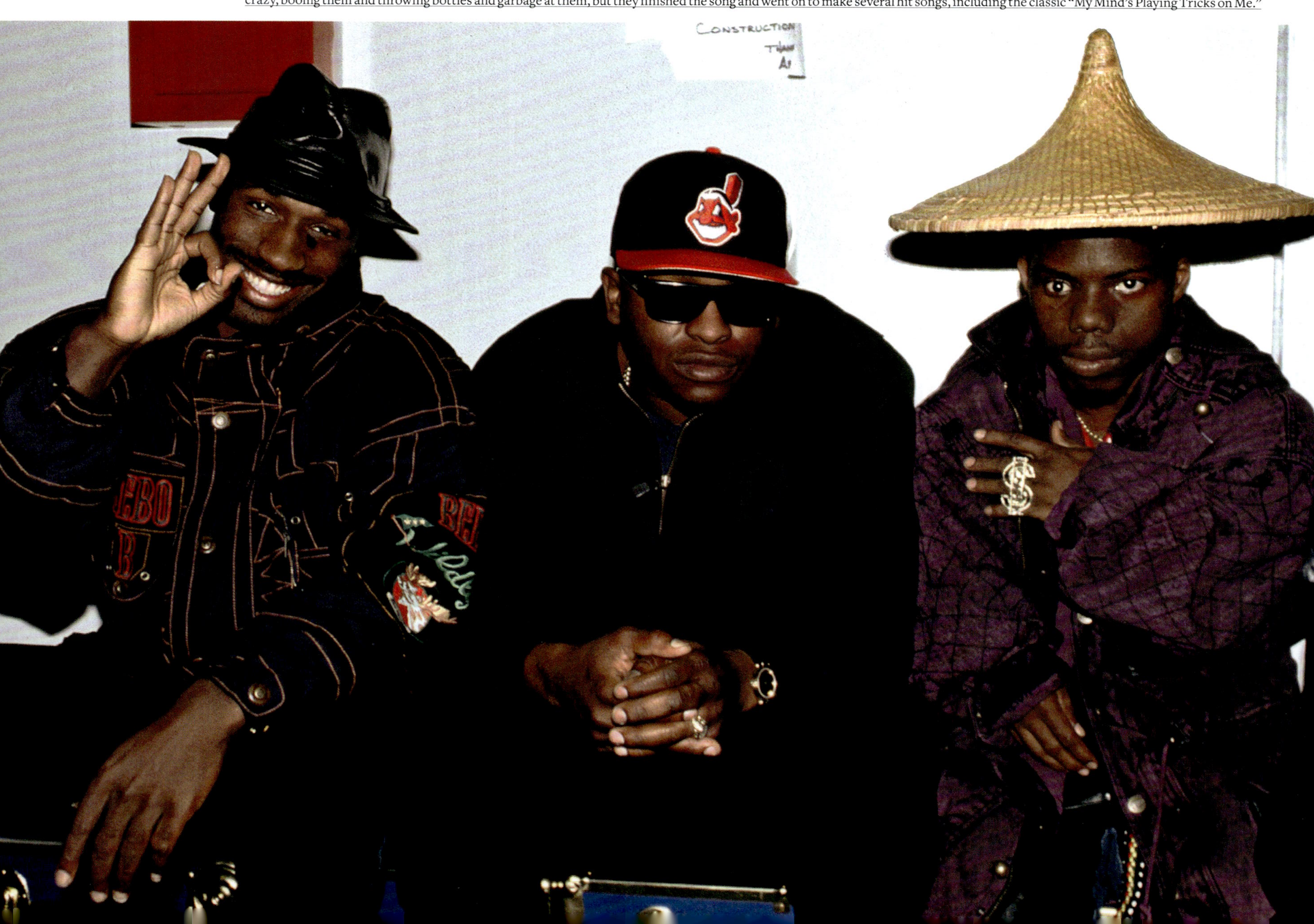

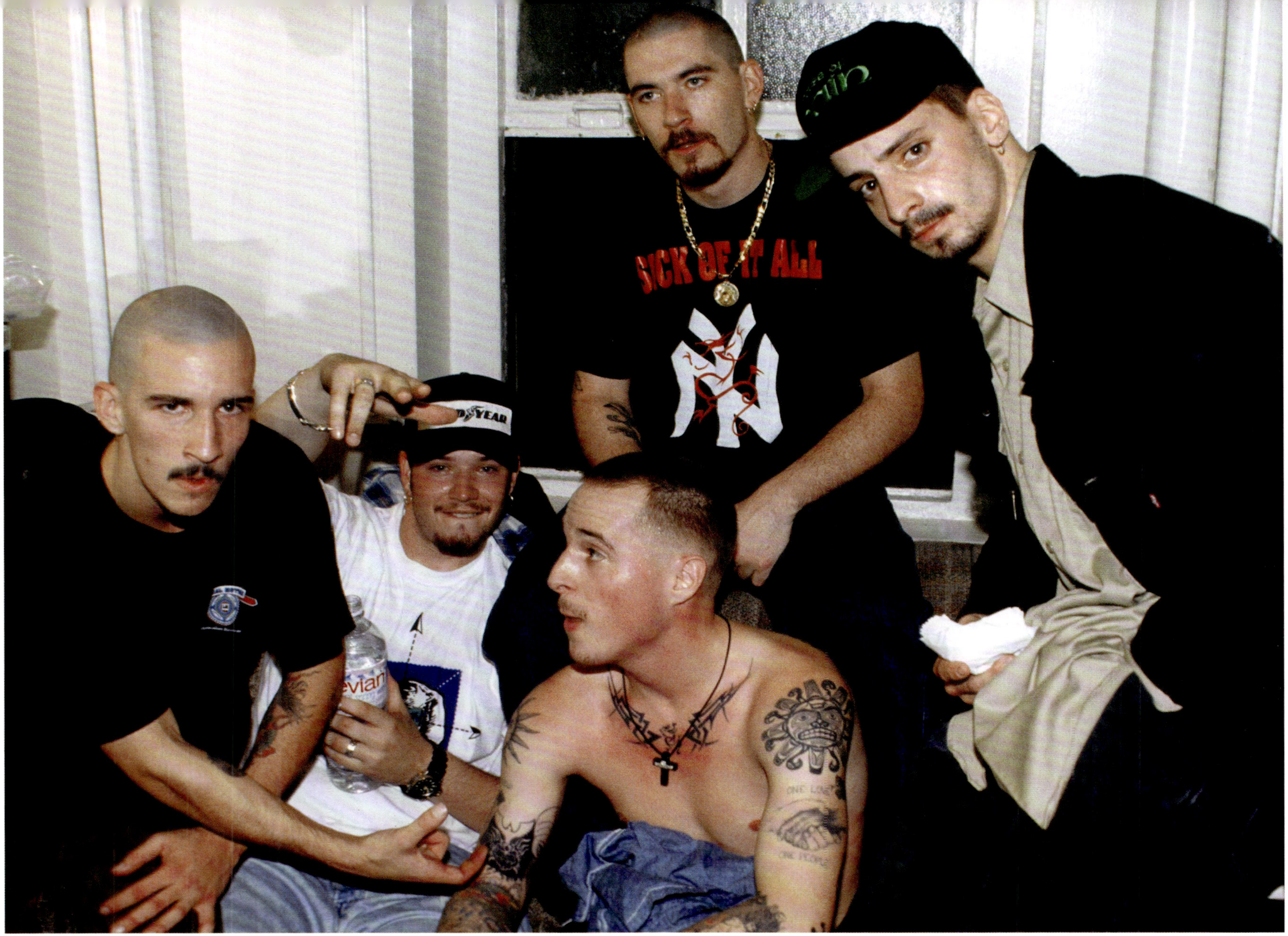

p.189 House of Pain, The Roxy, NYC, 1990s. Only three white groups—in my memory—had any impact in hip-hop. The Beastie Boys, 3rd Bass and House of Pain. HCP never tried to sound or look black, never had any desire to be other than what they were, loud, tough, drunk Irish guys having fun while performing, making music and videos. Not every hip-hop group was fun to shoot or hang out with. These guys were always a riot and were full of energy.

p.190 Das EFX (Dray and Skoob) had a style I called "speed rap." They had their own flow, cadence, intricate lyrics and lyrical style. NYC, 1992.

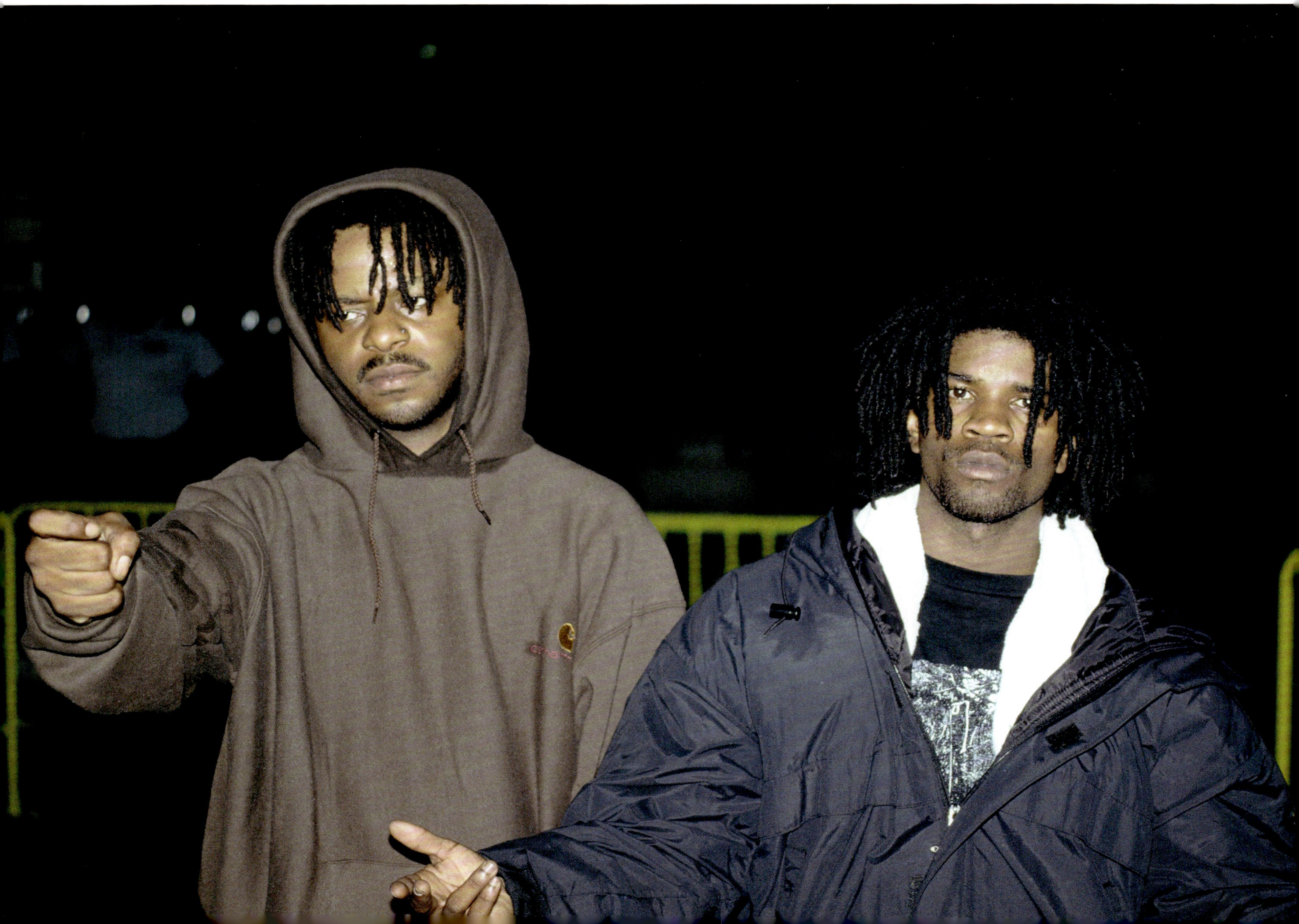

P.191 Illegal, Redman, Treach from Naughty By Nature. Illegal was the tough guy counterpoint to Kris Kross who they liked to diss. Newark, NJ, 1993.

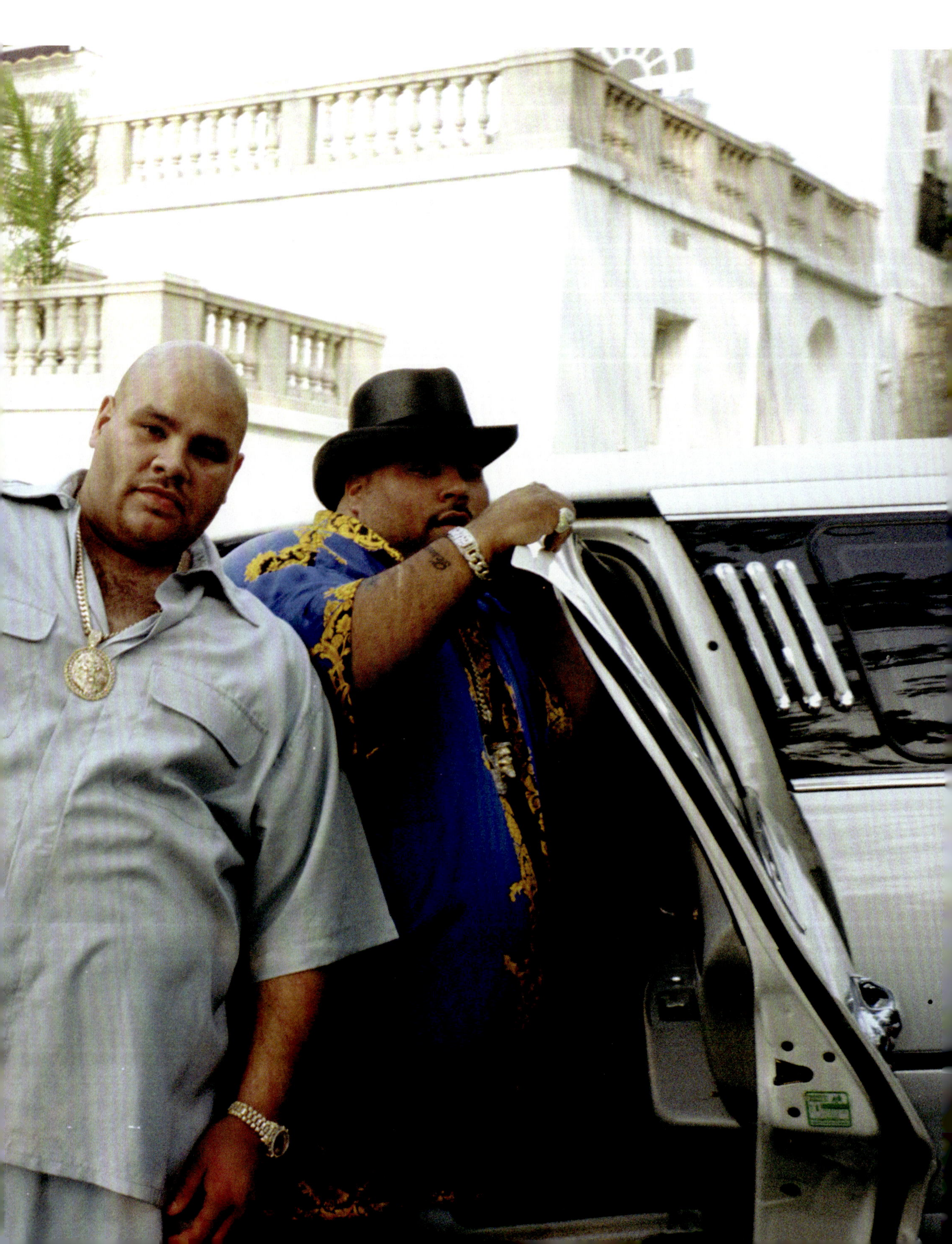

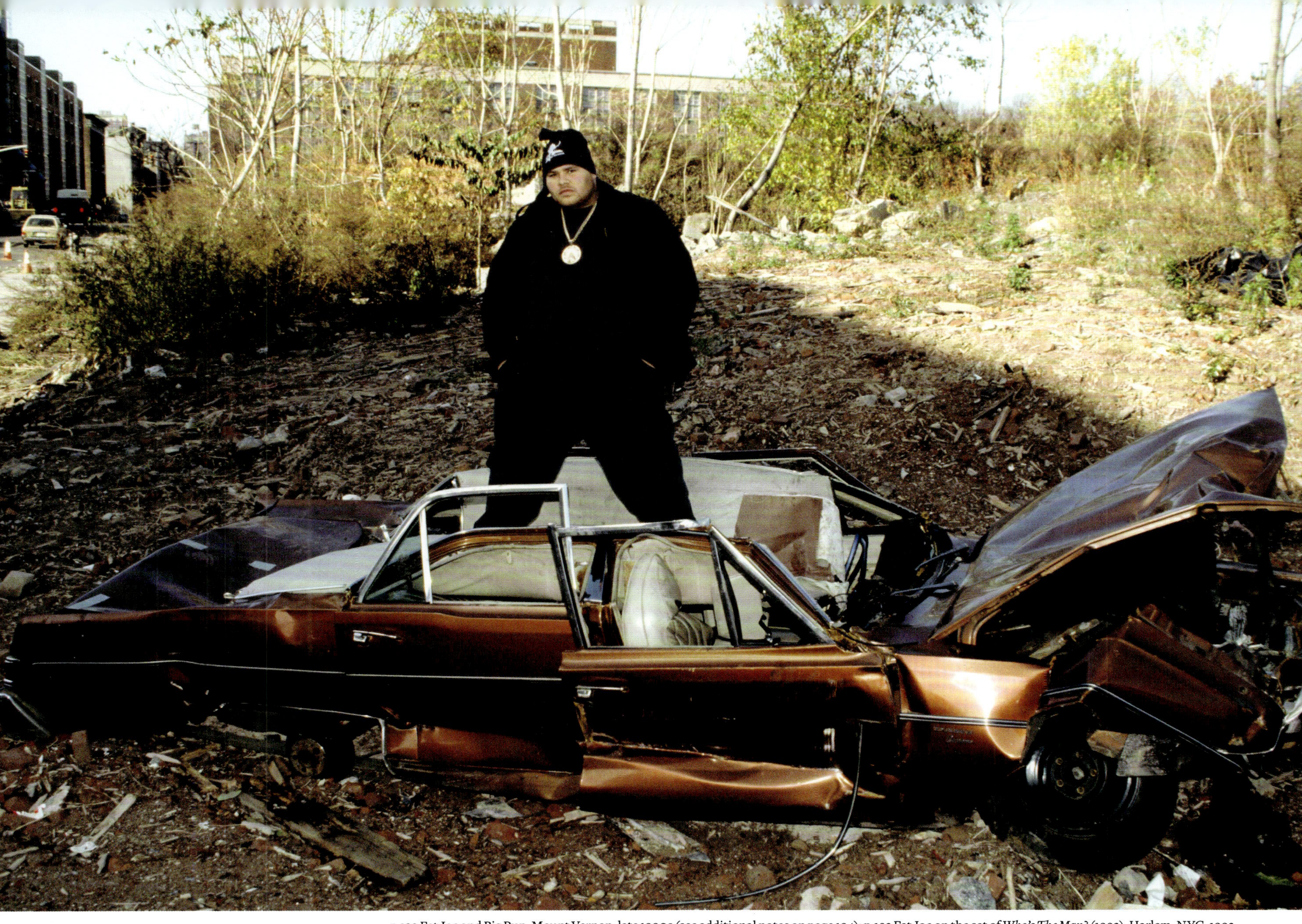

p.192 Fat Joe and Big Pun, Mount Vernon, late 1990s (see additional notes on page 194); p.193 Fat Joe on the set of *Who's The Man?* (1993), Harlem, NYC, 1992. Joe realized my off-kilter sense of humor with him crushing an abandoned car.

p.194-195 One of my all time favorite hip-hop portraits and my favorite photo of Big Pun. Shot at 3am during his last recording session, he passed only a few days later. I did this session for a Japanese hip-hop magazine. Pun was there with his wife and kids and Fat Joe. A memory seared into my brain was him gagging, unable to breathe, and Fat Joe and Pun's wife Liza stripping him naked and using towels soaked in cold water to shock him back to normal. Watching them struggle with his nearly 700-pound body expressed to me their intense love for him. Sony Studios, NYC, 2000.

Notes to page 192:

Fat Joe and the late Big Pun (1971-2000). I could write about these two and my dealings with them all day. Principals of their posse, Terror Squad, each Puerto Rican member had a tattoo of the Italian Al Pacino in his iconic role as Cuban drug kingpin Tony Montana. I am fond of saying that "you can't make this shit up." Probably no group other than Naughty By Nature and Public Enemy made me feel more like a part of their group than Terror Squad. Joe and Pun were like brothers and each had that raw, Bronx P-R sense of identity, with rawness and warmth in equal measure. In the background of this photo is the mansion of black legend Madam C.J. Walker.

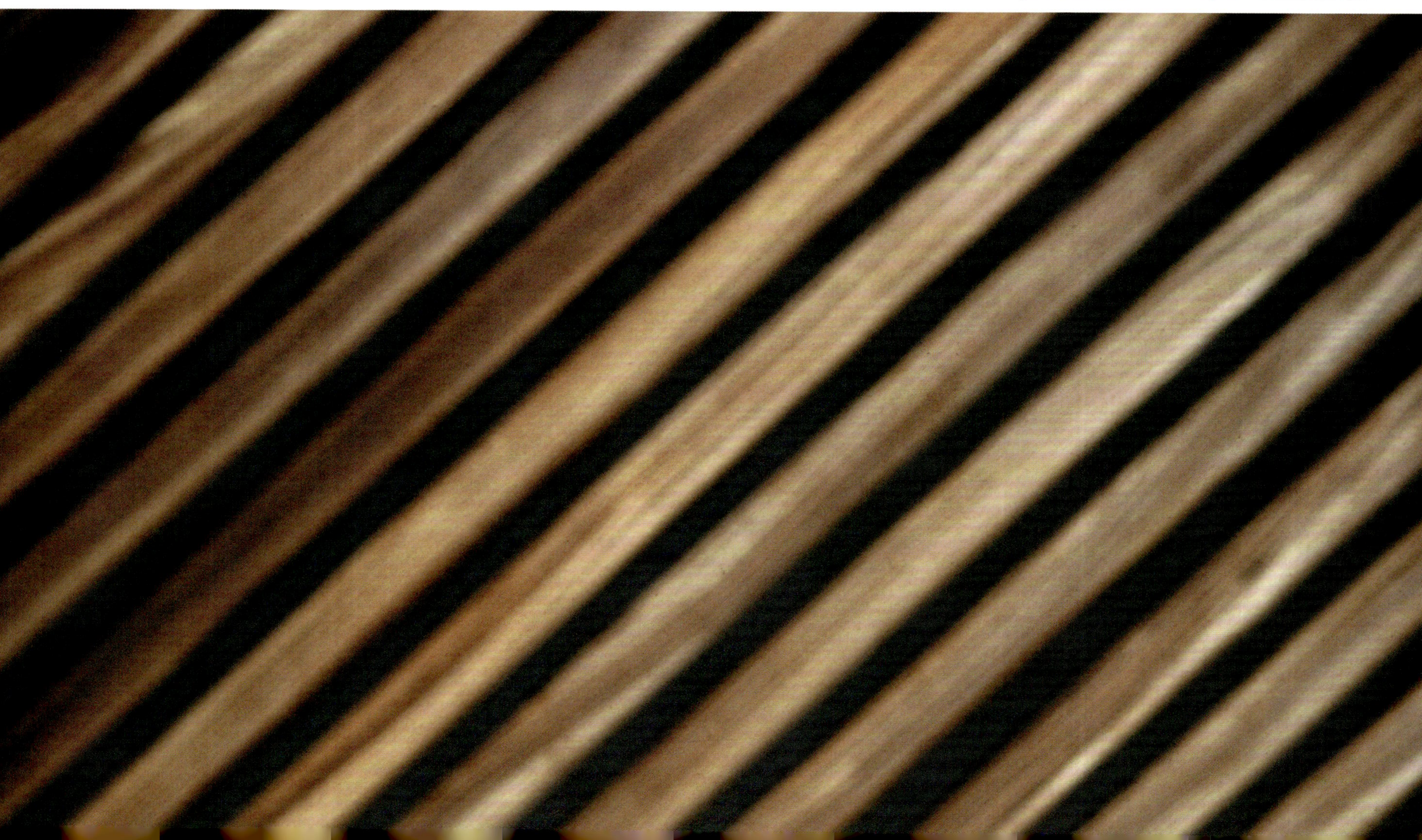

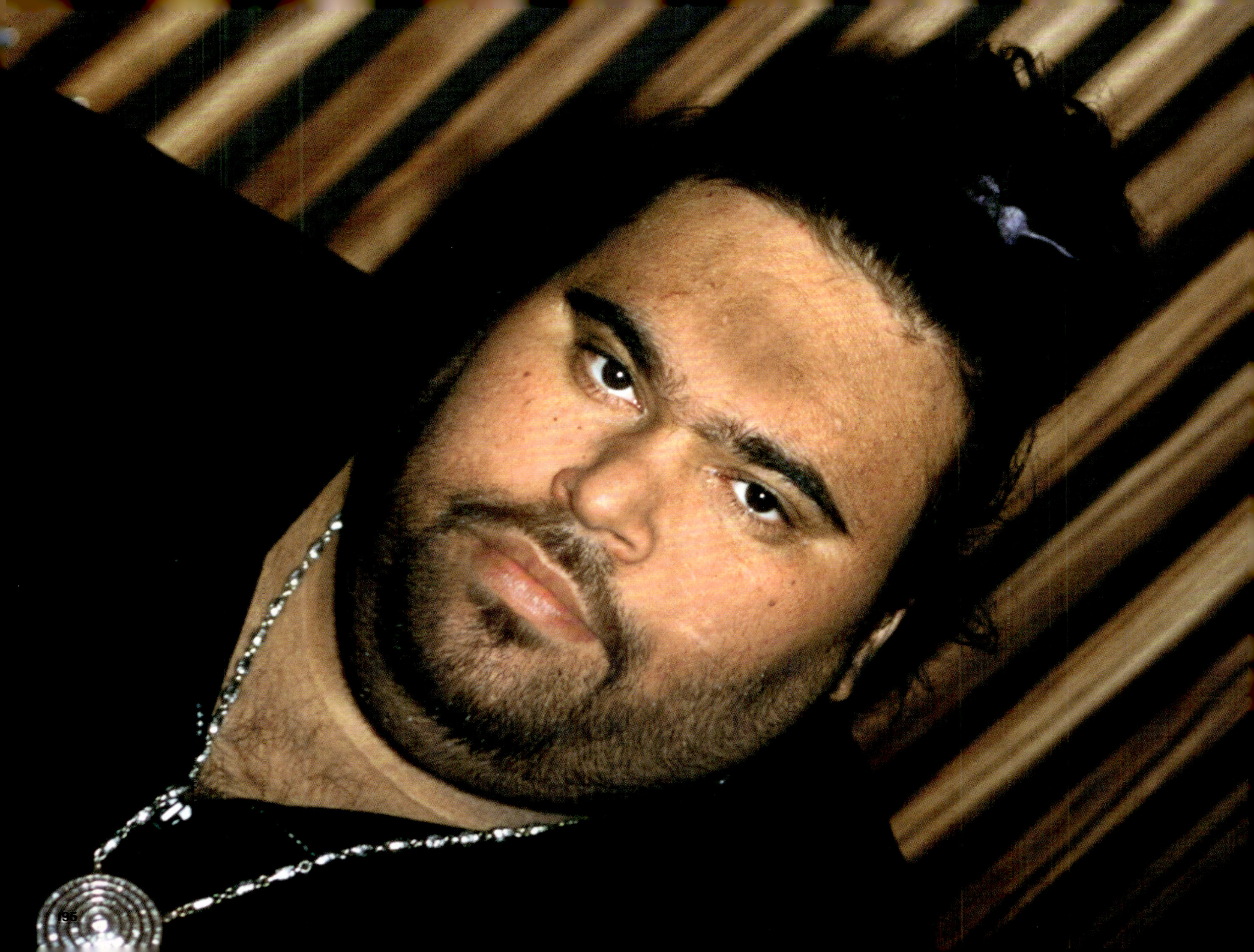

p.196 Five Pointz. A mecca for graffiti art in Long Island City, Queens, NYC, from the 90s until it was demolished in 2014.

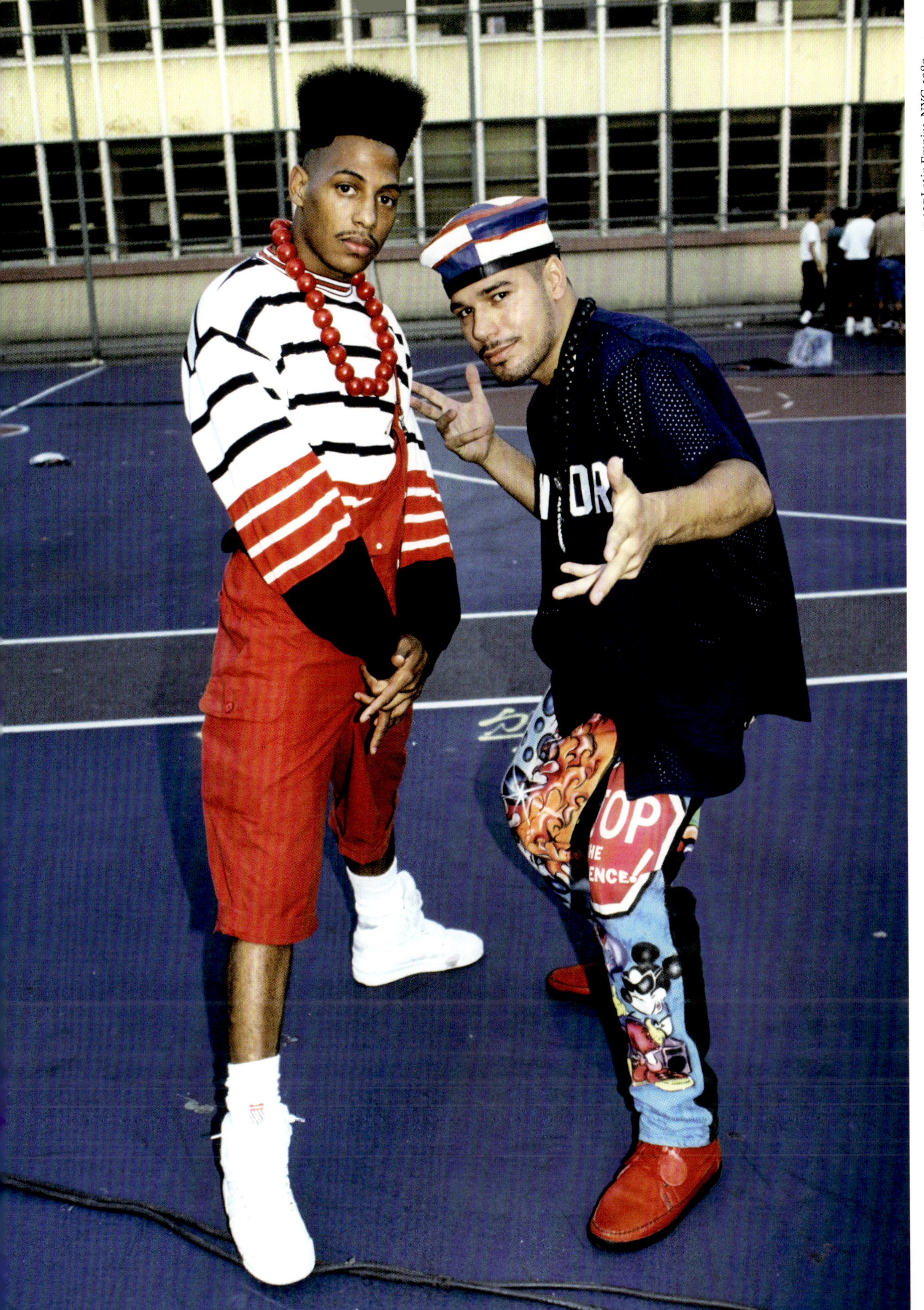

p.197 Latin Empire, NYC, 1989.

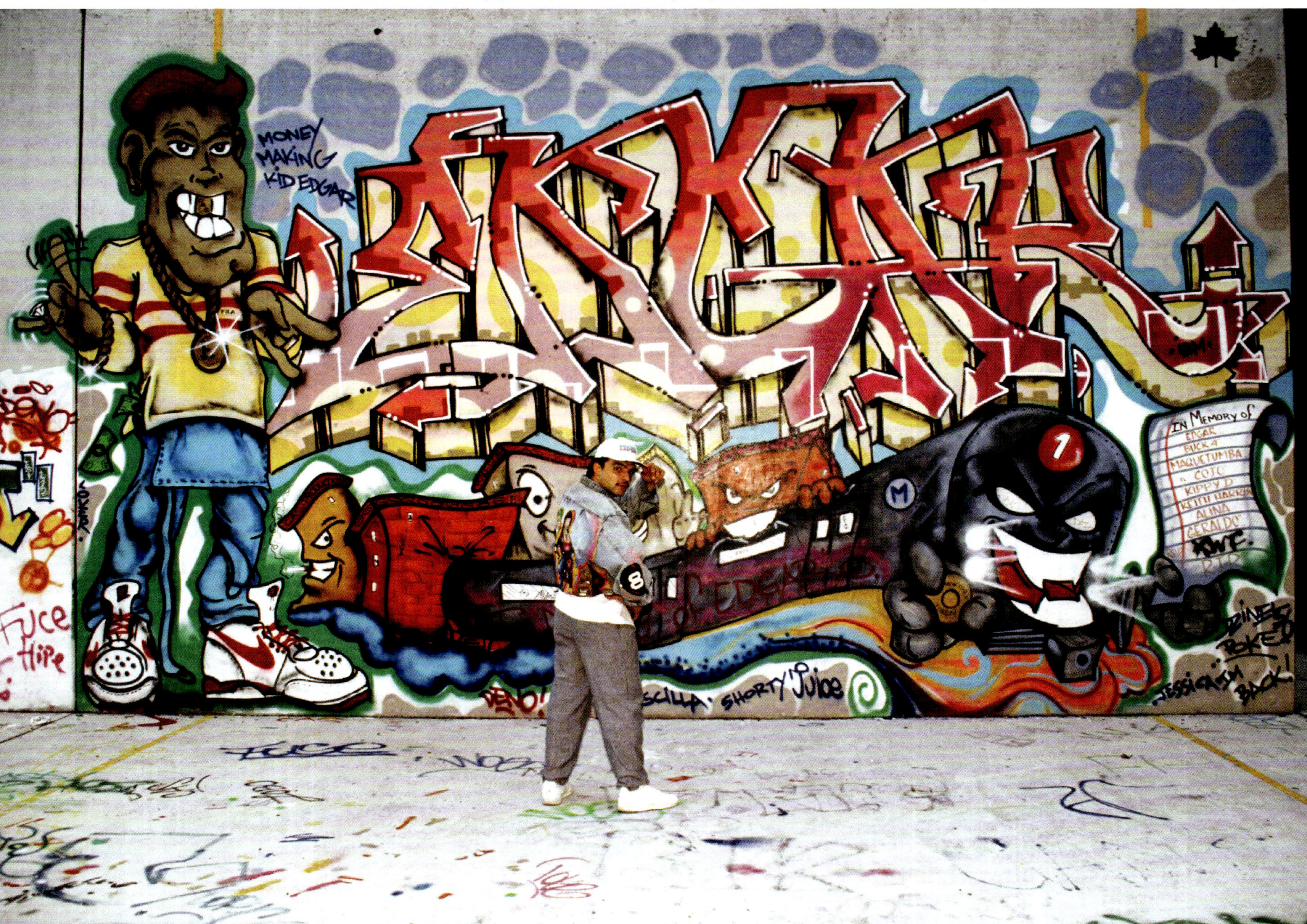

p.198 CAZ with mural "In Memory of Edgar," East 108th Street, East Harlem, NYC, 1988; p.199 Futura, near Financial District, NYC, 1991.

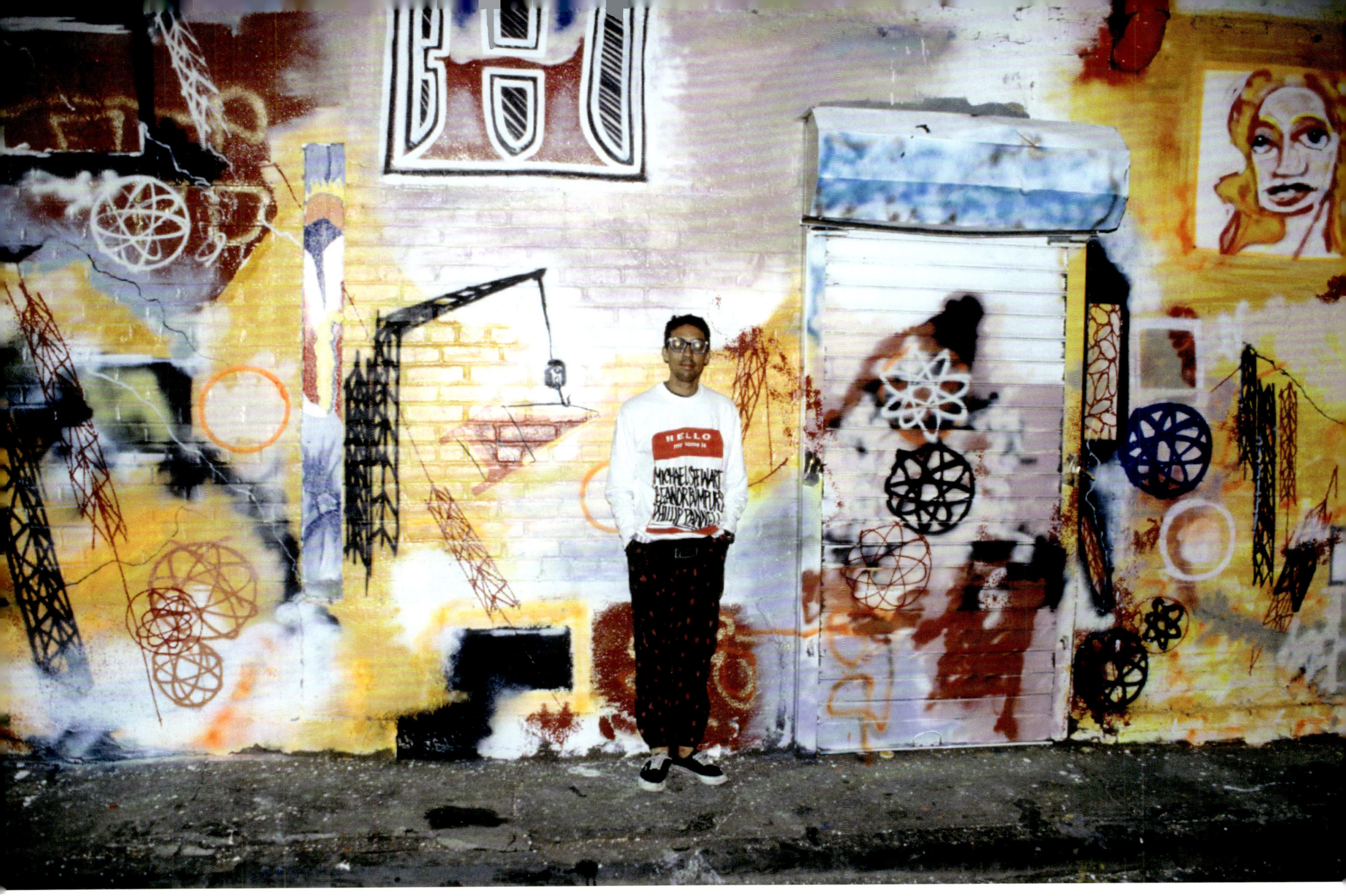

p.200 Scorpio and Melle Mel, Pyramids, NYC, 1991; Scorpio and Melle Mel at RAPMANIA, Apollo Theatre, Harlem, NYC, 1990; p.201 (Top) Brand Nubian: Sadat X, Lord Jamar, Alamo, Grand Puba, The Ritz, NYC, 1990; (Bottom) Cypress Hill, Naughty By Nature and Tim Dog, The Ritz, NYC, 1992.

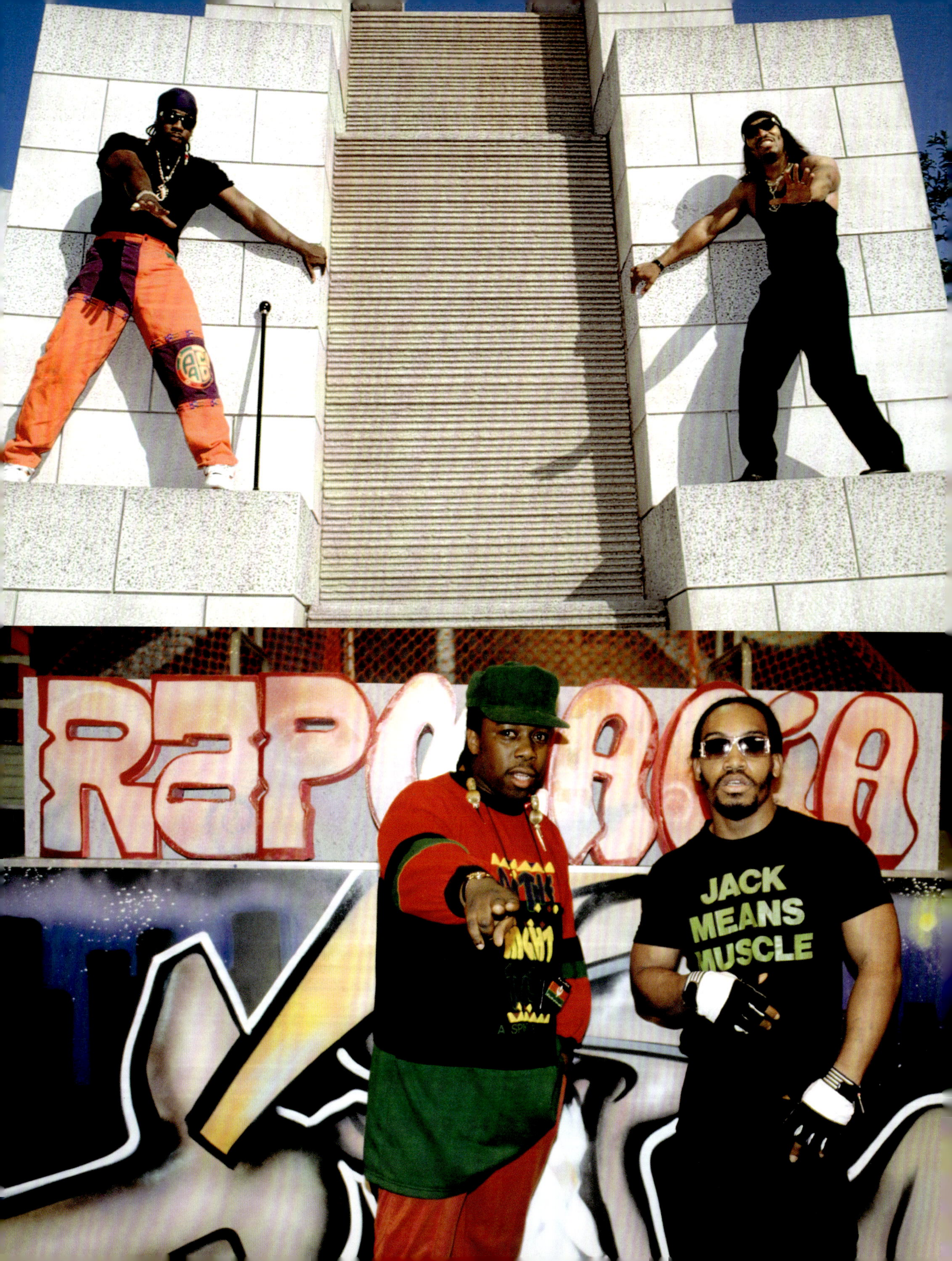
JACK
MEANS
MUSCLE

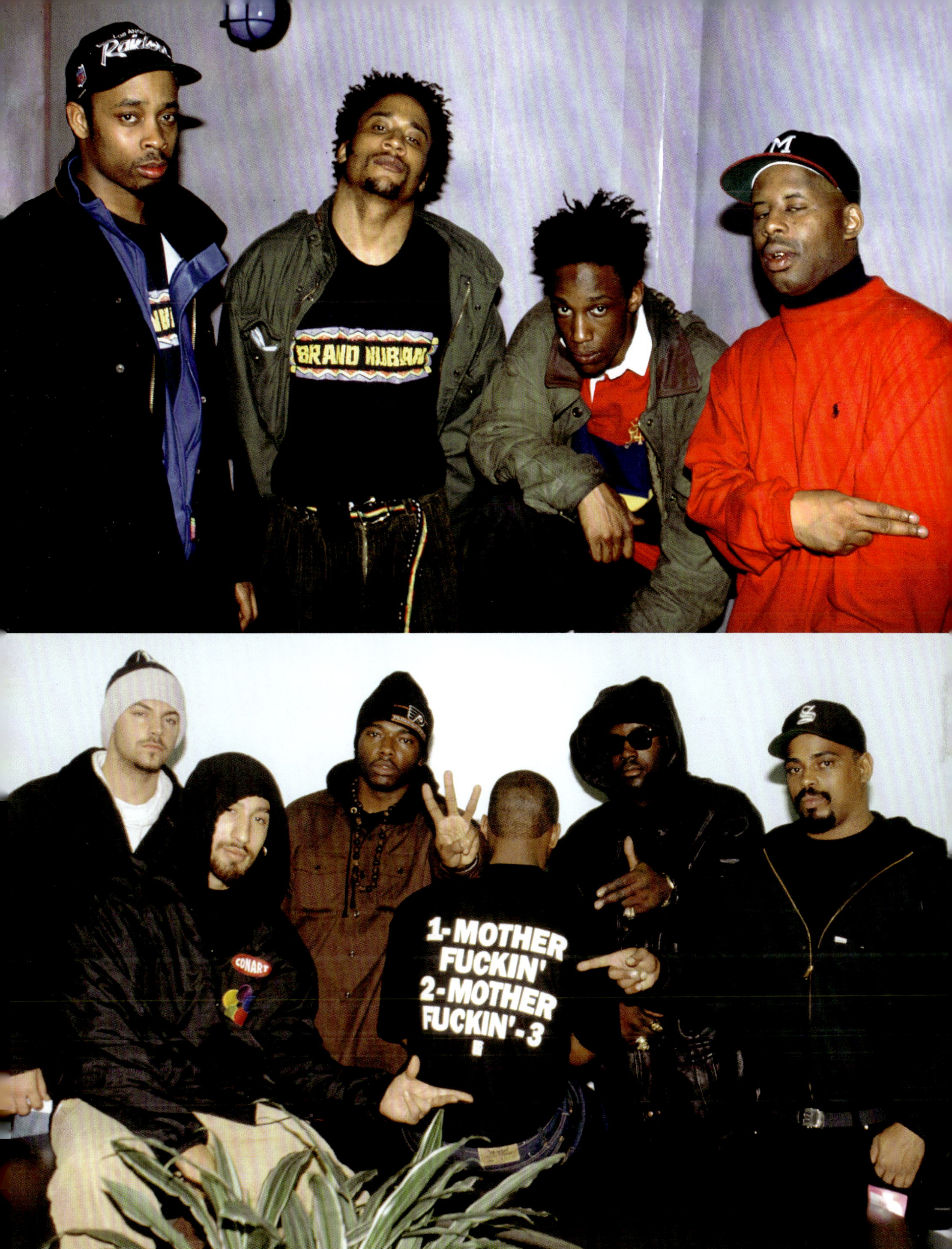
BRAND NUBIAN
1-MOTHER
FUCKIN'
2-MOTHER
FUCKIN'-3
CONART

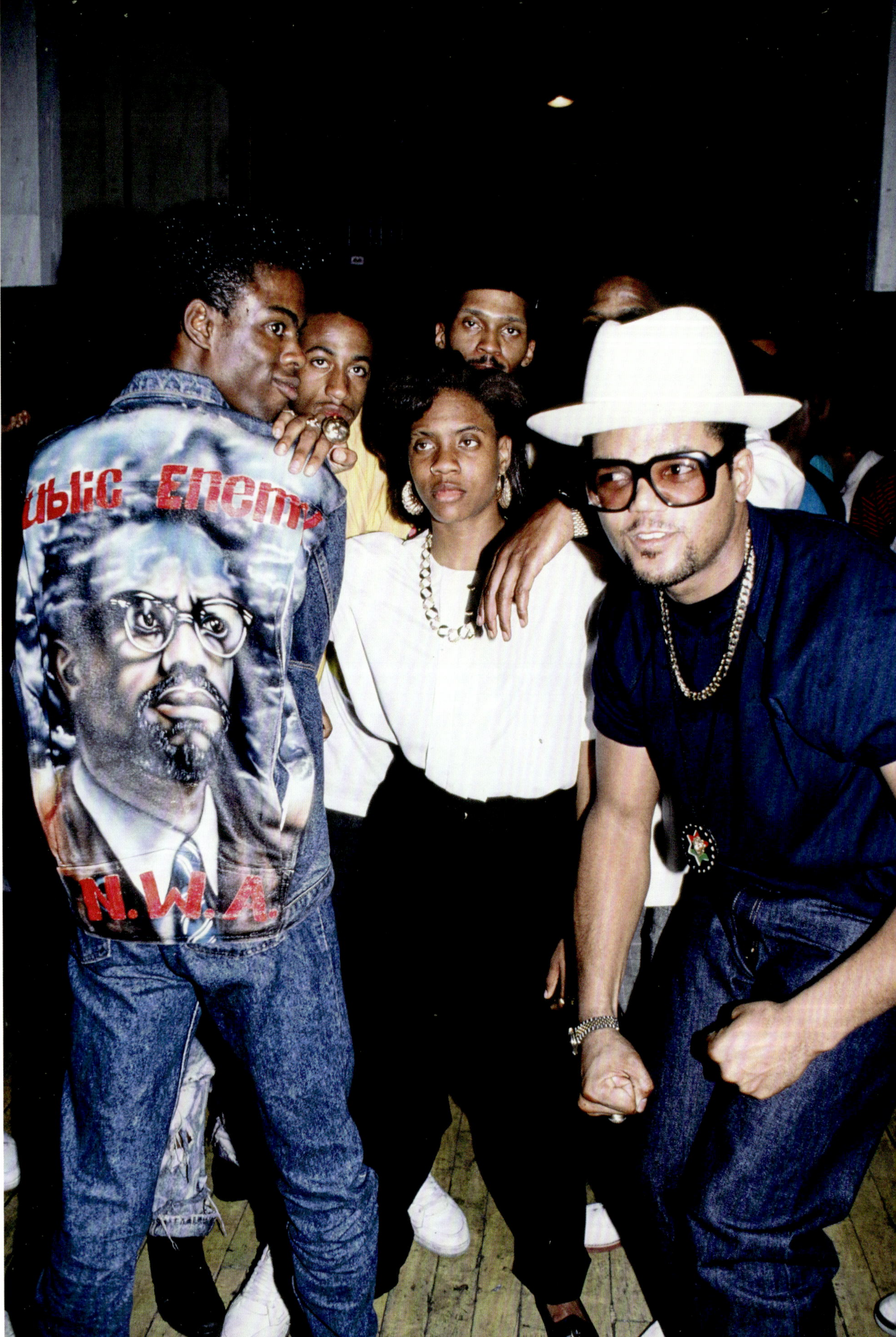

p.202 Chris Rock, MC Lyte & DMC, NYC, early 1990s;
p.203 (top) Isis (Lin Que & Queen Mother Rage). The female component of The X Clan, NYC, early 1990s; (bottom) Dead Prez, stic.man & M-1, 3rd. Eye Studio, NYC, 2000.

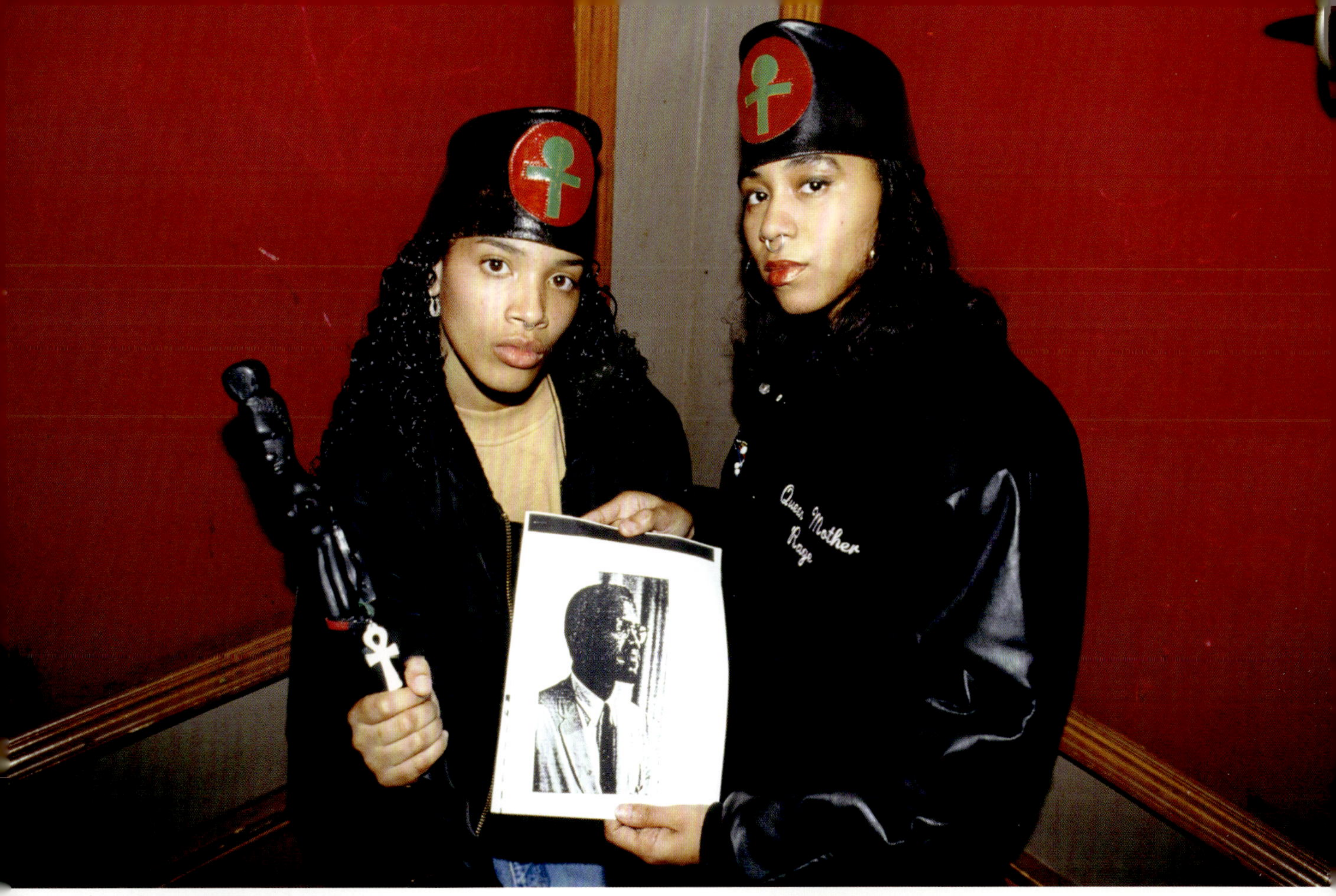

Queen Mother
Rage

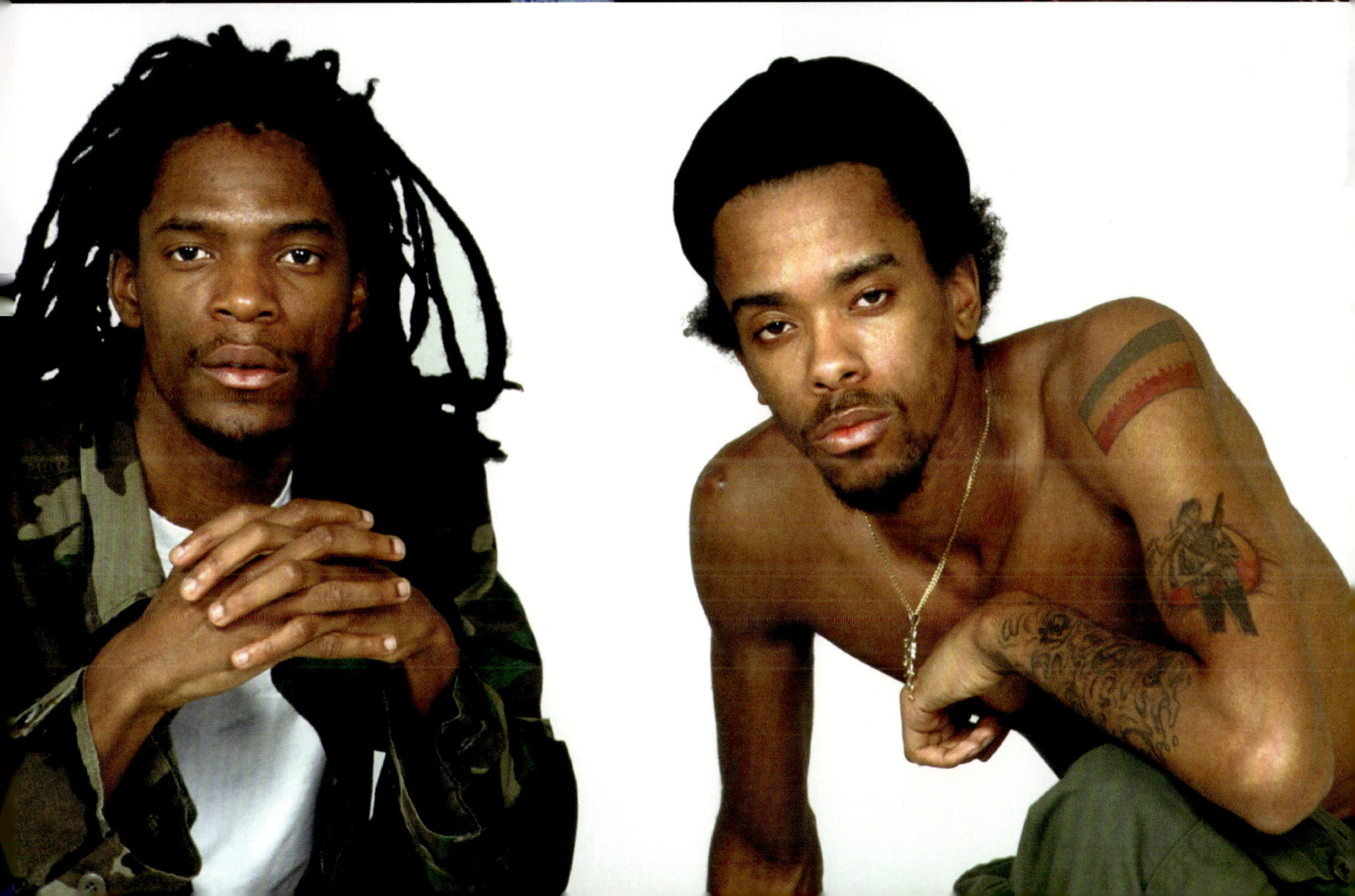

p.204 Ultramagnetic MCs, Apollo Theatre, Harlem, NYC, 1990s.

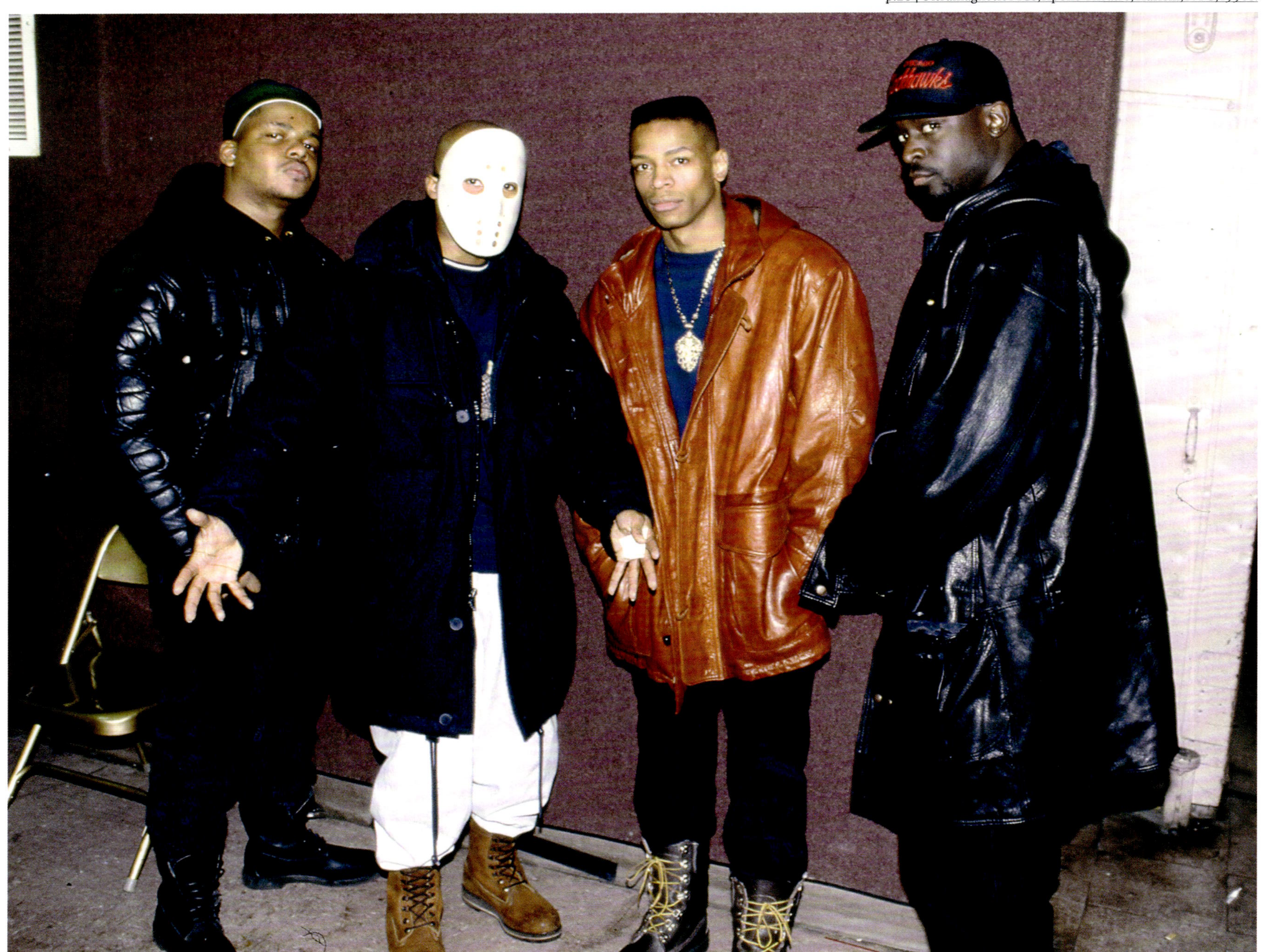

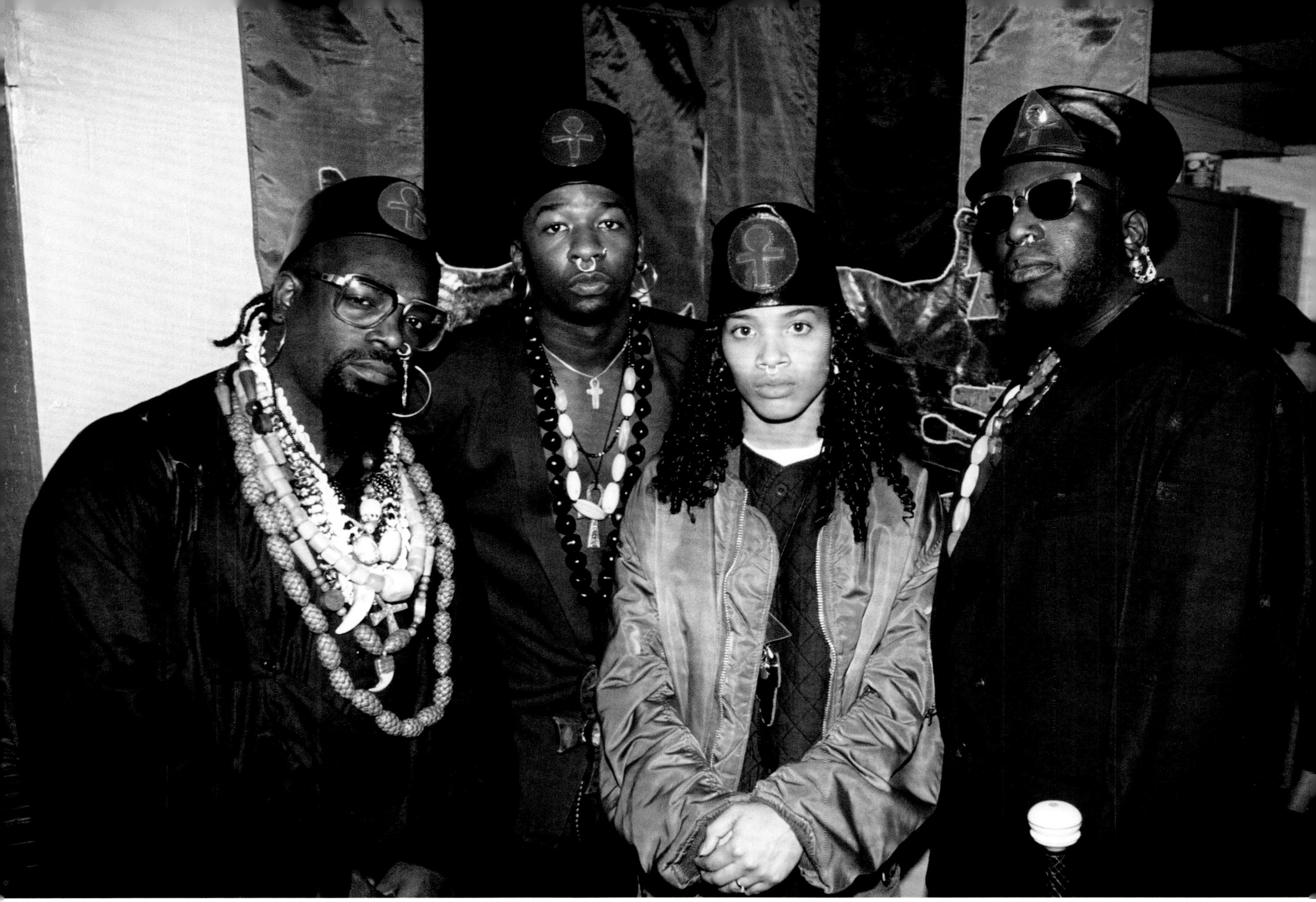

p.205 X Clan (Paradise, Brother J, Isis (Lin Que), & Professor X- S.O.B.'s, NYC, 90s.

p.206 Lamont "Big L" Coleman (1974-1999). He wrote the hip-hop classic "Ebonics" which is the Rosetta Stone of ghetto slang. Killed in a drive-by in Harlem at only 25 years old. Bronx, NYC, 1994; p.207 Rakim Allah. Much of the hip-hop world considers Rakim the best rapper/emcee/songwriter ever. Here he is pictured getting his "R The 18th Letter" tattoo. A rare privilege, allowing me to shoot him getting inked. Greenwich Village, NYC ,1997.

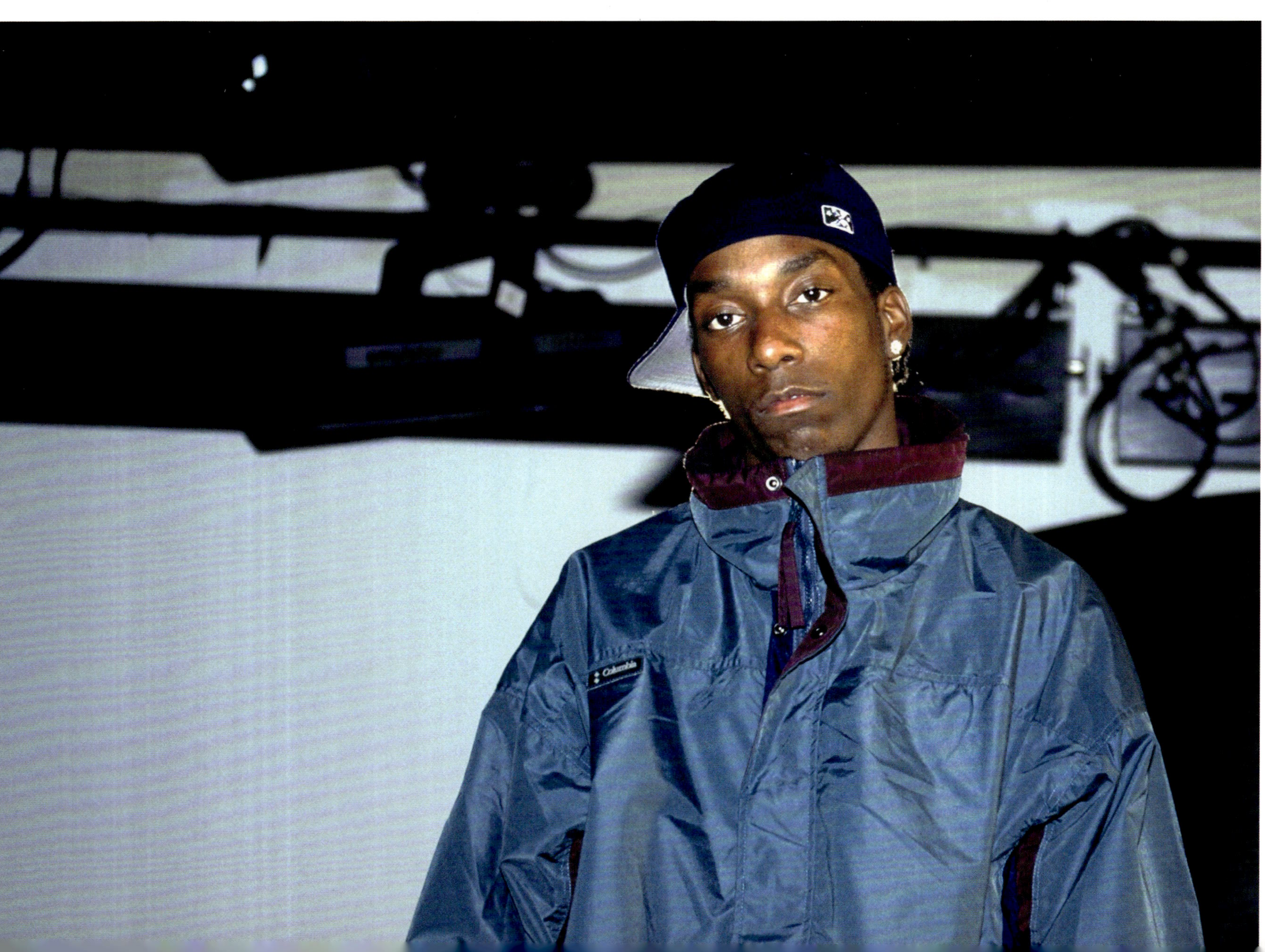

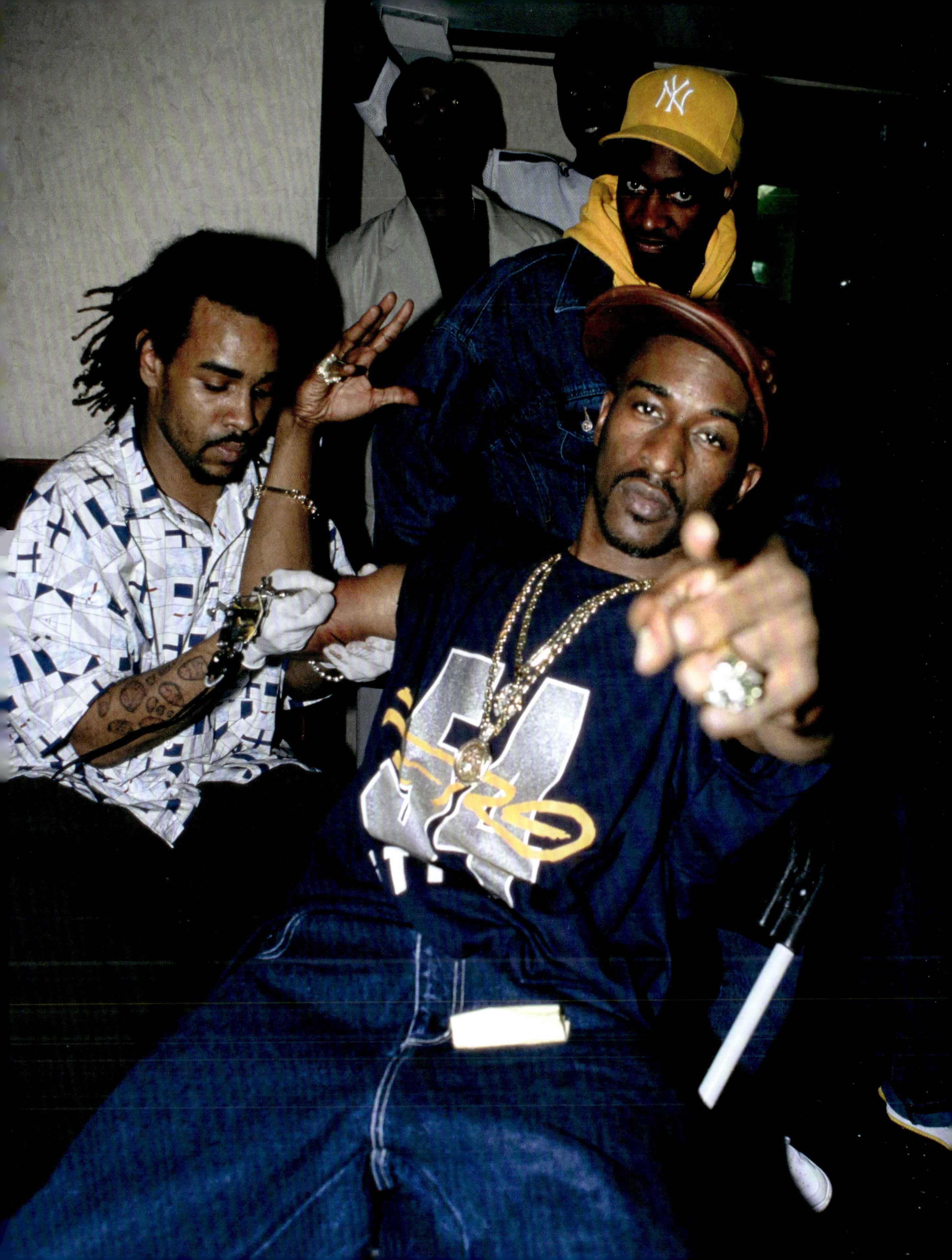

p.208 Goodie Mob (The Good Die Young, Mostly Over Bullshit), 3rd Eye Studio, NYC, 1991. Was part of an Atlanta, Georgia, collective called The Dungeon Family, which included Outkast. Under the fun in their lyrics was coded awareness; listen carefully to "Cell Therapy" (1995) to hear echoes of Steve Cokely. CeeLo Green was one of the stars of this posse. If many of our conversations had been overheard we would have been wiretapped and followed, but I'm not saying that wasn't the case. I had them in my studio two or three times.

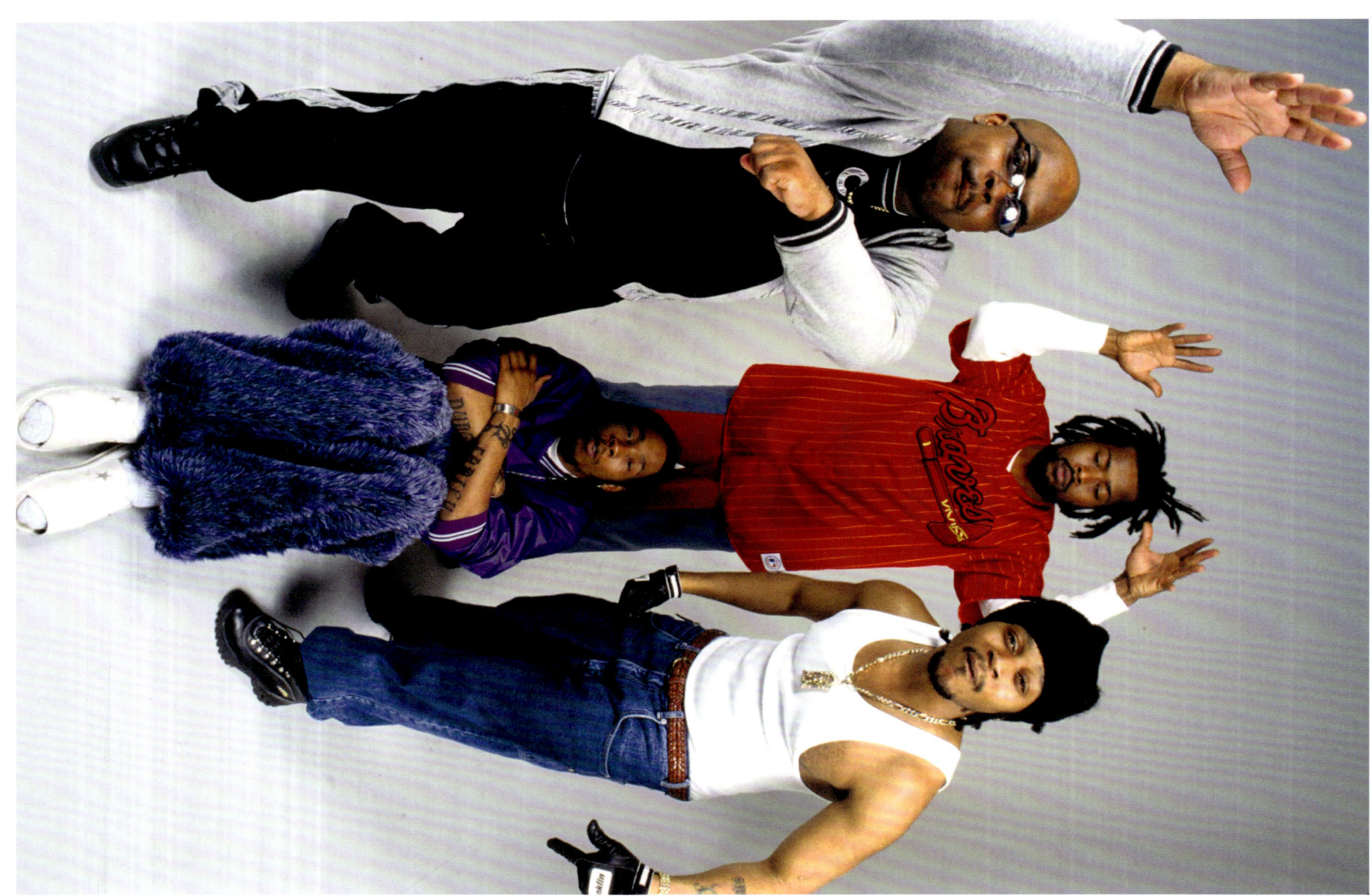

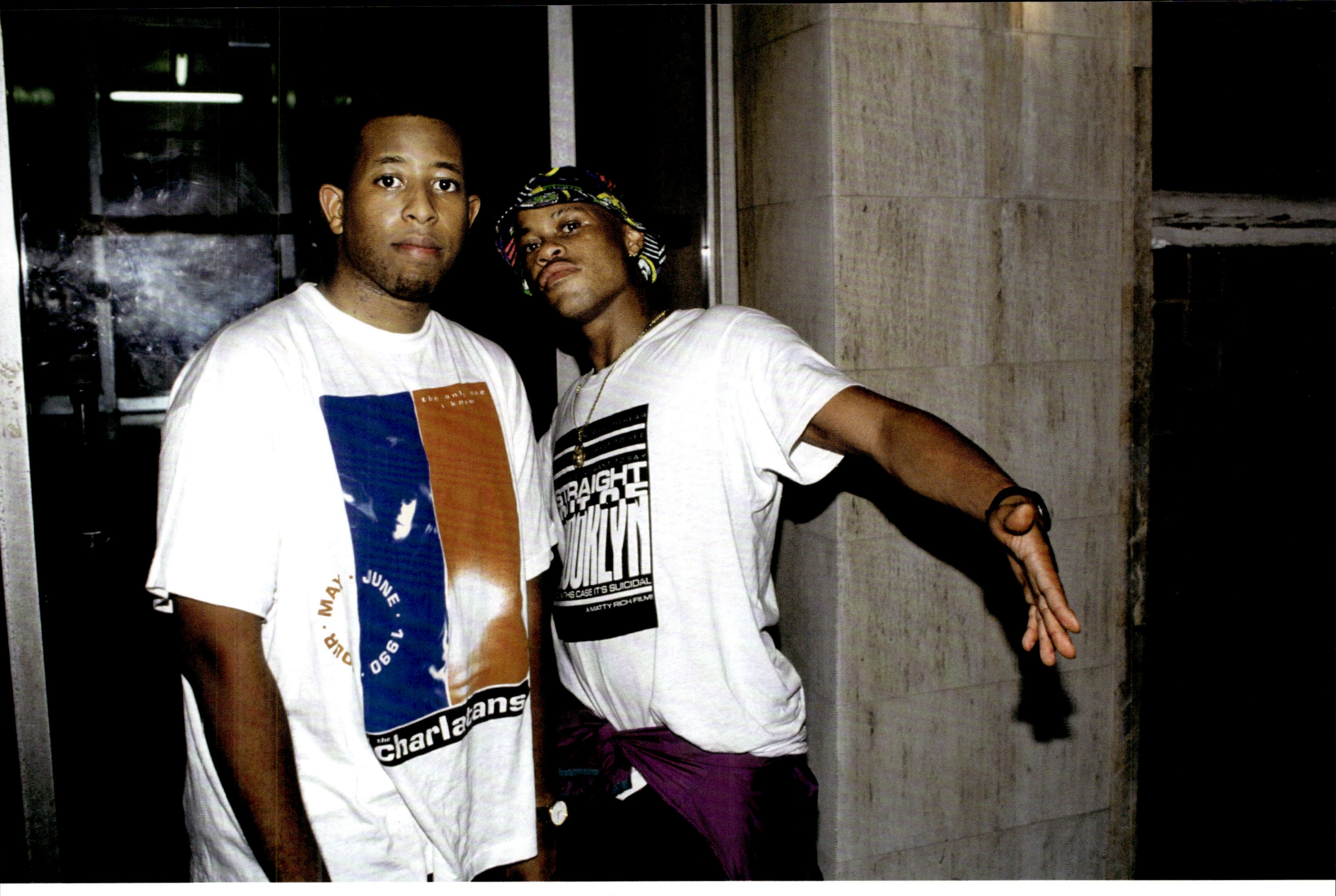

p.209 Gang Starr: DJ Premier and the late rapper Guru—Keith Edward Elam (1966-2010), NYC, early 1990s. I did a lecture with Guru a few months before he passed and I remember him hugging me tight, a sadness in his eyes, and telling me he is in a fight for his life. A friend videotaped us, but I have never seen the tape. He always called me "Uncle Ernie." Man, I miss him.

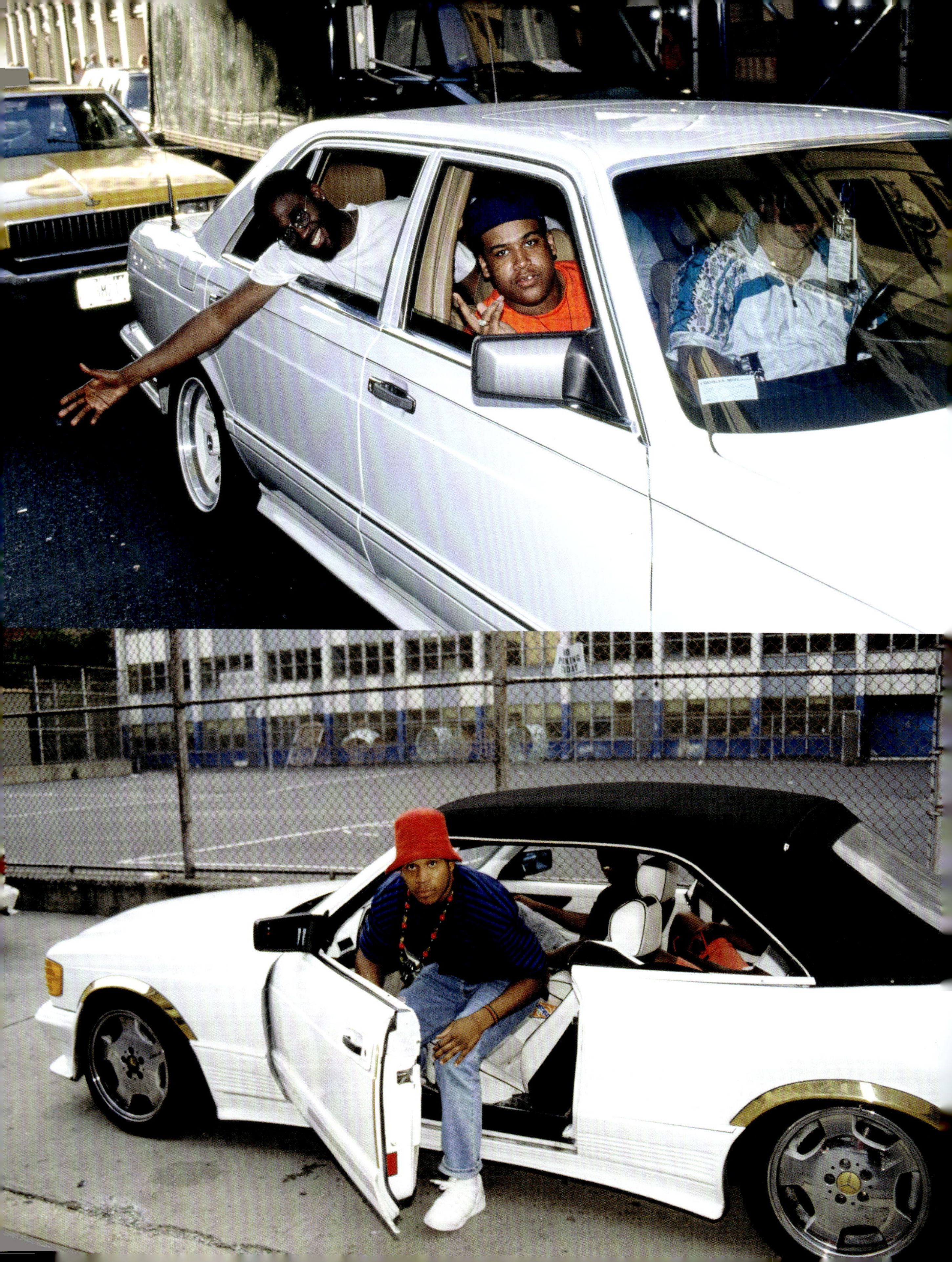

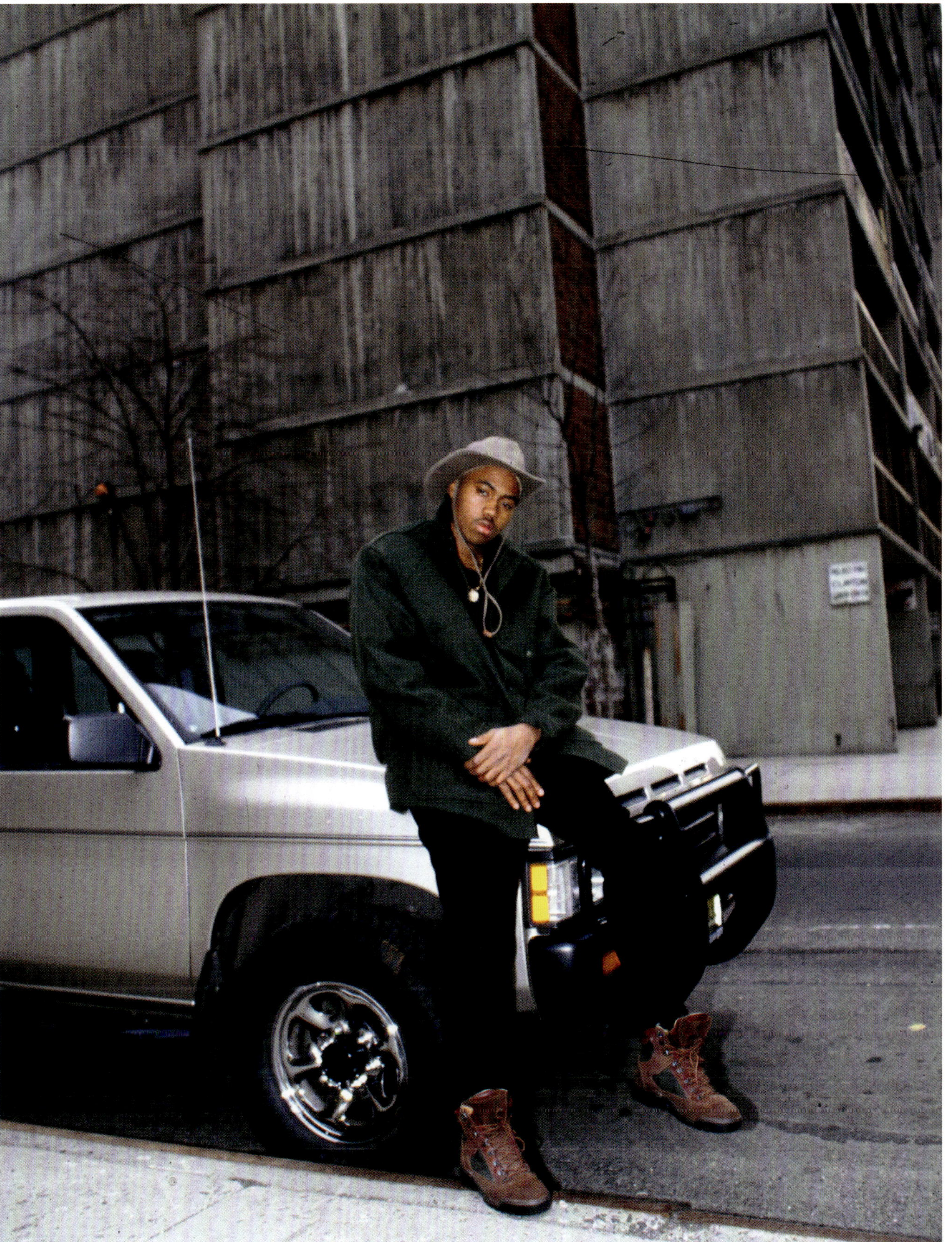

p.210 De La Soul in their hoopty, NYC, early 1990s; LL Cool J, 126th Street, Harlem, NYC, 1989; p.211 A young Nas sitting on my Pathfinder in our first of many photo shoots, NYC, 1990s.

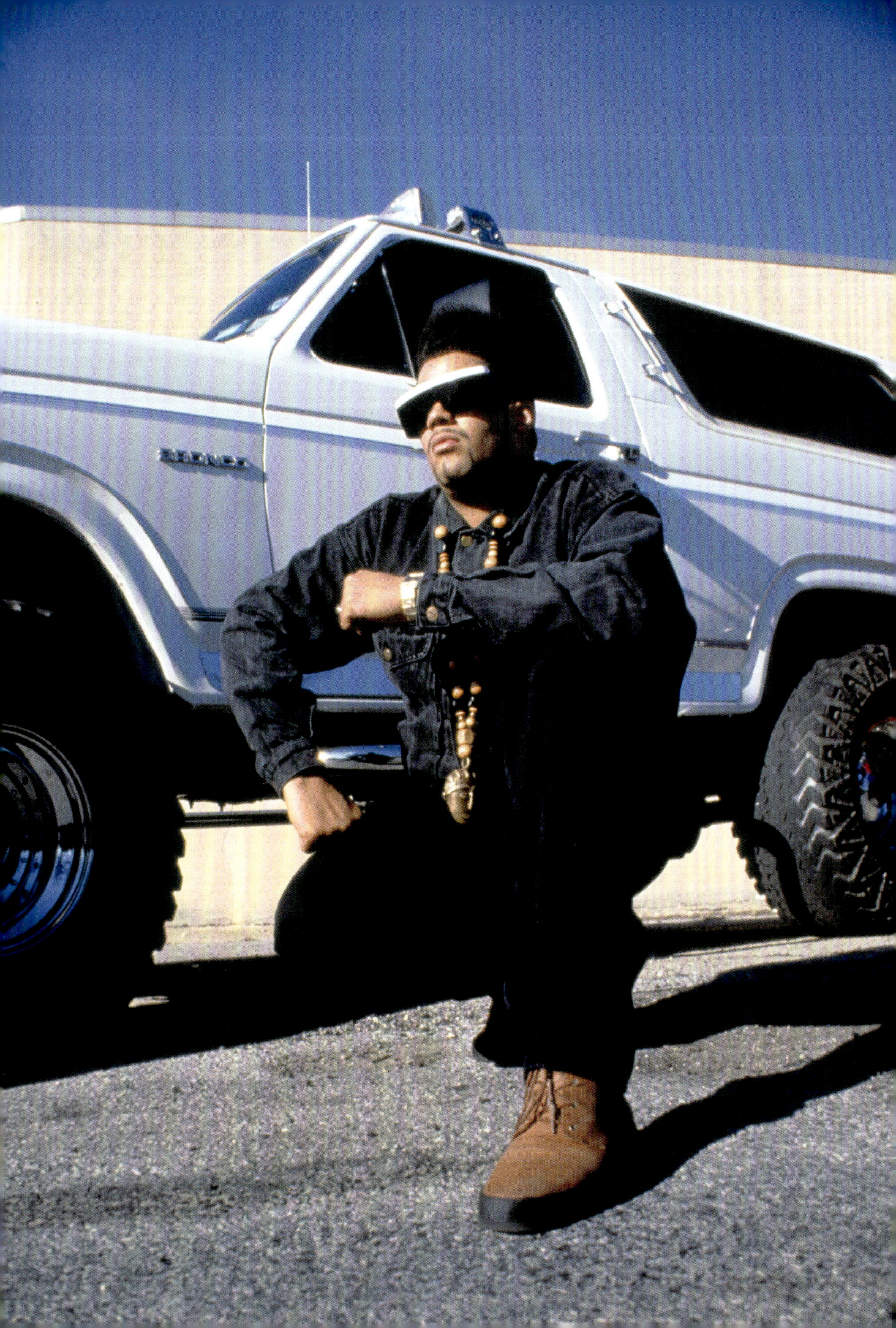
BRONCO

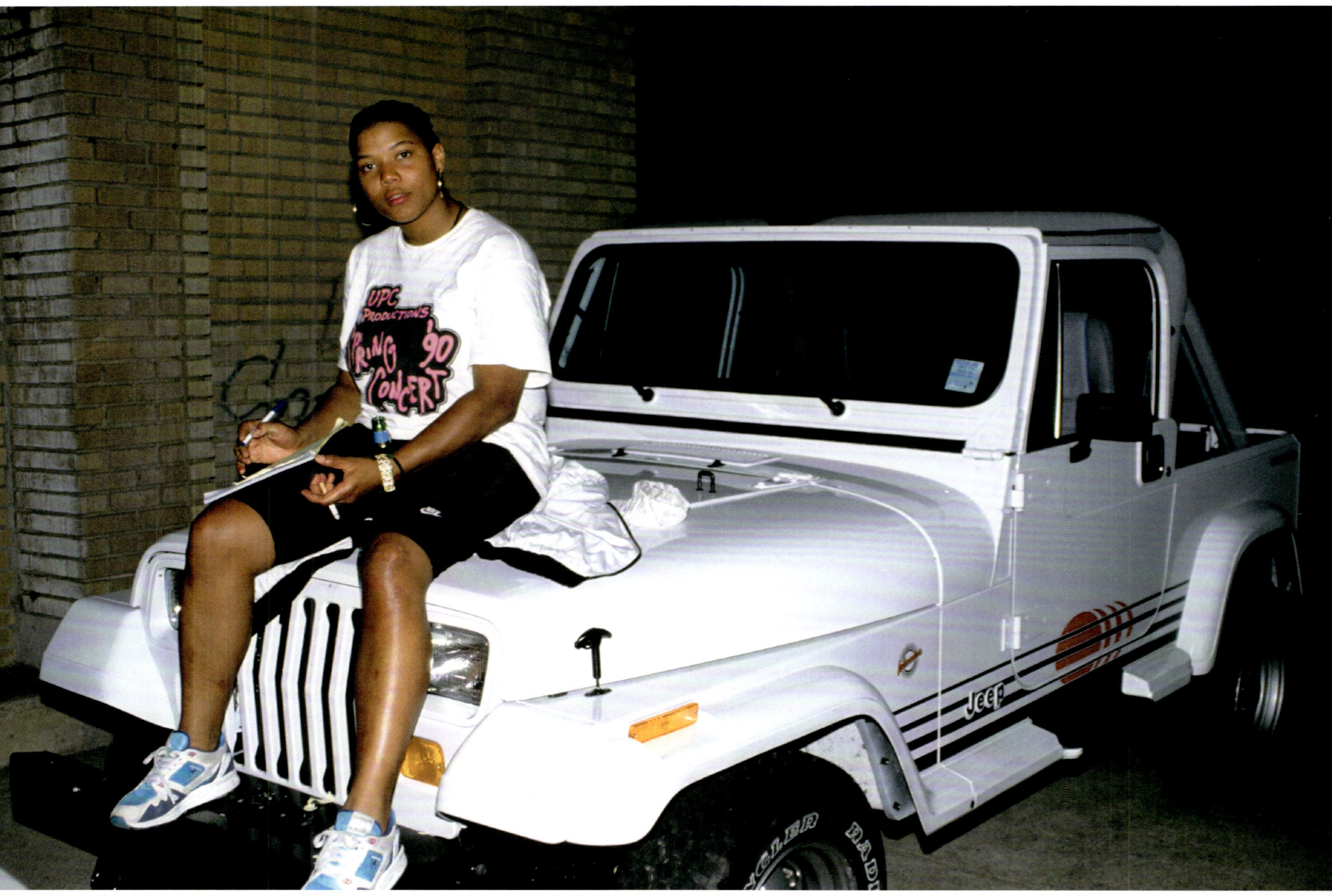

p.212 Public Enemy's DJ Terminator X posing for the cover of his album *Valley of The Jeep Beets*, Long Island, 1991.

p.213 Latifah sitting on her Jeep, writing her lyrics for *H.E.A.L. (Human Education Against Lies)*, a 1991 EP produced by KRS-One and D-Nice, Queens, NY, 1991.

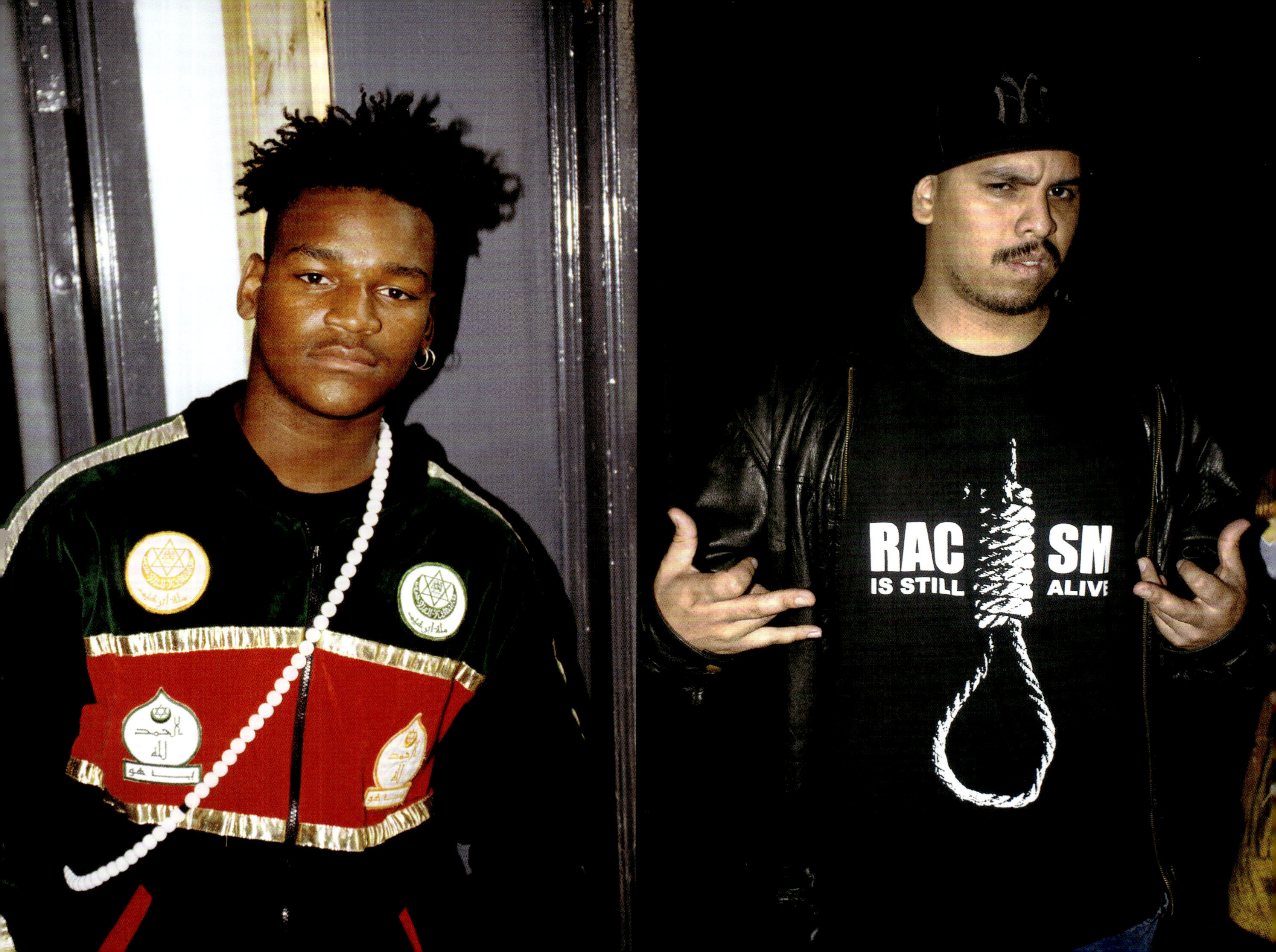
RAC SM
IS STILL ALIVE

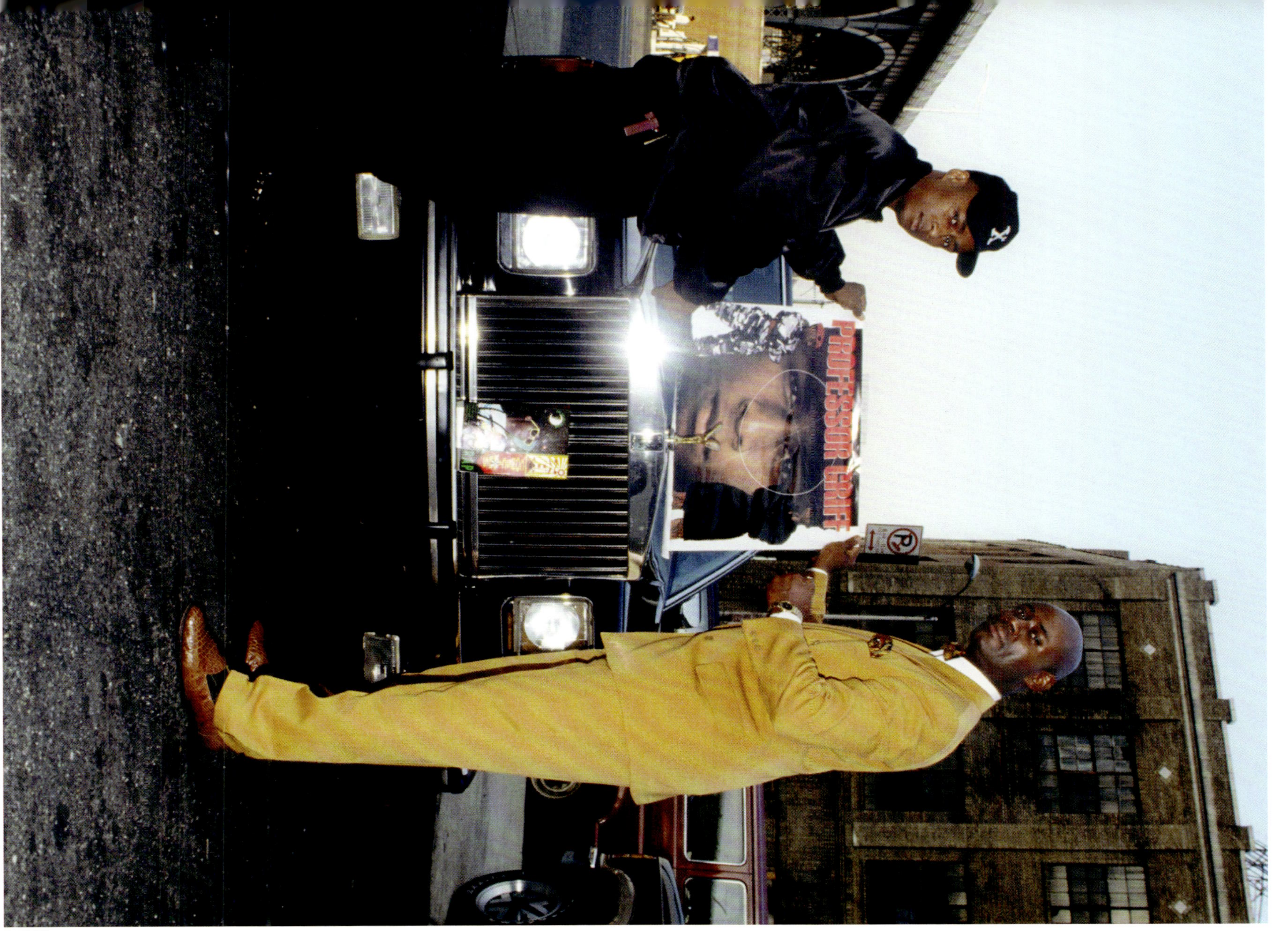

p.214 (top) Immortal Technique. Perhaps the most political, hardcore, conscious and lyrically gifted artist since The Last Poets. A friend, brother and comrade, fearless and focused. B.B. King's, NYC, 2000; (bottom) Percy Chapman aka Intelligent Hoodlum aka Tragedy aka Tragedy Kadafi, NYC, 1989; p.215 Public Enemy's Professor Griff with Minister Khalid Abdul Muhammad, Harlem, NYC, 1991 (see additional notes on page 216).

p.216 Lesane Parish Crooks, aka Tupac Amaru Shakur (1971-1996), NYC, 1991. I ran into him in the hallway of Madison Square Garden and did an impromptu photo session. I had met and photographed him before in Virginia when he was with Digital Underground; p.217 Tupac Shakur, Del the Funky Homosapien, Prince Paul and an unidentified associate in front of The Village Gate after Yo-Yo's Birthday Party. Greenwich Village, NYC early 1990's.

Notes to page 215:

Minister Khalid Abdul Muhammad (1948-2001) holding the album cover of Professor Griff's album *Kao's II Wiz*7*Dome* one early Sunday morning at The Cotton Club, Harlem. Muhammad's unforgettable intro on Public Enemy's "Night Of The Living Baseheads" (1988) is part of the reason the song is a hip-hop masterpiece: *Have you forgotten that once we were brought here, we were robbed of our name, robbed of our language. We lost our religion, our culture, our god...and many of us, by the way we act, we even lost our minds.*

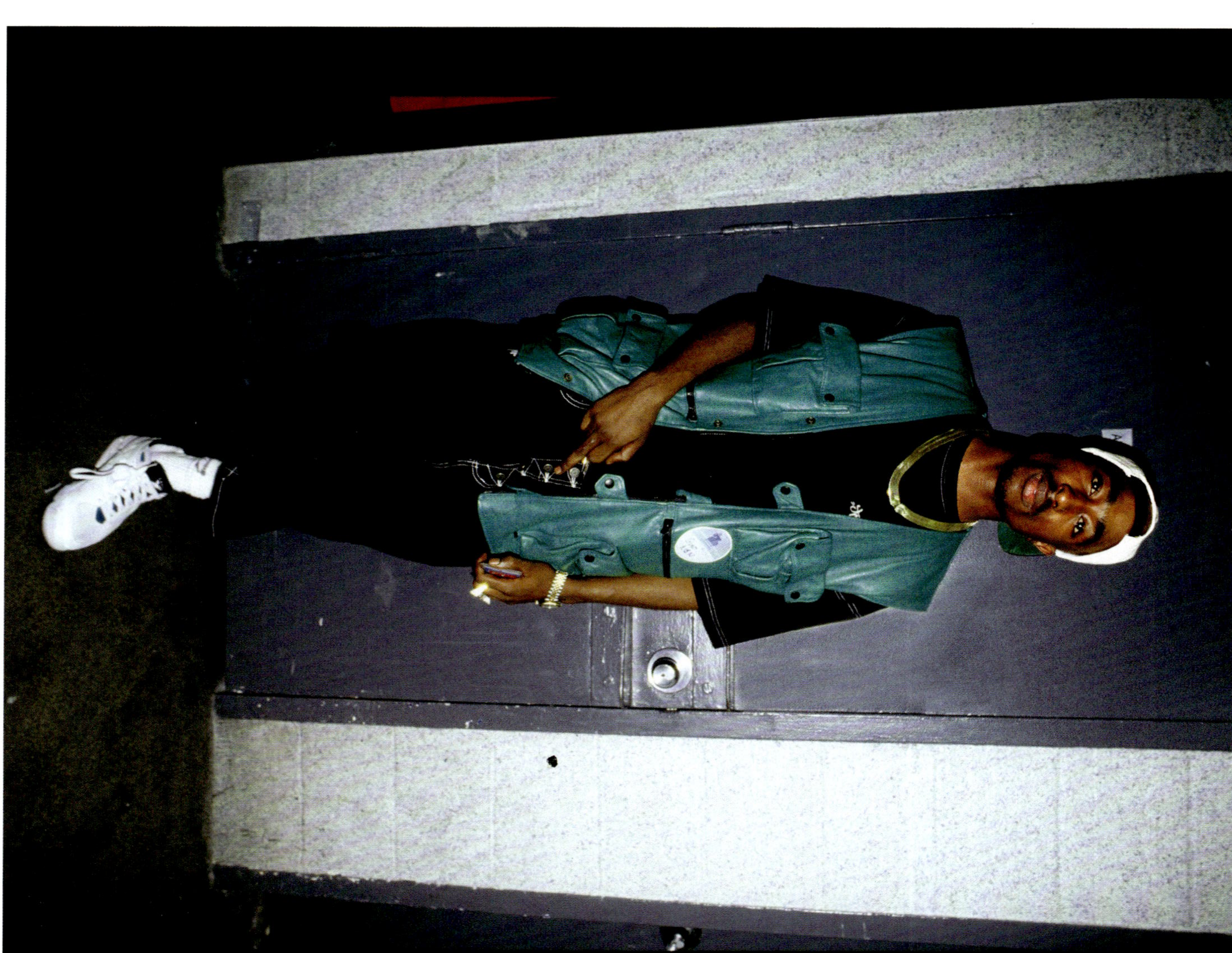

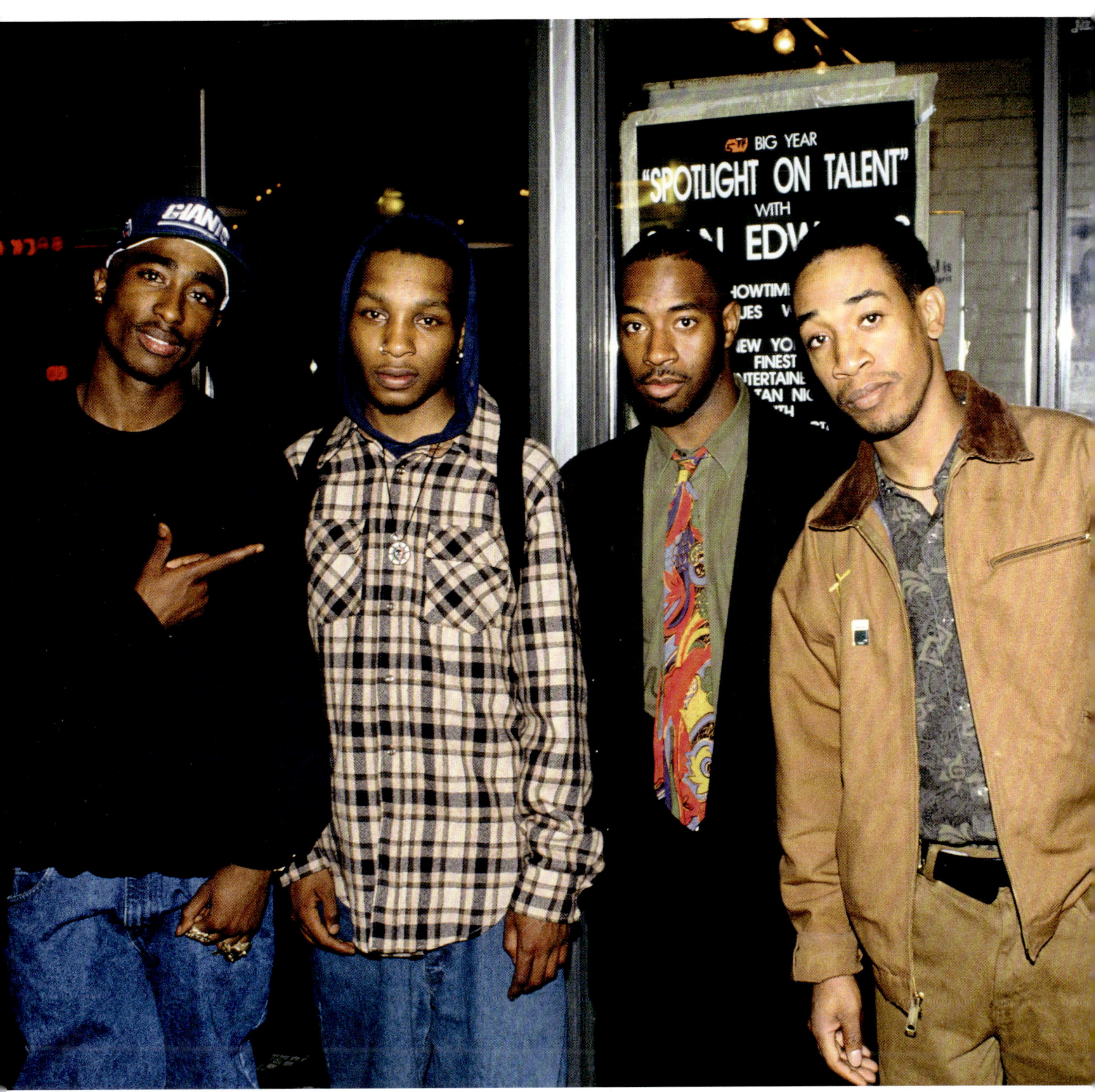
BIG YEAR
"SPOTLIGHT ON TALENT"
WITH
FINEST

p.218 Del the Funky Homosapien, NYC, 1990s.

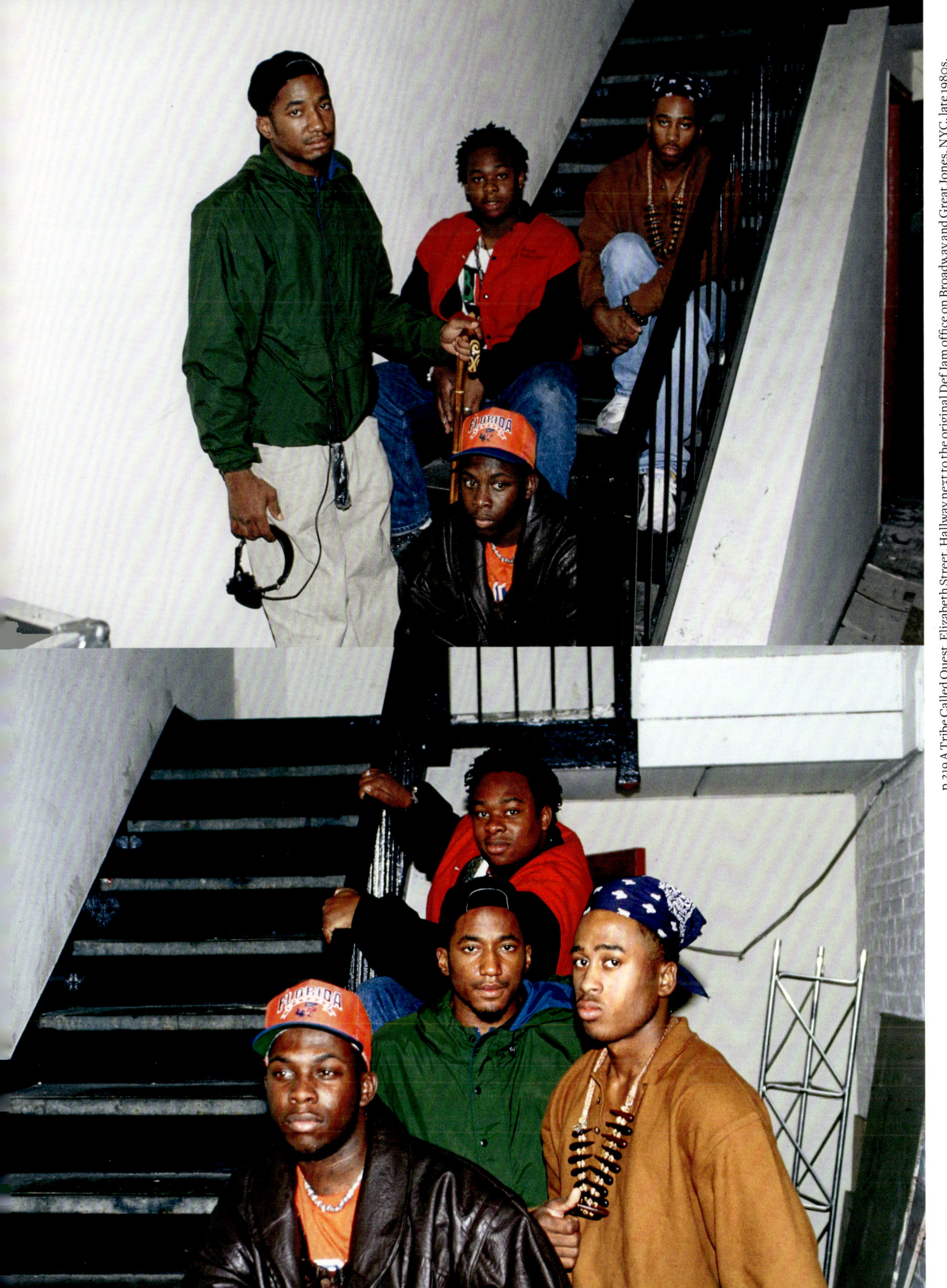

p.219 A Tribe Called Quest. Elizabeth Street, Hallway next to the original Def Jam office on Broadway and Great Jones, NYC, late 1980s.

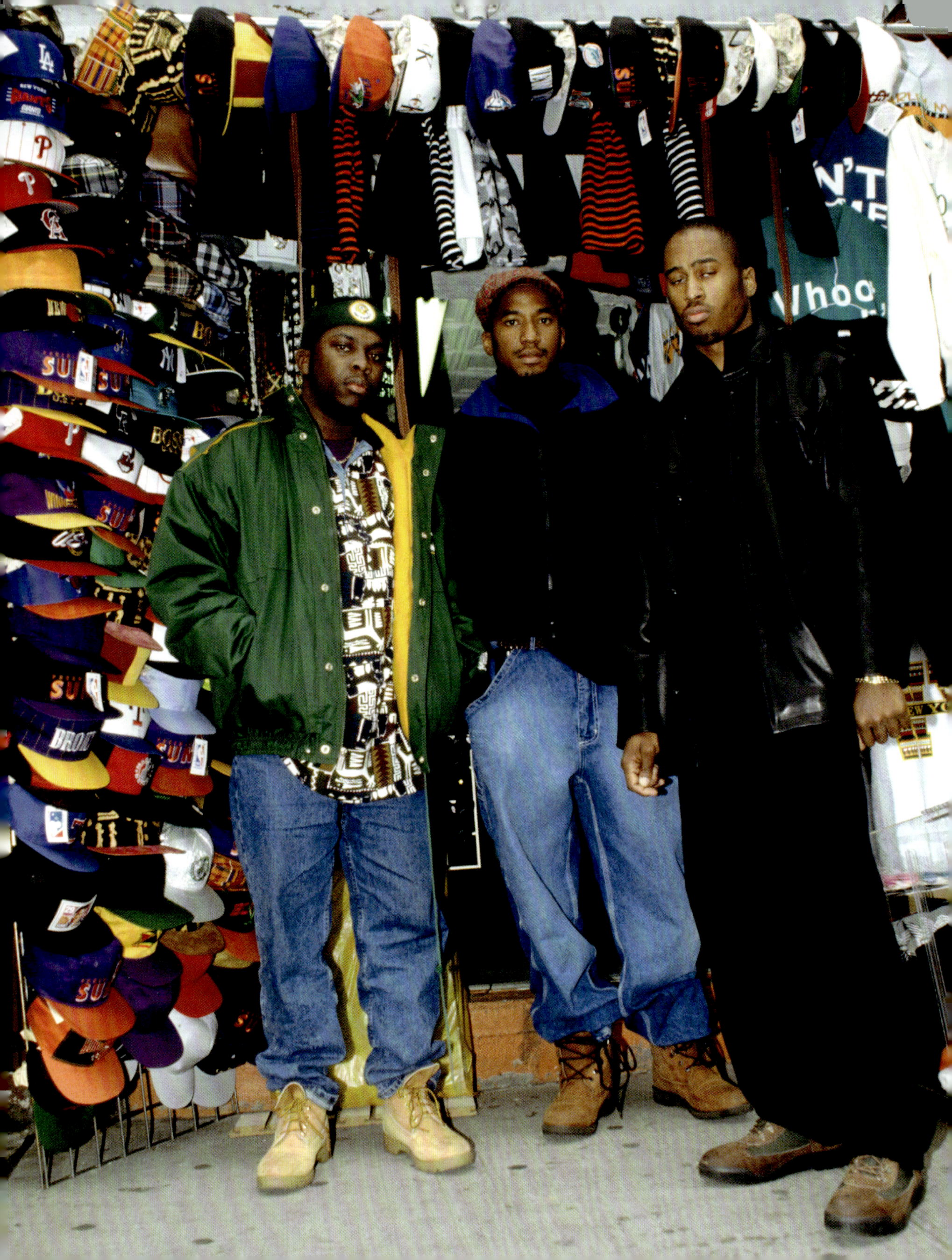
LA
Whoo,

p.220-221 A Tribe Called Quest, West 25th Street near their label, Jive Records, NYC, early 1990s.

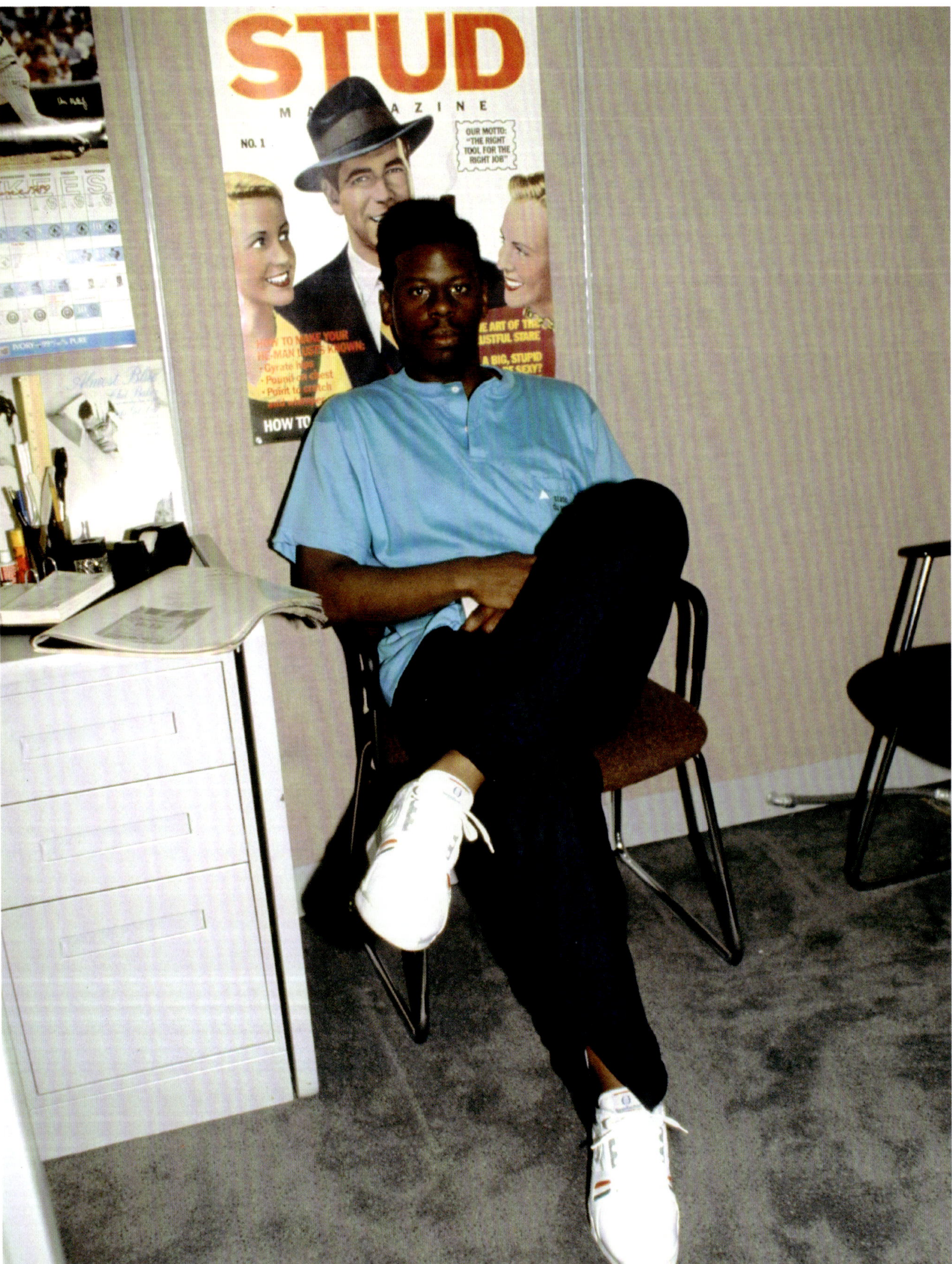

p.222 Schoolly D, at Jive Records, NYC, 1986; p.223 Flava Flav, Jungle Brothers, Schoolly D and Hank Shocklee, NYC, 2000.

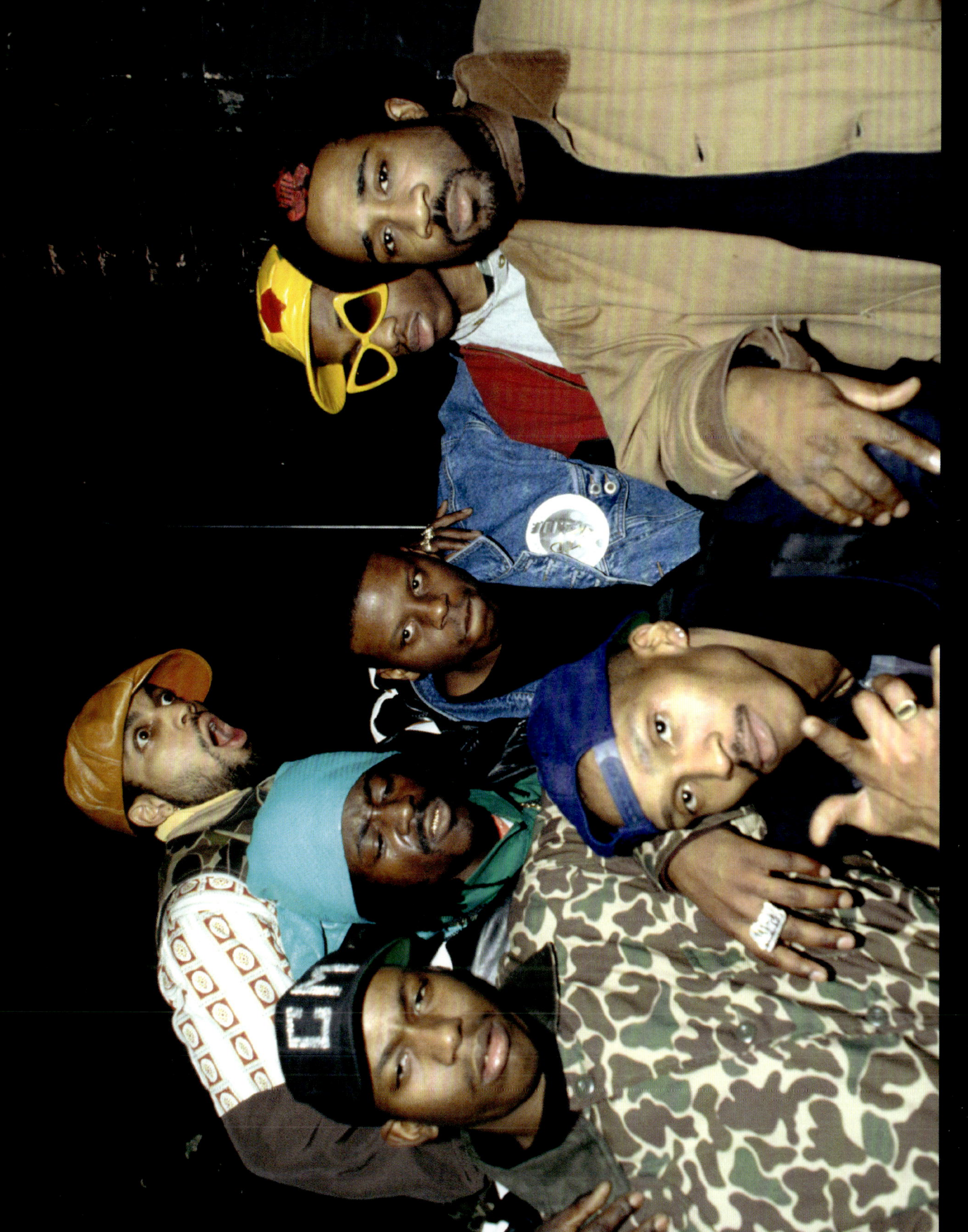

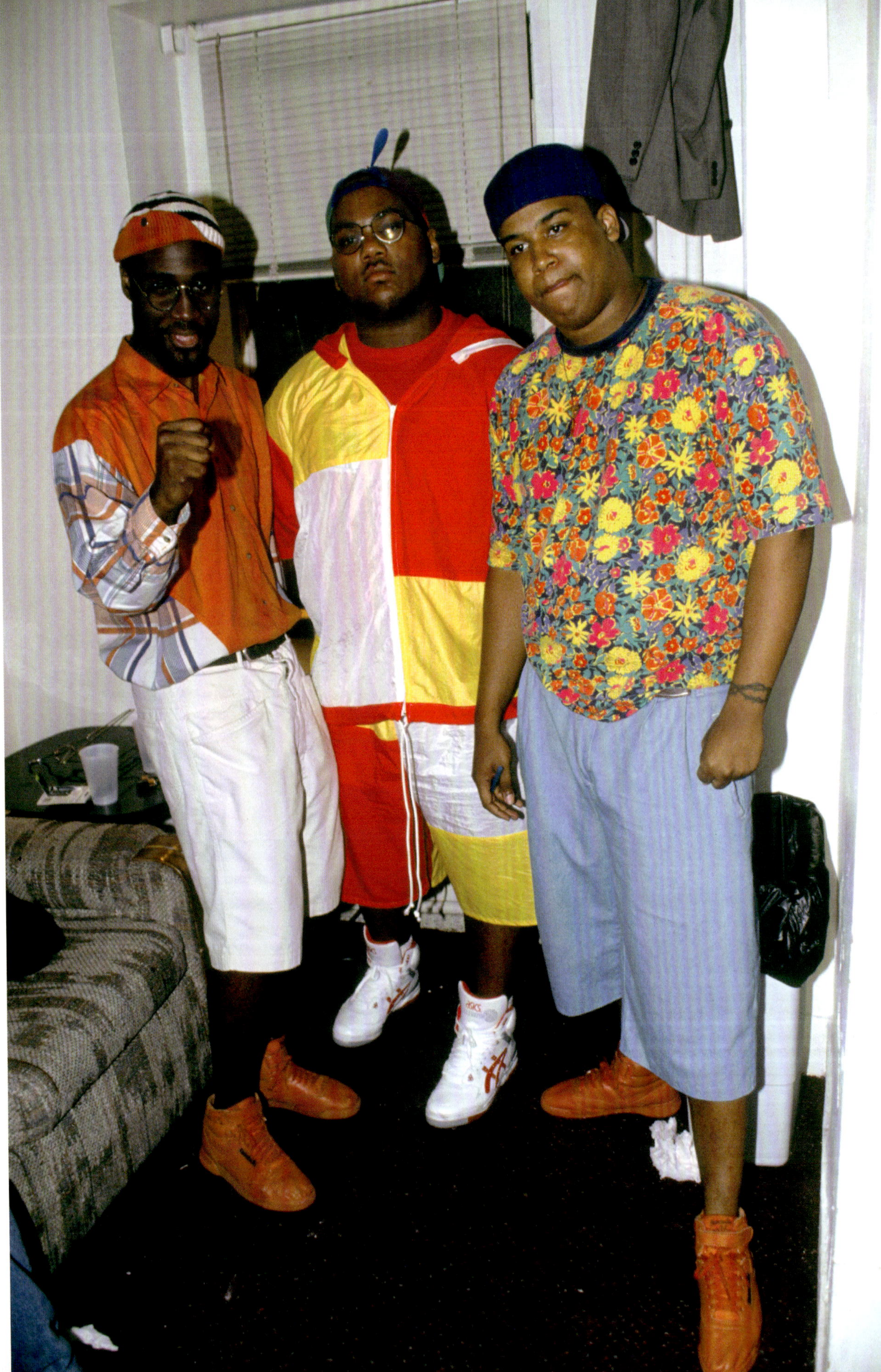

p.224 De La Soul, The Ritz, NYC, early 1990s. p.225 De La Soul, video shoot for "All Good?" (ft. Chaka Khan) which was a parody of *Car Wash* (1976). I was given a cameo in the video. New Jersey, 1999.
p.226 (top) Chaka Khan w Posdnous of De La Soul on the video shoot for "All Good?," New Jersey, 1999; (bottom) Erykah Badu and Isaac Hayes, NYC, 1999.
p.227 (top) BWP (Bitches With Problems), Dakota Studio, NYC, 1991; Brandy and Lil' Kim, NYC, 2000.

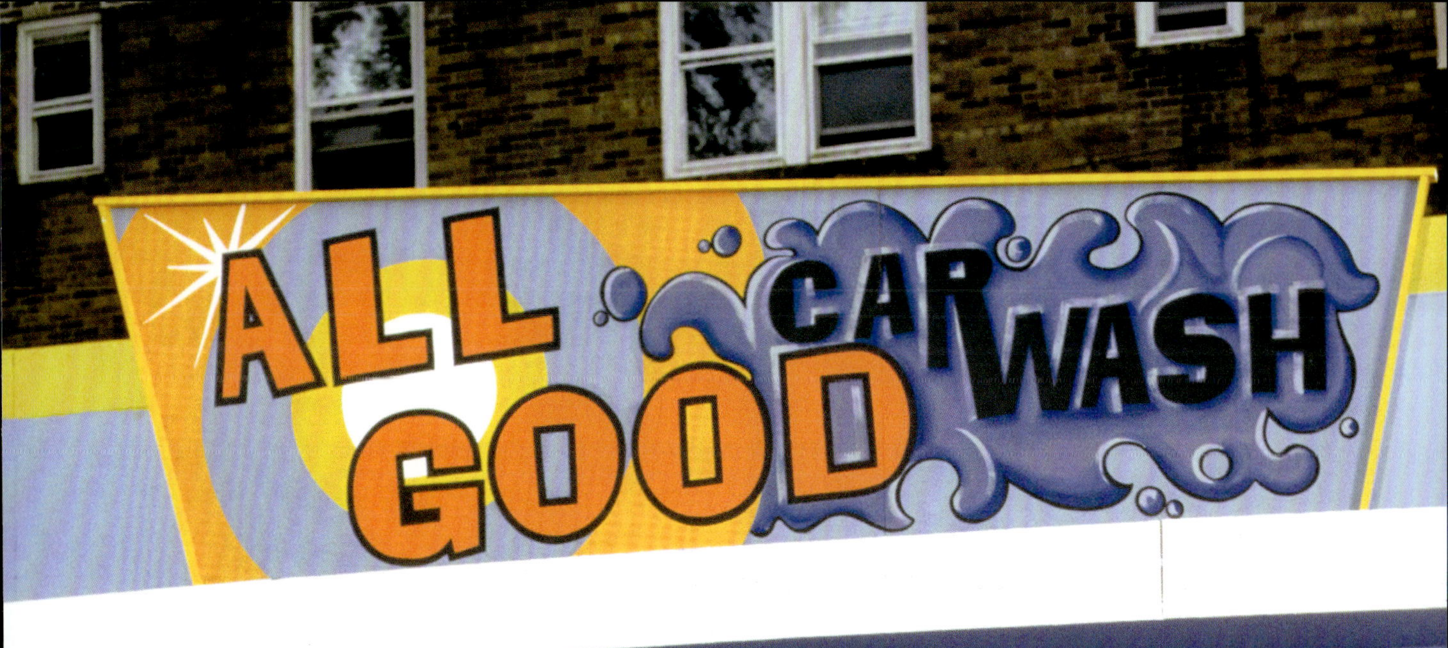
ALL GOOD
CAR WASH
322
OPEN

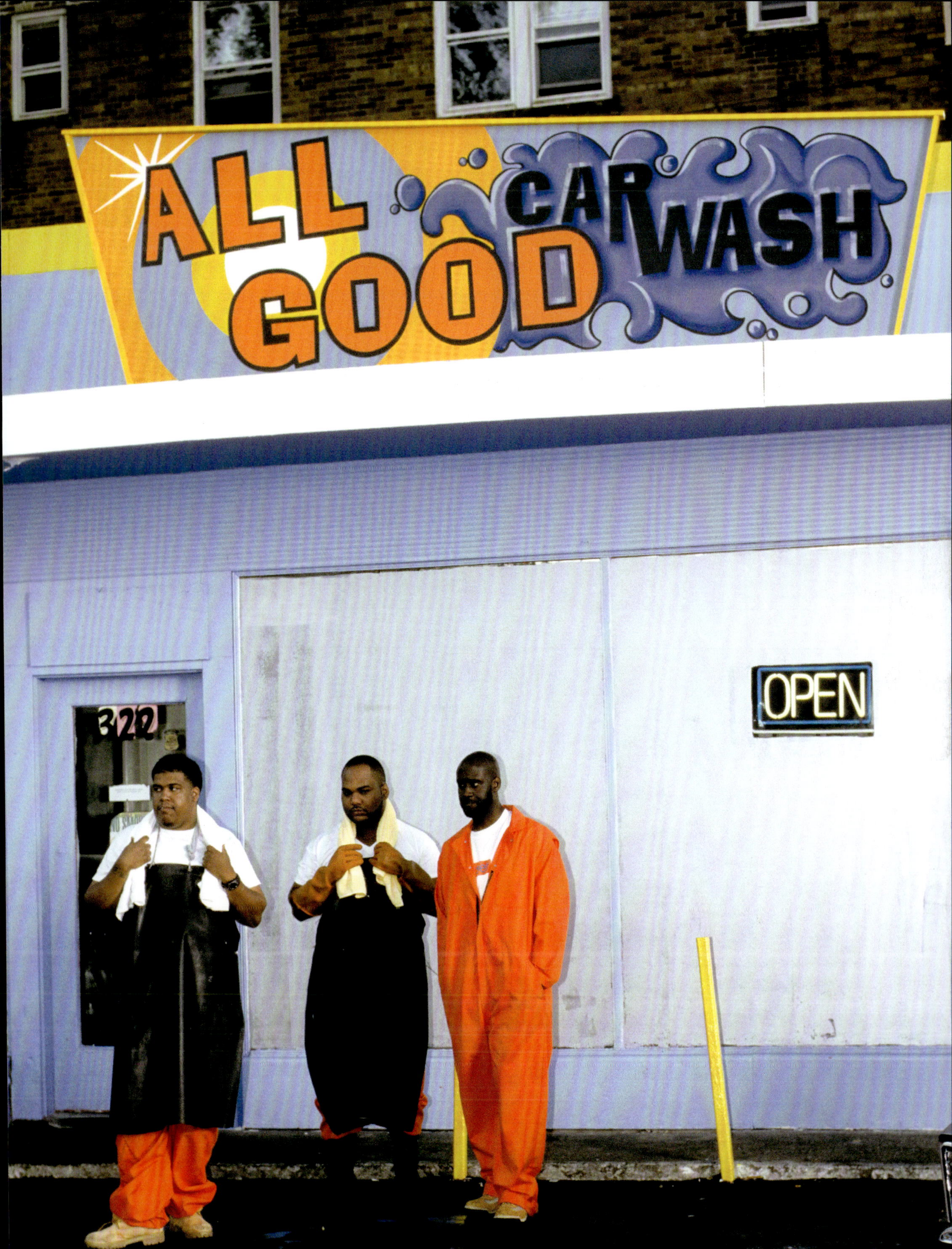

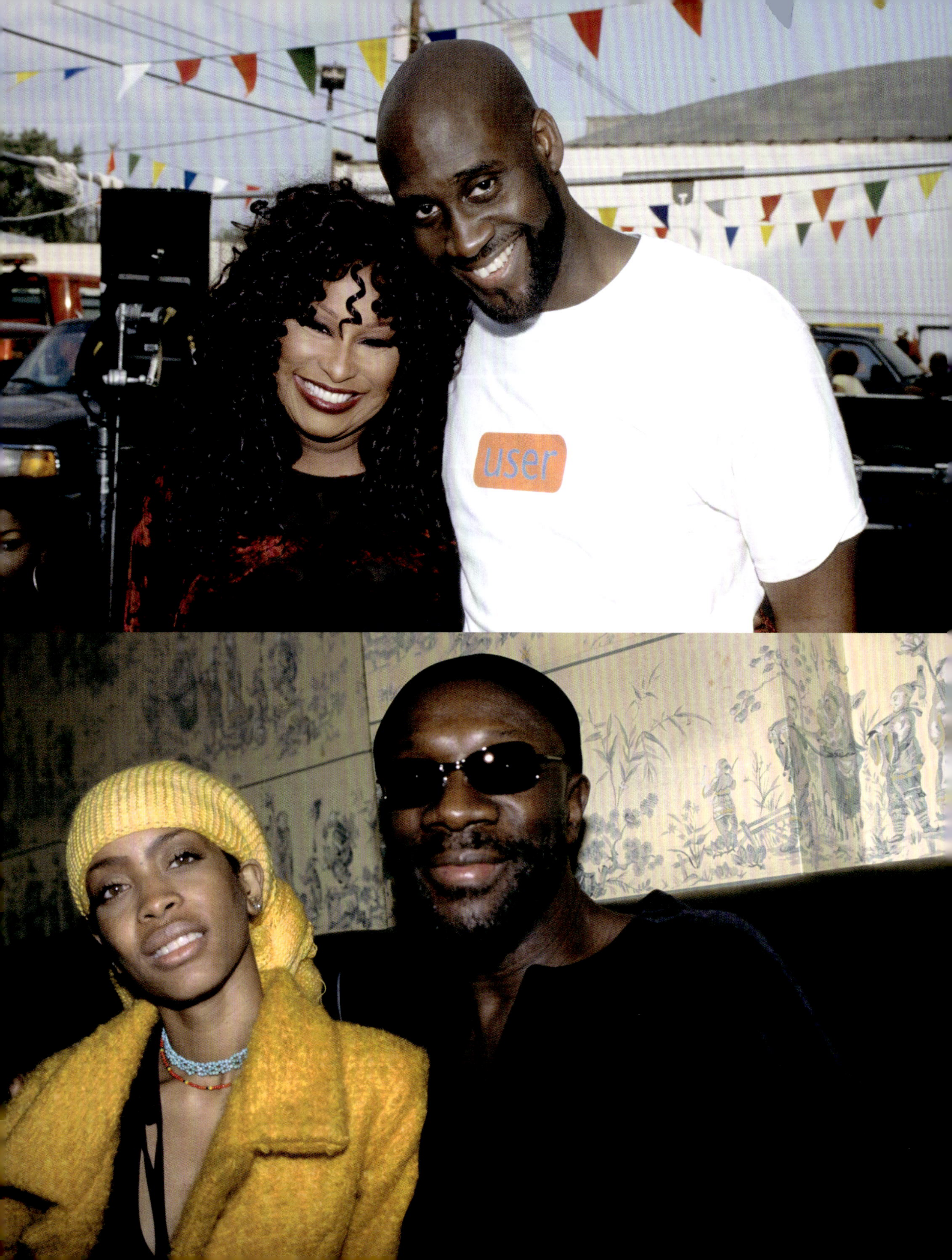
user

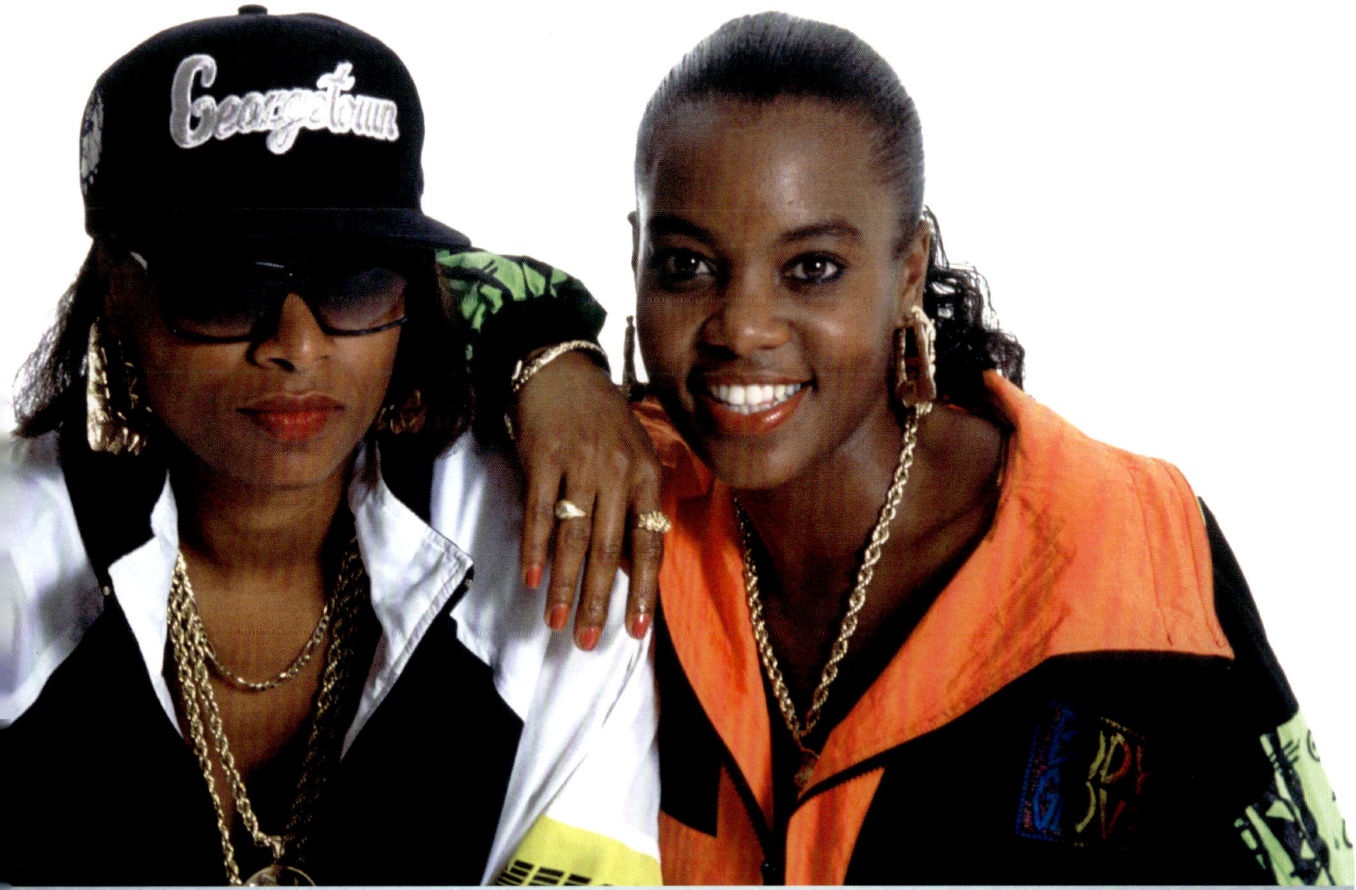

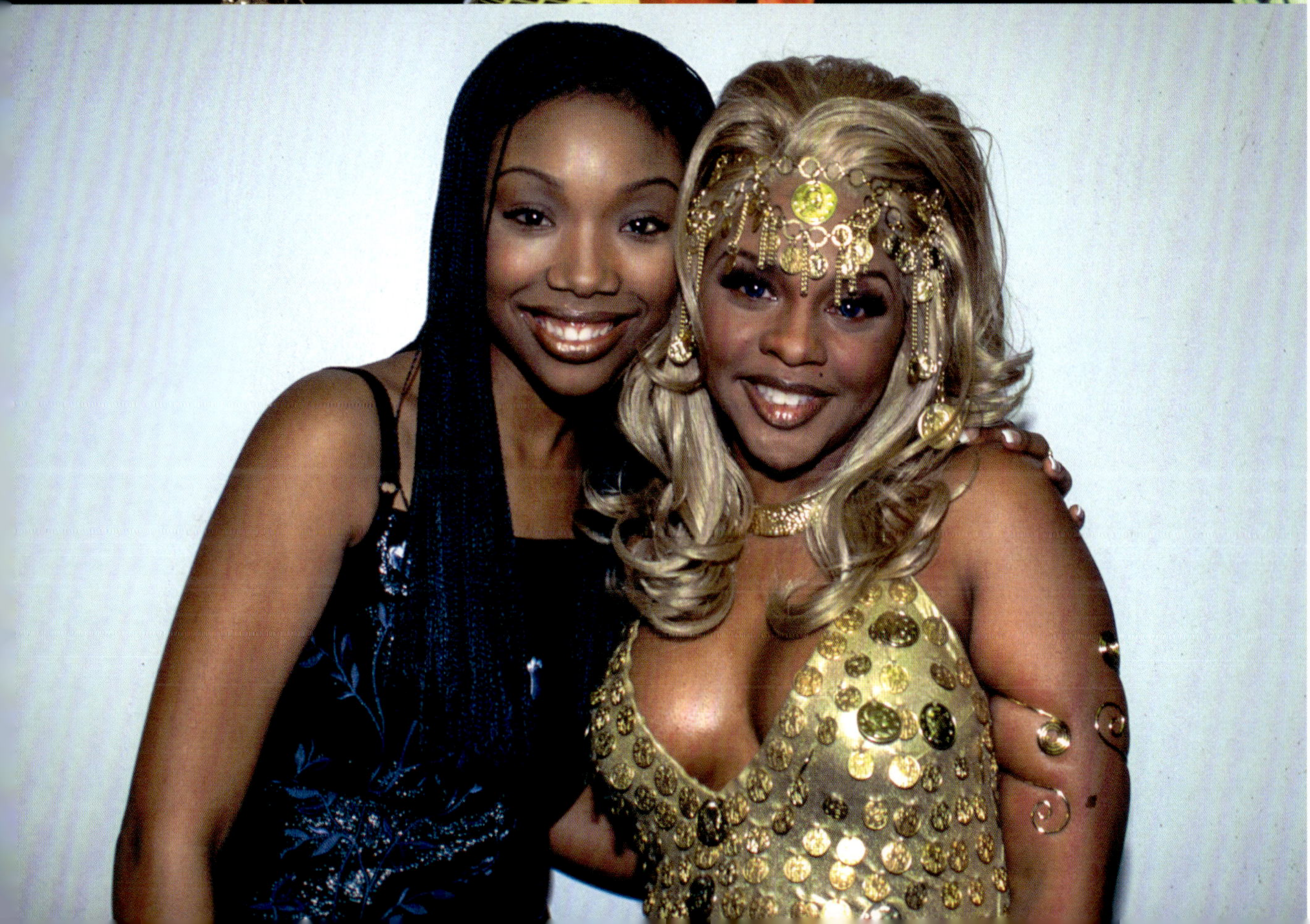

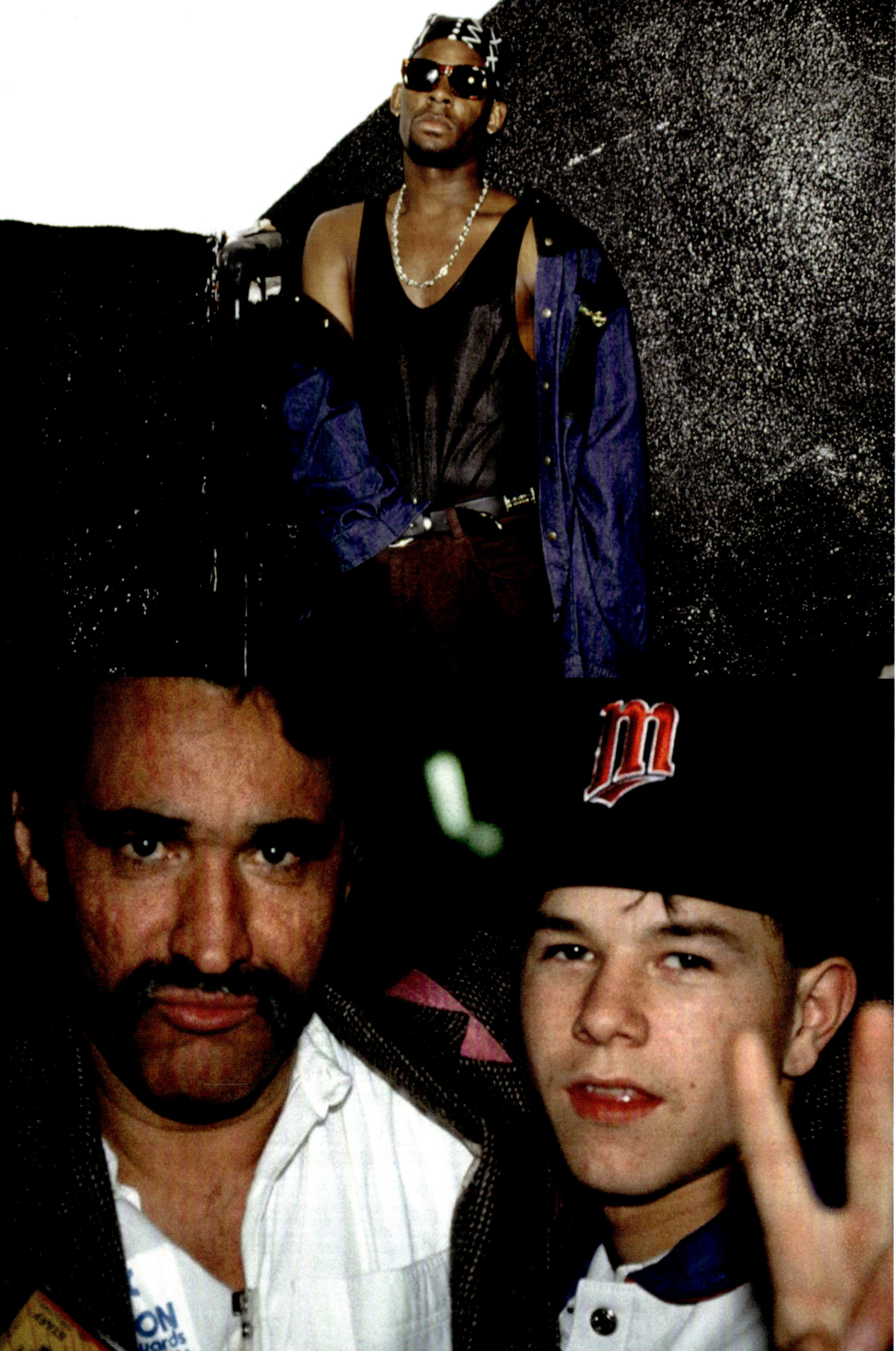

p.228 (top) R. Kelly playing pocket pool on the staircase of the Apollo Theatre, Harlem, NYC, early 1990s; (bottom) Ernie selfie with Marky Mark, Westbury Music Fair, New York, 1986.

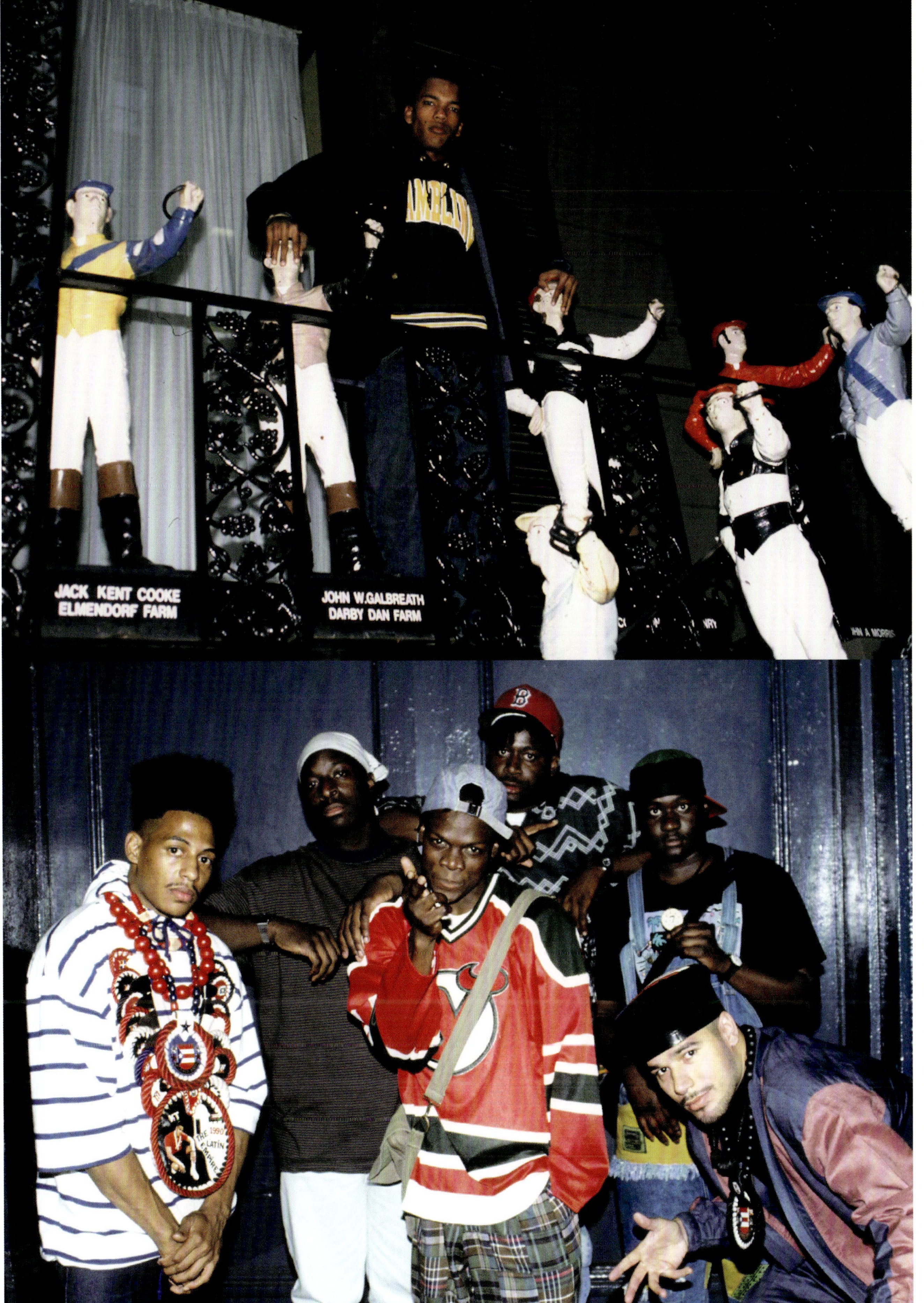

p.229 (top) Kam on balcony of the 21 Club, NYC, 1991. Making a parody of the usually black lawn jockeys by mushing the white lawn jockeys; (bottom) Latin Empire with Poor Righteous Teachers, Newark, NJ, 1990s.

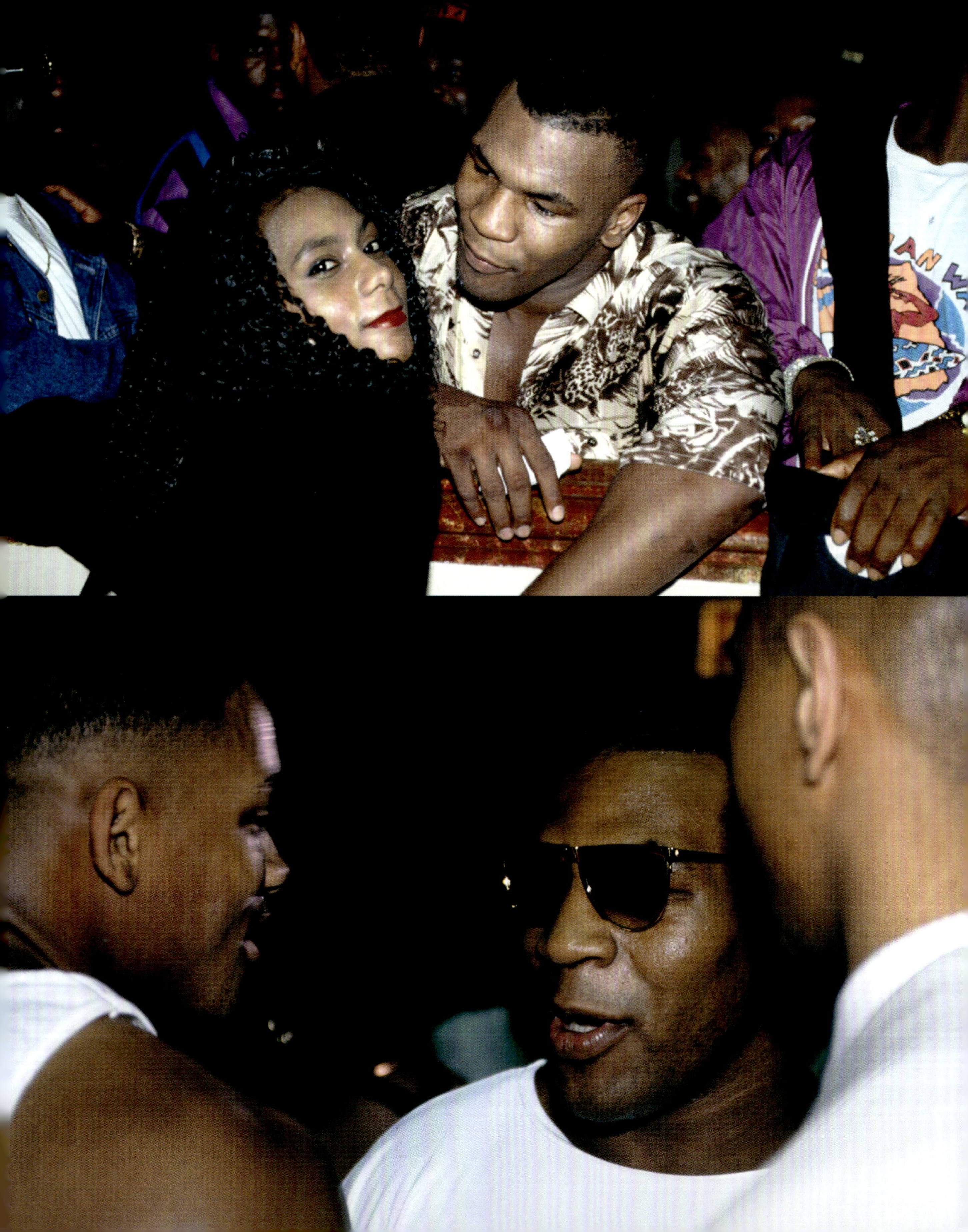

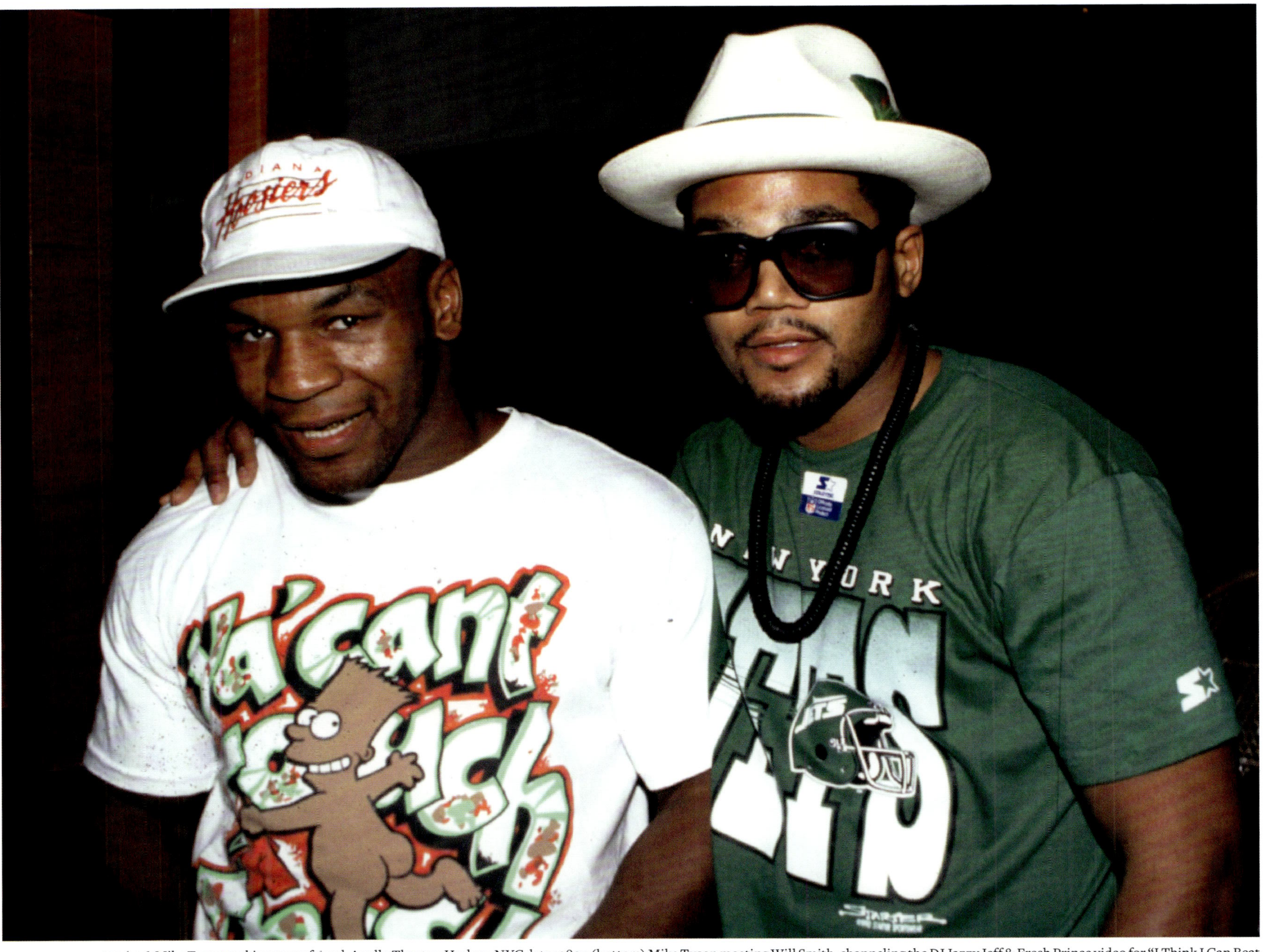

p.230 (top) Mike Tyson making a new friend, Apollo Theatre, Harlem, NYC, late 1980s; (bottom) Mike Tyson meeting Will Smith, channeling the DJ Jazzy Jeff & Fresh Prince video for "I Think I Can Beat Mike Tyson," Mark Jackson Charity Basketball Game, Queens, NY, 1989; p.231 Mike Tyson and DMC, Brooklyn, NY, 1989.

p.232 Guru, DJ Premier, and Jeru Da Damaja, Brooklyn, NY, early 1990s; p.233 Bell Biv Devoe, NYC, early 1990s.

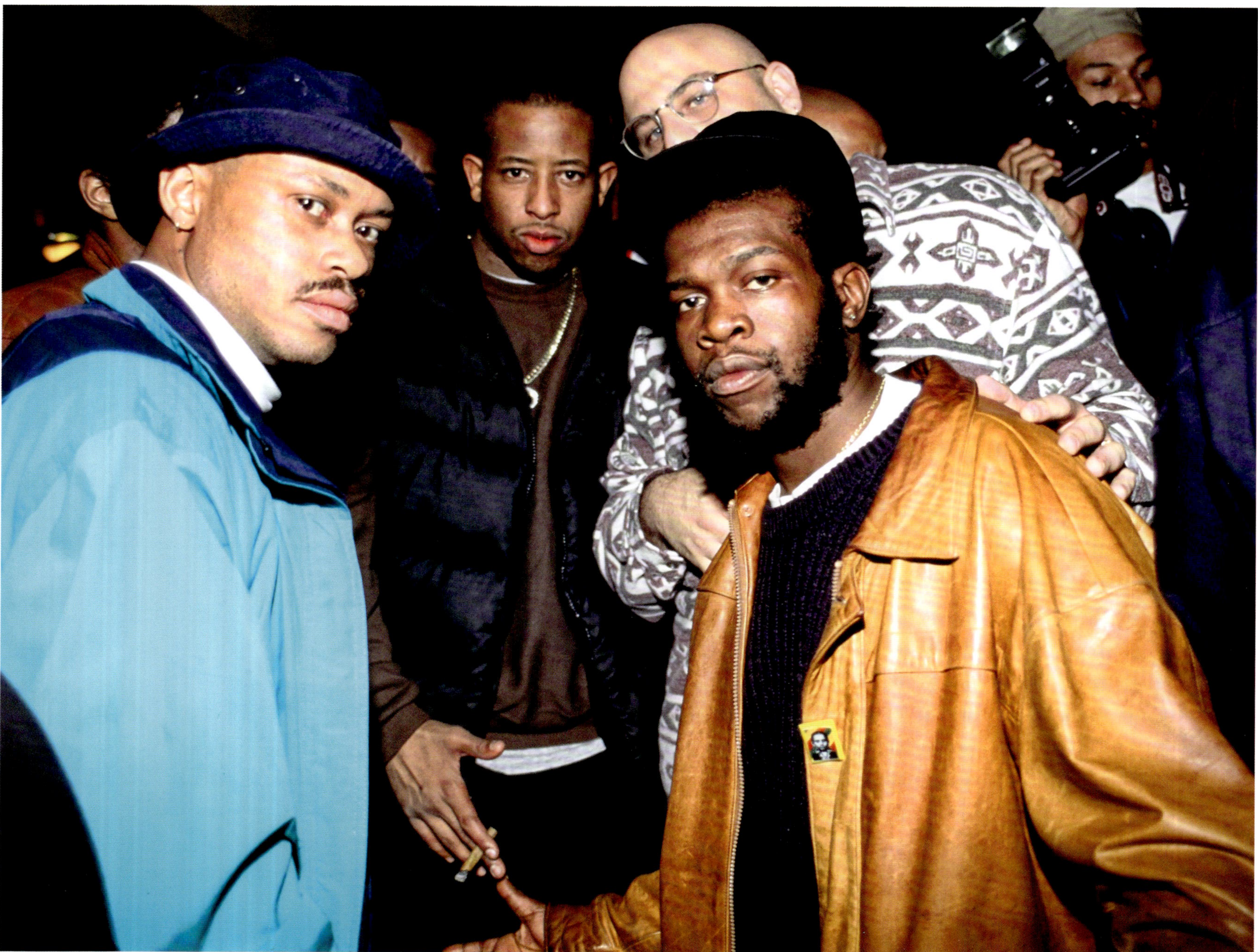

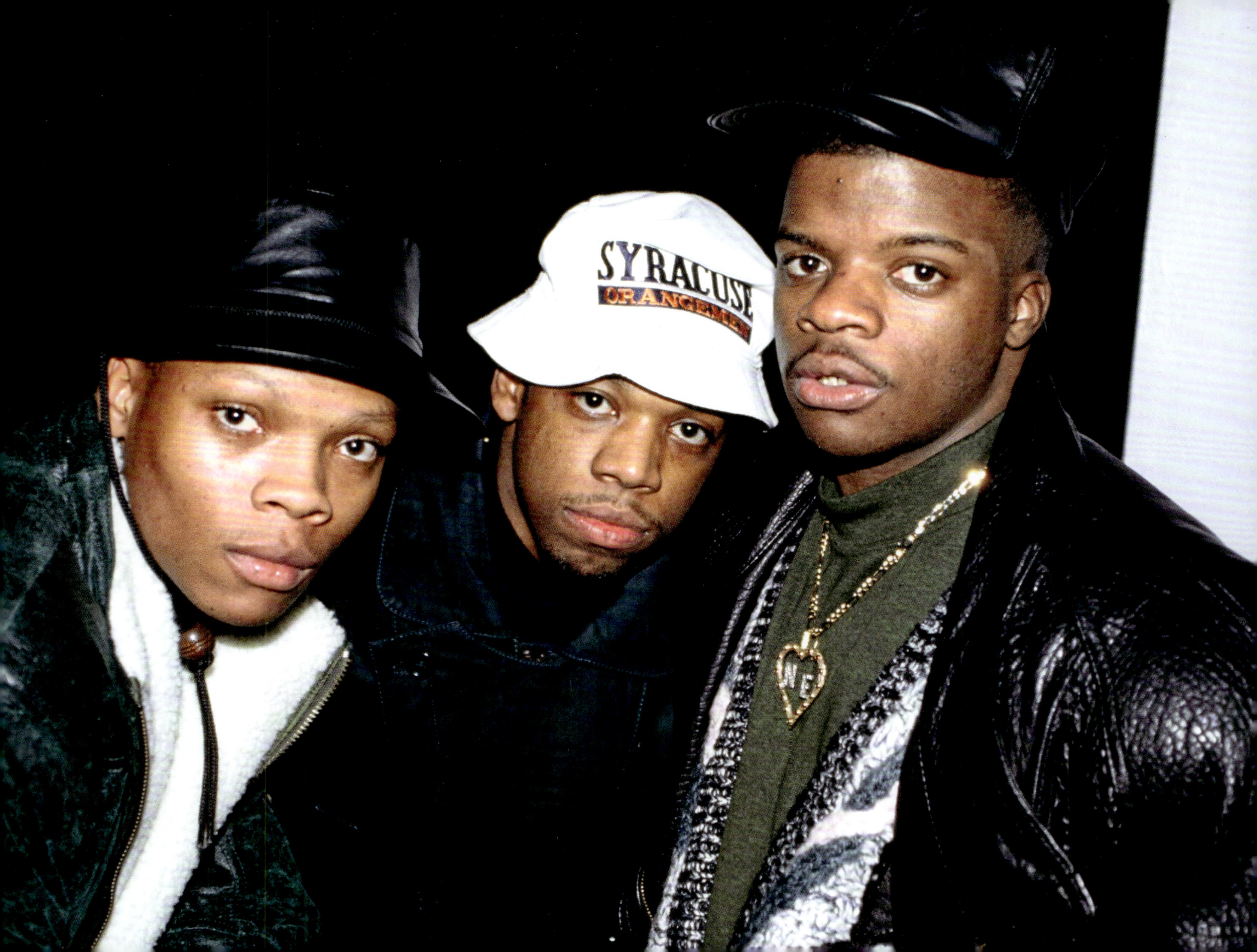
SYRACUSE
ORANGEMEN

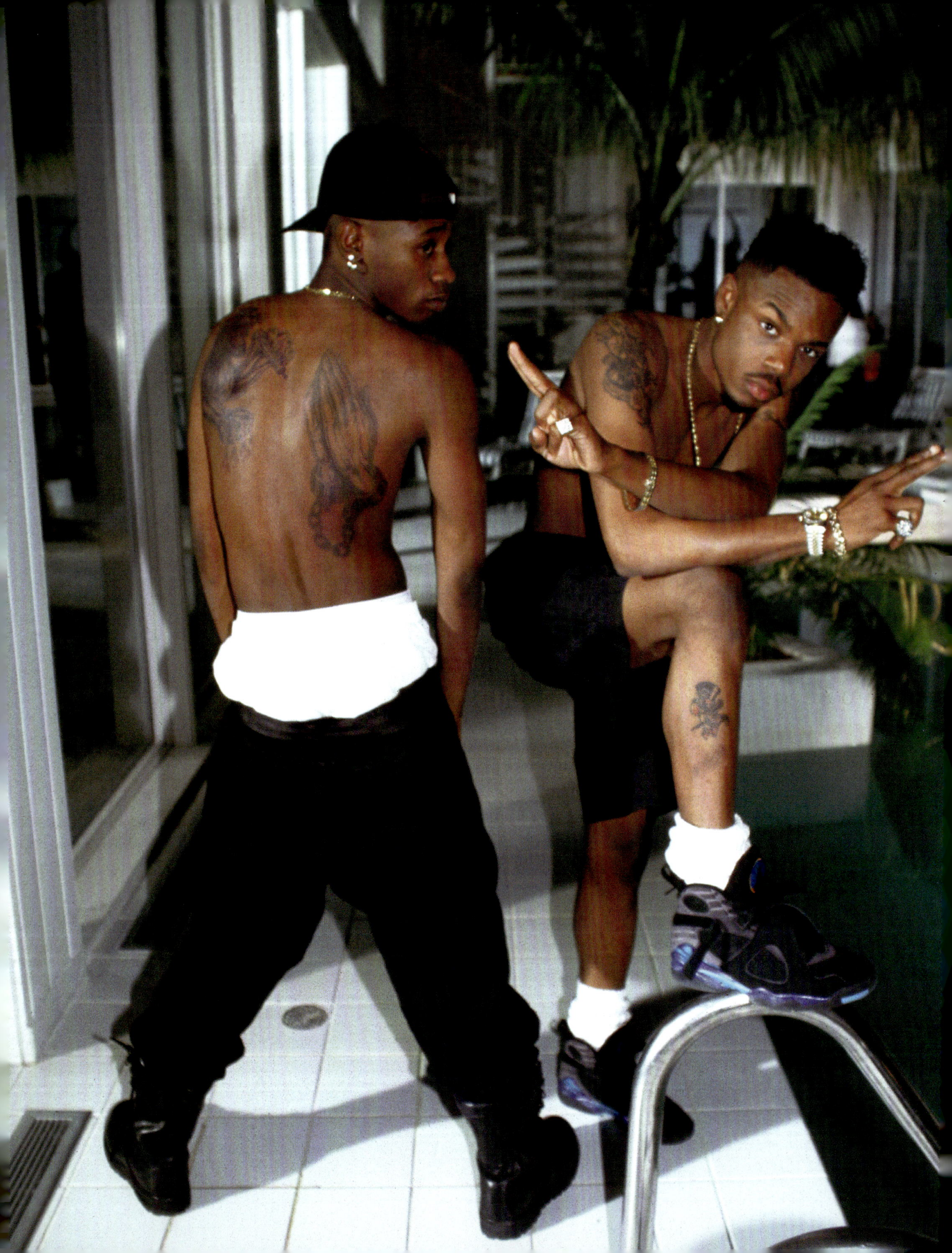

p.234–235 Jodeci during a video shoot in a mansion in Long Island, New York, 1990s.

p.236 Boyz II Men, Apollo Theatre, Harlem, NYC, early 1990s.

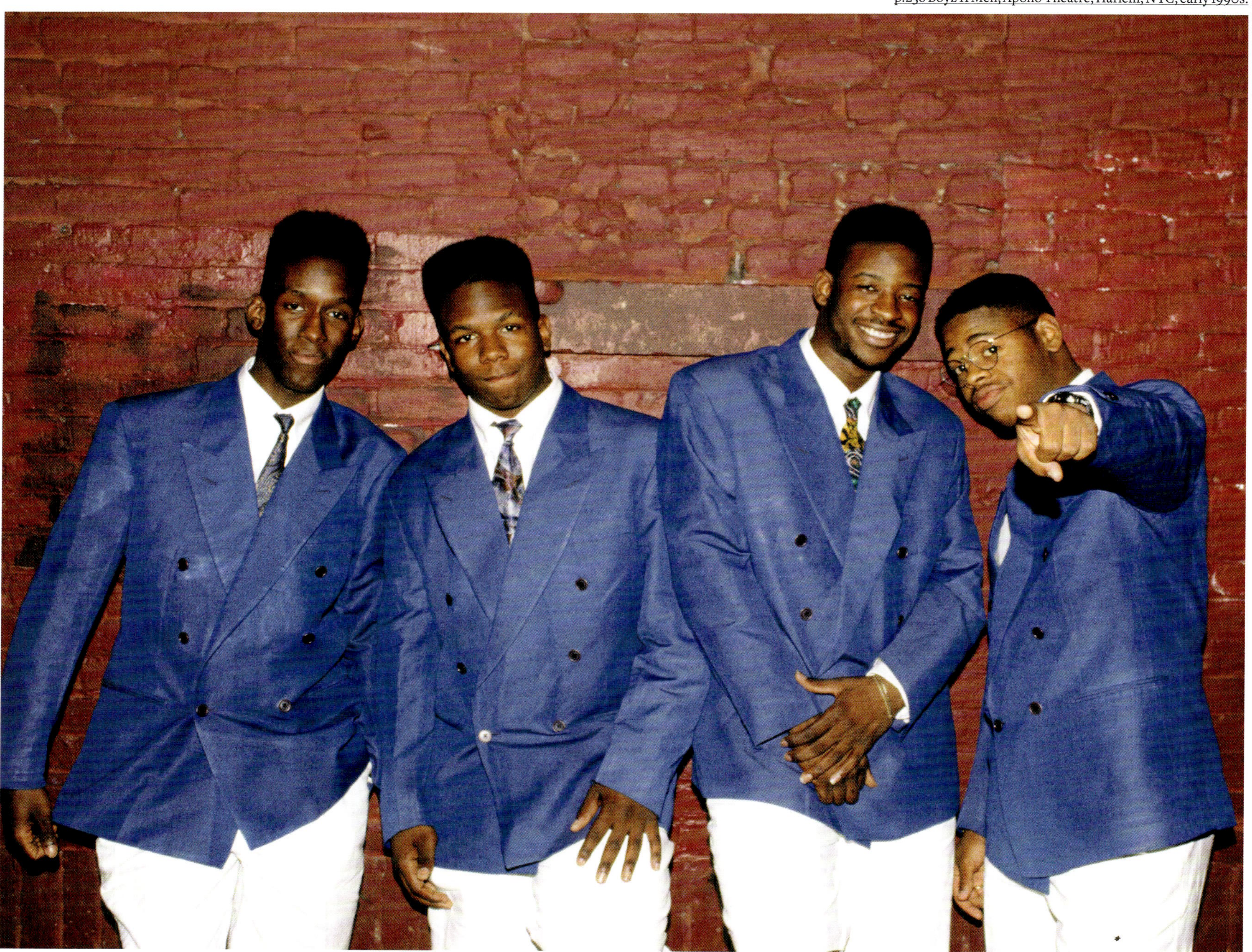

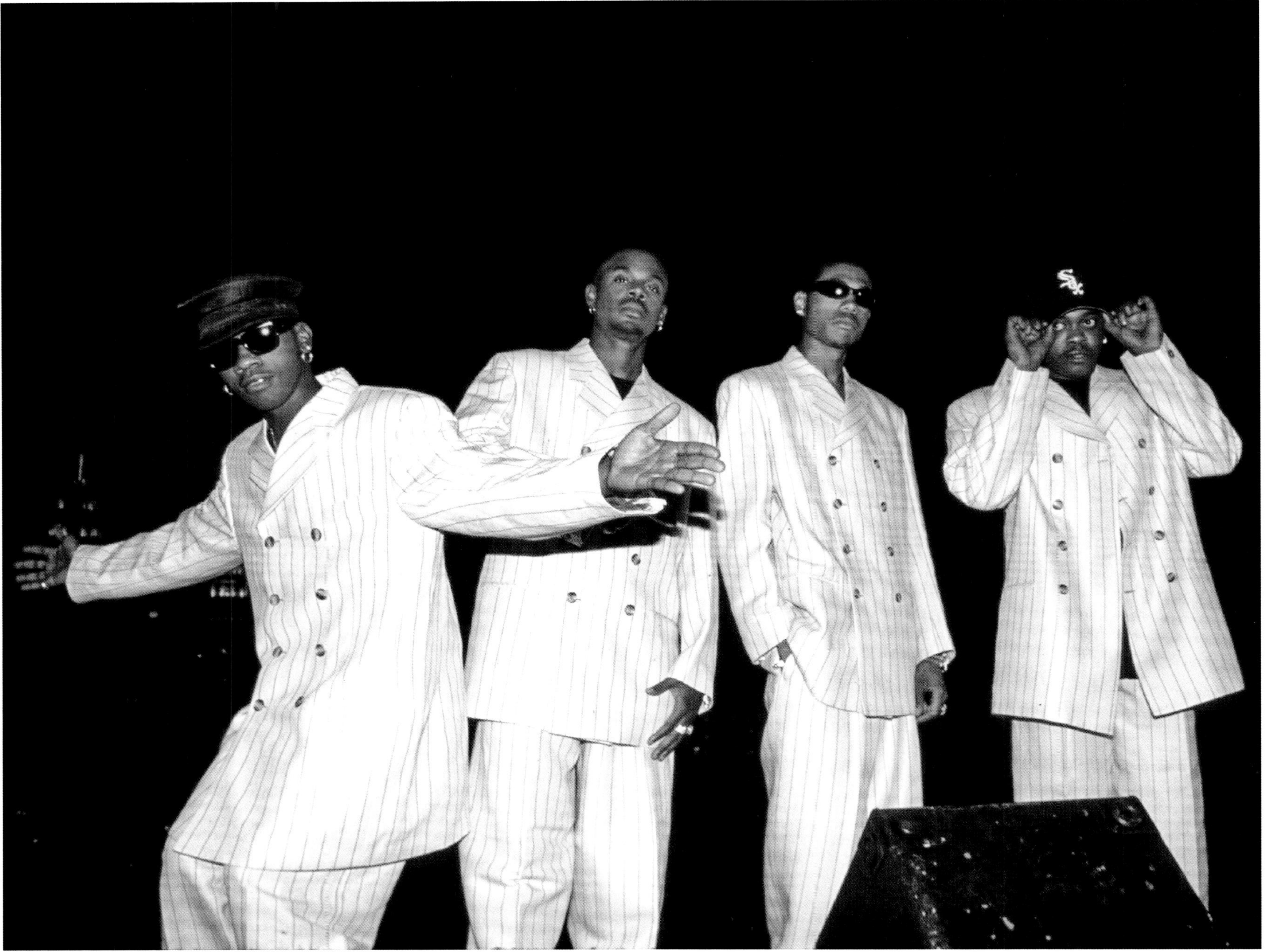

p.237 Jodeci video shoot for “Love You For Life,” NYC, 1995. Another cameo for me.

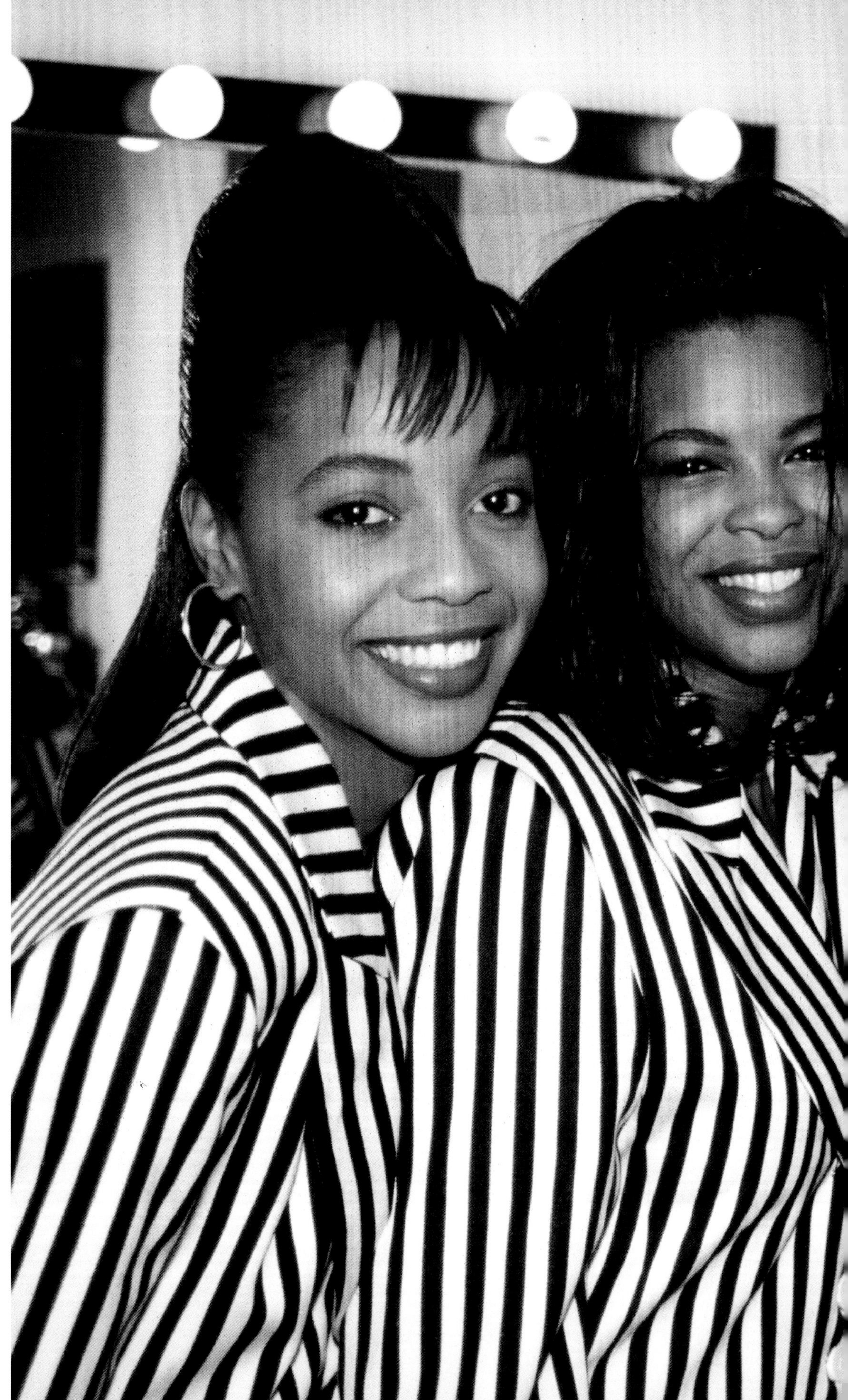

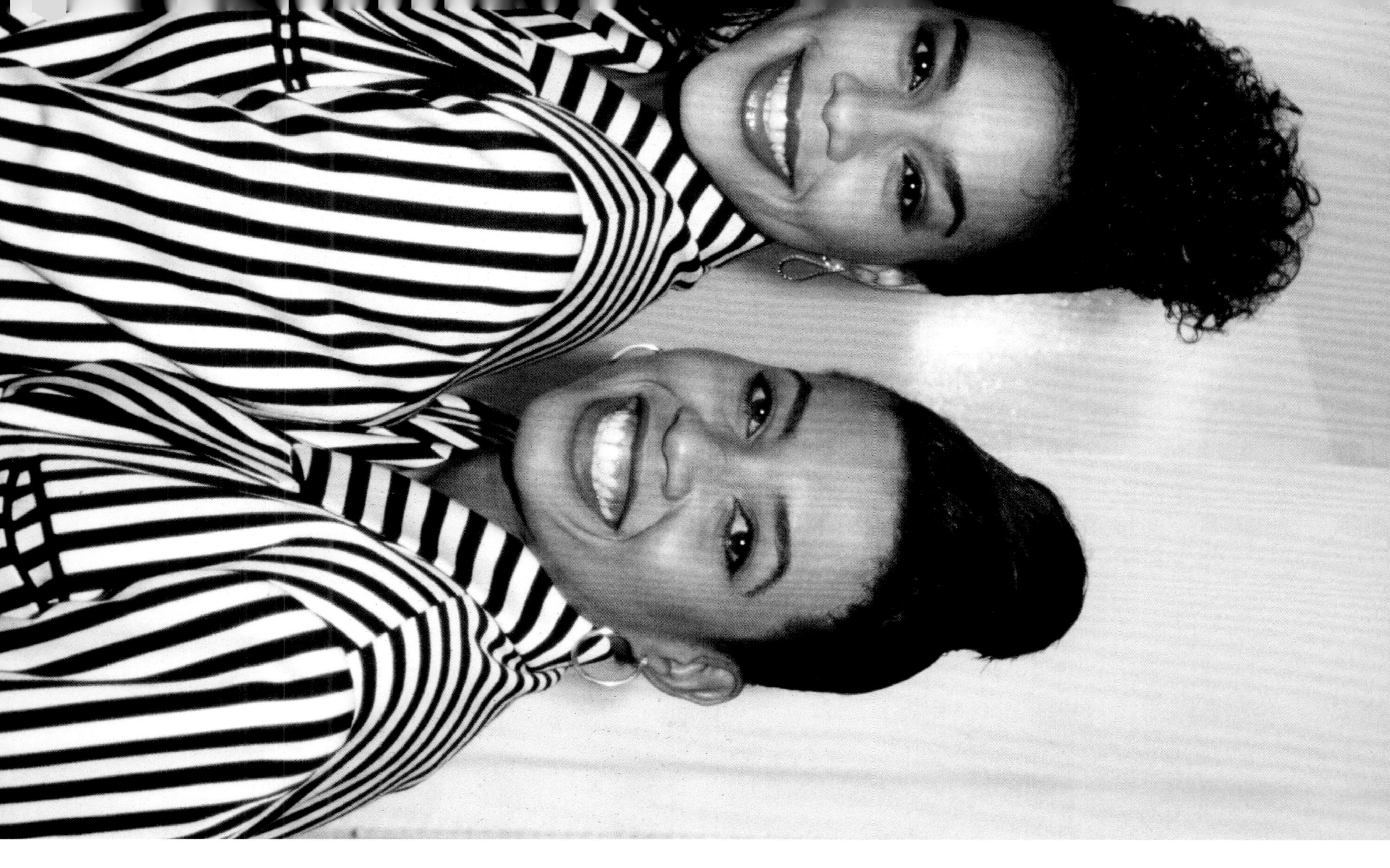

p.238–239 En Vogue in their dressing room, NYC, early 1990s.

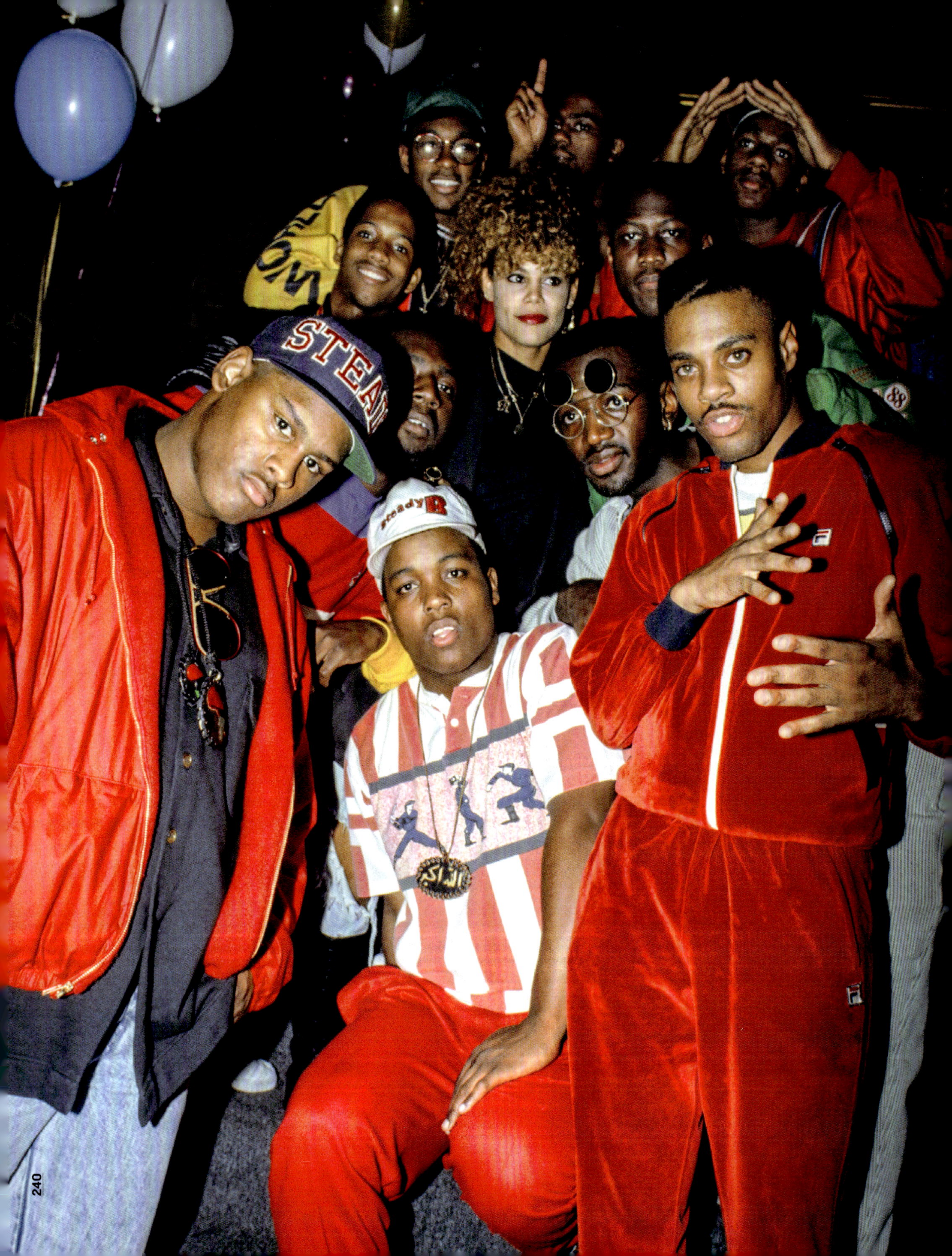

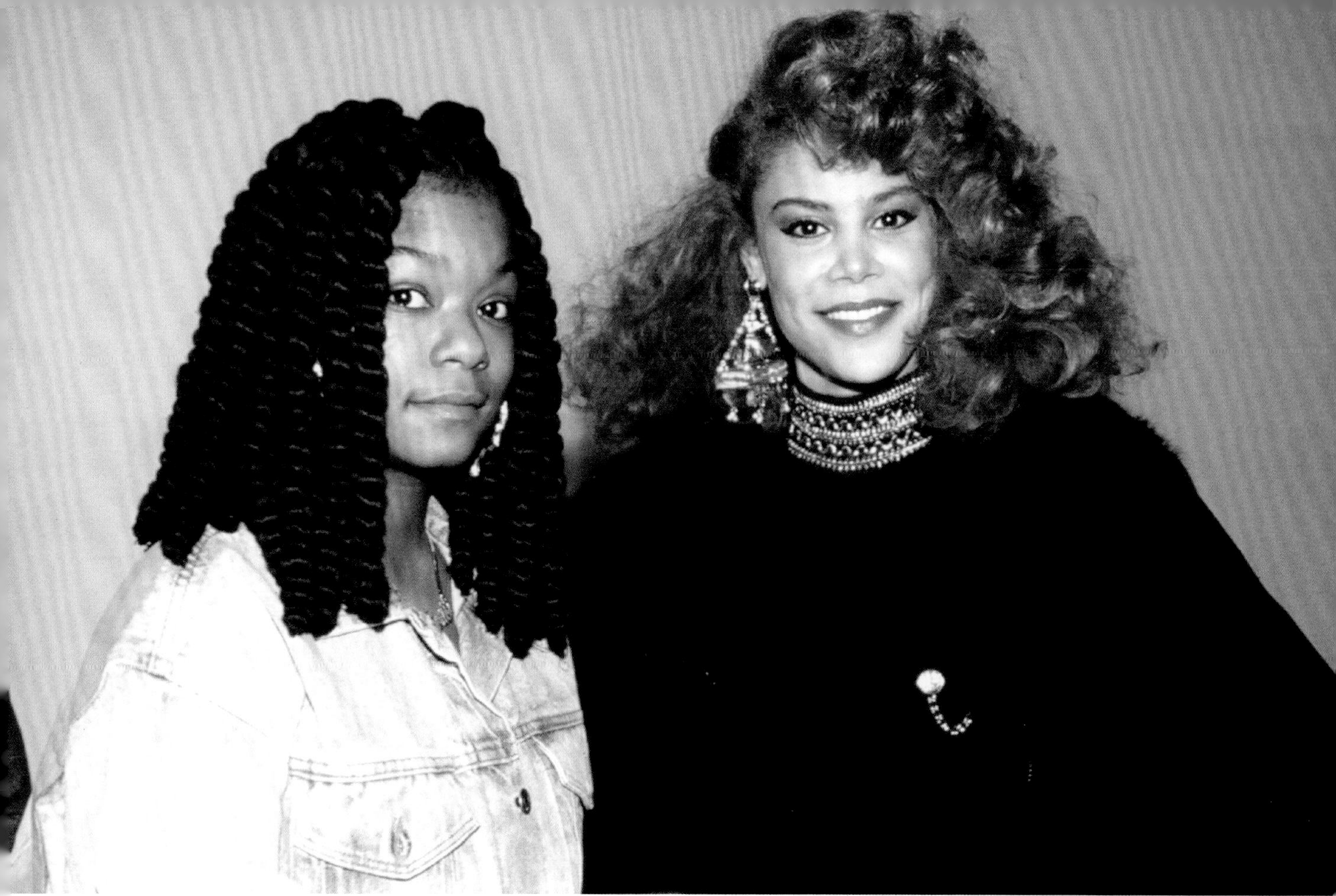

p.240 Steady B, Cool C (top right), the Real Roxanne, Jalil from Whodini and Whistle members at a *Word Up!* magazine party, NYC, 1987.

In 1996, Steady B of Hilltop Hustlers was sentenced to life in prison without parole for the murder of a female police officer during a botched bank robbery in Philadelphia. His accomplice, Cool C, was sentenced to death by lethal injection and is on death row at a Supermax prison.

p.241 Roxanne Shanté and The Real Roxanne (Adelaida Martinez), bitter rivals in one of the first public rap beefs. It took a lot of pleading for me to get this classic, one-of-a-kind photo. Roxanne Shanté went on to have a film based on her life on Netflix in 2018 and did numerous voiceovers. The Real Roxanne faded into obscurity. Rapfest, Times Square, NYC, 1989.

p.242 (Top) Boss (Lichelle Laws), Lexington Ave. Subway Station near Grand Central, NYC, early 1990s; (Bottom) Busta Rhymes, Hammerstein Ballroom, 1990s.

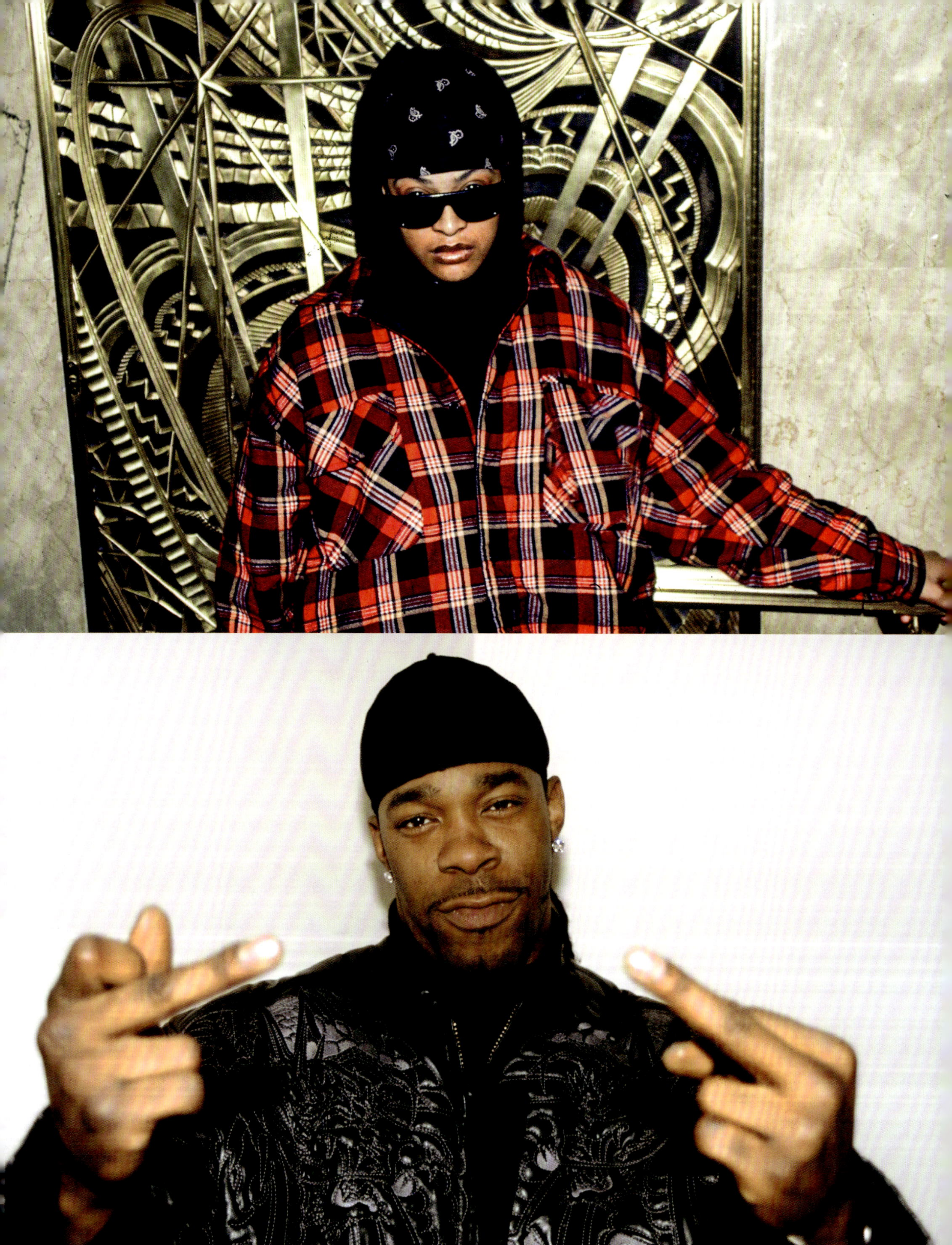

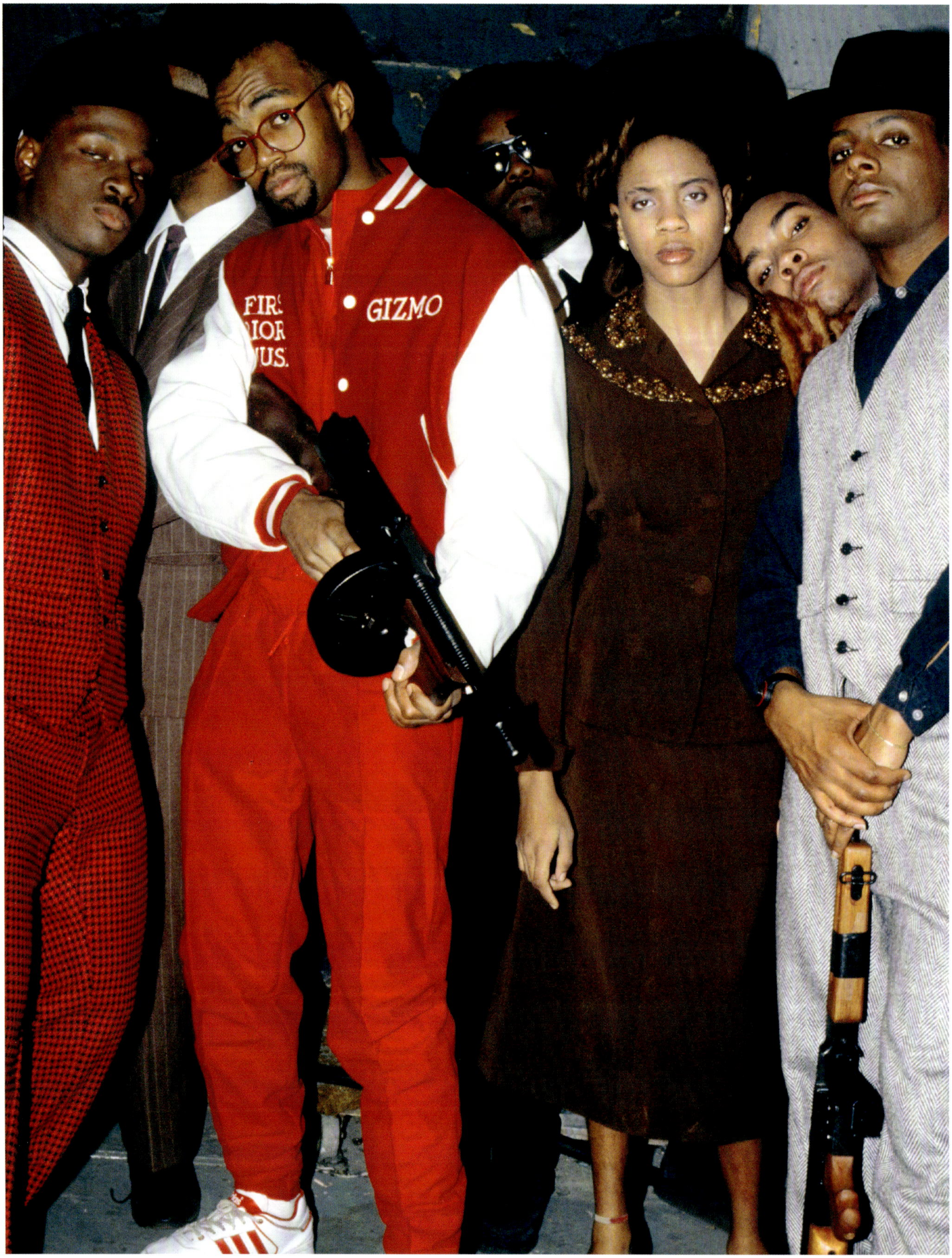

p.243 MC Lyte on the set of her "Lyte as a Rock" video shoot. I remember her car being broken into and the car radio stolen during the shoot. NYC, 1988.

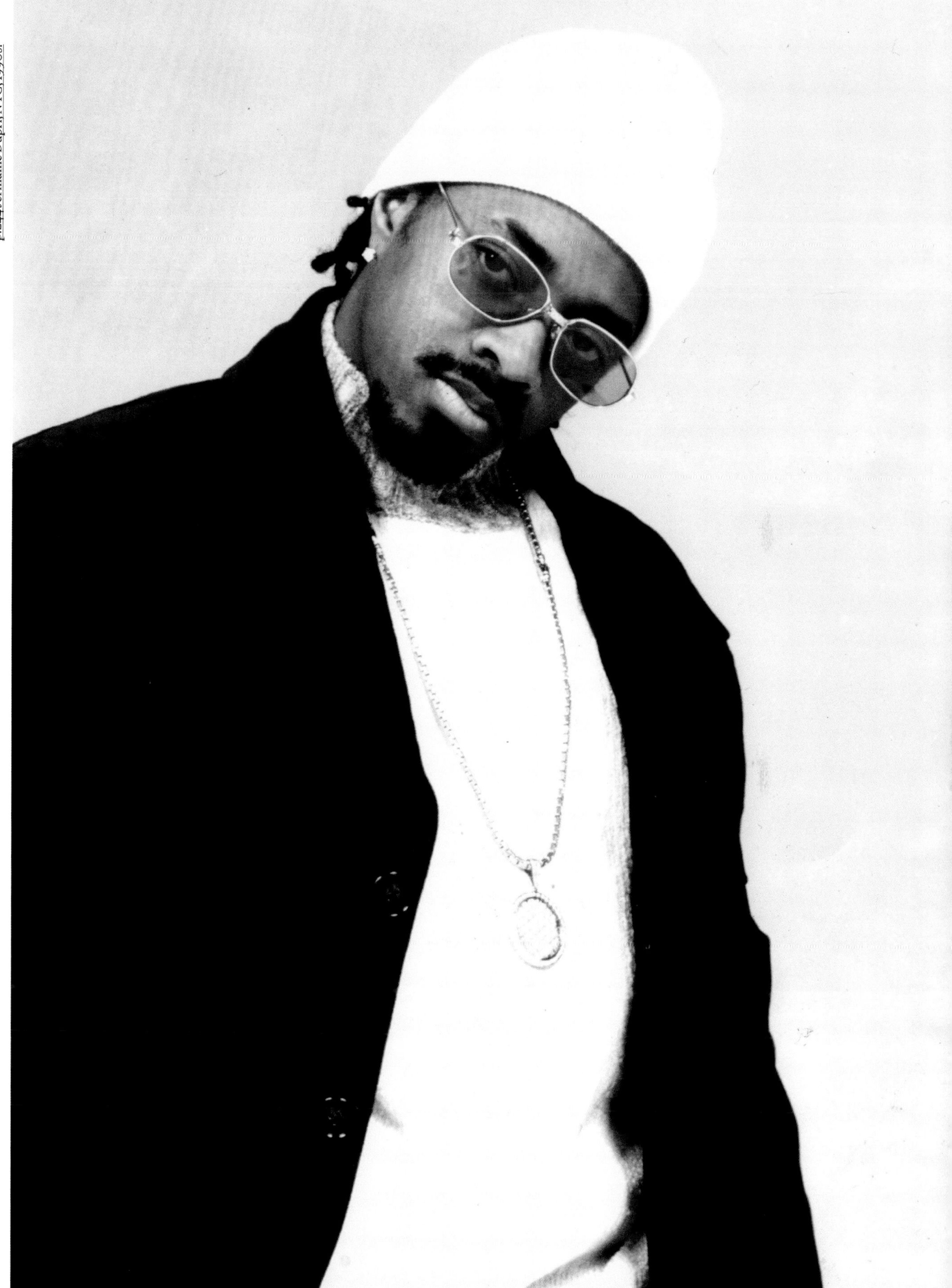

p.244 Jermaine Dupri, NYC, 1990s.

p.245 Marky Mark, NYC, 1991.

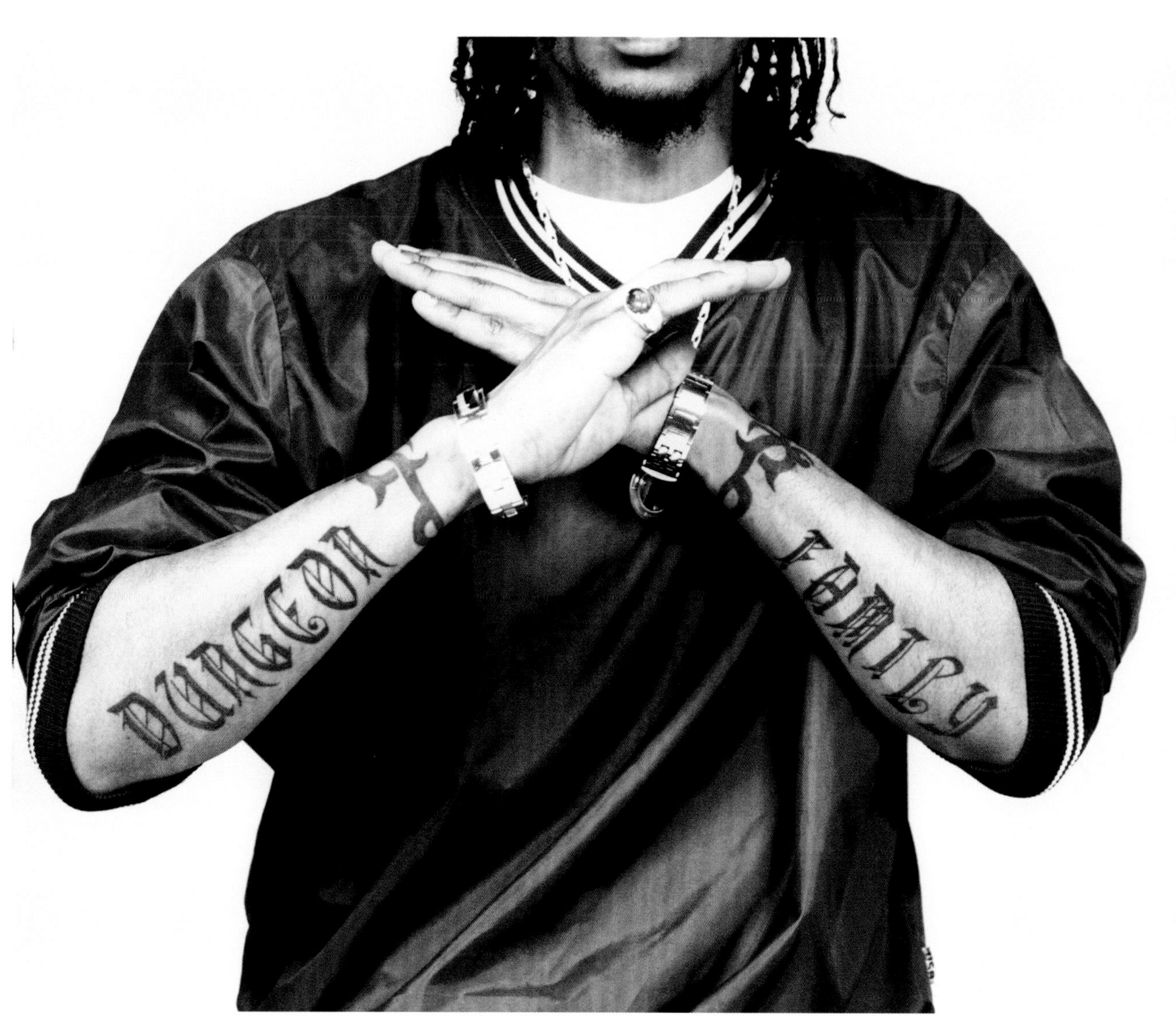
DUNGEON
FAMILY

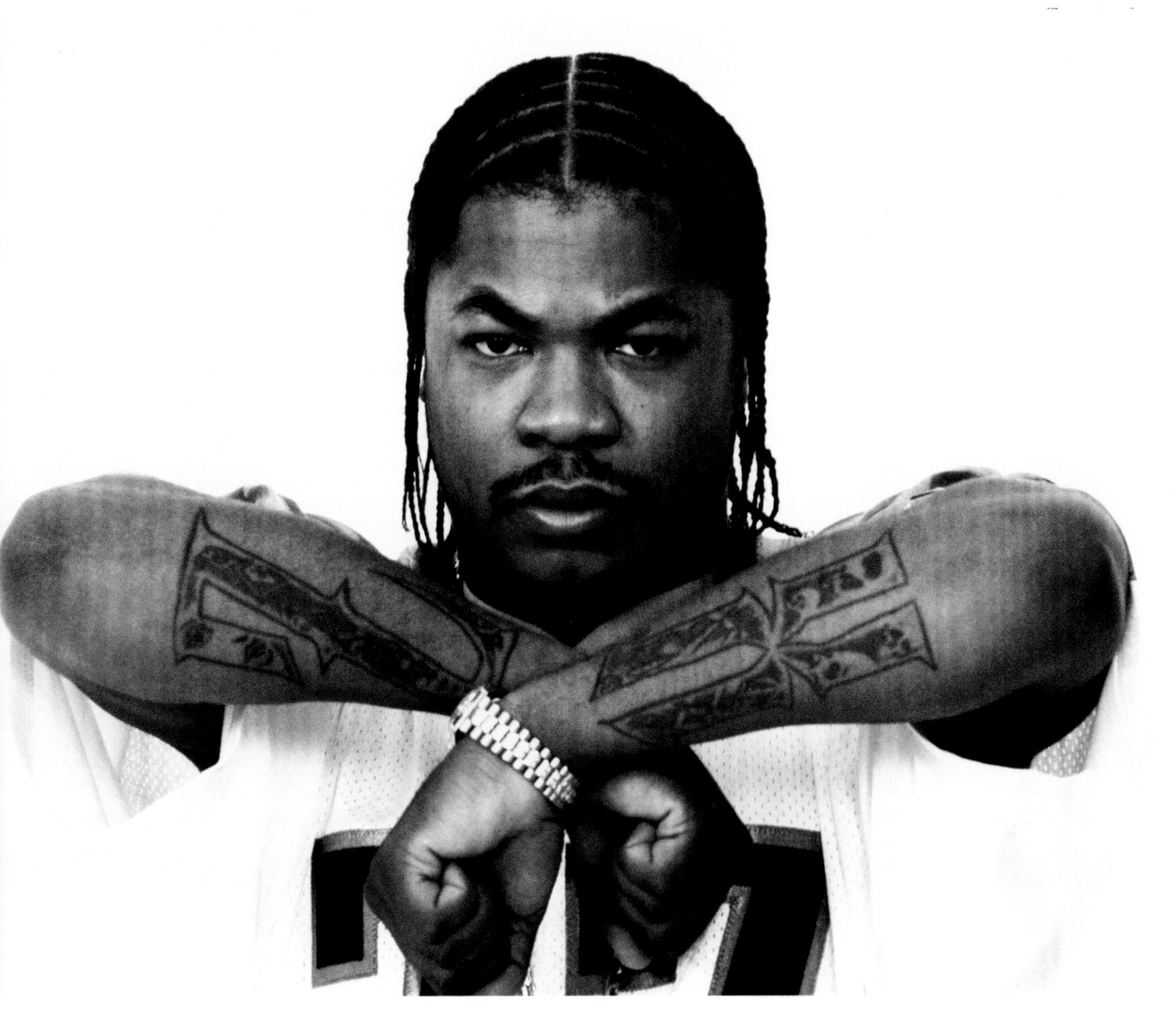

p.246 Gipp from Goodie Mob, which was one group from the Dungeon Family posse from Atlanta. I always tried to get photos of artists with their tattoos, NYC, 1990s; p.247 Xzibit, NYC, 1990s.

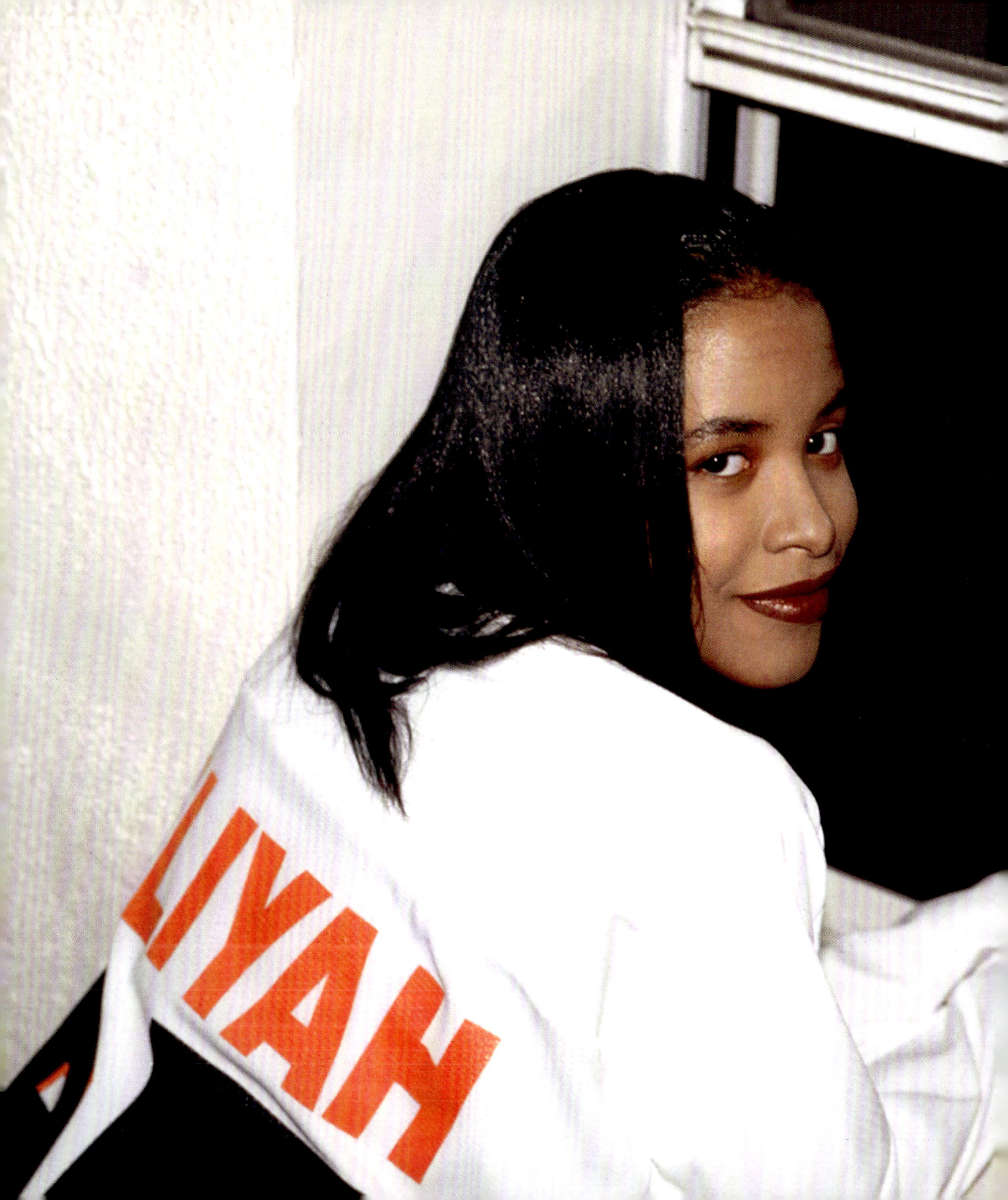
LIYAH

p.248-249 The singer Aaliyah (1979-2001) on her sixteenth birthday. The thing that makes this photo eerie is that she was looking out the window and the view is darkness. Her life was cut tragically short at the height of her career by a plane crash in 2001. Shot in the stairway of the Apollo Theatre, Harlem, NYC, 1995.

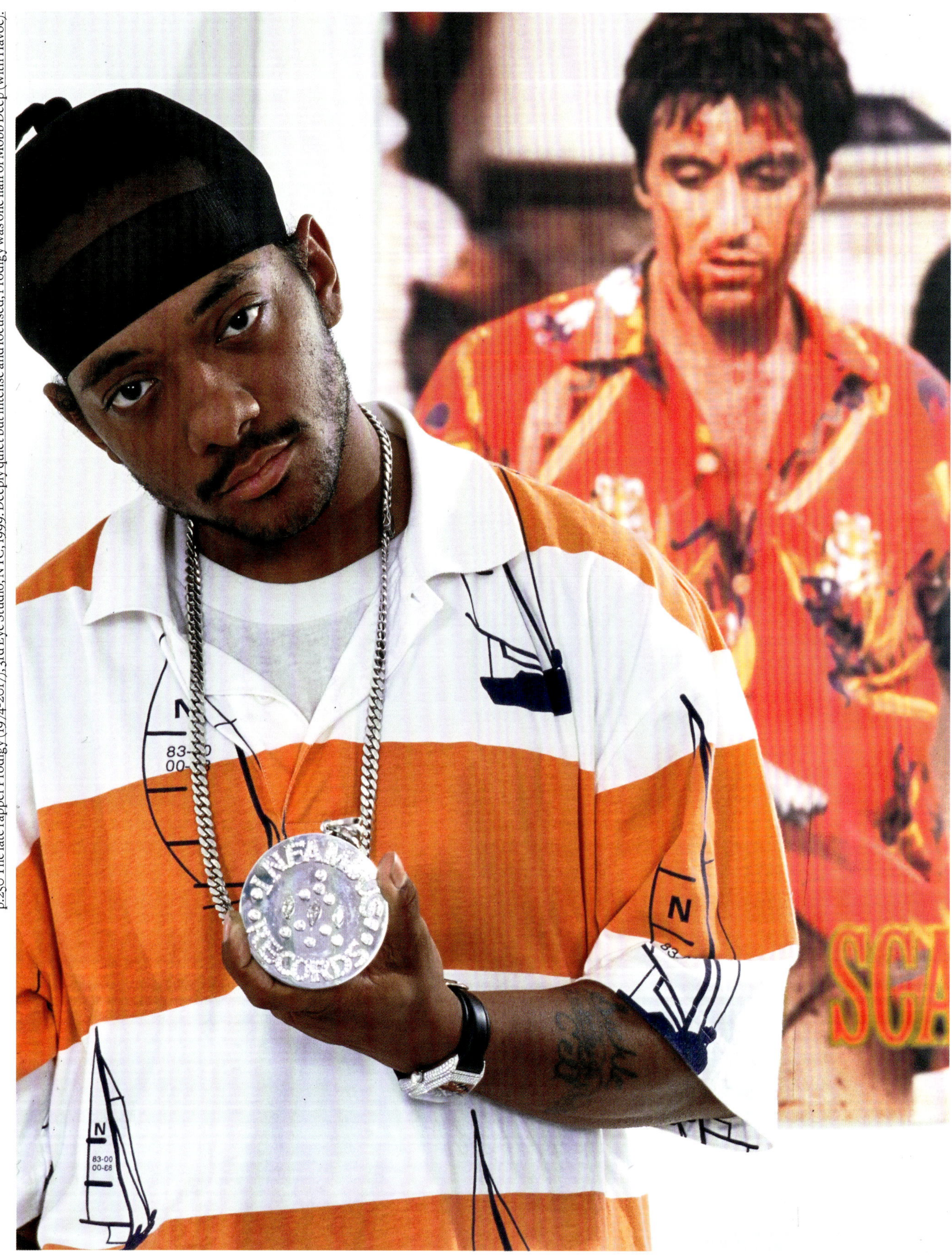

p.250 The late rapper Prodigy (1974-2017), 3rd Eye Studio, NYC, 1999. Deeply quiet but intense and focused, Prodigy was one half of Mobb Deep (with Havoc).

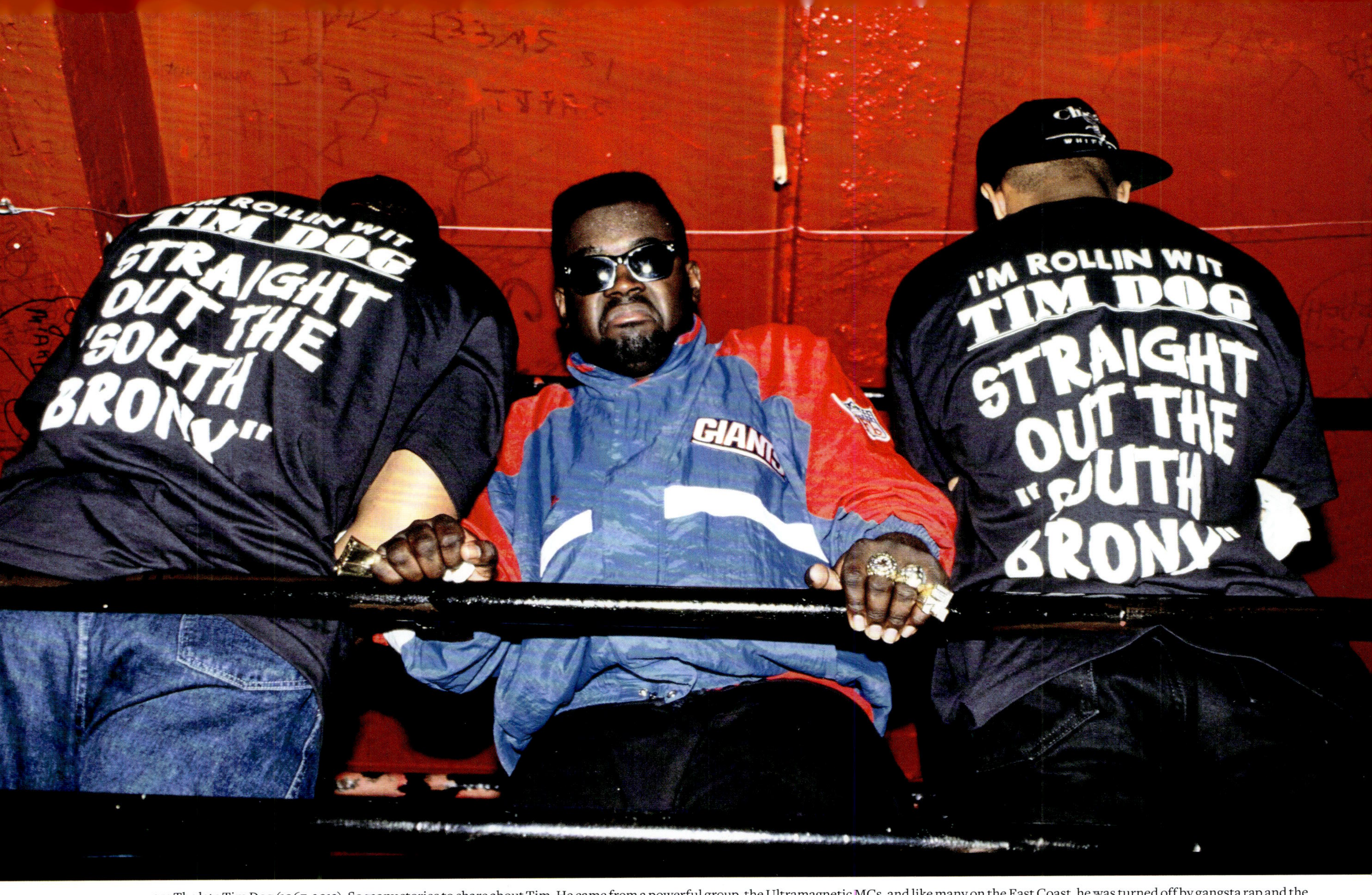

p.251 The late Tim Dog (1967-2013). So many stories to share about Tim. He came from a powerful group, the Ultramagnetic MCs, and like many on the East Coast, he was turned off by gangsta rap and the West Coast scene. He felt the East Coast deserved more respect from the major record companies for having created rap and hip-hop, and in 1990 recorded one of the most angry and cutting diss tracks in the history of the genre. He named names, groups and places rather than hinting at them. "Fuck Compton" became an instant classic and ignited the East Coast-West Coast rivalry. He asked me to shoot the cover for his single *Bronx Nigga* and when the label refused to pay me due to litigation from Eazy E's label, Tim paid me $1,000 cash out of his pocket, something damn few rappers would do. And I can't forget seeing his 50-man posse all wearing FUCK COMPTON t-shirts (I have a photo of that). I also did a shoot of him with a topless fan that was never released because she was white and he said he had enough headaches. NYC, early 1990s.

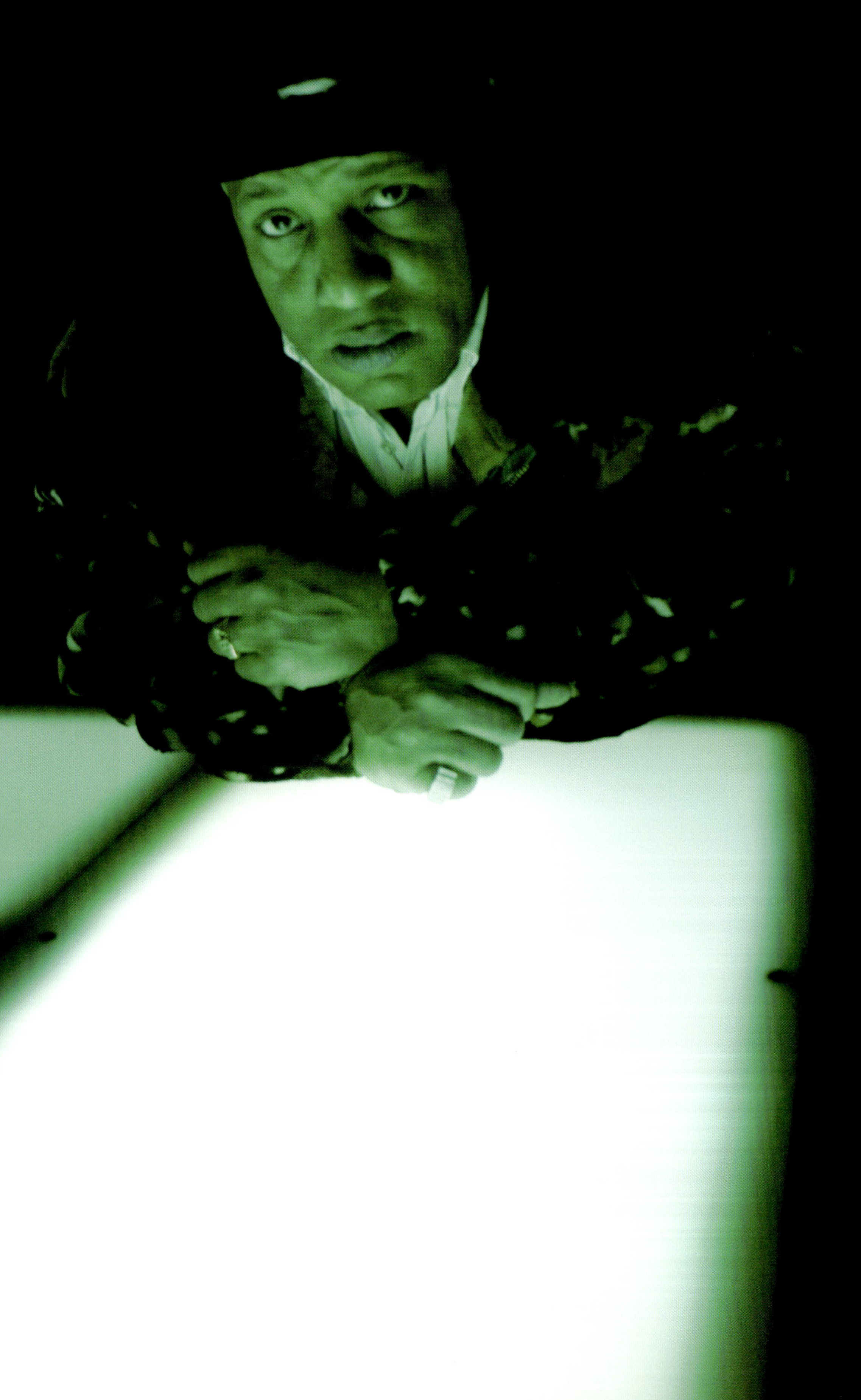

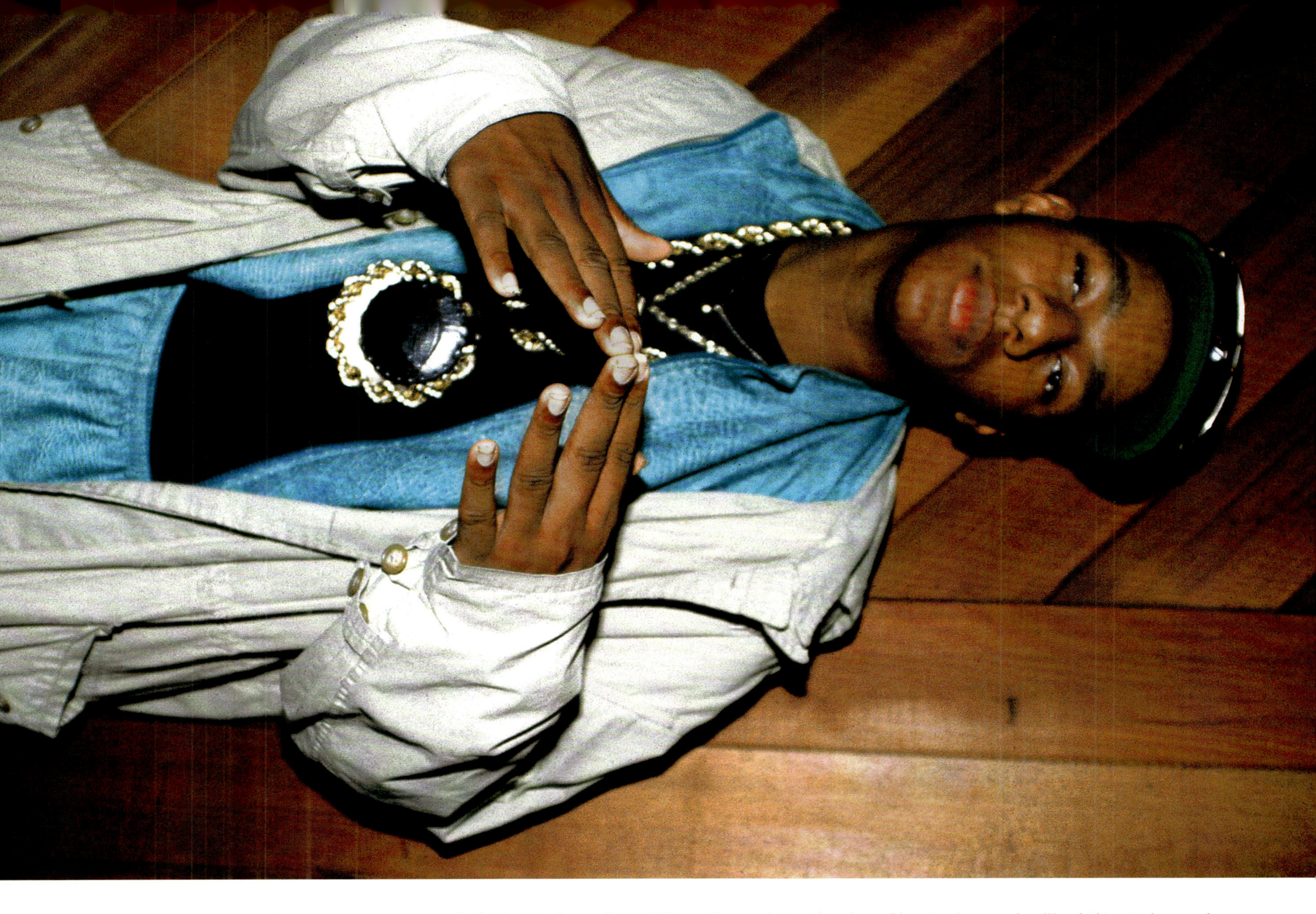

p.252 Late rapper and DJ Luvbug Starski (1960-2018). He is credited with coining the term "HIP HOP." A true pioneer and a Bronx legend, one of the artists that was truly well loved. This eerie photo was shot using the illumination from a light table. NYC, 2012; p.253 Cool C, who with Steady B was part of Philly's Hilltop Hustlers. He is also known for his involvement in the murder of Philadelphia police officer Lauretha Vaird, a single mom with two children during a botched bank robbery he committed (also with Steady B) in January 1996. He is currently on death row, not the label, the real thing. NYC, late 1980s.

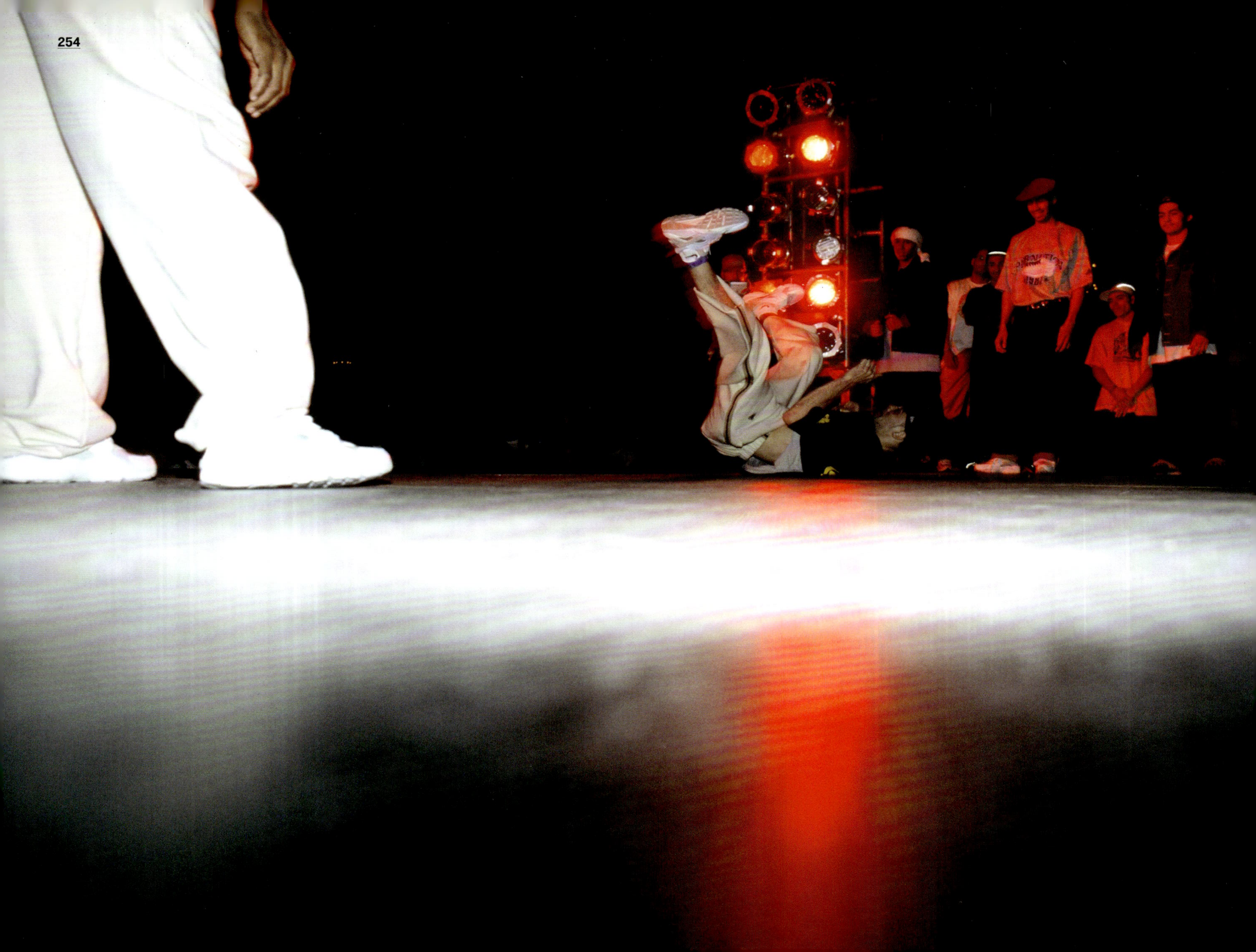

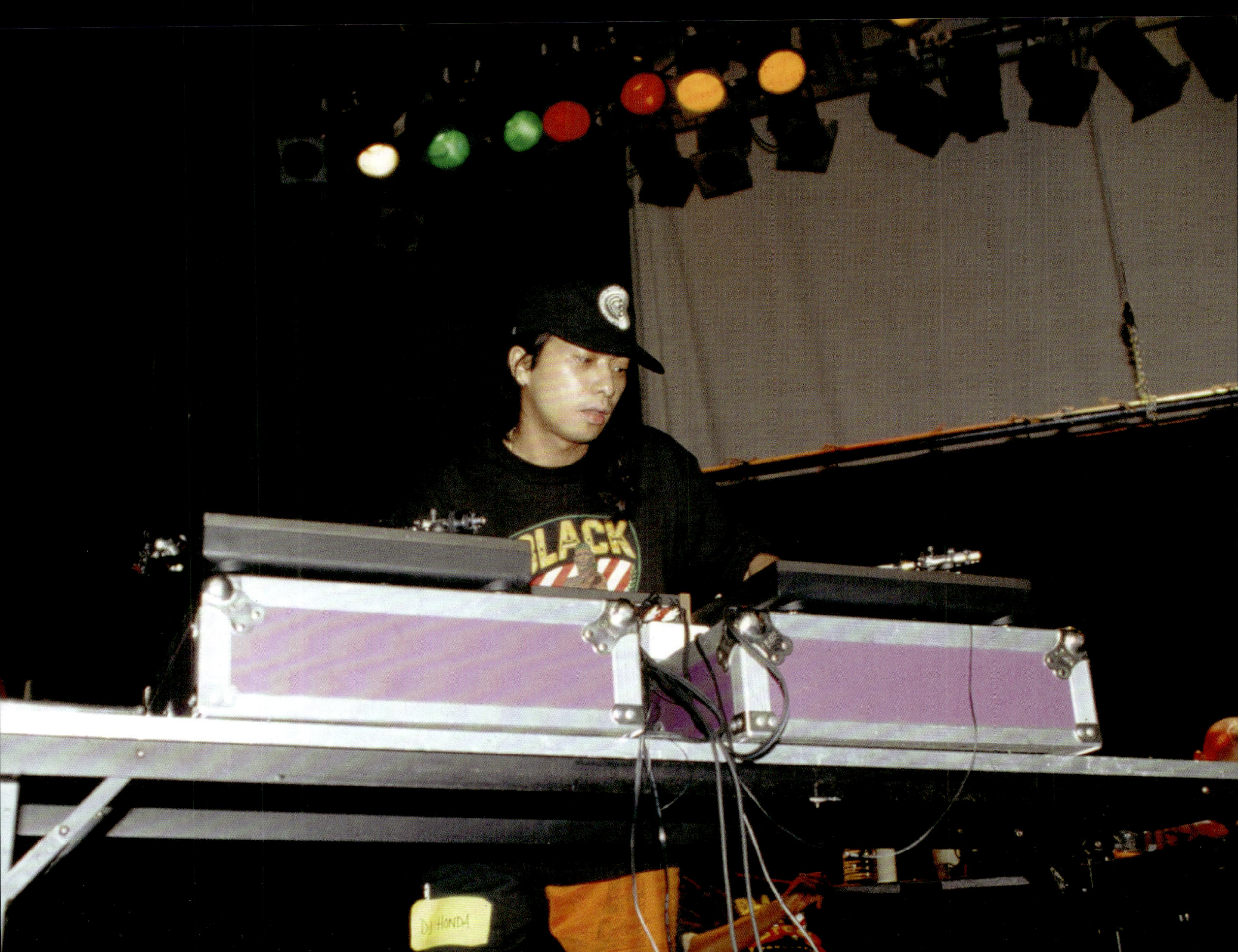
BLACK
DJ HONDA

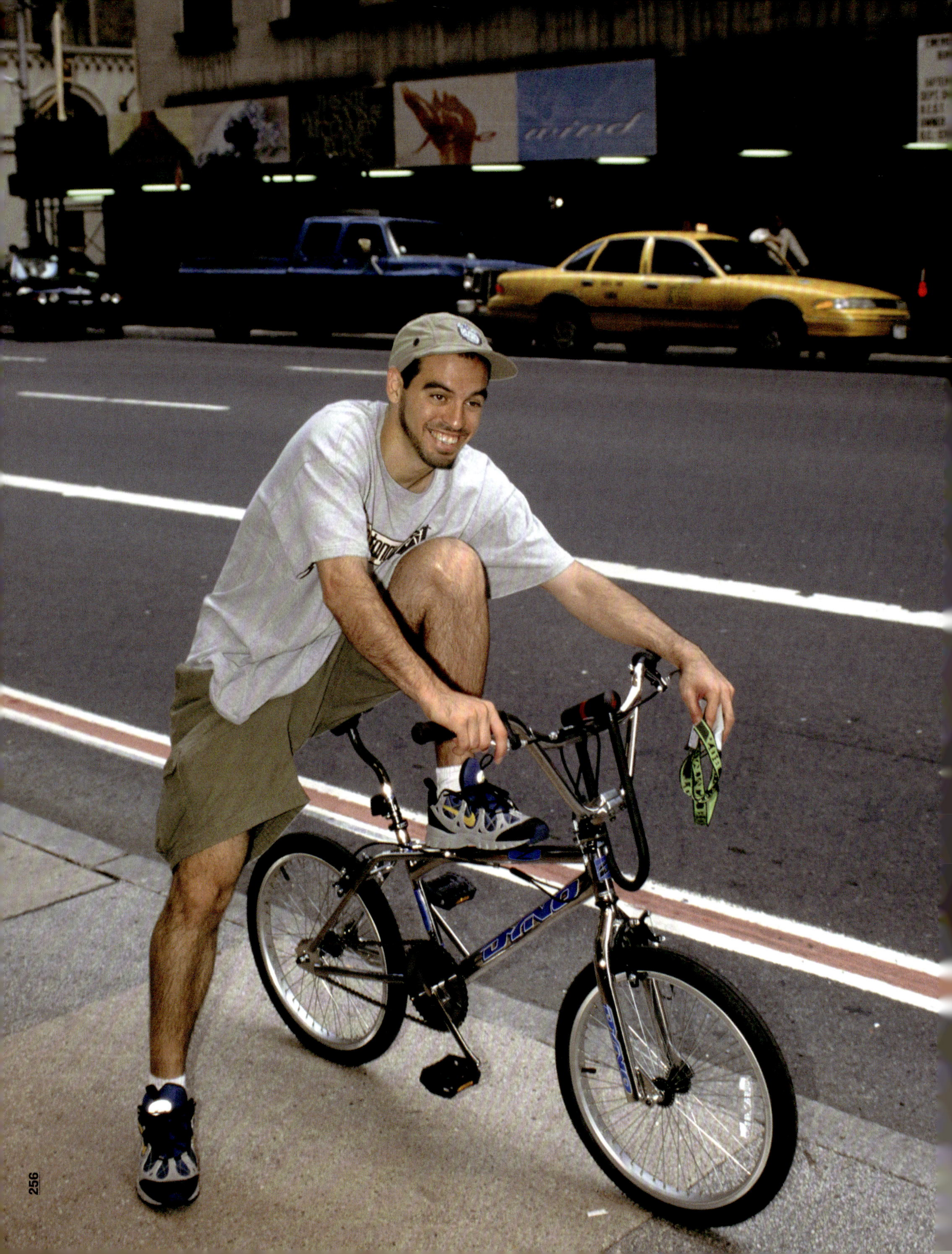
wired
DYNO

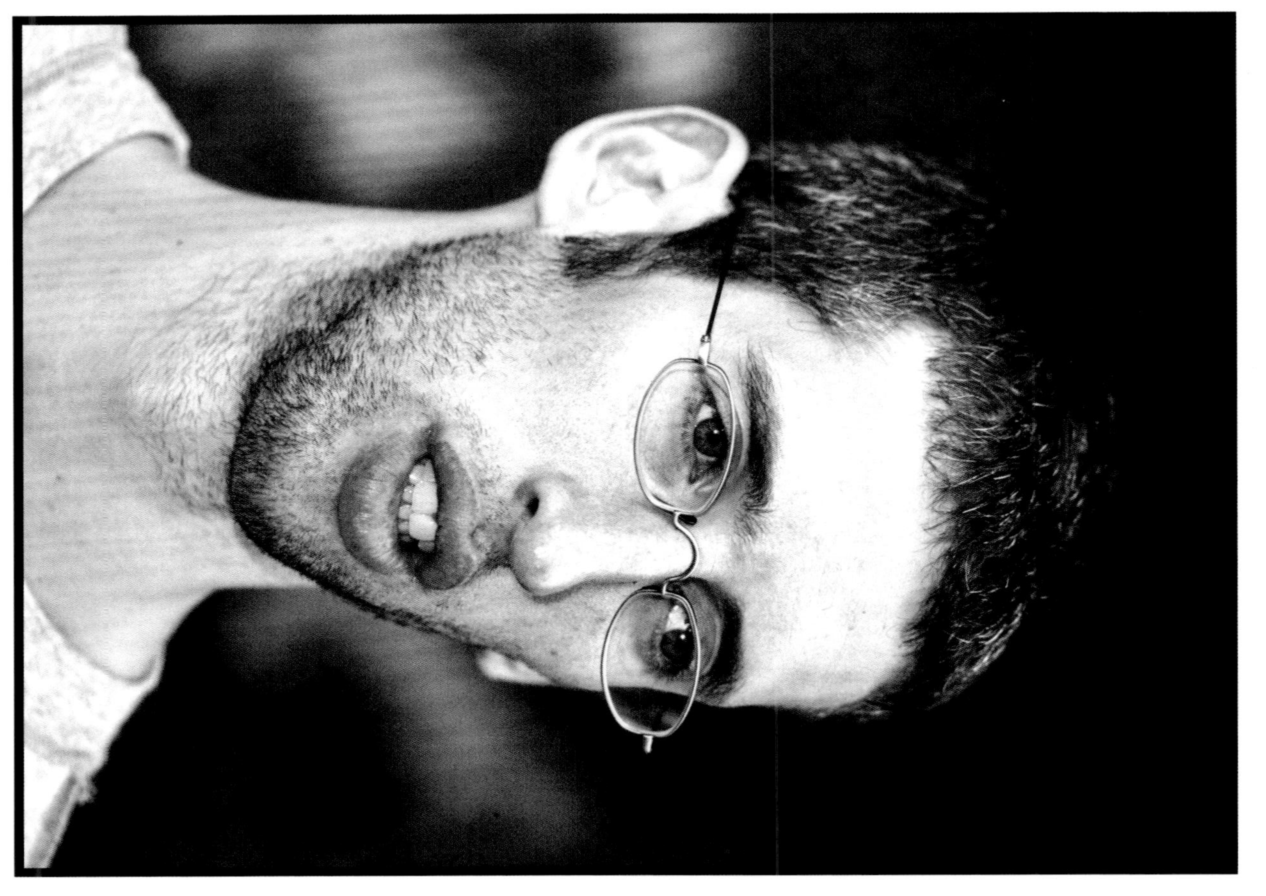

p.254 Rock Steady Crew, Brooklyn Museum, New York, 2002; p.255 DJ Honda, NYC, 2002.
p.256 Bobbito; and p. 257, DJ Stretch Armstrong, NYC, 1990s. Stretch Armstrong (Adrian Bartos) and Robert "Bobbito" Garcia hosted the influential *Stretch Armstrong and Bobbito Show* from WKCR-FM at Columbia University from 1990 to 1998.

p.258 (Top) Ed Lover and Andre "Doctor Dré" Brown on the set of the Ted Demme comedy feature film *Who's the Man* (1993) with Bushwick Bill of the Geto Boys. Harlem NYC 1993.

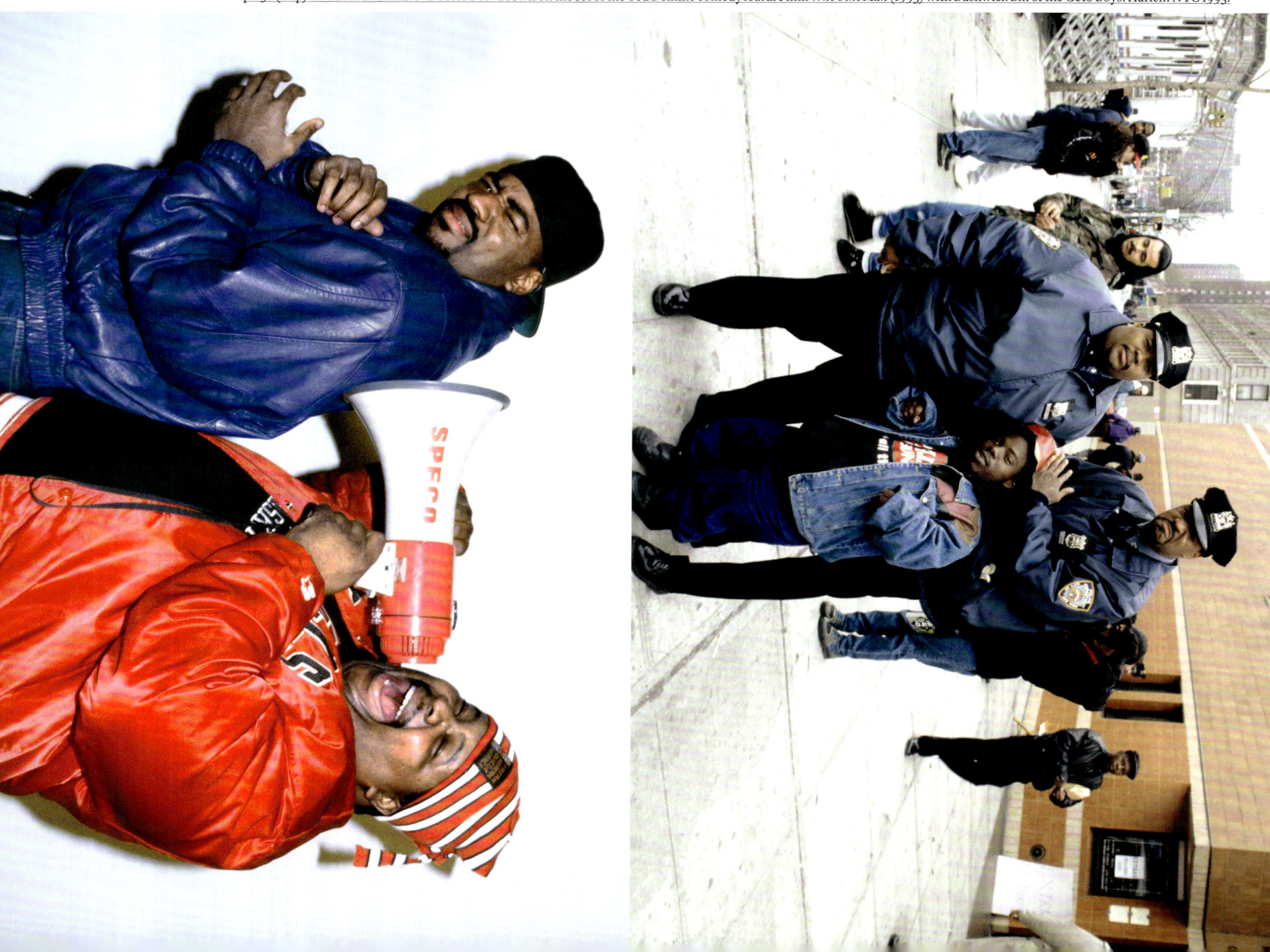

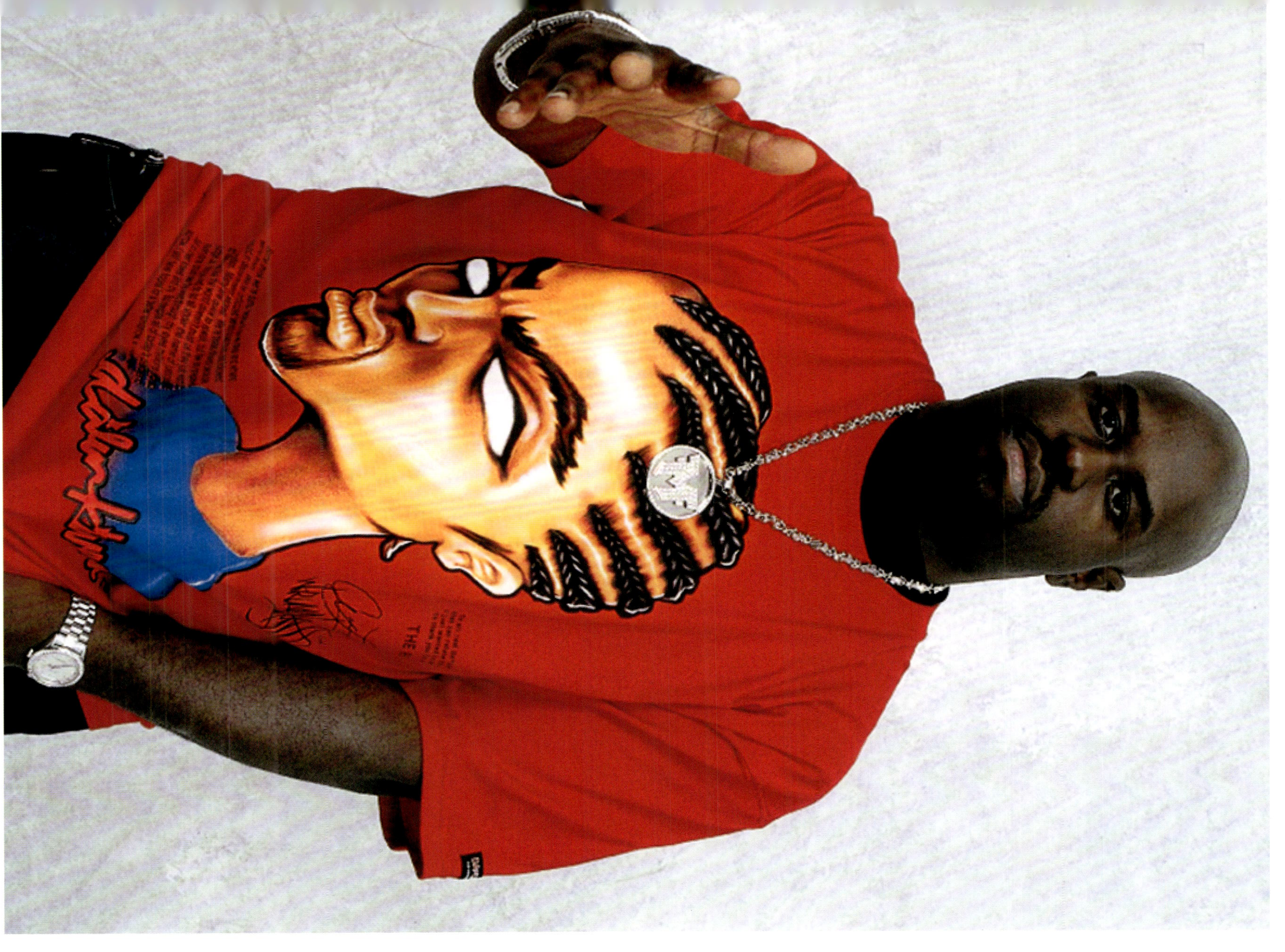

p. 258 (bottom) Ed Lover and Andre "Doctor Dré" Brown co-hosted the popular *Morning Show with Ed, Lisa and Dré* (with Lisa Blasberg) on Hot 97 (WQHT-FM) from 1993 to 1998. Brooklyn, 1994.
p. 259 Funkmaster Flex, a pioneering DJ on New York's Hot 97 (WQHT-FM), was instrumental in helping turn a middling pop station into the leading radio outlet for hip-hop and R&B by the mid 1990s. He first hosted *Friday Night Street Jam* in 1993. 3rd Eye Studio, NYC, 1999.

p.261 The beautiful Grammy recipient Mya Marie Harrison was a joy to work with. She had a great vibe, and was warm, funny and relaxed. Tribeca, NYC, 1999.

p.262 Portraits (clockwise from top left): Buju Banton, Kool G Rap, Shabba Ranks and Busy Bee, all NYC, 1990s.

p.263 Portraits (clockwise from top left): Usher Raymond, Cam'Ron, Beenie Man and Jadakiss, NYC, 1990s.

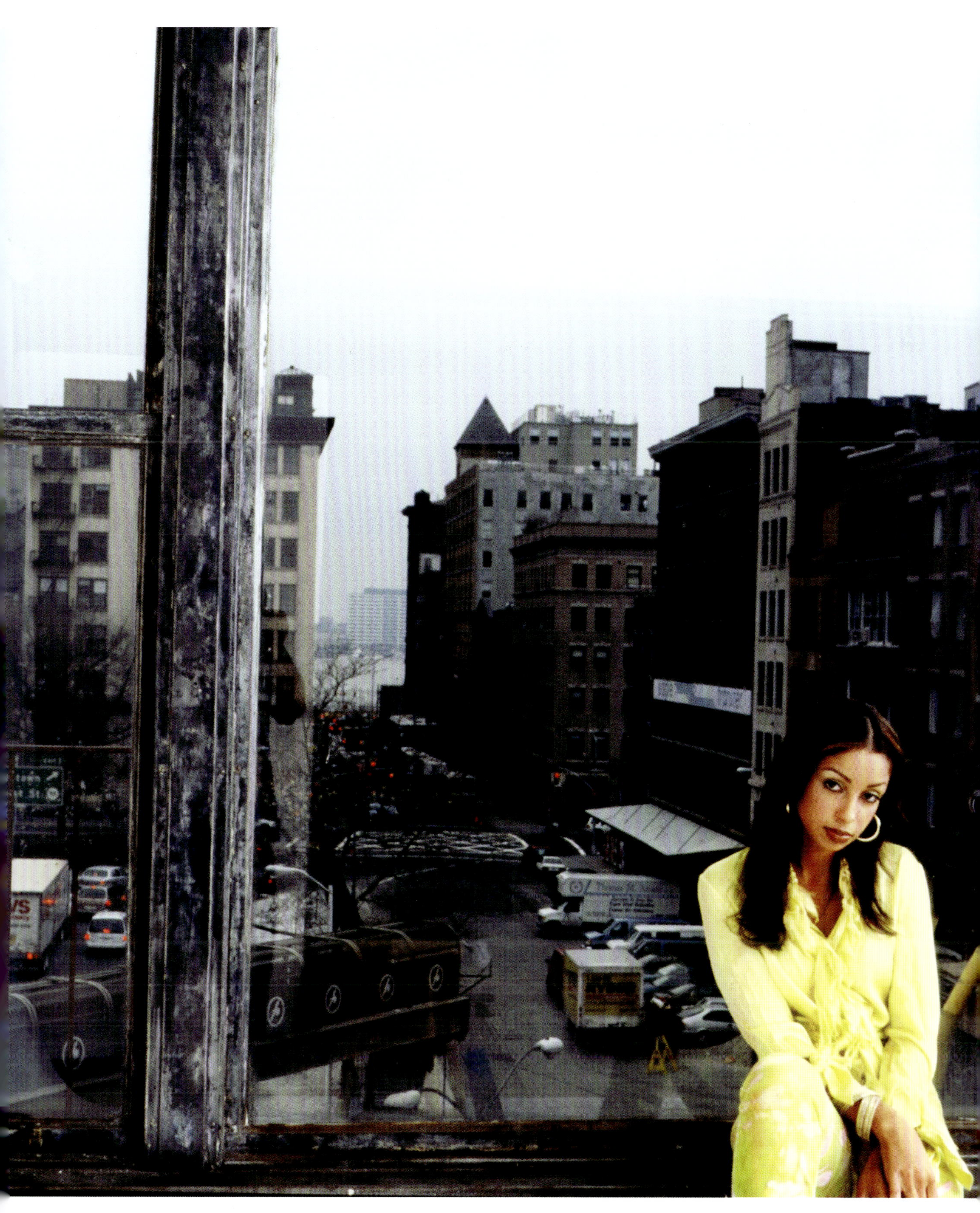

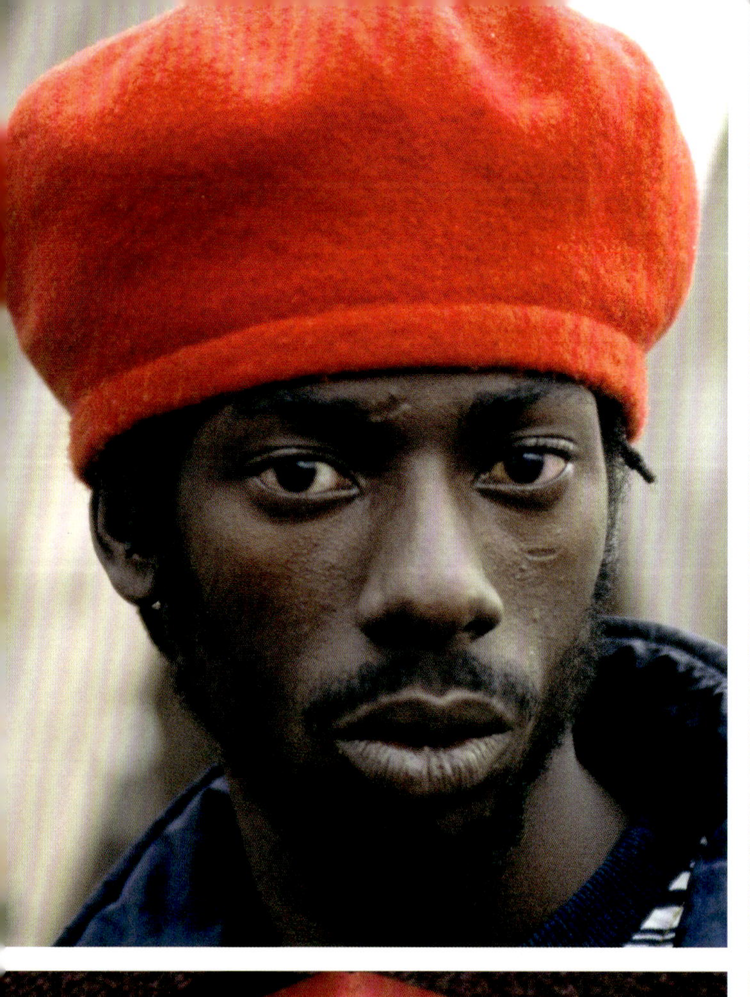

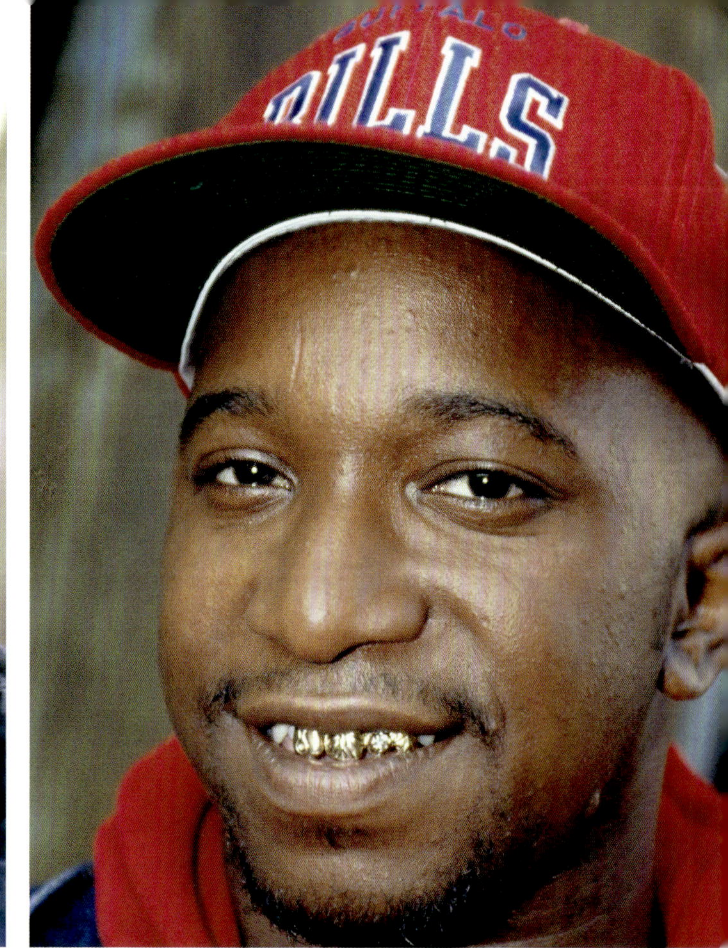

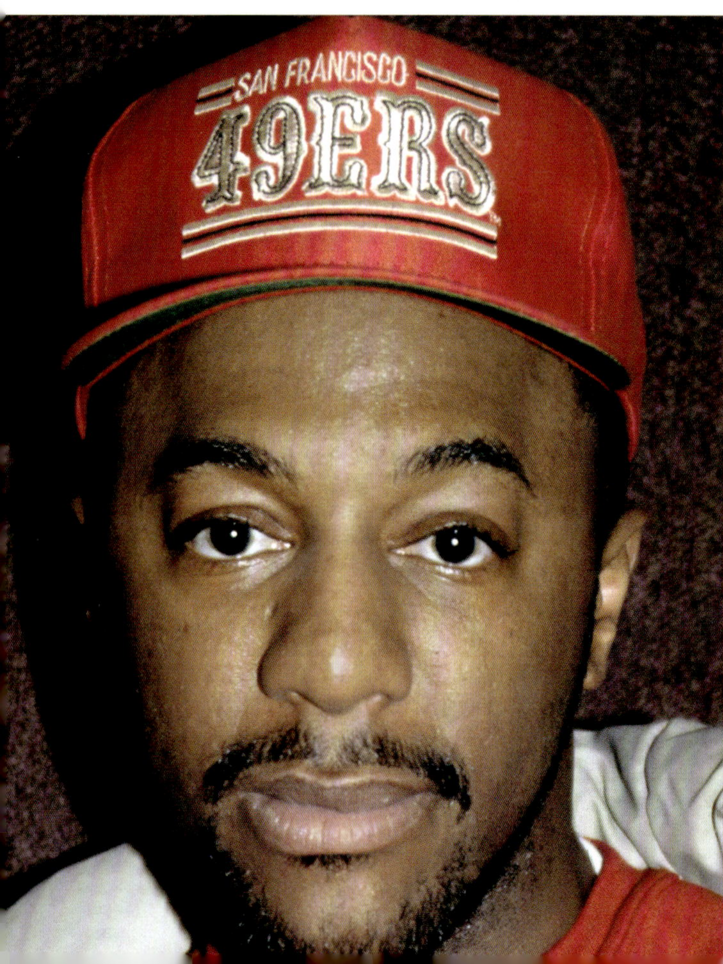
SAN FRANCISCO
49ERS

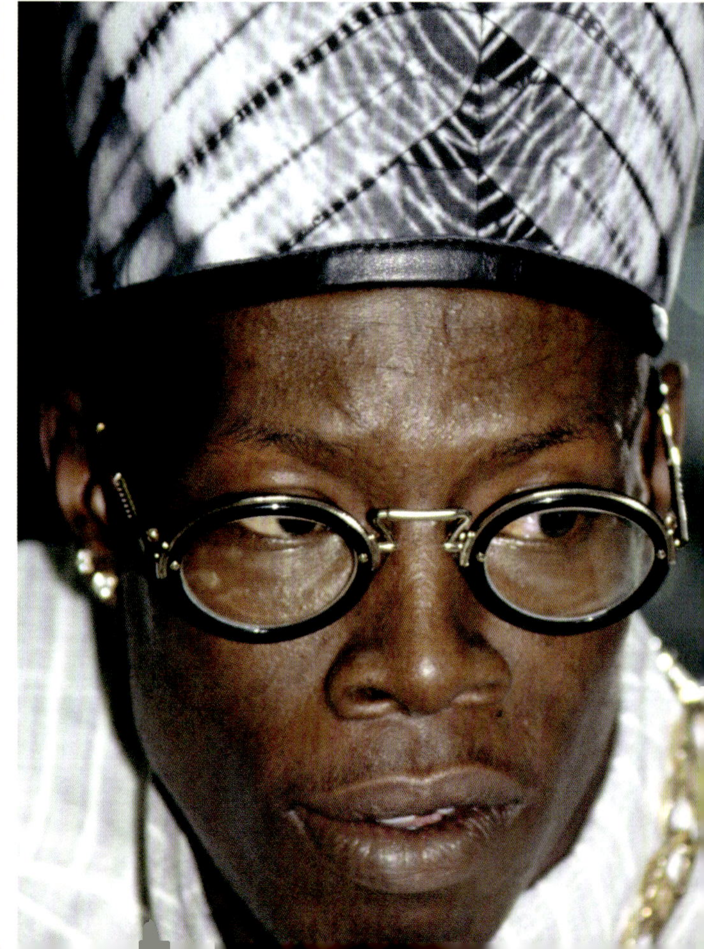

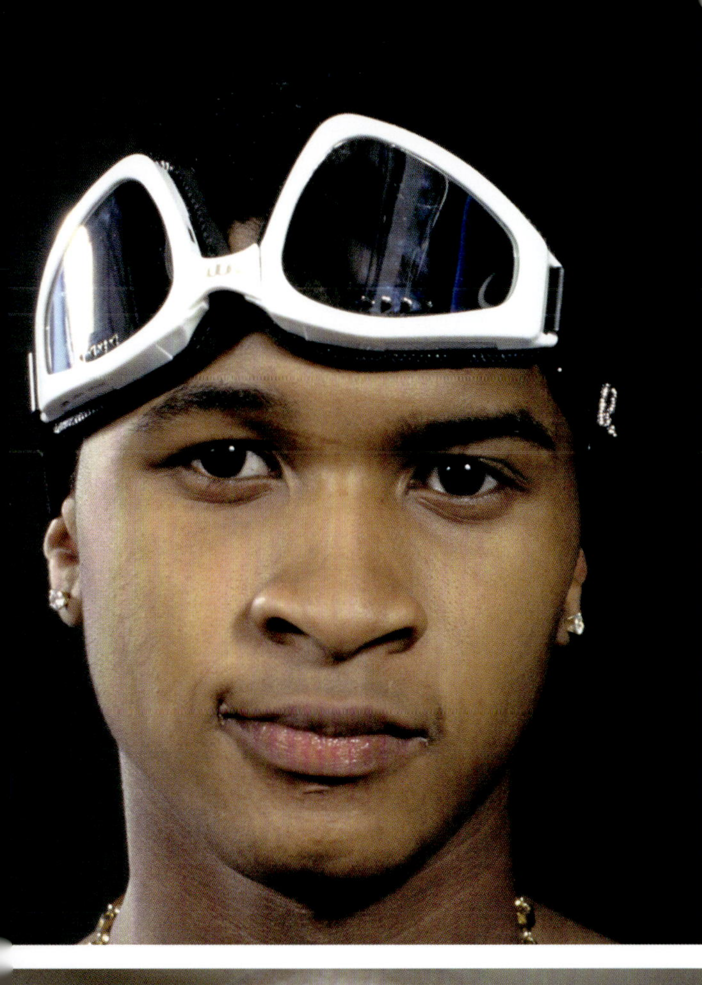

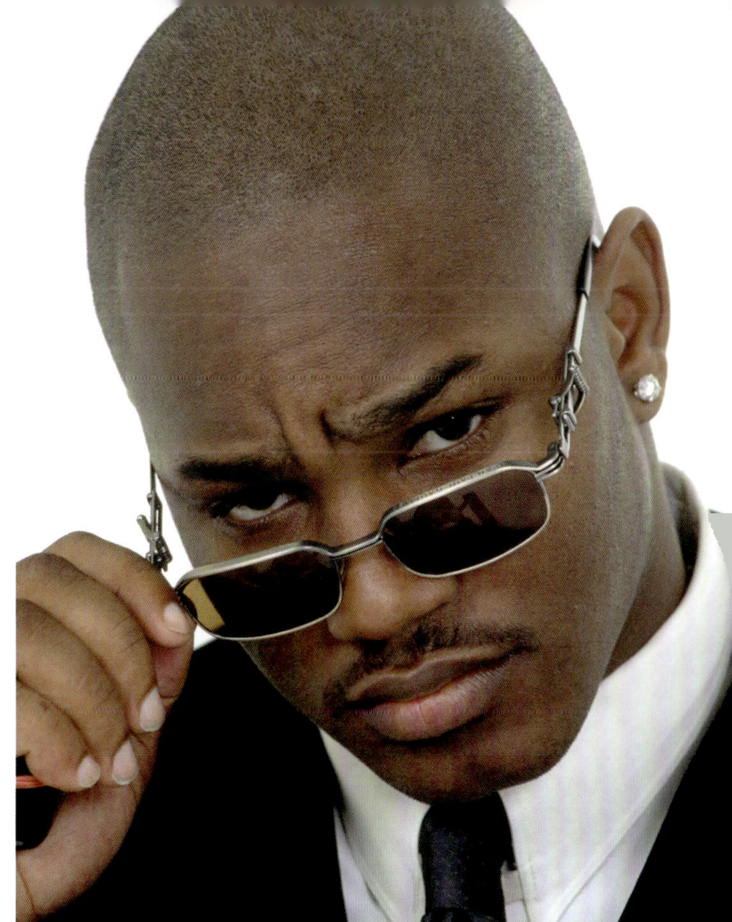

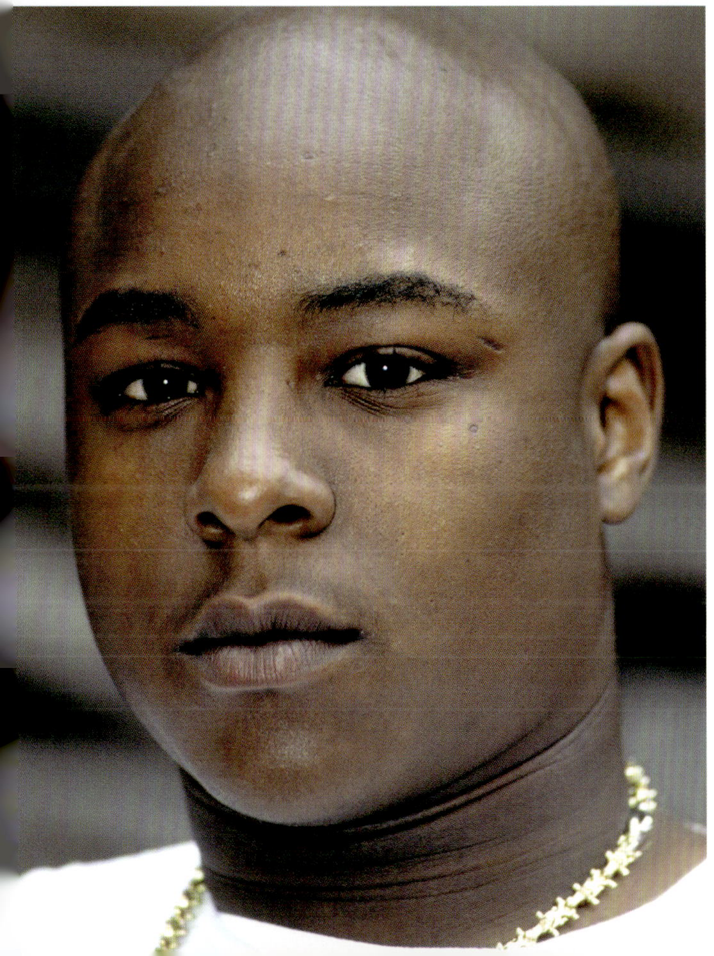

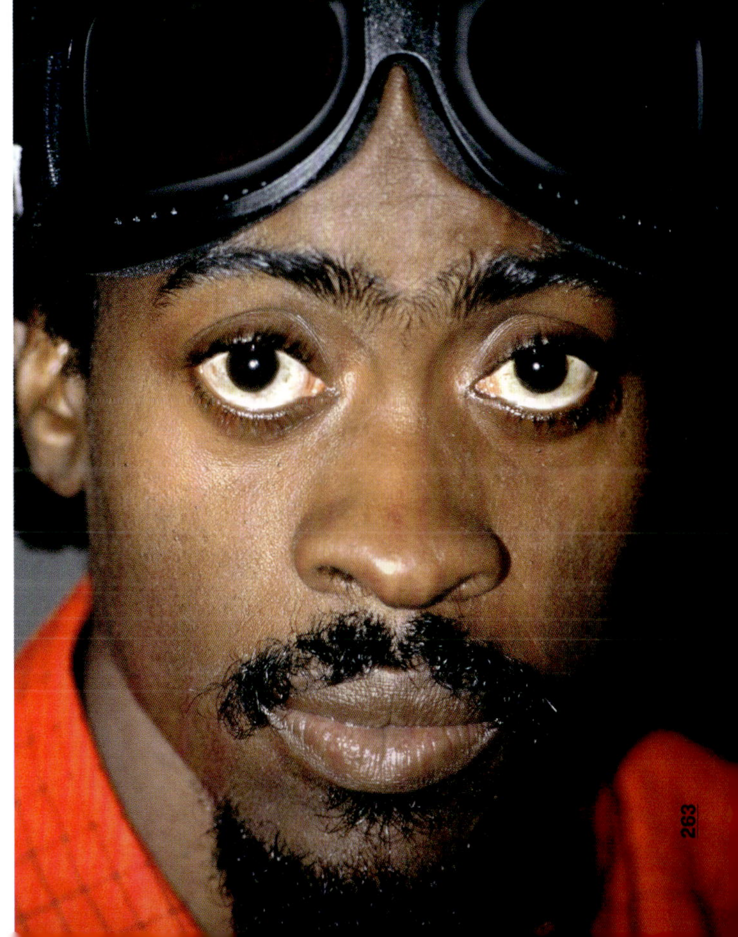

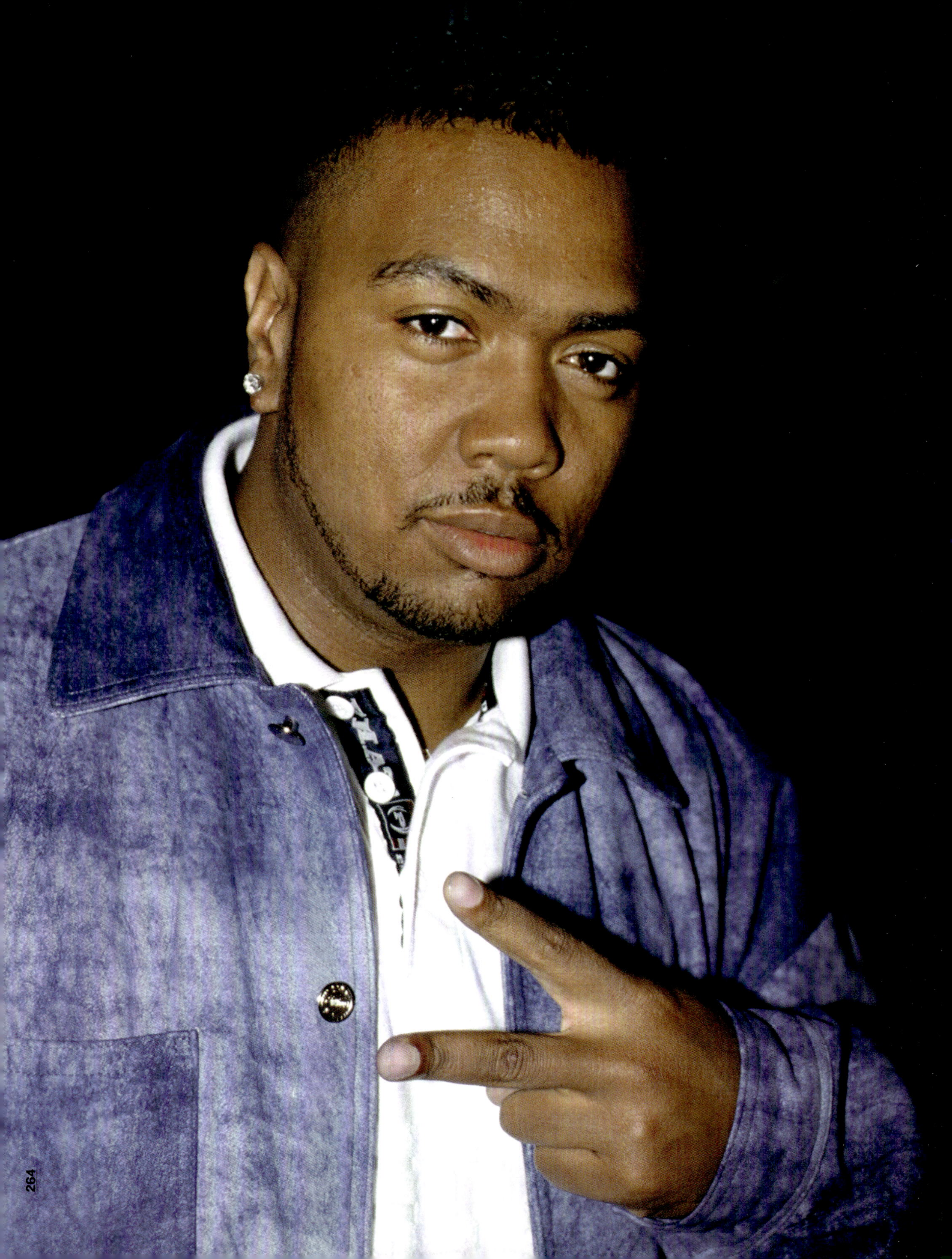

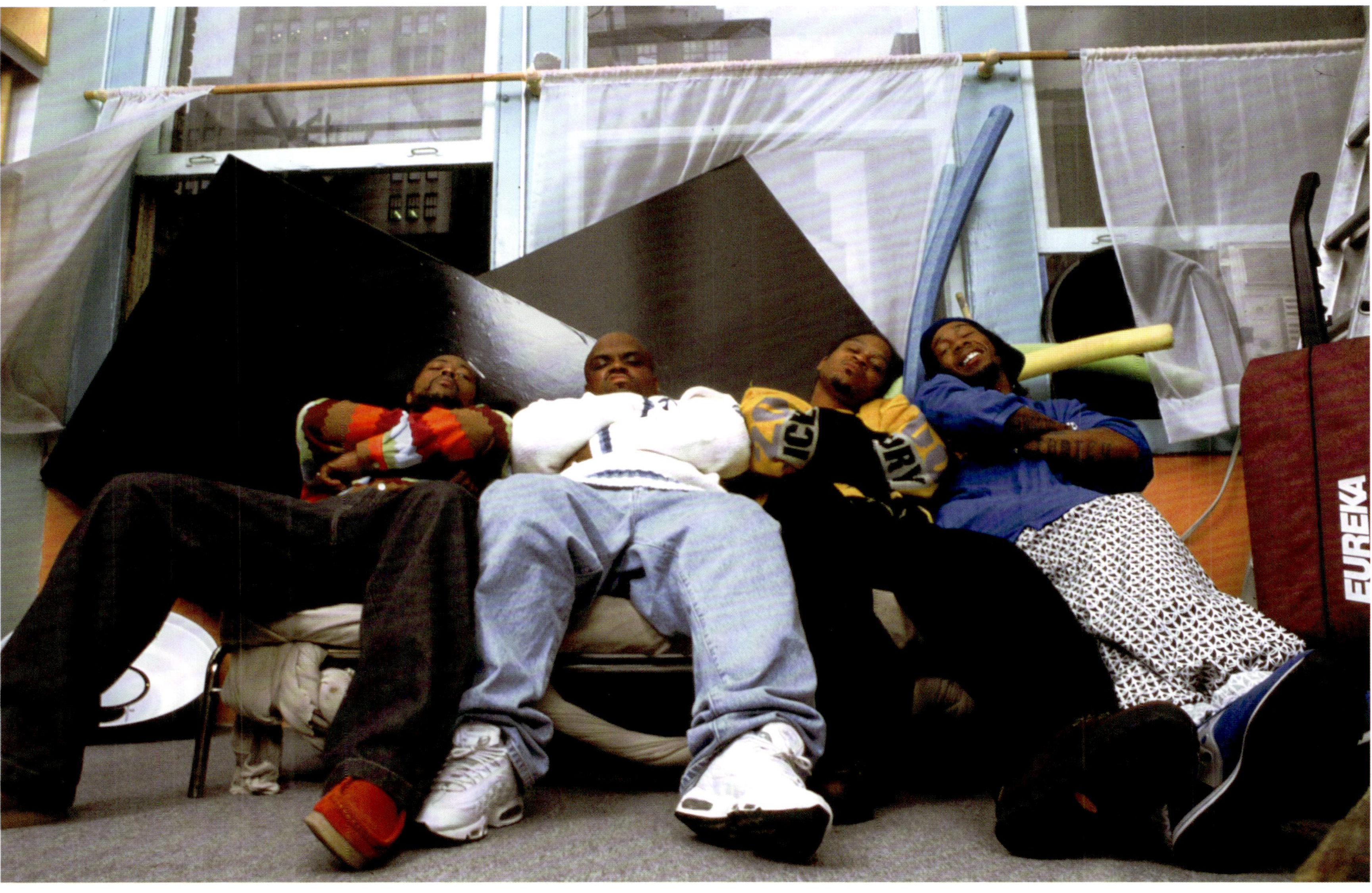

p.264 Timbaland, VH1 Music Awards, NYC, 2004; p.265 CeeLo Green and Goodie Mob, 3rd Eye Studio, 1999. One of the most humorous and laid back group shots done in my studio.

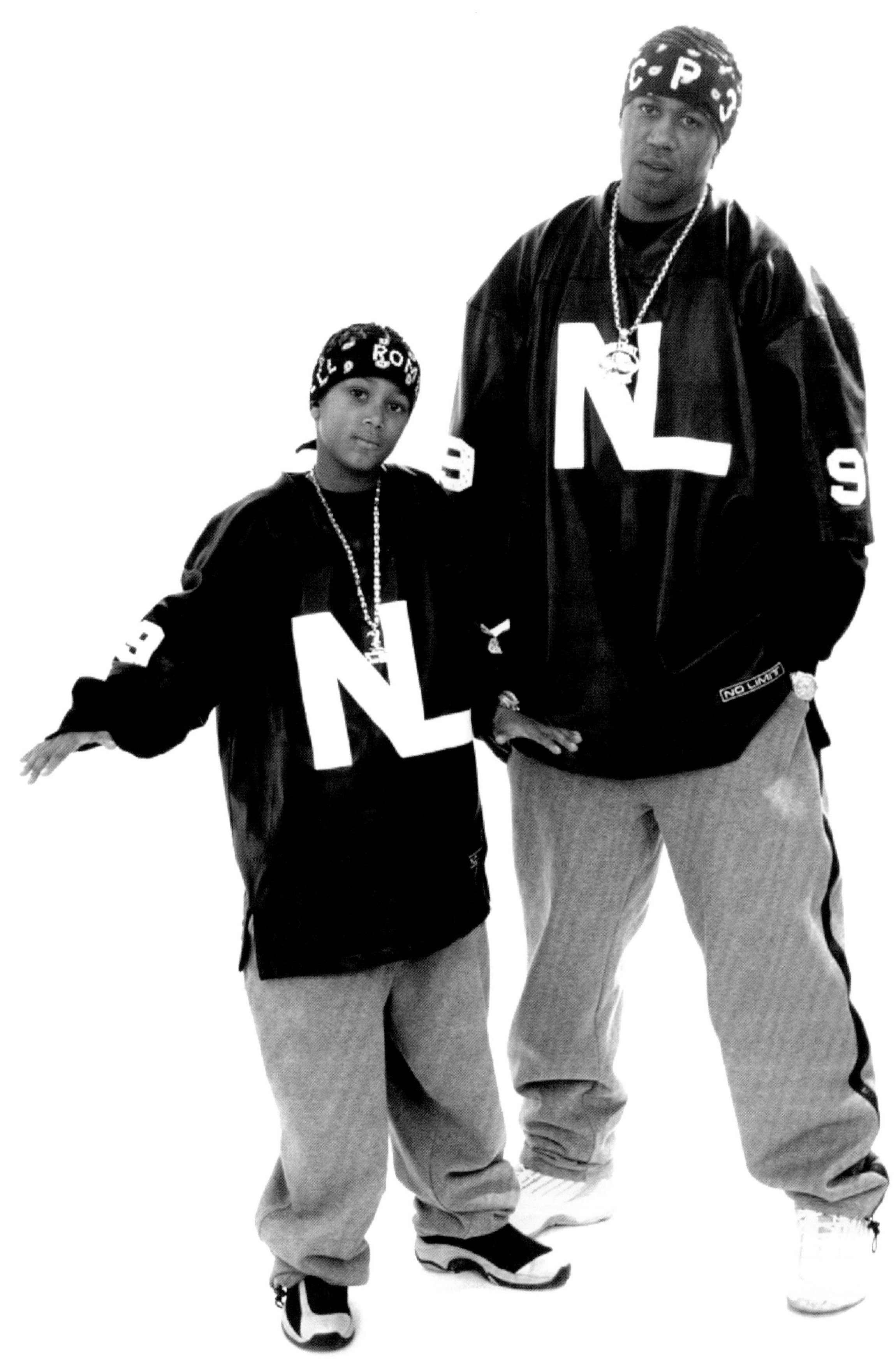
NL
9
9
NL
9
NO LIMIT

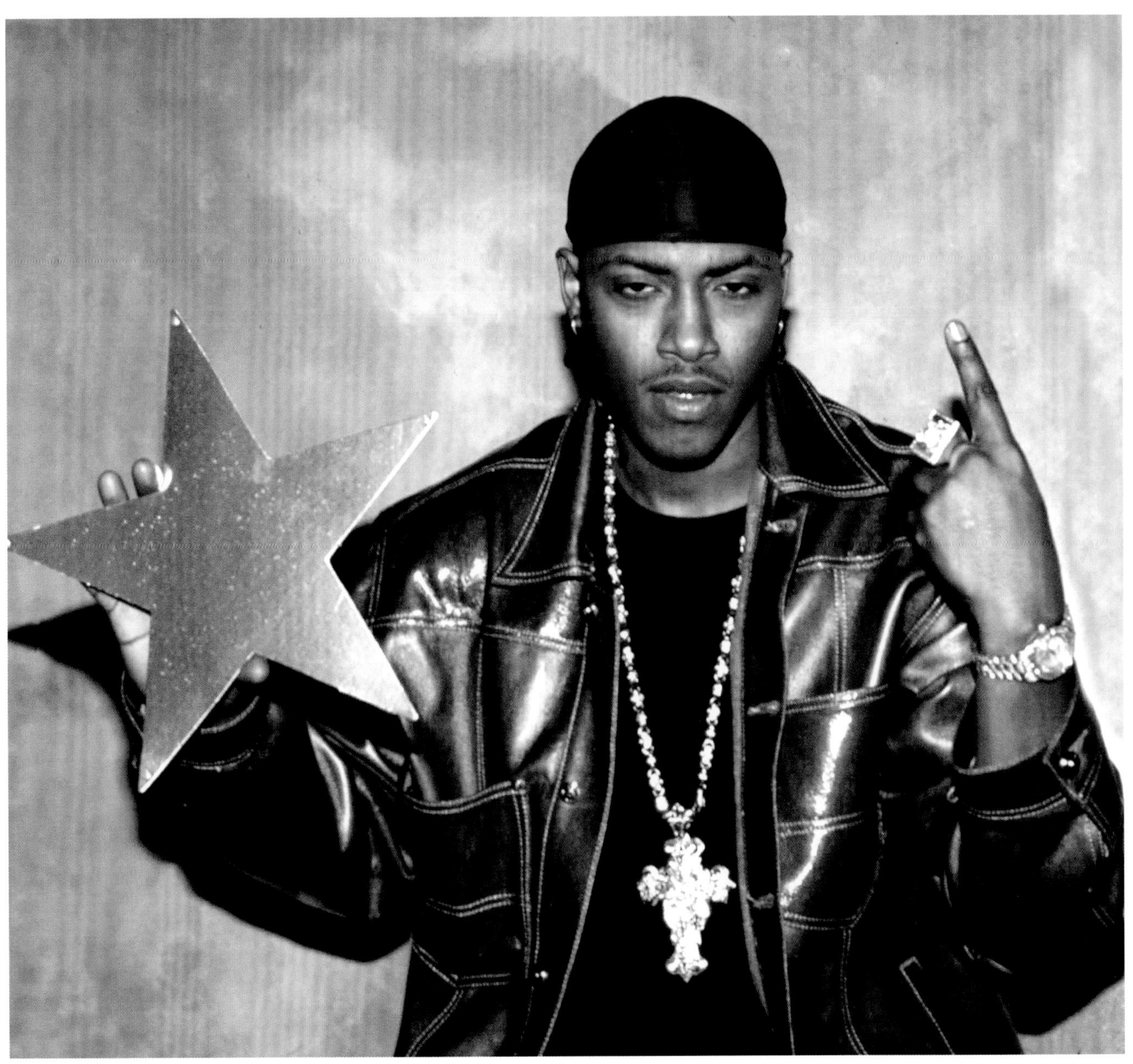

p.266 Lil' Romeo and his father Masta P. They spent a lot of time in my studio and the magazines seemed to not be able to get enough photos of Romeo, who was at that time competing with Lil' Bow Wow. And contrary to the hype, the two were friends. Masta P. was the only artist that ever grabbed a broom and a garbage bag and helped clean up my studio after a dozen hours of shooting.

p.267 Mystikal, Justin's Restaurant, NYC, 2007. He unfortunately spent most of his career battling charges of sexual abuse.

p.268 Outkast, NYC, 2000s; and p. 269, NYC, 1999. Part of the dynamic Dungeon Family from Atlanta, Georgia. These high-energy hit makers also had a sense of humor. Watch "Ms. Jackson" (2000) if you are in a sour mood.

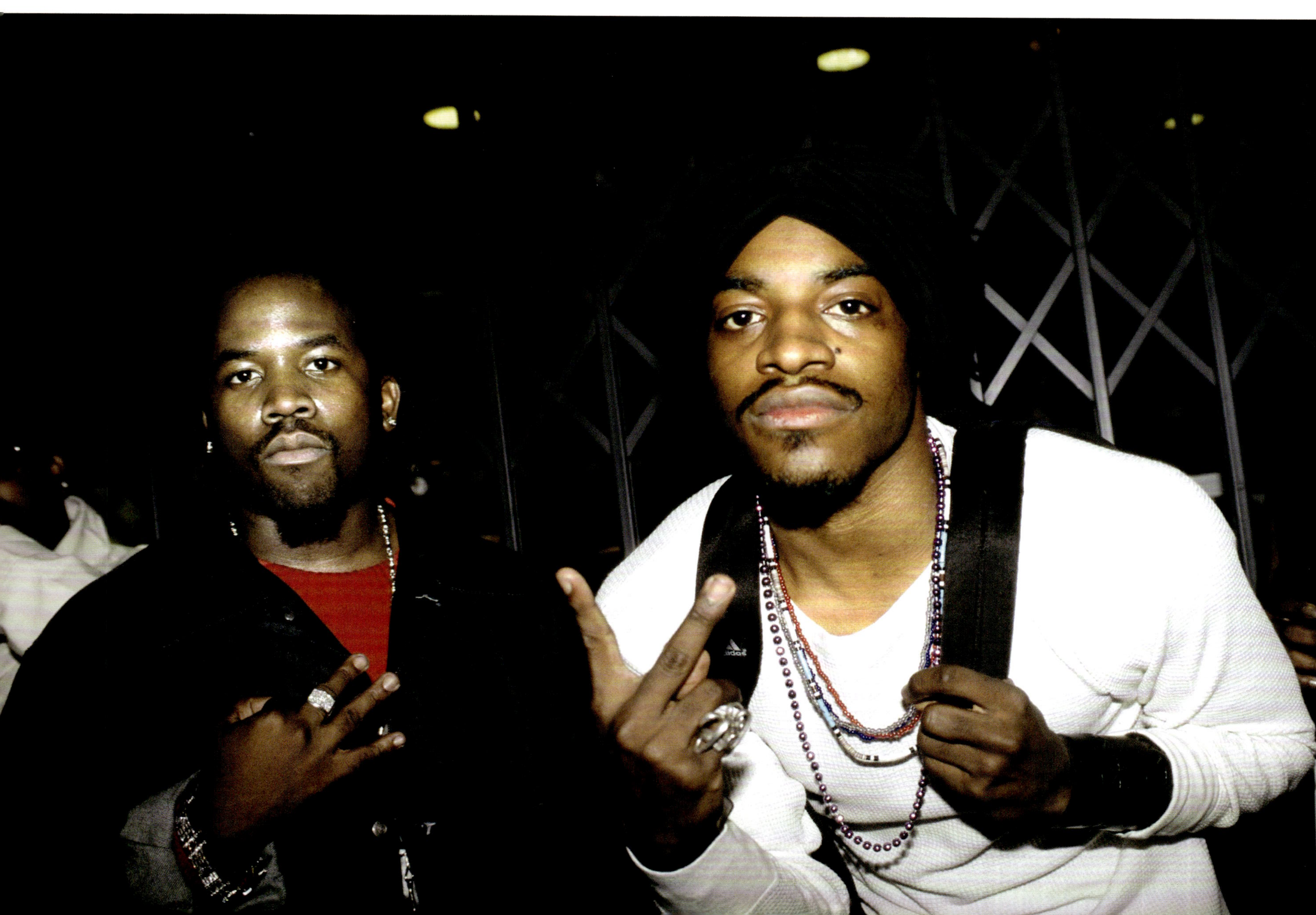

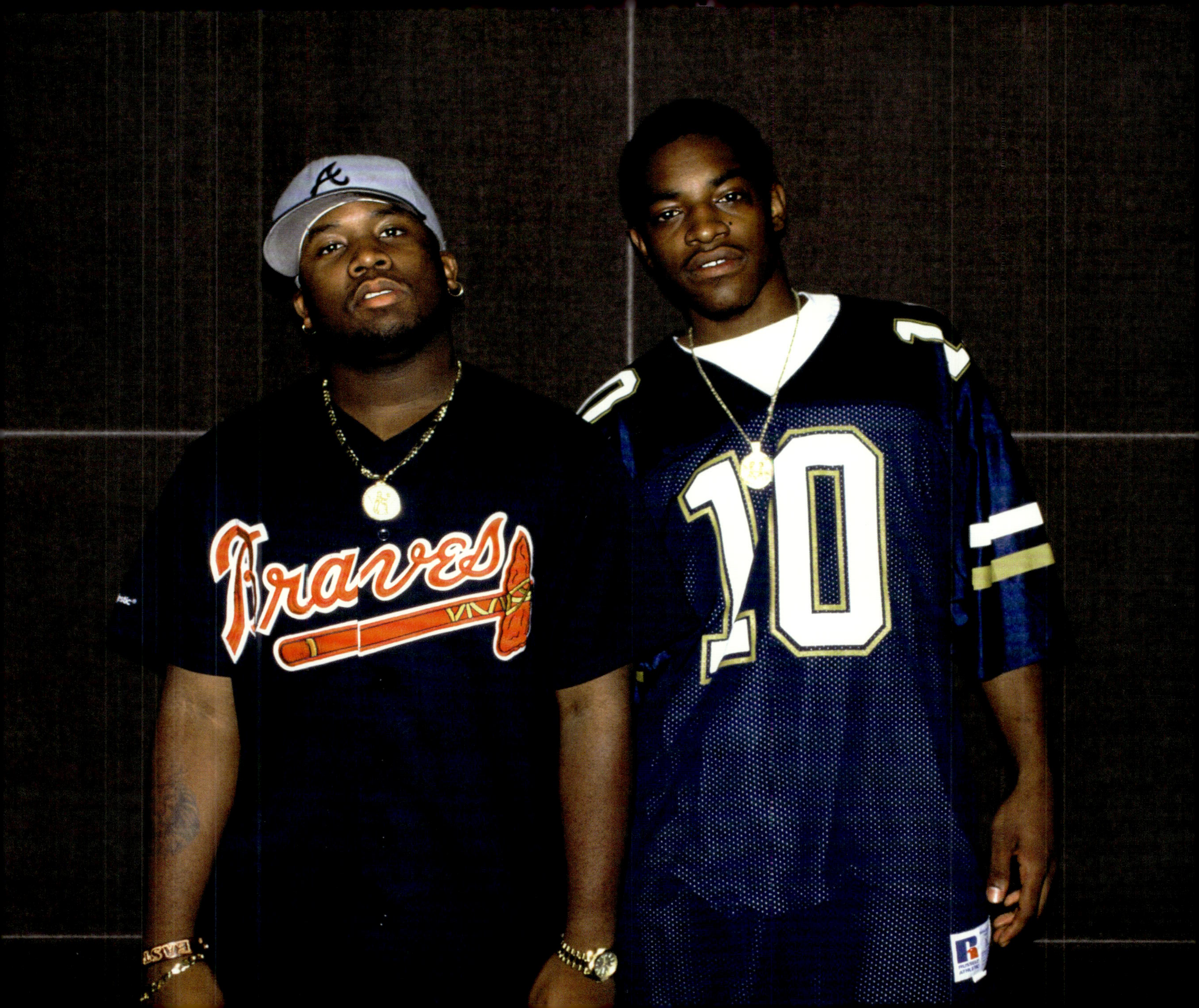
Braves
10

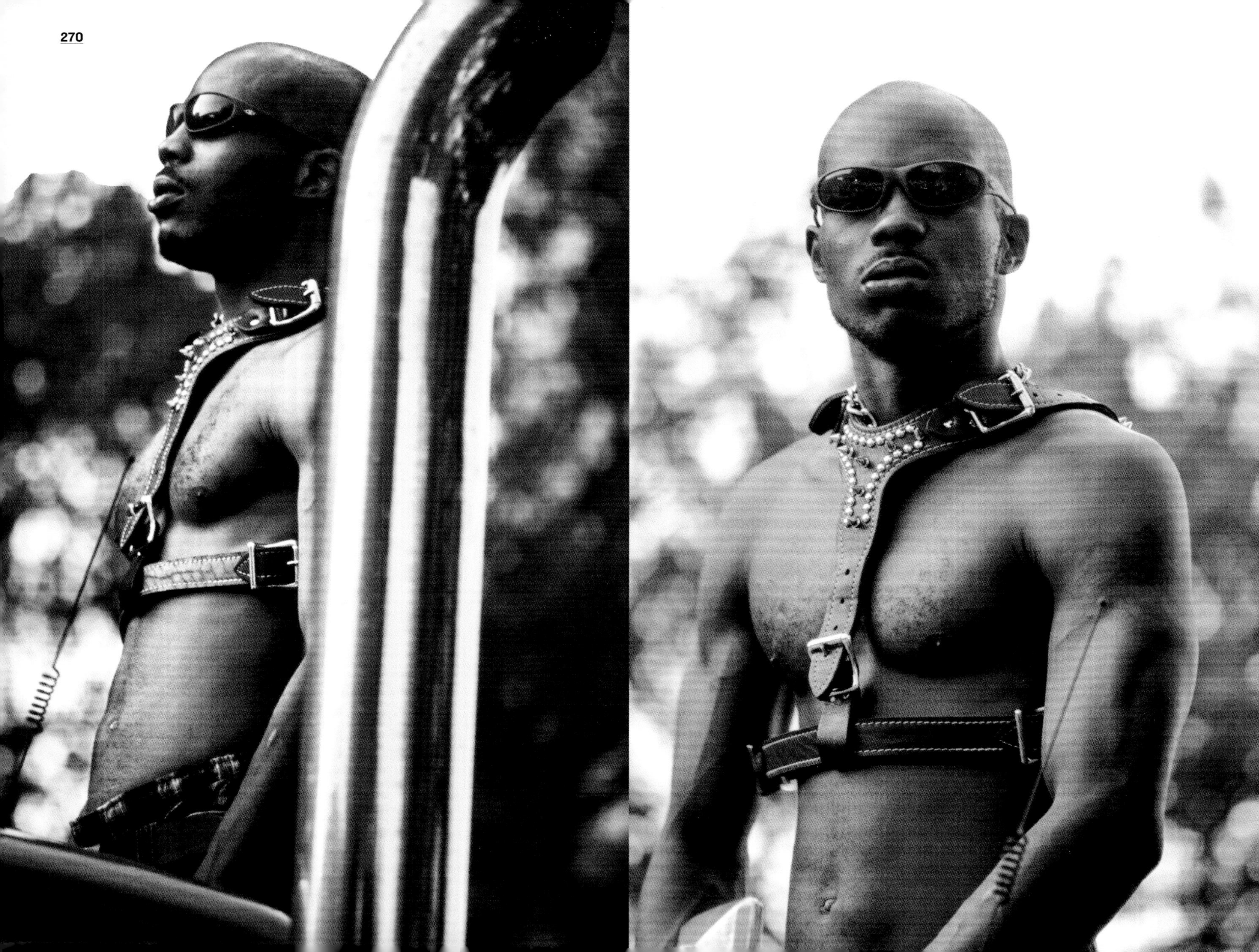

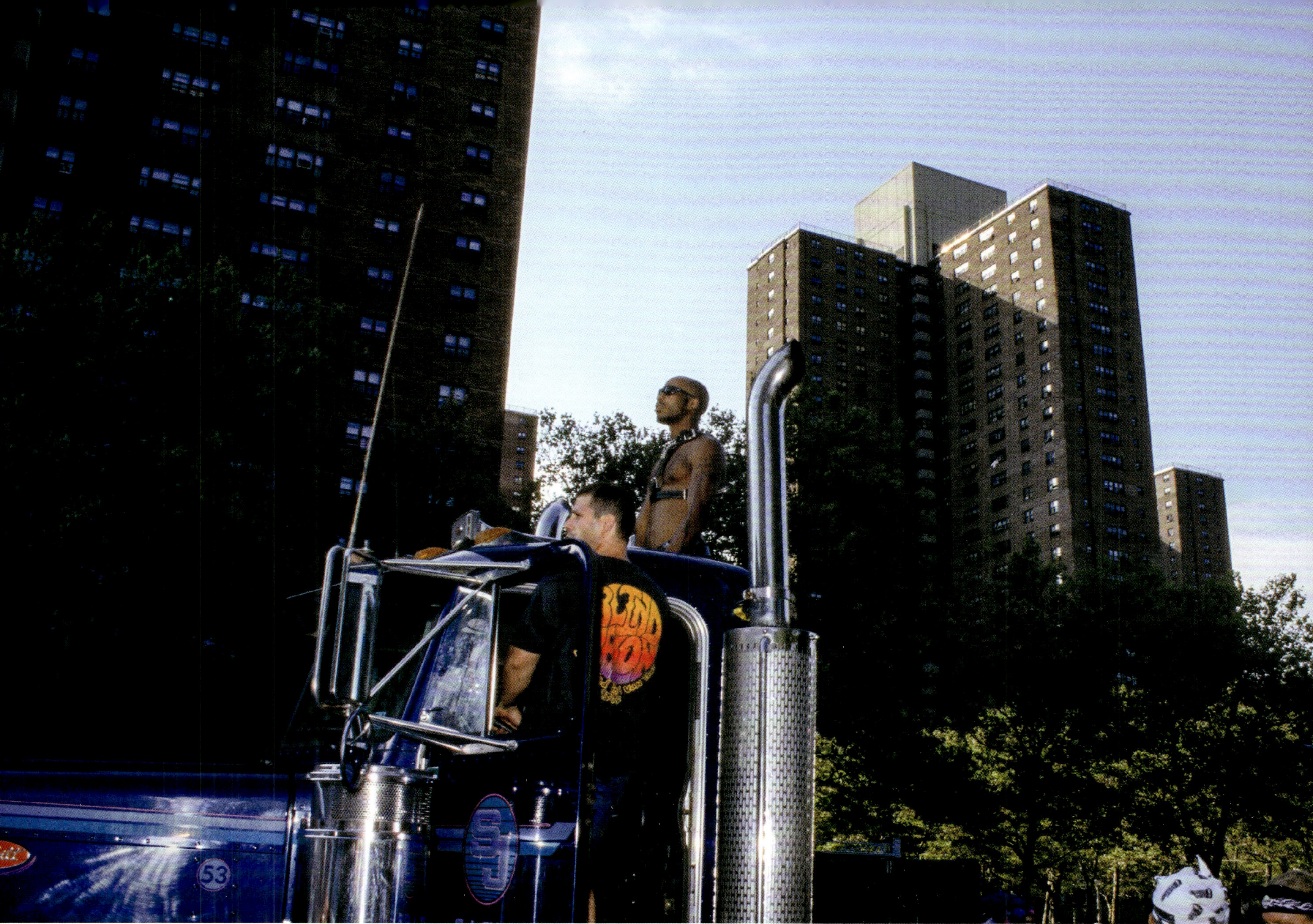

p.270–271, DMX, Washington Heights, NYC, 2003 (additional notes on p. 272)

p. 272 DMX, NYC, 2003. A complex man and a troubled one, but a very gifted artist, actor and songwriter. Washington Heights, NYC, early 2000s.

p.273 KRS-One, wearing a BDP jacket, NYC, early 1990s (see additional notes on page 279).

Notes to pages 270-271:

These are outtakes for DMX's video for "Where the Hood At?" (2003). The scenes with him atop the Mack truck and the bondage gear ended up on the cutting room floor, but many scenes shot in the Rucker Park Basketball Courts (across from the former Polo Grounds) made it into the video.

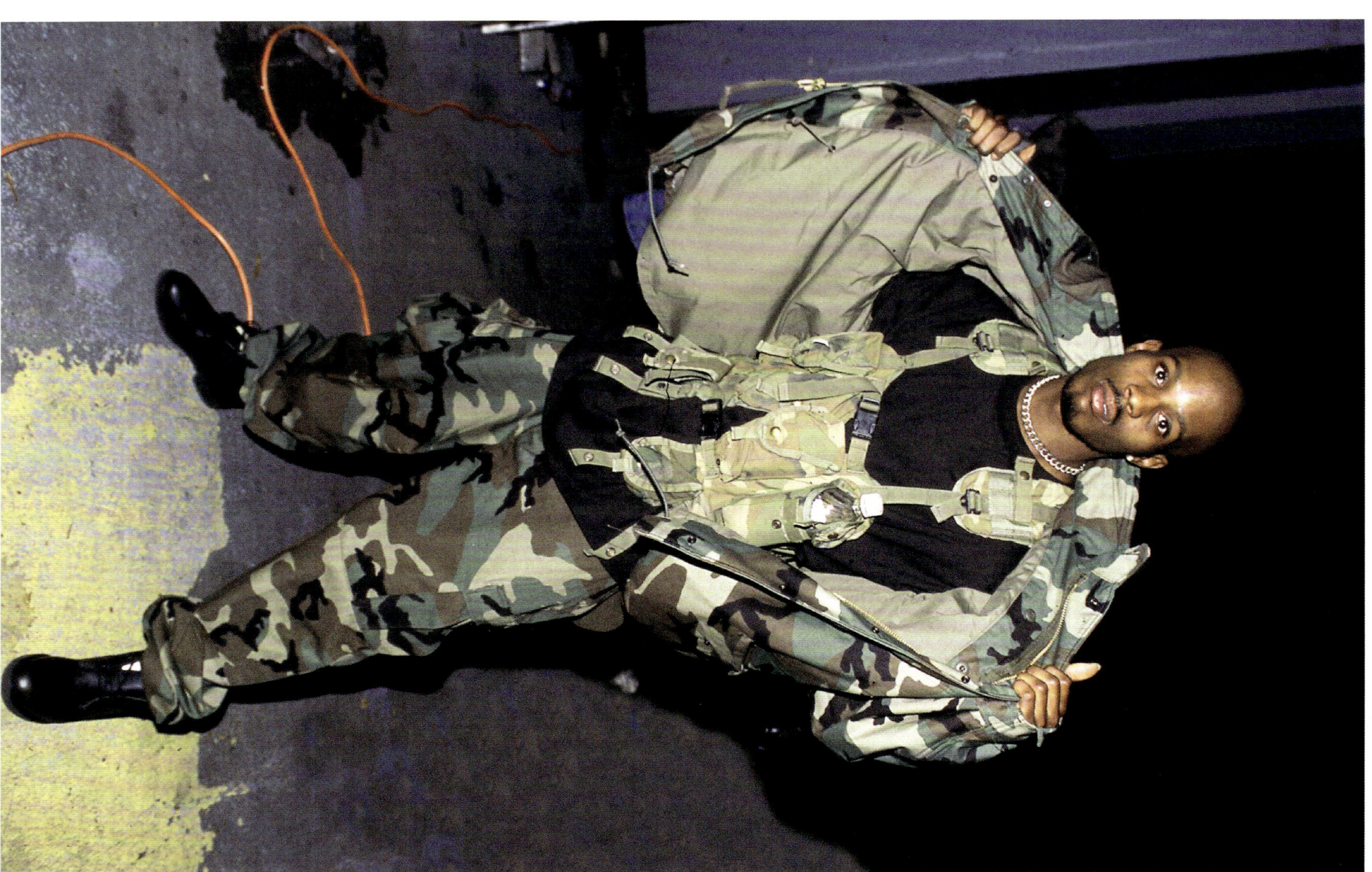

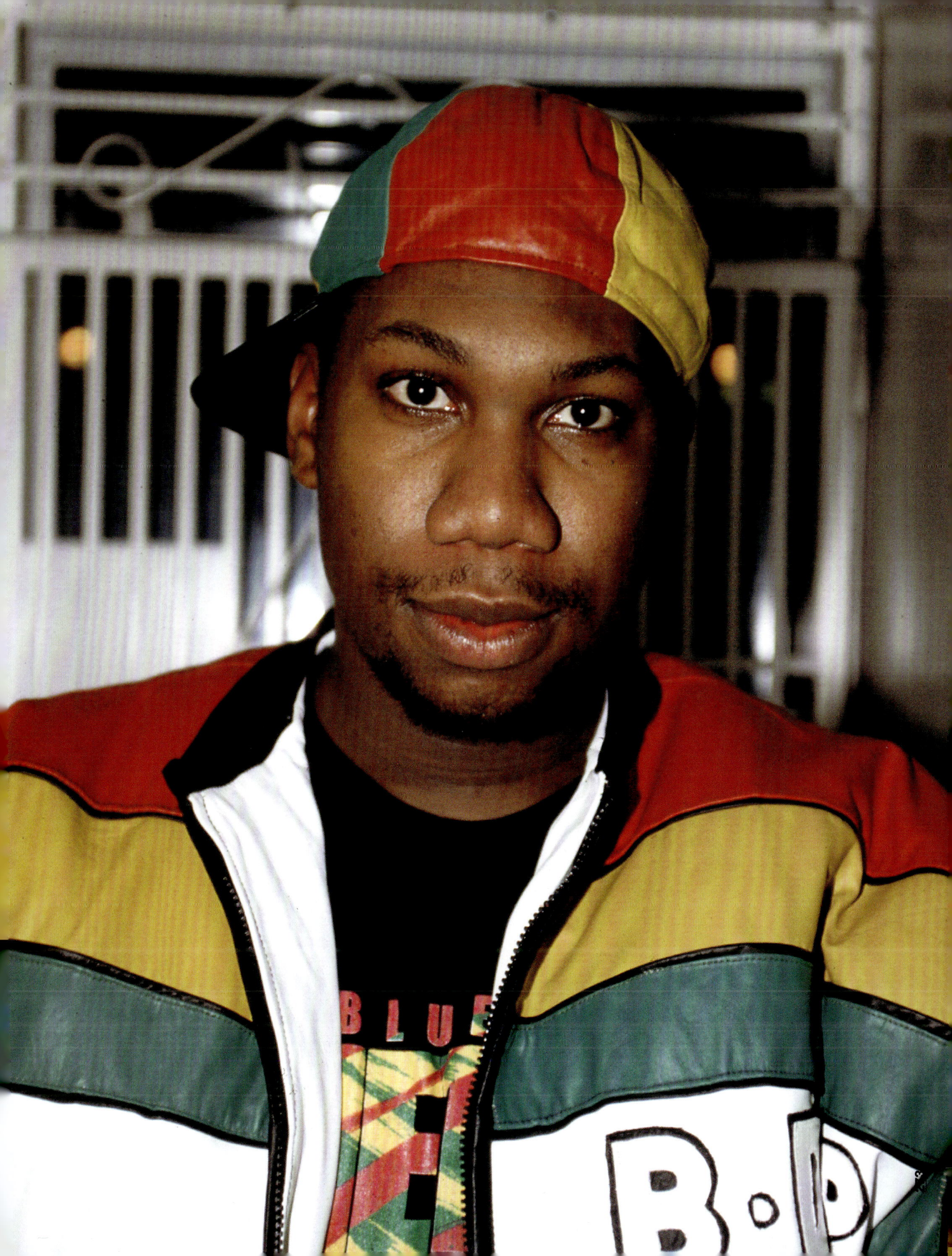
BLUE

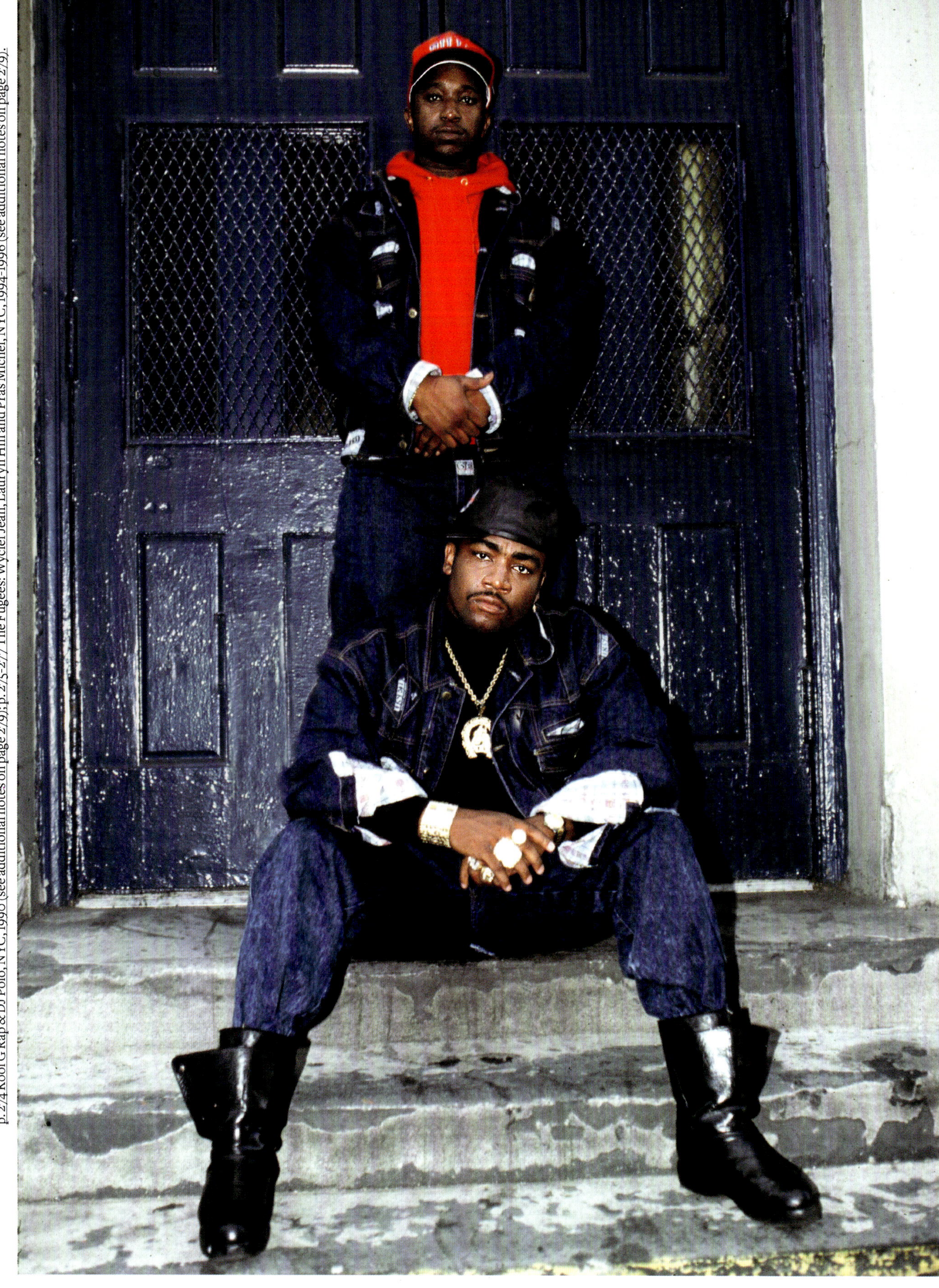

p.274 Kool G Rap & DJ Polo, NYC, 1990 (see additional notes on page 279); p.275-277 The Fugees: Wyclef Jean, Lauryn Hill and Pras Michel, NYC, 1994-1996 (see additional notes on page 279).

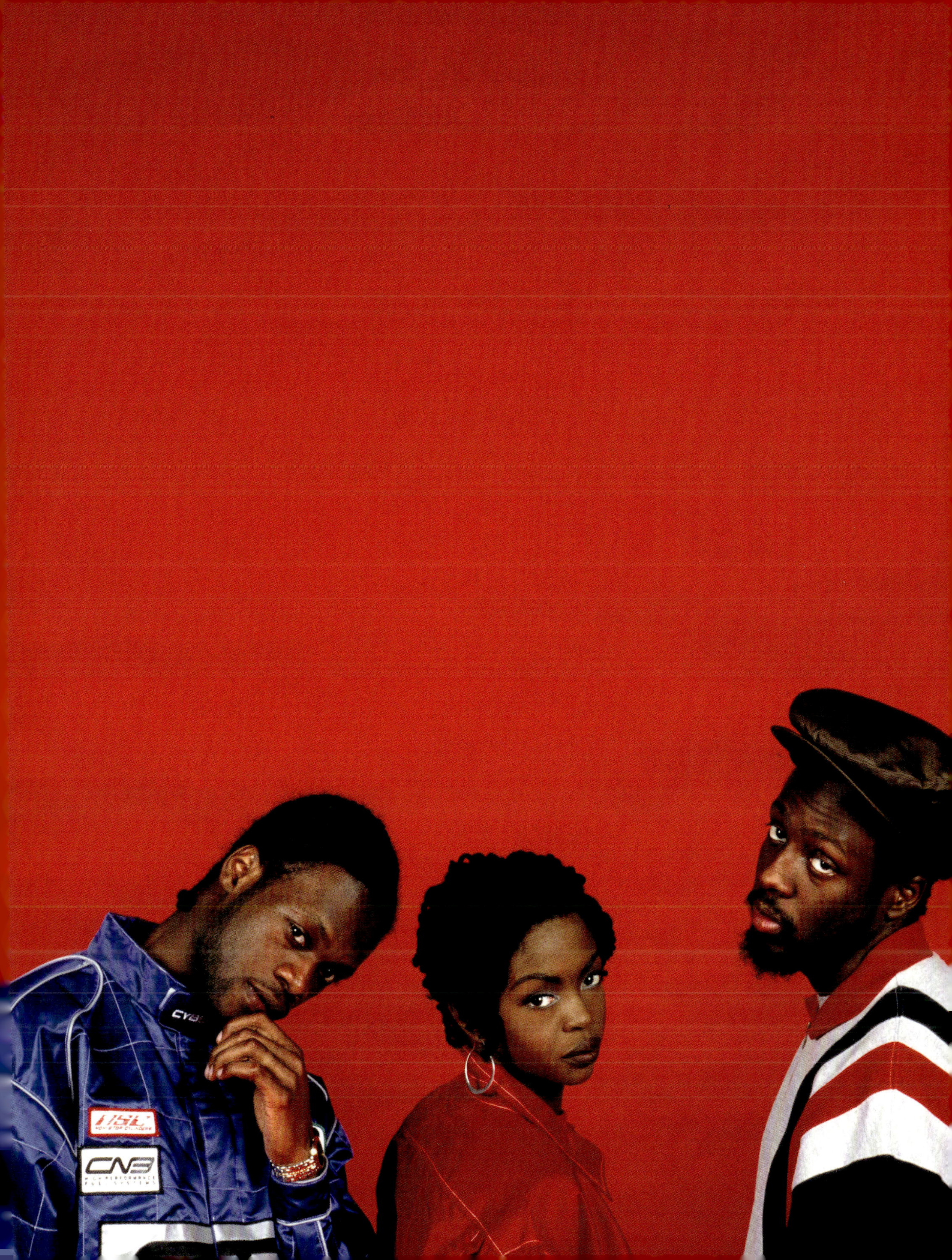

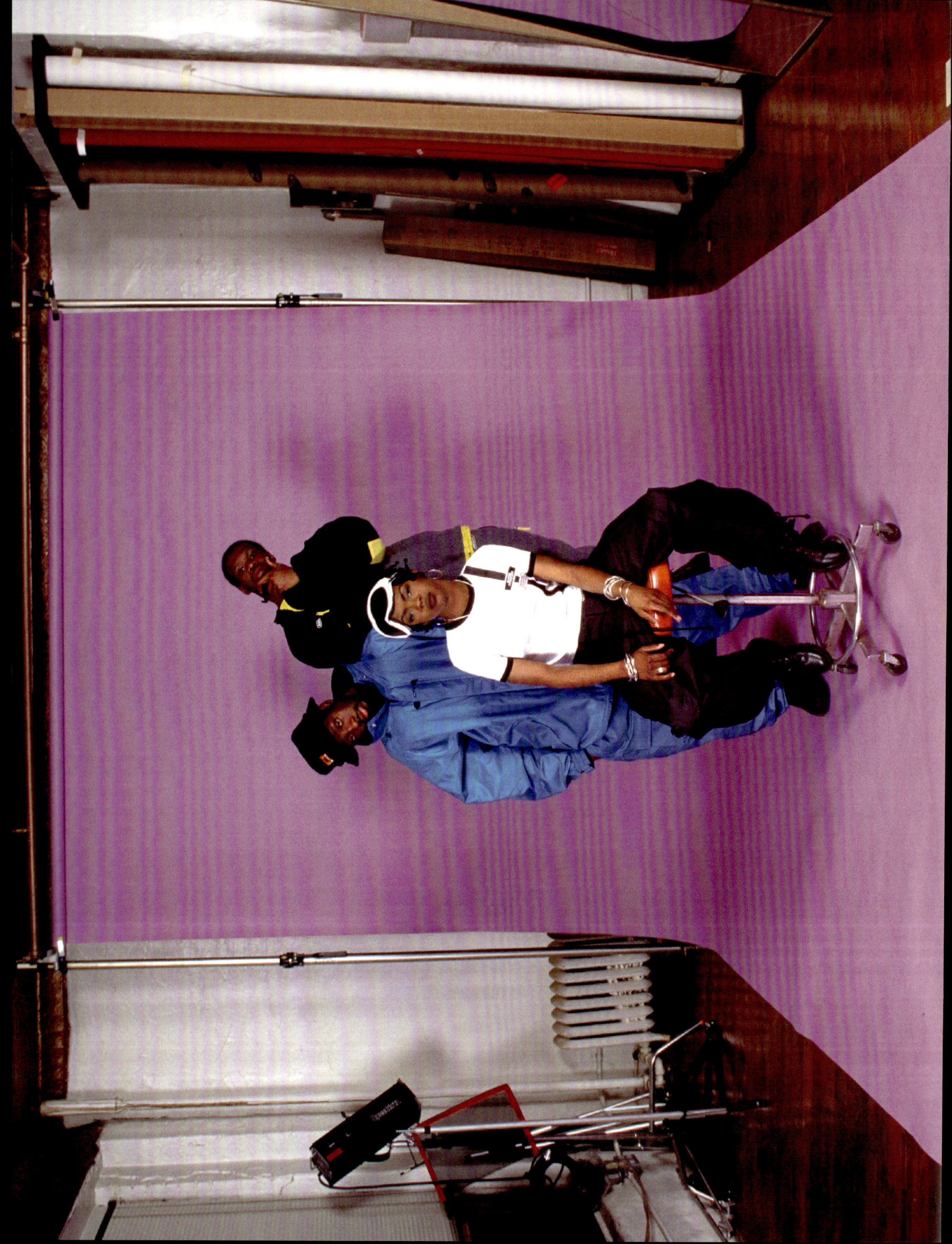

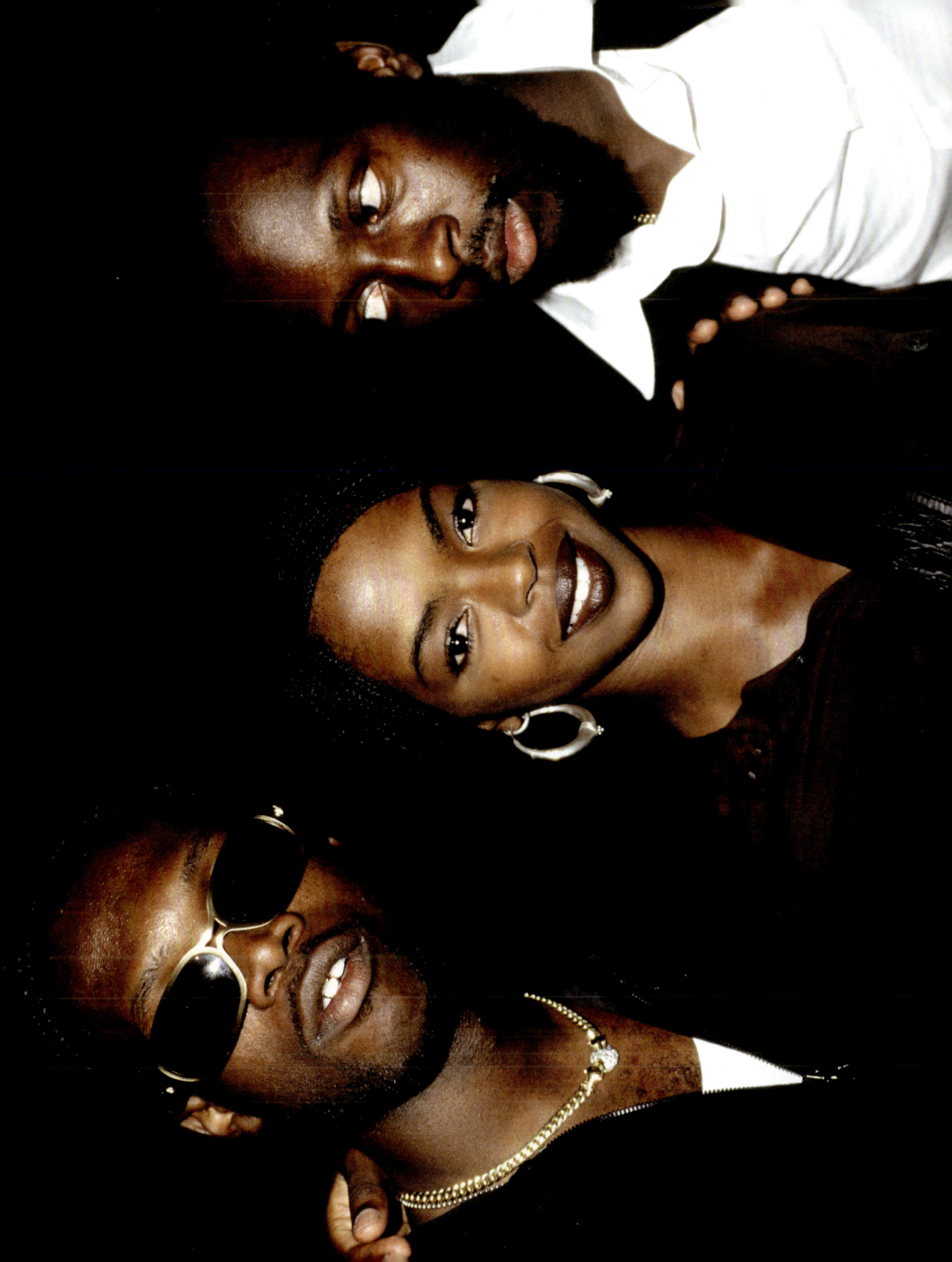

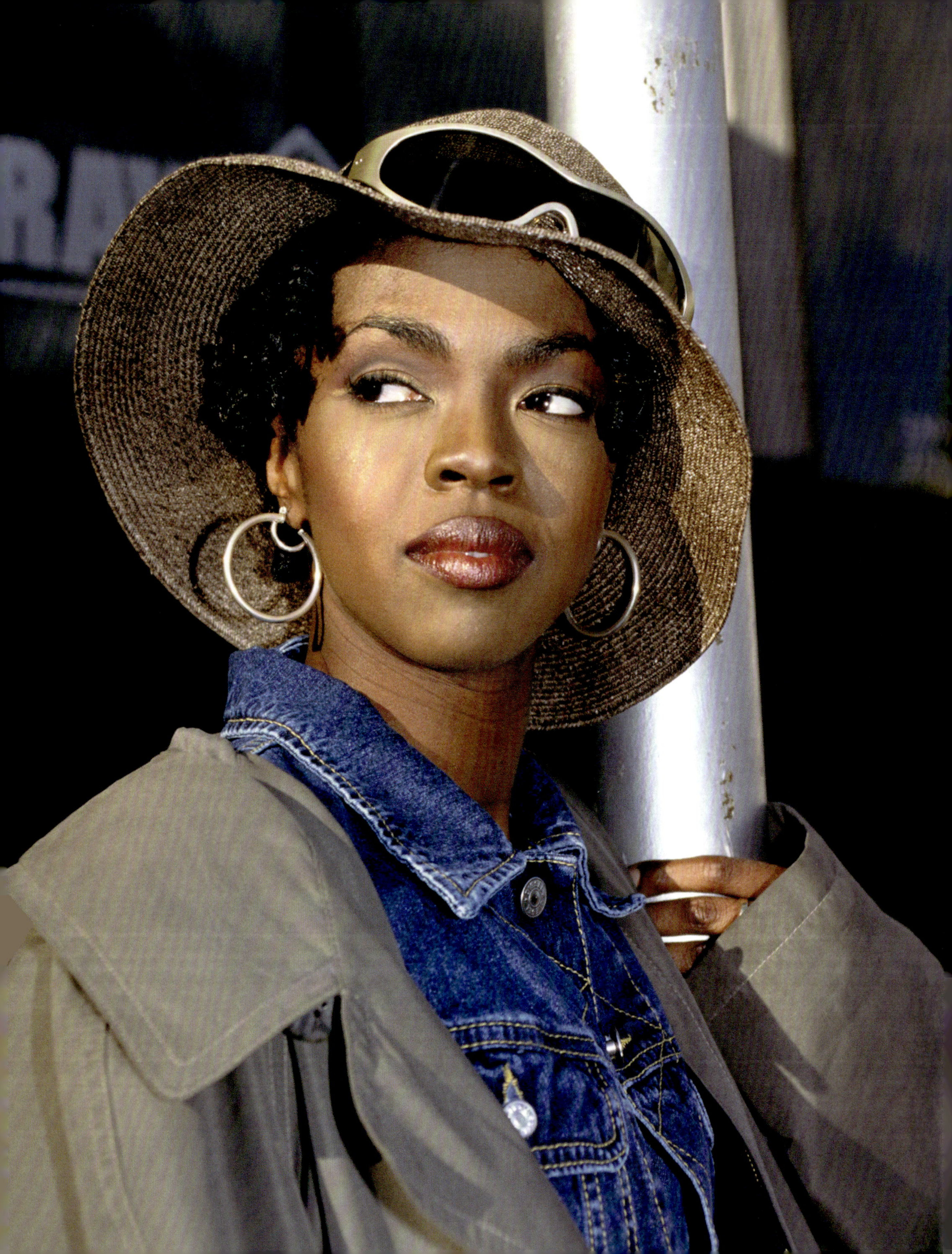

p.278 Lauryn Hill, 42nd Street, NYC, 1996. This is one of my favorite portraits ever. Shot this while hanging out with her during a break from shooting a video for the song "If I Ruled The World" that she did with Nas. I often told people that I had the largest studio in America, namely the streets of New York City.

Notes to page 273:
KRS-One, aka Blastmaster KRS-1, aka Tha Teacha, one of the best rappers/emcees if not the best ever. Founder of The Temple of Hip-Hop. Conscious, aware, unique and has always reflected the best of what hip-hop is and what hip-hop can be. The 1991 EP *H.E.A.L. (Human Education Against Lies)* and the BDP album *Edutainment* from 1990 were concept albums that explored the breadth and depth of what he called "Hip-hop Kulture." He honored me by choosing me to be a keynote speaker at "The Hip-hop Declaration of Peace" at the United Nations. Two little known facts about him: 1) His name was Krishna; 2) His mother was a Black Panther. And it is universally accepted that no one in hip-hop is better on stage, and only someone demented would want to go after him.

Notes to Page 274:
Point of fact: I saw a poster of the Beatles sitting in front of a blue door in the 1960s. When I was shooting Kool G Rap & Polo and saw the door, the poster popped into my head and I shot this both for its color scheme but also as a tribute to that original image. And we were lucky to find a clean area for them to sit on since NYC was in the first full week of a garbage strike. Kool G Rap was perhaps the first real gangsta rapper, but instead of bragging about his murderous habits or his massive drug sales, all of his songs are told as stories, not lived reality.

Notes to p. 275-277:
The Fugees (Wyclef Jean, Lauryn Hill and Pras Michel) were not taken seriously when they began. More people had more negative things to say about them than nearly any other group I knew of. "Haitians can't rap," "women can't rap," "rappers from New Jersey suck," and more. But their second album, *The Score* (1996), won two Grammys, and is one of the best selling albums in hip-hop history with 18 million copies sold worldwide, proving all the naysayers were wrong as hell. Lauryn Hill and Wyclef went on to great solo careers.

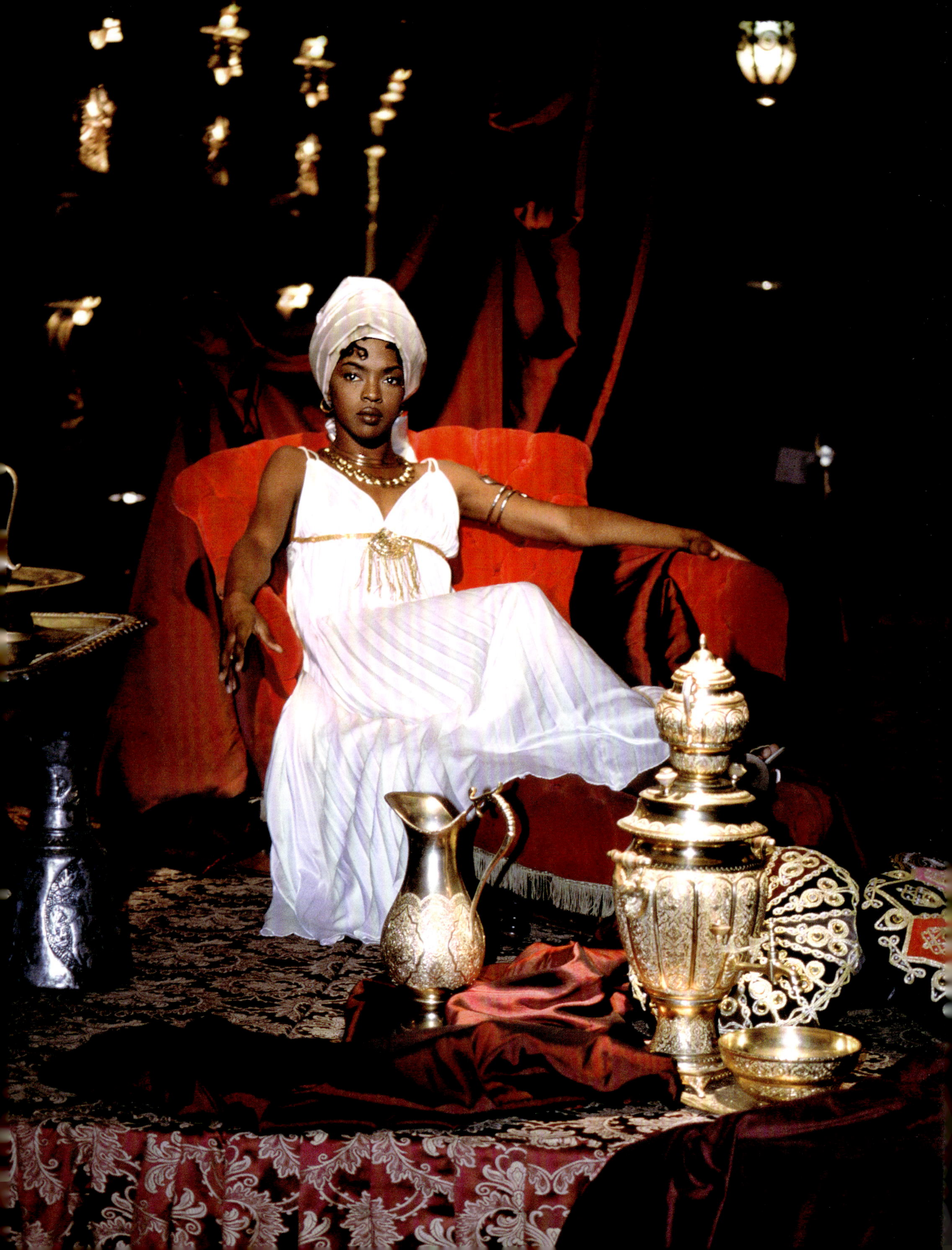

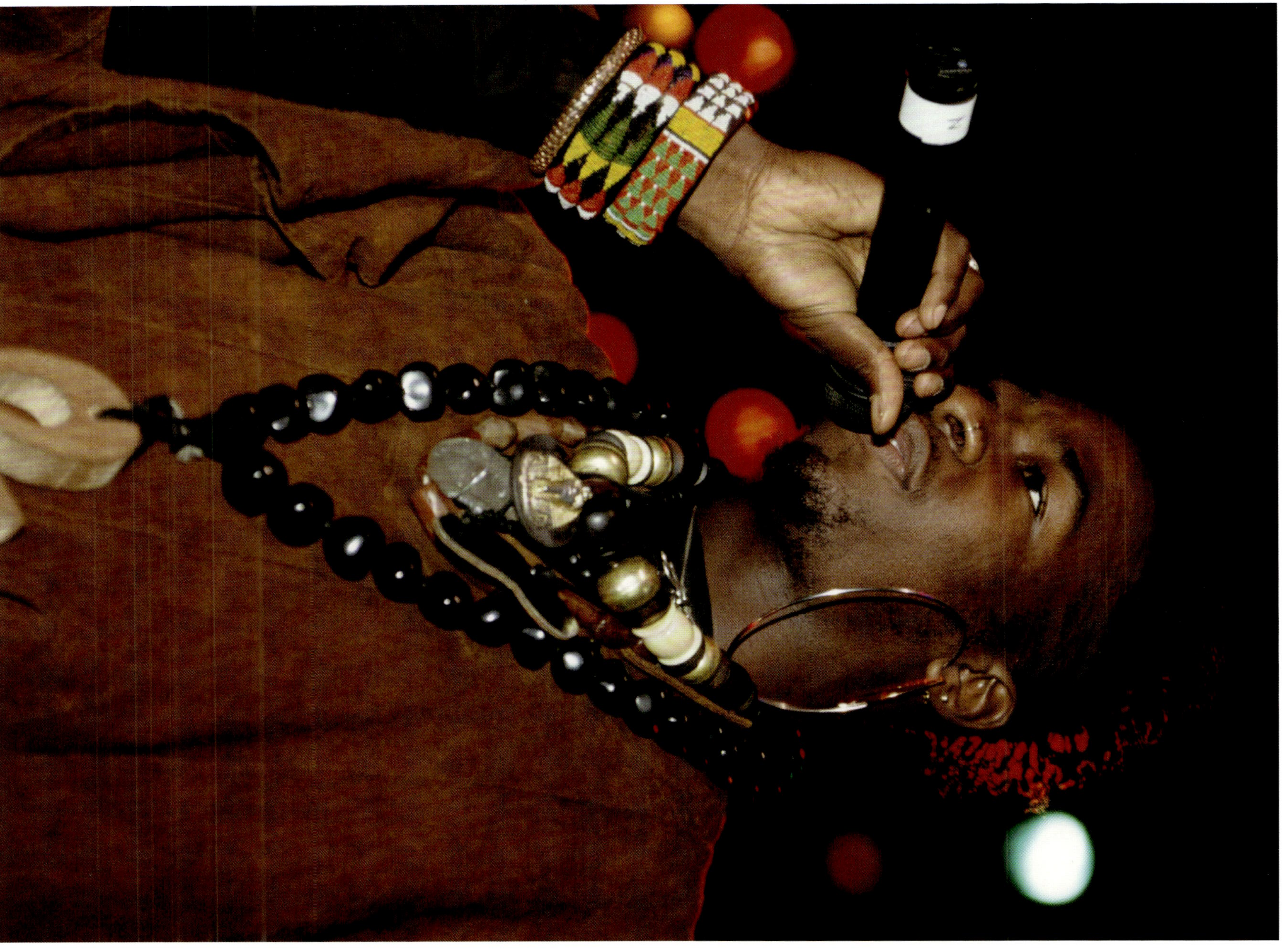

p.280 Lauryn Hill dressed as a princess during the video shoot for Bounty Killer's "Hip-Hopera" ft. the Fugees, United Palace, Washington Heights, NYC, 1996.

p.281 Brother J from The X Clan. One of the most underrated emcees from one of the most underrated groups in hip-hop. Newark, NJ, 1990s.

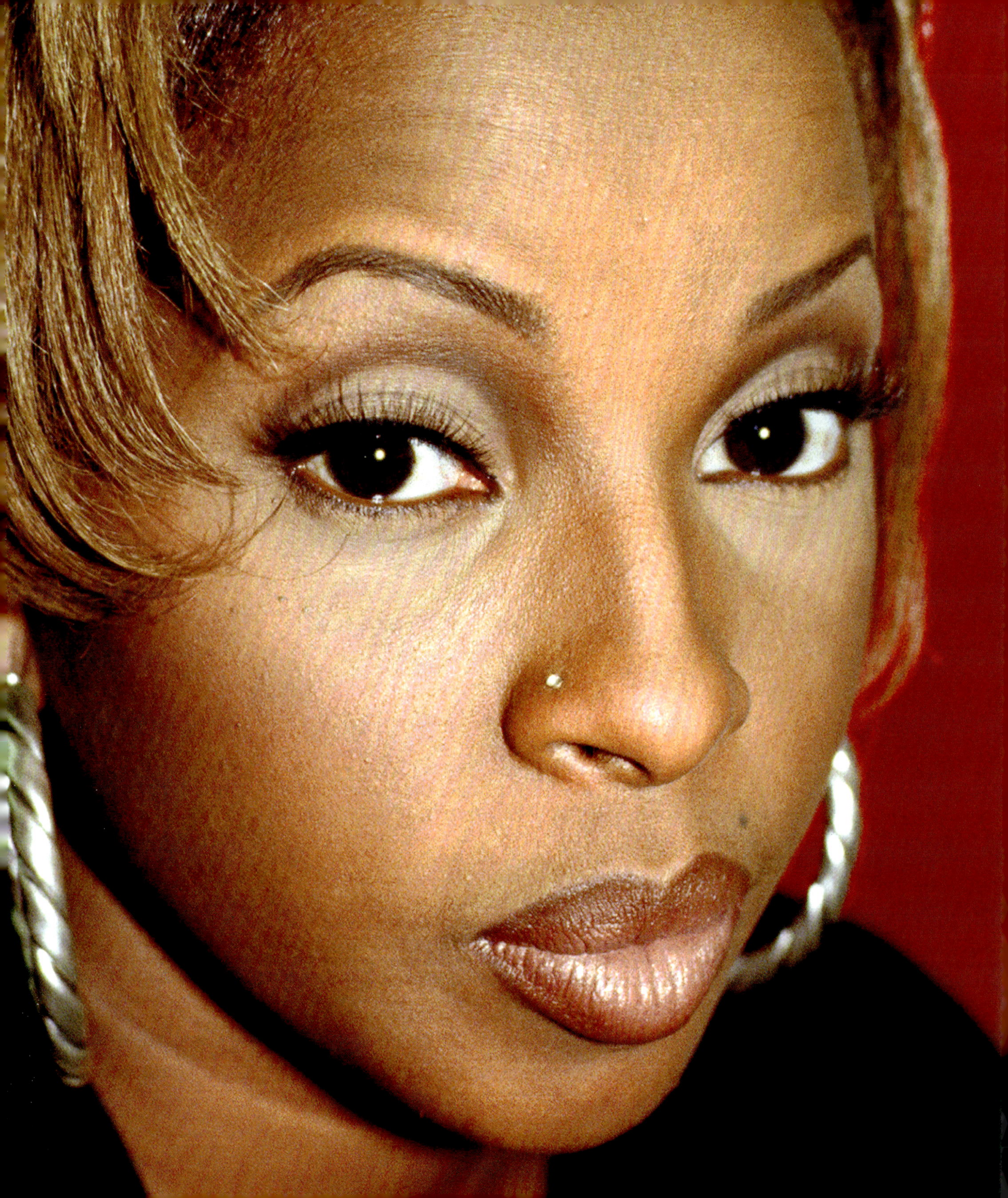

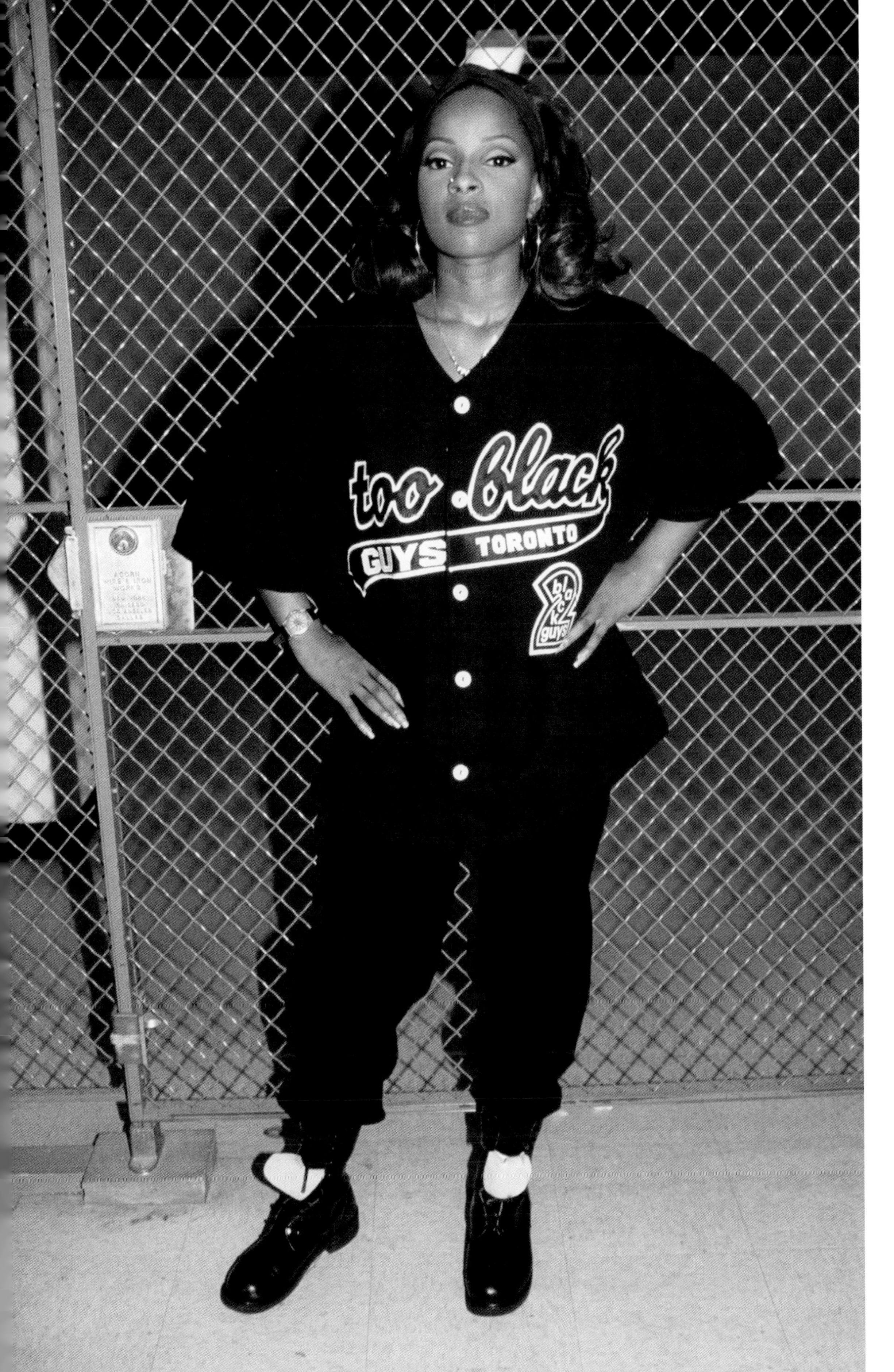

p.282–283 Mary J. Blige. It would take hours to describe all of the things she has accomplished. Singer, songwriter, record producer and actress; nine-time Grammy Award winner, three Golden Globe nominations, and two Academy Award nominations. And I have photos of her as a backup singer for Father MC in 1989. Eight of her studio albums have gone multi-platinum.

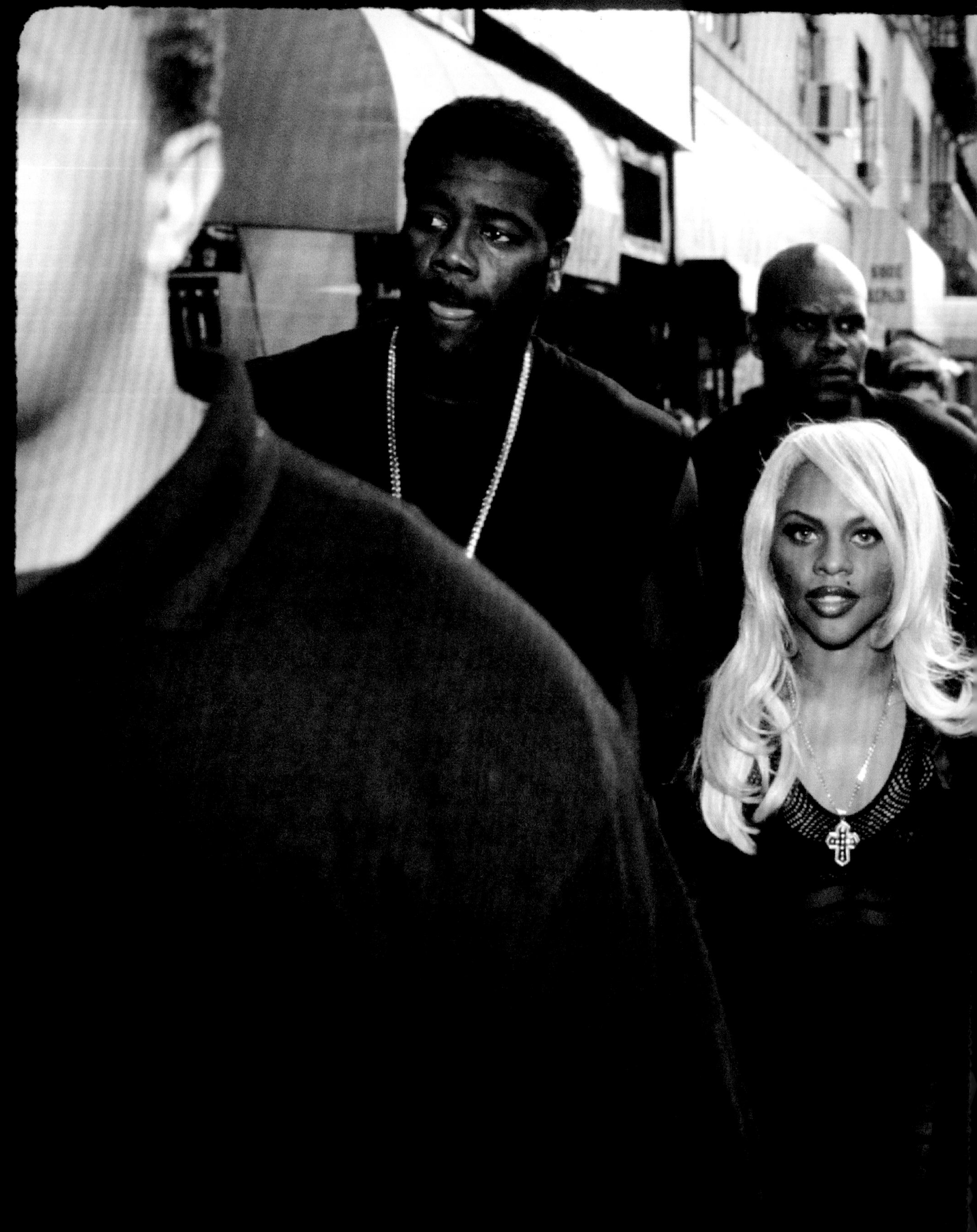

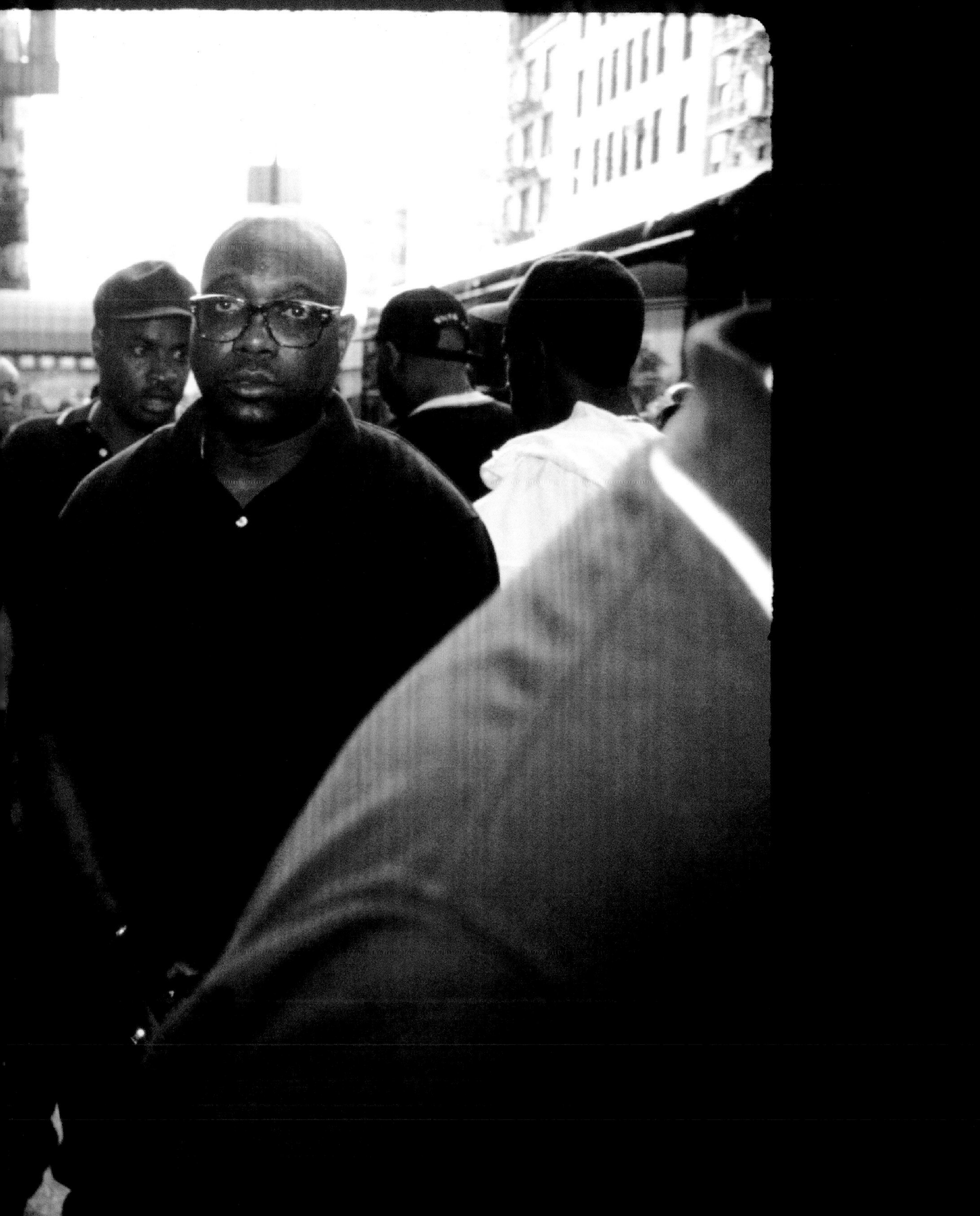

p.284-285 Lil' Kim surrounded by her bodyguards on her way to a video shoot with Sean "Puffy" Combs, NYC, 1998.
p.286-287 Lil' Kim studio shoot where we channeled 1920s flappers at the Savoy Ballroom or the Cotton Club, NYC, 1990s.

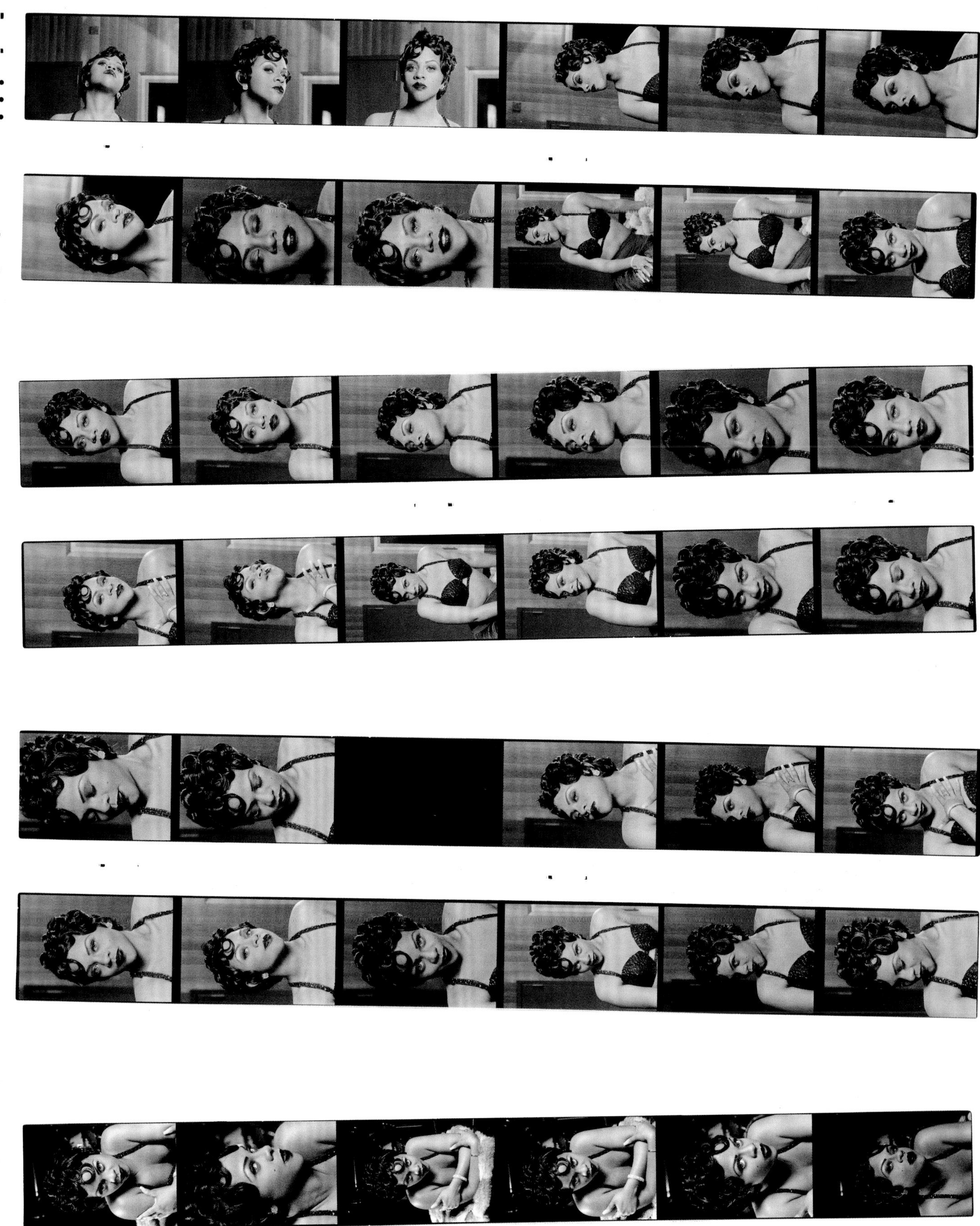

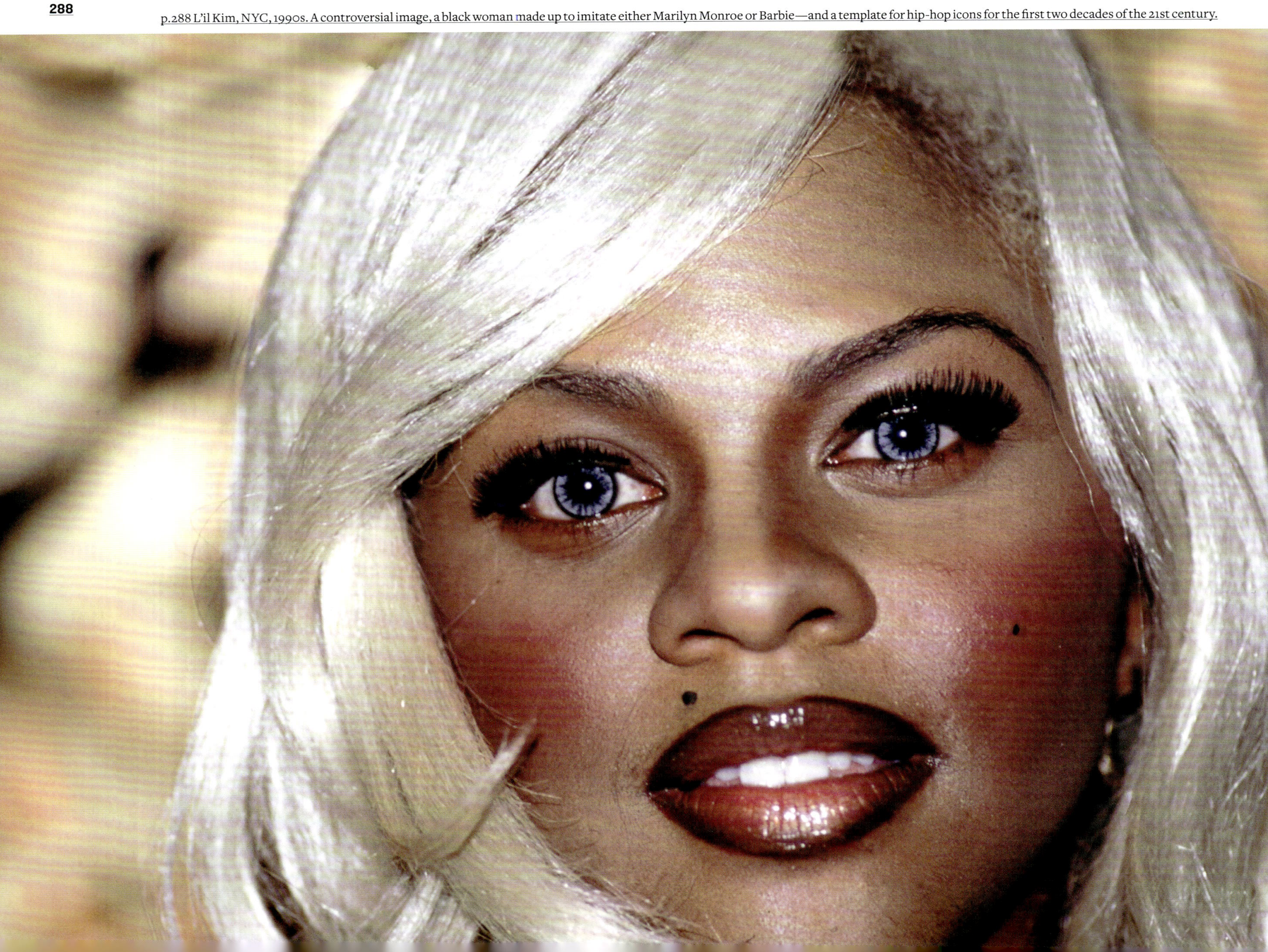

p.288 L'il Kim, NYC, 1990s. A controversial image, a black woman made up to imitate either Marilyn Monroe or Barbie—and a template for hip-hop icons for the first two decades of the 21st century.

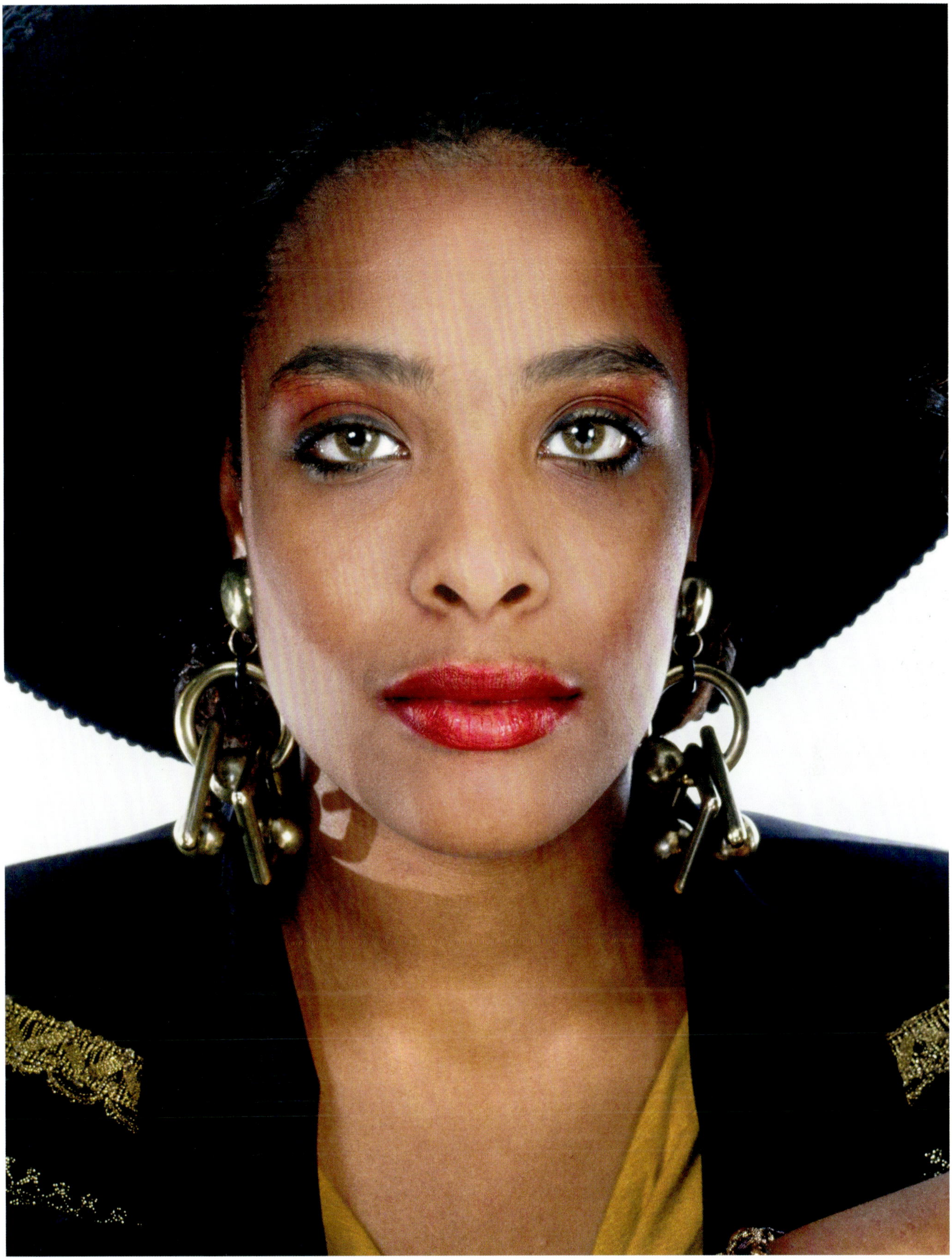

p.289 Dee Dee Roper aka DJ Spinderella from the group Salt-N-Pepa. Dakota Studios, NYC, 1990s.

p.290 SWV aka Sisters With Voices, Coko, Taj and Leelee. One of the bestselling girl groups of all time, with 25 million records sold. And I am grateful to their publicist Mary Moore for making sure I always had direct contact and access to them during their entire career. And I had a sensual photo of Taj on my business card back then too. NYC, 1990s; p.291 Missy Elliot, a joy to work with, fun, playful and high-energy, qualities she expresses abundantly in her videos. Shot this photo on the set of her music video for the song "Sock It 2 Me" which she did with Da Brat and Lil' Kim. Queensbridge, NYC, 1997.

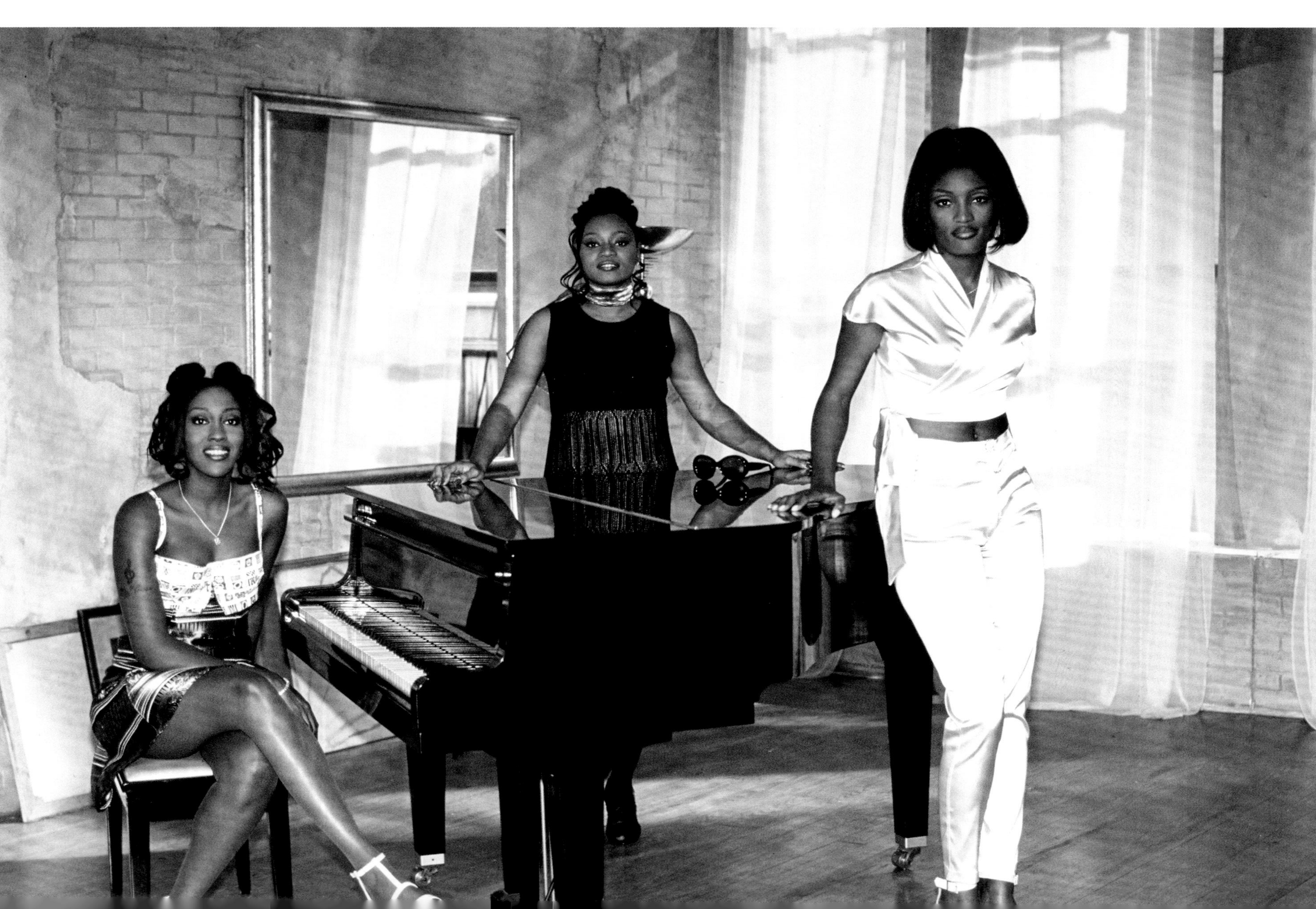

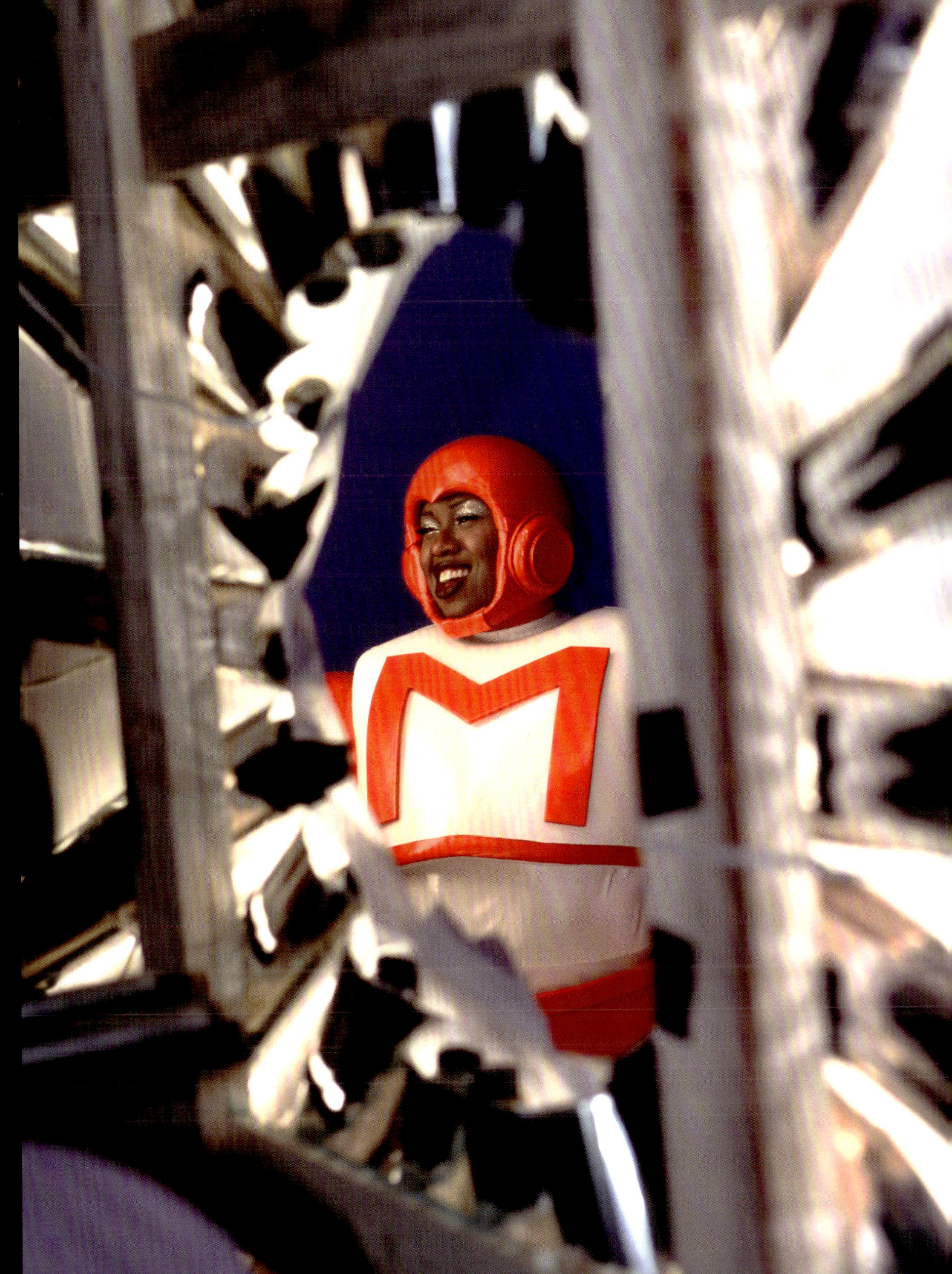

p.292 Da Brat, NYC, 1990s.

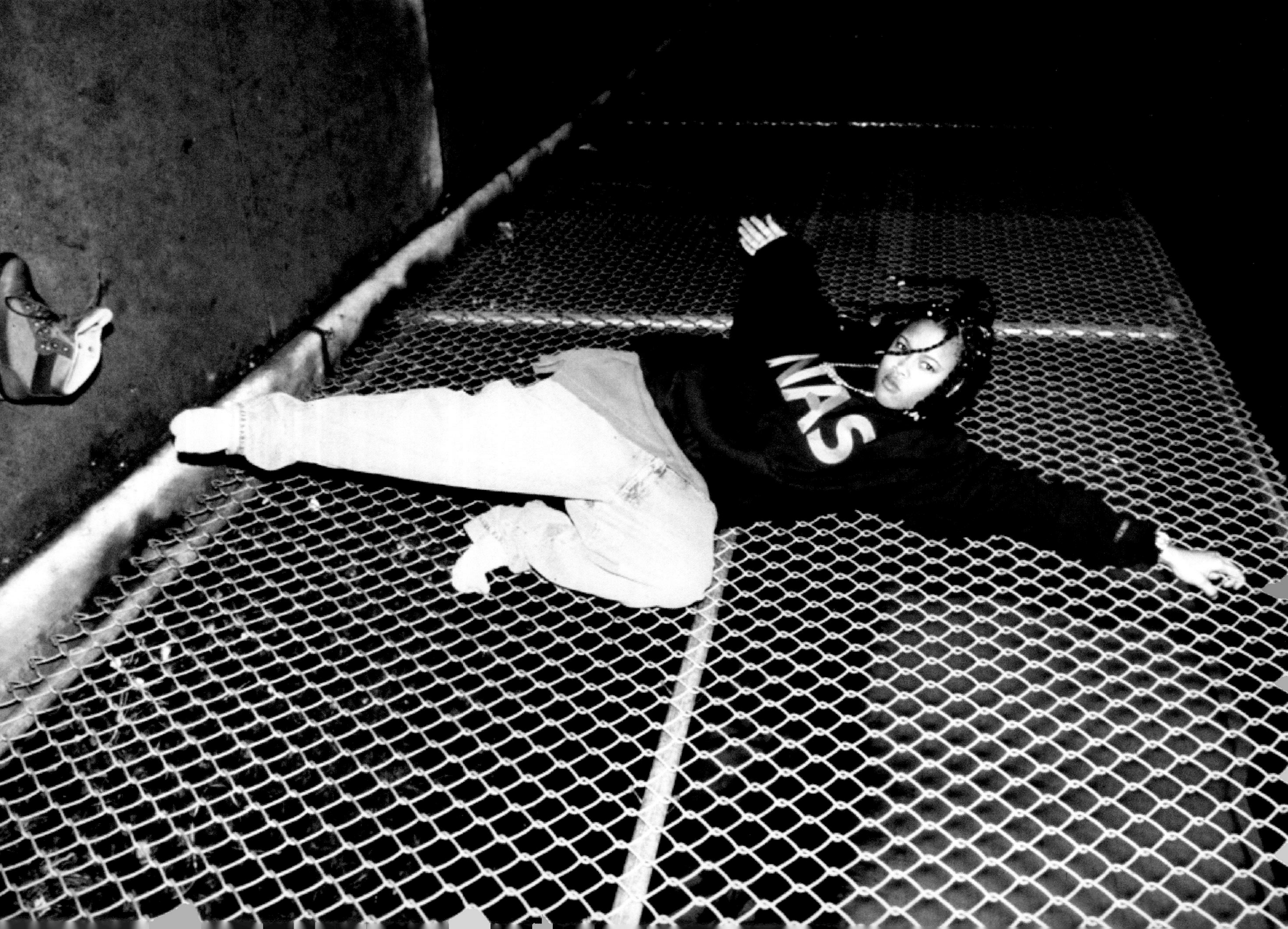

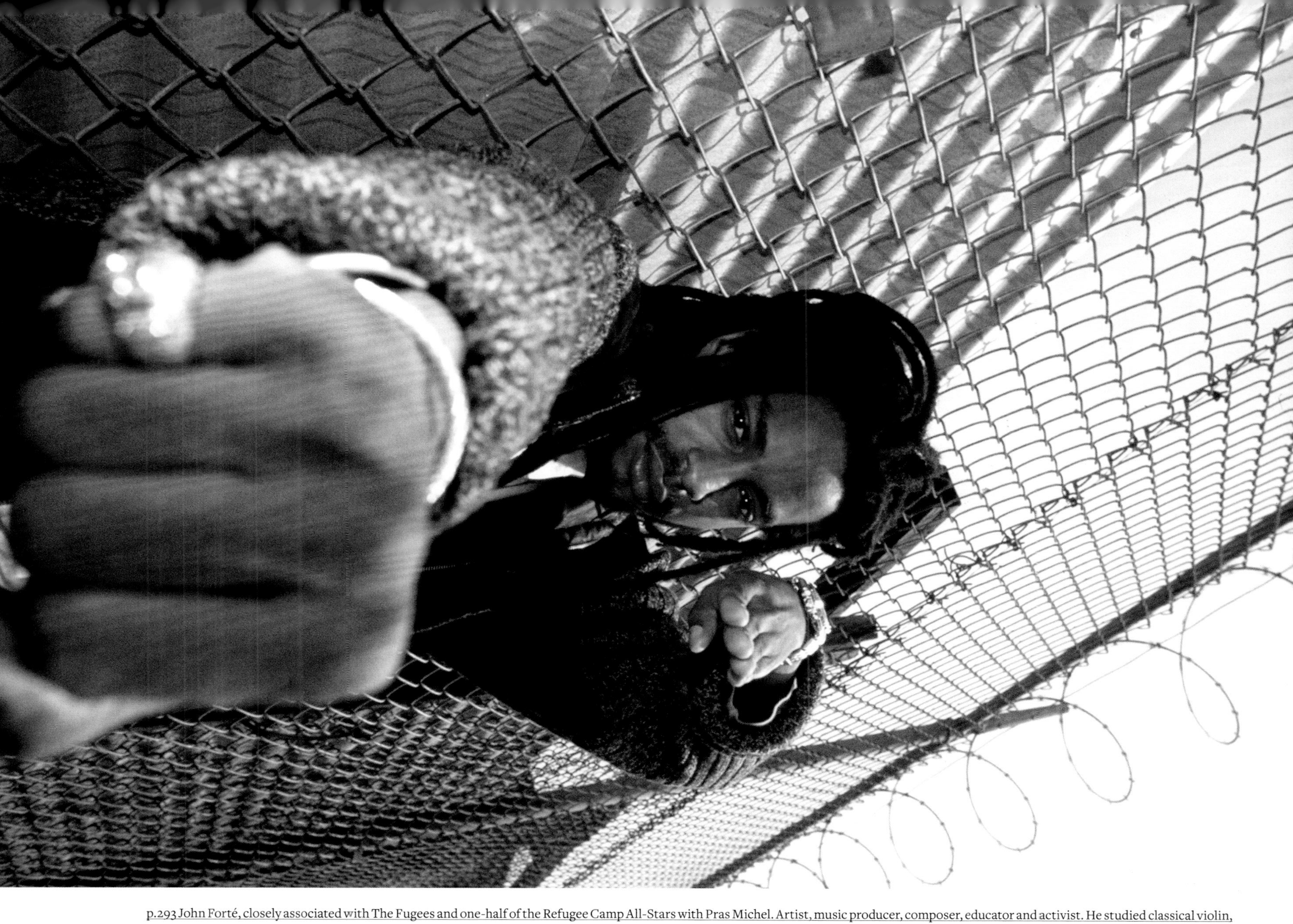

p.293 John Forté, closely associated with The Fugees and one-half of the Refugee Camp All-Stars with Pras Michel. Artist, music producer, composer, educator and activist. He studied classical violin, and was arrested at Newark Airport in New Jersey with over a million dollars' worth of liquid cocaine and sentenced to a minimum of 14 years. His sentence was later commuted by President G.W. Bush. As I always say, "you simply can't make this shit up." SoHo, NYC, 1999.

p. 294 John Forté with an early configuration of Destiny's Child with LaTavia Roberson and LaToya Luckett flanking Beyoncé Knowles and Kelly Rowland. Beyoncé went on to literally do and win everthing. "The Night I Had Dinner With Beyoncé," NYC, 1999.

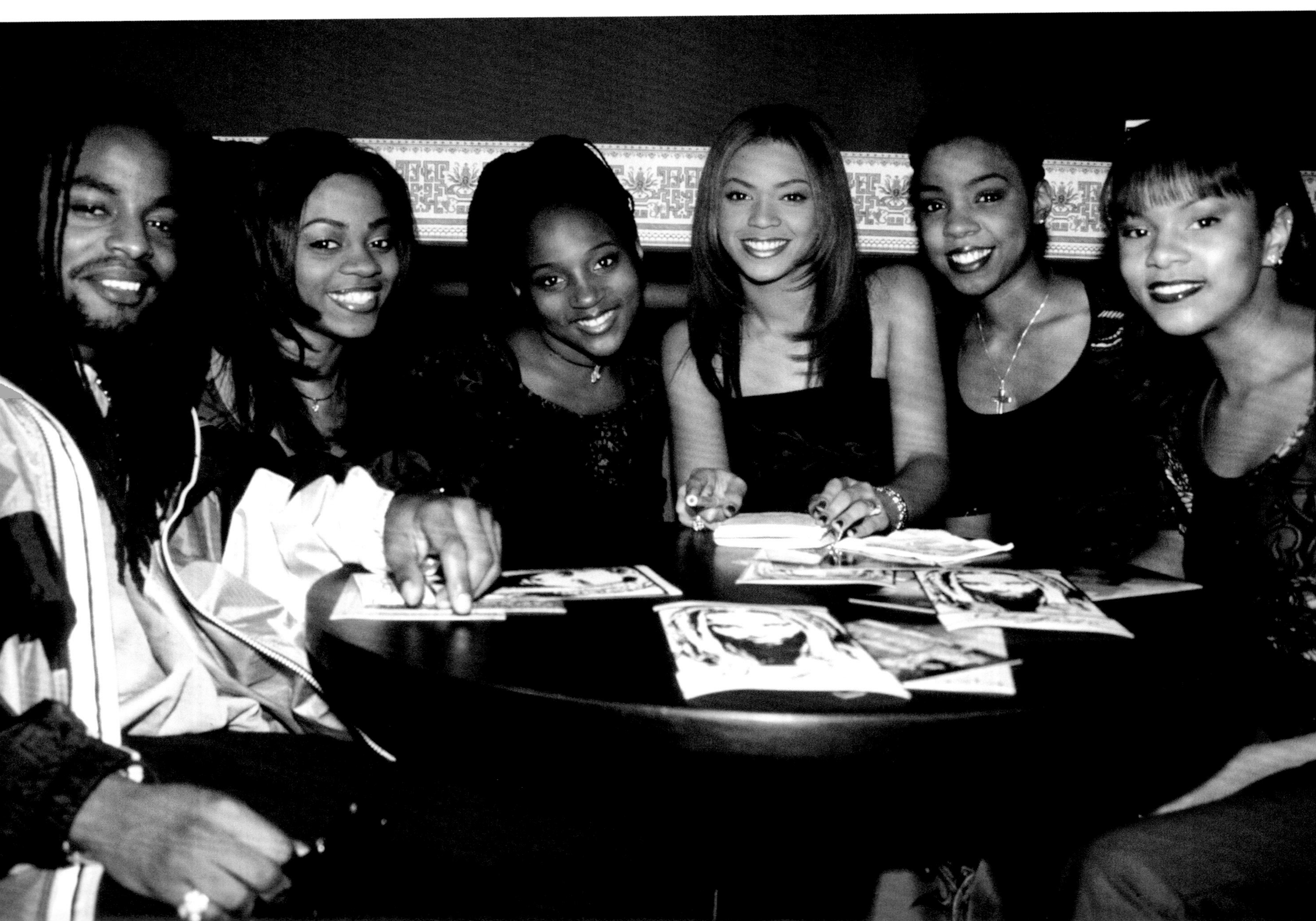

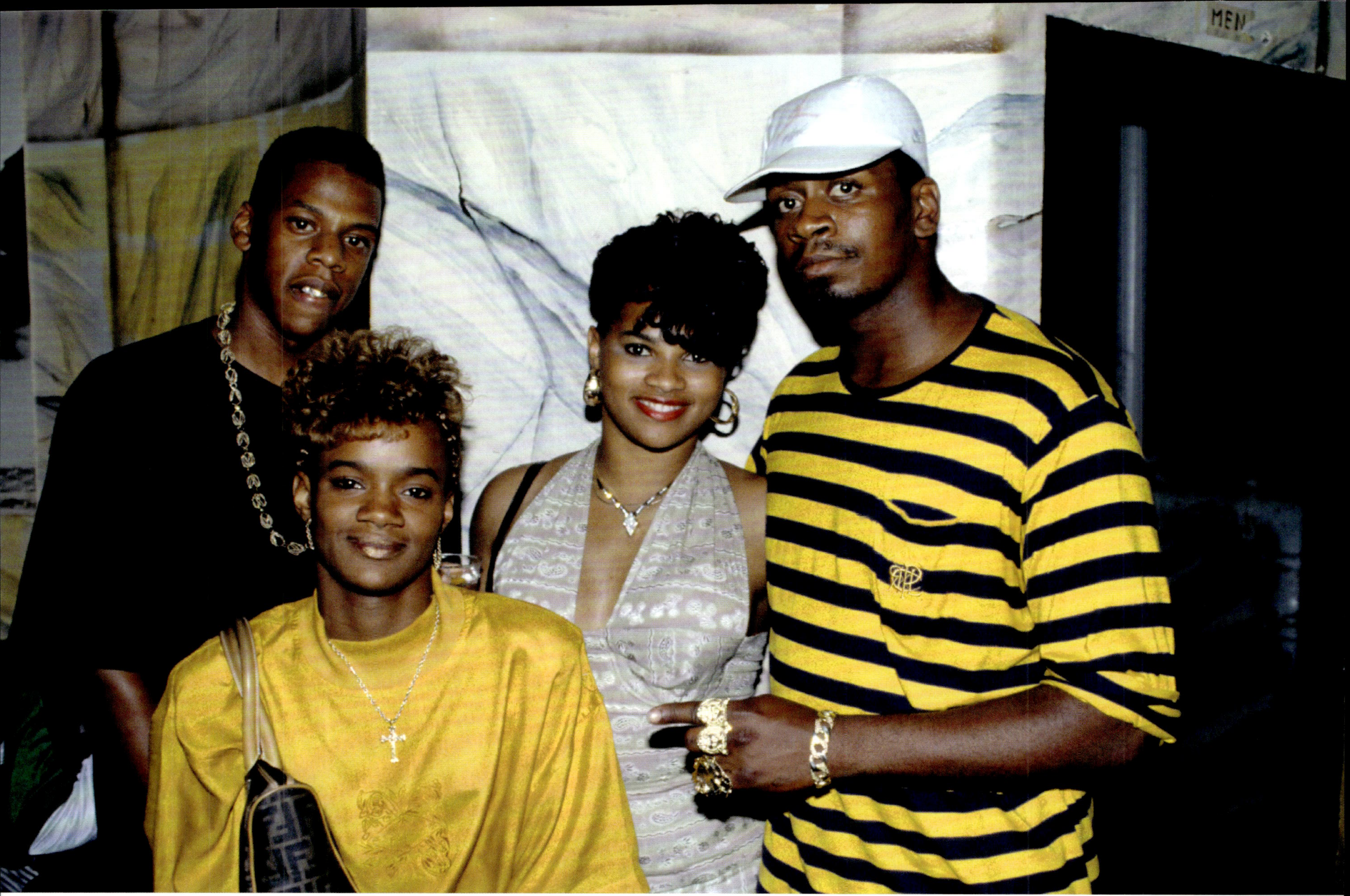

p.295 Jay-Z, Pepa from Salt-N-Pepa (in grey dress), Jaz-O (Jay-Z's mentor), and a friend. This was the night I met Jay-Z and he told me to "take my picture" because "I'm going to be running this shit, and I'm a great rapper." NYC, around 1986-1987.

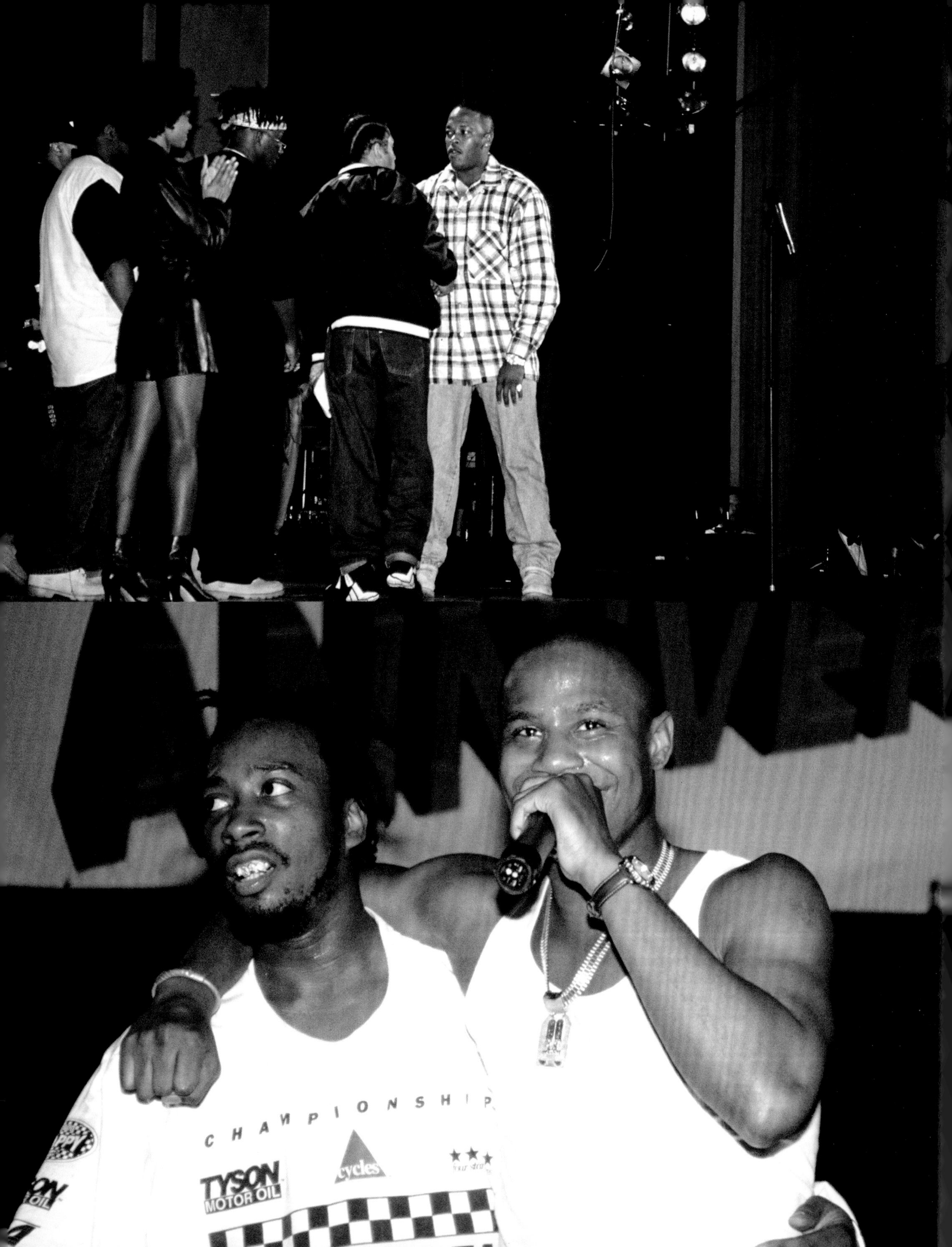
CHAMPIONSHIP
TYSON
MOTOR OIL
cycles

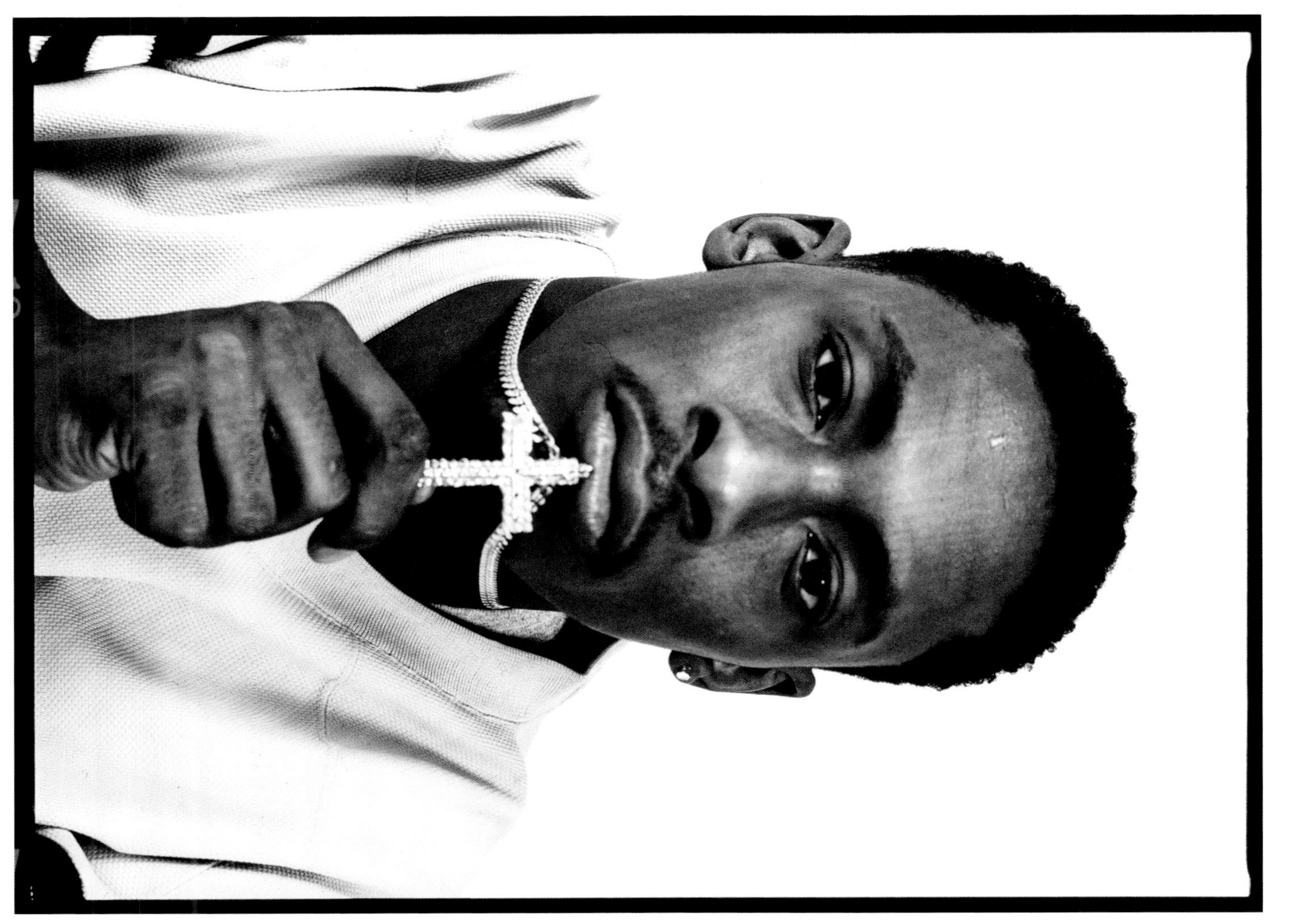

p.296 (Top) Dr. Dre, *The Source* Awards, NYC, mid-1990s; (Bottom) Old Dirty Bastard interrupts Doug E. Fresh's performance at *Vibe* magazine's second anniversary party and is promptly escorted off stage. NYC, August 1995; p.297 DJ Pete Rock, half of the group Pete Rock and C.L. Smooth, who are best known for "They Reminisce Over You (T.R.O.Y.)" from 1992, an homage to Trouble T-Roy (1967-1990), a dancer with Heavy D and Boyz who died in a fall in 1990; p.298-p.299 Snoop Dogg. Rapper, songwriter, gang member, actor, game show host, and comic. Next to Flava Flav perhaps the most recognizable rapper in the world. Sony Studios, 2000.

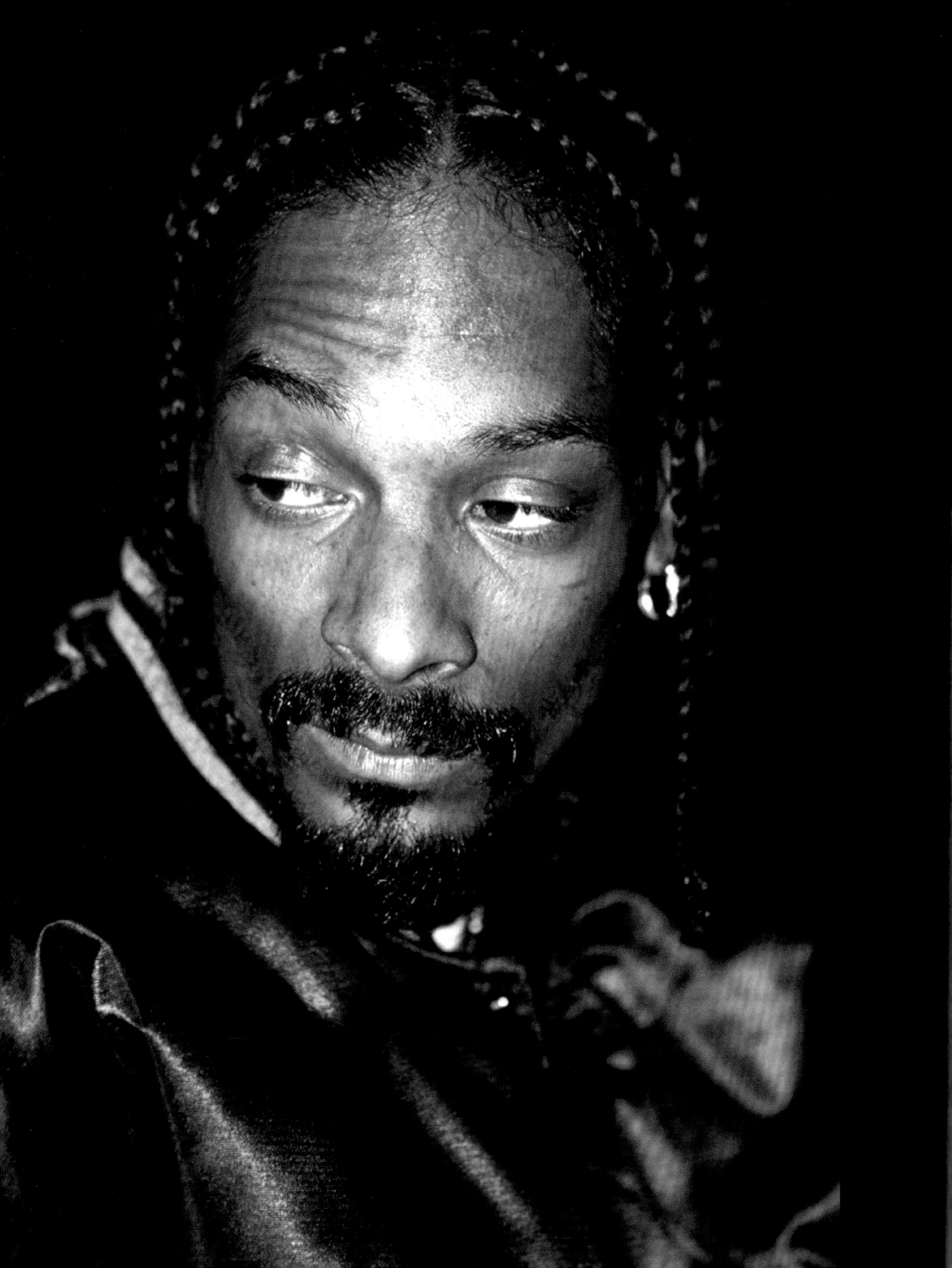

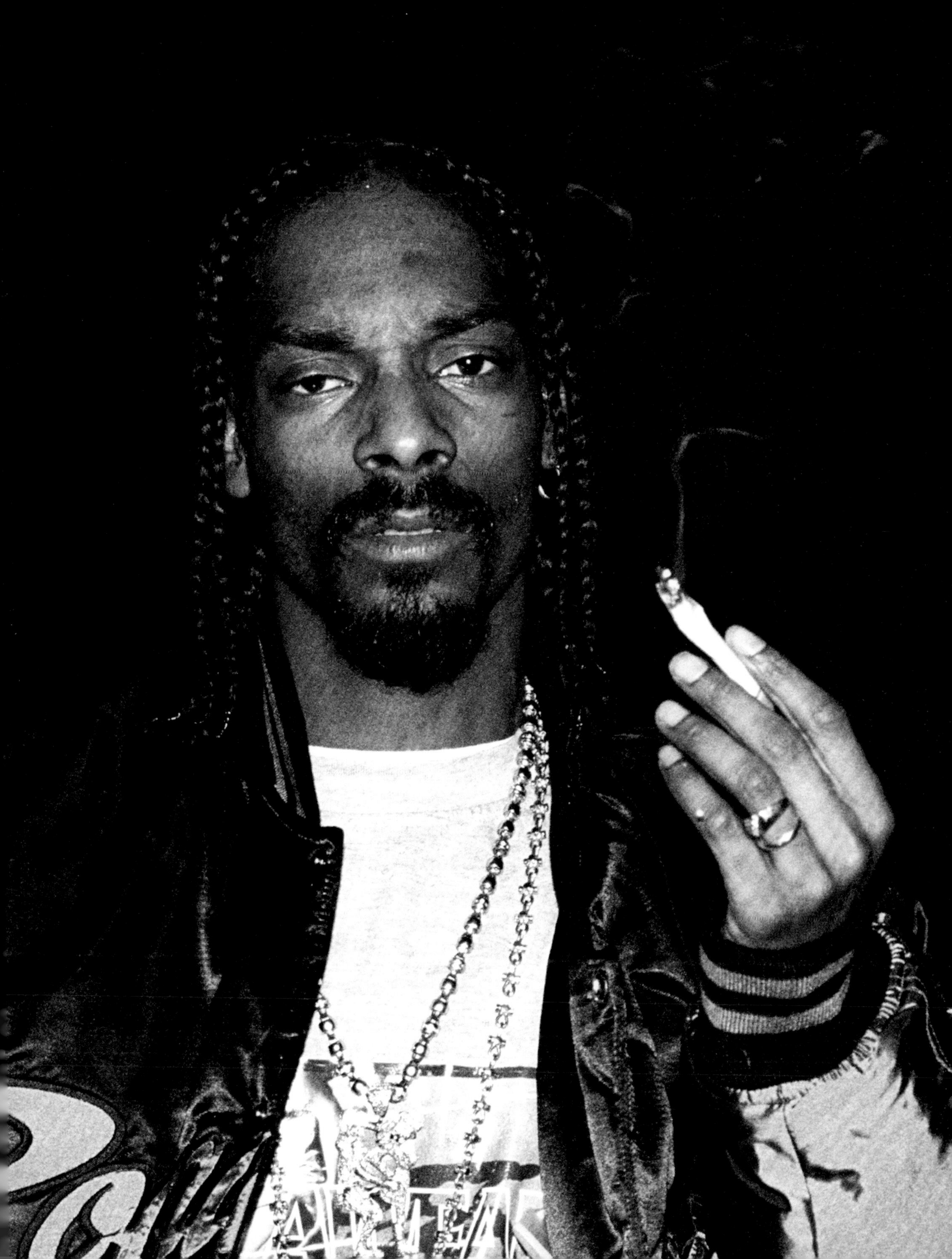

p.300 Method Man with young fans on a Sunday morning in the Apollo Theatre, Harlem, NYC, 2000s.

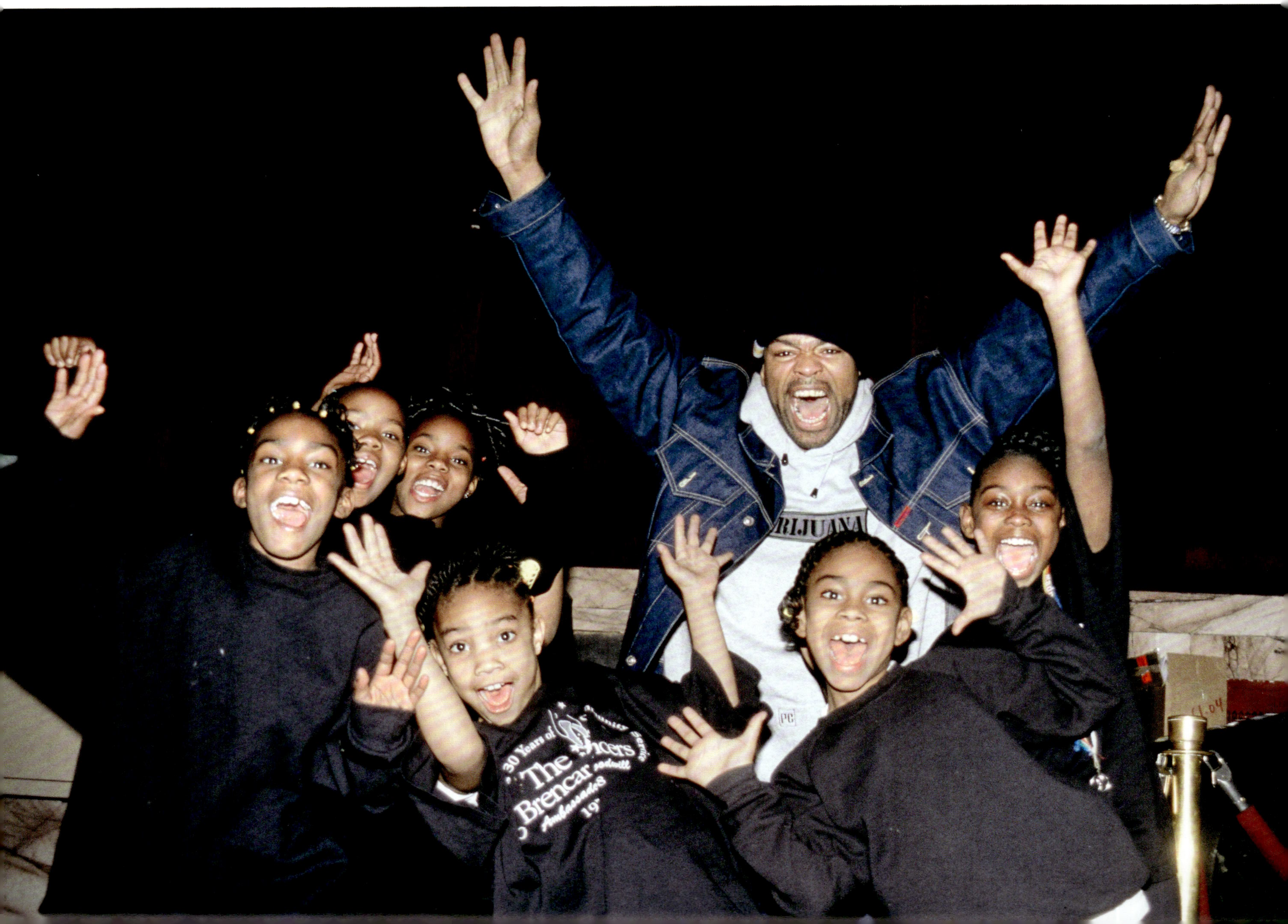

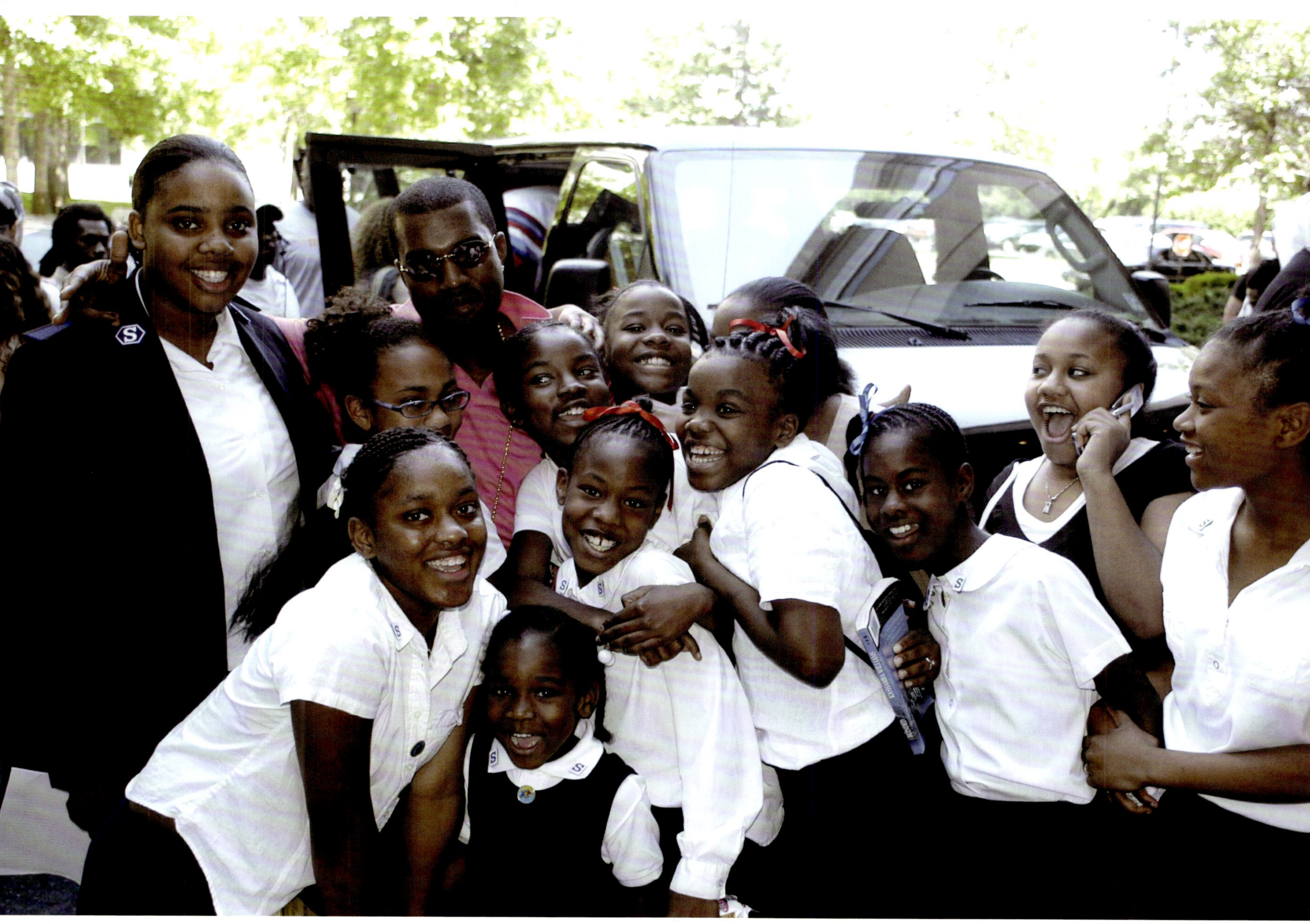

p.301 Kanye West in the pink polo shirt, smiling and embracing a group of young fans. New Jersey Meadowlands, 2004.

A poetic tribute to Brother Ernie Paniccioli by Jessica Care Moore

PULLING THE TRIGGER

In the beginning was the word
Poets with no mics
No radio and no hype
No magazines no rappers
with hooks
that sing.
The verse was the truth
And the meaning of
all things...

He was born in between

Brooklyn and Cree
armed with lenses, camera
and shoulder strap
He saw the history and importance of the boom bap
Captured the spirit of this sound
Inside his lens cap.
What he shot would shock the world with its
relevance
He understood the beauty of the crime
He brought the evidence
His foresight brought the news
Of future royalty
But the world stage didn't realize just
How this would come to be....

Birth of a nation
With no mammies
Just griots
Who broke bread and beats
The word unleashed
Blasted through neighborhood speakers
The church rocked shell toe sneakers

Ernie understood
one day the world would need us
The media would mistreat us
So he protected us
inside a different light

A light with perspective and love
Brilliance and humility
A light the devil recognizes as pure
Without pretension or zoom

Hip Hop was born
In a world of dark rooms

And we loved the jazz be-bop in you
The midnight marauder in you
The rock and roll nigga in you
The Africa Bambaataa in you
The flashy car, iced out confusion
They continue to try to pump in you.
We can still recognize your heart.
Your Pete Rock, RZA, DJ Premiere beats.
We can feel you inside Quest Love's drum licks

You helped me love my husband to the gangsta
dirty south music he creates

You make my whole house shake

They say you were born
in the Bronx
But you've been seen traveling through the
Children of Soweto
Bouncing to your truth in
The streets of Brazil
Dancing against the walls of Japan

How many decades can one man
Capture inside the pupil
of one eye?
Can you carry that much weight
With just two hands?

When you are a little girl
Listening to Run DMC and MC Lyte lacing up
Your thick laces
You think you can outrun the planet
You know that this is the soundtrack you walk to
Breathe to and learn to love to.
And like all little girls in love one day
You will figure out that even when it sounds pretty
Doesn't mean it won't hurt you
Catch you off guard
Like nodding your head to a song that portrays
You as simple, a ho, a sack chaser, an object.
So you deconstruct and play the track back
You find a way, despite your pain
To find the love in it.

Can you picture that?

It was the only thing that made sense when you
Dreamed of rocking the mic
While memorizing all the words to Fight The Power
Why you gave up beef after listening to Kris Parker
It's the reason why your Maurice Malone baggy jeans
used to hang low to hide your shape
so you could get respect
when your voice touched the mic
You understood violence
was a part of the world
So you armed yourself inside the music
Found solace.
Wrote your own stories, rocked your own bells
And Kangols
On the mic when Rakim killed 21 emcees, when Crazy
Legs spun in circles on the floor,
Armed with Keisha's complex graffiti, and Jam
Masters
Jay scratches.
You could outlive your circumstance
You can define yourself outside the label of ho.
Invisible and silenced in your country
You thought your track suit had wings

And this mystical thing
That pushed you close to the edge
Helped you escape the gunshots of your streets
With your headphones tight on your ears
You could hear liberation ancestors speak back
gritty speaking of tongues, a scientific language
Only you and your people understood

You never pictured someone taking your picture

While you were just trying to live
Contort your body into a b-girl stance
To help you get down the street
Or build your self-esteem

Ernie proves that we were here.
That we smiled and mean mugged
That we grew, switched rhyme styles
And some of us wear suits now
Own fashion labels and television shows

I wrote this for Ernie because
Legends aren't ever honored
or paid what they are worth
While they are still alive.

We are hypocrites
The world's beautiful antagonists
Hood historians, battle rhyme magicians,
Capitalistic, misogynists, debate champions,
Comedians, actors, poets, politicians, activists and
Hustlers
We bring balance
We are corn-rolled/faded up/parents
Afro puff blowing/patent leather/ trendsetting/funky
sweat hanging off a biggie t-shirt, late night
concert
going/
laughing aloud/crying when no one's looking/stage
loving/
revolutionary
creators
of the blue light in the basement party.

Children of the "Genesis"
Labeled by the labeling committee
Surviving so many storms.
Babies of the civil rights movement
Who stretched far beyond the norm

Thank you Ernie for
More proof of life.
For being our reflection in a world
Surrounded by false mirrors.
You are the grandmaster with your flash
The magnificent hills of sugar
Memorialized inside the mountain of your film

Thank you for taking our 35 millimeter picture
When no one else was looking.

We remember when radio didn't play us
And our street corner freestyles
Never went past our block, or that moment
You documented our time
standing still shots

And I pray you never quit, Ernie Paniccioli
Even when we betray our own portraits
Our incredible history
Turn our backs on our roots
Forget the fire

People are dying to be heard
To be seen
all over the world
And I gotta find a poem
To fit inside one of your pictures
One that matters more than this moment
Somewhere under my skin
Below my neck,
Inside my throat
Deep in the pit of my stomach

I don't know what the others will do
When the earth cracks in two
Or the sun finally gets too close
When the oceans, tornadoes, volcanoes,
Hurricanes and rainforests
Come for revenge
As we sip our morning paper
And read our premium coffee

When our addiction to nothing
Finally goes away.

But, I know you will be there

Shooting our pain
Exposing our possibilities
Loving our glory
Explaining our expressions
Our peace signs
Our war chants
Our subtleties
In black and white
Our complexities
In full color
Maybe it was your mother's love that saved you
Or the library that empowered you
Or living on the streets of New York City that
Propelled you
To keep shooting us
From a spiritual perspective
To honestly love what you were
Shooting
right before you decided
to pull the trigger.
I shot ya.

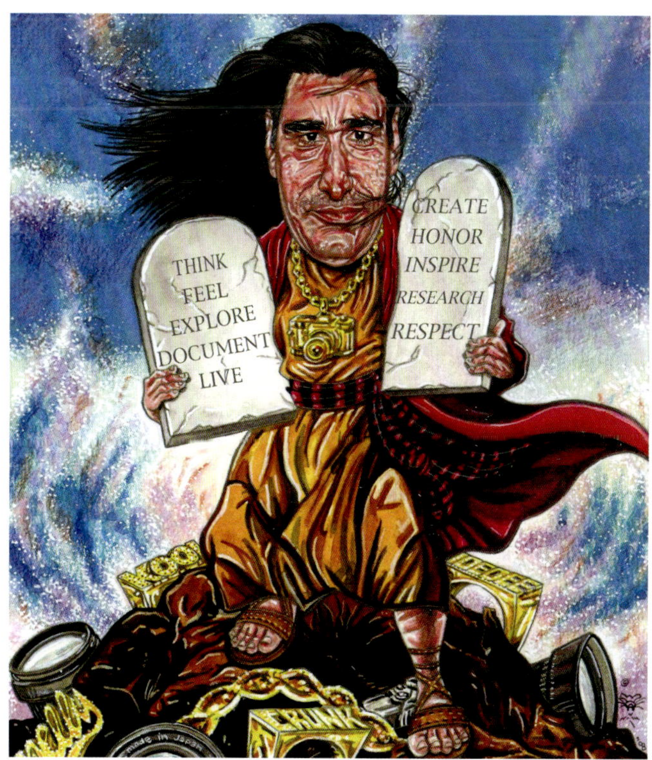

Jessica Care Moore is an American poet from Detroit, Michigan. Moore's poetry is featured on Nas' *Nastradamus* album, Jeezy's *Church in These Streets*, and Talib Kweli's *Attack The Block.*

p.303 Painting of me by Andre LeRoi Davis, aka Mr. Last Word. Most people picking up a copy of *The Source* would instantly flip to the last page to see Andre's parody of some rapper or group or DJ. The Last Word always inspired both laughs and thought. He told me he would often look to my photos in various magazines for inspiration. To be painted by him is a great honor. I call him The Hip-Hop Picasso.

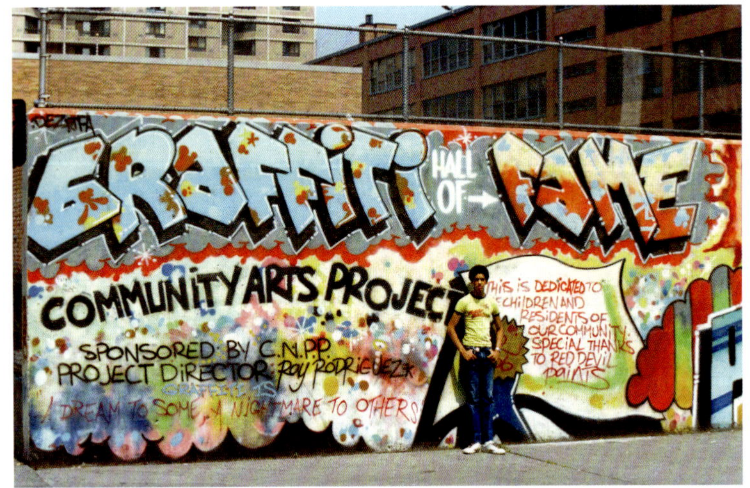

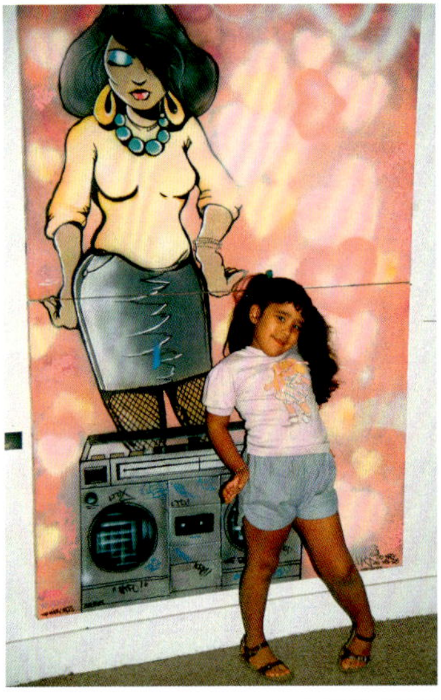

p.304 (clockwise from top) My son Krishna in front of the very first series of graffiti murals in The Graffiti Wall of Fame on 106th and Park Avenue, in 1983, when he was only 14 years old; my daughter Melissa Dawn in front of a painting by Porn at City Without Walls Gallery in Newark NJ in 1984; an ad I shot for Naughty By Nature's Naughty Gear Store on Halsey Street in Newark, New Jersey, 1990s.

Front Endpaper: Divine Sounds. Outdoor concert on the top of a truck overlooking Washington Heights, NYC, mid-1980s; KAOS aka David Gerena's graf jacket, The Roxy Roller Rink, NYC, 1979.

Back Endpaper: Graf jacket, East Harlem, NYC, 1979; Salt-N-Pepa, New Year's Eve party studio shoot, NYC, late 1980s.

The authorized representative in the EU for product safety and compliance is Mondadori Libri S.p.A., via Gian Battista Vico 42, Milan, Italy, 20123
www.mondadori.it

ACKNOWLEDGMENTS

My mother Julia and my brothers Raymond and Ernesto, R.I.P. My wife Angela, my brothers and sister, son and daughter and my three grandchildren. Brother William Dabney, who dreamed up the title of this book. Manny Martinez, Jamel Shabazz, Joe Conzo, Koe Rodriquez, Scott Figman, Matthew Kemp, Rayon Richards, Jabar Jordan, Jessica Care Moore, Nancy Wolff, Andre LeRoi Davis, Afrika Bambaataa, Yasiin Bey, Rakim, Melle Mel, KRS1, Kenny Yoda, Sun One, my Zulu family, and Charlie Sutton, who kept the mighty doors of The Apollo open to me.

My Canada Crew: Dalton Higgins, Jay Robi, Griz on The Grind, Sumita Bidaye, Matthew Creeasian, Bri Briskool Marie, Corey Bulpitt, Chris Wong, Girl 23 aka Larissa Healey, Q Rock, Che Kothari.

To my France Crew, especially Nadjib Ben Bella; and a special thanks to the guardians of my archive at Cornell University, Katherine Reagan and Ben Ortiz.

And the Rizzoli Crew: Ian Luna and Meaghan McGovern.

First published in the United States of America
by Rizzoli International Publications, Inc.
49 West 27th Street, New York, NY 10001
www.rizzoliusa.com

Editor: Ian Luna
Project Editor: Meaghan McGovern
Production: Kaija Markoe
Production Coordination: Kayleigh Jankowski
Recording and Transcription: Cindy Hansen of Transcription Professionals, and Edward Ng
Proofreader: Mary Ellen Wilson

Publisher: Charles Miers

Book Design: Eugene Lee

The Editor would like to extend his gratitude to
Michel LeBugle, Paula Kamen, Stan Wooh, and Nancy Wolff.

Printed in China
2025 2026 2027 2028 / 16 15 14 13 12 11 10
Library of Congress Control Number: 2018943558
ISBN: 978-0-7893-3441-1

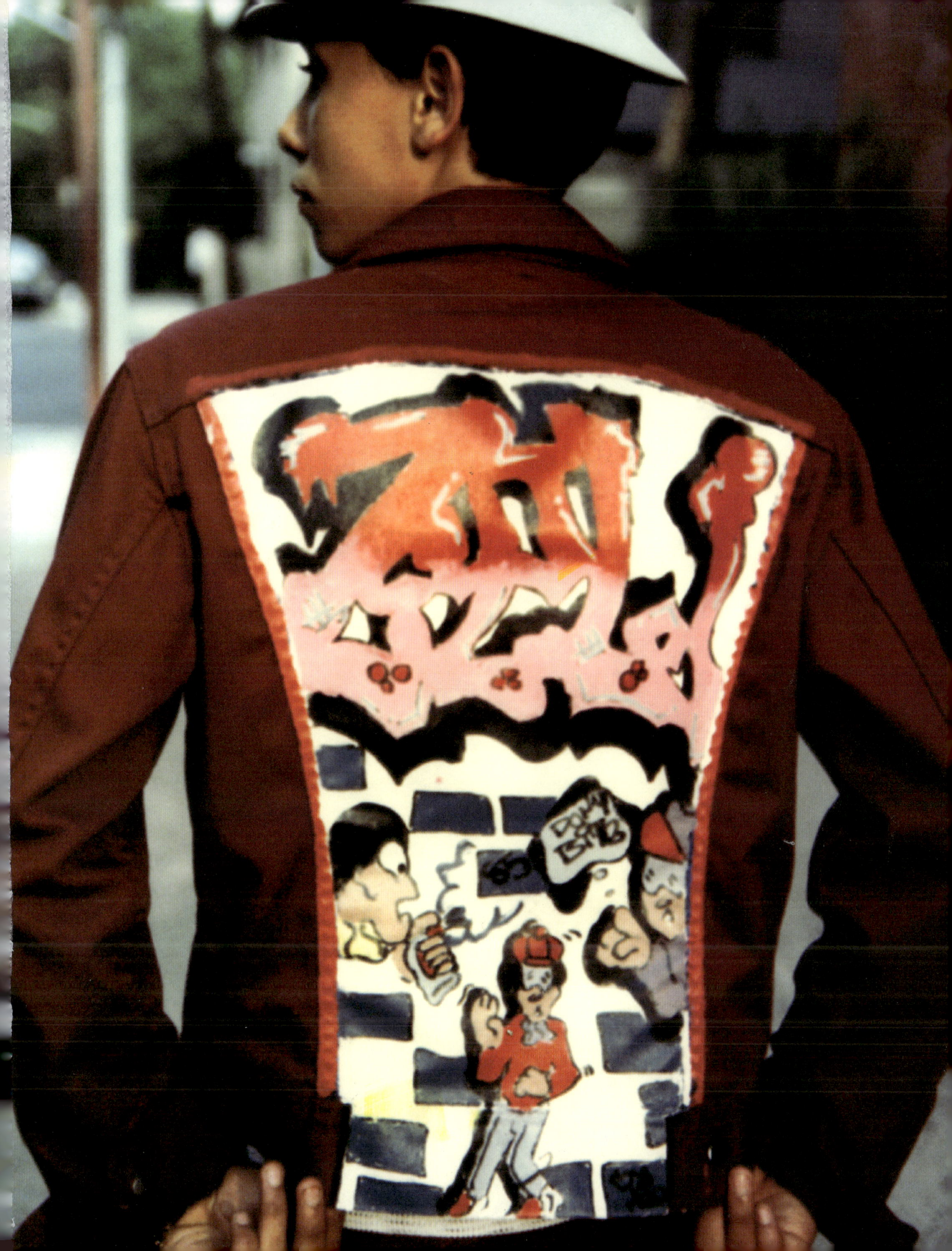

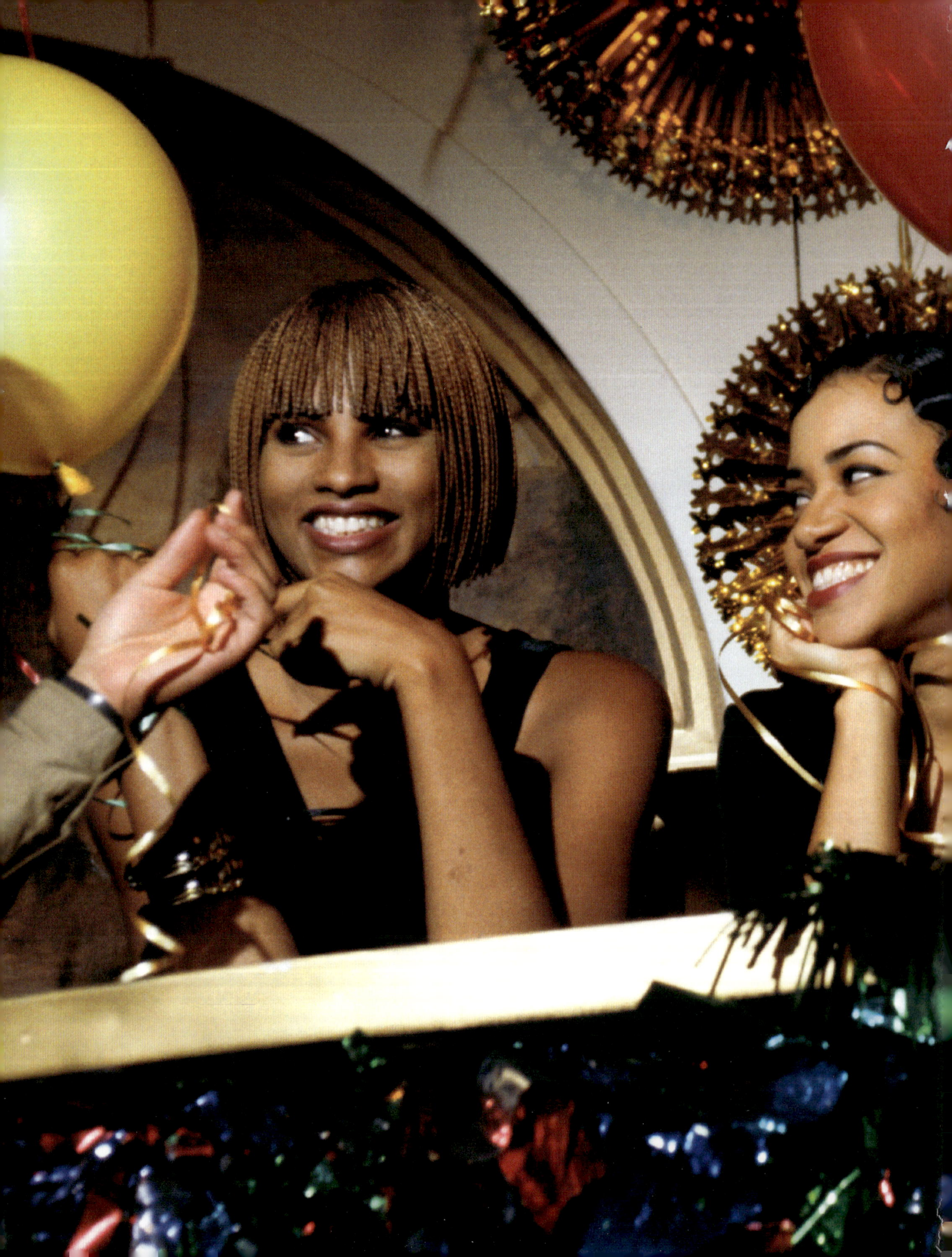